The Enduring Vision

The Enduring Vision

A HISTORY OF THE AMERICAN PEOPLE

VOLUME ONE: TO 1877

Concise Fifth Edition

Paul S. Boyer
University of Wisconsin, Madison

Clifford E. Clark, Jr.
Carleton College

Sandra McNair Hawley
San Jacinto College

Joseph F. Kett
University of Virginia

Neal Salisbury
Smith College

Harvard Sitkoff
University of New Hampshire

Nancy Woloch
Barnard College

Houghton Mifflin Company
Boston   New York

Publisher: Charles Hartford
Senior Sponsoring Editor: Sally Constable
Development Editor: Lisa Kalner Williams
Editorial Assistant: Arianne Vanni
Senior Project Editor: Bob Greiner
Editorial Assistant: Robert Woo
Senior Art and Design Coordinator: Jill Haber
Senior Composition Buyer: Sarah Ambrose
Senior Manufacturing Coordinator: Marie Barnes
Senior Marketing Manager: Sandra McGuire
Marketing Assistant: Molly Parke

Cover: *The Lackawanna Valley* by George Inness, 1856.
Gift of Mrs. Huttleston Rogers, Image © 2004 Board of Trustees,
National Gallery of Art, Washington, D.C.

Text Credits:
p. 43: Adapted from *Salem Possessed: The Social Origins of Witchcraft* by Paul Boyer and
Stephen Nissenbaum. Copyright © 1974 by the President and Fellows of Harvard
College. Reprinted by permission of Harvard University Press; p. 235: Reprinted with
permission of the McGraw-Hill Companies from *Ordeal By Fire: The Civil War and
Reconstruction*, Second Edition, by James M. McPherson. Copyright © 1992 by The
McGraw-Hill Companies; p. 339: Reprinted from John Hope Franklin, *Reconstruction
After the Civil War* (Chicago: University of Chicago Press, 1962), 231, with permission.

Printed in the U.S.A.

Library of Congress Catalog Number: 2005921390

Complete volume ISBN: 0-618-47382-3

Volume One ISBN: 0-618-47383-1

Volume Two ISBN: 0-618-47384-X

1 2 3 4 5 6 7 8 9-VH-09 08 07 06 05

Contents

Maps

Charts, Graphs and Tables

Preface

Much has changed in America and the world since we first began *The Enduring Vision* more than a decade ago. Some of these developments have been welcome and positive; others have been troubling and unsettling. In this new Concise Fifth Edition, we fully document the scope of these changes, for good or ill. But we have also taken care to stress the continuities that can provide assurance and inspire hope in troubled times.

For this Fifth Edition, we have reorganized sections of the chapter sequence so the narrative flows more smoothly and assures full coverage of recent events. Two chapters on the late nineteenth-century era, "The Transformation of Urban America" and "Daily Life, Popular Culture, and the Arts, 1860–1900," have been combined into one: Chapter 19, "Immigration, Urbanization, and Everyday Life, 1860–1900." Similarly, the two chapters on the 1930s have been consolidated into Chapter 24, "The Great Depression and the New Deal, 1929–1939." This allows us to convey more directly how the economic crisis and the reform energies of the 1930s played out across American society.

We also decided to shift some material among chapters to promote clarity and coherence. We moved the discussion of early twentieth-century foreign relations, including the Open Door notes to China and the building of the Panama Canal, into Chapter 22, "Global Involvements and World War I, 1902–1920," allowing us to trace America's expanding world role in those crucial years. Similarly, the diplomacy of the 1930s, which as the decade wore on focused heavily on the deepening foreign menace in Europe and Asia, formerly included in the chapter on the Great Depression and the New Deal, is now covered at the beginning of Chapter 25, "Americans and a World in Crisis, 1933–1945," which also deals with World War II.

Having restructured and tightened our treatment of earlier time periods, we were able to add a new concluding chapter. We now devote three full chapters to the eventful contemporary era, from Richard Nixon's resignation in 1974 to the present. The energy crises of the 1970s, the ferment and controversies of the Reagan years, the end of the Cold War, new patterns of immigration, the economic transformation associated with the rise of the service economy and the revolution in information processing, the deadly attack on America in September 2001, and even the war in Iraq in 2004 are now treated in full analytic detail.

New Interpretations, Expanded Coverage

The changes we have made in this latest edition of *The Enduring Vision* extend beyond simply a new chapter arrangement. We have been especially attentive to new work in social and cultural history, building on a strength of the book that instructors have long recognized.

As in earlier editions, our extensive coverage of environmental history, the land, and the West is fully integrated into the narrative, not simply mechanically "tacked on" to a traditional account.

This edition of *The Enduring Vision* pays even closer attention to the crucial role of science, technology, medicine, and disease. In addition, there is additional focus on American's emergence as a world power and the evolution of the nation's global role over time.

Learning And Teaching Ancillaries

The program for *The Enduring Vision*, Concise Fifth Edition includes a number of useful learning and teaching aids. These ancillaries are designed to help students get the most from the course and to provide instructors with useful course management and presentation tools.

The **Houghton Mifflin History Companion** is a collection of resources designed to complement the use of *The Enduring Vision,* Concise Fifth Edition. It is organized according to the chapters in the text and has four parts—the **Instructor Companion website**, the **Instructor Companion CD-ROM**, the **Student Study Companion**, and the **Student Research Companion**. The beginning of each chapter will feature an ***hc*** icon to remind you of these resources.

The **Instructor Companion website** and **Instructor Companion CD-ROM** features the **Instructor's Resource Manual with Test Items** in addition to hundreds of maps, images, audio and video clips, and PowerPoint® slides for classroom presentation. The Instructor Companion CD-ROM offers the same collection of maps and images with additional audio and video clips for classroom use and a computerized version of the Test Items.

The **Student Study Companion** is a free, online study guide to accompany *The Enduring Vision.* The Study Companion contains a variety of tutorial resources including ACE quizzes with feedback, flashcards, annotated links to history sites, and other interactivities. At the end of each chapter, the ***hc*** ACE Practice Test icon will refer you to the ACE quizzes on the Student Study Companion.

The **Student Research Companion** is a free, on-line tool with a wealth of interactive maps and primary sources. Students can use the maps for research, classroom assignments, or review of their geography skills. Primary sources provide a real-world introduction to historical evidence. The sources include headnotes that provide pertinent background information and questions that students can answer and e-mail to their instructors. At key sections of each chapter, ***hc*** Interactive Map and ***hc*** Primary Source icons will refer you to related interactive maps and primary sources on the Student Research Companion.

Please contact your local Houghton Mifflin sales representative for more information about the History Companion in addition to our other ancillary materials.

Acknowledgments

Any book, and this one in particular, is the result of the hard work of many people. I would particularly like to acknowledge the contributions of Jan Fitter and Margaret Manos on Volume Two of *The Enduring Vision,* Concise Fifth Edition. As always, the editorial staff at Houghton Mifflin has been outstanding. Particularly deserving of thanks are Sally Constable; Lisa Kalner Williams; Bob Greiner; Jane W. Sherman; and Sandra McGuire. Warm thanks go as well to my colleagues at San Jacinto College for their support and encouragement; to Jim Heil for his help in all matters digital; and to my daughter Lee Anne for her patience and support. The support of Tina Olivier, Maggie Seaton, Judy Wissing, and Ann Williamson has been invaluable, as are the memories of Kathy Heil and Barbara Rossi. I have also profited from working closely with the authors of the full text—again, many thanks for their patience and help.

As always, we couple our gratitude with the disclaimer that any errors are ours alone.

S.M.H

The Enduring Vision

1

Native Peoples of America, to 1500

Anasazi Wicker Basket with Turquoise Mosaic, Pueblo Bonito, Chaco Canyon. American Museum of Natural History

CHAPTER OUTLINE

The First Americans, c. 13,000–2500 B.C.

Cultural Diversity, c. 2500 B.C.–A.D. 1500

North American Peoples on the Eve of European Contact

hc This icon will direct you to additional study and research resources at http://college.hmco.com/history/us/boyer/enduring_concise/5e/students/index.html

The history of the Americas began thousands of years before Christopher Columbus's first voyage. Over that time, an indigenous American history unfolded, separate from that of the Old World of Africa, Asia, and Europe.

Some Native Americans eked out their existences in precarious environments, whereas others enjoyed prosperity; some lived in small bands, but others dwelled in large cities; some believed that the first humans came from the sky, and others thought that they originated underground. Wherever and however they lived, and whatever

This chapter focuses on three major questions:

▶ What prompted the transition from Paleo-Indian to Archaic ways of life for the earliest Americans?

▶ How did the Western Hemisphere's varied environments shape the diverse Native American cultures?

▶ What common values did Native Americans share despite their vast diversity?

they believed, native peoples together made North America a human habitat and gave it a history.

THE FIRST AMERICANS, c. 13,000–2500 B.C.

Precisely how and when the Western Hemisphere was settled remains uncertain. Although many Indians believe that their ancestors originated in the Americas, most scientific theories point to the arrival of peoples from northeastern Asia during the last Ice Age (c. 33,000–10,500 B.C.) when land linked Siberia and Alaska. As the Ice Age waned, Native Americans developed diverse cultures that nonetheless had many elements in common.

Peopling New Worlds

Two theories dominate views of the peopling of America. According to the first theory, Siberian hunters crossed the land bridge linking Alaska and Siberia around 10,500 B.C. and spread southward and eastward through a hunters' paradise of large animals. The second theory, based on recent ar-

chaeological finds, holds that the first humans arrived much earlier than 10,500, traveling by boat along the Asian-American coastline and establishing new homes as they moved southward. Findings at coastal sites as far south as Monte Verde, Chile, seem to support this view. Both theories seem in part correct, and scientists now believe that there were multiple migrations, both coastal and overland, as early as 13,000 B.C.

Most Native Americans descend from these early migrations, but a later surge of migration brought Athapaskan-speaking peoples to the Americas about 7000 B.C. Their descendants include the Apaches and Navajos. The arrival of non-Indian Inuits, Aleuts, and Eskimos after 3000 B.C. completed the peopling of the Americas.

Most Paleo-Indians lived in small bands of fifteen to fifty people. The band lived together for the summer but split into smaller groups of one or two families for fall and winter. Although they moved constantly, they remained within informal boundaries except when they traveled to favored quarries to obtain jasper or flint for making tools. Here they encountered other bands, with whom they traded and joined in religious ceremonies.

By 9000 B.C. many big-game species, including mammoths and mastodons, had vanished. Paleo-Indian hunters contributed to this extinction, as did a warming climate and environmental changes. Human beings were major beneficiaries of these changes.

Archaic Societies

Climatic warming continued until about 4000 B.C. with dramatic effects for North America. Sea levels rose, flooding the shallow continental shelf, and glacial runoff filled the Great Lakes, the Mississippi River basin, and other waters. As the glaciers receded northward, so did the cold, icy arctic or subarctic environments that had covered much of what is now the United States. Treeless plains and evergreen forests yielded to deciduous forests in the East, grassland prairies on the Plains, and desert in much of the West. An immense range of plants and animals covered the landscape.

The Archaic peoples, as archaeologists term native North Americans from 8000 B.C. to 1500 B.C., lived off wide varieties of smaller mammals, fish, and wild plants rather than big game. Greater efficiency in hunting and gathering permitted larger populations to inhabit smaller areas. In rich areas such as the East and Midwest, large populations lived in villages for virtually the entire year. For example, a year-round village that flourished near present-day Kampsville, Illinois, from 3900 to 2800 B.C. supported 100 to 150 people. Its residents procured fish and mussels from local lakes to supplement the deer, birds, nuts, and seeds available in the surrounding area.

Over time, Archaic Americans sharpened distinctions between women's and men's roles. Generally men fished and hunted while women foraged for wild plant products. However, both genders apparently served as religious healers.

As they foraged for wild plants, women gradually learned how to cultivate the plants and then developed tools for digging and grinding as well as effective methods of drying and storing seeds. By 5000 B.C.— well before farming reached Europe — some Native Americans were already practicing agriculture.

The most sophisticated of these early farmers lived in highland valleys in Mesoamerica, particularly Tehuacán. By 3000 B.C. they were cultivating squash, gourds, beans, chili peppers, and fruits. At the same time Tehuacán farmers began the long process of domesticating a lowlands plant called teosinte, which ultimately became maize, or corn. Maize agriculture spread rapidly; by 2500 B.C. maize was cultivated as far north as modern New Mexico and as far south as the Amazon basin. The earliest ears of maize were about the size of an adult human finger.

At the same time, Indians in the Andes were already cultivating potatoes, while their counterparts along the Pacific coast harvested squash, beans, and peppers. Initially these domesticated plants constituted only a small part of the Native American diet, essentially a supplement to meat, fish, and wild plants. Centuries would pass before stable societies based primarily on agriculture emerged.

CULTURAL DIVERSITY, c. 2500 B.C.–A.D. 1500

After 2500 B.C. dramatic transformations took place among agricultural peoples, particularly those who depended largely on cultivated crops. Intensive farming radically changed the environment, and larger populations linked by trade and religion evolved into formal confederacies and even hierarchical states joined by political and religious systems.

Mesoamerica and South America

Mesoamerican farmers rapidly developed more sophisticated agricultural systems, improving both the quality and quantity of their crops. In turn, the higher yields and improved nutrition led to the emergence of maize-based farming societies throughout Mesoamerica during the next eight centuries.

By 2000 B.C. some Mesoamerican farming societies were trading surplus crops to their nonfarming neighbors. Trade led to the development of wealthy and powerful urban centers that dominated surrounding communities. These chiefdoms generally dominated relatively small areas, but some developed into centralized states complete with taxes, public works, and armies. The capital of the largest early state, Teotihuacán, about fifty miles northeast of modern Mexico City, housed a population of a hundred thousand people. At its center was a complex of pyramids over which towered the Sun Pyramid, the largest structure in the Americas prior to the arrival of the Spanish. From 100 to 700 A.D., Teotihuacán dominated the Valley of Mexico, with trade networks extending throughout modern Mexico; its influence on the religion, government, and culture of its neighbors was enormous.

As Teotihuacán declined, the Maya rose. Living in kingdom-states that flourished from southern Mexico to Honduras, the Maya developed a highly accurate calendar; a numerical system; and a system of phonetic, hieroglyphic writing. Mayan codices (singular codex)—formed from bark paper glued into long folded strips—recorded religious

Sun Pyramid, Teotihuacán
Built over several centuries, this pyramid remained the largest structure in the Americas until after the Spanish arrived.

ceremonies, historical traditions, and astronomical observations.

In the fifteenth century two powerful empires emerged, the Aztecs of Mexico and the Inca of Peru. In 1428 the Aztec began asserting control over Lake Texcoco in the Valley of Mexico and its surrounding communities. After 1450 Aztec expansion became increasingly bloody as Aztec priests maintained that their gods demanded to be served human blood and hearts; warriors sought captives for human sacrifice.

Tenochtitlán, the Aztec capital, at its peak had some two hundred thousand inhabitants. At the center of the city was a massive temple complex. The Aztec borrowed freely from other Mesoamerican societies, taking writing from the Teotihuacán and the calendar from the Maya. To support the capital's population, the Aztec developed intensive agriculture based on artificially created islands anchored in Lake Texcoco; Aztec engineers developed an elaborate irrigation system to provide fresh water for both people and crops.

The Aztec collected taxes from conquered people living within a hundred miles of the capital; from those further away, they exacted tribute.

Aztec trading networks extended far from Tenochtitlán, reaching as far north as the American Southwest. However, Aztec expansion was cut short by the arrival of the Spanish in 1519.

Far to the south, the Inca empire was expanding as well. After 1548 Inca conquest created an empire that stretched along the Andes and its adjacent areas. The Inca were highly successful farmers, producing enormous quantities of potatoes, maize, beans, and meats. They constructed terraced irrigation systems on their uneven terrain, perfected freeze-drying and other preservation techniques, and built a vast network of roads and bridges. Inca expansion ended early in the sixteenth century when they were crushed by another even larger empire, the Spanish.

The Southwest

The Southwest (the modern American Southwest and most of northern Mexico) is an arid region of diverse landscapes; however, various peoples managed to establish stable supplies of water and become farmers. Although maize had reached the Southwest as early as 2500 B.C., not until the introduction of drought-resistant strains of the plant around 400 B.C. did large agricultural societies emerge. The two most influential of these were the Hohokam and the Anasazi.

Hohokam culture emerged in the third century B.C. when ancestors of Pima and Tohono O'odham Indians began farming in the Gila River and Salt River valleys of southern Arizona. The Hohokam people built elaborate canal systems for irrigation that enabled them to harvest two crops each year, an amazing feat in such an arid environment. The construction and maintenance of the canals demanded large, coordinated work forces. The Hohokams therefore built permanent villages of several hundred residents, and many such communities were joined in confederations linked by canals. The central village in each confederation coordinated labor, trade, and religious and political life for all.

The Hohokam way of life drew on Mesoamerican materials and ideas. From about the sixth century A.D., the larger Hohokam villages had ball courts and platform mounds such as those in Mesoamerica, and ball games became major public events. Mesoamerican art influenced Hohokam artists, who used clay, stone, turquoise, and shell. Archaeologists have found Mesoamerican items such as rubber balls, macaw feathers, and copper bells at Hohokam sites.

Anasazi culture originated during the first century B.C. in the Four Corners area where Arizona, New Mexico, Colorado, and Utah meet. Although they adopted village life and agriculture late, the Anasazis expanded rapidly in the eighth century A.D. and dominated a wide area.

The Anasazis had a distinctive architecture. They constructed their early dwellings, round pit houses, in the shape of *kivas,* the partly underground, circular structures where Anasazi men conducted religious ceremonies, Anasazi-style apartments and *kivas* are characteristic of the architecture of the modern-day Pueblo Indians of the Southwest.

From the tenth through the mid-twelfth century, an unusually wet period, the Anasazis expanded over much of what today is New Mexico and Arizona. Village populations grew to 1,000 or more. In Chaco Canyon in northwestern New Mexico, a cluster of twelve villages forged a powerful confederation numbering 15,000 people. Perfectly straight roads radiated from the canyon to satellite pueblos up to sixty-five miles away. The builders carved out stairs or footholds in the sides of steep cliffs. The largest village, Pueblo Bonito, had 1,200 inhabitants and two Great Kivas, each fifty feet in diameter. People traveled from outlying areas to Chaco Canyon for religious ceremonies. The Canyon was a major trade center, importing and exporting a wide range of materials from and to Mesoamerica, the Great Plains, the Mississippi Valley, and California.

Devastating droughts in the late twelfth and thirteenth centuries destroyed classic Anasazi culture. Suddenly, the amount of farmland was drastically reduced for a population that had grown rapidly during the preceding centuries. The Indians abandoned the great Anasazi centers and scattered. Other large agricultural communities, such as those of the Hohokam, also dispersed when droughts came. With farming peoples clustered in the few areas with sufficient water, the drier southwestern lands attracted the nonfarming Apaches and Navajos, whose arrival at the end of the thirteenth century ended their long migration from northwestern Canada.

The Eastern Woodlands

Long before they developed agriculture, Indians of the Eastern Woodlands, the vast forests from the Mississippi Valley to the Atlantic coast, experimented with village life and political centralization. By 1200 B.C. about 5,000 people had concentrated in a single village at Poverty Point on the Mississippi River in Louisiana. Two large mounds flanked the village, and six concentric embankments—the largest over half a mile in diameter—surrounded it. During the spring and autumn equinoxes, a person standing on the larger mound could watch the sun rise directly over the village center. Solar observations formed the basis for these Indians' religious beliefs as well as for their calendar.

Poverty Point lay at the center of a large political and economic unit. It imported quartz, copper, obsidian, crystal, and other sacred materials from long distances and distributed them to nearby communities. These communities almost certainly supplied the labor for the earthworks. The Olmec peoples of Mesoamerica clearly influenced the design and organization of Poverty Point. The settlement flourished for only three centuries and then declined, for reasons that are unclear. Nevertheless, it foreshadowed later Mississippi Valley developments.

A different mound-building culture, the Adena, emerged in the Ohio Valley in the fifth century B.C. Adena villages rarely exceeded 400 inhabitants, but the Adena people spread over a wide area and built hundreds of mounds, most of them containing graves. In Adena culture, a person's social and political status apparently determined his or her treatment in death: some corpses were cremated (burned), others were placed in round clay basins, and still others were given elaborate tombs.

During the first century B.C., Adena culture evolved into a more developed and widespread culture known as Hopewell. Hopewell ceremonial centers, larger and more elaborate than those of the Adena, mushroomed along the Ohio and Illinois river valleys. Some centers contained two or three dozen mounds within enclosures of several square miles. The graves of elites contained elaborate burial goods: freshwater pearls, copper ornaments, mica, quartz, or other sacred substances. Hopewell artisans used raw materials from throughout America east of the Rockies. Through trade networks Hopewell influence spread to communities as distant as places in modern-day Wisconsin, Florida, and New York.

The people who created the sophisticated Hopewell culture were primarily hunter-gatherers, not farmers. Although they did grow some crops, agriculture became a dietary mainstay for Woodlands people only between the seventh and twelfth centuries A.D.

The first full-time farmers in the East were the Mississippians, who lived on the flood plains of the Mississippi River and its major tributaries. Their culture incorporated elements from the Hopewell culture and new ideas from Mesoamerica into their own traditions. The volume of Mississippian craft production and of long-distance trade dwarfed those of the Hopewell and Adena cultures. Mississippian towns, containing hundreds or even thousands of people, were built around open plazas like those of central Mexico. Religious temples and elite residences stood atop large mounds next to the plazas. Religious ceremonies focused on worship of the sun as the source of agricultural fertility. Chiefs claimed to be related to the sun, and when they died, wives and servants were killed to accompany them to the afterlife. Artisans produced sophisticated work in clay, stone, shell, copper, and wood, largely for religious and funeral rituals.

Many Mississippian centers were built not by local people but by outsiders seeking to combine farming and riverborne trade. By the tenth century most Mississippian centers were part of larger confederacies based on trade and shared religious beliefs. Powerful "supercenters" and their chiefs dominated these confederacies. The most power-ful confederacy revolved around the magnificent city of Cahokia, near modern St. Louis; its influence extended from the Appalachians to the edge of the Plains and from the Great Lakes to the Gulf of Mexico.

A city of about 20,000 people, Cahokia covered more than 6 square miles and contained more than 120 earthworks. At its center a four-terraced structure called Monk's Mound covered fifteen acres (more than the Great Pyramid of Egypt) and rose 100 feet at its highest point. Surrounding the city, a 125-square-mile metropolitan area encompassed ten large towns and more than fifty farming villages. In addition, Cahokia dominated a giant network of commercial and political alliances extending over much of the American heartland. Like other Mississippian societies, Cahokia, influenced by ideas and crops from Mexico, erected ever-more-complex political, economic, and religious institutions. Many scholars believe that by the twelfth century, Cahokia was the capital of a potential nation-state. *hc* Primary Source: Cahokia

Cahokia reigned supreme for two and a half centuries, but by the thirteenth century, it and allied centers were beginning to suffer food shortages. Neighboring peoples challenged them militarily, and the inhabitants fled. By the fifteenth century, Indians in the central Mississippi Valley were living in small villages linked by mutual interdependence, not coercion. Similar temple-mound centers in the Southeast also declined, and although new centers rose, European diseases destroyed them after 1500.

The Mississippians profoundly affected native culture in the East. They spread not only new strains of corn and beans but also the techniques and tools to cultivate them. Only northern New England and the upper Great Lakes had growing seasons too short for corn to become a reliable crop.

Woodlands tribes employed slash-and-burn techniques, which were environmentally sound as well as economically productive. Indian men systematically burned hardwood forests to form open expanses of land. The grass and berry bushes that flourished there attracted deer and other game, while some areas of the ash-enriched soil were

Cahokia Mounds
This contemporary painting conveys Cahokia's grand scale. Not until the late eighteenth century did another North American city (Philadelphia) surpass the population of Cahokia, c. 1150.

planted in corn, beans, and pumpkins. After several years of abundant harvests, yields declined and the Indians repeated the process on another area; ground cover restored the fertility of the abandoned areas, permitting the Indians to return.

Nonfarming Societies

Along the Pacific coast, from Alaska to southern California, improvements in the production and storage of food enabled Indians to develop more settled ways of life than their Archaic forebearers. From the Alaskan panhandle to northern California, natives spent brief periods each year catching salmon and other fish. The Northwest Coast Indians dried and stored enough fish to last the year, and their seasonal movements gradually gave way to settled life in permanent villages of cedar-plank houses. In the Columbia Plateau, Indians built villages of pit houses and ate salmon through the summer. They left these communities in spring and fall for hunting and gathering.

By A.D. 1 many Northwest Coast villages numbered several hundred people. Trade and warfare strengthened the power of chiefs and other leaders, whose families had greater wealth and prestige than commoners. Leading families proclaimed their status in elaborate totem poles depicting supernatural beings linked to their ancestors and in potlatches, ceremonies in which the Indians gave away or destroyed much of their material wealth. The artistic and architectural achievements of Northwest Coast Indians awed Europeans. "What must astonish most [observers]," a French explorer wrote in 1791, "is to see painting everywhere, everywhere sculpture, among a nation of hunters."

At about the same time, Indians farther south, along the coast and in the interior valleys of what is now California, began to live in villages of one hundred or more people. Acorns dominated their diet, supplementing game, fish, and plants. After the fall harvest, Indians ground the acorns into meal, leached them of bitter tannic acid, and then roasted, boiled, or baked the nuts before eating or storing them. Intense competition for acorns forced California bands to define territorial boundaries rigidly and to combine several villages under a single chief. Chiefs conducted trade, diplomacy, and religious ceremonies with neighboring groups and, when necessary, led their people in battle.

The end of the Archaic period produced little change in the forbidding aridity of the Great Basin, encompassing present-day Nevada, western Utah, southern Idaho, and eastern Oregon. The area continued to support small hunting and gathering bands. Change came only in the fourteenth or fifteenth century A.D. when Paiute, Ute, and Shoshone Indians absorbed or displaced earlier inhabitants across the Great Basin. The newcomers' more efficient seed processing enabled them to support increased populations, which in turn occupied ever-larger territories.

NORTH AMERICAN PEOPLES ON THE EVE OF EUROPEAN CONTACT

In 1492 the entire Western Hemisphere had about 75 million people, clustered thickly in Mexico and Central America, the Caribbean islands, and Peru. Between 7 and 10 million Native Americans lived north of Mexico. Sparse nomad populations inhabited the Great Basin, the high plains, and the northern forests. Denser concentrations, however, thrived along the Pacific coast, in the Southwest and Southeast, in the Mississippi Valley, and along the Atlantic coast. Speaking many diverse languages and dialects, these people constituted several hundred Indian nations and tribes. But for all Native Americans, the most important social groups were the family, clan, and village.

Despite the vast diversity of Native American cultures, they shared many characteristics. Kinship, reciprocity, and communal control of resources lay at the base of Indian societies, while trade ensured that the bow and arrow, ceramic pottery, and certain religious practices existed in almost all Indian societies.

Kinship and Gender

Kinship and gender cemented societies north of Mesoamerica together. Ties to cousins, aunts, and uncles created complex patterns of social obligation.

Kinship bonds were more important in Indian society than the bonds within nuclear families, that is, among married couples and their children. Indians did not necessarily expect spouses to be bound together forever; but kinship lasted for life. Divorce thus did not threaten the social order. Customs regulating marriage varied, but strict rules prevailed. In most cultures young people married in their teens, generally after a period of sexual experimentation. Although male leaders sometimes took several wives, nuclear families never stood alone. Instead, strong ties of residence and deference bound each couple to one or both sets of parents, producing what social scientists call extended families.

In some Native American societies such as the Iroquois, the extended families of women took precedence over those of men. A new husband moved in with his wife's extended family. The mother's oldest brother was the primary male authority figure in a child's life. In many ways, a husband and father was simply the guest of his wife's family. Other Indian societies recognized men's extended families as primary, while still others did not distinguish sharply between the status of male and female family lines.

In addition, kinship was the basis for armed conflict. Indian societies typically considered homicide a matter to be resolved by the extended families of the victim and the perpetrator. If the perpetrator's family offered a gift that the victim's family considered appropriate, the question was settled. If not, the victim's kin might avenge the killing by armed retaliation. Chiefs or other leaders intervened to resolve disputes within the same village or tribe, but disputes between members of different groups could escalate into war. Densely populated societies that competed for scarce resources, as on the California coast, and centralized societies that attempted to dominate trade networks through

MAP 1.1

Locations of Selected Native American Peoples, A.D. 1500

Today's Indian nations were well established in homelands across the continent when Europeans first arrived. Many would combine with others or move in later centuries, either voluntarily or because they were forced. **hc** Interactive Map: Peopling of the Americas

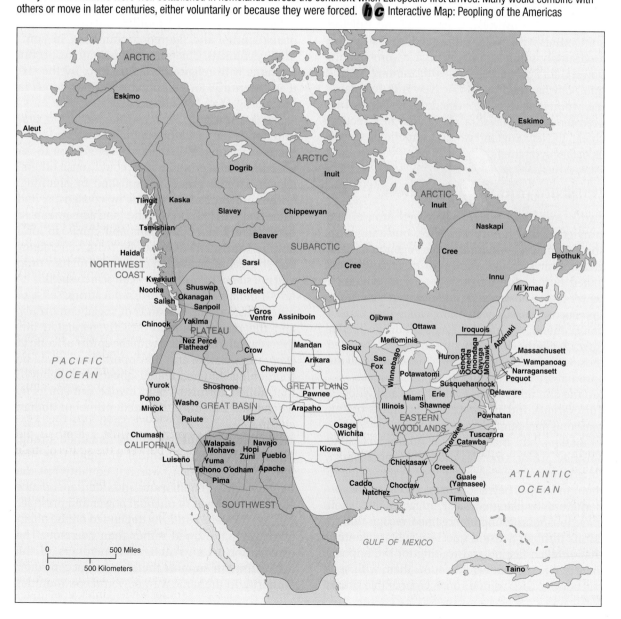

coercion, such as the Hopewell culture, experienced frequent and intense warfare. However, warfare remained a low-level affair in most of North America. An exasperated New England officer, writing of his effort to win Indian allies in the early seventeenth century, described a battle between two Indian groups as "more for pastime than to conquer and subdue enemies." He concluded that "they might fight seven years and not kill seven men."

Among almost all agricultural Indians except those in the Southwest, women did most of the cultivating. With women producing most of the food supply, some communities gave women more power than European societies did. Among the Iroquois of what today is upstate New York, for example, women collectively owned the fields, distributed food, and played a major role in selecting chiefs. In New England women sometimes served as *sachems,* or chiefs.

Spiritual and Social Values

Native American religions revolved around the conviction that nature was alive, pulsating with spiritual power—*manitou* in the Algonquian language. A mysterious, awe-inspiring force that affected human life for both good and evil, such power united all nature in an unbroken web. *Manitou* encompassed "every thing which they cannot comprehend," wrote the English Puritan leader Roger Williams. Belief in supernatural power led most Indians to seek constantly to conciliate all the spiritual forces in nature: living things, rocks, water, the sun and moon, even ghosts and witches. For example, Indians prayed to the spirits of animals that they hunted.

Indians had many ways of gaining access to spiritual power. One was dreaming; most Native Americans took seriously the visions that came to them in sleep. They also sought access to the supernatural by using physical ordeals to alter their consciousness. Young men gained recognition as adults through a vision quest—a solitary venture that entailed fasting and waiting for the appearance of a spirit that would endow them with special powers. Girls went through comparable rituals

at the onset of menstruation to initiate them into the spiritual world from which female reproductive power flowed. Entire communities often engaged in collective power-seeking rituals such as the Sun Dance (see Chapter 17).

Indians normally relied on those with special powers to understand the unseen. These medicine men and women were healers who used medicinal plants and magical chants, but their role went further. They interpreted dreams, guided vision quests and other ceremonies, invoked war or peace spirits, and figured prominently in community councils. Chiefs had to maintain respectful relations with religious leaders, who, by the sixteenth century, formed organized priesthoods in the Southeast and Southwest.

Native American societies demanded cooperation. From early childhood, Indians learned to be accommodating and reserved—careful not to reveal their feelings before they could sense others'. Indian parents generally punished by shaming. Communities made decisions by consensus, and leaders articulated slowly emerging agreements in passionate oratory. Shamans and chiefs, in John Smith's words, spoke in public "with vehemency and so great passions that they sweat till they drop and are so out of breath they can scarce speak."

All Indian cultures possessed a strong sense of order. Custom, the demands of social conformity, and the rigors of nature strictly regulated life. Everyday affairs mingled with the spiritual world at every turn. Nature and the supernatural could be frightening. Indians feared ghosts and believed that nonconformists could invoke evil spirits by witchcraft, the most dreaded crime in Indian cultures.

The principle of reciprocity remained strong. Although it involved mutual give-and-take, the purpose of reciprocity was not equality but the maintenance of equilibrium and interdependence among individuals of unequal power and prestige.

Most leaders' authority depended on the obligations they bestowed rather than coercion. The distribution of gifts obligated members of the community to support them and to accept their authority. In the same way, powerful communities

Chronology

c. 13,000 B.C. People present in America.

c. 10,500–9000 B.C. Paleo-Indians spread throughout Western Hemisphere.

c. 9000 B.C. Extinction of big-game mammals.

c. 8000 B.C. Archaic era begins.

c. 7000 B.C. Athapaskan-speaking peoples arrive in North America.

c. 5000 B.C. First domesticated plants grown.

c. 3000 B.C. First maize grown in Mesoamerica.

c. 3000–2000 B.C. Eskimo and Aleut peoples arrive in North America.

c. 2500 B.C. Archaic societies yield before diverse cultures. First maize grown in North America.

c. 1200 B.C. First chiefdoms emerge.

c. 1200 B.C. Poverty Point flourishes in Louisiana.

c. 400–100 B.C. Adena culture flourishes in Ohio Valley.

c. 250 B.C. Hohokam culture begins in Southwest.

c. 100 B.C. Anasazi culture begins in Southwest.

c. 100 B.C.–A.D. 600 Hopewell culture thrives in Midwest.

C. A.D. 1 Rise of chiefdoms on Northwest Coast and in California.

c. 100–700 Teotihuacán flourishes in Mesoamerica.

c. 600–1400 Mayan kingdoms flourish.

c. 700 Mississippian culture begins. Anasazi expansion begins.

c. 900 Urban center arises at Cahokia.

c. 1200 Anasazi and Hohokam peoples disperse in Southwest.

c. 1200–1400 Cahokia declines, inhabitants disperse.

1428 Rise of Aztec Empire.

1438 Rise of Inca Empire.

1492 Christopher Columbus reaches Western Hemisphere.

---

distributed gifts to weaker neighbors who reciprocated with tribute in the form of material goods and submission.

CONCLUSION *hc* ACE Practice Test

Native American history did not begin with Christopher Columbus's arrival. Despite what Europeans thought, they did not encounter an unchanging world of simple savages. Rather, for thousands of years native cultures and societies had transformed North America into a human habitat. Over millennia Indians learned the properties, uses, and values of plants, animals, soils, rocks, and minerals as well as the cycles of months, seasons, and years. Hunting camps, villages, cornfields, and trails transformed the landscape. Although occasionally wasteful—Plains Indians stampeding herds of bison over cliffs often killed far more animals than they could eat—Native Americans seem to have learned painful lessons from the collapse of the Anasazi and Cahokia cultures.

After 1500 a new attitude toward the land made itself felt in North America. Certain that God had given Christians dominion over nature, European newcomers claimed vast expanses of territory for their crowned heads. They divided the land into plots owned by an individual or family and valued it according to the wealth it produced, ignoring Indian strategies that had allowed natural resources to renew themselves. The modern society that has arisen on the Indians' ancient continent bears little resemblance to the world that Native Americans once knew.

FURTHER READING

The Cambridge History of the Native Peoples of the Americas (3 vols., 1996–2000). Authoritative essays by archaeologists and historians covering the entire expanse of Native American history.

Cheryl Claassen and Rosemary A. Joyce, eds. *Women in Prehistory: North America and Mesoamerica* (1997). Essays draw on archaeological evidence to examine women's roles and gender identity in a range of North American societies.

Thomas D. Dillehay, *The Settlement of the Americas: A New Prehistory* (2000). An excellent review of current scholarly debates on the earliest Americans.

Brian Fagan, *Ancient North America: The Archaeology of a Continent* (1991). An informative, comprehensive introduction to the continent's history before Europeans' arrival.

Alvin M. Josephy, Jr., *America in 1492: The World of the Indian Peoples Before the Arrival of Columbus* (1992). Outstanding essays on life in the Western Hemisphere on the eve of European contact.

Shepard Krech III, *The Ecological Indian: Myth and History* (1999). A controversial critique of the idea that Indians invariably lived in harmony with nature before Europeans arrived.

William C. Sturtevant, gen. ed., *Handbook of North American Indians* (20 vols. projected, 1978–). A reference work, still in progress, providing basic information on the history and culture of virtually every known native society.

Lawrence E. Sullivan, ed., *Native American Religions: North America* (1989). Essays focusing on religious life throughout the continent.

Bartholomew Gosnold Trading with Wampanoag Indians at Martha's Vineyard, Massachusetts, by Theodore De Bry, 1634

2

The Rise of the Atlantic World, 1400–1625

 This icon will direct you to additional study and research resources at http://college.hmco.com/history/us/boyer/enduring_concise/5e/students/index.html

At ten o'clock on a moonlit night the tense crew spotted a glimmering light. At two o'clock the next morning came the shout "Land! Land!" It was October 12, 1492. At daybreak Christopher Columbus went ashore, the royal standard of Spain fluttering, knelt to give thanks, and rose to claim the island that he named San Salvador for Spain.

Columbus's crew quickly learned to savor the tobacco grown on the islands and to trade with the local Taino Indians for golden ornaments. Certain he had reached Asia, and taking with him various souvenirs, including several "Indians," Columbus sailed home to tell of "a land to be desired and, once seen, never to be left."

Columbus's achievement was a critical step in the formation of an Atlantic world. After 1492 peoples from Europe, Africa, and North and South America became intertwined in elaborate webs of trade, colonization, religion, and wars. These interchanges constantly challenged

This chapter focuses on four major questions:

▶ How did trade and political centralization transform West Africa before the advent of the Atlantic slave trade?

▶ How did European monarchs use commerce and religion to advance their nations' fortunes?

▶ What role did the Columbian exchange play in the formation of an Atlantic world?

▶ Why did Native Americans sometimes welcome, and sometimes resist, European traders and colonizers?

customary ways of thinking and acting. They also led to far-reaching environmental changes as not only people but also plants and animals crossed the Atlantic in both directions, a process known as "the Columbian exchange." European nations sought to increase their wealth and power by conquering and exploiting the inhabitants of the Americas, whom they deemed noncivilized.

In much of what is now Latin America, the arrival of the Europeans led to conquest. In the future United States and Canada, however, European mastery came more slowly; more than one hundred years would pass before self-sustaining colonies were established. Nevertheless, from the moment of Columbus's landing on October 12, 1492, the American continents became the stage for the encounter of Native American, European, and African peoples in the emerging Atlantic world.

AFRICAN AND EUROPEAN PEOPLES

Even before the emergence of the Atlantic world in the fifteenth and sixteenth centuries, the four con-

tinents bordering the Atlantic were changing. In the Americas, societies rose and fell (see Chapter 1). In Africa, the growth of long-distance trade enabled some empires to flourish as a market economy developed alongside older social and religious customs. In Europe, ambitious monarchs joined forces with merchants to propel territorial expansion. At the same time, an intellectual revolution, the Renaissance, would help spawn a religious revolution, the Reformation.

Mediterranean Crossroads

Africans, Asians, and Europeans had met, traded, and warred on the Mediterranean Sea since ancient times. By 1400, West African gold enriched Turkish sultans, European guns strengthened North African rulers, and Indian spices stimulated Italian palates. Caravans laden with goods crossed the Sahara to North African ports, to be exchanged for goods carried from China and India across Central Asia. Seagoing merchants linked Africa with Asia, the Arabian peninsula with India and China. But before the fifteenth century, intercontinental travel and trade were unknown on the Atlantic Ocean.

Religion and politics intertwined with trade. From the seventh to the fourteenth centuries, Muslim conquerors spread Islam from Southeast Asia to West Africa and much of southern Europe. At the same time Christian rulers carried their faith deep into central and northern Europe. Islam and Christianity alike provided a common faith and identity to peoples spread across vast distances, reinforcing their emerging political and economic ties.

For centuries Christians and Muslims traded with one another in relative harmony. But, in the eleventh century, European Christians began a long series of crusades to take back formerly Christian lands in Europe and the Middle East from the Muslims. In turn, Muslim leaders declared *jihad* (holy war) against the Christians. The Spanish waged a long war of "reconquista" to drive Muslims from the Iberian Peninsula, a war that culminated in complete victory for Christian Spain in 1492.

Mali Horseman, c. 13th–14th century
This terra-cotta figure originated in Mali, one of several powerful empires in West Africa before the arrival of Europeans.

West Africa and Its Peoples

Before the beginning of Atlantic travel, the only link between sub-Saharan Africa and the Mediterranean was a broad belt of grassland, or savanna, that separates the desert from the forests to the south. Here caravan trade stimulated the rise of kingdoms and empires whose size and wealth rivaled any in Europe.

The richest grassland kingdoms rose in West Africa, with its ample stores of gold. Chief among these in the fifteenth century was Mali, whose Muslim rulers enjoyed access to a network of wealthy Muslim rulers and merchants. Mali's wealth rested on the careful cultivation of trade, and its fame extended throughout Africa, Europe, and the Middle East. Its best-known city, Timbuktu, was famed for its intellectual and academic vitality and its beautiful architecture.

However, Mali fell victim to internal strife early in the fifteenth century; a successor state, Songhai, prospered for less than a century before it was absorbed by Morocco.

Compared to the savanna empires, coastal West Africa was relatively insignificant. During the first millennium A.D., small Islamic states arose in Senegambia, at Africa's westernmost bulge, and in Guinea's coastal forests. The best-known state was Benin, where artisans fashioned magnificent ironwork for centuries.

Near the Congo River still farther south, four major kingdoms had arisen by the fifteenth century. The most powerful of these kingdoms was Kongo.

When most European nations adopted gold as the standard for their currencies in the fifteenth century, gold-rich Guinea's population soared. Thousands of newcomers from the savanna and Central Africa surged into Africa's "Gold Coast," and new states emerged to capitalize on the precious metal. None was as extensive or powerful as Mali or Ghana at their height.

West African leaders wielded sharply different amounts and kinds of political power. Grassland emperors claimed semigodlike status, which they only thinly disguised after adopting Islam. Rulers of smaller kingdoms depended on their ability to persuade, to conform to custom, and sometimes to redistribute wealth justly among their people.

In West Africa, kinship groups knitted societies together. Parents, aunts, uncles, distant cousins, and those who shared clan ties formed networks of mutual obligation. In centuries to come, the tradition of strong extended families would help enslaved Africans to endure the breakup of nuclear families by sale. West Africans saw marriage as a way for families to forge mutually beneficial alliances. A prospective husband made a payment to his bride's kin to acknowledge the relative prestige of his own and his bride's kin groups. Wives generally maintained lifelong links with their own kin group, and children traced descent through the mother's bloodline. These traditions buttressed women's standing in society.

The region's high mortality rate from famine and tropical disease epidemics was a driving force behind marriage. Children were an essential part of the labor force, contributing to a family's wealth by increasing its food production and the amount of land it cultivated. Men of means frequently married more than one wife in order to produce more children; women generally married soon after puberty.

Both men and women farmed. The high ratio of land to people enabled African farmers to shift their fields periodically and thus maintain high soil quality and productivity. Like many North American Indians, Africans relied on burning to clear fertile land, returning periodically to the same sites. In areas of coastal rain forest food crops such as yams, sugar cane, bananas, and eggplant flourished; so too did cotton. On the grasslands cattle raising and fishing complemented the cultivation of millet, sorghum, and rice.

By the fifteenth century the market economy took in many small farmers, who traded surplus crops for other food and cloth. Artisans wove cotton or raffia palm leaves, made clothing and jewelry, and crafted tools and religious objects.

Religion permeated African life. People believed that another world lay beyond the one they perceived through their five senses, a world the souls of most people passed to at death. Deities spoke to mortals through a variety of means, including priests, dreams, "speaking shrines," and magical charms. West African religions emphasized the importance of continuous revelations; consequently there was no fixed dogma or hierarchy such as characterized both Islam and Christianity. African religion also emphasized ancestor worship, venerating ancestors as spiritual guardians. Religious motifs saturated African art. West Africans used their ivory, cast-iron, and wood sculptures in ceremonies reenacting creation

myths and honoring spirits. A strong moralistic streak ran through African folktales. Oral reciters transmitted these stories in dramatic public presentations with ritual masks, dance, and music of a complex rhythmic structure. West African art and music powerfully influenced twentieth-century art and jazz.

Among Africans, Islam appealed primarily to merchants trading with Muslim North Africa and to grassland rulers eager to consolidate their power. By the sixteenth century, Islam had only just begun to affect the daily lives of grassland cultivators and artisans. Christianity, which accompanied the Portuguese to Africa in the fifteenth and sixteenth centuries, had limited impact on Africans until the nineteenth century.

European Culture and Society

When Columbus reached the New World in 1492, Europe was approaching the height of a cultural revival known as the Renaissance, the rebirth of classical Greek and Roman culture. Intellectuals and poets believed that their age marked a return to the ideals of the ancient Greeks and Romans. The writings of Muslim, Eastern Orthodox, and Jewish scholars provided a treasure trove of ancient texts in philosophy, science, medicine, geography, and other subjects. Scholars strove to reconcile Christian faith and ancient philosophy, to explore the mysteries of nature, to map the world, and to explain the motions of the heavens. Renaissance painters and sculptors created works glowing with idealized human beauty.

But European society was quivering with tension. The era's artistic and intellectual creativity stemmed partly from intense social and spiritual stress as Europeans groped for stability by glorifying order, hierarchy, and beauty. A concern for power and rank, or "degree," dominated European life in the fifteenth and sixteenth centuries. Gender, wealth, inherited position, and political power affected every European's status, and few lived beyond the reach of some political authority's claim to tax and rule. But this order was shaky. Conflicts between ranks, between religions, and between rich and poor threatened the balance, making

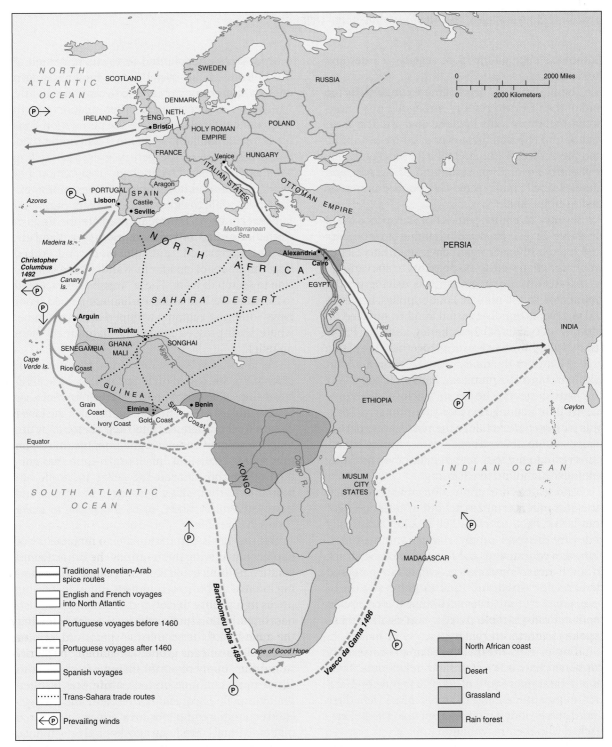

Map 2.1

Europe, Africa, and Southwestern Asia in 1500

During the fifteenth century, Portugal led the way in integrating Europe with Africa in a new Atlantic world. Several voyages near the end of the century extended Europe's reach to India and the Americas. *hc* Interactive Map: Western Africa and Atlantic Slave Trade.

Map labels:

NORTH ATLANTIC OCEAN
SCOTLAND
SWEDEN
RUSSIA
DENMARK
NETH.
IRELAND
ENG.
Bristol
HOLY ROMAN EMPIRE
POLAND
FRANCE
HUNGARY
Venice
ITALIAN STATES
OTTOMAN EMPIRE
PORTUGAL
Aragon
SPAIN
Lisbon
Castile
Azores
Seville
Madeira Is.
Mediterranean Sea
NORTH AFRICA
Alexandria
Cairo
PERSIA
Christopher Columbus 1492
Canary Is.
EGYPT
SAHARA DESERT
Nile R.
Red Sea
INDIA
Arguin
Timbuktu
SONGHAI
SENEGAMBIA
GHANA
MALI
Niger R.
Cape Verde Is.
Rice Coast
GUINEA
Grain Coast
Elmina
Benin
Ivory Coast
Gold Coast
Slave Coast
ETHIOPIA
Ceylon
Equator
KONGO
Congo R.
MUSLIM CITY STATES
INDIAN OCEAN
SOUTH ATLANTIC OCEAN
Bartolomeu Dias 1488
Cape of Good Hope
Vasco da Gama 1496
MADAGASCAR

Legend:

Traditional Venetian-Arab spice routes
English and French voyages into North Atlantic
Portuguese voyages before 1460
Portuguese voyages after 1460
Spanish voyages
Trans-Sahara trade routes
Prevailing winds

North African coast
Desert
Grassland
Rain forest

Scale: 0 — 2000 Miles / 0 — 2000 Kilometers

Europeans cling all the more eagerly to order and hierarchy.

Change lay at the heart of these conflicts. By the end of the fifteenth century, strong national monarchs in France and England had unified their realms and reduced the power of both the nobility and the Catholic Church. On the Iberian Peninsula, the marriage of King Ferdinand of Aragon and Queen Isabella had created the Spanish monarchy and a unified Spain.

Seventy to eighty percent of Europeans were peasants. Taxes, rents, and other dues to landlords and church officials were heavy. Poor harvests or war drove even well-to-do peasants to starvation.

By 1600 dramatic growth was driving up the population to 100 million. Food supplies, however, did not rise as rapidly. Peasant families survived on pitifully low yields of wheat, barley, and oats. Plowing, sowing, and harvesting together, they also grazed livestock on jointly owned "commons." But with new land at a premium, landlords, especially the English gentry, began to "enclose" the commons, thus making them private property. Peasants with no *written* title to their lands were particularly vulnerable. Those with strong titles, however, could either keep their land or profit by joining the landlord in enclosing.

Land scarcity and population growth worsened peasants' circumstances, as did a "little Ice Age" that lasted from roughly 1600 to 1800, drastically reducing the food supply. Hunger and malnutrition were widespread, and full-scale famine struck in some areas. Population growth led to increased demand for wood and thus to deforestation of large areas; the subsequent disappearance of wild foods and game accelerated the exodus of rural Europeans to towns and cities.

Though numerous, European towns usually contained only a few thousand inhabitants. London, a great metropolis of 200,000 people by 1600, was an exception. Large or small, towns were dirty and disease-ridden, and townspeople lived close-packed with their neighbors.

People of the times saw towns as centers of opportunity for the ambitious. Immigration from the countryside therefore swelled urban populations.

But peasants transplanted to towns remained at the bottom of the social order, unable to earn enough money to marry and to live independently.

The consequences of rapid population growth were acute in England, where the population doubled from 2.5 million in 1500 to 5 million by 1620. Some members of the gentry grew rich selling wool, but because of technological stagnation, per capita output and household income among textile workers fell. In effect, more workers competed for fewer jobs as European markets for English cloth diminished and as food prices rose. Land enclosure aggravated unemployment and forced large numbers of people to wander the countryside in search of work. These "vagabonds" seemed to threaten law and order. Parliament passed "Poor Laws" ordering vagrants whipped and sent home, where hard-pressed taxpayers maintained them on relief.

As in the New World and Africa, traditional society in Europe rested on long-term, reciprocal relationships. Reciprocity required the upper classes to act with self-restraint and dignity and the lower classes to show deference to their "betters." It demanded strict economic regulation, too, to ensure that sellers charged a "just" price—one that covered costs and allowed the seller to profit but barred him from taking advantage of buyers' and borrowers' misfortunes, or of shortages, to make "excessive" profits.

Yet the ideals of traditional economic behavior had been withering for centuries. By the sixteenth century, nothing could stop the practices of charging interest on borrowed money and of increasing prices in response to demand. New forms of business organization such as the joint-stock company, the ancestor of the modern corporation, steadily spread. Demand for capital investment grew, and so did the supply of accumulated wealth. Gradually, a new economic outlook arose that justified the unimpeded acquisition of wealth and unregulated economic competition. Its adherents insisted that individuals owed one another only the money necessary to settle each market transaction. This "market economy" capitalism stood counter to traditional demands for the strict regulation of economic activity to ensure social reciprocity and to maintain "just prices."

Sixteenth- and seventeenth-century Europeans therefore were ambivalent about economic enterprise and social change. A restless desire for opportunity kept life simmering with competitive tension. However, even those who prospered still sought the security and prestige of traditional social distinctions, and the poor longed for the age-old values that they hoped would restrain irresponsible greed.

Fundamental change in European society could also be seen in the rising importance of the nuclear family. Each member of the family—father, mother, children—had specific roles. The father exercised supreme authority; the wife bore and reared children and assisted her husband in the unending labor of providing for the family's subsistence. Children were laborers from an early age. The family was thus the principal economic unit in European society, and the household the primary social organization. Those who lived outside a household were viewed with extreme suspicion and became easy targets for accusations of theft or even witchcraft. The nuclear family represented a "little commonwealth" within which the father's rule mirrored God's rule over Creation and kings' lordship over their subjects. The ideal, according to a German writer, was that "wives should obey their husbands and not seek to dominate them; they must manage the home efficiently. Husbands . . . should treat their wives with consideration and occasionally close an eye to their faults." In practice, however, the father's domination often had to make room for the wife's management of family affairs and her assistance in running the farm or the workshop.

Religious Upheavals

Sixteenth-century Europeans believed in the biblical explanation of the origins of the world and its peoples. Christianity taught that Jesus Christ, God's Son, redeemed sinners through his crucifixion and resurrection. As real as God to European Christians was the devil, Satan, who lured people to damnation by tempting them to do evil. Jewish and Muslim European minorities shared Christians' worship of a single supreme being, based on the God of the Old Testament. But many sixteenth-century Europeans also believed in witchcraft, magic, and astrology.

The medieval Christian church taught that Christ had founded the church to save sinners from hell. Every time a priest said Mass, Christ's sacrifice was repeated, and divine grace flowed to sinners through sacraments that priests alone could administer—especially baptism, confession, and the Eucharist (communion). In most of Europe the "church" was a huge network of clergymen set apart from laypeople by ordination into the priesthood and by the fact that they did not marry. The pope, the "vicar (representative) of Christ," topped this hierarchy. His authority reached throughout most of central and western Europe.

The papacy wielded awesome spiritual power. Fifteenth- and sixteenth-century popes claimed the authority to dispense extra blessings, or "indulgences," to repentant sinners in return for "good works," such as donating money to the church. Indulgences also promised time off from future punishment in purgatory. Given people's anxieties over sin, indulgences were enormously popular. A German seller of indulgences even advertised that

> As soon as the coin in the cash box rings,
> The soul from purgatory's fire springs.

But the sale of indulgences provoked charges of materialism and corruption. In 1517 Martin Luther, a German friar, attacked the practice. When the papacy tried to silence him, Luther broadened his criticism to include the Mass, priests, and the pope. His revolt sparked the Protestant Reformation, which changed Christianity forever.

To Luther, the selling of indulgences was evil not only because it bilked people but also because the church did harm by falsely assuring people that they could "earn" salvation by doing good works. Luther believed instead that God alone chose whom to save and that believers should trust only

God's love, not the word of priests and the pope. Luther's own spiritual struggle and experience of being "born again" constituted a classic conversion experience—the heart of Protestant religion as it would be preached and practiced for centuries in England and North America.

Later reformers challenged Luther. For example, French theologian John Calvin insisted on the doctrine of predestination, in which an omnipotent God "predestined" most sinful humans to hell, saving only a few to exemplify his grace. Calvinists and Lutherans, as the followers of the two Reformation leaders came to be called, alike were horrified by radical Protestants such as the Anabaptists, who criticized the rich and powerful and restricted baptism to adults who had undergone a conversion.

Despite such differences, Protestants shared much common ground. Reading the Bible became an essential element of faith; translations into living languages made the Bible accessible, and the newly invented printing press allowed for wide circulation. Protestantism thus fostered education. Protestants also rejected the idea that priests had special powers; each individual had to assume responsibility for his or her own spiritual and moral condition. Finally, many Protestants felt displaced by the rapidly changing European world and yearned for greater simplicity. Thus Protestantism condemned the replacement of traditional reciprocity by marketplace values. Instead it nurtured individuals of strong moral determination and equipped them with the fortitude to survive and prosper amid the temptations of worldly wealth.

Challenged by the rise of Protestantism, the Catholic church displayed remarkable resilience. Indeed, the papacy vigorously attacked church corruption and combated Protestant viewpoints. The popes also sponsored a new religious order committed to the papacy, the Jesuits, whose members would distinguish themselves for centuries as teachers, missionaries, and royal advisers. This Catholic revival, known as the Counter-Reformation, created the modern Roman Catholic church.

The Reformation also split Europe geographically. Many northern and western European areas, including England, most of the German states, the Netherlands, and parts of France, become predominantly Protestant; most southern European states,—Portugal, Spain, and Italy—and most of France remained Roman Catholic.

The Reformation in England, 1533–1625

England's Reformation began when King Henry VIII, anxious for a male heir, tried to annul his marriage to Catherine of Aragon. When the pope refused to do so, Henry persuaded Parliament to annul the marriage and then to proclaim him "supreme head" of the Church of England (the Anglican church).

Religious strife troubled England for over a century after Henry's break with Rome. Under his son Edward VI (ruled 1547–1553), however, the English church veered sharply toward Protestantism. Then Henry's daughter Mary assumed the throne in 1553 and tried to restore Catholicism, in part by burning several hundred Protestants at the stake.

The reign of Mary's successor, Elizabeth I, who became queen in 1558, marked a crucial watershed. Most English people were now Protestant; *how* Protestant was the question. A militant Calvinist minority, the Puritans, demanded wholesale "purification" of the Church of England from "popish abuses." As Calvinists, they affirmed salvation by predestination, denied Christ's presence in the Eucharist, and believed that a learned sermon was the heart of true worship. They wished to free each congregation from outside interference and encouraged lay members to participate in parish affairs.

Puritanism appealed mainly to the growing middle sectors of English society—the gentry, university-educated clergymen and intellectuals, merchants, shopkeepers, artisans, and well-to-do peasants. Self-discipline had become central to both the worldly and the spiritual dimensions of these people's lives, and from their ranks would come the settlers of New England (see Chapter 3). Puritanism attracted few of the titled nobility, who enjoyed their wealth and privilege, and few of the desperately poor, who were struggling for mere survival.

Queen Elizabeth distrusted Puritan militancy until the pope declared her a heretic in 1570 and urged Catholics to overthrow her. By courting influential Puritans and embracing militant anti-Catholicism, Elizabeth maintained most Puritans' loyalty. But after her death, religious tensions came to a boil.

Under Elizabeth, most Puritans expected to transform the Church of England into independent congregations of "saints." However, Stuart monarchs, James I (ruled 1603–1625) and Charles I (ruled 1625–1649), bitterly opposed Puritan efforts to eliminate the office of bishop. Recognizing that Puritan attacks on bishops were a direct threat to his throne, he snapped, "No bishop, no king." Nonetheless James quietly tolerated Calvinists who did not dissent loudly.

EUROPE AND THE ATLANTIC WORLD, 1440–1600

At the start of the fifteenth century, European wealth was concentrated in the Mediterranean city-states such as Venice. By the seventeenth century, much of this wealth had shifted to the Atlantic states, where monarchs were consolidating their power over vast territories in Europe and the Americas. Portugal and Spain emerged as the first great Atlantic powers, leading a new European imperialism across the oceans of the world. From this imperialism would emerge both a trans-Atlantic slave trade and the colonization of new lands; these in turn would lead to a new Atlantic world.

Portugal and the Atlantic, 1440–1600

Merchants realized that they could increase their profits by trading directly with Asia and Africa. Leading the shift to an Atlantic world was Portugal.

Improved maritime technology permitted this European expansion. In the early fifteenth century shipbuilders added the triangular Arab sail to their heavy cargo ships, creating a highly maneuverable

African View of Portuguese, c. 1650–1700 A carver in the kingdom of Benin, on Africa's west coast, created this saltholder depicting Portuguese officials and their ship.

ship, the caravel, to sail the stormy Atlantic. Further, the growing use of the compass and astrolabe permitted mariners to calculate their bearings on the open sea. Hand in hand with the technological advances of this "maritime revolution," Renaissance scholars corrected ancient geographical data and drew increasingly accurate maps. The new geography and sophisticated use of Arabic mathematics sharpened Europeans' knowledge of the world.

Led by Prince Henry "the Navigator," Portugal was first to capitalize on these developments. He encouraged Portuguese seamen to pilot their caravels farther down the African coast searching for weak spots in Muslim defenses and for trade opportunities. By the time of Henry's death, the Portuguese had built a profitable slaving station at Arguin; shortly after, they had penetrated south of the equator. In 1488 Bartolomeu Días reached Africa's southern tip, the Cape of Good Hope, opening the possibility of direct trade with India, and in 1498

Vasco da Gama led a Portuguese fleet around the cape and on to India. For more than a century the Portuguese remained an imperial presence in the Indian Ocean and the East Indies (modern Indonesia). But far more significantly, they brought Europeans face to face with black Africans.

The "New Slavery" and Racism

Slavery was well established in fifteenth-century West Africa, as elsewhere. The grassland emperors as well as individual families depended on slave labor. But most slaves or their children were absorbed into African families over time. First Arabs, and then Europeans, however, turned African slavery into an intercontinental business. A fifteenth-century Italian reported that the Arabs

> have many Berber horses, which they trade, and take to the Land of the Blacks, exchanging them with the rulers for slaves. . . . These slaves are brought to the market town of Hoden. . . . [Some] are taken . . . and sold to the Portuguese lease-holders of Arguin. . . . Every year the Portuguese carry away from [Arguin] a thousand slaves.

The Portuguese exploited existing African commercial and social patterns, often trading slaves and local products to other Africans for gold. The local African kingdoms were too strong for the Portuguese to attack, and black rulers traded—or chose not to trade—according to their own self-interest.

The coming of the Portuguese slavers changed West African societies. Small kingdoms in Guinea and Senegambia expanded to "service" the trade, and some of their rulers became rich. Farther south, in modern Angola, the kings of Kongo used the slave trade to consolidate their power and adopted Christianity. Kongo flourished until attackers from the interior severely weakened it at the end of the sixteenth century. African kings and their communities used the slave trade to dispose of "undesirables," including troublesome slaves, lawbreakers, and persons accused of witchcraft. But most slaves were simply victims of raids or wars. Muslim and European slave trading greatly stimulated conflicts among communities in Africa.

Europeans had used slaves since ancient Greece and Rome, but ominous changes took place in European slavery once the Portuguese began making voyages to Africa. First, the new slave trade was a high-volume business that expanded at a steady rate as Europeans colonized the Western Hemisphere and established plantation societies there. Between 1500 and 1600, perhaps 250,000 African slaves would reach the New World, and 50,000 would perish en route. Between 1601 and 1621, 200,000 more would arrive. Before the Atlantic slave trade ended in the nineteenth century, nearly 12 million Africans would be shipped across the sea. Slavery on this scale had been unknown since the Roman Empire. Second, African slaves received exceptionally harsh treatment. In medieval Europe slaves had primarily performed domestic service, but by 1450 the Portuguese and Spanish had created large slave-labor plantations on their Atlantic and Mediterranean islands. Using African slaves who toiled until death, these plantations produced sugar for European markets. In short, the African slaves owned by Europeans performed exhausting, mindless labor. By 1600 the "new slavery" had become a brutal link in an expanding commerce that ultimately would encompass all major Western nations.

Finally, race became the explicit basis of the "new slavery." Africans' blackness and alien religion dehumanized them in European eyes. As racial prejudice hardened, Europeans found it easy to justify black slavery. European Christianity, moreover, made few attempts to soften slavery's rigors. Because the victims of the "new slavery" were physically distinctive and culturally alien, slavery became a lifelong, hereditary, and despised status.

Europeans Reach America, 1492–1541

The fascinating, contradictory figure of Christopher Columbus (1451–1506) embodied Europeans' varied motives for expansion. The son of an Italian weaver, Columbus became obsessed by the idea that Europeans could reach Asia by sailing westward across the Atlantic. Combining an overesti-

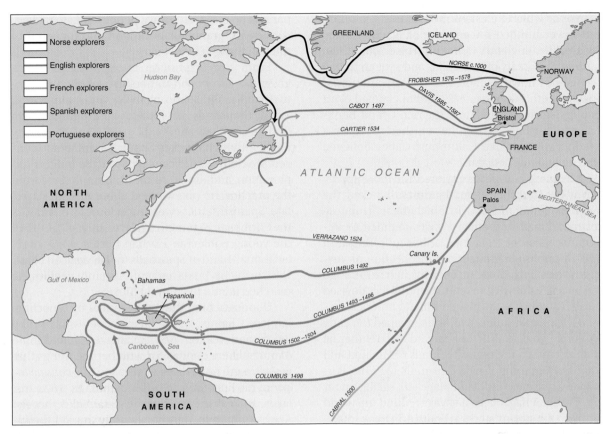

MAP 2.2
Major Transatlantic Explorations, 1000–1587
Following Columbus's 1492 voyage, Spain's rivals soon began laying claim to parts of the New World based on the voyages of Cabot for England, Cabral for Portugal, and Verrazano for France. Later English and French exploration focused on finding a passage to Asia around or through Canada.

mation of Asia's eastward thrust with an underestimation of the earth's circumference, he concluded that the world was much smaller than it actually is and that the open-sea distance from Europe to Asia was roughly 3,000 miles, not the actual 12,000 miles. Religious fervor led Columbus to dream of carrying Christianity around the globe, but he also hungered for wealth and glory.

Europeans had ventured far into the Atlantic before Columbus: besides the early Norse, fifteenth-century English fishers may have reached North America's coast. What distinguished Columbus was his persistence in hawking his "enterprise of the Indies" around Europe's royal courts. In 1492 the rulers of newly united Spain, Isabella of Castile and Ferdinand of Aragon, accepted Columbus's offer, hoping to break a threatened Portuguese monopoly on Asian trade. Picking up the westerly trade winds, Columbus's three small ships made landfall within a month off the North American coast at a small island that he named San Salvador.

Word of Columbus's discovery fired Europeans' imaginations. It also induced the Spanish and Portuguese to sign the Treaty of Tordesillas in 1494, dividing all future discoveries between themselves. Columbus made three further voyages, in the course of which he established Spanish colonies, but never fulfilled his promise of reaching Asia. Meanwhile, England's Henry VII (ruled 1485–1509) ignored the Treaty of Tordesillas and sent an Italian navigator known as John Cabot westward across the northern Atlantic in 1497. Cabot claimed Nova Scotia, Newfoundland, and the rich Grand Banks fisheries for England, but he vanished at sea on a second voyage. Like Columbus, Cabot believed that he had reached Asia.

The more Europeans explored, the more apparent it became that a vast landmass blocked the western route to Asia. In 1500 the Portuguese claimed Brazil, and other voyages outlined a continuous coastline from the Caribbean to Brazil. In 1507 a publisher brought out a collection of voyagers' tales, including one from the Italian Amerigo Vespucci. A shrewd marketer, the publisher devised a catchy name for the new continent: America.

Getting past America to Asia remained the early explorers' goal. In 1513 the Spaniard Vasco Núñez de Balboa crossed the narrow isthmus of Panama and chanced upon the Pacific Ocean. In 1519 the Portuguese mariner Ferdinand Magellan, sailing under the Castilian flag, began a voyage around the world through the stormy straits at South America's southern tip, now named the Straits of Magellan. He crossed the Pacific to the Philippines, only to die fighting with natives. One of his five ships and fifteen emaciated sailors returned to Spain in 1522, the first people to have sailed around the world. But Europeans desired an easier way to Asia's fabled wealth. The French dispatched Giovanni da Verrazano and Jacques Cartier to search for a "northwest passage" to Asia. Verrazano probed the North American coast from the Carolinas to Newfoundland while Cartier ascended the St. Lawrence River as far as Montreal. But they found neither gold nor a northwest passage.

ℏ𝒸 Primary Source: European Explorations in America

Spain's Conquistadors, 1492–1526

Columbus was America's first slave trader and the first Spanish *conquistador,* or conqueror. On His-

paniola he enslaved Native people and created *encomiendas,* grants for both land and the labor of the Indians who lived on it.

From the beginning, *encomienderos,* those given the *encomiendas,* harshly exploited the native people. As disease, overwork, and malnutrition killed thousands of Indians, Portuguese slave traders supplied shiploads of Africans to replace them. Although shocked Spanish friars sent to convert the Native Americans reported the Indians' exploitation, and King Ferdinand attempted to forbid the practice, no one worried about African slaves' fate. Spanish settlers were soon fanning out across the Caribbean in pursuit of slaves and gold. In 1519 the young nobleman Hernán Cortés (1485–1547) led a small band of Spaniards to the Mexican coast. Destroying his boats and enlisting Indian allies, he marched inland to conquer Mexico.

Upon reaching the Aztec capital of Tenochtitlán (see Chapter 1), the Spanish were stunned by its size and wealth. "We were amazed . . . and some of our soldiers even asked whether the things that we saw were not a dream," recalled one *conquistador* of his first glimpse of Tenochtitlán's pyramids, lakes, and causeways. But the golden gifts that the Aztecs offered in vain hopes of buying off the invaders were no dream. Recalled an Indian, "Their bodies swelled with greed. . . . They hungered like pigs for that gold."

The Spanish raided the imperial palace and treasury, melting down all the gold they could find. But the Aztecs regrouped and recaptured the city. Then an epidemic of smallpox, which the Aztecs and other Indians were ill-equipped to resist, plus reinforcements from Cuba, enabled Cortés to defeat the Aztecs. By 1521 the Spanish had begun to build Mexico City on the ruins of Tenochtitlán. Within twenty years, Central America lay at the Spaniards' feet. Thus was New Spain born.

Over the remainder of the sixteenth century, conquistadors and officials established a great Spanish empire stretching from Mexico to Chile. The Inca empire represented the most important conquest, thanks to smallpox and Inca unfamiliarity with European weapons. The human cost of the Spanish empire was enormous. When Cortés

MAP 2.3
The Spanish and Portuguese Empires, 1610
By 1610 Spain dominated Latin America, including Portugal's possessions. Having devoted its energies to exploiting Mexico and the Caribbean, Spain had not yet expanded into what is now the United States, aside from establishing outposts in Florida and New Mexico.

landed in 1519, central Mexico had been home to between 13 and 25 million people. By 1600 the population had shrunk to seven hundred thousand. Peru and other regions witnessed similar devastation in the greatest demographic disaster in world history.

The Columbian Exchange

The Spanish conquest came at enormous human cost. Disease, not war or slavery, was the greatest killer. Native Americans lacked resistance to European and African infections, especially the deadly, highly communicable smallpox. From the first years of contact with Europeans, terrible epidemics decimated Indian communities. In the West Indies the native population vanished within a half century, and disease opened the mainland for conquest as well. "The people began to die very fast, and many in a short space," an Englishman later remarked. From the early sixteenth century on, smallpox and other epidemics ravaged the defenseless Indians.

The "Columbian exchange"—the biological encounter of the Old and New Worlds—went beyond deadly germs. Europeans brought horses, cattle, sheep, swine, chickens, wheat, coffee, sugar cane, and numerous fruits and vegetables with them, as well as an astonishing variety of weeds. African slaves carried rice and yams across the Atlantic. The list of American gifts to Europe and Africa was equally impressive: it included corn, white and sweet potatoes, many varieties of beans, tomatoes, squash, pumpkins, peanuts, vanilla, chocolate, avocados, pineapples, chilis, tobacco, turkeys, canoes, kayaks, hammocks, snowshoes, and moccasins. European weeds and domesticated animals often, especially in North America, overwhelmed indigenous plant life and drove away native animals. Settlers' crops, intensively cultivated on land never allowed to lie fallow, frequently exhausted American soils. Nonetheless, the worldwide exchange of food products enriched human diets and made possible enormous population growth. Today, nearly 60 percent of all food crops worldwide trace their roots to the Native American garden.

Another dimension of the emergence of the Atlantic world was the mixing of peoples. Within Spain's empire, a great human intermingling occurred. From 1500 to 1600 about 300,000 Spaniards immigrated to the New World, 90 percent of them male. A racially mixed population developed, particularly in towns. Spaniards fathered numerous children with African or Indian mothers; most of the former were slaves. Such racial mixing would occur, although far less commonly, in French and English colonies as well.

The Americas supplied seemingly endless wealth for Spain. West Indian sugar plantations and Mexican sheep and cattle ranches enriched many. Much of Spain's wealth, however, was dug from the silver mines of Mexico and Peru. After

Navajo View of Spanish Colonizers
This pictograph—a painting or drawing on rock—was sketched in the early colonial period in Cañón del Muerto, Arizona.

1540 enormous amounts of silver flowed across the Atlantic, far more than the small Spanish economy could absorb, setting off inflation that eventually engulfed Europe. But, bent on dominating Europe, Spanish kings needed even more silver to pay for their ships and armies. Several times they went bankrupt, and in the 1560s their efforts to squeeze more taxes from their subjects provoked revolt in Spain's Dutch provinces. In the end, gaining access to American wealth cost the Spanish dearly.

FOOTHOLDS IN NORTH AMERICA, 1512–1625

Spain's New World wealth attracted other Europeans. Throughout the sixteenth century they sailed the North American coast, exploring, fishing, trading for furs, and smuggling. But except for a Spanish fort at St. Augustine, Florida, all sixteenth-century attempts at colonizing North America failed. Unrealistic dreams of easy wealth and pliant Indians brought French, English, and Spanish attempts to grief. Only the ravaging of the

Indians by disease, declining Spanish power, and rising French, Dutch, and English power finally made colonization possible.

In 1607–1608 the English and French finally established permanent colonies. By 1614 the Dutch had followed. Within a generation North America's modern history took shape as each colony developed an economic orientation and its own approach to Native Americans.

Spain's Northern Frontier, 1512–1625

The Spanish built their New World empire by subduing the Aztec, Inca, and other Indian states. The dream of finding even more wealth drew would-be conquistadors to lands north of Mexico.

Earliest came Juan Ponce de León, the conqueror of Puerto Rico, who trudged through Florida in search of gold and slaves twice, in 1512–1513 and in 1521, and then died in an Indian skirmish. The most astonishing early expedition began when 300 explorers left Florida in 1527 to explore the Gulf of Mexico. Indian attacks whittled their numbers until only a handful survived. Stranded in Texas, the survivors, led by Cabeza de Vaca, moved from Indian tribe to tribe, at first as slaves, later as traders and medicine men. They finally made their way south to Mexico in 1536.

Cabeza de Vaca inspired two would-be conquerors. Hernando de Soto and Francisco Vásquez de Coronado. In 1539–1543 de Soto and his party blundered from Tampa Bay to the Appalachians and back to southern Texas, scouring the land for gold and harrying the Indians. Although de Soto died without finding gold or conquering any Indians, his and other expeditions touched off epidemics that destroyed most of the remaining Mississippian societies. By the time Europeans returned to the southeastern interior late in the seventeenth century, only the Natchez people on the lower Mississippi River still inhabited their temple-mound center. Depopulated, the Cherokee, Creek, and neighboring Indians had adopted the less centralized village life of other eastern tribes.

As de Soto roamed the Southeast, the Southwest drew others with dreams of conquest, lured by rumors that the fabled Seven Golden Cities of Cíbola lay north of Mexico. In 1538 an expedition sighted the Zuñi pueblos and assumed them to be the golden cities. In 1540–1542 Francisco Vásquez de Coronado led a massive expedition bent on conquest. Coronado plundered several pueblos and roamed from the Grand Canyon to Kansas before returning to Mexico, carrying with him no gold but the bitter enmity of many Native Americans. Other expeditions to California and to the Colorado River proved equally fruitless.

For decades after these failures, Spain's principal interest in the lands north of Mexico lay in establishing a few strategic bases in Florida to keep out intruders. In 1565 Spain planted the first successful European settlement on mainland North America, the fortress of St. Augustine. Spanish missionaries moved north from the fortress to establish religious missions as far north as the Chesapeake Bay, but Indian resistance and epidemic disease ended their efforts shortly before 1600.

Meanwhile, in the 1580s, the Spanish had returned to the southwestern pueblo country,

preaching Christianity and scouting for wealth. In 1598 Juan de Oñate led 500 Spaniards into the upper Rio Grande Valley, where he proclaimed the royal colony of New Mexico. When Acoma Indians refused his demands for provisions in December 1598, Oñate ordered massive retaliation. In January Spanish troops captured the pueblo, killing more than eight hundred inhabitants. Oñate then forced surviving men to have one foot cut off and sent them, along with women and children, to become servants. Two prominent Acoma leaders also had their right hands amputated.

The new colony barely survived. In 1606 the Spanish replaced Oñate because of his excessive brutality. Determined to succeed, by 1630 Franciscan missionaries had established more than fifty pueblo missions stretching along the Rio Grande and had converted about 20,000 Indians. Eventually, the missions' demands for labor and their attempts to uproot native religions would provoke an Indian backlash. Spanish New Mexico began, then, amidst uneasy tensions between colonists and natives.

France: Initial Failures and Canadian Success, 1541–1610

France made its first attempt at colonizing North America in 1541, when ten ships sailed into the St. Lawrence Valley. Having alienated many of the Indians along the St. Lawrence in two previous expeditions, Jacques Cartier built a fortified settlement on Indian land and thus ended all possibility of peaceful Indian-French relations. Steady Indian attacks and scurvy (for which the Indians could have shown them a cure) drove the French off within two years.

This fiasco underlined one Spaniard's view that "this whole coast as far [south] as Florida is utterly unproductive." In 1562 French Huguenots (Calvinists) made the next French attempt at colonization, establishing a base in modern South Carolina. Two years later they founded a settlement in Florida, which the Spanish quickly destroyed. These failures as well as a civil war between French Catholics and Huguenots ended France's first attempts at colonization.

Meanwhile, French and other European fishermen worked the teeming Grand Banks fisheries off the coast of Newfoundland. Going ashore to dry their catch, French sailors bartered with Indians for beaver pelts; by the late sixteenth century, as European demands for beaver hats soared, a French-dominated fur trade blossomed.

Most traders, unlike explorers or colonizers, recognized the need for reciprocity in dealing with Native Americans; consequently trade flourished. Glass beads were a mainstay of this trade, since Indians believed they possessed spiritual power comparable to that of quartz, mica, and other sacred substances. By the seventeenth century specialized factories in Europe would be producing cloth and glass for the "Indian trade."

To deter potential competitors, the French dispatched Samuel de Champlain to establish the colony of New France at Quebec in 1608. Familiar with Indian politics and diplomacy, Champlain built alliances with the Montagnais and Algonquins of the St. Lawrence and with the Hurons of the lower Great Lakes by promising to help them defeat their enemies the Mohawks.

In July 1609 Champlain and Indian allies encountered a substantial Mohawk force near the southern tip of Lake Champlain (which the explorer had named for himself). In the ensuing Battle of Lake Champlain, more than fifty Mohawks died and a dozen were captured. The battle marked the beginning of a deadly era of trade, diplomacy, and warfare. Through their alliance with the Hurons, the French gained access to the thick beaver pelts of the interior in exchange for European goods and protection against the Mohawks and other Iroquois. These economic and diplomatic arrangements defined the course of New France's history for the rest of the seventeenth century.

England and the Atlantic World, 1558–1603

When Elizabeth I became queen in 1558, England, a minor power, stood on the sidelines as Spain and France grappled for European supremacy. Religious division and domestic instability preoccupied the English. They hoped to cure the country's economic woes by founding colonies overseas, but Spain blocked the way.

Meanwhile, England's position in Ireland had deteriorated. By 1565 English troops were fighting to impose Elizabeth's rule throughout the island, where a Protestant English government was battling Irish Catholic rebels aided by Spain. In a war that ground on through the 1580s, English troops drove the Irish clans from their strongholds and established "plantations," or settlements, of Scottish and English Protestants. The English resorted to starvation and mass slaughter to break the Irish spirit. Elizabeth's generals justified these atrocities by calling the Irish savages. The Irish experience gave England strategies that it later used against North American Indians, whose customs, religion, and method of fighting seemed to absolve the English from guilt in waging exceptionally cruel warfare.

England had two objectives in the Western Hemisphere in the 1570s. The first was to find the northwest passage to Asia, preferably one lined with gold. The second, as Sir Francis Drake said, was to "singe the king of Spain's beard" by raiding Spanish fleets and cities. The search for a northwest passage proved fruitless, but the English did stage spectacularly successful and profitable privateering raids against the Spanish. The most breathtaking enterprise of the era was Drake's voyage around the world in 1577–1580 in quest of sites for colonies.

In 1587 Sir Walter Raleigh, dreaming of founding an American colony where English, Indians, and even blacks freed from Spanish slavery could live together amicably, sponsored a colony on Roanoke Island, off the modern North Carolina coast. An earlier settlement (1585-1586) had failed, in part because the colonists refused to grow their own food, expecting the Indians to feed them, and had worn out their welcome. One hundred ten colonists, many of them members of families, reached Roanoke in late summer 1587. Almost immediately the colony's leader, John White, returned to England for more supplies, leaving behind the settlers.

Spain's attempt to crush England with the Great Armada in 1588 prevented White from returning to Roanoke until 1590. When he did, he found only rusty armor, moldy books, and the word CROATOAN carved into a post. To this day, no one knows exactly what happened to the "Lost Colony," although they were probably living among the nearby Croatoan Indians The miserable failure at Roanoke would postpone the establishment of English colonies for seventeen more years.

Roanoke's fate illustrated several stubborn realities. First, even a large-scale, well-financed colony could fail, given settlers' unpreparedness for the American environment. Second, Europeans falsely assumed that the Indians would feed them and thus neglected to carry enough food supplies to carry them through the first winter. Third, colonizing attempts would have to be self-financing: a fiscally strapped monarch such as Elizabeth would not throw good money after bad. Finally, conflict with Spain hung menacingly over every other European attempt to gain a foothold in North America.

England's victory over the Spanish Armada in 1588 preserved English independence and confirmed its status as a major Atlantic power.

The Beginnings of English Colonization, 1603–1625

Peace between England and Spain, concluded in 1604 by Elizabeth's successor, James I (ruled 1603–1625), opened the way for new colonization attempts in the New World. The Spanish not only agreed to peace but also renounced their claims to Virginia, leaving England a free hand.

But the problem of financing colonies remained. Neither the Crown nor Parliament would spend money on colonies, and Roanoke clearly showed how inadequate a private fortune could be. However, joint-stock companies, which could amass money through sales of stock, raised large sums of money with limited risk for the individual investor.

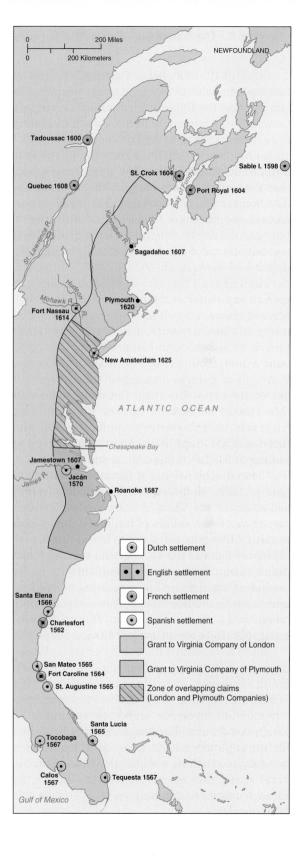

MAP 2.4

European Settlements in Eastern North America, 1565–1625

Except for St. Augustine, Florida, and Sante Fe, New Mexico, all European settlements founded before 1607 were abandoned by 1625. Despite the migration of 10,000 Europeans to North America's Atlantic coast by 1625, the total number of Spanish, English, French, and Dutch on the continent was then about 1,800, of whom two-thirds lived in Virginia.

On April 10, 1606, James I granted charters to two separate joint-stock companies, one based in London and the other in Plymouth. The Virginia Company of Plymouth received a grant extending from modern Maine to the Potomac River; the Virginia Company of London, a grant from Cape Fear north to the Hudson River. The grants overlapped, with the land in question to go to the first successful colonizer. The colonists would be business employees, not citizens of a separate political jurisdiction, and the stockholders of each company would regulate the colonists' behavior. Both companies dispatched colonists in 1607.

The Virginia Company of Plymouth sent 120 men to Sagadahoc at the mouth of the Kennebec River in Maine. The following year the colony disintegrated, the victim of Indian hostility (generally provoked) and the hard Maine winters. The company subsequently became dormant. The Virginia Company of London dispatched 105 settlers to a site on the James River near Chesapeake Bay that they named Jamestown. But the first colonists, who included many gentry, hunted for gold and failed to plant crops. When relief ships arrived in January 1608, they found only 38 survivors.

Near anarchy reigned at Jamestown until September 1608, when desperate councilors, representatives of the Virginia Company of London, turned to a brash soldier of fortune, Captain John Smith. Only twenty-eight, Smith found that his experiences fighting the Spanish and the Turks had prepared him well to assume control in Virginia. By instituting harsh discipline, organizing the settlers, and requiring them to build houses and plant food, he ensured Jamestown's survival. During the winter of 1608–1609, Smith lost just 12 men out of 200.

Smith also became the colony's best diplomat. After local Indians captured him late in 1607, Smith displayed such impressive courage that Powhatan, the leader of the nearby Powhatan Confederacy, arranged an elaborate ceremony in which Pocahontas, his daughter, "saved" Smith's life during a mock execution. Smith maintained satisfactory relations with the Powhatan Confederacy partly through his personality and partly through calculated demonstrations of English military strength.

When serious injuries forced Smith to return to England in 1609, discipline again crumbled. Expecting the Indians to furnish corn, the settlers had not laid away enough food for winter. One colonist reported that Jamestown residents ate dogs, cats, rats, and snakes in order to survive. He gruesomely added that "many besides fed on the corpses of dead men." Of the 500 residents at Jamestown in September 1609, only 100 lived to May 1610. An influx of new recruits and the imposition of military rule, however, enabled Virginia to win the First Anglo-Powhatan War (1610–1614) and, by 1611, to expand west to modern Richmond. The English population remained small—only 380 by 1616—and produced nothing of value for the stockholders.

Tobacco saved Virginia. John Rolfe, an Englishman who married Pocahontas, perfected a salable variety of tobacco for planting there, and by 1619 Virginia was exporting large, profitable amounts of the crop. Thereafter the Virginia Company poured supplies and settlers into the colony.

To attract labor and capital, the company awarded fifty-acre land grants ("headrights") to anyone paying his or her own passage or that of a laborer. By financing the passage of indentured servants, planters could accumulate large tracts of land. Thousands of single young men and a few hundred women became indentured servants, choosing the uncertainty of Virginia over poverty in England. In return for their passage, they worked a fixed term, usually four to seven years.

In 1619 the Virginia Company ended military rule and provided for an elected assembly, the House of Burgesses. Although the company could veto the assembly's actions, 1619 marked the beginning of representative government in North America. However, Virginia still faced three serious problems. First, local officials systematically defrauded shareholders, in the process sinking the company deeply into debt. Second, the colony's death rate soared. Malnutrition, salt poisoning, typhus, and dysentery (from drinking polluted river water), killed thousands of immigrants. Third, Indian relations worsened. After Powhatan's death in 1618, the new leader, Opechancanough, worried about the relentless expansion of the English colony. In 1622 the Indians killed 347 of the 1,200 settlers in a surprise attack. With their livestock destroyed, spring planting impossible, and disease spreading through crowded stockades, hundreds more colonists died in the ensuing months.

The Virginia Company sent more men, and Governor Francis Wyatt took the offensive. Using tactics developed during the Irish war, Wyatt destroyed the Indians' food supplies, conducted winter campaigns to drive them from their homes when they would suffer most, and fought (according to John Smith) as if he had "just cause to destroy them by all means possible." By 1625 the English had won the war, and the Indians had lost their best chance of forcing out the intruders.

But the struggle bankrupted the Virginia Company. After receiving complaints about its management, James I revoked its charter and made Virginia a royal colony in 1624. Only 500 Old World settlers lived there, including a handful of Africans of uncertain status. The roots from which Virginia's Anglo-American and African-American peoples grew were fragile indeed.

New England Begins, 1614–1625

After Virginia, the next permanent English settlements appeared in New England. Along the coast, a terrible epidemic devastated the Indian population by about 90 percent in 1616-18. In 1620 the Virginia Company of London granted a patent for a settlement to some English merchants headed by Thomas Weston. Weston dispatched eighteen families (102 people) in a small, leaky ship, the *Mayflower*. The colonists promised to send back lumber, furs, and fish for seven years, after which they would own the tract.

The expedition's leaders, and half its members, belonged to a small religious community from the northern English town of Scrooby. Separatist Puritans, they had earlier fled to the Netherlands to practice their religion freely. Fearing that their children were adopting Dutch ways, they decided to immigrate to America.

In November 1620 the *Mayflower* landed at Plymouth, outside the bounds of Virginia. Because they had no legal right to be there, the leaders forced the adult males in the group to sign the

Mayflower Compact before they landed. By this document they constituted themselves a "civil body politic"—a civil government—under James I's sovereignty and established the colony of Plymouth Plantation.

Weakened by their journey and unprepared for winter, half the Pilgrims, as they were later called, died within four months. Two Indians helped the others to survive: Squanto, a local Patuxet, and Samoset, an Abenaki from Maine who had traded with the English. To stop the Pilgrims from stealing their food, the Indians taught the newcomers how to grow corn. Squanto and Samoset also arranged an alliance between the Pilgrims and the local Wampanoag Indians, who were headed by Chief Massasoit. With firearms, the Pilgrims became the dominant partner, and the Wampanoags were forced to acknowledge English sovereignty.

Plymouth's relations with the Indians gradually worsened. Learning of the Virginia massacre of 1622, the Pilgrims militarized their colony and threatened their Indian "allies" with their monopoly of firepower. Although Massasoit remained loyal, this conduct offended many Wampanoags.

Relations with Native Americans also fostered economic self-sufficiency. After the colony turned from communal farming to individually owned plots, farmers began producing surplus corn, which they traded to Abenakis in Maine for furs. Within a decade, Plymouth had attracted several hundred colonists.

Plymouth colony had three lasting influences. It constituted an outpost of Puritans dissenting from the Church of England, proved that a self-governing society could exist in New England, and foreshadowed the aggressive methods that would give Europeans mastery over the Indians. Plymouth represented the vanguard of a massive migration of Puritans to New England in the 1630s (see Chapter 3).

The Enterprising Dutch, 1609–1625

The Dutch-speaking provinces of the Netherlands were among the most fervently Calvinist regions of Europe. Ruled by the Spanish during the sixteenth century and alienated by high taxes and religious intolerance, the Dutch rebelled in 1566. More than forty years later, in 1609, Spain and the Dutch Republic signed a truce. By then the Netherlands was a wealthy commercial power whose empire stretched from Brazil to South Africa to Taiwan. It would play a key role in colonizing North America.

In 1609 Henry Hudson sailed up the broad, deep river that today bears his name, and in the next year Dutch ships sailed up the Hudson to trade with Indians. In 1614 they began their New Netherlands colony by establishing Fort Nassau at the site of modern Albany, New York, and in 1625 planted another fort on an island at the mouth of the Hudson. Within two years Peter Minuit, director-general of the colony, bought the island from local Indians, named it Manhattan, and began a settlement christened New Amsterdam.

Furs, particularly beaver pelts, became the New Netherlanders' chief economic staple. The Mohawks as well as the other nations of the Iroquois Confederacy became the Dutch colonists' chief suppliers of furs and soon found themselves embroiled in competition with the French-supported Hurons.

CONCLUSION   *hc* ACE Practice Test

The sixteenth century saw the emergence of a new "Atlantic world" linking Europe, Africa, and the Americas. Commercial capitalism, nation-states, and post-medieval Christianity increasingly characterized "modern" Europe. Expansion and colonization strengthened these forces by providing fresh fields for investment and profit as well as new foundations for national power.

Africa benefited little from this new Atlantic world. By century's end the overwhelming demand for slave labor was shaping, and distorting, trade, politics, and warfare throughout West Africa, setting the stage for modern Africa's underdevelopment.

The other side of the Atlantic world fared little better, as indigenous peoples in the Americas reeled under the terrible violence of the Spanish conquest, their political, religious, and social institutions shattered. Movements of people, animals, plants and germs constituted a Columbian exchange that affected societies and environments of both exploiters and exploited.

As late as 1625, Europe's presence north of Mexico and the Caribbean was limited to a handful of Spanish outposts in New Mexico and Florida and

New Amsterdam

After the Dutch "purchase" of Manhattan Island, the fortified settlement of New Amsterdam grew only slowly, as this view from 1651 clearly shows. Except for the tip, the island remained farmland or forest. Corn brought by canoe-paddling Indians also helped feed the settlement. Note the windmill, where grain was ground.

Chronology

c. 1400–1600	European Renaissance.	**1558**	Elizabeth I becomes queen of England.
c. 1400	Mali challenged in West African grassland. Coastal West African kingdoms rise and expand.	**1565**	St. Augustine founded by Spanish.
1440	Portuguese slave trade in West Africa begins.	**1585–1590**	English colony of Roanoke established, then disappears.
1488	Bartolomeu Días reaches the Cape of Good Hope.	**1588**	England defeats the Spanish Armada.
1492	Christian "reconquest" of Spain. Columbus lands at San Salvador.	**1598**	Oñate founds New Mexico.
1517	Protestant Reformation begins in Germany.	**1603**	James I becomes king of England.
1519–1521	Hernán Cortés leads conquest of Aztec empire.	**1607**	English founds colonies at Jamestown and Sagadahoc.
1519–1522	Magellan's expedition circumnavigates the globe.	**1608**	Champlain founds New France.
		1609	Henry Hudson explores the Hudson River.
1532–1536	Pizarro leads Spanish conquest of Inca empire.	**1610–1614**	First Anglo-Powhatan War.
1534	Church of England breaks from Roman Catholic church.	**1614**	New Netherland colony founded.
1541–1542	Cartier attempts to colonize eastern Canada.	**1619**	Large exports of tobacco from Virginia begin. House of Burgesses, first elected assembly, established in Virginia.
1539–1543	De Soto attempts conquests in southeastern United States.	**1620**	Plymouth colony founded.
1540–1542	Coronado attempts conquests in southwestern United States.	**1622–1632**	Second Anglo-Powhatan War.
		1624	James I revokes Virginia Company's charter.

England's tenuous footholds in Virginia and at Plymouth Plantation. All the European colonies depended for success or security on stable relations with at least some Native Americans, and their early years were hardly a story of inevitable triumph.

FURTHER READING

Robert J. Berkhofer, Jr., *The White Man's Burden: Images of the American Indian from Columbus to the Present* (1978). A penetrating analysis of the shaping of European and American attitudes, ideologies, and policies toward Native Americans.

Nicholas Canny, ed., *The Origins of Empire (The Oxford History of the British Empire, vol. I; 1998).* Essays by leading authorities offer a comprehensive treatment of early English imperialism.

Alfred W. Crosby, Jr., *Ecological Imperialism: The Biological Expansion of Europe, 900–1900* (1986). An outstanding discussion of the environmental and medical history of European overseas expansion.

Philip Curtin, et al., eds., *African History from Earliest Times to Independence,* 2nd ed. (1995). Excellent overviews by leading historians in the field.

Olwen Hufton, *The Prospect Before Her: A History of Women in Western Europe,* vol. I: 1500–1800 (1995). An outstanding interpretive synthesis.

D. W. Meinig, *The Shaping of America, vol. I: Atlantic America, 1492–1800* (1986). A geographer's engrossing study of Europeans' encounter with North America and the rise of colonial society.

Sidney W. Mintz, *Sweetness and Power: The Place of Sugar in Modern History* (1985). The role of sugar as crop, commodity, food, and cultural artifact.

Anthony Pagden, *Lords of All the World: Ideologies of Empire in Spain, Britain, and France, c. 1500–c.1800.* A comparative discussion of imperialist thought in Europe's three most powerful overseas empires.

John Thornton, *Africa and Africans in the Making of the Atlantic World, 1400–1680,* 2nd ed. (1998). An insightful perspective on the place of West Africa and its peoples in the colonization of the Americas.

3

Expansion and Diversity: The Rise of Colonial America, 1625–1700

CHAPTER OUTLINE

 This icon will direct you to additional study and research resources at http://college.hmco.com/history/us/boyer/enduring_concise/5e/students/index.html

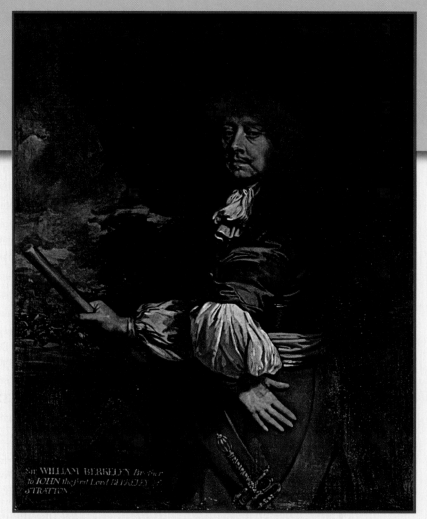

Portrait of Virginia's Governor William Berkeley, by Peter Laly, 1676

The seventeenth century witnessed a flood of English migration across the Atlantic. In 1600 no English person had lived along the North American seacoast. By 1700, however, about 225,000 people of English birth or ancestry were dwelling in what became the United States. Large numbers of Dutch, French, Spanish, Irish, Scottish, and German settlers joined them. A second wave carried 300,000 West Africans to the English colonies, about 10 percent of whom arrived in North America. Whereas English immigrants to America hoped to realize economic opportunity or religious freedom, Africans and their descendants were owned by others. The majority of Africans taken to the English colonies went to West Indies sugar plantations. A third demographic upheaval, the depopulation and uprooting of Native Americans, made these two other migrations possible. Epidemic disease did much of the work of destroying the Indians, but warfare played an important role as well. About 1 million Indians had died as a result of contact with Europeans by 1700.

Indian depopulation and European and African immigration transformed North America in the seventeenth century. Europeans expanded their territorial domains and established colonial societies from the St. Lawrence River to the Rio Grande, increasing the continent's cultural diversity.

English immigrants, and English capital, ensured that England would dominate the East coast as well as the Caribbean; by 1700 the English would force out the Dutch and leave France and Spain with lands less attractive to colonists. Four distinct regions emerged within England's mainland colonies: New England, the Chesapeake, Carolina, and the middle colonies, each shaped by its environment, the motives of white immigrants, and the concentrations of enslaved Africans.

THE NEW ENGLAND WAY

As England's religious and political environment grew worse in the 1620s, many Puritans became interested in colonizing New England. Large-scale Puritan migration would begin in 1630, as the intensely religious Puritans built a community based on religious ideals, the first utopian society in America.

A City upon a Hill, 1628–1632

In 1628 several Puritan merchants obtained a charter to settle north of the Separatist colony at Plymouth. Organized as the Massachusetts Bay Company, they moved the seat of their colony's government to New England, paving the way for Massachusetts to be self-governing.

This chapter focuses on four major questions:

▶ Why did colonial New Englanders abandon John Winthrop's vision of a "city upon a hill"?

▶ Why did indentured servitude give way to racial slavery in England's plantation colonies? Why were both these institutions more limited in the nonplantation colonies?

▶ What were the major factors facilitating French and Spanish colonial expansion?

▶ Why was England's North American empire so much larger and wealthier than those of France and Spain by 1700?

In 1630 the company dispatched a "great fleet," eleven ships and 700 passengers, to New England. As the ships crossed the Atlantic, Governor John Winthrop delivered a lay sermon, "A Model of Christian Charity," in which he explained how and why the new colony would differ from England itself.

Winthrop boldly announced that "we shall be as a city upon a hill, the eyes of all people are upon us." The settlers would build a godly community whose compelling example would shame England. The English government would then truly reform the church, and a revival of piety would create a nation of saints. Denouncing economic jealousy, Winthrop explained that God intended "in all times some must be rich and some poor." The rich would practice charity and mercy, and the poor show their faith in God's will by practicing patience and fortitude. In a godly state, the government would prevent the greedy among the rich from exploiting the poor and the lazy among the poor from burdening their fellow citizens. Winthrop's sermon expressed both traditional European ideas of social reciprocity (see Chapter 2) and the Puritans' dismay at the economic forces battering—and changing—English society.

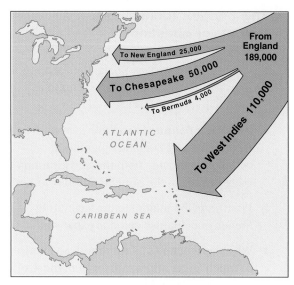

MAP 3.1
English Migration, 1610–1660
During the first phase of English transatlantic migration, the West Indies attracted more than twice as many colonists as went to the Chesapeake, and over four times as many as settled in New England.

The Pequot War, 1637

In contrast to the settlement of Virginia, the Puritan colonization of New England initially met little resistance from Native Americans, whose numbers had been drastically reduced by disease. Between 1616 and 1618 an epidemic killed 90 percent of New England's coastal Indians, and a second epidemic in 1643–1644 inflicted comparable casualties on Indians throughout the Northeast. The Massachusett Indians dwindled from 20,000 in 1600 to a few dozen in 1635 and sold most of their land. By 1675, New England's Native American population had shrunk from 125,000 in 1600 to about 10,000. During the 1640s Massachusetts Bay passed laws prohibiting Indians from practicing their own religion and encouraging missionaries to convert them to Christianity. Beginning in 1651 the Indians surrendered much of their independence and moved into "praying towns" such as Natick, a reservation established by the colony.

The expansion of English settlement farther inland, however, aroused Indian resistance. As settlers moved into the Connecticut River Valley, beginning in 1633, friction developed with the Pequots, who controlled the trade in furs and wampum with New Netherland. After tensions escalated into violence, the English waged a ruthless campaign against the Pequots, using tactics similar to those devised to break Irish resistance (see Chapter 2). In a predawn attack, troops led by Captain John Mason surrounded and set fire to a Pequot village at Mystic, Connecticut, and then cut down all who tried to escape. Several hundred Pequots, mostly women and children, were killed. The Puritans found the grisly massacre a cause for celebration. Wrote Plymouth's governor William Bradford, "It was a fearful sight to see them [the Pequots] thus frying in the fire and the streams of blood quenching the same . . . but the victory seemed a sweet sacrifice, and they [the English] gave the praise to God, who had wrought so wonderfully for them." By late 1637 Pequot resistance was crushed, and English settlement of the new colonies of Connecticut and New Haven could proceed unimpeded.

Dissent and Orthodoxy, 1630–1650

In England, Puritans had focused on their common opposition to Anglican practices. However, in America theological differences began to undermine the harmony that Winthrop had envisioned. Some Puritan ministers struggled to define orthodox practices—the "New England Way"—while others objected.

Education was a key means of establishing orthodoxy. Like most Protestants, Puritans insisted on familiarity with the Bible and, thus, literacy. Education should begin in childhood and should be promoted by each colony.

In 1647 the Massachusetts Bay colony passed the Old Deluder Act because "one chief project of that old deluder, Satan [is] to keep men from knowledge of the Scriptures." Every town of fifty or more households was to appoint one teacher

Attack on Mystic Fort
This print, published in an English participant's account of the war, shows English troops, backed by allied Indians, surrounding the Pequot village while soldiers prepare to burn it.

from whom all children could receive instruction, and every town of one hundred households or more was to maintain a grammar school with a teacher capable of preparing students for university-level learning. This law, echoed by other Puritan colonies, was New England's first step toward public education, although attendance remained optional and boys were more likely to be taught reading and writing than girls. In any case, the family remained the chief guardian of education.

An educated clergy was essential, and so in 1636 Massachusetts founded Harvard College to produce learned ministers. In its first thirty-five years, the college turned out 201 graduates, 111 of them ministers. These alumni made New England the only American colony with a college-educated elite during the seventeenth century.

Although agreeing that the church must be free of state control, Winthrop and other Massachusetts Bay leaders insisted that a holy commonwealth required cooperation between church and state. Therefore the colony required all adults to attend services and pay tithes to support their local church. Massachusetts thus had a state-sponsored or "established" religion. The use of a single building for both religious services and town business symbolized this relationship.

Some Puritans, however, dissented from their leaders' vision of social order and religious conformity. Roger Williams, who arrived in America in 1631, argued that civil government had to remain absolutely uninvolved with religious matters. Williams opposed compulsory church service and interference with private religious beliefs because he feared that the state would eventually corrupt the church and its saints.

Believing that the purpose of the colony was to protect true religion and to prevent heresy, political authorities declared Williams's opinions subversive and banished him in 1635. Williams went south to the edge of Narragansett Bay to a place that he later named Providence, which he purchased from the Indians. A steady stream of dissenters drifted to the group of settlements near Providence, forming Rhode Island in 1647. The only New England colony to practice religious toleration, Rhode Island grew to 800 settlers by 1650.

Anne Hutchinson presented the second major challenge to the New England Way. "A woman of haughty and fierce carriage, of a nimble wit and active spirit," Hutchinson maintained that her fellow Puritans were too certain that they could tell whether or not a person was a saint on the basis of his or her behavior. She reminded them that their creed stressed predestination, not good works, and argued that New England's ministers had gone astray. She ultimately claimed that only two of the colony's ministers were actually among the saints and denied that the others had any authority over saints such as herself.

Hutchinson's ideas directly attacked the clergy's authority to interpret and teach Scripture; critics charged that her beliefs would delude individuals into imagining that they were accountable only to themselves. Her followers were labeled Antinomians, meaning those opposed to the rule of law. Anne Hutchinson bore the additional liability of being a woman challenging traditional male roles in church and state. Her gender made her seem an especially dangerous foe.

Massachusetts Bay split into pro- and anti-Hutchinson forces. Her opponents prevailed, bringing Hutchinson to trial for sedition in 1637 before the Massachusetts Bay legislature (the General Court) and then for heresy before a panel of ministers. Hutchinson's knowledge of Scripture was so superior to that of her inquisitors that she might well have been acquitted had she not claimed to communicate directly with the Holy Spirit. Because Puritans believed that God had ceased to make known matters of faith by personal revelation since New Testament times, Hutchinson was condemned by her own words. Banished from the colony along with other antinomians, Hutchinson settled in Rhode Island and then moved to New Netherland, where she was killed in that colony's war with Indians in 1643. Her banishment effectively ended the last challenge capable of splitting congregationalism and ensured the survival of the New England Way for two more generations.

New restrictions on women's independence and on equality within Puritan congregations followed antinomianism's defeat. Increasingly, women were prohibited from assuming the kind of public religious role claimed by Hutchinson and were even required to relate their conversion experiences in private to their ministers rather than publicly before their congregations.

Economics as well as ideas posed serious threats to Winthrop's "city upon a hill." While most Puritans shared Winthrop's view of community, self-discipline, and mutual obligation, a large minority had come to America for prosperity and social mobility. The most visibly ambitious colonists were merchants, whose activities fueled New England's economy but whose way of life challenged its ideals.

Merchants fit uneasily into a religious society that equated financial shrewdness with greed. They often clashed with government leaders, who were trying to regulate prices so that consumers would not suffer from the chronic shortage of manufactured goods that afflicted New England. In 1635 the General Court forbade the sale of any item at above 5 percent of its cost. Led by Robert Keayne, merchants protested that they needed to sell some goods at higher rates to offset losses incurred by shipwreck and inflation. In 1639 authorities fined Keayne for selling nails at 25 percent above cost and forced him to apologize in front of his congregation.

Keayne symbolized the fear that a headlong rush for prosperity would lead New Englanders to forget that they were their brothers' keepers. Controversies such as these were part of a struggle for the New England soul. At stake was the Puritans' ability to insulate their city upon a hill from a market economy that threatened to strangle the spirit of community within a harsh world of frantic competition.

Power to the Saints, 1630–1660

Despite sharp limits on dissent, control of New England churches was broadly based. Male "saints"—those who had been saved—chose ministers, elected elders to handle finances, decided whom to admit to membership, and ignored Anglican bishops' authority.

While English Puritans accepted as saints any who correctly professed the Calvinist faith, repented their sins, and lived free of scandal, Massachusetts Puritans required that candidates for membership provide a convincing account of their conversion experience. Many were reluctant to do so, and the conversion relation became the New England Way's most vulnerable feature.

Political participation was also more broadly based in New England than elsewhere. There were no property requirements; every adult male "saint" enjoyed suffrage. By 1641, 55 percent of the colony's men could vote; in contrast, property requirements in England restricted the vote to less than 30 percent of adult males.

By 1634 each town had gained the right to send two delegates to the General Court; ten years later the elected deputies and the appointed Governor's Council separated to create a bicameral (two-chamber) legislature.

In England the basic unit of local government was the county court. By contrast, in New England the county court was primarily a court of law; the town meeting oversaw matters of local administration.

Towns were formed when a legislature granted land to several dozen heads of families. These individuals had almost unlimited freedom to lay out the settlement, design its church, distribute land among themselves, and make local laws. Generally, all adult male taxpayers, even nonsaints, participated in town meetings. In turn, the meetings ran the town and granted land rights to new settlers.

Most towns attempted to maintain communities of tightly clustered settlers by distributing only as much land as was necessary for each family to support itself. The remaining land would be distributed to future generations as needed. Forcing residents to live close together was an attempt to foster social reciprocity. New England's generally compact system of settlement made people interact with each other and established an atmosphere of mutual watchfulness that promoted godly order.

Women were a social force in Puritan communities. They created neighborhoods through the interactions of their daily lives, whether trading eggs for butter, exchanging information about local events, or attending births. As women confided in one another, they built and sustained networks of friendships and extended family relationships in each town that contributed to the enforcement of morals and the protection of the poor and vulnerable.

New England Families

"The little commonwealth"—the nuclear family— was the foundation of Puritan society. *"Well-ordered families,"* declared minister Cotton Mather in 1699, "naturally produce a *Good Order* in other *Societies.*" A well-ordered family was one in which wife, children, and servants dutifully obeyed the husband and in which the "true wife" thought of herself "in subjection to her husband's authority."

Puritans defined matrimony as a contract, not a sacrament; they were thus married by justices of the peace rather than ministers. As a civil institution, marriage could be dissolved by the courts in cases of desertion, bigamy, adultery, or physical cruelty. However, New England courts saw divorce as a remedy only for extremely wronged spouses, such as the Plymouth woman who found that her husband also had wives in Boston, Barbados, and England. Massachusetts courts granted just twenty-seven divorces from 1639 to 1692.

Because Puritans believed that healthy families were crucial to the community's welfare, they intervened whenever they discovered serious problems in a household. Courts disciplined unruly youngsters, disobedient servants, disrespectful wives, and irresponsible husbands. Churches also censured, and even expelled, spouses who did not maintain domestic tranquility.

New England wives enjoyed significant legal protections against spousal violence and nonsupport and had more freedom than their English counterparts to escape a failed marriage. But they suffered the legal disabilities borne by all women under English law. A wife had no property rights independent of her husband except by premarital agreement. Only if there were no other heirs or if a will so specified would a widow receive control of household property, although law entitled her to lifetime use of one-third of the estate.

New England's families enjoyed greater stability and lived longer lives than their English counterparts. The region's cold climate limited the impact of disease, especially in winter, when limited travel between towns slowed the spread of infection. Easy access to land contributed to a healthy diet, which strengthened resistance to disease and lowered death rates associated with childbirth. Life expectancy for Puritan men reached sixty-five, and women lived nearly that long. These life spans were ten years or more longer than those of England. More than 80 percent of all infants survived long enough to marry. Because so many of the 20,000 immigrants who arrived in New England between 1630 and 1642 came as members of families, an even sex ratio and a rapid natural increase of population followed.

Families were economically interdependent. Male heads of family managed the household's crops and livestock, conducted its business transactions, and represented it at town meetings. Wives bore and nurtured children and performed or oversaw work in the house, garden, and barn. Sons depended on parents to provide them with acreage for a farm, and parents encouraged sons to stay at home and work in return for a bequest of land later on. Young males often tended their fathers' fields until their late twenties before receiving their own land. The average family, raising four sons to adulthood, could count on thirty to forty years of work if their sons delayed marriage until age twenty-six. Families with many sons and daughters enjoyed a labor surplus and sometimes hired out their children to work for others. Although inefficient, this system of family labor was all that New Englanders could afford.

There were other benefits. Prolonged dependence for sons ensured that the family line and property would continue in the hands of capable, experienced men. Although daughters performed vital labor, they would marry into another family. Young women with many childbearing years ahead of them were the most valuable potential wives,

and first-generation women tended to marry by the age of twenty-one.

Saddled with the triple burdens of a short growing season, rocky soil salted with gravel, and an inefficient system of land distribution that forced farmers to cultivate widely scattered strips, the colonists nevertheless managed to feed their families and to keep ahead of their debts. Few grew wealthy from farming. For wealth, New Englanders turned lumbering, shipbuilding, fishing, and rum distilling into major industries that employed– perhaps one-fifth of all adults full-time. As its economy diversified, New England prospered. Increasingly concerned more with profit than prophecy, the Puritans discovered, to their dismay, that fewer of their children were emerging as saints. **ℏ𝒸** Primary Source: Cotton Mather

The Half-Way Covenant, 1662

As New England struggled for stability and conformity, old England fell into chaos and civil war. Alienated by years of religious harassment, Puritans gained control of the revolt, beheaded Charles I in 1649, and governed without a king for more than a decade. In 1660 a provisional English government recalled the Stuarts and restored Charles II to the throne.

The Stuart Restoration left American Puritans without a mission. Having conquered a wilderness and built their city upon a hill, they found that the eyes of the world were no longer fixed on them.

An internal crisis also gripped New England. First-generation Puritans had believed that they held a covenant, a holy contract, with God to establish a scripturally ordained church and to charge their descendants with its preservation. However, understandably reluctant to submit to a public review of their spirituality, relatively few second-generation Puritans were willing to join the elect by making the required conversion relation before the congregation. Through its passivity, the second generation expressed a preference for a more inclusive religious community, organized on traditional English practices. This generation also rejected the ritual of public conversion relation as an unnecessary source of division and bitterness that undermined Christian fellowship.

Because Puritan churches baptized only babies born to saints, first-generation Puritans faced the prospect that their own grandchildren would remain unbaptized unless the standards for church membership were lowered. They solved their dilemma in 1662 through a compromise known as the Half-Way Covenant, which permitted the children of all baptized members, including nonsaints, to be baptized. Church membership would pass down from generation to generation, but nonsaints would be "half-way" members, unable to take communion or to vote in church affairs. When forced to choose between a church system founded on a pure membership of the elect and one that embraced the entire community, New Englanders opted to sacrifice purity for community.

The Half-Way Covenant marked the end of the New England Way. Most adults chose to remain in "half-way" status for life, and the saints became a shrinking minority in the third and fourth generations. By the 1700s there were more female than male saints in most congregations. But because women could not vote in church affairs, religious authority stayed in male hands. Nevertheless, ministers publicly recognized women's role in upholding piety and the church itself.

Expansion and Native Americans, 1650–1676

Indians felt the English presence in many ways. The fur trade, initially beneficial to Native Americans of the interior, became a burden. Once Indians began hunting for trade instead of for their subsistence needs alone, they quickly depleted the supply of beavers and other fur-bearing animals. Because English traders advanced trade goods on credit before the hunting season began, many Indians fell into debt. Traders increasingly took Indian land as collateral and sold it to settlers.

English townspeople, eager to expand their agricultural output and provide for their sons, voted themselves much larger amounts of land after 1660. For example, Dedham, Massachusetts,

had distributed only 3,000 acres from 1636 to 1656; by 1668 it had allocated another 15,000 acres. Many farmers built their homes on their outlying tracts, crowding closer to the Indians' settlements and their hunting, fishing, and gathering areas.

Expansion put pressure on the natives and the land alike. By clearing trees for fields and for use as fuel and building material, the colonists were altering the entire ecosystem by the mid-1600s. Deer no longer grazed freely, and the wild plants on which the Indians depended for food and medicine could not grow. Deforestation not only dried the soil but also brought frequent flooding. Encroaching white settlers allowed their livestock to run wild, according to English custom. Pigs damaged Indian cornfields and shellfish-gathering sites. Cattle and horses devoured native grasses, which the settlers replaced with English varieties.

Powerless to reverse the alarming decline of population, land, and food supplies, many Indians became demoralized. Some turned to alcohol, which became increasingly available during the 1660s despite colonial attempts to suppress its sale to Native Americans. Interpreting the crisis as one of belief, other Indians converted to Christianity. By 1675 Puritan missionaries had established about thirty "praying towns." Supervised by missionaries, each praying town had its own Native American magistrate, and many congregations had Indian preachers. Although missionaries struggled to convert the Indians to "civilization"—English culture and ways of life—most Indians integrated the new faith with their native cultural identities, reinforcing the hostility of settlers who believed that all Indians were irrevocably "savage" and heathen.

Anglo-Indian conflict became acute in the 1670s because of pressure on the Indians to sell their land and to accept missionaries and the legal authority of white courts. Tension was especially high in the Plymouth colony, where Puritans had engulfed the Wampanoag tribe and forced a series of humiliating concessions from their leader Metacom, "King Philip," the son of the Pilgrims' onetime ally Massasoit.

In 1675 Plymouth hanged three Wampanoags for killing a Christian Indian. Then several other

Wampanoags were shot while burglarizing a farmhouse, touching off the conflict known as King Philip's War. In response to the escalation of violence, Metacom organized two-thirds of the Native Americans, including many praying Indians, into a military alliance. The war raged across New England. Metacom's forces, as well armed as the Puritans, devastated the countryside, wiping out twelve of New England's ninety towns and killing 600 colonists. The following year, 1676, saw the tide turn as Puritan militia destroyed their enemies' food supplies and sold hundreds of captives into slavery, including Metacom's wife and child. Perhaps 5,000 Indians starved or died in battle, including Metacom himself.

King Philip's War reduced southern New England's Indian population by almost 40 percent and eliminated open Indian resistance to white expansion. It also deepened whites' hostility toward all Native Americans, even the Christian Indians who had fought against King Philip. In 1677 ten praying towns were disbanded and all Indians were restricted to the remaining four. Missionary work ceased. "There is a cloud, a dark cloud upon the work of the Gospel among the poor Indians," mourned Puritan missionary John Eliot. In the face of poverty and discrimination, the remaining Indians struggled to maintain their communities and cultural identity.

Salem Witchcraft and the Demise of the New England Way, 1691–1693

After the Half-Way Covenant's adoption, social and economic changes continued to undermine the foundations of New England life. As they pursued economic gain more openly and as populations dispersed away from town centers, the fabric of community frayed. Friction easily arose between the townspeople still dwelling near the meetinghouse (who usually dominated politics) and the "outlivers," those living on outlying tracts of land, who were less influential because of their distance from town. The distribution of wealth was growing more uneven, especially in large, prosperous port cities. New England's rising involvement in international trade, moreover, encouraged competitiveness and impersonality. John Winthrop's vision of a religious community sustained by reciprocity and charity faded before the reality of a world increasingly materialistic and acquisitive—like the one that the early Puritans had fled.

Nowhere in New England did those trends converge more forcefully than in Salem, Massachusetts. Trade made Salem prosperous but destroyed the relatively equal society of the first generation. Such divisions were especially sharp in Salem Village, an economically stagnant district north of Salem Town; those who lived the eastern section farmed richer soils and benefited from Salem Town's commercial expansion, while those in the less fertile western half did not share this prosperity and lost the political influence that they had once held.

In late 1691 several Salem Village girls encouraged an African slave woman, Tituba, to tell fortunes and talk about sorcery. When the girls began behaving strangely, villagers assumed that they were victims of witchcraft. Pressed to identify their tormenters, they named two local white women and Tituba.

To this point the incident was not unusual; witchcraft beliefs remained strong in seventeenth-century Europe and its colonies. Generally, witches were women whose greed, pride, envy, or discontent drove them to sign pacts with the devil and use his supernatural power of evil to torment neighbors by causing illness, destroying property, or "possessing" their victims' minds and bodies. Witnesses usually accused these women of unfeminine behavior. A disproportionate number of the 342 accused witches in New England were women who had inherited or stood to inherit more property than the usual one-third of a husband's estate. In other words, most accused witches were assertive women who had or might have more economic power and independence than many men. To New Englanders, who felt it necessary to limit both female independence and economic individualism, they were dangerous. In most earlier witchcraft accusations, there was only one defendant and the case never went to trial. However, events in Salem would lead to a colony-wide panic.

MAP 3.2
The Geography of Witchcraft: Salem Village, 1692
Geographic patterns of witchcraft testimony mirrored tensions within Salem Village. Accused witches and their defenders lived mostly in the village's eastern division or in Salem Town, whereas their accusers overwhelmingly resided in the village's western sector. (Source: *Adapted from* Salem Possessed: The Social Origins of Witchcraft *by Paul Boyer and Stephen Nissenbaum. Copyright © 1974 by the President and Fellows of Harvard College. Reprinted by permission of Harvard University Press.)*

Map legend:
- **A** Accuser
- **D** Defender
- **W** Accused witch
- Roads and bridges
- Village boundary
- Internal division between village accusers and defenders

Map labels: SALEM VILLAGE, Meetinghouse, Ipswich R., SALEM TOWN, Salem Harbor, Courthouse, Gallows Hill, 2 Miles, 2 Kilometers

By April 1692 the girls had denounced two prosperous farm wives long considered saints in the local church and had identified the village's former minister as a wizard (male witch). Fear of witchcraft soon overrode considerable doubts about the girls' credibility and led local judges to sweep aside normal procedural safeguards. Specifically, the judges ignored legal bans on "spectral evidence," testimony that a spirit resembling the accused had been seen tormenting a victim. Thereafter charges multiplied until the jails overflowed with accused witches.

The pattern of hysteria and accusations reflected Salem Village's internal divisions. Most charges came from the western side of the village and were lodged against people from the eastern village and in Salem Town. Two-thirds of all accusers were girls aged eleven to twenty, and more than one-half had lost one or more parents in conflicts between Indians and settlers in Maine. They and other survivors had fled to Massachusetts, where most worked as servants in other families' households. They most frequently named as witches middle-aged wives and widows—women who had escaped the poverty and uncertainty that they themselves faced. At the same time, the "possessed" accusers gained momentary power and prominence by voicing the anxieties and hostilities of many others in their community and by virtually dictating the course of events in and around Salem for months.

Those found guilty of witchcraft tried to stave off death by implicating others. As the pandemonium spread, fear dissolved ties of friendship and family. A minister was condemned by his granddaughter, a mother by her seven-year-old daughter, and a husband and father by his wife and daughter. Fifty saved themselves by confessing, but twenty were condemned and executed.

By late 1692 doubts about the charges were surfacing. Clergymen objected to the emphasis on spectral evidence, crucial to most convictions. By accepting such evidence in court, minister

Increase Mather warned, the Puritans had fallen victim to a deadly game of "blind man's buffet" set up by Satan and were "hotly and madly mauling one another in the dark." In October Governor William Phips forbade any further imprisonments for witchcraft. One hundred were still in jail, and 200 more stood accused. In early 1693 Phips ended the terror by pardoning all those who were convicted or suspected of practicing witchcraft.

The witchcraft hysteria reflected profound anxieties over social change. The underlying causes of this tension became clear as Salem Village's communally oriented farmers directed their wrath toward Salem Town's competitive and individualistic merchants. This clash of values revealed the extent to which John Winthrop's city upon a hill had lost its relevance to new generations forced into economic enterprise by New England's harsh climate and meager natural resources.

In the aftermath of the Salem hysteria, younger New Englanders concluded that Winthrop's vision belonged to the past. Those reaching maturity after 1692 would be far less willing to accept restrictions on either personal or economic freedom. While they remained true to the forceful convictions of self-discipline of their Puritan roots, they would apply these qualities to the pursuit of material gain. Puritanism thus gave New England a distinctive and enduring regional identity.

CHESAPEAKE SOCIETY

Both Virginia and its Chesapeake neighbor Maryland were dedicated to the production of tobacco for export. This cash-crop economy was a striking departure from the New England model, as were the sharp social divisions between a handful of wealthy planters and the majority of indentured servants, poor white farmers, and black slaves.

State and Church in Virginia

James I planned to rule Virginia through appointed officials, but Virginians petitioned repeatedly for the restoration of their elected assembly, the first in the New World. James I's successor, Charles I, grudgingly relented in 1628, but only in order to induce the assembly to tax tobacco exports so as to transfer the cost of government from the crown to Virginia's taxpayers. After 1630, seeking more taxes, Virginia's royal governors called regular assemblies. During the 1650s the assembly split into two chambers, the elected House of Burgesses and the appointed Governor's Council. Later royal colonies also adopted this bicameral pattern.

Local government officials were appointed, rather than elected, during Virginia's first quarter-century. In 1634 Virginia adopted England's county-court system. Appointed by the royal governor, justices of the peace acted as judges, set local tax rates, paid county officials, and oversaw the construction and maintenance of roads, bridges, and public buildings. Thus south of New England, unelected county courts became the basic unit of local government.

In contrast to Puritan New England, Virginia had the Church of England as its established church. Anglican vestries governed each parish; elected vestrymen handled church finances, determined poor relief, and investigated complaints against the minister. Taxpayers were legally obliged to pay fixed rates to the Anglican church. Because of the large distances between settlements and churches as well as a chronic shortage of clergymen, few Virginians regularly attended services. In 1662 Virginia had just ten ministers to serve its forty-five parishes. Compared to New Englanders, Chesapeake dwellers felt religion's influence lightly.

Maryland

Beginning in the 1630s, grants by the crown to reward English politicians replaced joint-stock companies as the primary mechanism of colonization. The first such grant, or proprietorship, went in 1632 to Lord Baltimore (Cecilius Calvert); he named the large tract east of Chesapeake Bay Maryland in honor of England's Queen Henrietta Maria. Lord Baltimore enjoyed broad power, lessened only by the stipulations that an elected assembly had to approve all laws and that the crown would control both war and trade.

With Charles I's consent, Baltimore intended to make Maryland a refuge for England's Catholics, who could neither worship in public nor hold political office and who had to pay tithes to the Anglican church. To make Maryland a haven, Baltimore tried to install the old English manor system. In theory, a manor lord would employ a Catholic priest as chaplain and allow others to hear Mass and to receive the sacraments on the manor. In practice, this arrangement never worked, for relatively few Catholics settled in Maryland, which was overwhelmingly Protestant from the beginning. Cheap land lured settlers who did not need to become tenants on the manors, and Baltimore's scheme fell apart. By 1675 all sixty of Maryland's nonproprietary manors had become plantations.

Religious tension gradually developed in Maryland society. The Protestant majority dominated the elected lower house of government, but many Catholics had become large landowners, held high public office, and dominated the appointive upper house. Until 1642 Catholics and Protestants shared the chapel at St. Mary's, the capital, but they began to argue over its use. As antagonisms intensified, Baltimore drafted, and the assembly passed, the Act for Religious Toleration (1649).

Unfortunately, the toleration act did not secure religious peace. In 1654 the Protestant majority barred Catholics from voting; ousted Governor William Stone, a Protestant; and repealed the toleration act. Stone raised an army, both Protestant and Catholic, to regain the government but met defeat at the Battle of the Severn River in 1655. The victors imprisoned Stone and hanged three Catholic leaders. Maryland remained in Protestant hands until 1658. Although Lord Baltimore was restored to control that year (ironically, at the command of English Puritans), Protestant resistance to Catholic political influence continued to cause problems in Maryland.

Death, Gender, and Kinship

So few women immigrated to the Chesapeake that before 1650, only one-third of male servants could find brides and then only after completing their in-

MAP 3.3
Colonizing the Chesapeake, 1607–1660
The native-settler frontier moved slowly westward until after Indian defeat in the Third Anglo-Powhatan War (1644–1646). By 1700, when the European and African population reached 110,000, newcomers spread through the tidewater.
hc Interactive Map: Pattern of Settlement in Surry County

dentures. Female scarcity gave women an advantage in negotiating favorable marriages. Many female indentured servants married prosperous planters who paid off their remaining time of service.

Death ravaged Chesapeake society and left domestic life exceptionally fragile. In 1650 malaria joined the killer diseases typhoid, dysentery, and salt poisoning as the marshy lowlands of the tidewater Chesapeake became fertile breeding grounds for the mosquitoes that spread malaria. Life expectancy in the 1600s was twenty years lower in the Chesapeake than in New England. Servants died at appalling rates; 40 percent were dead within a decade of arrival and 70 percent before reaching age fifty.

Chesapeake widows often enjoyed substantial property rights. The region's men wrote wills giving their wives perpetual and complete control of their estates so that their own children could inherit them. Although a widow in such circumstances had a degree of economic independence, she faced enormous pressure to remarry, particularly a man who could produce income by farming her fields.

The lopsided sex ratio and high death rates contributed to slow population growth in the Chesapeake. Although perhaps 100,000 English immigrated to the Chesapeake between 1630 and 1700, the white population was just 85,000 in 1700. Change came gradually as children acquired childhood immunities, life spans lengthened, and the sex ratio evened out. By 1720 most Chesapeake residents were native born.

Tobacco Shapes a Region, 1630–1670

Chesapeake settlers were scattered across the landscape. A typical community included only 24 families in a twenty-five-square-mile area, a mere six people per square mile. (In contrast, New England often had 500 people squeezed onto one square mile.) Most Chesapeake inhabitants lived in a world of few friendships and considerable isolation; typical was Robert Boone, a Maryland farmer, who died at age seventy-nine "on the same Plantation where he was born in 1680, from which he never went 30 miles in his Life."

Isolated Chesapeake settlers shared a life governed by one overriding factor: the price of tobacco. After an initial boom, tobacco prices plunged 97 percent in 1629 before stabilizing at 10 percent of their original high. Tobacco was still profitable as long as it was grown on fertile soil near navigable water. As a result, 80 percent of Chesapeake homes were located along a riverbank.

Chesapeake society became increasingly unequal. A few planters used the headright system to build up large landholdings and to profit from their servants' labor. Wretchedly exploited—and poorly fed, clothed, and housed—servants faced a bleak future even when their indentures ended. Although some were able to claim fifty acres of land in Maryland, the majority who went to Virginia had no such prospects. Indeed, in Virginia after 1650 most riverfront land was held by large planters and speculators, and upward mobility became virtually impossible.

In 1660 Chesapeake tobacco prices plunged by 50 percent, setting off a depression that lasted fifty years. Despite losses, large planters earned some income from rents, interest on loans, and shopkeeping, and many landowners scrambled to sell corn and cattle in the West Indies. A typical family

Tobacco Label
The slave's central role in growing tobacco and serving his white master (here enjoying a smoke) is depicted.

in this depression era lived in a small wooden shack, slept on rags, and ate mush or stew cooked in the single pot. Having fled poverty in England or the West Indies, people often found utter destitution in the Chesapeake. Ex-servants in particular became a frustrated and embittered underclass that seemed destined to remain landless and poor.

Bacon's Rebellion, 1675–1676

By the 1670s these bleak conditions had locked most Virginia landowners into a losing battle against poverty and had left the colony's freedmen in despair. Both groups were capable of striking out in blind rage if an opportunity to stave off economic disaster presented itself. In 1676 this human powder keg exploded in violence.

Virginians had been free of serious conflict with the Indians since the end of the Third Anglo-Powhatan War in 1646. By 1653 tribes encircled by English settlements had begun agreeing to remain within boundaries set by the government—in effect, on reservations. White settlement continued to expand northward to the Potomac River, and by 1675 whites outnumbered Indians by a ten-to-one ratio.

In June 1675 a dispute between some Doeg Indians and a Virginia farmer escalated. A force of Virginia and Maryland militia pursuing the Doegs murdered fourteen friendly Susquehannocks and later executed five of their chiefs. The violence was now unstoppable. While Governor William Berkeley proposed defending the frontier by a costly system of forts, small farmers preferred the cheaper solution: a war of extermination against the Indians. Some 300 settlers elected Nathaniel Bacon, a distant relative of Berkeley and member of the Royal Council, to lead them against nearby Indians in April 1676. The expedition found only peaceful Indians but slaughtered them anyhow.

Returning to Jamestown in June 1676, Bacon asked for authority to wage war "against all Indians in general." The legislature voted for a program designed to appeal to both hard-pressed taxpayers and landless ex-servants. All Indians who had left their villages without permission (even if fleeing Bacon) were declared enemies, and their lands were forfeited. Bacon's troops could seize any "enemy" property and enslave Indian prisoners.

But Governor Berkeley soon had second thoughts about the slaughter and recalled Bacon and his 1,300 men. Forbidden to attack Indians, Bacon's forces turned against the government and burned Jamestown. The rebels offered freedom to any servants or slaves owned by Berkeley's allies who would join them and then looted enemy plantations. What had begun as Indian warfare was now a social rebellion. Before the uprising could proceed further, however, Bacon died of dysentery in late 1676, and his followers dispersed.

Bacon's Rebellion revealed a society under deep internal stress. Begun as an effort to displace escalating tensions among whites onto the Indians, it became an excuse to plunder other whites. Economic opportunism as well as racism had spurred the small farmers and landless ex-servants to rise up. This rebellion was an outburst of pent-up frustrations by marginal taxpayers and ex-servants driven to desperation by the tobacco depression.

Slavery

Chesapeake whites drew racialized boundaries between themselves and the region's growing African population and tried to avert class conflict by substituting black slaves for white servants.

Racial slavery developed in three stages. From 1619 to 1640, Anglo-Virginians carefully distinguished between whites and blacks in official documents, but did not assume that every African sold was a slave for life. Some Africans gained their freedom and a few even owned their own farms.

By 1640 blacks and some Indians were being treated as slaves, and their children inherited their status. Thus their situation had become inferior to that of indentured white servants. In the final phase, after 1660, laws defined slavery as a lifelong, inheritable status based on color. By 1705 strict legal codes defined the place of slaves in society and set standards of racial etiquette.

Slavery was a system for blacks and Indians only. Whites never enslaved their white enemies; rather, they reserved the complete denial of human rights for nonwhites. In order to stabilize Chesapeake society and to defuse the resentment of poor whites, planter elites created a caste system based on race. This system simultaneously defined nonwhites as unfit for freedom and created a common, exclusive identity among whites.

Slavery grew slowly in the Chesapeake, with fewer than a thousand slaves in Virginia and Maryland as late as 1660. However, by 1680 the slave population had grown to 12,000; by 1700 slaves would make up nearly one-fourth of the Chesapeake population and much of the labor force.

The rise of a direct slave trade with Africa increased the growing gap between whites and blacks. Before 1690, most blacks in the Chesapeake, having spent long periods in West African ports or other American colonies, were familiar with English ways and spoke some English. They could carve out space for themselves as free landowners. After 1690, as slaves poured into the Chesapeake direct from the West African interior, language and culture became barriers rather than bridges, reinforcing increased racism among whites.

Racism was enforced by the changing composition of the white population, increasingly American-born and evenly distributed between male and female. Whites shared a sense of common racial identity vis-à-vis an increasingly fragmented and seemingly alien black population.

By 1700 the Chesapeake had been transformed; profits had fallen, but life expectancy had risen. As nonwhites' condition deteriorated, Virginia and Maryland expanded their territories and their white colonists flourished.

THE SPREAD OF SLAVERY: THE CARIBBEAN AND CAROLINA

As European colonies expanded on the mainland, an even larger wave of settlement swept the West Indies. Between 1630 and 1642 nearly two-thirds of the English who emigrated to the Americas went to the Caribbean. Beginning in the 1640s both the French and the English followed the Spanish, Portuguese, and Dutch by using slave labor to produce

sugar on large plantations. The fastest-growing and most profitable sugar plantations were those of the English.

After 1670 large numbers of English islanders migrated to the Chesapeake and to Carolina, carrying with them the habits and prejudices of plantation slaveholding. By 1710 the population of Carolina, like that of the Caribbean colonies, was predominantly black and enslaved.

Sugar and Slaves: The West Indies

Initially, the English West Indies developed along lines similar to Virginia, with tobacco the dominant crop. Because a single worker could tend only three acres of tobacco, tobacco farming demanded a large population. By 1640 more colonists lived on England's five West Indian islands than in all of Virginia.

Tobacco, requiring little equipment beyond a curing shed, was cheap to raise, and tobacco cultivation gave individuals with little money a chance at upward mobility. Through the 1630s the West Indies remained a society with a large percentage of independent landowners, an overwhelmingly white population, and no extreme inequality of wealth.

Sugar cane soon changed that, revolutionizing the islands' economy and society. Encouraged by Dutch merchants, wealthy English planters began to raise this enormously lucrative crop. The demand for labor soared because sugar required triple the labor force of tobacco. African slaves soon replaced indentured white servants in the fields. Most planters preferred black slaves to white servants because they could be driven harder and maintained more cheaply. Also, African slaves could better withstand the tropical diseases of the Caribbean, they had no rights under contract, and they toiled until they died. Although slaves initially cost two to four times more than indentured servants, they were an economical long-term investment. Some English immigrants to the Caribbean copied the example already set by the Spanish and enslaved both Indians and Africans.

By 1670 the sugar revolution had transformed the British West Indies into a predominantly black

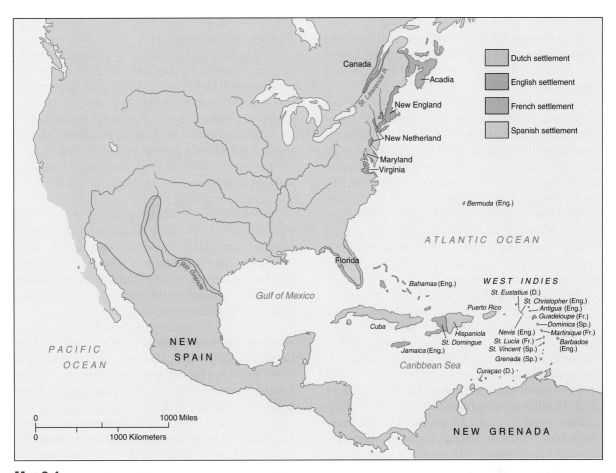

MAP 3.4
The Caribbean Colonies, 1660
By 1660 nearly every West Indian island had been colonized by Europeans and was producing sugar with slave labor,

and slave society. In 1713 slaves outnumbered whites by four to one; the slave population had leaped from 40,000 in 1670 to 130,000 in 1713, with the white population remaining stable at 33,000. Meanwhile, driven from the Indies by high land prices, thousands of English settlers went north to the mainland, settling in Carolina.

Rice and Slaves: Carolina

In 1663 Charles II bestowed the swampy coast between Virginia and Spanish Florida on several English supporters, making it the first of several Restoration colonies. The proprietors named their colony Carolina in honor of Charles (*Carolus* in Latin).

Settlers from New England and the West Indies had established outposts along the northern Carolina coast in the 1650s; the proprietors organized them into a separate district with a bicameral legislature. In 1669 one of the proprietors, Anthony Ashley Cooper, accelerated settlement by offering immigrants fifty-acre headright grants for every family member, indentured servant, or slave they brought in. The next year 200 Barbadian and English people began the settlement of southern

Carolina near modern Charleston, "in the very chops of the Spanish." In the settlement they called Charles Town, they formed the colony's nucleus, with a bicameral legislature distinct from that of the northern district.

Cooper and his secretary, John Locke, devised an intricate plan for Carolina's settlement and government. Their Fundamental Constitutions of Carolina attempted to ensure the colony's stability by decreeing that political power and social rank should accurately reflect settlers' landed wealth. Thus they invented a three-tiered nobility that would hold two-fifths of all land, make laws through a council of nobles, and dispense justice through manorial courts. Ordinary Carolinians were expected to defer to the nobility and pay them rent, although they would enjoy religious toleration and the benefits of English common law.

In the early years Carolina's population mainly consisted of small landowners. Southern Carolinians raised livestock, and colonists in northern Carolina exported tobacco, lumber, and pitch. In neither north nor south did the people realize enough profit to maintain slaves, and so self-sufficient white families predominated. But southern Carolinians eagerly sought a cash crop. In the early 1690s they found it—rice. Rice cultivation enriched the few settlers with capital enough to acquire the dikes, dams, and slaves necessary to grow it. By earning annual profits of 25 percent, successful rice planters within a generation became the only colonial mainland elite whose wealth rivaled that of the Caribbean sugar planters.

Treated inhumanely, white indentured servants did not survive in the humid rice paddies swarming with malaria-carrying mosquitoes. Thus planters imported an ever-growing force of African slaves, who possessed two major advantages. First, some had cultivated rice in Africa and possessed expertise vital to teaching whites how to raise the unfamiliar crop. Second, many Africans were immune to malaria and yellow fever, which were endemic in coastal regions of West Africa, and which they carried to North America. (Tragically, the antibody against malaria also tends to produce the sickle-cell trait, an often-fatal genetic condition.)

These two factors made commercial rice production possible in Carolina.

The typical rice planter, with 130 acres in cultivation, needed sixty-five slaves. Demand drove the proportion of slaves in southern Carolina's population from 17 percent in 1680 to 67 percent in 1720, when the region officially became South Carolina. By 1776 the colony, with at least 100,000 slaves, would have more bondsmen than any other mainland colony in the eighteenth century. It would be Britain's only eighteenth-century mainland colony with a black majority.

Rice thrived in a narrow coastal strip extending from Cape Fear (now in North Carolina) to Georgia. Malaria, carried in from Africa but to which many Africans had partial immunity, ravaged this hot, humid lowland. In the worst months planters' families escaped to the relatively healthful climate of Charles Town, while overseers supervised the harvest.

As the black majority increased, whites relied on force and fear to control their slaves. In 1696 Carolina adopted the galling restrictions and gruesome punishments of the Barbados slave code. Bondage in the mainland colony grew as cruel and harsh as in the West Indies.

White Carolinians' attitudes toward Native Americans likewise hardened. The most vicious result was the trade in Indian slaves. White Carolinians armed allied Indians, encouraged them to raid and capture unarmed Indians to the south and west, and sold the captives to the West Indies during the 1670s and 1680s. A recent study estimates that the Carolina traders enslaved tens of thousands of Indians. Once shipped to the West Indies, most Native Americans died because they lacked immunities to European and tropical diseases.

THE MIDDLE COLONIES

The Dutch and the Swedish established small commercial outposts between the Chesapeake and New England. The Dutch took over New Sweden, and in turn in 1664 England seized New Netherland; by 1681 England had used this territory as the basis for New York, New Jersey, and Pennsylvania, creating a fourth colonial region, the middle colonies.

Precursors: New Netherland and New Sweden

New Netherland became North America's first multiethnic society. Barely half the settlers were Dutch; most of the rest comprised Germans, French, Scandinavians, and Africans, both free and slave. In 1643 the population included Protestants, Catholics, Jews, and Muslims, speaking eighteen European and African languages. The trading company that had established the settlement struggled to control the settlers, whose get-rich-quick attitude sapped company profits as private individuals traded illegally in furs. Eventually, the company legalized the private trade.

Privatization rapidly increased the number of guns in the hands of New Netherland's Iroquois allies, giving them a distinct advantage over other tribes. As overhunting depleted local fur supplies and smallpox epidemics raged, the Iroquois encroached on Huron territory for pelts and captives (who were adopted into Iroquois families to replace the dead). After 1648 the Dutch-armed Iroquois destroyed the Hurons and attacked French settlements along the St. Lawrence. "They come like foxes, they attack like lions, they disappear like birds," wrote a French Jesuit.

Although the Dutch had allied with the Iroquois, relations with the nearer Indian neighbors were terrible. With greedy settlers and military weakness, New Netherland largely had itself to blame. In 1643 an all-out war erupted when Governor Willem Kieft massacred previously friendly Indians. By 1645 the Dutch had temporarily prevailed, but only by enlisting English help and by inflicting atrocities. The fighting cut New Netherland's Indian population from 1,600 to 700.

Another European challenger, Sweden, distracted the Dutch in their war with the Native Americans. In 1638 Sweden had planted a small fur-trading colony in the lower Delaware Valley that was diverting furs from New Netherland. In 1655 the Dutch colony's stern soldier-governor Peter Stuyvesant marched against New Sweden, whose 400 residents peacefully accepted Dutch annexation. But New Netherland paid dearly for its

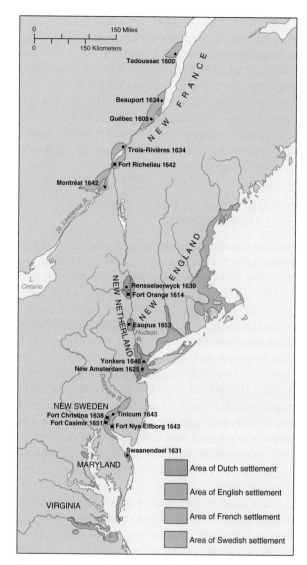

MAP 3.5

European Colonization in the Middle and North Atlantic, c. 1650

North of Spanish Florida, four European powers competed for territory and trade with Native Americans in the early seventeenth century. Swedish and Dutch colonization was the foundation upon which England's middle colonies were built.

victory. With the militia absent, the Algonquians destroyed scattered Dutch settlements and forced Stuyvesant to ransom white captives.

Although tiny, the Dutch and Swedish colonies were significant. New Netherland fell to the English in 1664, but the Dutch presence in what became New York has lent a distinctive flavor to American life. Even short-lived New Sweden left a mark, the log cabin, introduced to the continent by Finnish settlers in the Swedish colony. Above all, the Dutch and Swedish colonies bequeathed a religious and ethnic diversity that would continue in England's middle colonies.

English Conquests: New York and New Jersey

Like the Carolinas, New York and New Jerseys originated with Restoration-era proprietors hoping to grow rich from rents collected from settlers within a hierarchical society. New York marginally achieved this dream, but the New Jerseys did not.

In 1664, at war with the Dutch Republic, Charles II attacked the Dutch colony of New Netherland. Four hundred poorly armed Dutch civilians under Governor Peter Stuyvesant surrendered peacefully. Charles II made his brother James, duke of York, proprietor of the new English colony and renamed it New York. With James's ascension to the throne in 1685, he converted New York into a royal colony. By 1700 immigration had swelled the population to 20,000, of whom just 44 percent were descended from the original Dutch settlers.

New York's governors rewarded their influential political supporters with large land grants. By 1703 five families held 1.75 million acres, which they carved into manors and rented to tenants. By 1750 the enormous income they earned from rents had made the New York estate owners a landed elite second in wealth only to the Carolina rice planters.

Ambitious plans collided with American realities in New Jerseys, also carved out of New Netherland. In 1664 the duke of York awarded a group of supporters New Jerseys, at the time inhabited by a few hundred Dutch and Swedes and several thousand Delaware Indians. Within a decade thousands of troublesome New England Puritans settled in New Jerseys, and the proprietors sold the region to Quakers, who split the territory into East and West Jersey.

The Jerseys' Quakers, Anglicans, Puritans, Scottish Presbyterians, and Dutch Calvinists quarreled with one another and got along even worse with the proprietors. The governments collapsed between 1698 and 1701, and in 1702 the disillusioned proprietors surrendered their political powers to the crown, which made New Jersey a royal colony.

Quaker Pennsylvania

In 1681 Charles II paid off a huge debt by appointing a supporter's son, William Penn, as proprietor of the last unallocated tract of American territory at the king's disposal. Penn, a Quaker, thus founded the colony as a "holy experiment" based on the teachings of the English preacher George Fox. Penn also hoped for financial gain.

Quakers in late-seventeenth-century England stood well beyond the fringe of respectability. Challenging conventional foundations of social order, they appealed to those at the bottom of the economic ladder. But they also attracted some well-educated, well-to-do individuals disillusioned by the quarreling of rival religious faiths, including significant numbers of merchants. The members of this radical religious sect, which had been born in war-torn England during the 1640s and 1650s, called themselves the Society of Friends, but most others dubbed them Quakers.

At the heart of their founder George Fox's theology was the belief that the Holy Spirit, or "Inner Light," could inspire every soul. Mainstream Christians found this claim highly suspicious. Although trusting such direct inspiration, Quakers took pains to ensure that individual opinions would not be mistaken for God's will. Indeed, they felt confident that they understood the Inner Light only after having reached near-unanimous agreement through intensive discussion. In their religious services ("meetings"), Quakers sat silently until the Inner Light prompted one of them to speak. Quakers believed that the Inner Light could "speak in the fe-

William Penn's Map of Philadelphia, c. 1681
Central to Penn's master plan for Philadelphia was the idea that each residence should stand in the middle of its plot, encircled by gardens and orchards.

male as well as the male," and they thus accorded women unprecedented equality.

Quaker behavior often seemed disrespectful to government and to the social elite and thus aroused hostility. For example, Quakers refused to tip their hats to their social betters, insisting that spiritual state, not wealth or status, deserved recognition. Their refusal to bear arms appeared unpatriotic and cowardly, though they faced persecution and imprisonment with courage.

Care and planning made the Quaker migration to Pennsylvania one of the most successful initial transplantations of Europeans in any North American colony. After sending an advance party, Penn arrived in 1682. He named his new capital Philadelphia, the "City of Brotherly Love." Within five years, 8,000 English Quakers had joined him. Quakers migrated in family groups, and their high birthrate led to rapid population growth. (Pennsylvania's religious toleration attracted not only Quakers but also many other religious groups: Presbyterians, Baptists, Anglicans, and Catholics from England and Lutherans and radical sectarians from Germany.)

A victim of persecution, Penn hated intolerance and arbitrary governance. He offered Quakers the opportunity to make laws according to their ideals. His Frame of Government (constitution) featured a strong executive branch (a governor and governor's council) and a lower chamber (the assembly) with limited power. Friends, a majority in the colony, dominated the assembly, and Penn generally named Quakers to other positions. Hardly a democrat, Penn feared "the ambitions of the populace which shakes the Constitution" and intended to check the "rabble" as much as possible. To prevent wrangling and to achieve an orderly disposition of property, Penn personally oversaw land sales. He also designed a grid plan for Philadelphia, reserving park areas to keep it a "greene country towne." Penn sought peace with Native Americans by reassuring the Indians that the Quakers wished "to live together as Neighbours and Friends" and by buying land from them fairly.

Pennsylvania seemed an ideal colony—intelligently organized, well financed, tolerant, open to all industrious settlers, and at peace with the

Indians. Rich lands and a lengthy growing season produced bumper crops. West Indian demand for grain generated widespread prosperity. By 1700 Philadelphia had become a major port. In 1704 counties along the lower Delaware River, where Swedes and Dutch had settled long before Penn, gained the right to elect their own legislature and became the colony of Delaware.

However, by this time Penn's "peaceable kingdom" had bogged down in human bickering. In 1684 Penn had returned to England, and during his fifteen-year absence the settlers had quarreled incessantly. An opposition party had attacked his efforts to monopolize foreign trade and to collect a small annual fee from each landowner. Struggles between pro- and anti-Penn forces had deadlocked the government. Penn's return from 1699 to 1701 had restored some order, but before leaving again, he made the legislature unicameral (one chamber) and allowed it to initiate measures.

Religious controversy meanwhile had erupted in the 1690s when prominent Quaker preacher George Keith urged the Quakers to adopt a formal religious creed. Doing so would have changed the democratically functioning Quakers into a conventional clergy-dominated church. In 1692 a majority of Quakers had rejected Keith's views, and he had joined the Church of England. But Keith's departure had begun a major decline in the Quaker share of Pennsylvania's population. In 1748 Penn's sons, who inherited the proprietorship, would become Anglican, and Anglicans thereafter would hold the highest political offices, although Friends would still dominate the colony's assembly.

Although little had gone as planned in the middle colonies, they had succeeded. Before they were a quarter century old, the middle colonies had demonstrated that English America could benefit by encouraging pluralism. New York and New Jersey successfully integrated Dutch and Swedish populations; Pennsylvania, New Jersey, and Delaware refused to require residents to support any official church. But the virtual completion of English claim-staking along the Atlantic coast had set England on a collision course with France and Spain, which also were vying for American territory.

RIVALS FOR NORTH AMERICA: FRANCE AND SPAIN

Unlike England, with its compact seacoast colonial settlements in North America, France and Spain had cast enormous nets of widely separated trading posts and missions across the interior. The two Catholic nations had converted many Indians to Christianity and made them trading partners and allies. By 1720 scattered missionaries, fur traders, and merchants had spread French and Spanish influence across two-thirds of today's United States. The French government invested heavily in its American enterprise, but Spain, its empire decaying, made little effort to influence North American affairs. Local officials and settlers assumed the burden of extending imperial control for both powers.

France Claims a Continent

After briefly losing Canada to England (1629–1632), France resumed and extended its colonization there. Initially a privately held company, the Company of New France issued extensive tracts to large landlords, who in turn imported indentured servants or rented out small tracts. Nonetheless, Canada's harsh winters and short growing season sharply limited their numbers.

More successful were the traders and missionaries who spread beyond the settlements and relied on stable relations with the Indians to succeed. The lucrative opportunities offered by trade converted many would-be farmers into traders.

Jesuit missionaries followed the traders into the interior, spreading French influence westward to the Great Lakes. Ursuline nuns ministered to Native American women and girls nearer Quebec, ensuring that Catholic piety and morality reached all members of Indian families.

Under King Louis XIV (reigned 1661–1715), France sought to subordinate its American colony to French interests, following the doctrine of *mercantilism*. According to this doctrine, colonies should serve as sources of raw materials and as markets for manufactured goods so that the colonial power did not have to depend on rival nations for trade. The French hoped that New France would increase the fur trade, provide agricultural surpluses to ship to France's West Indies colonies, and export timber for those colonies and for the French Navy. To achieve this, the French government transformed New France into a royal colony, confronted and sought to stifle the Iroquois, and encouraged French immigration to Canada.

The Iroquois had long limited French colonial profits by intercepting convoys of fur pelts. In the 1660s Louis XIV had dispatched French troops to New France. The French Army had burned Mohawk villages. Sobered by the destruction, the Iroquois Confederacy had made a peace that permitted New France's rapid expansion of fur exports.

The French crown energetically built up New France's population, primarily by sending indentured servants to New France; army members stationed there were encouraged to stay, become farmers, and marry the "king's girls," female orphans shipped over with dowries. However, after 1673 immigration dwindled. Colonists who returned to France—more than two-thirds of the immigrants—told horrifying tales of disease, Canada's hard winter, and "savage" Indians. Natural increase would replace immigration as the chief source of population growth, guaranteeing slow development for New France.

Even male immigrants who stayed did not always fulfill the French vision of sturdy farmers. Many of them struck out westward from the St. Lawrence Valley, becoming *coureurs de bois,* independent and sometimes disreputable fur traders. These French traders obtained furs from the Indians in exchange for European goods, including guns. The coureurs lived among and married among the Indians, forging for France a precarious empire based on alliances with Canadian and Great Lakes Indians. Alarmed by the rapid expansion of England's colonies, France sought to contain the English colonies, and to prevent Spain from linking Florida with New Mexico, by dominating the North American heartland.

As early as 1672, fur trader Louis Jolliet and Jesuit missionary Jacques Marquette became the first Europeans known to have reached the upper Mississippi; they later paddled twelve hundred miles downstream to the Mississippi's junction with the Arkansas. Ten years later, the Sieur de La Salle, an ambitious dreamer and adventurer, descended the entire Mississippi to the Gulf of Mexico, ultimately claiming the entire Mississippi basin—half the territory of the present-day United States—for Louis XIV.

Having asserted title to Louisiana, as LaSalle christened this empire, the French began settling its southern gateway. The first colonizers arrived on the Gulf Coast in 1698; within a year the French had erected a fort near modern Biloxi, Mississippi; in 1702 the French founded a trading post where De Soto had faltered and called it Mobile. But Louisiana's growth would be delayed for another decade.

New Mexico: The Pueblo Revolt

After 1625 Spanish colonization in North America expanded on early bases in New Mexico and Florida. Although the colonies needed ties with friendly Native Americans to obtain land, labor, and security, such friendly relations proved hard to come by.

The Spanish sought to rule New Mexico by subordinating the Pueblo Indians to their authority. Franciscan missionaries established churches in the native communities (pueblos) and tried to force the Indians to attend mass and observe Catholic rituals and morality. Spanish landowners received *encomiendas* that allowed them to exploit Indian labor. Finally, the Spanish drove a wedge between the Pueblo Indians and their nonfarming trade partners, the Apaches and the Navajos. Corn once used to trade was now claimed as tribute by the Spanish. In response the Apaches raided both pueblos and Spanish settlements, driving most of the pueblo dwellers to stronger ties with the Spanish.

Spanish rule began to chafe, especially after 1660. Drought withered Pueblo crops, leaving populations vulnerable to disease and starvation. The Pueblo population plummeted from eighty thousand in 1600 to barely seventeen thousand by the 1670s. Compounding the misery, Apaches riding horses stolen from the Spanish raided and plundered the pueblos. Desperate Indians turned to traditional beliefs and ceremonies to restore the spiritual balance and bring rainfall and peace. Determined to suppress this "witchcraft," Franciscan missionaries entered sacred kivas, destroyed religious objects, and publicly whipped Native religious leaders and their followers.

In 1675, Governor Juan Francisco Trevino ordered the kivas sacked and religious leaders arrested. Three leaders went to the gallows; a fourth hanged himself; forty-three others were jailed, whipped, and sentenced to be sold as slaves. When armed warriors from several pueblos converged on Santa Fe to demand the prisoners' release, Governor Trevino complied.

But Indian resentment against the Spanish still blazed. Pueblo leaders began planning to overthrow the Spanish. At the head of the revolt was Popé, who had been arrested in 1675. Other leaders included disillusioned Christian converts and individuals of mixed Pueblo-Spanish ancestry. Most had tried to reconcile Christianity and Spanish rule with their Indian identities, but the deteriorating conditions and Spanish intolerance had turned them against Catholicism.

The Pueblo Revolt began in August 1680 as Popé and cohorts attacked Spanish colonists residing near Taos and killed sixty-eight of the seventy. Joined by Indians from neighboring pueblos, they laid siege to New Mexico's capital, Santa Fe. The rebels destroyed the churches and killed nearly four hundred colonists and missionaries. The Spanish fled, not to return for twelve years.

Led by a new governor, Diego de Vargas, the Spanish returned in 1692, using both violence and threats of violence to re-establish their rule. Spanish control of New Mexico remained limited as the Europeans abolished the *encomienda* and reined in the Franciscans. Pueblo suspicion of the Spanish remained, but there were no more revolts. Instead the Indians accepted the limited Spanish control and sustained their cultural identities within the boundaries of colonial rule.

Diego de Vargas
As the newly appointed governor of New Mexico, Vargas led Spain's reoccupation of New Mexico, beginning in 1692.

Florida and Texas

The Spanish fared no better in Florida. Periodic rebellions swept the Spanish settlements, and beginning in the 1680s Indian slave raiders allied to the English killed or captured thousands of Florida Natives and sold them to English slave traders. Even before a new round of warfare erupted in Europe at the turn of the century, Spain was ill prepared to defend its beleaguered North American empire.

English expansion threatened Florida, while the French establishment of Louisiana dashed Spanish hopes of linking Florida to New Mexico. To offset the French, Spanish authorities proclaimed the province of Tejas (Texas) in 1691, but no permanent Spanish settlements appeared there until 1716.

Chronology

1628	Massachusetts Bay colony founded.	**1663**	Half-Way Covenant adopted.
1630–1642	The great English migration to North America.	**1664**	English conquer New Netherland; establish New York and New Jersey.
1633	First English settlements in Connecticut.	**1670**	Charles Town, Carolina, established. Virginia defines slavery as a lifelong, inheritable racial status.
1634	Lord Baltimore founds Maryland.		
1636	Roger Williams founds Providence, Rhode Island. Harvard College established.	**1675–1676**	King Philip's War in New England.
1637	Antinomian crisis in Massachusetts Bay. Pequot War in Connecticut.	**1676**	Bacon's Rebellion in Virginia.
		1680	Pueblo revolt begins in New Mexico.
1638	New Sweden established.	**1681**	William Penn founds Pennsylvania.
1642–1648	English Civil War.	**1682**	La Salle claims Louisiana for France.
1644–1646	Third Anglo-Powhatan War in Virginia.	**1691**	Spain establishes Texas.
1649	Maryland's Act for Religious Toleration. King Charles I beheaded.	**1692–1700**	Spain "reconquers" New Mexico.
		1692–1693	Salem witchcraft trials.
1655	New Netherland annexes New Sweden.	**1698**	First French settlements in Louisiana.
1660	Restoration in England; Charles II becomes king.		
1661	Maryland defines slavery as a lifelong, inheritable racial status.		

CONCLUSION *hc* ACE Practice Test

By 1700 the movement of peoples and goods transformed the map of North America. Europeans spread far and wide among colonial regions; trade linked some regions to others and all to Europe. Strong Indian groups such as the Creek and Iroquois enhanced their economic and political standing; others either reconciled themselves to coexistence with the Europeans or fled in order to avoid contact with them.

Within the English colonies, four distinct regions emerged. In New England, Puritanism lost its sharp edges as colonists reconciled their religious views with the realities of a commercial economy. In the Chesapeake, tobacco planters replaced white indentured servants with African slaves. Carolina, the third region, prospered with the introduction of slavery from the West Indies. In the middle colonies, ethnic and religious pluralism generally prevailed as colonists embraced the market economy. Planters and merchants rose to prominence in each region, but most whites lived on family farms.

The English colonies far outnumbered their French or Spanish counterparts. By 1700 England's mainland population, including slaves, stood at 250,000, compared to 15,000 in the French colonies and 4,500 in the Spanish.

French and Spanish colonists depended more on friendly relations with Native Americans for their livelihoods and security than did the English. Most French colonists lived in the St. Lawrence Valley, while most Spanish colonists clustered along the Rio Grande Valley in New Mexico. Both numbers and isolation precluded the Southwest's development as a major center of colonization.

By 1700 there were clear differences between the colonies of the major European powers in North America, differences that would shape American history during the century that followed.

FURTHER READING

Ira Berlin, *Many Thousands Gone: The First Two Centuries of Slavery in North America* (1998). A major study comparing the experiences and cultures of three distinct cohorts of mainland slaves, from the earliest arrival through the age of the American Revolution.

Paul Boyer and Stephen Nissenbaum, *Salem Possessed: The Social Origins of Witchcraft* (1974). A study of the witchcraft episode as the expression of social conflict in one New England community.

James Deetz and Patricia Scott Deetz, *The Times of Their Lives: Life, Love, and Death in Plymouth Colony (2000)*. An examination of everyday life in New England using archaeological and documentary evidence and offering some surprising conclusions.

Allison Games, *Migration and the Origins of the English Atlantic World* (1999). An in-depth study of English emigrants to the Chesapeake, New England, and the Caribbean in the second quarter of the seventeenth century.

Jack P. Greene, *Pursuits of Happiness: The Social Development of Early Modern British Colonies and the Formation of American Culture* (1988). A brilliant synthesis of the colonial history of English America.

Allan Greer, *The People of New France* (1997). An excellent brief introduction to the social history of French North America.

Andrew L. Knaut, *The Pueblo Revolt of 1680: Conquest and Resistance in Seventeenth-Century New Mexico* (1995). A comprehensive, insightful account of Pueblo-Spanish relations during the seventeenth century.

Edmund S. Morgan, *American Slavery, American Freedom: The Ordeal of Colonial Virginia* (1975). A classic analysis of the origins of southern slavery and race relations.

Mary Beth Norton, *Founding Mothers and Fathers: Gendered Power and the Forming of American Society* (1996). A major study of female and male power in the seventeenth-century colonies.

Mrs. Harme Gansevoort (Magdalena Bouw), by Pieter Vanderlyn, c. 1740

The Bonds of Empire, 1660–1750

 This icon will direct you to additional study and research resources at http://college.hmco.com/history/us/boyer/enduring_concise/5e/students/index.html

With the English Civil War's end in 1646, the flow of English settlers to America became a torrent. New colonies soon dotted the Atlantic seaboard from French-held Canada to Spanish-controlled Florida. Although English immigrants peopled most of these colonies, significant numbers of Germans, Irish, Scottish, Dutch, and French arrived and contributed to the emerging American culture. So, too, did the increasing African-American population, which slowly became English-speaking and Christian.

**This chapter focuses on
four major questions:**

▶ How did the Glorious Revolution shape relations between England and its North
American colonies?

▶ What were the most important consequences of British mercantilism for the
mainland colonies?

▶ What factors explain the relative strengths
of the British, French, and Spanish empires
in North America?

▶ What were the most important effects of the
Enlightenment and the Great Awakening for
the British colonies?

A generation of imperial crisis and war against
the French from 1685 until 1713 forged among
Anglo-America's whites a strong sense of shared allegiance to the English crown and of deeply felt
Protestant heritage. During the peace that prevailed from 1713 to 1744, two vital but conflicting
currents of European culture challenged British-
American provincialism. The first was the Enlightenment, a movement among the educated public
characterized by a faith in reason and an appreciation of natural science. Joining and opposing this
movement was a second current, a religious revival
that pulsed across Protestant Europe in the 1730s
and 1740s, a movement known as the Great Awakening in the American colonies.

Beginning with a series of Navigation Acts late
in seventeenth century, England tightened the
bonds linking the colonies' economic fortune with
its own. These policies, coupled with the astonishing population growth of the colonies, enabled
British North America to achieve a level of growth
and prosperity unequaled elsewhere in the Americas. Accompanying the steadily accelerating move-

ment of goods was the movement of ideas and
news that made the British Empire a world power
and sharply distinguished its colonies from their
French and Spanish neighbors.

REBELLION AND WAR, 1660–1713

After the Restoration, England undertook a con-
certed effort to expanded overseas trade and to
subordinate its colonies to English commercial interests and political authority. The fall of the Stuart
dynasty in 1689 and a succession of international
wars hindered but did not halt this effort.

Royal Centralization, 1660–1688

The sons of a king executed by Parliament, the last
Stuart monarchs, Charles II and James II, disliked
representative government. They tried to rule England as much as possible without Parliament and
eyed American colonial assemblies suspiciously.

As Duke of York during his brother Charles's
rule, James showed his disdain for colonial assemblies almost as soon as he became the proprietor of
New York. Calling elected assemblies "of dangerous
consequence," he forbade legislatures to meet
from 1664 to 1682. Charles himself often appointed high-ranking army officers as colonial
governors. Technically civilians, these officers
commanded the militia and used it to crush civilian dissent. In his twenty-five-year reign, more
than 90 percent of the governors whom Charles II
appointed were army officers, a serious violation of
the English tradition of holding the military accountable to civilian authority. When James became king, he continued the policy.

Ever resentful of outside meddling, New Englanders resisted such centralization of power. In
1661 the Massachusetts assembly declared its citizens exempt from all English laws and royal decrees
except declarations of war. Ignoring the Navigation
Acts, New Englanders welcomed Dutch traders.

Provoked, Charles targeted Massachusetts for
punishment. In 1679 he carved a new royal terri-

tory, New Hampshire, from Massachusetts. In 1684 he declared Massachusetts a royal colony and revoked its charter, the very foundation of the Puritan city upon a hill. Puritan minister Increase Mather called on the colonists to resist, even to the point of martyrdom.

James II's accession to the throne intensified royal centralization in America. In 1686 the new king merged five separate colonies—Massachusetts, New Hampshire, Connecticut, Rhode Island, and Plymouth—into the Dominion of New England, later adding New York and the Jerseys. Under the new system, these colonies' legislatures ceased to exist. Sir Edmund Andros, a former army officer, became the Dominion's governor.

Andros's arbitrary actions ignited burning hatred. He limited towns to one annual meeting and jailed prominent citizens in order to crush protests. He forced a Boston Puritan congregation to share its meetinghouse with an Anglican minister. And Andros enforced the Navigation Acts. "You have no more privileges left you," Andros reportedly told a group of colonists, "than not to be sold for slaves."

Tensions also ran high in New York, where Catholics held high political and military posts under the Duke of York's rule. Anxious colonists feared that these Catholic officials would betray the colony to France. When Andros's local deputy allowed harbor forts to deteriorate, New Yorkers suspected the worst.

The Glorious Revolution in England and America, 1688–1689

Puritans in England also worriedly monitored Stuart displays of pro-Catholic sympathies. The Duke of York himself became a Catholic in 1676, and Charles II converted on his deathbed. Both rulers violated English law by allowing Catholics to hold high office and to worship openly. James II had Anglican bishops who denounced these practices tried as state enemies.

The English tolerated James II's Catholicism only because his heirs, daughters Mary and Anne, remained Anglican. But in 1688 his second wife bore a son, who would be raised—and perhaps

would rule—as a Catholic. Aghast at the idea, English political leaders asked Mary and her husband, William of Orange (the Dutch Republic's leader), to intervene. When William and Mary led a small army to England in November 1688, royal troops defected to them, and James II fled to France.

This bloodless coup, the "Glorious Revolution," created a "limited monarchy" as defined by England's Bill of Rights of 1689. The monarchs promised to summon Parliament annually, to sign its bills, and to respect civil liberties. Neither the English nor Anglo-Americans would ever forget this vindication of limited representative government. Anglo-Americans struck their own blows for political liberty as well when Massachusetts, New York, and Maryland rose up against their Stuart-appointed rulers.

News of the Glorious Revolution electrified Massachusetts Puritans, who arrested Andros and his councilors. (He tried to flee in women's clothing but was caught when a guard spotted this "lady" in army boots.) Acting in the name of William and Mary, the Massachusetts elite resumed its own government. The new monarchs allowed Connecticut and Rhode Island to resume election of their own governors and permitted Massachusetts to absorb the Plymouth colony. But Massachusetts enjoyed only a partial victory. The colony's new royal charter of 1691 reserved to the crown the appointment of the governor. Moreover, property ownership, not church membership, became the criterion for voting. Worst of all, the Puritan colony had to tolerate Anglicans, who were proliferating in the port towns.

New York's counterpart of the anti-Stuart uprising was Leisler's Rebellion. In May 1689 the city militia, under Captain Jacob Leisler, had seized the harbor's main fort, begun to repair its defenses, and called elections for an assembly. Andros's deputy, his authority strangled, had sailed for England. In 1691 Leisler, still riding high, denied newly arrived English troops entry to key forts for fear that they were loyal to James II. But after a brief skirmish, Leisler was arrested and charged with treason for firing on royal troops. New Yorkers who considered themselves ill treated by Leisler packed the jury, and both he and his son-in-law were convicted and hanged.

Arbitrary government and fears of Catholic plots had also brought turmoil to Maryland by 1689, where the Protestant-dominated lower house and the Catholic upper chamber were feuding. When the Glorious Revolution had toppled James II, Lord Baltimore, away in England, had dispatched a courier to Maryland, commanding obedience to William and Mary. But the courier died en route. Maryland's Protestants widely suspected that their proprietor was a traitor who supported James II.

Protestant rebel John Coode organized the Protestant Association to secure Maryland for William and Mary. In July 1689 Coode and his co-conspirators seized the capital, removed Catholics from office, and requested that the crown take over the colony. Maryland became a royal province in 1691 and made the Church of England an established religion in 1692. Catholics, composing less than one-fourth of the population, lost the right to vote and to worship in public. In 1715 the fourth Lord Baltimore joined the Church of England and regained the proprietorship of Maryland. Maryland remained a proprietary colony until 1776.

The revolutionary events of 1688–1689 reestablished the colonies' legislative government and ensured Protestant religious freedom. William and Mary allowed colonial elites to reassert local control and encouraged Americans to identify their interests with England, laying the foundation for an empire based on voluntary allegiance, not raw force.

A Generation of War, 1689–1713

The Glorious Revolution ushered in a quarter century of war that convulsed both England and the colonies. In 1689 England joined a European coalition against France's Louis XIV and plunged into the War of the League of Augsburg (which Anglo-Americans called King William's War).

In 1690, the war spread to North America, as New Yorkers and Yankees launched an invasion of England's enemy, New France. The invasion deteriorated into cruel but inconclusive border raids by both sides. The Iroquois, allied to the English, bore the brunt of the war. French forces, enlisting the aid of virtually every other tribe from Maine to the Great Lakes, played havoc with Iroquois land and peoples. By 1700 one-fourth of the Iroquois warriors had been killed or taken prisoner or had fled to Canada. In twelve years the Iroquois population fell from 8,600 to 7,000. By comparison, English and Dutch casualties were fewer than 900, while the French probably lost no more than 400. In 1701 the Iroquois agreed to let Canada's governor settle their disputes with other Indians and to remain neutral in future wars. Thereafter, playing French and English off against each other, the Iroquois maintained control of their lands, rebuilt their population, and held the balance of power along the Great Lakes.

In 1702 a new European war pitted England against France and Spain. During what the colonists called Queen Anne's War, Anglo-Americans became painfully aware of their own military weakness. French and Indian raiders from Canada destroyed New England towns, while the Spanish invaded southern Carolina and nearly took Charles Town in 1706. Colonial vessels fell to French and Spanish warships. English forces, however, gained control of the Hudson Bay region, Newfoundland, and Acadia (henceforth called Nova Scotia). The peace signed in 1713 allowed Britain to keep these lands but left the French and Indians in control of their interior.

These wars had a profound political consequence. Anglo-Americans, newly aware of their military weakness, realized how much they needed the protection of the Royal Navy, and consequently they became more loyal than ever to the English crown. War thus reinforced the Anglo-American sense of British identity.

COLONIAL ECONOMIES AND SOCIETIES, 1660–1750

The arrival of peace in 1713 shifted the competition among England, France, and Spain from the military to the economic. Britain and France sought to integrate their colonies into single colonial empires; Spain attempted to do so, but found its power north of Mexico and the Caribbean severely limited.

Mercantilist Empires in America

A set of political-economic assumptions known as mercantilism supplied the framework for the new imperial economies. The term refers to European policies that aimed at guaranteeing prosperity by making the European country (England, France, or Spain) as self-sufficient as possible—by eliminating its dependence on foreign suppliers, damaging its foreign competitors' commerce, and increasing the national stock of gold and silver by selling more goods abroad than it bought.

A series of Navigation Acts governing commerce between Britain and its colonies embodied mercantilism. In 1651 the English Parliament passed the first Navigation Act to exclude the Dutch from English trade. During the Restoration, Parliament enacted the Navigation Acts of 1660 and 1663; they barred colonial merchants from exporting such commodities as sugar and tobacco to anywhere but England and from importing goods on non-English ships. Another major measure, the Molasses Act of 1733, sought to integrate Caribbean sugar growers into the imperial economy by slapping heavy import taxes on non-British imports and thus creating in effect a protective tariff. By 1750 a long series of Navigation Acts was affecting the colonial economy in four major ways.

First, the laws limited imperial trade to British-owned ships whose crews were three-quarters British (which was broadly defined to include all colonists, even blacks). This new shipping restriction helped Britain to become Europe's foremost shipping nation and laid the foundations for an American merchant marine. By the 1750s Americans owned one-third of all imperial vessels. The swift growth of this merchant marine diversified the colonial economy and made it more self-sufficient. The expansion of colonial shipping hastened urbanization. By 1770 New York and Philadelphia had become major ports, and one-third of the British merchant marine was American built.

Second, the Navigation Acts barred the colonies' export of "enumerated goods" unless they first passed through England or Scotland. Among these were tobacco, rice, furs, indigo, and naval stores (masts, hemp, tar, and turpentine). Parliament did not restrict grain, livestock, fish, lumber, or rum, which constituted 60 percent of colonial exports. Furthermore, American tobacco exporters received a monopoly on the British tobacco market. Parliament also refunded taxes on tobacco and rice later shipped from Britain to other countries—amounting eventually to about 85 percent of American tobacco and rice.

Third, the navigation system encouraged economic diversification. Parliament paid modest bounties to Americans producing silk, iron, dyes, hemp, lumber, and other products that Britain would otherwise have had to import from foreign countries. Parliament also erected protective tariffs against foreign goods.

Finally, the Navigation Acts made the colonies a protected market for low-priced consumer goods from Britain. As a result, the share of British exports bound for America rose from just 5 percent in 1700 to almost 40 percent by 1760. Mercantilism had given rise to a "consumer revolution" in British America.

Britain's fellow mercantilists in France and Spain enjoyed no such growth or prosperity. France's Canadian colonies had few materials other than furs to export, and they imported primarily wine and brandy. The French government actually lost money in the fur trade by sending sizable amounts of cloth, firearms, and other manufactured commodities to their Indian allies; the large army that France kept stationed in North America was also a drain on the French treasury. French Canada continued to lack the private investment, commercial infrastructure, consumer market, and manufacturing capacity that British North America was rapidly developing. The French did achieve some economic success in the West Indies, where sugar planters (in defiance of mercantilist principles) turned their cane into molasses and then sold much of the molasses to New England merchants. Louisiana remained unprofitable, a drain upon French resources.

Spain's economic record was even more dismal. The revival of the Spanish and Latin American economies during the eighteenth century did not extend north of Mexico, where many Spanish colonists turned to smuggling goods to and from Spain's rivals as a source of income. On the frontier between Spanish Texas and French Louisiana, for example, a thriving contraband trade generated substantial profits that helped keep the colonies afloat.

These economic successes and failures mirrored what was happening in the European mother countries. In both France and Spain, most wealth was in the form of land held by the nobility and the Catholic church; there was almost no liquidity. In contrast, England's economy was a commercial-mercantile one. More and more wealth was in the hands of merchants, who used it as capital to invest in commercial enterprises, trade, and manufacturing. Britain's navy protected that trade while the Bank of England ensured a stable money supply. Great Britain was well on the way to becoming the world's first industrial nation, and her colonies benefited accordingly; indeed, the colonies' per capita income from 1650 to 1770 rose twice as fast as that of Britain.

Immigration, Population Growth, and Diversity

Demographic differences reinforced Britain's economic advantages. The British colonies' non-Indian population outnumbered that of France by a nearly 17 to 1 ratio, and that of the Spanish colonies by a whopping 66 to 1 margin. By 1750 the British North American colonies boasted more than 1.1 million inhabitants, the French colonies 60,000, and the Spanish colonies an almost negligible 19,000.

Potential Spanish immigrants generally chose the wealthier Latin American colonies as their destination. Spain saw its settlements north of Mexico primarily as a buffer against French or English expansion, and consequently maintained a heavy military presence.

Poverty kept most French people from immigrating, and tales of harsh Canadian winters and wretched Louisiana conditions often deterred those who might otherwise have tried their luck in the New World. French Canada's population growth was primarily the result of natural increase; to populate Louisiana, the French government dispatched paupers and criminals and encouraged the large-scale importation of slaves. By 1732 two-thirds of lower Louisiana's 5,800 people were slaves.

Unlike their French and Spanish rivals, the British colonies could offer potential immigrants good farmland and a healthy economy. Equally important, the British willingly accepted non-British immigrants—as long as they were not Catholics—including a handful of Jews. Thus immigration as well as natural increase swelled the population of British North America.

After 1700, when life expectancy and family size in the South rose to levels typical of those of the North, Anglo-America's growth far outpaced Britain's. Colonial women had an average of eight children and forty-two grandchildren, compared to five children and fifteen grandchildren for their British counterparts. In 1700 England's population outnumbered the colonies' by twenty to one; by 1775 the ratio would be only three to one.

In the eighteenth century continuing immigration contributed significantly to colonial population growth. In the forty years after Queen Anne's War, 350,000 newcomers had reached the colonies. The percentage of English-born immigrants among whites decreased sharply. Ironically, enslaved Africans, some 140,000 in number, constituted the largest group of newcomers. Most were from Africa's west coast, and all had survived a sea crossing of sickening brutality. Ship captains closely calculated how many slaves they could jam into their vessels. Kept below deck in near-darkness, surrounded by filth and stench, numbed by depression, the Africans frequently fell victim to disease.

By mid-century blacks constituted 20 percent of the North American colonies' population. Although slavery remained primarily a southern institution, 15 percent of all slaves lived north of Maryland; by 1750 one in seven New Yorkers was a slave.

West Indian and Brazilian slave buyers often outbid the mainland colonists, who of necessity not

Architect's Plan of a Slave Ship
This plan graphically depicts the crowded, unsanitary conditions under which enslaved Africans were packed like cargo and transported across the Atlantic.

only bought a higher proportion of female slaves but also protected their investments by maintaining slaves' health. As a result, slaves on the mainland, unlike their Caribbean or Brazilian counterparts, often formed families and enjoyed relatively long life spans. Natural increase among African-Americans almost equaled that of whites, and in some places American-born slaves outnumbered those born in Africa. As the number of creole (American-born) slaves grew, sharp differences between them and African-born blacks arose. Creoles enjoyed the advantage of knowing the English language, the local environment, and the ways of their masters. They often translated this advantage into greater autonomy. Wealthier planters in particular used African-born slaves as field hands while training creoles to perform household duties such as repairing and driving carriages, preparing and serving meals, sewing, and caring for their children.

Between 1630 and 1700 approximately 2,000 English settlers arrived in the colonies annually, constituting 90 percent of all European immigrants. After 1713 the flood slowed to a trickle of 500 English immigrants a year. Rising employment and wages in England made emigration less attractive, but economic hardships elsewhere in the British isles and on the Continent guaranteed a steady stream of immigrants, greatly increasing ethnic diversity among white North Americans.

More than 100,000 newcomers in this era were from Ireland. Two-thirds of these were "Scots-Irish," the descendants of sixteenth-century Scottish Presbyterian settlers of northern Ireland. The Scots-Irish generally immigrated as complete

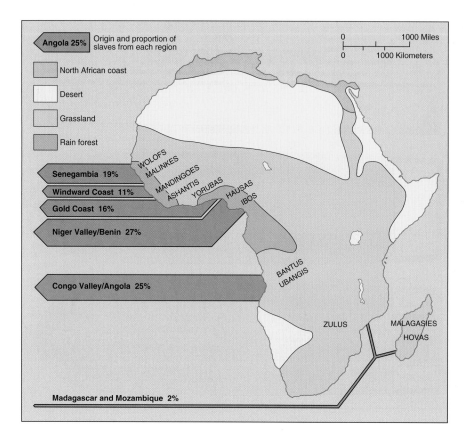

MAP 4.1
African Origins of North American Slaves, 1690–1807
Virtually all slaves brought to English North America came from West Africa, between Senegambia and Angola. Most were captured or bought inland and marched to the coast, where they were sold to African merchants who in turn sold them to European slave traders.

families. In contrast, 90 percent of Irish Catholic immigrants consisted of unmarried males who, once in America, often abandoned their faith to marry Protestant women.

Germany contributed some 125,000 settlers, the majority seeking escape from desperate poverty. One-third were "redemptioners" who had sold themselves or their children as indentured servants. Lutherans and Calvinists predominated, but a significant minority belonged to small, pacifist sects that desired above all to be left alone.

Immigrants shunned areas where land was scarce and expensive because most of them were poor. Philadelphia became the immigrants' primary port of entry. By 1775 the English accounted for only one-third of Pennsylvania's population.

Indentured servants had to work one to four years for a master who might exploit them cruelly.

Servants could be sold or rented out, beaten, kept from marrying, and sexually harassed; attempted escape usually meant an extension of service. At the end of their term, most collected "freedom dues," which helped them to marry and to acquire land. **hc** Primary Source: Excerpts on Virginia Law

The piedmont, a broad, rolling upland stretching along the eastern slope of the Appalachians, drew many immigrants. Upper New York, Pennsylvania, and Maryland attracted large numbers of Germans and Scots-Irish. Charles Town became a popular gateway for immigrants who later moved westward to the Carolina piedmont to become small farmers. In 1713 few Anglo-Americans lived more than fifty miles from the Atlantic, but by 1750 one-third of the colonists resided in the piedmont.

Not all of the white immigrants came voluntarily. Between 1718 and 1783 some thirty thousand

English convicts arrived in North America; some were murderers, most thieves. They were sold as servants. Relatively few committed crimes in the colonies, and some established themselves as successful backcountry farmers.

English-descended colonists did not relish the arrival of so many foreigners. Benjamin Franklin wrote:

> Why should the Palatine boors [Germans] be suffered to swarm into our settlements, and, by herding together, establish their language and manners, to the exclusion of ours? Why should Pennsylvania, founded by the English, become a colony of aliens, who will shortly be so numerous as to Germanize us instead of us Anglicizing them, and will never adopt our language or customs any more than they can acquire our complexion?

Franklin also objected to the slave trade because, he argued, it would increase America's black population at the expense of industrious whites. He uncharitably suggested that colonists reciprocate by sending rattlesnakes to Britain.

Rural White Men and Women

Because the vast majority of colonial landowners had just enough acreage for a working farm, most could not provide land for their children when they married. Moreover, with longevity increasing, children often did not receive their inheritances until middle age or later; and, because families were large, a farmer's wealth was typically divided into small portions. Under these circumstances, a young man typically worked from about age sixteen to twenty-three as a field hand to save money just to buy farm equipment, and a young husband generally had to rent land until he reached his mid-thirties. Land ownership came fastest to those farmers who took part-time work to increase their savings. Carpentry, fur trapping, and wintertime jobs such as draining meadows and fencing land supplemented farm incomes.

MAP 4.2

Immigration and British Colonial Expansion, to 1755

Black majorities emerged in much of the Chesapeake tidewater and the Carolina-Georgia low country. Immigrants from Germany, Ireland, and Scotland predominated among the settlers in the piedmont. A significant Jewish population emerged in the seaports.

The payment of mortgages was slow. A farmer could expect to earn 6 percent cash income per year, which barely equaled mortgage interest. After making a down payment of one-third, a husband and wife generally paid the next third through their inheritances. The final third would be paid when the children reached their teens and helped to double the regular farm income. Most colonial parents found themselves free of debt only as they reached their late fifties.

Rural families depended somewhat on barter and much more on what wives and daughters manufactured: soap, preserved food, knitted goods, yarn, and the products of dairy, orchard, and garden. In this way women made significant contributions to the family's cash income and well-being. Legal constraints, however, bound colonial women. A woman's most independent decision was her choice of a husband. Once married, she lost control of her dowry. Nevertheless, widows controlled substantial property—an estimated 8 to 10 percent of all property in eighteenth-century Anglo-America—and some ran large estates or plantations.

Colonial Farmers and the Environment

As English settlement expanded, the environment east of the Appalachians changed rapidly. Eighteenth-century settlers cleared forest land in order to plant crops in its fertile soil. New England farmers also cleared from their land innumerable large rocks, debris from the last Ice Age. The felled trees provided timber to construct houses, barns, and fences and to burn as fuel for cooking and heating. Urban dwellers bought their firewood and construction timber from farmers and planters. Six years after Georgia's founding, a colonist noted that there was "no more firewood in Savannah; . . . it must be brought from the plantations [and is] already right expensive."

Removal of trees (deforestation) deprived large forest creatures such as bears, panthers, and wild turkeys of their habitat, while the planted land provided free lunch for rabbits, mice, and possums. Deforestation removed protection from winds and

A New England Woman's Cupboard
Modest prosperity enabled some married women to exercise power as consumers and even to express their individuality. Hannah Barnard, a Hadley, Massachusetts, farm woman, commissioned this cupboard for storing linens and other fine textiles, in about 1720.

sun, producing warmer summers and harsher winters and, ironically, reinforcing the demand for firewood. By hastening the runoff of spring waters, deforestation led to heavier flooding and, where water could not escape, to larger swamps. Volatile temperatures and water levels rapidly reduced the number of fish in colonial streams and lakes. By 1766 naturalist John Bartram noted that fish "abounded formerly when the Indians lived much on them" but that "now there is not the 100th or perhaps the 1000th [portion] to be found."

Deforestation also dried and hardened the soil; colonial crops had even more drastic effects. Native Americans had rotated their crops to protect against soil depletion, but many colonial farmers lacked enough land to do so—and many more were unwilling to sacrifice short-term profits for long-term benefits. As early as 1637 a dismayed New England farmer found that his soil "after five or six years [of planting corn] grows barren beyond belief and puts on the face of winter in the time of summer." Tobacco yields in the Chesapeake region declined in fields planted only three or four consecutive years. As Chesapeake tobacco growers abandoned tidewater fields and moved to the piedmont, they hastened erosion. By 1750, in order to remain productive, many shifted from tobacco to wheat.

Well-to-do Europeans had already turned to conservation and "scientific farming." North American colonists ignored such techniques. Some could not afford to implement them, and virtually all believed that America's vast lands, including those still held by Indians, would sustain them and future generations indefinitely.

The Urban Paradox

Cities were colonial America's economic paradox. Although they shipped the livestock, grain, and lumber that enriched the countryside, at the same time they were caught in a downward spiral of declining opportunity.

After 1740 the 4 percent of colonists in cities found economic success elusive. Philadelphia, New York, and Boston faced escalating poverty. Debilitating ocean voyages left many immigrants too weak to work, and every ship from Europe carried widows and orphans. The cities' poor rolls, moreover, always bulged with the survivors of mariners lost at sea; unskilled, landless men; and women (often widows) and children from the countryside. High population density and poor sanitation left colonial cities vulnerable to the rapid spread of contagious diseases. As a result, half of all city children died before twenty-one, and urban adults averaged ten fewer years of life than rural residents.

Even the able-bodied found cities economically treacherous. Traditionally, artisans trained apprentices and employed them as journeymen until they could open their own shops. After 1750, however,

more employers released their workers when business slowed. And from 1720 onward recessions hit frequently, creating longer spells of unemployment. As urban populations ballooned, wages shrank, while the cost of rent, food, and firewood shot up.

After 1700 urban poverty became a major problem. In Boston, for example, the proportion of the population too poor to pay taxes climbed steadily. New York did not build its first poorhouse until 1736, but 4 percent of its population needed public assistance by 1772. The percentage of Philadelphia families listed as poor jumped from 3 percent in 1720 to 11 percent by 1760.

Wealth remained highly concentrated. New York's wealthiest 10 percent owned about 45 percent of the property throughout the eighteenth century; Boston and Philadelphia followed similar patterns. Both status and wealth were becoming increasingly polarized in urban America.

In the South most cities were little more than large towns, although Charles Town was North America's fourth-largest city. South Carolina's capital offered gracious living to wealthy planters during the months of heat and insect infestations on their plantations. But shanties on the city's outskirts sheltered a growing crowd of destitute whites. Like their counterparts in northern port cities, Charles Town's poor whites competed for work with urban slaves whose masters rented out their labor. Racial tensions simmered.

Middle-class urban women faced less manual drudgery than their rural counterparts. Nonetheless, they managed complex households, often including servants and other nonfamily members. Although they raised poultry and vegetables, sewed, and knitted, urban women generally purchased their cloth and most of their food. Household servants, usually young single women or widows, helped with cooking, cleaning, and laundering. Wives also worked in family businesses, usually located in the owner's home.

Widows and less affluent wives took in boarders and often spun and wove cloth for local merchants. Grim conditions in Boston forced many widows with children to look to the community for relief. Although their Puritan ancestors had seen providing care for poor dependents a matter of Christian charity, affluent Bostonians turned an increasingly wary eye toward the needy.

Slavery's Wages

Masters could usually afford to keep slaves healthy, but they rarely made their human chattels comfortable. Slave upkeep generally cost 60 percent less than the maintenance of indentured servants. White servants ate 200 pounds of beef or pork a year; slaves, 50 pounds. A master would spend as much providing beer and hard cider for a servant as food and clothing for a slave. Adult slaves received eight quarts of corn and one pound of pork weekly and were expected to grow vegetables and to raise poultry.

Slaves worked for a longer portion of their lives than whites. Slave children worked part-time from the age of seven and full-time as early as eleven. African-American women performed hard work alongside men and tended tobacco and rice crops even when pregnant. Most slaves toiled until they died, although those in their sixties rarely did hard labor.

Both Africans and creoles maximized opportunities within this harsh system. House slaves demanded that guests tip them for shining shoes and stabling horses; they also expected gifts on holidays. In the Carolina and Georgia rice country, the task system gave slaves some control of their work. Under tasking, each slave spent a half day caring for a quarter acre, after which his or her duties ended. Ambitious slaves used the rest of the day to keep hogs or to grow vegetables for sale in Charles Town.

The gang system used on tobacco plantations gave Chesapeake slaves less free time than their counterparts in Carolina. However, despite Carolina slaves' greater autonomy, racial tensions ran high, especially as blacks began to outnumber whites. For example, a law of 1735 imposed severe restrictions on slave clothing. Of far greater concern were large gatherings of blacks uncontrolled by whites. In 1721 Charles Town enacted a 9 p.m. curfew for blacks; Carolina's assembly placed all lo-

cal slave patrols under the colonial militia. Slaves responded with increased instances of arson, theft, flight, and violence.

By midcentury slaves constituted 20 percent of New York City's population and formed a majority in Charles Town and Savannah. Skilled urban slaves hired themselves out and kept part of their wages. By 1770 one-tenth of Savannah's slaves were living in rented rooms away from their owners. Despite substantial personal freedom, they remained slaves. Although city life afforded them some freedom of association, it did not extend to them the opportunities of their owners.

Tensions erupted in 1739 when a slave uprising known as the Stono Rebellion jolted South Carolina. Stealing guns and ammunition from a store at the Stono River Bridge, one hundred slaves headed for Florida crying "Liberty!" Along the way they burned seven plantations and killed twenty whites. Within a day, however, mounted militiamen surrounded the runaways, cut them down, and spiked a rebel head on every milepost back to Charles Town. Whites expressed their fears in a new slave code stipulating constant surveillance for slaves. The code threatened masters with fines for not disciplining slaves and required legislative approval for manumission (the freeing of individual slaves). The Stono Rebellion thus accelerated South Carolina's emergence as a racist and fear-ridden society. The rebels' failure showed slaves that armed uprisings were suicidal. But slaves would continue to resist by feigning stupidity, running away, committing arson or sabotage, or poisoning masters. Not until 1831 would significant slave violence of a comparable scale erupt on the mainland.

Racial tensions wracked cities as well as plantations. In 1712 rebellious slaves in New York City killed nine whites; as a result thirteen slaves were hanged, one was starved to death, three were burned at the stake, one was broken on the wheel, and six committed suicide. In 1741 a wave of thefts and fires attributed to slaves in New York led to the torture and hanging of thirteen slaves, the burning of thirteen more, and the sale of seventy to the West Indies.

The Rise of the Colonial Elites

For white colonial Americans, wealth defined status. "A man who has money here, no matter how he came by it, he is everything," wrote a Rhode Islander in 1748. Once wealthy, a man was expected to be responsible, dignified, and generous and to act as a community leader—to act like a gentleman. His wife was expected to be a skillful household manager and a refined, yet deferential hostess—a lady.

Before 1700 class structure in the colonies was relatively invisible; the rural elite spent its resources on land, servants, and slaves instead of conspicuous luxuries. A traveler visiting one of Virginia's richest planters noted that his host owned only "good beds but no curtains and instead of cane chairs . . . stools made of wood." After 1720, however, the display of wealth became more ostentatious. The greater gentry—the richest 2 percent of the population—built splendid estate homes such as New Jersey's Low House and Virginia's Shirley Mansion. The lesser gentry, or second-wealthiest 2 to 10 percent, lived in more modest fieldstone or wood-frame houses, and middle-class farmers typically inhabited one-story wooden buildings with four small rooms.

The gentry also exhibited their wealth after 1720 by imitating European "refinements." They wore costly English fashions, drove carriages, and bought expensive china, books, and furniture. They pursued a gracious life by studying foreign languages, learning formal dances, and cultivating polite manners. Horse racing replaced cockfighting as a preferred spectator sport. A few young colonial males received English educations.

COMPETING FOR A CONTINENT, 1713–1750

Europeans transformed North America in the first half of the eighteenth century as they expanded their territorial claims, opened new areas for settlement, and engaged in more intensive trade and warfare with Native Americans. In turn, Native Americans welcomed some of these developments and resisted others.

France and Native Americans

Louisiana became a principal focus of France's imperial efforts. New Orleans, established in 1718, became the colony's capital and port. France hoped to use the Choctaw Indians as allies, but by the 1730s the tribe had become bitterly divided between pro-English and pro-French factions.

Louisiana's sluggish export economy forced settlers and slaves to find other means of support. Like the Indians, they hunted, fished, gathered wild plants, and cultivated gardens. And red, white, and black Louisianans traded with one another. Indians provided corn, tallow, and above all deerskins to merchants in return for blankets, kettles, axes, chickens, hogs, guns, and alcohol. Indians from west of the Mississippi brought horses and cattle, usually stolen from Spanish ranches in Texas. West African slaves, familiar with cattle from their homelands, managed many of Louisiana's herds; some became rustlers and illicit traders of beef.

French settlements in Upper Louisiana, usually referred to as Illinois, were somewhat better off. Wheat became Illinois' major export, a more stable and profitable crop than the plantation commodities grown further south. However, the colony's remote location limited exports and attracted few whites. It continued to depend on Native American allies to defend it from Indian enemies.

French attention also turned to the Ohio Valley, which, thanks to Iroquois neutrality, had become a refuge for dislocated Native American tribes such as the Kickapoos, Shawnees, and Delawares. In order to counter growing English influence and to secure commercial and diplomatic ties with the Indians, the French expanded their trade. Several French posts, including Detroit, ballooned into sizable villages of Indian, French, and mixed-ancestry residents. Nonetheless, increased English trade in the area led most Indians to prefer an independent course.

Although the French were generally more successful than the English among the Indians, the French never won over the Chickasaws, who were supported by Carolina and whose frequent attacks made life miserable for the French and their Indian allies. Another southeastern tribe, the Creeks, played French, Spanish, and British off against one another, while the Fox Indians kept French traders from direct contact with Sioux tribes. In 1729–1730 the French brutally suppressed the Natchez Indians, the last of the Mississippian peoples, in order to open up land in Louisiana for tobacco and sugar cultivation.

By 1744 French traders had explored as far west as North Dakota and Colorado, buying beaver pelts and Indian slaves on the Great Plains. These traders and their competitors spread trade goods, including guns, to Native Americans throughout central Canada and the Plains. Meanwhile, Indians in the southern Plains and Great Basin had acquired horses from the thousands left behind by fleeing Spaniards after the Pueblo Revolt of 1680. Horses and guns enabled tribes such as the Lakota Sioux and Comanche to move onto the Plains and build a new, highly mobile way of life based on the pursuit of the buffalo. Widely scattered settlements along the Mississippi in modern-day Illinois and Missouri completed France's domain, an immense territory precariously dependent on often shaky relations with Native Americans.

Native Americans and British Expansion

The depopulation and dislocation of Native Americans made possible the colonies' rapid expansion. Epidemic diseases, environmental changes, war, and political pressure opened new land for Europeans. In Carolina, imperial wars and the trade in Indian slaves soon produced violence. Between 1711 and 1713 clashes between the Tuscaroras and the white settlers led to the death or enslavement of about one-fifth of the tribe; most survivors migrated northward to upstate New York to become the sixth nation of the Iroquois Confederacy.

More clashes between settlers and Indians quickly followed, as the Yamasee led a series of attacks on English settlements between 1715 and 1716 in retaliation for a series of abuses. Only by relying on the aid of the Cherokees and by arming four hundred slaves did the colony crush the uprising.

The defeat of the Yamasees in turn left their Catawba allies wedged uncomfortably between the English to the south and the Iroquois to the north. They turned to the English for help. In return for land and promises to defend the colony against other Indians, the Catawbas received guns, food, and clothing. Although this gave the Catawba at least temporary security, the rapidly increasing white population and the competition for resources sharply limited Catawba autonomy.

To the North, the Iroquois tried to accommodate the English and consolidate their own power. Late in the seventeenth century the Iroquois had entered into a series of agreements, known as the Covenant Chain, to relocate Indians whose lands the colonists desired. These tribes were moved to areas of New York and Pennsylvania, on the periphery of the Iroquois' homeland, to serve as buffers against English expansion. By agreeing to the covenant, and by incorporating the Tuscaroras into their confederacy, the Iroquois created a center of Native American power distinct from, but cooperative with, the British. Pennsylvania coerced the Delawares into selling more than 50,000 acres between 1729 and 1734. Then the colony's leaders produced a patently fraudulent treaty, dated to 1686, in which the Delawares promised to sell their land as far west as a man could walk in a day and a half. In 1737 the colony hired three men to walk west as fast as they could. They covered nearly 60 miles, forcing the Delawares to cede 1,200 square miles of land in what became known as the Walking Purchase. The Delawares were forced to move, and the proprietors made a huge profit from land sales.

Indians elsewhere along the westward-moving frontier faced pressure from settlers on one side and the Iroquois on the other. For example, having earlier abandoned some villages that white settlers were encroaching on, the Catawbas of the Carolina piedmont, facing a dramatic decrease in wild game, moved westward and ran into the Iroquois.

British Expansion in the South: Georgia

In 1732 Parliament chartered a new colony, Georgia. It was to be a refuge for debtors, whose settlement would buffer South Carolina against attacks from Spanish Florida. Further, the new English colony would export expensive commodities such as wine and silk. To fulfill these plans, Parliament even spent money on the colony, the only North American colony except Nova Scotia in which the British government invested.

James Oglethorpe, who dominated the provincial board of trustees, shaped Georgia's early years. He established the port of entry, Savannah, in 1733. By 1740 nearly 3,000 colonists resided in Georgia. Almost half were non-English, immigrants from Germany, Switzerland, and Scotland, and most had their overseas passage paid by the government. A small number of Jews were among the early settlers. Thus Georgia began as the last English colony.

Idealism and concerns about security led Oglethorpe to ban slavery from Georgia. "If we allow slaves," he wrote to the trustees, "we act against the very principles by which we associated together, which was to relieve the distressed." Oglethorpe thought that slavery degraded blacks, made whites lazy, and presented a terrible risk. He worried that reliance on slave labor could result in a slave revolt. Parliament thus made Georgia the only colony where slavery was forbidden.

Oglethorpe's well-intentioned plans failed. Few debtors arrived because of Parliament's restrictions on their release from prison. Limitations that Oglethorpe had secured on settlers' rights to enlarge or sell their holdings discouraged immigrants, as did the ban on slavery. Georgia exported neither wine nor silk; only rice proved profitable. After a decade of struggle against economic reality, Oglethorpe yielded. In 1750 slavery became legal, and restrictions on landholdings ended. As a result, Georgia boomed.

Spain's Tenacity

While trying to maintain an empire in the face of Native American, French, and British adversaries, Spain spread its language and culture over much of North America, especially the Southwest. To repopulate New Mexico with settlers after the Pueblo Revolt (see Chapter 3), Spain handed out huge land grants and constructed fortifications, primarily for defense against the Apaches. Settlers typically built houses on small lots around the church plaza, farmed separate fields nearby, grazed livestock, and shared community woodlands and pasture. Livestock-raising *ranchos* (ranches) monopolized vast amounts of land along the Rio Grande and blocked the establishment of further towns. On these *ranchos* mounted herders of cattle and sheep (*vaqueros*) created the way of life later adopted by the American cowboy, featuring lariat and roping skills, cattle drives, and roundups.

By 1750 New Mexico contained just 5,200 Spanish and 13,500 Pueblos. Integrated into New Mexico society, most Pueblos practiced both Catholicism and their traditional religion. Along the frontier, Navajos and Apaches made peace with New Mexico to gain support against raids by Utes from the north and Comanches from the east.

To counter growing French influence among the Comanches and other Native Americans on the southern plains, Spain colonized Texas. In 1716 the Spanish established four missions. The most successful of the missions was at San Antonio de Bexar, where friars constructed a fortified building known as the Alamo. The Spanish presence in Texas remained light, however; by midcentury only 1,200 Spaniards lived there under constant threat of Indian raids.

By 1750 the French and Spanish empires had reached their limits in North America. Spain controlled much of the Southeast and Southwest, and France claimed the Mississippi, Ohio, and Missouri River valleys. Spain also maintained a precarious hold on Florida. Both empires, spread thin,

MAP 4.3
French and Spanish Occupation of North America, to 1750
While British colonists concentrated themselves on the Atlantic seaboard, the French and Spanish together established themselves thinly over two-thirds of the present-day United States. **hc** Interactive Map: European Claims in North America

depended heavily on Indian goodwill. In contrast, British North America, compact and aggressively expansionist, was generally antagonistic toward Native Americans.

The Return of War, 1739–1748

Imperial rivalries between England, on the one hand, and France and Spain, on the other, prevailed after 1713. In 1739 Britain launched a war against Spain. James Oglethorpe led a massive but unsuccessful assault on St. Augustine in 1740; Spanish troops and refugees slaves from South Carolina likewise failed in a counterattack on Georgia two years later. By then, the Anglo-Spanish War had merged with one in Europe, the War of the Austrian Succession (1739–1748), known as King George's War to the colonists. In this conflict, four thousand New Englanders besieged the French fortress at Louisbourg, at the mouth of the St. Lawrence, and captured it after seven intense weeks of fighting. But the war was inconclusive and in 1748 Britain returned Louisbourg to the French under terms of the peace treaty ending the conflict. The memory of how their sacrifices were for naught rankled New Englanders thereafter.

PUBLIC LIFE IN BRITISH AMERICA, 1689–1750

During the early and middle eighteenth century, the ties linking Britain and its colonies extended far beyond the movement of goods and peoples. England's new Bill of Rights was the foundation of government and politics in the colonies. English thinkers inspired the Enlightenment, while English preacher George Whitefield sparked a generation of colonists to transform the practice of Protestantism in British America. Significantly, these developments involved many more colonists than before as active participants in politics, in intellectual discussions, and in new religious movements. This wider participation signaled the emergence of a new phenomenon in colonial life, the "public."

Colonial Politics

The colonial elite dominated politics as well as society. Governors appointed members of the greater gentry to serve on councils and as judges in the highest courts. The upper gentry, along with militia majors and colonels, also dominated among the representatives elected to the legislatures' lower houses (the assemblies). Members of the lesser gentry sat less often in the legislatures, but they commonly served as justices of the peace in the county courts.

Outside New England property restrictions barred 80 percent of white men from running for the assembly. In any case few ordinary citizens could have afforded the high costs of elective office. Assemblymen received meager living expenses, which did not cover the cost of staying at the capital, much less make up for six to ten weeks of missed work. Even members of the gentry grumbled about legislative duty, many of them viewing it as "a sort of tax . . . to serve the public at their own Expense besides the neglect of their business." Consequently, political leadership fell to a small number of wealthy families with a tradition of public service.

The colonies generally set liberal qualifications for male voters, but all excluded women, blacks, and Indians from voting. In seven colonies voters had to own land (usually forty to fifty acres), and in the others they had to have enough property to furnish a house and to work a farm. Most of the 40 percent who could not meet these requirements were indentured servants, single sons living with parents, or young men just beginning family life. Most white males in Anglo-America could vote by age forty, whereas across the Atlantic, two-thirds of all Englishmen and 90 percent of Irishmen could never vote.

Rural voting participation was low, averaging 45 percent. Governors called elections randomly so that after years without an election one could be called on short notice. Voters in isolated areas often did not know of an upcoming election. Voting took place at the county seat, and many voters did not risk traveling long distances over poor roads to reach the voting place. In many colonies voters stated their preference publicly, often face to face with the candidates, a practice that discouraged dissenters. There were no political parties to stimulate popular interest or to mobilize voters. Candidates nominated themselves and ran on their reputations, not on issues.

In view of these factors, political indifference was widespread. For example, to avoid paying legislators' expenses, many Massachusetts towns refused to elect assemblymen. From 1731 to 1760 one-third of South Carolina's elected assemblymen neglected to take their seats. Apathy might have been even greater had not candidates plied voters with alcohol. George Washington dispensed almost two quarts of liquor for each voter when first elected to Virginia's assembly in 1758.

Only in the major seaports did political life flourish. Here greater population density, better communications, and the use of secret ballots (except in New York) accounted for a relatively high voter turnout. Furthermore, the cities' acute economic difficulties stimulated political participation among voters, ever hopeful that government might ease their problems.

In 1735 New York became the site of a celebrated trial. Newspaper printer John Peter Zenger was charged with seditiously libeling the colony's governor. Zenger's acquittal on the charge broadened political discussion and participation beyond a small circle of elites. It also established truth as a defense against the charge of libel, opening the way toward greater freedom of the press in the future.

The most important political development after 1700 was the rise of the assembly as the dominant force in colonial government. Except in Connecticut and Rhode Island, the crown or proprietors chose colonial governors, who in turn named a council, or upper legislative house. Only in the lower house, or assembly, could members of the gentry defend their interests. Until 1689 governors and councils drafted laws, and the assemblies generally followed passively. Thereafter assemblies assumed a more central role in politics as colonial leaders argued that their legislatures should exercise the same rights as Parliament. Indeed, they viewed their assemblies as miniature Houses of Commons and believed that colonial governors should be as restricted as monarchs. Parliament's victory in the Glorious Revolution convinced Americans that their governors had limited powers and should defer to the assemblies.

The lower houses refused to permit meddling in their procedures, took control over taxes and budgets, and kept a tight rein on executive salaries. Governors remained vulnerable to such financial pressure: they received no salary from Britain and relied on the assemblies for income. This "power of the purse" often forced governors to sign laws opposed by the crown.

Moreover, Britain's lack of interest in colonial politics allowed the assemblies to seize considerable power. The Board of Trade, established by Parliament in 1696 to monitor American affairs, had neither the staff, the energy, nor the vision to maintain royal authority by supporting embattled governors. This vacuum in royal power allowed the colonies to become self-governing in most respects except for regulating trade, printing money, and declaring war. This autonomy, reinforced by self-assertive assemblies, would haunt British authorities when they attempted to exercise more direct rule after 1763 (see Chapter 5).

THE ENLIGHTENMENT

Eighteenth-century Anglo-America was probably the world's most literate society. Ninety percent of New England's adult white males and 40 percent of its women could write well enough to sign documents. In other colonies the literacy rate varied from 35 to 50 percent. In contrast, in England it stood at just over 30 percent. Nevertheless, ordinary Americans' reading encompassed only a few books: an almanac, a psalter, and the Bible. They inhabited a world of oral culture, in which ideas and information were passed through the spoken word—in conversations, debates, and sermons.

However, members of the gentry, well-off merchants, and educated ministers lived in a world of print culture. Though costly, books and writing paper opened eighteenth-century European civilization to men and women of these classes who could read. And a rich, exciting world it was. Great advances in natural science seemed to explain the laws of nature, human intelligence appeared poised to triumph over ignorance and prejudice, and life itself would surely become more pleasant. For those with time to read and think, an age of optimism and progress had dawned: the Enlightenment.

American intellectuals drew inspiration from Enlightenment ideals, which combined confidence in reason with skepticism toward beliefs not based on science or logic. Enlightenment thought drew on the work of the English physicist Sir Isaac Newton (1642–1727), who explained how gravitation ruled the universe. Newton's work demonstrated the harmony of natural laws and stimulated others to search for rational principles in medicine, law, psychology, and government.

No American more embodied the Enlightenment spirit than Benjamin Franklin (1706–1790). Born in Boston, Franklin migrated to Philadelphia at age seventeen, bringing considerable assets: skill as a printer, ambition, and insatiable curiosity. In 1732 Franklin began publishing *Poor Richard's Almanack,* a collection of proverbs that made him famous. By age forty-two he had saved enough money to retire from printing and to devote himself to science and community service.

To Franklin, science and community service were intertwined; true science would make everyone's life more comfortable. For example, his experiments in flying a kite during a thunderstorm proved that lightning was electricity and led to the invention of the lightning rod. In 1743 Franklin organized the American Philosophical Society to encourage "all philosophical experiments that let light into the nature of things, tend to increase the power of man over matter, and multiply the conveniences and pleasures of life." By 1769 the society had blossomed into an intercolonial network of amateur scientists.

Although some plantation owners, among them Thomas Jefferson, championed the Enlightenment, it flourished in the seaboard cities, where the latest ideas from Europe circulated and gentlemen and artisans met in small societies to investigate nature. To these individuals, the Royal Society in London, the foremost learned society in the English-speaking world, represented the ideal. The Enlightenment thus initially strengthened ties between British and colonial elites. Its adherents envisioned progress as gradual and proceeding from the top down. They trusted reason far more than they trusted the common people, whose judgment seemed too easily deranged.

Just as Newton inspired the scientific bent of Enlightenment intellectuals, the English philosopher John Locke's *Essay Concerning Human Understanding* (1690) led many to embrace "reasonable" or "rational" religion. Locke contended that ideas are not inborn but are acquired by investigation of, and reflection on, experience. Enlightenment intellectuals believed that the study of the harmony and order of nature provided the best argument for God, a rational Creator. A handful insisted that where the Bible conflicted with reason, one should follow reason. Those—including Franklin and Jefferson—who took the argument furthest were called Deists. They concluded that God, having created a perfect universe, did not miraculously intervene in its workings but instead left it alone to operate according to natural law.

Most colonists influenced by the Enlightenment considered themselves Christians but feared Christianity's excesses, particularly persecution in the name of religion and "enthusiasts" who emphasized emotion over reason. Mindful of Locke's caution that no human can be absolutely certain of anything but his or her own existence, they distrusted zealots and sectarians and believed that religion's value lay in the encouragement of virtue and morality, not in theological hair-splitting.

In 1750 the Enlightenment's greatest contributions to American life lay in the future, when Anglo-Americans would draw on the Enlightenment's revolutionary ideas as they declared independence and created a new nation. In the meantime, a series of religious revivals known as the Great Awakening would challenge the Enlightenment's most basic assumptions.

The Great Awakening

Rationalists viewed the world as orderly and predictable. Many Americans, however, had neither worldly goods nor orderly and predictable lives. A diphtheria epidemic in 1737–1738 that killed every tenth child under sixteen from New Hampshire to Pennsylvania starkly reminded the colonists how fragile life was and turned their thoughts to religion.

A quickening of religious fervor in scattered places in the 1730s became passionate revivalism throughout Anglo-America in 1739. This "Great Awakening" cut across lines of class, status, and education. Above all, the Great Awakening represented an unleashing of anxiety and longing among ordinary people living in a world of oral culture—anxiety about sin, longing for salvation. And it was the spoken word that brought the answers that they craved. But for all—colonial elites comfortable in the print world and commoners accustomed to the oral world—religion was primarily a matter of emotional commitment.

In contrast to rationalists, who stressed the human potential for betterment, the ministers of the Great Awakening emphasized the corruption of human nature, the fury of divine wrath, and the need for immediate repentance. Although well aware of contemporary philosophy and science, Congregationalist minister Jonathan Edwards drove home this message with breathtaking clarity. In 1735 during a revival in Northampton, Massachusetts, Edwards preached his great sermon "Sinners in the Hands of an Angry God." "The God that holds you over the pit of Hell, much as one holds a spider or other loathsome insect over the fire, abhors you," Edwards intoned. "His wrath toward you burns like fire; He looks upon you as worthy of nothing else but to be cast into the fire."

Other colonial ministers—Presbyterian William Tennent and Dutch Reformed Theodore Frelinghuysen—had anticipated Edwards's fire-and-brimstone style. Pulling the diverse threads of revival together was the arrival in 1739 of the charismatic English cleric George Whitefield. A man of overpowering presence and a booming voice, Whitefield attracted some crowds exceeding 20,000. On a tour through the colonies Whitefield inspired thousands, mainly young adults, to seek salvation. Within four years of Whitefield's arrival, 20 percent of Connecticut colonists under age forty-five had been "saved" after listening to Whitefield.

Whitefield's powerful allure awed even his critics. But divisions over the revivals developed in Whitefield's wake. For example, after leaving Boston in October 1740, Whitefield invited Gilbert Tennent (William's son) to follow "in order to blow up the divine flame lately kindled there." Denouncing Boston's established clergy as "dead Drones" and lashing out at elites, Tennent built a following among the poor and downtrodden.

Exposing colonial society's divisions, Tennent and other radicals corroded support for revivals among established ministers and officials. Increasingly, lines hardened between the revivalists, the "New Lights," and the rationalist clergymen, or "Old Lights," who dominated the Anglican, Presbyterian, and Congregational churches. In 1740 Gilbert Tennent hinted that most Presbyterian ministers lacked saving grace and were bound for hell, and he urged parishioners to abandon them for the New Lights. By sowing doubts about ministers, Tennent undermined one of the foundations of the social order, for if people could not trust their ministers, whom *could* they trust? Old Light rationalists fired back. In 1742 Charles Chauncy, a Boston Congregationalist, condemned revivals as an epidemic of the "enthusiasm" that enlightened intellectuals so hated. Chauncy especially blasted enthusiasts who mistook the ravings of their overheated imaginations for direct communications from God.

The Great Awakening thus split American Protestantism. In 1741 Old and New Light Presbyterians formed rival branches that reunited in 1758 when the revivalists emerged victorious. The Anglican church lost many members to New Light Presbyterians and Baptists. Congregationalists also splintered badly; by 1760 New Lights had seceded from one-third of all churches and formed separate parishes.

In Massachusetts and Connecticut, where the Congregational church was established by law, the secession of New Light parishes provoked bitter conflict. Old Lights denied new parishes legal status and tried to force New Lights into paying tithes to their former churches. Many New Lights were expelled from the legislature. In Windham County, Connecticut, an extra story was added to the jail to hold the New Lights arrested for failure to pay tithes.

The Great Awakening peaked in 1742 but New Lights made steady gains into the 1770s, and the revival's long-term effects far exceeded its immediate impact. First, the revival started a decline in the influence of older sects such as the Quakers, Anglicans, and Congregationalists. In turn, the number of Presbyterians and Baptists increased after 1740, and that of Methodists rose steadily after 1770. These churches have since dominated American Protestantism. Second, the Great Awakening stimulated the founding of new colleges unscarred by religious wars. The College of New Jersey (Princeton, 1746), King's College (Columbia, 1754), the College of Rhode Island (Brown, 1764), Queen's College (Rutgers, 1766), and Dartmouth (1769) trace their roots to this era. Third, the revival drew many African-Americans and Native Americans to Protestantism for the first time. Its oral and communal nature and emphasis on piety, rather than learning, blended aspects of both groups' traditional cultures. The Great Awakening marked the real emergence of black Protestantism as New Lights reached out to slaves, some of whom joined white churches and even preached at revival meetings. Meanwhile,

Reverend Samson Occom, Mohegan Indian Preacher
Born in a wigwam in Connecticut, Occom converted to Christianity under the influence of the Great Awakening and preached to other Native Americans. But he grew disillusioned with the treatment of his people by whites and, after the American Revolution, joined an exodus of Indians from New England to upstate New York.

a few New Light preachers became missionaries to Indians still residing in the colonies. Some Christian Indians, such as the Mohegan Samson Occom, became preachers themselves.

The Great Awakening, moreover, gave women added prominence in colonial religion. For several decades ministers had praised women—the majority of church members—as the embodiment of Christian piety. Now some New Light sects, mainly Baptist and Congregationalist, granted women the right to speak and vote in church meetings. Some women, like Anne Hutchinson a century earlier, presided over prayer meetings that included women, men, and sometimes even slaves. Although some of these women's activities were suppressed, none was prosecuted as Hutchinson had been. The Great Awakening also fostered religious tolerance by blurring theological differences among New Lights. Indeed, revivalism's emphasis on inner experience, rather than doctrinal fine points, helped to prepare Americans to accept the denominational pluralism that emerged after the Revolution.

Historians disagree about whether the Great Awakening had political effects. Although New Lights flayed the wealthy, they neither advocated a social revolution nor developed a political ideology. Yet by empowering ordinary people to criticize those in authority, the revivals laid the groundwork for political revolutionaries a generation later who would preach that royal government had grown corrupt and unworthy of obedience.

CONCLUSION *hc* ACE Practice Test

By 1750 Britain's mainland colonies bore little resemblance to those of a hundred years earlier. Prosperity and a rapidly increasing population characterized the colonies. They also benefited from the emergence of representative government as result of the Glorious Revolution. Educated Anglo-Americans joined the intellectual ferment of the Enlightenment, while the Great Awakening, with its European origins, signaled the colonies' emergence from provincial isolation.

In stark contrast, French and Spanish colonies still faltered. Lightly populated by Europeans, they were remote from the more dynamic centers of Atlantic commerce and did little to enrich their home countries. Both depended heavily on Indian allies for military survival.

However, tensions filled British America. Vast discrepancies in wealth and opportunity fostered a rebellious spirit among the less well-off, while the Enlightenment and the Great Awakening revealed deep ideological and religious divisions. Racial antagonisms fueled both slave resistance and Anglo-Indian warfare, and the revived imperial warfare of 1739–1748 added to the uncertainties of colonial life.

Chronology

1651–1733	England enacts Navigation Acts.	**1718**	New Orleans founded.
1660	Restoration of the English monarchy.	**1729–1730**	French war on Natchez Indians in Louisiana.
1686–1689	Dominion of New England.	**1732**	Georgia founded.
1688–1689	Glorious Revolution in England.	**1735**	John Peter Zenger acquitted of seditious libel in New York.
1689	Uprisings in Massachusetts, New York, and Maryland; royal authority established.		Jonathan Edwards leads revival in Northampton, Massachusetts.
1689–1697	King William's War (in Europe, War of the League of Augsburg).	**1737**	"Walking Purchase" of Delaware Indians in Pennsylvania.
1690	John Locke, *Essay Concerning Human Understanding.*	**1739**	Great Awakening begins with George Whitefield's arrival in British colonies.
1693	Spain begins offering freedom to English slaves escaping to Florida.		Stono Rebellion in South Carolina.
1701	Iroquois Confederacy's Grand Settlement with England and France.	**1739–1740**	Anglo-Spanish War.
1702–1713	Queen Anne's War (in Europe, War of the Spanish Succession).	**1743**	Benjamin Franklin founds American Philosophical Society.
1711	Tuscarora War in Carolina.	**1740–1748**	King George's War (in Europe, the War of the Austrian Succession).
1715–1716	Yamasee War in Georgia.	**1750**	Slavery legalized in Georgia.
1716	San Antonio de Bexar founded.		

FURTHER READING

Bernard Bailyn and Philip D. Morgan, eds., *Strangers within the Realm: Cultural Margins of the First British Empire* (1991). Leading historians examine the interplay of ethnicity and empire in North America, the Caribbean, and the British Isles.

Jon Butler, *Becoming American: The Revolution Before 1776* (2000). A provocative discussion of the British colonies, arguing that they became a distinctive modern society between 1680 and 1770.

W. J. Eccles, *France in America*, rev. ed. (1991). An interpretive overview of French colonization in North America and the Caribbean by a distinguished scholar.

Ronald Hoffman et al., eds., *Through a Glass Darkly: Reflections on Personal Identity in Early America* (1997). Essays that explore issues of personal identity for individual Americans during the seventeenth and eighteenth centuries.

John J. McCusker and Russell R. Menard, *The Economy of British America, 1607–1789*, rev. ed. (1991). A comprehensive discussion of the colonial economy in light of current scholarship.

James H. Merrell, *Into the Woods: Negotiators on the Pennsylvania Frontier* (1999). A brilliant, innovative study of intercultural diplomacy as practiced by Indians and colonists.

Philip D. Morgan, *Slave Counterpoint: Black Culture in the Eighteenth-Century Chesapeake and Lowcountry* (1998). The definitive study of African-American life in Britain's southern colonies.

Daniel K. Richter, *Facing East from Indian Country: A Native History of Early America* (2001). A highly original examination of colonial American history from the perspective of Native Americans.

Laurel Thatcher Ulrich, *The Age of Homespun: Objects and Stories in the Creation of an American Myth* (2001). A pathbreaking study that uses New England women's work with textiles as a window into economic, gender, and cultural history.

David J. Weber, *The Spanish People in North America* (1992). A masterful synthesis of Spanish colonial history north of the Caribbean and Mexico.

5

The Boston Massacre, 1770, engraving by Paul Revere

Roads to Revolution, 1750–1776

 This icon will direct you to additional study and research resources at http://college.hmco.com/history/us/boyer/enduring_concise/5e/students/index.html

By 1763 Britain had defeated France, its chief competitor for preeminence in North America, and stood at the height of eighteenth-century imperial power. British rule ran undisputed from the Atlantic seacoast to the Mississippi River and from northernmost Canada to the Florida straits. Ironically, this greatest of British triumphs would turn into one of the greatest of British defeats.

The imperial reorganization that war and conquest made necessary after 1763 radically altered Britain's relationship with its American colonies. Conflict arose between Britain and the colonies when Parliament, searching for ways to pay off the enormous debt accumulated during the war, attempted to tighten control over colonial affairs. The colonists, accustomed to legislating for themselves, widely resisted this effort to centralize decision making in

This chapter focuses on four major questions:

▶ How and why did their joint triumph in the Seven Years' War lead to a rupture between Britain and its American colonies?

▶ Why did differences over revenue-raising measures lead to a more fundamental conflict over political authority between Britain and the colonists?

▶ How did the imperial crisis lead nonelite colonists to become politically active?

▶ What were the major factors that led most colonists to abandon their loyalty to Britain and choose independence instead?

London. American leaders interpreted Britain's clampdown as calculated antagonism, intended to deprive them of both prosperity and relative independence.

Other groups had their own perspectives, shaped as much by social-economic tensions as by constitutional crisis. In port cities crowds of poor and working people clashed with British authority in sometimes violent demonstrations, in concert with or in defiance of elite radicals. In remote "backcountry" areas settlers used the language and ideas of urban radicals to resist domination by large landowners and seaboard elites. Throughout the colonies women brought their own perspective to the unfolding crisis.

Colonial resistance to British policies also reflected democratic stirrings in America and throughout the North Atlantic world. Among the products of this democratic urge were both the American Revolution, which erupted in 1776, and the French Revolution, which began in 1789 and sparked unrest over much of Europe and the Americas.

Despite their apprehension, colonial politicians expressed their opposition peacefully from 1763 to 1775, through legislative resolutions and commercial boycotts. Even after fighting erupted, the colonists agonized for more than a year about whether to sever their political relationship with England—which even native-born Americans sometimes referred to affectionately as "home." Of all the world's colonial peoples, none became rebels more reluctantly than Anglo-Americans did in 1776.

THE TRIUMPH OF THE BRITISH EMPIRE, 1750–1763

King George's War (see Chapter 4) did nothing to avert a showdown between Britain and France. The conflict resumed in 1756 and ended in 1763. Known as the Seven Years' War, it was a major turning point in both American and European history.

A Fragile Peace, 1750–1754

Since neither Britain nor France emerged from King George's War as the dominant power in North America, each prepared for another war. The Ohio Valley became the tinderbox for conflict. When France started building a chain of forts in order to regain control of the Virginia and Pennsylvania Indian trade, Virginia sent a twenty-one-year-old surveyor, George Washington, to demand that the French abandon their forts. In 1754 French troops drove Washington and his militiamen back to their homes.

In mid-1754 seven colonies sent delegates to Albany, New York, to plan their mutual defense. They bought Iroquois neutrality with wagonloads of presents and endorsed a plan for a colonial confederation, the Albany Plan of Union. However, the Plan collapsed because no colonial legislature would surrender control over its powers of taxation. Nonetheless, the Albany Plan provided a precedent for future American unity.

The Seven Years' War in America, 1754–1760

Although France and Britain remained at peace in Europe until 1756, Washington's unsuccessful conflict with the French had created a virtual state of war in North America. In 1754 Britain dispatched General Edward Braddock and 1,000 regulars to take Fort Duquesne, at the headwaters of the Ohio River.

Scornful of colonial soldiers, Braddock expected his disciplined regulars to make short work of the French. On July 9, 1755, about 850 French and Indians ambushed Braddock's 2,200 Britons and Virginians near Fort Duquesne. After three hours of steady fire, the British regulars broke and

MAP 5.1
The Seven Years' War in America
After experiencing major defeats early in the war, Anglo-American forces turned the tide against the French by taking Fort Duquesne and Louisbourg in 1758. After Canada fell in 1760, the fighting shifted to Spain's Caribbean colonies.

retreated, leaving Washington's Virginians to cover the withdrawal. Nine hundred regular soldiers and colonists died, including Braddock.

In 1756–1757 New France's daring commanding general Louis Joseph Montcalm maintained the offensive. Anglo-Americans outnumbered Canadians twenty to one, but Montcalm benefited from large numbers of French regulars, Indian support (including that of the neutral but usually British-leaning Iroquois), and full-scale mobilization of the Canadian population. The Anglo-American colonies supported the war grudgingly, providing few and usually poorly trained troops. French-armed Shawnees, Delawares, and Mingos struck hard at settlers in Western Pennsylvania, Maryland, and Virginia. These attacks halted English expansion and prevented the three colonies from joining the war against France for three years.

However, 1758 proved a turning point for the British. First, Indian support for the French evaporated, largely because France appeared to hold a decisive margin. Their withdrawal enabled Britain to easily capture Fort Duquesne and win control of the Ohio Valley. Second, British minister William Pitt took over Britain's military affairs. The imaginative and single-minded Pitt reinvigorated the military campaign. Hard pressed in Europe by France and its allies (which after 1761 included Spain), Pitt believed that mobilizing colonial forces was the key to crushing New France. Keeping fewer than 4,000 British regulars in North America, he promised that Parliament would bear the cost of maintaining colonial troops.

Pitt's offer to free Americans from the war's financial burden generated unprecedented support. In 1758 and again in 1759 the colonies organized 21,000 troops. As a result, Britain took the offensive and captured Louisbourg and Fort Duquesne in 1758 and Quebec in September 1759. In 1760, with Montreal's surrender, French resistance ended.

The End of French North America, 1760–1763

In the Treaty of Paris of 1763 France ceded all its territories on the North American mainland. Several thousand French colonists, scattered from Quebec to Louisiana, became British or Spanish citizens. However, one group, the Acadians of Nova Scotia, suffered tremendous dislocation. British subjects since 1713, they had refused to swear loyalty to Britain during the war and had been driven from their homes. The British deported the Acadians, nearly 5 percent of Canada's French population, to more southerly colonies such as Pennsylvania and Maryland. Impoverished and facing intense anti-French, anti-Catholic prejudice, most fled to Louisiana, where they became known as the Cajuns.

Under the Treaty of Paris, Britain received all French lands east of the Mississippi; Spain acquired the port of New Orleans and all French lands west of the Mississippi. Spain traded Florida to Britain in return for Cuba. Thus Spain's New World empire actually increased in size, but France's virtually vanished, shrinking to a handful of islands. Britain's North American empire quadrupled in size.

The effects of King George's War and the Seven Years' War were ironically mixed. On one hand, shedding their blood in a common cause led British and Americans to rely on each other as never before. However, the conclusion of both wars planted the seeds of misunderstanding, suspicion, and open hostility between the former compatriots.

IMPERIAL REVENUES AND REORGANIZATION, 1760–1766

Even as the Seven Years' War wound down, tensions developed between Britain and its colonies, largely the result of British plans to finance its greatly enlarged empire by a series of revenue measures whose enforcement bypassed local authorities. In the wake of the Stamp Act, protest swelled against not only the cost of the new measures but also against what many colonists saw as a dangerous extension of Parliamentary power.

The new revenue measures followed the ascension to the British throne of George III (ruled 1760–1820). The new king was determined to play a major role in government, but he proved ill-suited to

MAP 5.2
European Powers in North America, 1763
The Treaty of Paris (1763) divided France's North American empire between Britain and Spain. Hoping to prevent unnecessary violence between whites and Indians, Britain forbade any new white settlements west of the Appalachians' crest in the Proclamation of 1763.

nizing street demonstrations and appealing directly to the populace. Poor and working people, especially in economically strapped New England, defied colonial elites as well as British authorities and resorted to violence.

Friction Among Allies, 1760–1763

An extraordinary coalition of Britons, colonists, and Native Americans had defeated France, but deep-seated tensions among these allies were evident both during and after the war. British officers complained that colonial troops not only fought poorly but also tended to return home, even in the midst of campaigns, when their terms were up or when their pay lagged. In turn, colonial soldiers complained that British officers treated their troops "little better than slaves."

Tensions flared as well between British officers and colonial civilians. Officers groused about colonial unwillingness to provide food or shelter; colonists resented the officers' arrogance. Pennsylvania Quakers, pacifist by conviction, refused to vote funds for the war effort, while New York and Massachusetts saw the quartering of British troops on their soil as an encroachment on their English liberties. In the meantime, British authorities viewed these actions as affronts to the king's prerogative and as threats to the defense of British territories. Moreover, Pitt's promise to reimburse the colonies for their military expenses enraged Britons. Wartime spending had brought substantial profits to colonial farmers, artisans, and merchants. And some merchants had continued their illicit trade with the French West Indies, simultaneously violating the Navigation Acts *and* trading with the enemy. Britain's national debt had nearly doubled during the war, to more than £123 million. In contrast, the total colonial debt amounted to less than £1 million. Staggering under debt and taxes, the British thought it outrageous to repay the Americans for defending themselves.

Many colonists felt equally burdened. Wartime profits had gone to pay for British goods as thousands of people purchased what they had previously produced. Britain's manufacturing sector

the task of building political coalitions or pursuing consistent policies. His frequent and abrupt changes in leadership worsened relations with the colonists.

The colonists' protests reflected class and other divisions within their society. Most elites expressed themselves in carefully worded arguments intended for Parliament. Artisans, businessmen, and some planters used inflammatory language, orgaflourished—and then the wartime boom ended when peace returned. Now accustomed to new middle-class life-styles, colonists went into debt, and British creditors obliged by extending repayment terms from six months to a full year. Newly prosperous colonists found themselves mired in debt and even bankruptcy, and many began to suspect Britain of plotting to "enslave" the colonies in order to protect its own merchants and manufacturers.

Worse, Britain's victory over the French generated new Indian-white conflicts that drove the British debt even higher. No longer able to play the two imperial powers off against each other, Indians feared the consequences. They were right. To cut costs after the war, the British had stopped distributing food and ammunition to their Indian allies. Meanwhile, colonial squatters were moving onto Indian lands, raising both fears and tensions.

In early 1763 the Delaware Indian religious prophet Neolin called for Indians to repudiate European culture, goods, and alliances. Other Native Americans in the Great Lakes and the Ohio Valley regions wished for the return of the French so that they could again play the European powers off against each other. Pontiac, an Ottawa Indian, and other leaders forged an anti-British coalition that sacked eight British forts and besieged British positions at Detroit and Pittsburgh. Short on food and ammunition, suffering a smallpox epidemic (deliberately spread by the British), and recognizing that the French would not return, the Indians surrendered in early fall.

But the British victory over the Indians was indecisive. Hoping to end the frontier fighting, the British government issued the Proclamation of 1763, which asserted royal control of land transactions, settlements, and trade of non-Indians west of the Appalachians and recognized existing Indian land titles everywhere west of the "proclamation line," which ran down the crest of the Appalachian Mountains. Although the policy calmed Indian fears, it angered the colonies by subordinating their western land claims to imperial authority and slowing colonial expansion.

Pontiac's rebellion also led the British government to station 10,000 regular troops in North America to occupy the western lands that France had ceded and to intimidate the Indians. The cost of administering British North America reached almost £440,000 yearly. Britons believed it perfectly reasonable for the colonists to help offset this expense. The colonists, however, struggling with their own postwar economic recession, saw it as none of their responsibility.

Although partially offsetting the colonies' unfavorable balance of payments with Britain, these troops raised fears of a peacetime "standing army" that could threaten American liberty. With the French menace gone, increasing numbers of colonists viewed Indian lands to the west as the key to future prosperity. The British troops that enforced the Proclamation Act of 1763 thus became not protectors but threats to that future.

The Writs of Assistance, 1760–1761

To halt American trade with the enemy in the French West Indies during the Seven Years' War, Britain had cracked down on colonial smuggling. In 1760 the royal governor of Massachusetts authorized the use of the writ of assistance to seize illegally imported goods. A general search warrant, the writ permitted customs officials to enter any ship or building where smuggled goods might be hidden. Because it required no evidence of probable cause for suspicion, the writ was considered unconstitutional by most English legal authorities. The writ also threatened the privacy of family residences, from which most merchants conducted business.

The writ of assistance proved a powerful weapon against smuggling. Merchants in Boston, the colonies' smuggling capital, hired James Otis to challenge the device's constitutionality. The former prosecuting attorney for Boston's vice-admiralty court, Otis had resigned to protest the use of the writ. Before the Massachusetts Supreme Court in 1761, he argued that "an act against the Constitution is void"—even an act of Parliament. But the court, noting the use of an identical writ of assistance in England, ruled against the merchants.

Despite having lost his case, Otis had stated with clarity the colonial conception of Parliament's role under the British constitution. Most British politicians assumed that Parliament's laws themselves were part of the unwritten constitution and that Parliament could in effect alter the constitution at will. But like most colonists, Otis believed that Parliament had no authority to violate the traditional "rights of Englishmen" and that there were limits "beyond which if Parliaments go, their Acts bind not."

The Sugar Act, 1764

In 1764, three years after Otis's court challenge, Parliament passed the Sugar Act to offset part of Britain's North American military expenses. In ending the long-standing exemption of colonial trade from revenue-raising measures, the Sugar Act triggered new tension between Britain and the colonies. (The Navigation Acts, in contrast, had been intended not to raise revenue but to benefit the imperial economy indirectly by stimulating trade and protecting English manufacturers from foreign competition.)

The Sugar Act amended the Molasses Act of 1733, which constituted a 6 pence per gallon tariff on French-produced molasses. Colonists commonly bribed customs inspectors $1^{1}/2$ pence per gallon to look the other way when they unloaded smuggled molasses. In designing the Sugar Act, British officials, well aware of the widespread bribery, wrongly assumed that the colonists would willingly pay a lower, 3-pence-per-gallon tax.

Colonists found other features of the Sugar Act equally objectionable. The act brought a wide range of colonial commerce under imperial control. It stipulated that the colonists had to export certain raw commodities *through* Britain instead of going directly to foreign ports, as they had been doing.

The Sugar Act also complicated the requirements for shipping colonial goods. A captain had to fill out a confusing series of documents certifying the legality of his trade. The absence of any document left his cargo liable to seizure. The law's petty regulations made it virtually impossible for

many colonial shippers to avoid committing technical violations of the act.

Finally, the Sugar Act discarded many traditional English protections for a fair trial. First, the law allowed customs officials to transfer smuggling cases from the colonial courts, in which juries decided the outcome, to vice-admiralty courts, in which a judge delivered the verdict. Because the act awarded vice-admiralty judges 5 percent of any confiscated cargo, it gave them a financial incentive to find defendants guilty. Second, until 1767 the law required all cases to be heard in the vice-admiralty court at Halifax, Nova Scotia, and reversed normal procedure by presuming the guilt of the accused and requiring the defendant to prove innocence.

The Sugar Act was no idle threat—the navy enforced it vigorously. A Boston resident complained that "no vessel hardly comes in or goes out but they find some pretence to seize and detain her."

Americans continued to smuggle molasses rather than pay the three-pence tax until 1766, when the British lowered the duty to a penny, making it cheaper to pay the tax than to smuggle. After that the tax brought in about £30,000 a year.

Generally, opposition to the Sugar Act remained fragmented; the act provoked most opposition in the most heavily affected colonies—Massachusetts, New York, and Pennsylvania. Other colonies, unaffected, protested very little. Although its immediate impact was minor, the Sugar Act heightened colonial awareness of the new direction of imperial policies and its implications.

The Stamp Act, 1765

Revenues raised by the Sugar Act did little to ease Britain's financial crisis. Britons groaned under the second-highest tax rates in Europe and looked resentfully at the lightly taxed colonists, who paid an average of 1 shilling per person compared to their 26 shillings per person. Most agreed with Prime Minister George Grenville that fairness demanded a larger colonial contribution.

In March 1765, to force colonists to pay their share of imperial expenses, Parliament passed the

Stamp Act Protest
A Boston crowd burns bundles of the special watermarked paper intended for use as stamps.

Stamp Act. The law obliged Americans to purchase and use specially marked or stamped paper for newspapers, customs documents, wills, contracts, and other public legal documents. Violators faced prosecution in vice-admiralty courts, without juries. Grenville projected yearly revenues of £60,000 to £100,000, which would defray up to 20 percent of North American military expenses. Unlike the Sugar Act, an *external* tax levied on imports, the Stamp Act was an *internal* tax levied directly on property, goods, and services in the colonies. External taxes regulated trade and fell primarily on merchants and ship captains, but internal taxes were designed to raise revenue and had far wider effects. The Stamp Act would tax anyone who made a will, bought or sold property, purchased newspapers, or borrowed money.

William Pitt and others objected to such an internal tax, arguing that the colonies taxed themselves through their elected assemblies. But to Grenville and his supporters, the tax seemed a small price for the benefits of empire, especially since Britons had paid a similar tax since 1695. Grenville agreed with Stamp Act opponents that Parliament could not tax British subjects unless they enjoyed representation in that body. He contended, however, that the colonists, like many other British adult males who did not vote for members of Parliament, were *virtually* represented. Theoretically, with virtual representation, every member of Parliament considered the welfare of *all* subjects, not just his constituents, in deciding issues. No Briton was represented by any particular member of the House of Commons; but all imperial subjects, including Americans, could depend on each member of Parliament to protect their well-being.

Grenville and his supporters also held that the colonial assemblies had no powers other than those Parliament allowed them. This view clashed directly with the stance of the many colonists who had argued for decades that their assemblies exercised legislative power equivalent to that of Britain's House of Commons.

The Stamp Act made many colonists believe that they had to confront parliamentary taxation head-on or surrender any claim to meaningful self-government. However much they admired Parliament, few Americans thought that it represented them. While virtual representation might apply to England and Scotland, they argued, it certainly did not extend across the Atlantic. In the American view, unless a lawmaker shared his constituents' interests, he would have no personal stake in opposing bills contrary to their welfare. Thus the colonists favored *actual,* rather than virtual, representation.

To the colonists, the Stamp Act demonstrated both Parliament's indifference to their interests and the shallowness of virtual representation. Nonetheless they conceded that Parliament possessed *limited* powers of legislation, and they accepted the parliamentary regulation of imperial trade.

In a speech opposing the Sugar Act, James Otis had expressed Americans' basic argument: "that by [the British] Constitution, every man in the dominions is a free man; that no parts of His Majesty's dominions can be taxed without consent; that every part has a right to be represented in the supreme or some subordinate legislature." In essence, the colonists saw the empire as a loose federation (union) in which their legislatures possessed considerable autonomy.

Resisting the Stamp Act, 1765–1766

In 1765 a political storm generated by the Stamp Act rumbled through all the colonies. The tempest caught up nearly every member of colonial society, but before it ended, elite leaders had assumed direction of the resistance movement.

Patrick Henry, a twenty-nine-year-old Virginia lawyer with a gift for fiery oratory, expressed the rising spirit of resistance in late May. He persuaded Virginia's House of Burgesses to adopt strong resolutions denying Parliament's power to tax the colonies. Garbled accounts of his resolutions and speeches—he probably never said, "Give me liberty or give me death"—electrified other colonists. By year's end, eight other colonial legislatures had rejected parliamentary taxation.

Meanwhile, active resistance took shape. In Boston by late summer, middle-class artisans and businessmen had created the Loyal Nine to fight the Stamp Act. They recognized that the stamp distributors, who alone could sell the specially watermarked paper, represented the law's weak link. If public pressure could force them to resign before the tax went into effect on November 1, the Stamp Act would not work.

Boston's preeminence in opposing Parliament was no accident. Bostonians lived primarily by trade and distilling, and in 1765 they were not living well. The heavy tax on molasses burdened rum producers, and the Sugar Act's trade restrictions dried up the wine-import business and interfered with the direct export of New England products to profitable overseas markets. Moreover, its shipbuilding and fishing industries were declining; taxes, unemployment, and poverty had skyrocketed; and the city was recovering from a disastrous fire that had left every tenth family homeless.

This widespread economic distress produced an explosive situation. There was good reason to blame British policy for hard times. Furthermore, poor and working class Bostonians were accustomed to gathering in large crowds to express themselves politically. The high point of each year was Pope's Day, November 5, when thousands commemorated the failure of a supposed Catholic plot in 1605 to blow up Parliament and to kill King James I. Crowds from the North End and the South End of Boston burned gigantic effigies of the pope as well as of local political leaders and generally poked fun at the "better sorts."

The morning of August 14, 1765, found a likeness of Boston's stamp distributor, Andrew Oliver, swinging from a tree. Oliver did not take the hint to resign, so at dusk several hundred Bostonians demolished a new building of his at the dock. The mob then surged toward Oliver's house and vandalized it. Oliver announced his resignation the following morning.

Anger against the Stamp Act unleashed spontaneous, contagious violence. For example, in late August rioting Bostonians demolished the elegant home of Lieutenant Governor and Chief Justice Thomas Hutchinson. To many financially pinched citizens, Hutchinson symbolized the British policies that crippled Boston's economy and threatened their livelihoods. The lieutenant governor and other wealthy officials "rioted in luxury," their homes and fancy furnishings dwarfing the annual income of workingmen. (Ironically, Hutchinson privately opposed the Stamp Act.)

Meanwhile, groups calling themselves Sons of Liberty were forming throughout the colonies. Elite leaders of these groups sought to curb violence, fearful that attacks on one set of elites could lead to attacks on all elites. The Sons of Liberty focused their actions against property and carefully left avenues of escape for their victims; they forbade their members to carry weapons in order to avoid harming royal soldiers or officials. The only victims of violence would be martyrs from their own ranks.

In October 1765 representatives from nine colonies met in New York City in the Stamp Act Congress. There the colonies agreed on, and boldly articulated, the principle that Parliament had no authority to levy taxes outside Britain or to deny any person a jury trial. The united front of the Stamp Act Congress was far more effective than the one earlier intercolonial meeting, the Albany Congress of 1754. But while emboldening and unifying the colonies, declarations of principle such as the Stamp Act Congress resolutions seemed futile to many colonists, in view of Parliament's earlier refusal to consider their objections to the stamp duties.

By late 1765 most stamp distributors had resigned or fled, and, without the watermarked paper required by law, most customs officials and court officers refused to perform their duties. In response, legislators compelled them to resume operations by threatening to withhold their pay. At the same time, merchants obtained sailing clearances by insisting that they would sue if their cargoes spoiled while delayed in port. By late December the colonial courts and harbors were again functioning.

In these ways colonial elites assumed control of the public outcry against the Stamp Act. Respectable gentlemen kept an explosive situation under control by taking over leadership of local Sons of Liberty, by coordinating protest through the Stamp Act Congress, and by having colonial legislatures resume normal business. But the Stamp Act remained in effect. To force its repeal, New York's merchants agreed on October 31, 1765, to boycott all British goods. Others followed. Because the colonies purchased 40 percent of England's manufactures, this nonimportation strategy triggered panic within England's business community. Its members descended on Parliament to warn that continuing the Stamp Act would result in bankruptcies, unemployment, and political unrest. *hc* Primary Source: Charleston Sons of Liberty

The Declaratory Act, 1766

Meanwhile, the Marquis of Rockingham had succeeded George Grenville as prime minister. Rockingham hesitated to advocate repeal, but parliamentary support for repeal gradually grew—the result of practicality, not principle. In March 1766 Parliament revoked the Stamp Act. Simultaneously, however, Parliament passed the Declaratory Act, affirming parliamentary power to legislate for the colonies "in all cases whatsoever."

Because Americans interpreted the Declaratory Act as merely a face-saving measure on Parliament's part, they ignored it. In truth, however, the House of Commons intended that the colonists take the Declaratory Act literally to mean that they were not exempt from *any* parliamentary statute, including a tax law. The Stamp Act crisis thus ended in a fundamental disagreement between Britain and America over the colonists' political rights.

Although philosophical differences between Britain and America remained unresolved, most colonists put the events of 1765 behind them. Still loyal to "Old England," Anglo-Americans concluded that their resistance to the law had slapped Britain's leaders back to their senses. Yet the crisis led many to ponder British policies and actions more deeply than ever.

Ideology, Religion, and Resistance

The Stamp Act crisis had caused some Anglo-Americans to discern for the first time a sinister quality in the imperial relationship with Britain. To understand these perceptions, some educated colonists turned to philosophers, historians, and political writers. Many more looked to religion.

The colonists were familiar with John Locke and other Enlightenment political thinkers. Locke argued that in a state of nature, people enjoyed the "natural rights" of life, liberty, and property. To form governments to protect these rights, people entered into a "social contract." A government that encroached on natural rights broke its contract with the people. In such cases the people could resist their government. To many colonial leaders, Locke's concept of natural rights justified opposition to Parliament's arbitrary legislation.

The political writers read most widely in the colonies included a group known as oppositionists. According to John Trenchard and Thomas Gordon, among others, Parliament—the freely elected representatives of the people—formed the foundation of England's unique political liberties and protected them against the inherent corruption and tyranny of executive power. But since 1720, the oppositionists argued, prime ministers had exploited the treasury to provide pensions, contracts, and profitable offices to politicians and had bought elections by bribing voters. Most members of Parliament, they held, no longer represented the true interests of their constituents; instead, they had sold their souls for financial gain and joined a "conspiracy against liberty." Referring to themselves as the "country party," these oppositionists feared that a power-hungry "court party" of nonelected officials close to the king was using a corrupt Parliament to gain absolute power.

Influenced by such ideas, a number of colonists believed they detected a diabolical conspiracy underlying British policy. Joseph Warren of Massachusetts observed that the Stamp Act "induced some to imagine that the minister designed by this to force the colonies into a rebellion, and from thence to take occasion to treat them with severity and, by military power, to reduce them to servitude." Over the next decade a flood of pamphlets denounced British efforts to "enslave" the colonies. To many Americans, such an assault on liberty and natural rights justified opposition to British policies and actions.

Many colonists also followed the lead of Massachusetts assemblyman Samuel Adams, who expressed hope that America would become a "Christian Sparta." By linking religion and ancient history, Adams combined two potent rhetorical appeals. Virtually every colonial American was steeped in Protestantism, and those whose education had gone beyond the basics had imbibed Greek and Latin learning as well as seventeenth-century English literature. These traditions, Americans believed, confirmed the legitimacy of their cause.

Thomas Jefferson of Virginia was typical of educated men of the day in revering the classical Greeks and Romans for their virtuous devotion to liberty. The pamphlets and speeches of gentlemen such as Jefferson, John Dickinson, and Patrick Henry resounded with quotations from the ancients that served as constant reminders of the righteous dignity of their cause. But appeals to ordinary Americans drew on deeper wellsprings of belief, notably the religious fervor that the Great Awakening had stirred.

Beginning with the Stamp Act crisis, many Protestant clergymen summoned their flocks to stand up for God and liberty. Exhorted one minister, "We are bound in conscience to stand fast in the liberty with which Christ has made us free." (Most Anglican ministers, whose church the king headed, tried to stay neutral or opposed the protest.) Clergymen who exalted the cause of liberty exerted an enormous influence on popular opinion. Far more Americans heard or read sermons than had access to newspapers or pamphlets. A popular theme was how God sent the people woes only to strengthen and sustain them until victory. Even Virginia gentlemen not known for their piety felt moved by such messages and ordered their families to comply with the days of "fasting and public humiliation" proclaimed by the clerical leaders. Moreover, protest leaders' calls to boycott British luxuries meshed neatly with ministers' traditional warnings against frivolity and wastefulness. Few Americans could ignore the unceasing public reminders that solidarity against British tyranny and "corruption" meant rejecting sin and obeying God.

The ebbing of the Stamp Act crisis removed the urgency from such extreme views. But the alarm raised by British actions was not easily quieted. After a gap of two years it would become clear that British and American views of the colonies' place in the empire remained far apart.

RESISTANCE RESUMES, 1766–1770

Repeal of the Stamp Act temporarily quieted colonial protests, but Britain's search for new revenue soon revived them. British leaders denounced the colonists for evading their responsibilities, leaving most colonists convinced that the Stamp Act had not been an isolated mistake but part of a deliberate design to undermine colonial self-government. Growing numbers in Britain likewise questioned economically costly policies and actions that seemed to threaten Britons as well as colonists.

Opposing the Quartering Act, 1766–1767

In August 1766 George III dismissed the Rockingham government and summoned William Pitt to form a cabinet. An opponent of taxing the colonies, Pitt had the potential to repair the Stamp Act's damage; the colonists respected him highly. However, Pitt's health collapsed in March 1767, and Charles Townshend, the Chancellor of the Exchequer (treasurer), became the effective leader.

Just as Townshend took office, a conflict arose with the New York legislature over the Quartering Act of 1765, which ordered colonial legislatures to pay for certain goods used by British soldiers stationed within their borders—candles, window-panes, mattress straw, and a small liquor ration. The act applied only to troops in settled areas, not on the frontier. It did not force citizens to accept soldiers in private homes or require legislatures to erect barracks. The law aroused resentment, however, because it constituted an *indirect* tax. That is, although it did not empower royal officials to collect money directly from the colonists, it obligated assemblies to raise revenue by whatever means they considered appropriate. The act fell lightly on the colonies except New York, where more soldiers were stationed than in any other province. New York refused to grant the supplies.

New York's resistance unleashed a torrent of anti-American feeling in Parliament, still bitter after revoking the Stamp Act. Townshend responded by drafting the New York Suspending Act, which threatened to nullify all laws passed by the colony after October 1, 1767, if it refused to vote the supplies. By the time George III signed the measure, New York had already appropriated the funds. Nonetheless, the conflict over the Quartering Act demonstrated that British leaders would not hesitate to defend Parliament's authority through the most drastic of all steps: interfering with American self-government.

The Townshend Duties, 1767

This new wave of British resentment toward the colonies coincided with an outpouring of frustration over the government's failure to cut taxes from wartime levels. Discontent seethed among the landed gentry, whose members took advantage of their domination of the House of Commons to slash their own taxes in 1767. This move cost the government £500,000 and prompted Townshend to propose laws that would tax imports entering America and increase colonial customs revenues.

Townshend sought to tax the colonists by exploiting a loophole in their arguments against the Stamp Tax. Americans had emphasized their opposition to *internal* taxes but had said nothing about *external* taxes—Parliament's right to tax imports as they entered the colonies. Townshend interpreted this silence as evidence that the colonists accepted Britain's right to impose external taxes. But a now much wiser George Grenville predicted, "They will laugh at you for your distinctions about regulations of trade." Brushing aside such warnings, Parliament passed Townshend's Revenue Act of 1767 (popularly called the Townshend duties) in the summer. The new law taxed glass, paint, lead, paper, and tea imported into the colonies.

On the surface Townshend's case for external taxation was convincing, as the colonists had long accepted parliamentary regulation of trade and had in principle acknowledged taxation as a form of regulation. But the Townshend duties differed significantly from what Americans considered a legitimate way of regulating trade through taxation. To the colonists, charging a duty was a lawful way for British authorities to control trade only if it excluded foreign goods by making them prohibitively expensive. The Revenue Act of 1767, however, set moderate rates that did not price goods out of the colonial market; clearly, its purpose was to collect money for the treasury. Thus from the colonial standpoint, Townshend's duties were taxes just like the Stamp Act duties.

Townshend had an ulterior motive for establishing an American source of revenue. Traditionally, colonial legislatures set colonial royal governors' salaries and often refused to pay them until the governors signed bills that they opposed. Townshend hoped that the Revenue Act would establish a fund to pay governors' and other royal officials' salaries, freeing them from the assemblies' control. In effect, he would strip the assemblies of their most potent weapon, the power of the purse, and tip the balance of power away from elected representatives and toward appointed royal officials.

The Revenue Act never yielded the income that Townshend had anticipated. Of all the items taxed, only tea produced any significant revenue— £20,000 of the £37,000 expected. And because the measure would serve its purpose only if the colonists could afford British tea, Townshend eliminated £60,000 in import fees paid on East Indian tea entering Britain before transshipment to America. On balance, the Revenue Act *worsened* the British treasury's deficit by £23,000. By 1767 Britain's financial difficulties were more an excuse for political demands to tax the colonies than a driving force. From Parliament's standpoint, the conflict with America was becoming a test of national will over the *principle* of taxation.

The Colonists' Reaction, 1767–1769

Resistance to the act remained weak until December 1767, when John Dickinson published *Letters from a Farmer in Pennsylvania*. These twelve essays, which appeared in nearly every colonial newspaper, emphasized that Parliament had no right to tax trade for the simple purpose of raising revenue. No tax designed to produce revenue could be considered constitutional unless a people's elected representatives voted for it. Dickinson's writings convinced Americans that their arguments against the Stamp Act also applied to the Revenue Act.

In early 1768 the Massachusetts assembly asked Samuel Adams to draft a "circular letter" to other legislatures. Possessing a flair for the push and shove of local politics, Adams had helped organize the Sons of Liberty in Boston. Adam's circular letter denounced taxation without representation and the threat to self-governance posed by Parliament's making governors and royal officials independent of the legislatures. Nevertheless, the document acknowledged Parliament as the "supreme legislative Power over the whole Empire" and advocated no illegal activities.

Virginia's assembly warmly approved Adams's eloquent measure and sent out a more strongly worded letter of its own, urging all the colonies to oppose imperial policies that would "have an immediate tendency to enslave them." But most colonial legislatures reacted indifferently to these letters. In fact, resistance might have disintegrated had not the British government overreacted to the circular letters.

Indeed, parliamentary leaders saw even the mild Massachusetts letter as "little better than an incentive to Rebellion." Disorganized because of Townshend's sudden death in 1767, the king's Privy Council (advisers) directed Lord Hillsborough, the first appointee to the new post of secretary of state for the colonies, to express the government's displeasure. Hillsborough ordered the Massachusetts assembly to disown its letter, forbade all overseas assemblies to endorse it, and commanded royal governors to dissolve any legislature that violated his instructions.

The tactic backfired. Protesting Hillsborough's bullying, many legislatures previously indifferent to the Massachusetts letter adopted it enthusiastically. The Massachusetts House of Representatives voted 92–17 not to recall its letter. Royal governors responded by dismissing legislatures in Massachusetts and elsewhere, playing into the hands of Samuel Adams and others who wished to ignite widespread opposition to the Townshend duties.

Increasingly outraged, the colonists still needed an effective means of pressuring Parliament for repeal. Nonimportation seemed especially promising because it offered an alternative to violence and would distress Britain's economy. Thus in August 1768 Boston's merchants adopted a nonimportation agreement, and the tactic spread southward. "Save your money, and you save your country!" trumpeted the Sons of Liberty, which reorganized after two years of inactivity. However, not all colonists supported nonimportation. Many merchants continued to import British goods until early 1769. The boycott probably kept out about 40 percent of British imports while encouraging colonists to resist British policies more actively.

Wilkes and Liberty, 1768-1770

British merchants and artisans, hit hard by the exclusion of 40 percent of imports, demanded repeal of the Townshend duties. Their protests became part of a larger movement in the 1760s against the policies of George III and a Parliament dominated by wealthy landowners. John Wilkes, a fiery London editor whose newspaper regularly and irreverently denounced the king, became both leader and focal point of the protest. A member of Parliament, Wilkes was tried for seditious libel and acquitted, to great popular acclaim. George III's government then shut down his newspaper and persuaded members of the House of Commons to deny Wilkes his seat. After publishing another slashing attack on the king, Wilkes fled to Paris.

In 1768 Wilkes returned to England, defying an arrest warrant, and again ran for Parliament. By then government policies, including the Townshend Acts, had unleashed a flood of protests against the "obnoxious" government ministers, a flood that swept along manufacturers and merchants as well as weavers and other workers. They all rallied around the cry "Wilkes and Liberty."

When the newly elected Wilkes was once again arrested 20,000 to 40,000 angry "Wilkesites" massed on St. George's Fields, outside the prison where he was being held. Soldiers and police responded to rock-throwing demonstrators by opening fire on them, killing eleven protesters. The "massacre of St. George's Fields" furnished martyrs to the protesters, and Wilkes received enormous outpourings of public support from the North American colonies as well as from Britain. Twice more elected from his prison cell, and twice more denied his seat, Wilkes maintained a regular correspondence with Boston's Sons of Liberty. Bostonians cheered his release from prison in April 1770 with a massive celebration honoring this "illustrious martyr to liberty."

The Wilkes furor sharpened the political ideas of government opponents on both sides of the Atlantic. English voters sent petitions to Parliament proclaiming that its refusal to seat Wilkes was an affront to the electorate's will and calling "virtual representation" a sham. To guard against further arbitrary government actions, some formed the Society of the Supporters of the Bill of Rights "to defend and maintain the legal, constitutional liberty of the subject[s of the King]." Emboldened by the Wilkes and Liberty movement, William Pitt, Edmund Burke, and others forcefully denounced the government's colonial policies. The colonists themselves concluded that Parliament and the government represented a small but powerful minority whose authority they could legitimately question.

Women and Colonial Resistance

Nonimportation convinced the British—and the colonists—that all Americans were determined to sustain resistance, and it demonstrated that the American cause rested on foundations of impeccable morality and sensible moderation. It also provided a unique opportunity for women to join the protest.

White women had been widening their participation in public affairs gradually for several decades. For example, women far outnumbered men among white church members, and they were hailed as superior to most men in piety and morality. During the Stamp Act crisis, upper-class women had attended political rallies and expressed their political opinions in discussion and in correspondence.

Calling themselves Daughters of Liberty, upper-class female patriots assumed a highly visible role during the Townshend crisis. Convinced that colonial women could exert a persuasive moral influence on public opinion, American leaders encouraged them to protest the Revenue Act's tax on tea. Accordingly, in early 1770 more than three hundred "mistresses of families" in Boston denounced the consumption of the beverage. In some ways nonconsumption was more effective than nonimportation, for the colonists' refusal to consume imports would chill merchants' economic incentive to import British goods.

Nonconsumption agreements therefore became popular and were extended to include other goods, mainly clothes. Again, women played a vital role because the boycott would fail unless the colonists replaced British imports with apparel of their own making. Responding to leaders' pleas for an expansion of domestic cloth production, women of all social ranks organized spinning bees. These attracted intense publicity as evidence of American determination to fight parliamentary taxation. The colonial cause, noted a New York woman, had enlisted "a fighting army of amazons . . . armed with spinning wheels." Spinning bees not only helped to undermine the masculine prejudice that women had no place in public life but also endowed spinning and weaving, previously considered routine tasks, with political virtue. For many colonists, the area of supposed feminine virtues widened from religion to include politics.

Such female activities as the spinning bees and boycotts of tea dramatically demonstrated that American protests extended beyond a few male merchants and crowds of angry men into the heart of American households and congregations. And they showed that American women could and would participate more broadly in politics.

Customs "Racketeering," 1767–1768

Townshend also sought to increase revenues by extending British surveillance of colonial trade. In 1767 he induced Parliament to create the American Board of Customs Commissioners to strictly enforce the Navigation Acts. At the same time, Parliament increased the number of port officials, funded a colonial coast guard to catch smugglers, and provided money for secret informers. Townshend's hope was that the new system would end widespread bribery of customs officials by colonial shippers and merchants by bringing honesty, efficiency, and greater revenue to overseas customs operations. Instead the law quickly drew protests because of the ways it was enforced and because it reversed traditional legal process by assuming the accused to be guilty until proved otherwise.

The rapid expansion of the customs service in 1767 coincided with new provisions that awarded an informer one-third of the value of all goods and ships appropriated through a conviction of smuggling. The fact that fines could be tripled under certain circumstances provided an even greater incentive to seize illegal cargoes. Smuggling cases were heard in vice-admiralty courts, where the probability of conviction was extremely high. The prospect of accumulating a small fortune proved too tempting to most commissioners.

Revenue agents commonly perverted the law by filing charges for technical violations of the Sugar Act even when no evidence existed of intent to conduct illegal trade. They most often exploited the provision that declared any cargo illegal unless it had been loaded or unloaded with a customs officer's written authorization.

Customs commissioners also fanned anger by invading sailors' traditional rights. Long-standing maritime custom allowed crews to supplement their incomes by making small sales between ports. Anything stored in a sailor's chest was considered private property, exempt from the Navigation Acts. But after 1767 revenue agents treated such belongings as cargo, thus establishing an excuse to seize the entire ship. Under this policy, crewmen saw arrogant inspectors break open their trunks and then lost trading stock worth several months' wages. Sailors waited for chances to get even. Not surprisingly, after 1767 inspectors increasingly fell victim to riots dominated by vengeful sailors.

John Hancock
A prominent anti-British merchant, Hancock was also a popular political leader in pre-Revolutionary Boston.
Photograph ©2005 Museum of Fine Arts, Boston.

In these ways the commissioners embarked on a program of "customs racketeering" that constituted legalized piracy. This program fed an upsurge in popular violence. Above all, customs commissioners' use of informers provoked retaliation. The *Pennsylvania Journal* in 1769 scorned these agents as "dogs of prey, thirsting after the fortunes of worthy and wealthy men." Informers aroused hatred in those whom they betrayed. Nearly all instances of tarring and feathering in these years represented private revenge against informers, not political reprisals.

Nowhere were customs agents and informers more detested than in Boston, where citizens retaliated in June 1768. When customs agents seized colonial merchant John Hancock's sloop *Liberty* on a technicality, a crowd tried to prevent the towing of Hancock's ship and then began assaulting customs officials. Swelling to several hundred, the mob drove all revenue inspectors from the city.

THE DEEPENING CRISIS, 1770–1774

Hancock's case made Americans rethink their acceptance of the principle that Parliament had limited authority to pass laws for them. By 1770 it was clear that measures such as the Sugar Act and the act creating the American Board of Customs Commissioners endangered property rights and civil liberties as much as taxes. Realizing this fact, many Americans began to reject any legislation without representation. By 1774 a consensus had emerged that Parliament had no lawmaking authority over the colonies except the right to regulate imperial commerce.

The Boston Massacre, 1770

British authorities responded to the violence directed at customs commissioners by dispatching 4,000 British troops to Boston in 1768. But the violence only escalated, intersecting with intra-colonial tensions and extending the crisis beyond the port cities.

Bostonians' resentment of British authority boiled over on February 22, 1770, when a customs informer fired birdshot at several children throwing rocks at his house and killed an eleven-year-old boy. Samuel Adams organized a burial procession to maximize the horror at a child's death, relying on grief to unite the community in opposition to British policies. "My Eyes never beheld such a funeral," wrote his cousin John Adams. "A vast Number of Boys walked before the Coffin, a vast Number of Women and Men after it. . . . This Shows there are many more Lives to spend if wanted in the Service of their country."

Although the army had played no part in the shooting, it became a target for Bostonians' rage. A week after the funeral, tension erupted at the guard post protecting the customs office. When an officer tried to disperse a crowd led by Crispus Attucks, a seaman of African and Native American ancestry, the mob responded with a barrage of flying objects. One soldier, knocked down by a block of ice, fired, and the others opened fire. Their volley killed five people, including Attucks.

Royal authorities moved quickly to defuse the crisis by isolating the army on a fortified island in the harbor and putting soldiers who had fired on trial. Patriot leader John Adams defended the accused British troops by claiming that they had been provoked by a "motley rabble," an accusation that resonated with Boston's "respectable" middle- and upper-class elites. Only two soldiers were found guilty; they received the relatively mild punishment of branding on their thumbs.

Burning hatreds underlay the Boston Massacre—a name designed to invoke the St. George's Fields Massacre two years earlier. For the first time colonists had to confront the stark possibility that a tyrannical British government was determined to coerce and suppress them through armed force.

Lord North's Partial Retreat, 1770

Meanwhile, in January 1770 Lord North had become prime minister. An able administrator, North favored eliminating most of the Townshend duties to end the commercial boycott, but he insisted on retaining the tax on tea to underscore British authority. In April 1770 Parliament again yielded to colonial pressure and repealed most of the Townshend duties.

This partial repeal presented a dilemma to American politicians. They considered it intolerable that taxes remained on tea, the most profitable item for the royal treasury. In July 1770 the general nonimportation movement collapsed, but the Sons of Liberty resisted external taxation by voluntary agreements not to drink British tea. Revenue from the tea tax consequently fell to only one-sixth the anticipated amount, far too low to pay royal governors' salaries. Yet American leaders remained dissatisfied. The tea duty was a galling reminder that Parliament still claimed broad authority.

Meanwhile, the British government, aware of officers' excesses, began to rein in the powers of the American Board of Customs Commissioners. The smuggling charges against John Hancock were dropped; the prosecution feared that if Hancock appealed a conviction, honest officials in England would take action against customs officials who had violated his rights.

The Committees of Correspondence, 1772–1773

In the fall of 1772 Lord North prepared to implement Townshend's goal of paying royal governors from customs revenue, freeing them from the control of the colonial assemblies. With representative government deeply threatened, Samuel Adams persuaded Boston's town meeting to request that every Massachusetts community appoint people to exchange information and to coordinate measures to defend colonial rights. Within a year most Massachusetts communities had established "committees of correspondence," and the idea spread throughout New England.

The committees of correspondence, the colonists' first attempt to maintain close political cooperation over a wide area, allowed Samuel Adams to conduct a campaign of political education for all New England. He sent messages for each local committee to read at its town meeting, which debated the issues and adopted formal resolutions. The system made tens of thousands of citizens consider evidence that their rights were endangered and committed them to take a stand. Adams's most successful venture in whipping up public alarm came in June 1773 when he published letters from Massachusetts governor Thomas Hutchinson, obtained by Benjamin Franklin, advocating "an abridgement of what are called English liberties" and "a great restraint of natural liberty." The Hutchinson correspondence confirmed Americans' suspicions that a plot was afoot to destroy their basic freedoms.

Patrick Henry, Thomas Jefferson, and Richard Henry Lee had proposed in March 1773 that Virginia establish committees of correspondence, and within a year every province but Pennsylvania had such committees. By early 1774 a communications web linked colonial leaders.

In contrast to the brief, intense Stamp Act crisis, the dissatisfaction spawned by the Townshend duties persisted and gradually poisoned relations between Britain and America. In 1765 strong ties of loyalty and affection had disguised the depth of the division over taxation. By 1773, however, colonial allegiance was becoming tenuous.

Backcountry Tensions

On the Appalachian frontier, tensions among natives, recent settlers, and colonial authorities underlined a continuing sense of emergency. Rapid population growth had spurred the migration of people and capital to the frontier, where colonists sought access to Indian lands. Land pressures and the lack of adequate revenue from the colonies left the British government helpless to enforce the Proclamation of 1763. The government could neither maintain garrisons at many of its forts, enforce laws and treaties, nor provide gifts to its native allies. Rising violence by colonists against Indians often went unpunished.

Under such pressures, Britain and the Iroquois, in the Treaty of Fort Stanwix (1768), turned land along the Ohio River that was occupied by the Shawnees, Delawares, and Cherokees over to the Virginia and Pennsylvania governments, resolving the two colonies' overlapping land claims in Ohio at the Indians' expense. The Shawnees assumed leadership among the Ohio Indians, who, with the Cherokees, were convinced that appeasement would not stop colonial expansion.

The treaty heightened rather than eased frontier tensions, especially in the Ohio country. Colonists moving westward into what they called Kentucky collided with Shawnee and Mingo Indians, and Virginia in 1774 launched Lord Dunmore's War. After Virginia's victory at Point Pleasant, Virginia gained uncontested rights to all land south of the Ohio River in exchange for giving up all claims north of the river. Resentment continued to fester on both sides, and fighting would resume when war broke out between Britain and the colonies.

Other frontier disputes led to conflict among the colonists themselves. Settlers in western Massachusetts in the early 1760s, for example, found their titles challenged by New Yorkers. In 1766, threatened with eviction, the New Englanders staged an armed uprising. And in 1769 New Hamp-

shire settlers calling themselves the Green Mountain Boys began guerrilla warfare against New York landlords. The independent government that they formed ultimately became that of Vermont.

Expansion also provoked conflict between frontier settlers and their own colonial governments. In North Carolina westerners, underrepresented in the assembly, found themselves exploited by dishonest officeholders appointed by eastern politicians. Twenty-five hundred armed westerners, known as Regulators, clashed with 1,300 North Carolina militia on May 16, 1771, at the battle of Alamance Creek. Although the Regulator uprising disintegrated, it crippled the colony's subsequent ability to resist British authority. A Regulator movement also arose in South Carolina, in this case to counter the government's unwillingness to prosecute bandits who terrorized the settlers. Fearful that the colony's slave population might revolt if the militia was dispatched, South Carolina's government yielded to the Regulators by establishing new courts and allowing jury trials in recently settled areas.

Although unrelated, these episodes reflected the tensions generated by a land-hungry white population willing to use violence against Native Americans, other colonists, and British officials. As Anglo-American tensions mounted in older settled areas, the westerners' anxious mood spread.

The Tea Act, 1773

Smuggling and nonconsumption had taken a heavy toll on Britain's East India Company, the holder of the legal monopoly on importing tea into the British Empire. By 1773, as tons of tea rotted in warehouses, the East India Company was teetering on the brink of bankruptcy. But Lord North could not let the company fail because by maintaining British authority in India at its own expense, the East India Company had become a vital component in the British imperial structure.

If the company could control the colonial market, North reasoned, it could increase its profits and its survival would be guaranteed. Americans consumed vast amounts of tea but by 1773 were purchasing just one-quarter of it from the company. In May 1773, to save the beleaguered East India Company, Parliament passed the Tea Act, which eliminated all import duties on tea entering England and thus lowered the selling price to consumers. To reduce the price further, the Tea Act also permitted the company to sell tea directly to consumers rather than through wholesalers. These provisions reduced the cost of East India Company tea in the colonies to well below the price of smuggled tea. Parliament expected economic self-interest to overcome American scruples about buying taxed tea.

But the Tea Act alarmed many Americans, who recognized that the revenues raised by the law would place royal governors' purses beyond the reach of the colonial assemblies. The law also threatened to seduce Americans into accepting parliamentary taxation in return for a frivolous luxury. The committees of correspondence decided to resist the importation of tea by pressuring the East India Company's agents to refuse acceptance or by preventing the landing of East India Company cargoes.

In Boston on November 28, 1773, the first ship came under jurisdiction of the customhouse, to which duties would have to be paid within twenty days or the cargo would be seized from the captain and the tea would be claimed by the company's agents and placed on sale. When Samuel Adams, John Hancock, and others asked customs officers to issue a special clearance for the ship's departure (to avoid the seizure and sale), Governor Hutchinson refused.

On the evening of December 16, 1773, Samuel Adams convened a meeting in Old South Church, at which he told 5,000 citizens about Hutchinson's insistence on landing the tea, warned them that the grace period would expire in a few hours, and proclaimed that "this meeting can do no more to save the country." About fifty young men disguised as Indians and armed with "tomahawks" headed for the wharf, followed by the crowd. Thousands lined the waterfront to watch them heave forty-five tons of tea overboard; for an hour the only sounds echoing through the crisp, moonlit night were the steady chop of hatchets breaking open wooden chests and

the soft splash of tea on the water. Their work finished, the participants left quietly. They had assaulted no one and damaged nothing but the tea.

TOWARD INDEPENDENCE, 1774–1776

The calm that followed the Boston Tea Party was the calm before the storm. The British government was more determined than ever to quash colonial insubordination, while colonial leaders were equally determined to defend self-government and liberty. The empire and its American colonies were on a collision course, but the colonists hesitated at a declaration of independence. In the meantime, African-Americans, both free and slave, pondered how to realize their own freedom.

Liberty for Black Americans

Throughout the imperial crisis, African-American slaves quickly responded to calls for liberty and equality. In 1772 a British court decision electrified much of the black population. A Massachusetts slave, James Somerset, whose master had taken him to England, sued for his freedom; Lord Chief Justice William Mansfield ruled that Parliament had never explicitly established slavery and therefore no court could compel a slave to obey an order depriving him of his liberty.

Although the decision applied only in England, Massachusetts slaves petitioned the legislature to apply it in the colony as well. In the Chesapeake area, dozens of slaves ran away from their masters and sought passage on ships bound for England. As Anglo-American tensions mounted in 1774, many slaves began to anticipate the arrival of British troops as their path to liberation. White Chesapeake colonists began to fear that war would lead to slave rebellion.

Bearing out such fears in 1775, Virginia's royal governor, Lord Dunmore, promised freedom to any slave who enlisted in the cause of restoring royal authority. Nearly a thousand slaves responded to Dunmore's proclamation before angry colonists forced him to flee the colony. Perhaps more important, both whites and blacks began to see a clear link between British forces and slave liberation.

The Coercive Acts

Boston's "Tea Party" enraged the British. Only "New England fanatics" could imagine that cheap tea oppressed them, fumed Lord North. A Welsh member of Parliament declared that "the town of Boston ought to be knocked about by the ears, and destroy'd." The great orator Edmund Burke pled in vain for the one action that could end the crisis: "Leave America . . . to tax herself." But the British government swiftly asserted its authority through the passage of four Coercive Acts, which, along with the Quebec Act, became known to many colonists as the "Intolerable Acts."

The first Coercive Act, the Boston Port Bill, was passed on April 1, 1774. It ordered the navy to close Boston harbor unless the town arranged to pay for the ruined tea by June 1. The impossibly short deadline was meant to ensure the harbor's closing, which would plunge Boston into economic distress. The second Coercive Act, the Massachusetts Government Act, revoked the Massachusetts charter and made the colony's government less democratic. The upper house would be appointed for life by the crown, not elected annually by the assembly. The royal governor gained absolute control over the appointment of judges and sheriffs. Finally, the new charter limited town meetings to one year. Although these changes brought Massachusetts government into line with other colonies, the colonists interpreted them as hostile toward representative government.

The final two Coercive Acts—the Administration of Justice Act and a new Quartering Act—rubbed salt into the wounds. The first of these permitted any person charged with murder while enforcing royal authority in Massachusetts to be tried in England or in another colony. The second went beyond the Quartering Act of 1765 by allowing the governor to requisition *empty* private buildings for quartering, or housing, troops. These measures, coupled with the appointment of General Thomas Gage, Britain's military commander in North America, as governor of Massachusetts, struck New Englanders as proof of a plan to place them under a military despotism.

Americans learned of the unrelated Quebec Act at the same time as the Coercive Acts. Intended to cement loyalty to Britain among conquered French-Canadian Catholics, the law established Roman Catholicism as Quebec's official religion. Protestant Anglo-Americans, who associated Catholicism with arbitrary government, took alarm. Furthermore, the Quebec Act gave Canada's governor sweeping powers but established no legislature. It also allowed property disputes to be decided by French law, which used no juries. The law extended Quebec's territorial claims south to the Ohio River and west to the Mississippi, a vast area populated by Indians and some French and claimed by several colonies.

The "Intolerable Acts" convinced New Englanders that the crown planned to corrode traditional English liberties throughout North America. Once the Coercive Acts destroyed these liberties in Massachusetts, many believed, the Quebec Act would serve as a blueprint for extinguishing representative government in other colonies. Parliament would replace all colonial governments with ones like Quebec's. Elected assemblies, freedom of religion for Protestants, and jury trials would vanish.

Intended only to punish Massachusetts, the Coercive Acts thus pushed most colonies to the brink of revolution. Repeal of these laws became the colonists' nonnegotiable demand. The Declaration of Independence would refer to these laws six times in listing colonial grievances justifying the break with Britain.

The First Continental Congress

In response to the "Intolerable Acts," the committees of correspondence of every colony but Georgia sent delegates to a Continental Congress in Philadelphia. The fifty-six delegates who assembled on September 5, 1774, included the colonies' most prominent politicians: Samuel and John Adams of Massachusetts; John Jay of New York;

Joseph Galloway and John Dickinson of Pennsylvania; and Patrick Henry, Richard Henry Lee, and George Washington of Virginia. They were determined to find a way to defend American rights without war.

The Continental Congress endorsed the Suffolk Resolves, extreme statements of principle that proclaimed that the colonies owed no obedience to the Coercive Acts, advocated a provisional government until restoration of the Massachusetts charter, and vowed that defensive measures should follow any attack by royal troops. The Continental Congress also voted to boycott British goods after December 1, 1774, and to stop exporting goods to Britain and its West Indies possessions after September 1775. This agreement, called the Continental Association, would be enforced by locally elected committees of "observation" or "safety." But not all the delegates embraced such bold defiance. Jay, Dickinson, Galloway, and other moderates who dominated the middle-colony contingent feared that a confrontation with Britain would spawn internal colonial turmoil. They vainly opposed nonimportation and unsuccessfully sought support of a plan for an American legislature that would share with Parliament the authority to tax and to govern the colonies.

Finally, the delegates summarized their principles and demands in a petition to George III. They conceded to Parliament the power to regulate colonial commerce but argued that parliamentary efforts to impose taxes, enforce laws through admiralty courts, suspend assemblies, and revoke charters were unconstitutional. By addressing the king rather than Parliament, Congress was imploring George III to end the crisis by dismissing the ministers responsible for passing the Coercive Acts.

From Resistance to Rebellion

Most Americans hoped that resistance would jolt Parliament into renouncing its claims of authority over the colonies. Only a minority of the colonial elite charged that Congress had made the "breach with the parent state a thousand times more ir-reparable than it was before," as one colonist observed. In England George III saw rebellion in Congress's actions. His instincts, like those of American loyalists—people loyal to England—were correct: a revolution was indeed brewing.

To solidify defiance, American resistance leaders used coercion against waverers and loyalists ("Tories"). Committees elected to enforce the Continental Association became vigilantes, compelling merchants to burn British imports, browbeating clergymen who preached pro-British sermons, and pressuring Americans to free themselves of dependence on British imports by adopting simpler diets and homespun clothing. In colony after colony, moreover, the committees assumed governmental functions by organizing volunteer military companies and extralegal legislatures. By spring 1775 colonial patriots had established provincial "congresses" that rivaled existing royal governments.

In April 1775 events in Massachusetts shattered the uneasy calm. Citizens had collected arms and organized militia units ("minutemen") to respond instantly in an emergency. The British government ordered Massachusetts's Governor Thomas Gage to quell the "rude rabble" and to arrest the patriot leaders. Aware that most of these had fled Boston, Gage, on April 19, 1775, sent 700 British soldiers to seize colonial military supplies stored at Concord. Two couriers, William Dawes and Paul Revere, alerted nearby towns of the British troop movements. At Lexington on the road to Concord, about 70 minutemen faced the British on the town green. After a confused skirmish in which eight minutemen died and a single redcoat was wounded, the British marched to Concord. They found few munitions but encountered a swarm of armed Yankees. When some minutemen mistakenly concluded that the town was being burned, they exchanged fire with British regulars and touched off a running battle that continued most of the sixteen miles back to Boston. By day's end the redcoats had lost 273 men.

These engagements awakened the countryside. Within a day some 20,000 New Englanders were besieging the British garrison in Boston. In the

New England interior the Green Mountain Boys under Ethan Allen overran Fort Ticonderoga on Lake Champlain on May 1, partly with the intent of using its captured cannon in the siege of Boston. That same day the Continental Congress reconvened in Philadelphia. Most delegates still opposed independence and agreed to send a "loyal message" to George III. The resulting Olive Branch Petition presented three demands: a cease-fire in Boston, repeal of the Coercive Acts, and negotiations to establish guarantees of American rights. Yet the same delegates who pleaded for peace voted to establish an "American continental army" and to appoint George Washington as commander, measures that the British could only see as rebellious.

The Olive Branch Petition reached London along with news of the Continental Army's formation and of the battles of Breed's Hill and Bunker Hill just outside Boston. Although the British dislodged the Americans in the clashes, they suffered 2,200 casualties, compared to colonial losses of only 311. After Bunker Hill the British public wanted retaliation, not reconciliation.

A View of the Town of Concord, 1775, by an unknown artist
British troops enter Concord to search for armaments. A few hours later, hostilities with the townspeople would erupt.
hc Interactive Map: The First Battles

Common Sense

Most Americans still clung to hopes of reconciliation. Even John Adams, who believed separation inevitable, said that he was "fond of reconciliation, if we could reasonably entertain Hopes of it on a constitutional basis." Like many elites, Adams recognized that war would entail arming common people, many of whom reviled all men of wealth. Such an outcome would threaten rule by colonial elites as well as by Britain.

The majority of Americans who resisted independence blamed evil ministers, rather than the king, for unconstitutional measures and expected saner heads to rise to power in Britain. On both counts they were wrong. Americans exaggerated the influence of Pitt, Burke, Wilkes (who finally took his seat in 1774), and their other friends in Britain. In March 1775 when Burke proposed that Parliament acknowledge the colonists' right to raise and dispose of taxes, a thumping majority of Parliament voted him down. In August George III declared the colonies to be in "open and avowed rebellion," and in December Parliament outlawed all trade with them.

Americans' sentimental attachment to the king, the last emotional barrier to independence, crumbled in January 1776 with the publication of Thomas Paine's *Common Sense*. Paine had immigrated to the colonies from England in 1774 with a penchant for radical politics and a gift for plain and pungent prose. Paine told Americans what they had been unable to bring themselves to say: that at the root of the conspiracy against American liberty was not corrupt politicians but the very institutions of monarchy and empire. Further, America did not need its British connection. "The commerce by which she [America] hath enriched herself are the necessaries of life, and will always have a market while eating is the custom in Europe," Paine argued. And, he pointed out, the events of the preceding six months had made independence a reality. Finally, Paine linked America's awakening nationalism with a sense of religious mission: "We have it in our power to begin the world over again. A situation, similar to the present, hath not happened since the days of Noah until now." America,

Paine wrote, would be a new *kind* of nation, a model society free of oppressive English beliefs and institutions.

Common Sense, "a landflood that sweeps all before it," sold more than 100,000 copies in three months, one copy for every fourth or fifth adult male in the colonies. By spring 1776 Paine's pamphlet had dissolved lingering allegiance to George III and removed the last psychological barrier to independence.

Declaring Independence

John Adams described the movement toward independence as a coach drawn by thirteen horses, which could not reach its destination any faster than the slowest were willing to run. New England was already in rebellion, and Rhode Island declared itself independent in May 1776. The middle colonies hesitated to support revolution because they feared, correctly, that the war would largely be fought over control of Philadelphia and New York. The South began to press for separation. In April North Carolina authorized its congressional delegates to vote for independence, and in June Virginia followed suit. On July 2 the Continental Congress formally adopted the Virginia resolution and created the United States of America.

The drafting of a statement to justify the colonies' separation from England fell to Virginia's Thomas Jefferson. Congress made two important changes to Jefferson's first draft: it inserted the phrase "pursuit of happiness" instead of "property" in the document's most famous sentence, and it deleted a condemnation of George III for forcing the slave trade on unwilling colonists. Congress then approved Jefferson's manuscript on July 4, 1776. Even though parliamentary authority had been the focal point of dispute since 1765, the Declaration of Independence never mentioned Parliament by name because Congress was unwilling to imply that Parliament held any authority over America. Jefferson instead focused on George III, citing "repeated injuries and usurpations" against the colonies. He added that the king's "direct object [was] the establishment of an absolute tyranny over these states."

Like Paine, Jefferson elevated colonial grievances to a struggle of universal dimensions. In the tradition of Enlightenment thought, Jefferson argued that Britain had violated its contract with the colonists, giving them the right to replace it with a government of their own. His emphasis on the equality of all individuals and their natural entitlement to justice, liberty, and self-fulfillment expressed the Enlightenment's deep longing for government that rested on neither legal privilege nor the exploitation of the majority by the few—and deliberately ignored the existence of slavery.

Jefferson addressed the Declaration of Independence as much to Americans uncertain about the wisdom of independence as to world opinion. Above all, he wanted to convince his fellow Americans that social and political progress were impossible within the British Empire. But the Declaration omitted key groups: blacks, poor white men,

and women. All of the colonies countenanced slavery, severely restricted the rights of free blacks, used property qualifications to determine voting rights, and relegated women to second-class status. Jefferson also put Indians beyond the pale when he accused the King of having unleashed "the merciless Indian savages" on innocent colonists.

Thus the Declaration expressed the sentiments of a minority of colonists at the same time that it set out the hopes of thousands upon thousands more. The struggle for independence from Britain had merged with a quest for equality and personal independence that would eventually transcend class, race, and gender. The declaration never claimed that perfect justice and equal opportunity existed; instead, it challenged the Revolutionary generation and all who followed to bring this ideal closer to reality.

Chronology

Year	Event
1744–1748	King George's War.
1756–1763	The Seven Years' War.
1760	George III becomes king of Great Britain. Writs of assistance.
1763–1766	Indian uprising in Ohio Valley and Great Lakes.
1763	Proclamation of 1763. Treaty of Paris divides France's North American empire between Britain and Spain.
1764	Sugar Act.
1765	Stamp Act followed by colonial resistance. First Quartering Act.
1766	Stamp Act repealed. Declaratory Act.
1767	Revenue Act (Townshend duties). American Board of Customs Commissioners created.
1768	Massachusetts "circular letters." John Hancock's ship *Liberty* seized by Boston customs commissioner. St. George's Field Massacre in London First Treaty of Fort Stanwix.
1770	Townshend duties, except tea tax, repealed. Boston Massacre.
1772–1774	Committees of correspondence formed.
1772	Somerset decision in England.
1773	Tea Act and Boston Tea Party.
1774	Coercive Acts and Quebec Act. First Continental Congress meets in Philadelphia and adopts Suffolk Resolves. Continental Association.
1775	Battles of Lexington and Concord. Lord Dunmore offers freedom to Virginia slaves joining British forces. Olive Branch Petition. Battles at Breed's Hill and Bunker Hill.
1776	Thomas Paine, *Common Sense.* Declaration of Independence.

CONCLUSION 🅗🅒 ACE Practice Test

In 1763 the defeat of French forces in North America left Britain at the head of the world's most powerful empire. Just over a decade later, war between Britain and her North American colonies shattered that empire. In attempting to centralize imperial authority and to force the colonists to contribute more to the British treasury, English officials had failed to take account of the Americans' stubborn self-reliance. The colonists persistently tried to return the empire to what it had been before 1763, a loosely knit structure in which they enjoyed a large measure of autonomy.

The conflict between empire and colonies quickly became a struggle over fundamental issues: who had the authority, as representatives of the people, to tax the colonists? What authority did Parliament have over the colonies? And finally, why should the colonists, entirely capable of self-government, continue to accept the institution of monarchy?

Americans followed varying paths to independence. For many elites and members of the middle class, the primary issue was commerce and profits. For many frontier and urban dwellers, the issue was their refusal to continue to see others as their superiors—they shared the anti-authoritarian, republican sentiments that were beginning to sweep through the Atlantic world.

The reluctant revolutionaries faced two daunting tasks: winning independence on the battlefield from Europe's greatest imperial power and implementing the ideals of the Declaration of Independence. Neither would be easy.

FURTHER READING

Fred Anderson, *Crucible of War: The Seven Years' War and the Fate of Empire in British North America, 1754–1766* (2000). A meticulous but engaging study of the war as a turning point in the history of British North America.

Bernard Bailyn, *The Ideological Origins of the American Revolution* (1967). Pulitzer Prize-winning examination of the political heritage that shaped colonial resistance to British authority.

Linda Colley, *Britons: Forging the Nation, 1707–1837* (1992). A major study of the formation of political identity in Great Britain, providing an important perspective on relations between the empire and its North American colonies.

Edward Countryman, *The American Revolution* (1985, revised ed. 2003) An outstanding introduction to the Revolution.

Eric Hinderaker, *Elusive Empires: Constructing Colonialism in the Ohio Valley, 1673–1800* (1997). A study of the multifaceted competition among Native Americans, Europeans, and European Americans for control of a critical American region.

Woody Holton, *Forced Founders: Indians, Debtors, Slaves, and the Making of the American Revolution* (1999). A major reinterpretation of the causes of the Revolution in one colony, emphasizing the role of internal conflicts across lines of class, race, and economic interest.

Pauline Maier, *American Scripture: Making the Declaration of Independence* (1997). A fine study of the immediate context in which independence was conceived and the Declaration was drafted and conceived.

Mary Beth Norton, *Liberty's Daughters: The Revolutionary Experience of American Women, 1750–1800* (1980). A wide-ranging discussion of the experiences and roles of women in eighteenth-century colonial society and the American Revolution.

Gordon S. Wood, *The American Revolution: A History* (2002). A concise interpretive overview of the Revolutionary Constitutional period by one of its leading historians.

Alfred F. Young, *The Shoemaker and the Revolution: Memory and the American Revolution* (1999). A fascinating study of ordinary people's participation in the Revolution, of how later generations of Americans interpreted and memorialized their role.

6

Securing Independence, Defining Nationhood, 1776–1788

hc This icon will direct you to additional study and research resources at http://college.hmco.com/history/us/boyer/enduring_concise/5e/students/index.html

George Washington, by John Trumbull, 1780
The Metropolitan Museum of Art, Bequest of Charles Allen Munn, 1924 (24.109.88). Photograph © 1989 The Metropolitan Museum of Art, New York.

The Revolution would teach Americans a hard lesson: that *proclaiming* a new nation, as they had done so proudly in 1776, was much easier than *making* a new nation, which they struggled to do from 1776 to 1788.

Before 1775 the outlooks of inhabitants of the different colonial regions had been narrow. With little opportunity and less necessity to work together, each colonist had regarded his own colony as superior to all others. But eight years of war transformed the colonists' narrow view and made them into American citizens. Only through the collective hardships of the War for Independence did the colonists learn to see each other not just as military allies but as fellow citizens.

Independence and peace in 1783, however, gave Americans a false security. Major problems remained unsolved. Americans were divided over how to distribute political power. Not until 1789 would they begin to overcome these challenges. The ratification of the constitution in 1787 marked a triumph for those favoring more centralization of power at the national level.

THE PROSPECTS OF WAR

The Revolution was both a struggle that pitted Americans against Britain and a civil war between Americans. Those opposed to independence represented one of several factors in Britain's favor as the war began; others included a larger population and superior military resources and preparation. The colonies, on the other hand, were far from Britain and enjoyed the intense commitment to independence from patriots and the Continental Army.

Loyalists and Other British Sympathizers

When independence came in July 1776, many colonists remained unconvinced of its necessity. About 20 percent of all whites actively opposed the rebellion or supported it only when threatened with fines and imprisonment. These opponents of the Revolution called themselves loyalists, but Whigs labeled them Tories.

Loyalists, like Whigs, typically opposed parliamentary taxation of the colonies. Many loyalists thus found themselves fighting for a cause with which they did not entirely agree, and as a result many switched sides during the war. Maryland loyalist Reverend Jonathan Boucher expressed a widespread apprehension: "For my part, I equally dread a Victory by either side." But loyalists believed that separation was illegal and was not necessary to preserve the colonists' constitutional rights. Above all, they revered the crown and equated any failure to defend their king with a sacrifice of personal honor.

This chapter focuses on three major questions:

▶ What were the most critical factors that allowed Americans to defeat the British?

▶ What changes did the Revolution promote in relationships among Americans of different classes, races, and genders?

▶ In what ways did the first state constitutions and the Articles of Confederation reflect pre-Revolutionary ideas about political power and authority? In what ways did they depart from older ideas?

The mutual hatred between Whigs and Tories was intense. Each side saw its cause as sacred, and those who opposed it as traitors. The worst atrocities of the war were committed by Americans against each other.

Loyalist strength in an area depended on how well prominent local Whigs had convinced voters that the king and Parliament were endangering representative government. From 1772 to 1776 elites in New England, Virginia, and South Carolina mobilized citizens by organizing public meetings and repeatedly explaining the issues. The majority opted for resistance; by 1776 loyalists constituted barely 5 percent of whites in these areas. In contrast, elites in New York and New Jersey remained reluctant to declare allegiance to either side, and their indecision resulted in divided communities. These two states provided half of the 21,000 Americans who would fight in loyalist units.

A second major factor in loyalist strength was the geographic distribution of recent British immigrants, who identified closely with their homeland. These newcomers included thousands of British veterans of the French and Indian War who had remained in the colonies, usually in New York. Further, the 125,000 British immigrants who arrived between 1763 and 1775 formed major centers of loyalist sympathy. In New York, Georgia, and the Carolina piedmont, where these newcomers clustered, loyalists probably constituted 25 to 40 percent of the white population in 1776.

Canada's religious and secular elites comprised another pro-British white minority. The Quebec Act of 1774 had guaranteed the Canadians' religious freedom and their continued use of French civil law. Remembering the bitter denunciations of this measure by their southern neighbors, French Catholics initially feared that Protestant Anglo-Americans would be far less tolerant. When Continental armies attacked Quebec to "free" Canada from British tyranny, they were welcomed by large numbers of French and English Canadians. But British forces repulsed the invasion and maintained a hold on the region until the war's end.

Other North Americans supported the British cause more from self-interest than from loyalty to the crown. For example, a few German, Dutch, and French religious congregations believed that their rights would be safer under royal rule than in a new nation dominated by Anglo-Americans. Generally, however, non-British whites supported the Revolution. **hc** Primary Source: Loyalist Widow

The rebels made no attempt to win over the three small mainland colonies—Nova Scotia and East and West Florida—whose populations consisted largely of recent immigrants and British troops. The West Indies, dependent on British markets for their sugar, also spurned independence.

Black slaves and Native Americans also widely supported the British. As in Virginia, hundreds of South Carolina slaves sought refuge on British ships before the outbreak of war. During the war itself at least 20,000 slaves would run away from southern plantations to sign on as laborers or soldiers in the Royal Army. Deeply alienated from white society, southern slaves realized that the Revolution would not benefit them. In contrast, most African-Americans in the north supported the rebels in hopes of hastening their own liberation.

Finally, most Indians, recognizing the threat that expansion-minded colonists posed, likewise supported the British. Of the handful of tribes that sided with the colonists, the most prominent were two Iroquois tribes, the Oneidas and the Tuscaroras.

Stockbridge Indian Serving with the Continental Army
Like other Native Americans in locales long dominated by whites, the Stockbridge Indians of western Massachusetts contributed substantially to the patriots' military effort.

The Opposing Sides

Britain entered the war with what should have been two major advantages. First, Britain's 11 million people greatly outnumbered the 2.5 million colonists, one-third of whom were either slaves or loyalists. Second, Britain possessed the world's largest navy and one of its best armies. During the war the army's size more than doubled, from 48,000 to 111,000 men, and Britain hired 30,000 Hessian mercenaries and enlisted 21,000 loyalists to supplement its own fighting force.

Despite a smaller population, the new nation mobilized about 220,000 troops—compared to the 162,000 Britons, loyalists, and Hessians who served in the British army. However, most Americans served only short terms; the nation would have been hard pressed without the contributions of its French allies in the late stages of the war. Further, peacetime budget cuts after 1763 had weakened British seapower and thus Britain's ability to crush the rebellion. Midway through the war, half of Britain's ships languished in dry dock, awaiting repairs. Of 110,000 new sailors, the navy lost 42,000 to desertion and 20,000 to disease or wounds. In addition, American privateers cost Britain's merchant marine dearly. During the war U.S. Navy ships and privateers would capture more than 2,000 British merchant vessels and 16,000 crewmen.

Britain could ill afford such losses, for supplying its troops in North America was a Herculean task. Although at various times the British army controlled all the major American cities, British soldiers seldom ventured into the agricultural hinterland and thus could not easily round up supplies. Virtually all the food consumed by the army, one-third of a ton per soldier per year, was imported from Britain. Seriously overextended, the navy barely kept the army supplied and never effectively blockaded American ports.

Maintaining public support presented another serious problem for Britain. The war more than doubled the British national debt, adding to the problems of a people already paying record taxes. Resentful of this tax burden, the politically influential landed gentry would not vote against their pocketbooks forever.

The new United States faced different but equally severe problems. First, one-fifth of its population was openly pro-British. Second, state militias lacked the training to fight pitched battles. Their hit-and-run guerrilla tactics could not bring victory, nor could avoiding major battles and allowing the British to occupy population centers. Moreover, the U.S. dependence on guerrilla warfare would convince potential European allies that the Americans could not drive out the British and would doom American efforts to gain foreign loans diplomatic recognition, and military allies.

The Continental Army would thus have to fight in European fashion, relying on precision movements of mass formations of troops. Victory would depend on rapid maneuvers to crush an enemy's undefended flank or rear. Attackers would need ex-

ceptional skill in close-order drill to fall on an enemy before it could re-form and return fire. After advancing within musket range, opposing troops would stand upright and fire at each other until one line weakened. Discipline, training, and nerve would be essential if soldiers were to hold their line as comrades fell around them.

In contrast to Britain, which had a well-trained army with a tradition of bravery under fire, the Continental Army had neither an inspirational heritage nor experienced officers in 1775. In the war's early years, it suffered heartbreaking defeats. However, to win, the Continentals did not have to destroy the British army but only to prolong the rebellion until Britain's taxpayers lost patience. Until then, American victory depended on the ability of one man to keep his army fighting despite defeat—George Washington.

George Washington

Few generals looked and acted the role as much as Washington. He spoke with authority and comported himself with dignity. At six feet two inches, he stood a half foot taller than an average contemporary. Powerfully built, athletic, and hardened by a rugged outdoor life, he could inspire troops to heroism.

Washington's military experience had begun at age twenty-two, when he had commanded a Virginia regiment raised to resist French claims in the Ohio Valley (see Chapter 5). Vastly outnumbered, he had lost his first battle. A year later at Braddock's defeat, Washington had assumed the point of greatest danger, had had two horses shot out from under him, and had his hat shot off and his coat ripped by bullets. But Washington's mistakes and lost battles had taught him lessons that easy victories might not have. He had discovered the dangers of overconfidence and the need for determination. He had also learned that Americans fought best when led by example and treated with respect.

In 1758, with Virginia's borders secured, Washington had resigned his commission and become a tobacco planter. He had sat in the House of Burgesses, where others respected him and sought his opinion. An early opponent of parliamentary taxation, he had also served in the Continental Congress. In the eyes of the many who valued his advice and his military experience, Washington was the logical choice to head the Continental Army.

WAR AND PEACE, 1776–1783

Each side initially won important victories in the North. West of the Appalachians, revolutionary forces prevailed over the British and their Indian allies. However, it was the American and French victory at Yorktown in 1781 that decided the war and gained British recognition of American independence.

Shifting Fortunes in the North, 1776–1778

In March 1776 the British evacuated Boston and moved south to New York, which they wished to use as a base for conquering New England. Under two brothers, General William Howe and Admiral Richard, Lord Howe, 130 warships carried 32,000 troops to New York City in the summer of 1776. Defending the city were 18,000 poorly trained soldiers under Washington. On August 27, 15,000 British troops nearly annihilated 10,500 American troops on Long Island, just across a river from New York City. But Washington executed a masterly night evacuation, saving 9,500 troops and most of his artillery from capture.

In mid-September 1776 the Continental Army counted 16,000 men. Over the next three months the British killed or took prisoner one-quarter of these troops and drove the survivors across New Jersey. By early December, when Washington retreated from New Jersey into Pennsylvania, he commanded fewer than 7,000 men fit for duty. Thomas Paine called these demoralizing days "the times that try men's souls."

Washington took the offensive before military and national morale collapsed. On Christmas night 1776 he attacked a Hessian garrison at Trenton, New Jersey, and captured nearly 1,000 Germans with the loss of only 4 men. On January 3, 1777, Washington attacked Princeton, New Jersey, killing or capturing one-third of his 1,200 British opponents and losing only 40. The American victories at Trenton and Princeton had important consequences. First, they boosted civilian and military morale. Second, they undermined the Howes' plans to rally loyalists and skeptics to Britain's cause and forced the British evacuation of New Jersey in early 1777. Washington established winter quarters only twenty-five miles from New York City.

The rebel militia meanwhile drove thousands of New Jersey loyalists, who had been plundering Whig property, into British-held New York, where many joined the Royal Army. The New Jersey militia became a police force dedicated to rooting out political dissent. It disarmed known loyalists, jailed their leaders, and constantly watched suspected Tories. Ironically, the failure by British commanders to prevent widespread looting by their troops undermined New Jersey loyalists' support for the crown. Facing constant danger of arrest, most loyalists who remained in New Jersey bowed to the inevitable and swore allegiance to the Continental Congress.

Shortly after the battles of Trenton and Princeton, the Marquis de Lafayette, a young French aristocrat, joined Washington's staff. Lafayette was twenty years old, idealistic, brave, infectiously optimistic—and closely connected to the French court. His arrival indicated that France might recognize American independence and declare war on Britain. However, the French first wanted proof that the Americans could win a major battle.

That victory came quickly. In summer 1777 the British planned a two-pronged attack to crush New York State and to isolate New England. Two British columns, one from Montreal and the other from Quebec, were to link up near Albany. Complicating an already intricate scheme, General William Howe launched another major campaign that summer aimed at the American capital, Philadelphia. Because of Howe's fateful decision, no British troops would be able to come to the aid of the Canadian columns.

The first British column, moving south from Montreal under Lieutenant Colonel Barry St. Leger,

MAP 6.1
The War in the North, 1775–1778
Following the British evacuation of Boston, the war shifted to New York City, which the British held from 1776 to 1783. In 1777 Britain's success in taking Philadelphia was offset by defeat in upstate New York. The hard-fought battle of Monmouth Court House, New Jersey, ended the northern campaigns in 1778.

encountered a Continental force holding a choke-point at Fort Stanwix. Unable to defeat the rebels after a three-week siege, the British retreated north. Meanwhile, the second British column, led by General John Burgoyne, became stranded in western New York, his supply lines overextended and his 8,300 troops depleted by combat and hunger. General Horatio Gates of the Continental Army gathered a force of 17,000 rebels and attacked Burgoyne near Saratoga. Burgoyne's troops, surrounded and outnumbered, surrendered on October 17, 1777.

Saratoga was as important diplomatically as militarily. Already pro-American and favorably impressed by the shrewd diplomacy of Benjamin Franklin as American ambassador, the French court received news of the victory at Saratoga as proof that the Americans could win the war and thus deserved diplomatic recognition. In February 1778 France formally recognized the United States. Four months later France went to war with Britain. Spain and Holland ultimately joined the war as French allies. Facing a coalition of enemies, Britain had no allies.

The colonies' allies made their presence felt. Between 1779 and 1781 Spanish troops prevented the British from taking the Mississippi Valley, and beginning in 1781 French troops contributed to rebel victories. Moreover, Britain sent thousands of soldiers to Ireland and the West Indies to guard against a French invasion, further stretching already depleted manpower reserves. The French and Spanish navies, which together approximately equaled the British fleet, won several large battles, and punctured the Royal Navy's blockade.

In late August 1777 British general Howe landed 18,000 troops near Philadelphia. With Washington at their head and Lafayette at his side, 16,000 Continentals paraded through the imperiled city.

The armies collided on September 11, 1777, at Brandywine Creek, Pennsylvania. After the Continentals crumbled in the face of superior British discipline, Congress fled Philadelphia, allowing Howe to occupy it. In early October Howe defeated the Americans a second time, at Germantown. In four bloody weeks 20 percent of the Continentals were killed, wounded, or captured.

In December 1777 the 11,000 Continental survivors marched to their winter headquarters at Valley Forge. They were short on rations and chilled to the bone; one-fourth of them had worn out at least one shoe. Washington later recalled, "You might have tracked the army from White Marsh to Valley Forge by the blood of their feet." As the British rested comfortably in Philadelphia, eighteen miles away, the Continentals huddled, exhausted and hungry, in crude huts.

The army slowly regained its strength but still lacked training. The Saratoga victory had resulted from the Americans' overwhelming numbers, not their superior skill. Meeting Howe on an even basis, the Continentals had lost badly—twice. The key skills of marching and maneuvering were nonexistent. Then in February 1778 the Continental Army's fortunes rose when a German soldier of fortune and drillmaster, Friedrich von Steuben, reached Valley Forge. An administrative genius and immensely popular, he turned the army into a formidable fighting force.

Just how formidable became clear in June 1778. The British, now under General Henry Clinton, evacuated Philadelphia and marched toward New York. The Continentals caught up on June 28 at Monmouth Court House, New Jersey. The battle blazed for six hours, with the Continentals throwing back Clinton's best units. The British finally broke off contact and slipped away under cover of darkness. Never again would they win easy victories against the Continental Army.

The Battle of Monmouth ended the contest for the North. Clinton occupied New York, which the Royal Navy made safe from attack. Washington kept his army on watch nearby, while Whig militia hunted down the last few Tory guerrillas.

The War in the West, 1776–1782

West of the Appalachians and along New York and Pennsylvania's western borders, a different kind of war unfolded. The numbers engaged along the frontier were small, but the stakes were enormous. In

1776 few Anglo-Americans had any clear idea of the country's western boundaries. By 1783 when the Peace of Paris concluded the war, the new nation would claim the Mississippi River as its western border. So although the frontier campaigns would not determine the war's outcome, they would significantly shape the future of the United States.

Frontier fighting first erupted in the South when Cherokees had begun attacking frontier settlements from Virginia to Georgia in 1776. Within a year retaliatory expeditions had burned most Cherokee towns and forced the Cherokees to cede most of their lands in South Carolina and large tracts in North Carolina and Tennessee. Elsewhere in the region the warfare lasted longer. Kentucky saw fierce fighting as rebels under Colonel George Rogers Clark established control of the Ohio River Valley from Pittsburgh to the

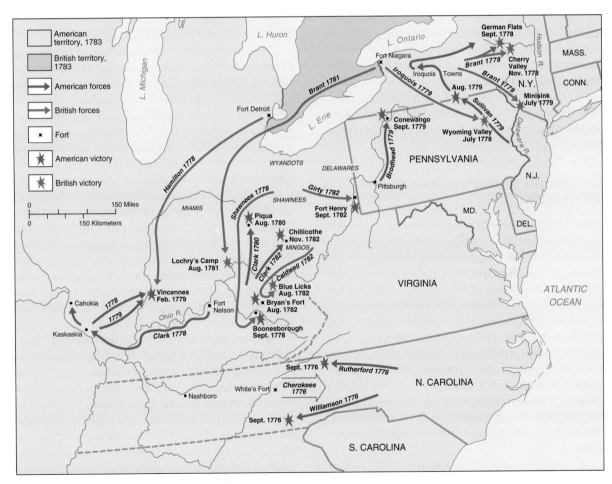

MAP 6.2
The War in the West, 1776–1782
Carolina militiamen drove attacking Cherokees far back into the Appalachians in 1776. George Rogers Clark's victory at Vincennes in 1779 gave the United States effective control of the Ohio Valley. In retaliation for raids on New York and Pennsylvania, John Sullivan inflicted widespread starvation on the Iroquois by burning their villages and winter food supplies in 1779.

Mississippi after defeating both the British and Native Americans.

In the East pro-British Iroquois under the gifted Mohawk leader Joseph Brant devastated the New York and Pennsylvania frontiers in 1778. General John Sullivan led a Continental force, with Tuscarora and Oneida allies, against the Iroquois. Victorious at what is now Elmira, New York, in 1779, Sullivan and his forces burned two dozen Iroquois villages and destroyed a million bushels of corn. The Iroquois fled north to Canada, and hundreds starved to death. Sullivan had destroyed the heartland of the Iroquois; their population declined by one-third during the Revolutionary War. Although Brant's warriors laid waste to Pennsylvania and New York in one final spasm of fury in 1780, the Iroquois never recovered.

Although its impact on the war itself was minimal, the intense fighting west of the Appalachians would play a major role in shaping the American future.

American Victory in the South, 1778–1781

After 1778 the British focus shifted to the South. France and Spain's entry had embroiled Britain in an international struggle that raged from India to Gibraltar and from the West Indies to the North American mainland. If the British could secure the South, they could easily shuffle forces between the West Indies and the mainland. And the South looked like an easy target: in 1778, 3,500 British troops had taken Savannah, Georgia, without difficulty, and Clinton expected a southern invasion to tap a huge reservoir of loyalist support. British strategy called for seizing key southern ports and, aided by loyal militiamen, moving back north, pacifying one region after another.

At first the plan unfolded smoothly. Sailing from New York with 4,000 men, General Clinton captured Charles Town, South Carolina, in May 1780. He left the mopping-up operation to Lord Charles Cornwallis. Clinton's miscalculation of loyalist strength rapidly became apparent. Southern

Tories used the British occupation to take revenge for their harsh treatment under rebel rule, and patriots struck back. The war engulfed the lower South and became intensely personal, with individuals choosing sides not for political reasons but for simple revenge.

The southern campaign also sparked a mass exodus of slaves; 25,000 Georgia and South Carolina slaves sought freedom in British-held territory. The British had no intention of emancipating slaves and made every effort to return them to their owners. Nonetheless, fear of slave rebellion caused many former loyalists to abandon their British ties and welcome the rebels' return to power.

Meanwhile, battles between British troops and Continental regulars led to a string of Continental defeats. America's worst loss of the entire war came at Camden, South Carolina, in August 1780. General Horatio Gates's combined force of professionals and militiamen faced Cornwallis's army. The militiamen fled after the first volley, and the badly outnumbered Continentals were overrun. Washington sent General Nathanael Greene to confront Cornwallis. Under Greene, the rebels lost three major battles in 1781 but won the campaign anyhow. Greene gave the patriot militiamen the protection that they needed to hunt down loyalists, stretched British supply lines until they snapped, and inflicted heavy casualties. Greene's dogged resistance forced Cornwallis to abandon the Carolina backcountry and to lead his battered troops into Virginia.

Still secure in New York, Clinton wanted Cornwallis to return to Charles Town, but Cornwallis had other plans. He established a base at Yorktown, Virginia, where the York and James rivers empty into Chesapeake Bay. He hoped to fan out into Virginia and Pennsylvania but never got the chance. On August 30, 1781, a French fleet dropped anchor off the Virginia coast and landed troops near Yorktown. Lafayette joined them, and Washington led his Continental Army south to tighten the noose. Trapped and besieged at Yorktown, Cornwallis's 6,000 troops lasted three weeks against 8,800 Americans and 7,800 French. On October 19, 1781, they surrendered.

MAP 6.3
The War in the South, 1778–1781
By 1780 Britain held the South's major cities, Charles Town and Savannah, but could not establish control over the backcountry because of resistance from Nathanael Greene's Continentals. By invading Virginia, Lord Cornwallis placed himself within striking distance of American and French forces, a decision that rapidly led to the British surrender at Yorktown in October 1781.

 Interactive Map: War in the South

Peace at Last, 1781–1783

"Oh God!" Lord North exclaimed on hearing of Yorktown. "It's all over." Indeed, Cornwallis's surrender had extinguished the overtaxed people's will to fight and forced the government to begin peace negotiations. Talks opened in Paris in June 1782, with John Adams, Benjamin Franklin, and John Jay as America's principal diplomats.

Military realities largely dictated the terms of

the peace treaty. Britain recognized American independence and promised the evacuation of all royal troops from U.S. soil. The British had little choice but to award the new nation the vast territory east of the Mississippi, for by 1783 there were 20,000 Anglo-American settlers living west of the Appalachians and George Rogers Clark's victories had given Americans control of the Northwest.

The settlement favored the United States but left some problems unresolved. In a separate treaty Britain transferred East and West Florida back to Spain, but the designated boundaries were ambiguous. Further, the Peace of Paris contained seeds of future British-American controversy: although the United States promised to urge state legislatures to compensate loyalists for property losses, several states would later refuse to comply. Missing from the treaty was any reference to the Native Americans, most of whom had supported the British. The treaty left them to deal with the new American republic on their own. Not surprisingly, many Indians did not acknowledge the new nation's claims to sovereignty over their territory.

Independence carried a heavy price. At least 5 percent of free males—white, black, and Native American—aged sixteen to forty-five had died fighting the British. One out of six loyalists and several thousand slaves had fled into exile. And the peace left two important issues unsettled: what kind of society the United States would become and what sort of government it would possess.

THE REVOLUTION AND SOCIAL CHANGE

Two forces shaped the Revolution's social effects: the principles articulated in the Declaration of Independence and the dislocations caused by the war. These factors combined to change relationships between members of different classes, races, and genders momentously. Increasingly, elites had to earn rather than expect the respect of nonelite whites. The Revolution dealt slavery a body blow in the North, enlarging the number of free blacks and extending their political rights. White males ac-

knowledged the wartime contributions of white women, foreshadowing a national debate over gender relations. Native Americans, occupying desirable lands, posed the greatest challenge to Revolutionary ideas of liberty and equality.

Egalitarianism Among White Males

Between 1700 and 1760 social relations between elites and common people had grown more formal, distant, and restrained. Members of the colonial gentry lived sumptuously to emphasize their position. By the late 1760s, however, many in the upper class were wearing homespun clothing in support of boycotts of British goods. When the Virginia planters organized militia companies in 1775, they dressed in plain hunting shirts so that even the poorest farmer would not find his humble appearance too embarrassing to enlist. Elites maintained the appearance, if not the substance, of equality. Nonetheless, many elites continued to believe that the lower classes should defer to those with the wealth and education necessary to govern.

The war accelerated the erosion of class differences by forcing gentry-officers to respect ordinary men serving as privates. Indeed, the soldiers demanded to be treated with consideration, especially in light of the ringing statement of the Declaration of Independence that "all men are created equal." Soldiers followed commands, but not if they were addressed and treated as inferiors.

The men who expected officers to recognize their worth as individuals carried their new self-esteem and insistence on respect back into civilian life. Personal pride gradually translated into political behavior and beliefs, and candidates took care not to scorn the common people. The war thus fundamentally democratized Americans' political assumptions. The gentry's sense of social rank also diminished as they met men who rose through ability and observed middle-class farmers and artisans handling duties previously thought above their station. This egalitarianism did not extend to propertyless males, women, and nonwhites, but it did undermine the tendency to believe that wealth or family background conferred a special claim to public office.

In short, Revolutionary-generation Americans insisted that virtue and sacrifice, not wealth, defined worth. They came to see the "natural aristocracy"—those who demonstrated fitness for government service by their personal accomplishments—as ideal candidates for political office. This natural aristocracy included self-made men such as Benjamin Franklin as well as those, like Thomas Jefferson and John Hancock, born into wealth.

The imperial crisis of the 1760s and 1770s had pulled elites in a democratic direction. Popularly elected assemblies dominated by the elites had led the fight against royal governors and their appointees who enforced laws and policies dangerous to liberty. Colonists believed that even elected executives could not be trusted with power. History had confirmed the belief that those in power tended to become either corrupt or dictatorial. Thus revolutionaries proclaimed the need to strengthen legislative power at the expense of executive.

A Revolution for Black Americans

The wartime condition of African-Americans contradicted the ideals of equality and justice for which Americans fought. About 500,000 black persons, composing one-fifth of the total population, inhabited the United States in 1776. All but 25,000 were slaves. Free blacks could not vote, lived under curfews, and lacked the guarantees of equal justice afforded to even the poorest white criminal. Grudging toleration was all that free blacks could expect, and few slaves ever became free.

The war nevertheless presented new opportunities to African-Americans. Some slaves took advantage of the confusion of war to run off and pose as freemen. A 1775 ban on black soldiers was collapsing by 1777. All states but Georgia and South Carolina eventually recruited blacks. Approximately 5,000 African-Americans, mainly from the North, served in the Continental Army. Most were slaves serving with their masters' consent, usually in racially integrated units.

Manpower demands, not a white commitment to equal justice, largely opened these opportunities. In fact, until the mid-eighteenth century most in the Western world saw slavery as part of the natural order. By the 1760s, however, some American opposition to slavery had blossomed. The Quakers led the way; by 1779 most Quaker slaveowners had freed their slaves. The Declaration of Independence's broad assertion of natural rights and human equality spurred a larger attack on slavery. By 1804 all the states from Pennsylvania north, except New Hampshire, had abolished slavery.

The antislavery movement reflected the Enlightenment's emphasis on gradual change. By priming public opinion to favor a weakening of the institution over time, leaders sought to bring about its demise. Most state abolition laws provided for gradual emancipation, typically declaring free all children born of a slave woman after a certain date, often July 4. (These individuals still had to work, without pay, for their mother's master for up to twenty-eight years.) Furthermore, Revolutionary leaders did not press for decisive action against slavery in the South, where the institution was embedded in the economy. They feared that widespread southern emancipation would either bankrupt or disrupt the Union. They argued that the United States, deeply in debt, could not finance immediate abolition in the South and that any attempt to do so without compensation would drive the region to secession.

Although slavery gnawed at Whig consciences even in the South, no state south of Pennsylvania abolished slavery. Most, however, passed laws making it easier to free slaves. Between 1775 and 1790 the number of free blacks in Virginia and Maryland rose from 4,000 to 21,000, or about 5 percent of all African-Americans residing there.

These "free persons of color" faced a future of destitution and second-class citizenship. Most had used up their cash savings to purchase their freedom and were past their physical prime. They found few whites willing to hire them or to pay equal wages. Most free blacks remained poor laborers or tenant farmers. But a few became landowners or skilled artisans. Benjamin Banneker of Maryland, a self-taught mathematician and astronomer, served on the survey team that laid out Washington, D.C., and published a series of almanacs. Phillis Wheatley, a slave in a Boston merchant family, gained her freedom in 1773, the same year her poems were published to acclaim in England.

Most states granted important civil rights to free blacks during and after the Revolution. For example, male free blacks who met property qualifications gained the right to vote everywhere by the 1780s. Most northern states repealed or stopped enforcing curfews and other restrictive laws; most also guaranteed free blacks equal treatment in court.

The Revolution neither ended slavery nor brought equality to free blacks, but it did begin a process by which slavery could be extinguished. In half the nation, public opinion no longer condoned human bondage, and southerners increasingly saw slavery as a necessary evil, implicitly admitting its immorality. The shift proved short-lived, as the trend toward egalitarianism faded in the 1790s.

White Women in Wartime

"To be adept in the art of Government is a prerogative to which your sex lay almost exclusive claim," wrote Abigail Adams to her husband, John, in 1776. One of the era's tartest political commentators and her husband's confidante and best friend, Adams had no public role. Indeed, most Americans in the 1780s believed that a woman's duty lay in maintaining her household and rearing her children.

Women greatly broadened their involvement in the cause, creating a wide range of support activities during the war. Female "camp followers," many of them soldiers' wives, cooked, laundered, and nursed the wounded for both sides. A few women disguised themselves as men and joined the fighting. Women who remained at home managed families, households, farms, and businesses on their own. Despite—and because of—enormous struggles, women gained confidence in their ability to think and act on matters traditionally reserved for men. Although women's public roles and visibility increased during the Revolution, the question was to what extent the new nation would make these gains permanent.

Native Americans and the Revolution

Revolutionary ideology held out at least abstract hope for African-Americans and women, but it made no provisions for the many Indians who sought to maintain political and cultural independence. Moreover, in an overwhelmingly agrarian society, the Revolution's promise of equal economic opportunity for all set the stage for territorial expansion beyond settled areas, thereby threatening Indian lands. Even where Indians retained land, the influx of settlers posed dangers in the form of deadly diseases, farming practices hostile to Indian subsistence, and alcohol. Indians were all

Phillis Wheatley, African-American Poet
Though a slave, Wheatley was the best-known poet in America at the time of the Revolution. Despite her fame, Wheatley died in poverty in 1784.

the more vulnerable because during the wars between 1754 and 1783, their population east of the Mississippi had fallen by about one-half and many villages had been uprooted.

In the face of these uncertainties, Native Americans continued to incorporate aspects of European culture into their lives. From the early colonial period, they had adopted European-made goods of cloth, metal, and glass while retaining some of their traditional clothing, tools, and weapons. Indians also participated in the American economy by occasionally working for wages or selling food, craft items, and other products. Such interweaving of old and new characterized Indian communities throughout the newly independent states.

Thus Native Americans did not hold stubbornly to traditional ways, but they did insist on retaining control of their communities and ways of life. In 1745 some Iroquois had told an Anglo-American missionary, "We are Indians and do not wish to be transformed into white men. The English are our Brethren, but we never promised to become what they are." In the Revolution's aftermath, it remained unclear whether the new nation would accommodate Native Americans on these terms.

FORGING NEW GOVERNMENTS, 1776–1787

Despite their unity against British authority, the revolutionaries differed sharply among themselves over basic questions of social and political order. Elite republicans feared democracy as "mob rule," while urban workers feared that elites profited at their expense. Rural colonists emphasized decentralization of power. The revolutionaries' early attempts at creating state and national governments reflected these conflicts.

From Colonies to States

In establishing the Revolutionary state governments, the patriots relied heavily on the colonial experience. For example, most favored bicameral

legislatures. Colonial legislatures in the royal provinces had consisted of two houses: an appointed upper chamber (council) and an elected lower chamber (assembly). These two-part legislatures resembled Parliament's division into the House of Lords and the House of Commons and symbolized the assumption that a government should represent aristocrats and commoners separately. Despite the Revolution's democratic tendencies, few questioned the long-standing practice of setting property requirements for voters and elected officials. Property ownership, they argued, enabled voters and officeholders to think and act independently.

Americans generally agreed, too, that their elected representatives should exercise independent judgment rather than simply carry out the popular will. The idea of political parties as instruments for identifying and mobilizing public opinion was alien to the Revolutionary era, which equated parties with "factions"—selfish groups that advanced their interests at the expense of the public good. Candidates campaigned on the basis of their reputation and qualifications, not issues. In general, they did not present voters with a clear choice between policies calculated to benefit rival interest groups. Thus voters did not know how candidates stood on specific issues and found it hard to influence government actions.

As in the colonial era, eleven of thirteen legislatures in the 1780s were bicameral and most were divided equally among all counties or towns, regardless of population distribution. A minority of voters normally elected a majority of assemblymen. The most radical constitution, Pennsylvania's, tried to establish election districts roughly equal in population so that a minority of voters could not elect a majority of legislators. Nine states reduced property requirements for voting, but none abolished them. In most states the majority of officeholders continued to be appointed.

The persistence of these features should not obscure the pathbreaking nature of the state constitutions. First, their adoption required ratification by the people. Second, they could be changed only by popular vote. Above all, counter to the

British view of a constitution as a body of customary practices, the state constitutions were *written* compacts that defined and limited rulers' powers. As a final check on government power, the Revolutionary constitutions contained bills of rights outlining fundamental freedoms beyond government control. Governments would no longer serve as the final judge of the constitutionality of their activities.

Contrary to political elites' predilections, the imperial crisis of the 1760s and 1770s had pulled them into a democratic tide The assemblies, the most democratic parts of colonial government, had led the fight against British policy. Colonists had embarked on the Revolution dreading executive officeholders and convinced that they could not trust even elected governors. Their recent experience seemed to confirm the "country party" view (see Chapter 5) that those in power tended to become corrupt or dictatorial. Thus revolutionary statesmen proclaimed the need to strengthen legislatures at the governors' expense.

Accordingly, the state constitutions strictly limited executive power. In most states the governor became an elected official, and elections were held far more frequently than before—usually every year. In the majority of states legislatures, not governors, appointed judges and other officials. Stripped of the veto and most appointive powers, governors became figureheads.

Having weakened the executive branch and vested more power in the legislatures, the state constitutions also made the legislatures more responsive to the will of the people. Nowhere could the governor appoint the upper chamber. Eight states allowed voters to select *both* houses of the legislature. Pennsylvania and Georgia abolished the upper house and substituted a unicameral (one-chamber) legislature. The Whigs' assault on executive power reflected bitter memories of arbitrary royal governors and underscored the influence of country-party ideologues who had warned against executives' usurpation of authority.

But Revolutionary leaders considered themselves republicans, not democrats. To them, "democracy" suggested mob rule and the concentration of power in the hands of an ignorant mass.

"Republicanism" presumed that government would be entrusted to leaders chosen for their talents and wisdom. Most republicans believed that government should balance the interests of different classes to prevent any one group from gaining absolute power. They also rejected monarchy—having blasted one king in the Declaration of Independence, they were not about to enthrone another. Nonetheless, republicans had difficulty reconciling their preference for strong, elite leadership with most Americans' pervasive distrust of executive power.

Initially, elites had to accept state governments dominated by elected legislatures. Gradually, however, well-to-do landowners, merchants, and lawyers reasserted their desires for centralized authority and the political prerogatives of wealth. For example, in 1780 an elite-dominated convention in Massachusetts pushed through a constitution with stiff property qualifications for voting and holding office and a strong governor with considerable appointment and veto power. Georgia and Pennsylvania had reverted to bicameral legislatures by 1790. Other states raised property qualifications for the upper chamber to make room for men of "Wisdom, remarkable integrity, or that Weight which arises from property."

Troubled far less by differences among social classes and restrictions on the expression of popular will than by the prospect of tyranny, some elites nevertheless feared that deep-seated and permanent social divisions could jeopardize republican liberty. In Virginia between 1776 and 1780, Thomas Jefferson drafted a series of bills to promote equality. He also attacked two legal bastions of the British aristocracy, primogeniture and entail. Primogeniture required that the eldest son inherit all property if there was no will; entail dictated that an heir and his descendants keep an estate intact—that is, neither sell nor divide it. Jefferson hoped that this legislation would ensure a continuous division of wealth and prevent wealthy families from amassing huge landholdings. By 1791 no state provided for primogeniture, and only two allowed entails.

These years also witnessed the end of most state-established churches. Religiously conservative New Hampshire, Connecticut, and Massachusetts resisted this reform until 1817, 1818, and 1833, respectively, but in every state where the Anglican church was established, such status was abolished by 1786. Jefferson's Statute for Religious Freedom (1786) resoundingly defended religious freedom. "Truth is great," he proclaimed, "and will prevail if left to itself."

In 1782 Thomas Paine wrote that the American Revolution was intended to ring in "a new era and give a new turn to human affairs." In this ambitious declaration, Paine expressed the heart of the republican ideal: that *all* political institutions would be judged by whether they served the public good, not the interests of a powerful few. More than anything else, this way of thinking made American politics revolutionary.

Formalizing a Confederation, 1776–1781

Americans' first national government reflected their fears of centralized authority. In 1776 John Dickinson drafted a proposal for a national government, and in 1777 Congress sent a weakened version of this document, the Articles of Confederation, to the states for ratification.

The Articles reserved to each state "its sovereignty, freedom and independence" and made Americans citizens of their states first and of the United States second. John Adams later explained that the Whigs never thought of "consolidating this vast Continent under one national Government" but created instead "a Confederacy of States, each of which must have a separate government."

Under the Articles, the national government consisted of a unicameral congress, elected by the state legislatures, in which each state had one vote. Congress could request funds from the states but could not tax without every state's approval, nor could it regulate interstate or overseas commerce. The Articles provided for no executive branch. Rather, congressional committees oversaw financial, diplomatic, and military affairs. Nor was there a judicial system by which the national government could compel allegiance to its laws.

All thirteen states had approved the Articles by March 1781, and they became law. The new government represented an important step in the process of defining the role of national sovereignty in relation to the sovereignty of individual states and in creating a formal government. Nonetheless, misgivings about centralized power left the new government severely limited in the views of nationally minded elites.

Finance, Trade, and the Economy, 1777–1786

Perhaps the greatest challenge facing the Confederation was putting the nation on a sound financial footing. Winning the war cost $160 million, far more than taxation could raise. The government borrowed from abroad and printed paper money, called Continentals. But from 1776 to 1791 lack of public faith in the government destroyed 98 percent of the Continentals' value—an inflationary disaster. Congress turned to Robert Morris, a wealthy Philadelphia merchant who became the nation's superintendent of finance in 1781. Morris proposed a national import duty of 5 percent to finance the congressional budget and to guarantee interest payments on the war debt, but the duty failed to pass because one state, Rhode Island, rejected it.

In 1783, hoping to panic the country into creating a regular source of national revenue, Morris and New York congressman Alexander Hamilton engineered a dangerous gamble, later known as the Newburgh Conspiracy. They secretly persuaded some army officers, encamped at Newburgh, New York, to threaten a coup d'état unless the treasury obtained the taxation authority necessary to raise funds for their pay, which was months late. George Washington forestalled the conspiracy by appealing to his officers' honor. Morris probably never intended a mutiny to take place, but his risk-taking demonstrated the new nation's perilous financial straits and the vulnerability of its political institutions.

When peace came in 1783, Morris found it impossible to fund the government adequately. After

MAP 6.4
State Claims to Western Lands and State Cessions to the Federal Government, 1782–1802
Eastern states' surrender of land claims paved the way for new state governments in the West. Georgia was the last state to cede its western lands, in 1802.

New York blocked another congressional tax measure sent to the states, state contributions to Congress fell steadily. By the late 1780s the states lagged 80 percent behind in providing the funds that Congress requested.

Nor could the Confederation pry trade concessions from Britain. Before independence, New England had depended heavily on exports to the West Indies. After independence, Britain had slapped strict limitations on U.S. commerce, allowing British shippers to increase their share of the Atlantic trade at American expense.

This loss of trade contributed to an economic depression that gripped the nation beginning in 1784.

New Englanders suffered greatly in these hard times. While facing high taxes to pay off war debts, they also confronted tightening credit and the loss of major overseas markets and even whaling grounds. Despite opening new routes or smuggling, by 1791 the number of seamen in fishing and whaling had fallen by more than 40 percent. Young men voted with their feet, migrating to the frontier or to cities and leaving many young women without marriage prospects.

Southerners also faced major problems as the markets for tobacco and rice failed to rebound to their prewar levels; in 1770 the South had provided nearly two-thirds of American exports, by 1790 that figure had fallen to less than half. Increased production of wheat and hemp did little to help and may even have hurt the South —these crops required fewer laborers than tobacco, leaving slave owners with large numbers of underemployed and restless slaves. Combined with Native American and Spanish resistance to westward expansion, these factors underlined nagging uncertainties about the South's future.

On the other hand, Mid-Atlantic farmers actually grew more prosperous from exporting grain to famine-stricken areas of Europe, and the region quickly recovered from the Revolution's ravages.

The Confederation and the West, 1785–1787

The postwar settlement and administration of western lands posed another formidable challenge to the new government. Settlers and speculators were determined to possess these lands, and Native Americans were equally determined to keep them out. At the same time, Britain and Spain sought to contain the new nation's territorial expansion.

After the states surrendered claims to more than 160 million acres north of the Ohio River, Congress, in the Ordinance of 1785, established uniform procedures for surveying the region. The law made the basic unit of settlement a township six miles square, subdivided into thirty-six sections of 640 acres each, with one section reserved as a source of income for public schools. A subsequent law, the Northwest Ordinance of 1787, defined the land north of the Ohio River as the Northwest Territory, provided for its later division into states, and forbade slavery in the territory. The Northwest Ordinance outlined three steps for admitting states to the Union. First, Congress would appoint a territorial governor and judges. Second, as soon as 5,000 adult males lived in a territory, the people would write a temporary constitution and elect a legislature. Third, when the population reached 60,000,

the settlers would write a state constitution, which Congress would approve before granting statehood.

The Ordinance of 1785 and the Northwest Ordinance became the Confederation's major contributions to American life. They set the principles for surveying the frontier, allowed territorial self-government at an early stage of settlement, and provided reasonable standards for statehood. They became models for organizing territories west of the Mississippi River and established precedents for banning slavery from certain territories. However, because Indians, determined to bar white settlement, controlled virtually the entire Northwest, Congress's ordinances had no immediate effect.

The Northwest Territory offered enough rich land to guarantee future citizens landownership, thus satisfying the republican belief that opening the West would prevent the rise, east of the Appalachians, of a large class of tenant farmers and poor laborers lacking the property needed to vote. Such a development would poison politics through class conflict and would undermine republican equality. However, standing in the way of such republican dreams were some 150,000 Native Americans already inhabiting the western territories and struggling to preserve their way of life.

At postwar treaty negotiations U.S. commissioners told Native Americans, "You are a subdued people. . . . We claim the country by conquest." Under threat of continued warfare, some Indian leaders initially yielded. Through treaties the Iroquois lost about one-half their land in New York and Pennsylvania, while the Delawares and Shawnees were obliged to recognize American sovereignty over their lands. But most Indians repudiated the treaties, denying that their negotiators had the authority to give up their nations' lands.

The Indians' resistance also stemmed from their confidence that the British would provide the arms necessary to defy the Americans. Britain had refused to abandon seven forts along the nation's northwestern frontier, ostensibly because Tories remained uncompensated for property losses. In April 1784 the British colonial office secretly ordered Canada's governor to hold onto the forts,

MAP 6.5
The Northwest Territory, 1785–1787
The Ordinance of 1785 provided for surveying land into townships of thirty-six sections, each supporting four families on 160-acre plots (approximately 25 people per square mile). In 1787 the Northwest Ordinance stipulated that states would ultimately be created in the region.

hoping to reestablish Britain's claim to the Northwest Territory.

The Mohawk Joseph Brant led Indian resistance to white settlement. Courageous, skilled in diplomacy, and well educated, he organized the northwestern Indians into a military alliance in 1786 to keep out white settlers. But Brant and his followers, who had relocated beyond American reach in Canada, could not win support from other Iroquois such as the Senecas of Jenuchshadago, who remained in New York. Trying to take advantage of disarray among the Indians, colonial militia raided the Northwest Territory, forcing the tribes to abandon southern Indiana and Ohio. Whites followed on their heels: New Englanders founded the Ohio River town of Marietta in the spring of 1788

and Pennsylvanians pushed slightly further west to establish Cincinnati.

The Confederation faced similar problems in the Southeast, where Spain and its Indian allies worked to block American encroachment on their land. The Spanish found an ally in the shrewd Creek diplomat Alexander McGillivray, who was determined to regain Creek territory held by Georgia. McGillivray negotiated a secret treaty with Spain that promised the Creeks weapons to protect themselves "from the Bears and other fierce Animals." In 1786, after Creeks expelled occupants of the disputed lands, Georgia quickly accepted McGillivray's offer of a cease-fire.

The Spanish also attempted to prevent American infiltration by denying western settlers permission to ship crops down the Mississippi River to New Orleans. After the Spanish closed New Orleans to Anglo-American commerce in 1784, John Jay went to Spain to negotiate trading privileges at New Orleans. Although he failed to win concessions, he returned with a treaty that opened Spanish markets to eastern merchants at the price of relinquishing American export rights through New Orleans. In 1786 Congress rejected this Jay-Gardoqui Treaty, but westerners and southerners, whose interests seemed to have been sacrificed to benefit northern commerce, felt betrayed.

TOWARD A NEW CONSTITUTION, 1786–1788

Despite the United States' enormous strides in establishing itself as an independent nation, impatience with the national government's limitation continued to grow among those seeking to establish the Republic on a more solid economic and military footing. Impatience became anxiety when protesting Massachusetts farmers defied local authorities. A national convention called to consider amendments to the Articles instead created a radical new frame of government, the Constitution; its ratification in 1788 set a new course for America.

Shays's Rebellion, 1786–1787

The Jay-Gardoqui treaty revealed deep-seated tensions beneath the surface appearance of American national unity. New England, which had never recovered from the loss of its West Indies markets, remained mired in the depression that had begun in 1784. Dominated by commercially minded elites, the Massachusetts legislature voted in 1786 to pay off its Revolutionary debt, necessitating a huge tax hike. Compounding these difficulties was a shortage of the specie (gold and silver coin) demanded by bankers, merchants, and tax collectors. Thousands of small family farmers groaned under this cycle of debt.

In contrast, the mid-Atlantic and southern states enjoyed rising prosperity, thanks to in-creased tobacco and food exports, and were easily paying off their war debts. Despite this general prosperity, a growing minority of nationalists were unhappy with the Confederation. Merchants and shippers wanted a strong central government that could secure trading privileges abroad and ensure America's standing in an Atlantic economy still dominated by Britain. Land speculators and western settlers wanted a more activist policy against Spain, Britain, and Native Americans. Urban artisans hoped for a stronger national government that would protect them from foreign competition by imposing high tariffs. The spark that ignited this tinderbox flared first in Massachusetts. Farmers in the western part of the state, already struggling with a narrow profit margin and facing demands for payment in specie, which they lacked, held public meetings to discuss "the Suppressing of tyrannical government." This time, however, tyranny stemmed from the state house in Boston, not Parliament in London. Late in 1786 Daniel Shays, a Revolutionary War officer and hard-pressed farmer, led 2,000 angry men in an attempt to shut down the courts and to prevent foreclosures and tax auctions. Although routed by the state militia, Shays's followers won control of the Massachusetts legislature in 1787, cut taxes, and secured a pardon for Shays.

Although Shays's Rebellion caused little bloodshed and never raised a serious threat of anarchy, critics of the Confederation painted it and similar, less radical movements elsewhere as a taste of the disorder to come under the weak national government. By threatening to seize weapons from a federal arsenal at Springfield, Massachusetts, the Shaysites had unintentionally reminded nationalists how vulnerable to "mobocracy" the United States had become. Meanwhile, rumors that Spain had offered westerners export rights at New Orleans if they would secede from the Union sowed fears that the United States was on the verge of coming apart.

Instead of igniting a popular uprising, Shays's Rebellion encouraged aggressive nationalists to push for wholesale reform of the Republic's legal and institutional structure. Delegates from five

James Madison
Although one of the Philadelphia Convention's youngest delegates, Madison of Virginia was among its most politically astute. He played a central role in the Constitution's adoption.

states had met at Annapolis, Maryland, intending to discuss ways to promote interstate commerce. With chaos looming in Massachusetts, they called instead for a general convention to propose amendments to the Articles of Confederation. Congress asked the states to appoint delegations to meet in Philadelphia.

The Philadelphia Convention, 1787

In May 1787 fifty-five delegates, from every state but Rhode Island, began gathering at the Pennsylvania State House (later called Independence Hall) in Philadelphia. Among them were men of established reputation—George Washington, Benjamin Franklin, Robert Morris—as well as talented new-

comers such as Alexander Hamilton and James Madison. Most were wealthy, were in their thirties or forties, and had legal training. Nineteen owned slaves. Most important, they shared a "continental" or "nationalist" perspective. Thirty-nine had served in Congress and knew firsthand the weaknesses of the Articles. They were convinced that without a strong national government, the country would fall victim to foreign aggression or simply disintegrate.

Two basic issues confronted the convention. First, should the delegates merely tinker with the Articles, or should they draw up a new frame of government? Second, how could any government balance the conflicting interests of large and small states? Thirty-six-year-old James Madison of Virginia proposed answers to both questions.

Madison's Virginia Plan, introduced by fellow Virginian Edmund Randolph in late May, boldly called for a national government, not a confederation of states. It gave Congress virtually unrestricted rights of legislation and taxation, power to veto state laws, and authority to use military force against states. As delegate Charles Pinckney of South Carolina immediately saw, the Virginia Plan was designed "to abolish the State Govern[men]ts altogether." The Virginia Plan specified a bicameral legislation and made representation in both houses of Congress proportional to each state's population. The voters would elect the lower house, which would then choose delegates to the upper house from nominations submitted by the state legislatures. The houses would jointly name the country's president and judges. But opposition to Madison's plan surfaced immediately, particularly his call for proportional representation, which favored Virginia, the largest state.

On June 15 William Paterson of New Jersey offered a counterproposal, the New Jersey Plan. It featured a unicameral legislature in which each state had one vote, just as under the Articles. It went even further than the Virginia Plan by defining congressional laws and treaties as the "supreme law of the land."

The New Jersey Plan exposed the convention's greatest problem: the question of representation.

The Virginia Plan gave the four largest states—Virginia, Massachusetts, New York, and Pennsylvania—a majority in both houses. The New Jersey Plan allowed the seven smallest states, with only 25 percent of the U.S. population, to control Congress. By early July the convention was stalemated. To end the impasse, the delegates appointed a "grand committee" dedicated to compromise. This panel adopted a proposal by the Connecticut delegation: an equal vote for each state in the upper house and proportional representation in the lower house. The convention accepted the compromise on July 17 and in two months overcame the remaining hurdles.

Despite their differences over representation, both Madison's and Paterson's proposals would have strengthened the national government at the states' expense, although other delegates remained wary of undermining the sovereignty of the states. Hard bargaining created the new Constitution's delicate balance between the desire for a stronger national government and the fear that all governments tended to become despotic.

As finally approved on September 17, 1787, the Constitution of the United States was an extraordinary document. In addition to reconciling the interests of large and small states, it balanced the delegates' desire for a strong national government against their fear of tyranny. It increased national authority in several ways. It vested in Congress the authority to levy and collect taxes, to regulate interstate commerce, and to conduct diplomacy. Under the Constitution, all acts and treaties of the United States would become "the supreme law of the land." State officials would have to uphold the Constitution, even against acts of their own states. The national government could use military force against any state.

In effect, the Constitution abandoned the principle on which the Articles of Confederation had rested: that the United States was a federation of independent republics known as states. However, the Constitution's framers restrained the new national government in two key ways. First, they established three distinct branches within the new government—the legislative, the executive, and the judicial. Second, they designed a system of checks and balances to prevent one branch from dominating the others. States' equal representation in the Senate offset proportional representation by population in the House, and each chamber could block hasty measures demanded by the other. Further, the president could veto acts of Congress, but to prevent capricious use of the presidential veto, a two-thirds majority in each house could override a veto. The president would conduct diplomacy, but only the Senate could ratify treaties. The president appointed his cabinet, but only with Senate approval. Congress could, by joint vote, remove the president and his appointees from office, but only for "high crimes," not for political disagreements.

To further guarantee the independence of each branch, the Constitution provided that the members of one branch would not choose those of another, except judges, whose independence was protected by lifetime appointments. For example, an electoral college, composed of members chosen by the various state legislatures, would select the president. State legislatures would also elect senators, whereas popular vote would determine delegates to the House of Representatives.

In addition to checks and balances, the Constitution embodied a novel form of federalism—a system of shared power and dual lawmaking by the state and national governments—to limit central authority. Not only did the state legislatures have a key role in electing the president and senators, but the Constitution could be amended by the votes of three-fourths of the state legislatures. This system differed greatly from Madison's original plan to establish a national government entirely independent of and superior to the states. Federalism assumed that the national government would limit its activities to foreign affairs, national defense, regulation of commerce, and coining of money. Most other political matters were left to the states. The states could otherwise act autonomously on purely internal matters, including slavery.

The Philadelphia convention faced a dilemma: were slaves property or persons? In general, southern states regarded slaves as property; however, since slaves constituted substantial portions of the southern population, southern delegates wanted to count them as persons in determining representation in the lower house. Many northern delegates from the states that were abolishing slavery hesitated to give southern states a political edge by counting as persons slaves who had neither civil nor political rights. At the same time, northern delegates, themselves property owners, balked at questioning southern notions of property rights. Thus they agreed to allow three-fifths of all slaves to be counted for congressional representation and forbade any state's people from taking action to prevent the return of runaway slaves to another state. The Constitution did limit slavery by not repudiating the Northwest Ordinance's restrictions on slavery and by permitting Congress to ban the importation of slaves after 1808.

Although leaving much authority to the states, the Constitution established a national government clearly superior to the states in several spheres and abandoned the notion of a confederation of virtually independent states. Having thus strengthened national authority, the convention faced the issue of ratification. Two factors argued against submitting the Constitution to the state legislatures for ratification. First, the state legislatures would probably reject the Constitution, which shrank their power relative to the national government. Second, most of the framers believed that the government had to rest on the consent of the American people themselves. The Constitution's opening words—"We the People of the United States"—embodied this view. In the end the Philadelphia Convention provided for ratification by special state conventions composed of delegates elected by the people. Approval by nine such conventions would enable the new government to operate.

Under the Constitution, the framers expected the nation's "natural aristocracy" to continue exercising political leadership; but did they also intend to rein in the democratic currents that the Revolution had set in motion? In one respect they did—by curtailing the power of popularly elected state legislatures. However, the Constitution did not try to control faction and disorder by suppressing liberty—a "remedy," wrote Madison, that would have been "worse than the disease." The House of Representatives did provide one crucial democratic element in the new government. Equally important, the Constitution recognized the American people as the ultimate source of political legitimacy. By making the Constitution amendable and by dividing political power among competing branches of government, the framers made it possible for the national government to be slowly democratized.

The Struggle over Ratification, 1787–1788

At first the Constitution had little national support. Many Americans hesitated to accept the idea of a radically restructured government. To quiet fears of centralized national authority, the Constitution's supporters shrewdly dubbed themselves Federalists, a term implying that the Constitution successfully balanced the relationship between state and national governments.

The Constitution's opponents became known as Antifederalists, a negative-sounding name that conveyed little of their fears that the Constitution *did not* balance the power of the state and national governments. By augmenting national authority, they believed, the Constitution would ultimately doom the states.

Antifederalist arguments reflected the deep-seated Anglo-American suspicion of any concentration of power, a suspicion that had driven events from the Stamp Act Congress through the War of Independence and the early years of the new republic. Unquestionably, the Constitution gave the national government unprecedented authority in an age when most writers on politics agreed that the sole means of preventing despotism was restraining the power of government officials. Distant from the people, especially in an era when news traveled slowly, the national government would be far less responsive to the popular will than state governments would be. "The vast Continent of America cannot be long subjected to a Democracy if consolidated into one Government. You might as well attempt to rule Hell by Prayer," wrote a New England Antifederalist. Furthermore, no one could be sure that the untried scheme of checks and balances would work. And the Constitution contained no guarantees that the new government would protect the liberties of individuals or the states. The absence of a bill of rights prompted Madison's nationalist ally and fellow Virginian George Mason, the author of the first state bill of rights in 1776, to oppose the Constitution.

The Antifederalists confronted several major disadvantages. For one thing, the Federalists included most of the country's wealthiest and most honored men, including Washington and Franklin. In addition, the majority of newspapers were Federalist and did not hesitate to bias their reporting. Finally, the Antifederalists, largely drawn from state and local leaders, lacked their opponents' contacts and experience at the national level. Ultimately, however, Federalist superiority in funds and political organizing proved decisive. The Antifederalists failed to create a sense of urgency among their supporters, assuming that most would automatically rally to them. However, only one-quarter of the voters turned out to elect delegates to the state ratifying conventions, and most had been mobilized by Federalists.

Federalist delegates prevailed in eight state conventions between December 1787 and May 1788, in all cases but one by margins of two-thirds or more. Such lopsided voting in favor of the Constitution reflected Federalist aggressiveness more than popular support. In a Pennsylvania Antifederalist's words, the Federalists rammed through approval in some states "before it can be digested or deliberately considered." Only Rhode Island and North Carolina rejected the Constitution; Rhode Island would not enter the union until 1790.

But unless the large states of Virginia and New York ratified, the new government would be unworkable. Antifederalism ran high in both, especially among small farmers, who believed that the Constitution favored city dwellers and monied interests. Prominent Antifederalists included New York's governor George Clinton and Virginia's Richard Henry Lee, George Mason, Patrick Henry, and future president James Monroe.

On June 21, 1788, the Constitution became the law of the land when the ninth state, New Hampshire, ratified. Debate continued in Virginia, where the Federalists won wide support from settlers in the western part of the state who wanted a strong national government capable of ending Indian raids along the Ohio River. Western Virginians' votes, combined with Madison's logic and tidewater planters' support, ruled the day. On June 25 the Virginia delegates ratified by a narrow 53 percent majority.

The struggle was even hotter in New York. Antifederalists controlled the state convention and probably would have voted down the Constitution had not news arrived of New Hampshire's and Virginia's ratification. Federalists, led by Alexander Hamilton and John Jay, hinted strongly that if the convention rejected the Constitution, New York City would secede and join the Union alone, leaving upstate New York a landlocked enclave. Alarmed, a number of Antifederalists switched sides and New York ratified on July 26 by a 30 to 27 vote.

Despite the defeat, the Antifederalists left an important legacy. At Antifederalist insistence, the Virginia, New York, and Massachusetts conventions ratified the Constitution with requests that the new charter be amended to include a bill of rights protecting Americans' basic freedoms. Widespread support for a bill of rights made it a major item on the new government's agenda, even as states were choosing members of Congress and presidential electors were unanimously designating George Washington president of the United States.

Antifederalists in New York also stimulated one of the greatest works of political analysis ever written: *The Federalist,* a series of eighty-five newspaper articles by Alexander Hamilton, James Madison, and John Jay. Although *The Federalist* papers did little to influence the New York vote, they provided a glimpse of the framers' intentions in designing the Constitution and thus powerfully shaped the American philosophy of government. The Constitution, insisted *The Federalist*'s authors, had two main purposes: to defend minority rights against majority tyranny and to prevent a stubborn

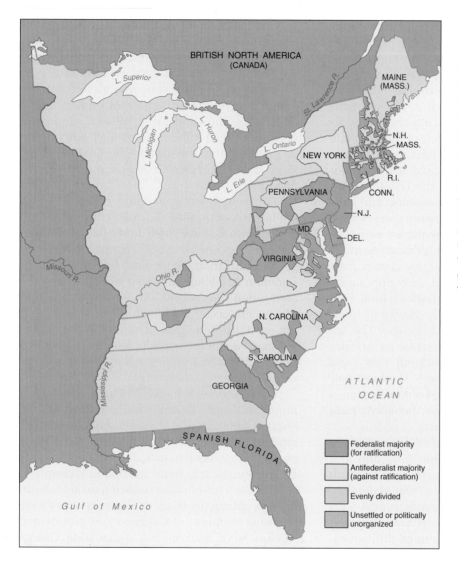

MAP 6.6
Federalist and Antifederalist Strongholds, 1787–1790
Federalists drew their primary backing from densely populated areas along major transportation routes, where trade, mobility, and frequent contact with people in other states encouraged a nationalistic identity. Antifederalist support came from interior regions where geographic isolation bred a localistic perspective. However, some frontier regions, among them Georgia and western Virginia, voted for a strong central government that would push back the Indians or the Spanish.

Federalist majority (for ratification)

Antifederalist majority (against ratification)

Evenly divided

Unsettled or politically unorganized

minority from blocking measures necessary for the national interest. There was no reason to fear that the Constitution would allow a single economic or regional interest to dominate. In the most profound essay in the series, Federalist No. 10, Madison argued that the nation's size and diversity would neutralize the attempts of factions to steer unwise laws through Congress.

Madison's analysis was far too optimistic, however. The Constitution did indeed afford enormous

scope for special interests to influence government. The great challenge for Madison's generation would be maintaining a government that provided equal benefits to all but special privileges to none.

CONCLUSION   *hc* ACE Practice Test

With the entry of Rhode Island into the Union in May 1790 the thirteen colonies were finally unified in a single nation. Eight years of devastating war,

Chronology

1775	Virginia governor Lord Dunmore promises freedom to any slave assisting in the restoration of royal authority.	**1781**	Articles of Confederation become law. Battle of Yorktown; British general Charles Cornwallis surrenders.
1776	British troops evacuate Boston. British defeat American forces under George Washington in fighting around New York City. American victory in Battle of Trenton.	**1782**	Paris peace negotiations begin.
		1783	Peace of Paris. Newburgh Conspiracy.
1777	American victory in Battle of Princeton. British surrender at Saratoga. Battle of Brandywine Creek; British occupy Philadelphia. American defeat at Battle of Germantown. Congress approves Articles of Confederation.	**1784**	Spain closes New Orleans to American trade. Economic depression begins.
		1785	Ordinance of 1785.
		1786	Congress rejects Jay-Gardoqui Treaty. Joseph Brant organizes Indian resistance to U.S. expansion. Virginia adopts Thomas Jefferson's Statute for Religious Freedom.
1778	France formally recognizes the United States. France declares war on Britain. Philadelphia evacuated by British; Battle of Monmouth Court House (New Jersey). British occupy Savannah. Joseph Brant leads Iroquois attacks in western Pennsylvania and New York.	**1786–1787**	Shays's Rebellion in Massachusetts.
		1787	Northwest Ordinance. Philadelphia Convention; federal Constitution signed.
1779	Spain declares war on Britain. George Rogers Clark's recapture of Vincennes. John Sullivan leads U.S. raids on Iroquois.	**1788**	Alexander Hamilton, James Madison, and John Jay, *The Federalist*. Federal Constitution becomes law.
1780	British seize Charles Town.		

which had swept across most of the country, gave civilians and soldiers a shared national identity that would have been unthinkable as late as 1774. Whether fighting or providing supplies and other support, colonists had become Americans.

The democratic ideals unleashed by the Revolution inspired some and appalled others. For many, democracy was central to the new nation's identity, the wellspring of its very essence. Others saw democracy as dangerous, needing to be checked by men of power and virtue. By itself, the Constitution did not make America a democracy; rather it created the legal and institutional framework within which Americans could struggle to attain democracy. Thus it became a fundamental part of America's enduring vision.

FURTHER READING

Colin G. Calloway, *The American Revolution in Indian Country: Crisis and Diversity in Native American Communities* (1995). A powerful study of eight distinct societies, from Canada to Florida, that demonstrates the variety of Indian experiences during and immediately after the Revolution.

Stephen Conway, *The British Isles and the War for American Independence* (2000). A thorough study of the effect on Britain and Ireland of the war in America.

Saul Cornell, *The Other Founders: Anti-Federalism and the Dissenting Tradition in America, 1788–1828* (1999) The definitive study of opponents to ratification of the Constitution and their continuing influence on politics during the early Republic.

Elizabeth A. Fenn, *Pox Americana: The Great Small-pox Epidemic of 1775-82* (2001). A pathbreaking study arguing for the importance of smallpox in shaping the Revolutionary War as well as Native American-European conflicts across the continent.

Sylvia R. Frey, *Water from the Rock: Black Resistance in a Revolutionary Age* (1991). A major study of southern African-Americans during and after the Revolution.

Linda K. Kerber, *Women of the Republic: Intellect and Ideology in Revolutionary America* (1980). A major study of women and of ideologies of gender during the Revolutionary and early republican eras.

Robert Middlekauff, *The Glorious Cause: The American Revolution, 1763–1789* (1982). A comprehensive account of military and political developments through the Philadelphia Convention.

Jack N. Rakove, *Original Meanings: Politics and Ideas in the Making of the Constitution* (1996). A thorough study of the Constitution's framing, rooted in historical context.

Charles Royster, *A Revolutionary People at War: The Continental Army and American Character* (1980). An illuminating analysis of how revolutionary Americans created and fought in an army.

Gordon Wood, *The Radicalism of the American Revolution* (1991). A sweeping interpretation of the Revolution's long-term effects on American society.

7

Launching the New Republic, 1789–1800

CHAPTER OUTLINE

Constitutional Government Takes Shape, 1789–1796

Hamilton and the Formulation of Federalist Policies, 1789–1794

The United States on the World Stage, 1789–1796

The Emergence of Party Politics, 1793–1800

Economic and Social Change

 This icon will direct you to additional study and research resources at http://college.hmco.com/history/us/boyer/enduring_concise/5e/students/index.html

Judith Sargent Stevens (Murray), by John Singleton Copley, c. 1770

Nothing more vividly illustrates the fragility of the new American nation than attempts by Spanish agents to draw westerners into a series of conspiracies that would have led to the secession of land west of the Appalachians and their absorption into the Spanish empire. Spanish offers of citizenship, land, and protection against both the British and Native Americans and of unrestricted export privileges through New Orleans glittered, especially when compared to what westerners saw as their abandonment by the newly formed government. Among those who listened attentively to the Spanish, and who accepted Spanish gold to "consider" their offer, was Daniel Boone.

This chapter focuses on four major questions:

▶ What were the principal features of Hamilton's economic program? What were its opponents' primary objections?

▶ Why was the United States at odds with Spain, France, and Britain at various times in the 1790s?

▶ What issues divided Federalists and Republicans in the election of 1800?

▶ What were the major factors that led to the declining position of nonwhites in the new republic?

An aspiring young lawyer, known more for his temper and wild behavior, also responded to Spain's siren song; later, as president of the United States, Andrew Jackson probably rejoiced that the Spanish had not taken him seriously.

The new United States government had more to worry about than Spain's courtship of westerners—a weak economy hampered by the inability to obtain credit abroad and British, Spanish, and Indian challenges to control of the frontier.

During the 1790s Americans fought bitterly over the social and economic course the new nation should take, and these conflicts were heightened by sharply different reactions to the French Revolution. By 1798 voters had split into two distinct parties, each viewing the other as a threat to liberty. Only when the election of 1800 had been decided—by the narrowest of margins—did it seem certain that the United States would endure.

CONSTITUTIONAL GOVERNMENT TAKES SHAPE, 1789–1796

Putting the new Constitution into effect got off to a slow start, largely because of miserable travel conditions. Congress was a month late in convening, and George Washington took his presidential oath on April 30. Late or not, the new government faced questions unanswered by the Constitution's framers. "We are in a wilderness," wrote James Madison, "without a footstep to guide us."

Defining the Presidency

No office in the new government aroused more suspicion than the presidency. Many feared that the president's powers could make him a king. But George Washington's reputation for honesty checked public apprehension, and Washington himself tried to calm fears of unlimited executive power.

The Constitution mentioned the executive departments of the federal government only in passing, required Senate approval of presidential nominees to head these bureaus, and made all executive personnel liable to being impeached or to being charged with wrongdoing in office. Otherwise, Congress was free to establish the organization and accountability of what became known as the cabinet. The first cabinet consisted of four departments, headed by the secretaries of state, treasury, and war and by the attorney general. A proposal to forbid the president's dismissal of cabinet officers without Senate approval was defeated. This outcome reinforced presidential authority to make and carry out policy; it also separated executive and legislative powers beyond what the Constitution required and made the president a more equal partner of Congress.

President Washington suggested few laws to Congress, seldom criticized opponents of government policy, and generally limited his public statements to matters of foreign relations and military affairs. He deferred to congressional decisions on domestic policy whenever possible and vetoed only two measures in his eight-year tenure. To reassure the public that he was above favoritism and conflicts of interest, Washington balanced his cabinet with southerners and northeasterners. When Secretary of State Thomas Jefferson opposed policies of Secretary of the Treasury Alexander Hamilton, Washington implored Jefferson not to resign, even though the president supported Hamilton. Like most republican leaders, Washington believed that the proper role for ordinary citizens was not to set policy through elections but to choose well-educated men to make laws in the people's best interest, independently of direct popular influence.

Only reluctantly did Washington accept reelection in 1792. He dreaded dying while in office and setting the precedent for a lifetime presidency. He realized that "the preservation of the sacred fire of liberty and the destiny of the republican model of government are . . . *deeply,* perhaps *finally,* staked on the experiment entrusted to the hands of the American people." Should he contribute to that experiment's failure, Washington feared, his name would live only as an "awful monument."

National Justice and the Bill of Rights

The Constitution authorized Congress to establish federal courts below the level of the Supreme Court but provided no plan for their structure. The absence of a comprehensive bill of rights, moreover, had led several delegates at Philadelphia to refuse to sign the Constitution and had been a major Antifederalist point of attack. The task of dealing with these gaps fell to Congress.

In 1789 many citizens feared that federal courts would ride roughshod over local customs. Every state had a blend of judicial procedures suited to its needs, and any attempt to force the states to abandon their legal heritage would have produced counterdemands for narrowly restricting federal justice.

In passing the Judiciary Act of 1789, Congress quieted popular apprehensions by establishing in each state a federal district court that operated according to local procedures. As the Constitution stipulated, the Supreme Court exercised final jurisdiction. Congress's compromise respected state traditions while offering wide access to federal justice.

Behind the movement for a bill of rights lay Americans' long-standing fear that a strong central government would lead to tyranny. Many Antifederalists believed that the best safeguard against tyranny would be to strengthen the powers of the state governments at the expense of the federal government, but many more Americans wanted simply to guarantee basic personal liberties. From

the House of Representatives, James Madison played the leading role in drafting the ten amendments that became known as the Bill of Rights when ratified in December 1791.

Madison insisted that the first eight amendments guarantee personal liberties, not strip the national government of authority. The First Amendment safeguarded the most fundamental freedoms of expression—religion, speech, press, and political activity. The Second Amendment ensured that each state could form its own militia. Like the Third Amendment, it sought to protect citizens from what Americans saw as the most sinister embodiment of tyranny: standing armies. The Fourth through the Eighth Amendments limited the police powers of the states by guaranteeing fair treatment in legal and judicial proceedings. The Ninth and Tenth Amendments reserved to the people or to the states powers not allocated to the federal government, but Madison headed off proposals to limit federal power more explicitly.

With the Bill of Rights in place, the federal judiciary established its authority. In the case of *Chisholm* v. *Georgia* (1793), the Supreme Court ruled that a nonresident could sue a state in federal court. In 1796 the Court declared its right to determine the constitutionality of federal statutes in *Hylton* v. *United States* and to strike down state laws in *Ware* v. *Hylton.* But in 1794 Congress decided that the *Chisholm* case had encroached too far on states' authority and overturned the decision through a constitutional amendment. Ratified in 1798, the Eleventh Amendment revised Article III, Section 2, so that private citizens could not undermine states' financial autonomy by using federal courts to sue another state's government in civil cases and claim money from that state's treasury.

By endorsing the Eleventh Amendment, Congress expressed its recognition that federal power could threaten vital local interests. The same awareness had ruptured the nationalist coalition that had written the Constitution, secured its ratification, and dominated the First Congress. Alexander Hamilton had embarked on a bold program that alienated many nationalists by demonstrating that federal policies could be shaped to reward special interests.

HAMILTON AND THE FORMULATION OF FEDERALIST POLICIES, 1789–1794

Washington's reluctance to become involved with legislation enabled Secretary of the Treasury Alexander Hamilton to set domestic priorities. Hamilton emerged as an imaginative and dynamic statesman by formulating a sweeping program for national economic development.

Alexander Hamilton and His Objectives

Born in the West Indies in 1755, Hamilton had arrived in New York in 1772 to enroll at King's College (now Columbia University), where he had passionately defended American rights. He entered the Continental Army in 1775, and rising quickly to become a member of Washington's staff and a confidante of the commander in chief. Born outside the thirteen colonies, he had little appreciation for Americans' fears of centralized authority.

Hamilton's financial policies had two goals: to strengthen the nation against foreign enemies and to lessen the threat of disunion. The possibility of war with Britain, Spain, or both presented the most immediate danger. To finance a war, the Republic would have to borrow, but because Congress under the Articles had failed to redeem or pay interest on the Revolutionary debt, the nation had little credit. Thus the country's economy seemed unequal to fighting a major European power.

Hamilton also feared that the Union might disintegrate because he believed that Americans tended to think first of local loyalties and interests. To him, the Constitution represented a close victory of national over state authority. Now he worried that the states might reassert power over the new government. If they succeeded, he doubted whether the nation could prevent ruinous trade discrimination between states, deter foreign aggression, and avoid civil war.

His view of human nature as well as his wartime experiences shaped Hamilton's political be-

Alexander Hamilton, by John Trumbull, 1792
Hamilton's self-confident pride clearly shines through in this portrait, painted at the height of his influence in the Washington administration.

liefs. He shared the conviction of many nationalists that the vast majority of the Republic's population, like the rest of humanity, would never display the degree of self-sacrifice and virtue that he had shown. Hamilton concluded that the federal government's survival depended on building support among politically influential citizens through a direct appeal to their financial interests. Private ambitions would then serve the national welfare.

Charming and brilliant, vain and handsome, a notorious womanizer, thirsty for fame and power, Hamilton exemplified the worldly citizens whose fortunes he hoped to link to the Republic's future. To his opponents, however, Hamilton embodied the dark forces luring the Republic to doom—a man who, Jefferson wrote, believed in "the necessity of either force or corruption to govern men."

Report on the Public Credit, 1790

In 1789 Congress directed the Treasury Department to evaluate the Revolutionary debt. Hamilton seized the opportunity to devise policies to strengthen the nation's credit, enable it to defer paying its debt, and entice the upper class to place its prestige and capital at the nation's service. In January 1790 Congress received his Report on the Public Credit. It listed $54 million in U.S. debt: $42 million owed to Americans and the rest to foreigners. Hamilton estimated that on top of the national debt, the states had debts of $25 million that the United States had promised to reimburse.

Hamilton recommended that the federal government "fund" the national debt by raising $54 million in new securities to honor the Revolutionary debt. Purchasers of these securities could choose from several combinations of federal "stock" and western lands. Those who wished could retain their original bonds and earn 4 percent interest. All these options would reduce interest payments on the debt. Creditors would approve this reduction because their investments would become more valuable and secure. The report proposed that the federal government use the same means to pay off state debts remaining from the Revolution.

Hamilton exhorted the government to use the money earned by selling federal lands in the West to pay off the $12 million owed to Europeans as soon as possible, but he suggested that the remaining $42 million owed to Americans be made a permanent debt. If the government paid only the interest on its bonds, investors would hold them for long terms. The sole burden on taxpayers would be the small annual interest. Thus the United States could uphold its credit at minimal expense without ever having to pay off the debt itself.

A permanent debt, Hamilton believed, would tie the economic fortunes of the nation's creditors to the government. In an age of notoriously risky investments, the federal government would protect the savings of wealthy bond holders through conservative policies but still pay an interest rate competitive with that of the Bank of England. The guarantee of future interest payments would link the interests of the moneyed class to those of the nation.

Hamilton's proposals provoked controversy. Many members of Congress objected that those least deserving reward would gain the most. The original owners of more than 60 percent of the debt certificates issued by the Continental Congress had long since sold at a loss, often out of dire necessity. Wealthy speculators, anticipating Hamilton's intentions, had snapped up large holdings at the expense of the unsuspecting original owners and would reap huge gains.

To Hamilton's surprise, Madison became a chief opponent of reimbursing current holders at face value. Sensing disapproval of the plan in Virginia, Madison tried but failed to obtain compensation for original owners who had sold their certificates. Hamilton's policy generated widespread resentment by rewarding rich profiteers while ignoring wartime sacrifice by ordinary citizens.

Opposition to assuming the state debts also ran high, especially in the South. But Hamilton saved his proposal by exploiting Virginians' desire to relocate the national capital in their region. They hoped that moving the capital would keep Virginia the nation's largest, most influential state. Essentially, Hamilton traded the votes necessary to locate the capital along the Potomac for enough votes to win his battle for assumption.

Enactment of the Report on the Public Credit reversed the nation's fiscal standing. By 1792 the United States' soaring fiscal reputation allowed some U.S. bonds to sell at 10 percent above face value.

Creating a National Bank, 1790–1791

Having restored full faith in greatly undervalued certificates, Hamilton had in effect expanded the capital available for investment. Now he intended to direct that money toward projects to diversify the national economy through a federally chartered bank.

In his Report on the National Bank in 1790 Hamilton proposed that the Bank of the United States raise $10 million through a public stock offering. Fully four-fifths of the control of the bank would fall to private hands. Private investors could purchase shares by paying for three-quarters of their value in government bonds. In this way the bank would capture a substantial portion of the recently funded debt and make it available for loans; it would also receive steady interest payments from the Treasury. Shareholders would profit handsomely.

Hamilton argued that the Bank would cost taxpayers nothing and greatly benefit the nation. It would provide a safe place for federal deposits, make inexpensive loans to the government when taxes fell short, and relieve the scarcity of hard cash by issuing paper notes. Further, the bank would regulate the business of state banks and, above all, provide much-needed credit for economic expansion.

Hamilton also called for American economic self-sufficiency. An admirer of the way that factory expansion had stimulated British wealth, he wanted to encourage industrialization in the United States. His Report on Manufactures of December 1791 advocated protective tariffs on imports to foster domestic manufacturing, which would in turn attract immigrants and create national wealth. He also called for assisting the merchant marine against British trade restrictions by reducing duties on goods brought into the country on U.S. ships and by offering subsidies for fishermen and whalers.

Hamilton's critics denounced the national bank as a dangerous scheme that gave a small elite special power to influence the government. These critics believed that the Bank of England had undermined the integrity of the government in Britain. Shareholders of the Bank of the United States could just as easily become tools of unscrupulous politicians. Members of Congress who owned bank stock would likely vote in support of the bank even at the cost of the national good. To Jefferson, the bank represented "a machine for the corruption of the legislature [Congress]."

Constitutional issues presented the bank's opponents with their strongest argument. The Constitution did not authorize Congress to issue charters of incorporation; in fact, the constitutional conven-

tion had rejected such a proposal. Unless Congress adhered to a "strict interpretation" of the Constitution, critics argued, the central government might oppress the states and trample individual liberties. Strict limits on government powers seemed the surest way to prevent the United States from degenerating into a corrupt despotism, as Britain had.

Congress approved the bank by only a thin margin. Dubious about its constitutionality, Washington asked Jefferson and Hamilton for advice. Jefferson distrusted banking and did not want to extend government power beyond the letter of the Constitution. But Hamilton urged Washington to sign the bill. Because Article I, Section 8, of the Constitution specified that Congress could enact all measures "necessary and proper," Hamilton contended that the only unconstitutional activities were those *forbidden* to the national government. Washington accepted Hamilton's argument, and in February 1791 the Bank of the United States obtained a twenty-year charter. Washington's acceptance of a "loose interpretation" of the Constitution marked an important victory for advocates of an active, assertive national government.

Hamilton's Legacy

Hamilton built a political base by appealing to people's economic self-interest. His "rescue" of the national credit provided huge gains for speculators, merchants, and other urban "moneyed men" who by 1790 held most of the Revolutionary debt. As holders of bank stock, these same groups had reason to use their prestige on behalf of national authority. Moreover, federal assumption of state debts liberated taxpayers from crushing burdens in New England, New Jersey, and South Carolina, while Hamilton's promotion of industry, commerce, and shipping won favor with the Northeast's budding entrepreneurs and hard-pressed artisans.

Supporters of Hamilton's policies called themselves Federalists in order to associate themselves with the Constitution. But they actually favored a centralized ("consolidated") national government, not a truly federal system that left substantial power to the states. They dominated public opinion in the states that were most benefited by assumption and enjoyed considerable support in Pennsylvania and New York.

Hamilton's economic program sowed dissension in areas where it provided little advantage. Resentment ran high among those who felt that the government was rewarding special interests. Southerners especially detested Hamilton's program. Southern states had generally paid off their Revolutionary debts, and few southerners still held Revolutionary certificates. Moreover, the Bank of the United States had few southern stockholders and allocated little capital for southern loans.

Hamilton's plan offered little to the West, where agriculture promised exceptional profit once the right of export through New Orleans was guaranteed. Even in New York and Pennsylvania, Hamilton's policies generated some dissatisfaction. Resentment of a supposedly national program that benefited eastern "moneyed men" and Yankees who refused to pay their debts gradually united westerners, southerners, and many people in the mid-Atlantic into a political coalition. Challenging the Federalists for control of the government, these opponents called for a return to true republicanism.

As outlined in his Report on the Subject of Manufactures (1791), Hamilton admired efficiently run factories. Not only would manufacturing provide jobs, promote immigration, and expand the applications of technology, it would also offer "greater scope for the talents and dispositions of men." Jefferson and his followers idealized white, landowning family farmers as bulwarks of republican liberty and virtue. "Those who labour in the earth are the chosen people," wrote Jefferson (ignoring the fact that those who labored in the earth he owned at Monticello were slaves). The debate between advocates of these points of view would continue for the next two centuries.

The Whiskey Rebellion, 1794

Hamilton's program helped to ignite a civil insurrection called the Whiskey Rebellion. Severely testing federal authority, this uprising posed the young republic's first serious crisis.

To augment national revenue, Hamilton had proposed an excise tax on domestically produced whiskey. He maintained that such a tax would not only distribute the expense of financing the national debt evenly but also improve the country's morals by lowering liquor consumption. Although Congress passed Hamilton's program in March 1791, many doubted that Americans, who drank an average of six gallons of hard liquor per adult per year, would submit tamely to sobriety.

Western Pennsylvanians found the new tax especially burdensome. Unable to ship their crops to world markets through New Orleans, most local farmers habitually distilled their rye or corn into alcohol, which could be carried across the Appalachians at a fraction of the price charged for bulky grain. Hamilton's excise tax, equal to 25 percent of whiskey's retail value, would wipe out frontier farmers' profit.

Because the law specified, in addition, that federal courts would try all cases of alleged tax evasion, any western Pennsylvanian indicted for non-compliance would have to travel 300 or so miles to Philadelphia. Not only would the accused face a jury of unsympathetic easterners, but he would also have to shoulder the cost of a long journey and lost earnings as well as fines and penalties if convicted. The discovery that Treasury Department officials rarely enforced the law outside western Pennsylvania was another major grievance.

In a scene reminiscent of colonial protests against Britain, large-scale resistance erupted in July 1794. One hundred men attacked a U.S. marshal serving delinquent taxpayers with summonses to appear in court in Philadelphia. A crowd of 500 burned the chief revenue officer's house following a shootout with federal soldiers. Roving bands torched buildings, assaulted tax collectors, and raised a flag symbolizing an independent country that they hoped to create from six western counties.

Echoing elites' denunciation of colonial protests, Hamilton blasted the rebellion as simple lawlessness. Washington concluded that a federal failure to respond strongly would encourage outbreaks in other frontier areas where lax enforcement had allowed distillers to escape paying taxes. The president accordingly mustered 12,900 militiamen to march west under his command, but opposition evaporated once the troops reached the Appalachians. Of 150 suspects later seized, 20 were sent in irons to Philadelphia.

The Whiskey Rebellion was a milestone in determining the limits of public opposition to federal policies. In the early 1790s many Americans assumed that it was still legitimate to protest unpopular laws by using the methods that they had employed against British policies. By firmly suppressing the first major challenge to national authority, President Washington served notice that citizens could change the law only through constitutional procedures—by making their dissatisfaction known to their elected representatives and, if necessary, by electing new representatives.

THE UNITED STATES ON THE WORLD STAGE, 1789–1796

By 1793 disagreements over foreign affairs had become the primary source of friction in American public life. The division created by controversy over Hamilton's economic program hardened into ideologically oriented factions that disagreed vehemently over whether American foreign policy should favor industrial and mercantile interests or those of farmers, planters, and small businessmen. Complicating American policy-making was the French Revolution, which had electrified all Europe in 1789 and touched off a series of wars between France and her neighbors that would last until 1815.

As part of the Atlantic world, the United States could not avoid entanglement in these wars, despite the desire of most Americans to remain uninvolved. The ambitions of key American interest groups frequently conflicted with those of the warring Atlantic powers. Increasingly foreign policy became caught up in domestic politics, intensifying the emerging partisanship.

Spanish Power in Western North America

Spain enjoyed a brief resurgence of imperial success in the late eighteenth century. Shifting from a policy of conquest to one of trade, the Spanish made peace with the nomadic Plains tribes—the Comanches, Utes, Navajos, and Apaches—that had threatened their New Mexico and Texas settlements.

These reforms were part of a larger Spanish effort to counter potential rivals for North American territory and influence. Russian fur traders had made substantial inroads along the Northwest Coast as early as the 1740s, and British and American traders followed in the 1780s. All three nations used American furs in the rapidly burgeoning and hugely profitable "China trade," and their mounting influence threatened Spain's northwestern frontier.

To counter these threats, Spain flung colonists and missionaries northward along the California coast from San Diego to Sonoma (north of San Francisco). In "New California," the missions fared better than the handful of settlers. However, epidemic and venereal diseases carried by the Spanish raged among the native coastal tribes; between 1769 and 1830 the Indian population plummeted from about 72,000 to about 18,000. Priests sought to "civilize" the survivors by placing them in missions, imposing rigid discipline, and putting them to work in vineyards and other enterprises. Having strengthened its positions in Texas, New Mexico, and California, Spain turned its attention to the area later known as Arizona in hopes of dominating North America from the Pacific to Louisiana. However, resistance from Native Americans such as the Hopi and the Yuma thwarted these hopes.

Challenging American Expansion, 1789–1792

East of the Mississippi River, on the Trans-Appalachian frontier, rivalries also multiplied. Spain, Britain, the United States, and Native Americans jockeyed for advantage in an area that all considered central to their interests.

To gain the loyalty of American settlers it could not keep out of its southeastern lands, Spain offered them citizenship. In turn, many of the new settlers began toying with the idea of secession in order to gain access to New Orleans and world markets. In 1788 Tennessee conspirators boldly advertised their flirtation with Spain by naming a large district after the governor of Spanish Louisiana. Most westerners accepted Spanish favors and gold in return only for vague promises of goodwill, but such incidents showed how susceptible to foreign manipulation and even subversion many were.

President Washington tried to keep tight control of foreign policy. Recognizing that the complex western problems would not easily yield, he pursued patient diplomacy to "preserve the country in peace if I can, and to be prepared for war if I cannot." The prospect of peace improved in 1789 when Spain unexpectedly opened New Orleans to American commerce. Secessionist sentiment subsided.

In the 1790s the Spanish bribed many well-known political figures in Tennessee and Kentucky, including James Wilkinson, one of Washington's former generals. Thomas Scott, a Congressman from western Pennsylvania, schemed with the British. The admission of Vermont (1791), Kentucky (1792), and Tennessee (1796) as states was meant in part to strengthen their sometimes shaky loyalty to the Union.

Washington then moved to weaken Spanish influence in the West by neutralizing Spain's most important ally, the Creek Indians. The Creeks numbered more than 20,000, including perhaps 5,000 warriors, and were fiercely hostile toward Georgian settlers, whom they called "the greedy people who want our lands." Under terms of the 1790 Treaty of New York, American settlers could occupy the Georgia piedmont but not other Creek territory. Washington insisted that Georgia restore to the Chickasaws and Choctaws, Creek allies, a vast area along the Mississippi River that Georgia had already begun selling off to land speculators.

Washington tried to force peace through military action against Britain's Indian allies in the Northwest. But two military campaigns, in 1790 and 1791, failed to force peace and cost the United States 1,100 men.

The Washington administration tried to pacify other Indians through a benevolent policy. Alarmed by the chaos on the frontier, where trespassers invaded Indian lands and the native peoples rejected U.S. claims to sovereignty, the government formally recognized Indian title as secure and inalienable except by the "free consent" of the Indians themselves. To reinforce this policy, Congress passed laws to prohibit trespassing on Indian lands, to punish crimes committed there by non-Indians, to outlaw alcohol, and to regulate trade. The administration also encouraged Indians to become "civilized." By adopting private property and a strictly agricultural livelihood, officials believed, Indians would find a place in American society—and make land available for non-Indians.

Indians, however, were unwilling to give up their traditional ways entirely and to assimilate into an alien culture. And most whites did not want to integrate Native Americans into their society. Consequently, the United States continued to pressure Indians to sell their lands and to move farther west. Washington's frontier policy became a wreck. Matters worsened in 1792 when the Spanish persuaded the Creeks to renounce the Treaty of New York and resume hostilities. Ultimately, the damage to U.S. prestige from these setbacks convinced many Americans that only an alliance with France could counterbalance the combined strength of Britain, Spain, and the Indians.

France and Factional Politics, 1793

One of the most momentous events in history, the French Revolution, began in 1789. Americans watched sympathetically as the French abolished nobles' privileges, wrote a constitution, and repelled invading armies. In 1793, after becoming a republic, France proclaimed a war of all peoples against all kings and assumed that the United States would eagerly enlist.

White southern slave owners were among France's fiercest supporters. In 1791 slaves in the French colony of Saint Domingue rebelled against slavery and against French rule, a bloody uprising that took a heavy death toll among French planters and send thousands fleeing to the United States. Fearful Southern whites believed that the British had intentionally sparked the bloodshed and would do the same in the American South.

Northern Federalists damned revolutionary France as an abomination—"an open Hell," thundered Massachusetts Federalist Fisher Ames, "still ringing with agonies and blasphemies, still smoking with sufferings and crimes." Conservative and religiously oriented, New Englanders detested the French government's disregard for civil rights and its adoration of reason over the worship of God. Middle Atlantic businessmen, perhaps less religious but no less conservative, condemned French leaders as evil radicals who incited the poor against the rich.

After 1790 economics led to sharp differences between northern and southern reactions to the French Revolution. Growing antagonism toward France among northern merchants reflected their awareness that their prosperity depended on good relations with Britain. Virtually all the nation's merchant marine operated from northern ports, and the largest share of U.S. foreign trade was with Britain. Fearful that an alliance with France would provoke British retaliation against this valuable commerce, northerners argued that the United States could win valuable concessions by demonstrating friendly intentions toward Britain.

Southerners had no such reasons to favor Britain. They perceived American reliance on British commerce as a menace to national self-determination and wished to divert most U.S. trade to France. Southern spokesmen such as Jefferson and Madison demanded discriminatory duties on British cargoes. These recommendations threatened ties with Britain, which sold more manufactured goods to the United States than to any other country. Federalist opponents of a discriminatory tariff warned that the English would not stand by while a weak French ally pushed them into depression. If Congress adopted trade retaliation, Hamilton predicted, "an open war between the United States and Great Britain" would result.

Pro-French feelings were also high in the western states, especially after France went to war against Spain and Great Britain in 1793. Westerners hoped that a French victory would remove Spanish and British roadblocks to expansion, put an end to Indian wars, and open the Mississippi for navigation.

After declaring war with Spain and Britain in 1793, France sought to enlist the United States in the war and to strengthen the treaty of alliance between the two nations. France dispatched Edmond Genet as minister to the United States with orders to recruit American mercenaries to conquer Spanish territories and to attack British shipping. Much to France's disgust, President Washington issued a proclamation of neutrality on April 22, 1793.

Meanwhile, Citizen Genet (as he was known in French Revolutionary style) had arrived on April 8. He found numerous southern volunteers for his American Foreign Legion despite official U.S. neutrality. Making generals of George Rogers Clark of Kentucky and Elisha Clarke, Genet ordered them to seize New Orleans and St. Augustine. Clark openly defied the neutrality proclamation by advertising for recruits, and Clarke drilled 300 soldiers along the Florida border. However, the French failed to provide adequate funds for either campaign, and in 1794 both expeditions disintegrated.

However, Genet did not need funds to outfit privateers, whose crews were paid from captured plunder. By summer 1793 nearly 1,000 Americans were at sea in a dozen ships flying the French flag. These privateers seized over eighty British ships and towed them to American ports, where French consuls sold the ships and cargoes at auction.

Avoiding War, 1793–1796

Although Washington swiftly closed the nation's harbors to Genet's buccaneers, the episode provoked an Anglo-American crisis. Britain decided that only a massive show of force would deter American aggression. Thus on November 6, 1793, Britain's Privy Council issued orders confiscating foreign ships trading with the French islands in the Caribbean. The orders were kept secret until most U.S. ships carrying winter provisions to the Caribbean left port so that their captains would not know that they were sailing into a war zone. The Royal Navy seized more than twenty-five U.S. ships.

Meanwhile, the U.S. merchant marine suffered another galling indignity—the drafting of its crewmen into the Royal Navy. Thousands of British sailors had fled to American ships looking for an easier life than the tough, poorly paying British system. In late 1793 British naval officers began inspecting American crews for British subjects, whom they then impressed (forcibly enlisted) as the king's sailors. Overzealous commanders sometimes exceeded orders by taking U.S. citizens—and in any case Britain did not recognize its former subjects' right to adopt American citizenship. Impressment struck a raw nerve in most Americans.

The British, along with Spain and Native Americans also challenged the United States for control of the West. In February 1794, Canada's governor denied U.S. claims north of the Ohio River and urged Indians to destroy every white settlement in the Northwest. Britain soon erected Fort Miami near Toledo, Ohio. That same year Spain encroached on U.S. territory by building Fort San Fernando at what is now Memphis, Tennessee.

Hoping to halt the drift toward war, Washington launched a desperate diplomatic initiative, sending Chief Justice John Jay to Great Britain and Thomas Pinckney to Spain. The president also authorized General Anthony Wayne to negotiate a treaty with the Indians of the Ohio Valley.

The Indians scoffed at Washington's peace offer until "Mad Anthony" Wayne led 3,000 regulars and militiamen deep into their homeland, ravaging every village in reach. On August 20, 1794, Wayne's troops routed 400 Shawnees at the Battle of Fallen Timbers, two miles from Britain's Fort Miami. Wayne's army staged a provocative victory march past the British garrison and then built Fort Defiance to challenge British authority in the Northwest. Indian morale plummeted. In August 1795 Wayne compelled twelve Ohio Valley tribes to sign the Treaty of Greenville, which opened most of Ohio to white settlement and temporarily ended Indian hostilities.

Negotiating the Treaty of Greenville
In this detail of a contemporary painting believed to have been done by a member of General Wayne's staff, Chief Little Turtle of the Miamis speaks to Wayne, who stands with one hand behind his back.

Wayne's success allowed John Jay a major diplomatic victory in London: a British promise to withdraw troops from American soil. Jay also gained American access to West Indian markets, but only by bargaining away U.S. rights to load cargoes of sugar, molasses, and coffee from the Caribbean. On other points the British remained unyielding. Few Americans would interpret Jay's Treaty as preserving peace with honor.

Jay's Treaty left Britain free not only to violate American neutrality but also to restrict U.S. trade with French ports. Moreover, Jay did not succeed in ending impressment. He also failed to gain compensation for slaves taken by the British during the Revolution, an outcome especially galling to southerners. In 1795 the Federalist-dominated Senate ratified the treaty by just one vote.

Jay's Treaty probably represented the most that a weak, politically divided United States could extract from Britain. A major achievement for the Washington administration, Jay's Treaty also stimulated American trade as British governors in the West Indies used the treaty's ratification as an excuse to open their harbors to U.S. ships. Other British officials permitted Americans to develop a thriving commerce with India. Within a few years of 1795, American exports to the British Empire had shot up 300 percent.

On the heels of Jay's Treaty came an unqualified diplomatic triumph engineered by Thomas Pinckney. Ratified in 1796, the Treaty of San Lorenzo (also called Pinckney's Treaty) with Spain gave westerners unrestricted, duty-free access to world markets via the Mississippi River. Spain also promised to recognize the thirty-first parallel as the United States' southern boundary, to dismantle all fortifications on American soil, and to discourage Indian attacks against western settlers.

By 1796 the Washington administration had defended the nation's territorial integrity, restored peace to the frontier, opened the Mississippi for western exports, reopened British markets to U.S. shipping, and kept the nation out of a European war. However, as the outcry over Jay's Treaty showed, foreign policy had left Americans far more divided in 1796 than in 1789.

THE EMERGENCE OF PARTY POLITICS, 1793–1800

Since before the American Revolution, many Americans viewed political parties as corrupt and dangerous. However, by the midpoint of Washington's administration, these same Americans had split into two political parties, Federalists and Republicans. A battle raged over the very future of representative government, culminating in the election of 1800, whose outcome would determine whether the nation's political elite could make room for ordinary citizens to play a more active role in deciding government policy.

Ideological Confrontation, 1793–1794

The French Revolution led many Americans to reassess their political values. The Revolution's radical turn in 1793–1794, which sent thousands to the guillotine, polarized public opinion, generally along regional lines.

Federalists trembled at the thought of "mob rule" in the nation's future. They took alarm when artisans in New York and Philadelphia used the French revolutionary slogan "Liberty, Equality, Fraternity" and exalted pro-French political leaders such as Jefferson. Citizen Genet's recruitment of hundreds of Americans to fight for France reinforced their fears. Federalists worried that all of this was just the tip of a revolutionary iceberg.

By the mid-1790s Federalist leaders had concluded that it was dangerous to involve the public deeply in politics. The people were undependable, too easy a prey for rabble-rousers like Genet. As Senator George Cabot of Massachusetts said, "The many do not think at all." Federalists saw democracy as "government by the passions of the multitude" and argued that personal merits, not policy, should decide elections. Elected officials should rule in the people's name, but independent of direct popular influence.

A very different perspective on government and politics surfaced in urban areas and in the South, Republicanism. Republican ideology stressed the corruption inherent in a powerful government dominated by a few highly visible men. Southern Republicans insisted that only the distribution of power among virtuous, independent citizens would protect liberty. They argued that self-interest could be pursued virtuously in a republic in which property and wealth were widely available. Jefferson, Madison, and their Republican compatriots viewed the American and French revolutions as the gateway to a new human community in which self-interested individuals recognized their common interest in maintaining a stable society responsive to all.

It might seem strange to see southern slave owners embracing republicanism, with its emphasis on equality and liberty, but southerners saw no such anomaly. They understood that the liberty and equality that they advocated were intended for white men only, no matter how universal the terms in which the ideas were expressed. With their own labor force consisting of enslaved blacks, not free wage workers, southern elites did not fear popular participation in politics. Unlike northern Federalists, then, southern planters faced the future with optimism and viewed attempts to inhibit widespread political participation as unworthy of educated gentlemen.

Ambition also drove Jefferson, Madison, and likeminded Americans to rouse ordinary citizens' concerns about civic affairs. Although the awe in which Washington was held precluded open criticism of him or his policies, Jefferson, Madison, and other Republicans hoped to hold the Federalists accountable to a public that could remove them from office for misguided or unpopular policies. Jefferson, although a wealthy land and slave owner, said, "I am not among those who fear the people; they and not the rich, are our dependence for continued freedom."

The Virginian's increasing frustration prompted him to resign from Washington's cabinet in 1793, widening the political split. Each side saw itself as the guardian of republican virtue and the other as an illegitimate "faction."

In October 1791 organized efforts to turn public opinion against the Federalists began with the publication of an opposition newspaper, the *National Gazette.* Then in 1793–1794 popular dissatisfaction with government policies led to the formation of several dozen Democratic (or Republican) societies. Their membership ranged from planters and merchants to artisans and sailors. Conspicuously absent were clergymen, the poor, and nonwhites. Sharply critical of Federalists, the societies spread dissatisfaction with the Washington administration's policies.

Federalists interpreted the societies' emotional appeals to ordinary people as demagoguery and denounced their followers as "democrats, mobocrats, & all other kinds of rats." They feared that the societies would become revolutionary organizations. Washington privately warned that "if [the clubs] were not counteracted . . . they would shake the government to its foundation." By criticizing them, Washington abandoned his nonpartisanship and aligned himself with the Federalists, a move that would cost him dearly.

The Republican Party, 1794–1796

Neither Jefferson nor Madison belonged to a Democratic society. However, the clubs' criticism of the administration galvanized into political activity many who would later support Jefferson and Madison's Republican party.

In 1794 party development reached a decisive stage. Shortly after Washington aligned himself with Federalist policies, supporters of Jefferson who had begun to call themselves Republicans won a slight majority in the House of Representatives. The election signaled their transformation from a faction to a broad-based party, the Republican party, capable of coordinating national political campaigns.

Federalists and Republicans alike used the press to mold public opinion. American journalism came of age in the 1790s as the number of newspapers multiplied from 92 to 242. By 1800 newspapers had perhaps 140,000 paid subscribers (about one-fifth of the eligible voters), and their secondhand readership probably exceeded 300,000. Newspapers of both camps, libelous and irresponsible, cheapened public debate through fear mongering and character assassination. Republicans stood accused of plotting a reign of terror and scheming to turn the nation over to France. Federalists faced charges of favoring hereditary aristocracy and planning to establish an American dynasty by marrying off John Adams's daughter to George III. But despite the mutual distrust thus created, newspaper warfare stimulated citizens to become politically active.

Underlying the inflammatory rhetoric was the Republican charge that the Federalists were bent on enriching the wealthy at taxpayers' expense. Although most Republican leaders were themselves well born, Republicans asserted that the Federalists planned to create a privileged order of men and to re-create the atmosphere of a European court through highly publicized formal dinners and balls. Although wrong in claiming that opponents wanted to introduce aristocracy and monarchy, the Republicans correctly identified the Federalists' fundamental assumption: that citizens' worth could be measured in terms of their money.

Accusations that he secretly supported a plot to establish a monarchy enraged Washington. "By God," Jefferson reported him swearing, "he [the president] would rather be in his grave than in his present situation. . . . He had rather be on his farm than to be made *emperor of the world*." Alarmed by the furor over Jay's Treaty, Washington dreaded the nation's polarization into hostile factions. Lonely and surrounded by mediocre men after Hamilton returned to private life, Washington decided in spring 1796 to retire after two terms and called on Hamilton to give a sharp political twist to a farewell address.

In the farewell message Washington vigorously condemned political parties. Partisan alignments, he insisted, endangered the republic's survival, especially if they became entangled in foreign policy disputes. Aside from fulfilling existing treaty obligations and maintaining foreign commerce, the United States had to avoid "political connection" with Europe and its wars. If the United States gathered its strength under "an efficient government," it could defy any foreign challenge; but if it was drawn into Europe's quarrels and corruption, the republican experiment would be doomed. Washington and Hamilton thus turned the central argument of republicanism against their Republican critics. They also evoked a vision of a United States virtuously isolated from foreign intrigue and power politics, an ideal that would remain a potent inspiration until the twentieth century.

Washington left the presidency in 1797 and died in 1799. He went out amid a barrage of criticism. The nation's political division into Republicans and Federalists meanwhile hardened into a two-party system.

The Election of 1796

As the election of 1796 approached, the Republicans cultivated a large, loyal body of voters, the first time since the Revolution that the political elite effectively mobilized ordinary Americans. The Republican constituency included the Democratic societies, workingmen's clubs, and immigrant-aid associations.

Immigrants became a prime target for Republican recruiters. During the 1790s the United States absorbed 20,000 French refugees from Saint Domingue and 60,000 Irish. Although few immigrants could vote, the Irish exerted critical influence in Pennsylvania and New York, where public opinion was so closely divided that a few hundred voters could tip the balance.

In 1796 the presidential candidates were Vice President John Adams, whom the Federalists supported, and the Republicans' Jefferson. Republican strength in the South offset Federalist strength in New England, leaving Pennsylvania and New York as crucial "swing" states where the Irish vote might tip the scales. In the end Jefferson carried Pennsylvania but not New York and lost the presidency by three electoral votes. The Federalists kept control of Congress. But by a political fluke, Jefferson became vice president under the constitutional provision (quickly changed by the Twelfth Amendment) that the candidate receiving the highest number of electoral votes would become president and the candidate amassing the next-highest number would become vice president.

President Adams's brilliance, insight, and idealism have seldom been equaled among American presidents. He was more comfortable, however, with ideas than with people, more theoretical than practical, and rather inflexible. He inspired trust and admiration but could not command loyalty or stir the electorate. As Benjamin Franklin observed, Adams was "always an honest man, often a wise one, but sometimes, and in some things, absolutely out of his senses." He was utterly unsuited to unify the country.

The French Crisis, 1798–1799

To Adams's initial good fortune, French provocations produced a sharp anti-Republican backlash. France interpreted Jay's Treaty as an American attempt to assist the British in their war against France. Learning of Jefferson's defeat, the French ordered the seizure of American ships; within a year they had plundered more than 300 U.S. vessels. The French also ordered that every American captured on a British naval ship, even those involuntarily impressed, be hanged.

Seeking to avoid war, Adams dispatched a peace commission to France. The French foreign minister, Charles de Talleyrand, refused to meet with the Americans, instead promising through three unnamed agents ("X, Y, and Z") that talks could begin after he received $250,000 and France obtained a $12 million loan. This barefaced demand for a bribe became known as the XYZ Affair. Outraged Americans adopted the battle cry "Millions for defense, not one cent for tribute."

The XYZ Affair discredited Republican foreign policy views. The party's leaders compounded the damage by refusing to condemn French aggression and opposing Adam's call for defensive measures. While Republicans tried to excuse French behavior, the Federalists rode a wave of patriotism to an enormous victory in the 1798 congressional elections.

Congress responded to the XYZ Affair by arming fifty-four ships to protect U.S. commerce. The new warships joined what became known as the Quasi-War—an undeclared Franco-American naval conflict in the Caribbean from 1798 to 1800, during which U.S. forces seized ninety-three French privateers at the loss of just one ship. The British navy meanwhile extended the protection of its convoys to the U.S. merchant marine. By early

1799 the French no longer posed a serious threat at sea.

Meanwhile, the Federalist-controlled Congress tripled the regular army to 10,000 men in 1798, with an automatic expansion of land forces to 50,000 in case of war. But the risk of a land war with France was minimal. What Federalists actually wanted was a strong military force ready in case of a civil war, for the crisis had produced near-hysterical fears that French and Irish malcontents were hatching treasonous conspiracies.

The Adams administration was aware of continuing French intrigue in the West in hopes of establishing an independent pro-French nation west of the mountains. In 1798 the State Department heard that France had created "a party of mad Americans ready to join with them at a given Signal" in the West.

The Alien and Sedition Acts, 1798

The Federalists insisted that the possibility of war with France demanded stringent legislation to protect national security. In 1798 the Federalist Congress passed four measures known collectively as the Alien and Sedition Acts. Although President Adams neither requested nor wanted the laws, he deferred to Congress and signed them.

The least controversial of the four laws, the Alien Enemies Act, was designed to prevent wartime espionage or sabotage. It outlined procedures for determining whether a hostile country's citizens, when staying in America, posed a threat to the United States; if so, they would be deported or jailed. It also established principles to respect the rights of enemy citizens. This law would not be used until the War of 1812.

The second of the laws, the Alien Friends Act, enforceable in peacetime until June 25, 1800, authorized the president to expel foreign residents whose activities he considered dangerous. It required no proof of guilt. Republicans maintained that the law's real purpose was to deport immigrants critical of Federalist policies. Republicans also denounced the third law, the Naturalization Act. This measure increased the residency requirement for U.S. citizenship from five to fourteen years (the last five continuously in one state) to reduce Irish voting.

Finally came the Sedition Act, the only one of these measures enforceable against U.S. citizens. Although its alleged purpose was to distinguish between free speech and attempts to encourage the violation of federal laws or to seed a revolution, the act defined criminal activity so broadly that it blurred distinctions between sedition and legitimate political discussion. Thus it forbade an individual or a group "to oppose any measure or measures of the United States"—wording that could be interpreted to ban any criticism of the party in power. Another clause made it illegal to speak, write, or print any statement that would bring the president "into contempt or disrepute." A newspaper editor could therefore face imprisonment for criticizing Adams or his cabinet. Juries heard sedition cases and could decide whether a defendant had intended to stir up rebellion or merely to express political dissent. However one regarded it, the Sedition Act interfered with free speech. The Federalists wrote the law to expire in 1801 so that it could not be used against them if they lost the next election.

The real target of all this Federalist repression was the opposition press. Four of the five largest Republican newspapers were charged with sedition just as the election of 1800 was getting under way. The attorney general used the Alien Friends Act to drive the Irish journalist John Daly Burk underground. After failing to deport Scottish editor Thomas Callender, an all-Federalist jury sent him to prison for criticizing the president. Federalist leaders intended that a small number of highly visible prosecutions would intimidate journalists and candidates into silence during the election. The attorney general charged seventeen persons with sedition and won ten convictions. Among the victims was Republican congressman Matthew Lyon of Vermont, who spent four months in prison for publishing an article blasting Adams.

Vocal criticism of Federalist repression erupted only in Virginia and Kentucky. In summer 1798 militia commanders in these states mustered their

regiments to hear speeches demanding that the federal government respect the Bill of Rights. Entire units signed petitions denouncing the Alien and Sedition Acts. Young men stepped forward to sign the documents on drumheads, a pen in one hand and a gun in the other. Older officers who had fought in the Continental Army looked on approvingly. It was not hard to imagine rifles replacing quill pens as the men who had led one revolution took up arms again.

Ten years earlier opponents of the Constitution had warned that giving the national government extensive powers would endanger freedom. By 1798 these predictions had come true. Shocked Republicans realized that with the Federalists in control of all three branches of government, neither the Bill of Rights nor the system of checks and balances protected individual liberties. In this context the doctrine of states' rights was advanced as a way to prevent the national government from violating freedoms.

James Madison and Thomas Jefferson anonymously wrote two manifestos on states' rights that the assemblies of Virginia and Kentucky endorsed in 1798. Madison's Virginia Resolutions and Jefferson's Kentucky Resolutions proclaimed that state legislatures retained both their right to judge the constitutionality of federal actions and an authority called interposition, which enabled them to protect the liberties of their citizens. A set of Kentucky Resolutions adopted in November 1799 added that states could "nullify" objectionable federal laws. The authors intended interposition and nullification to protect residents from being tried for breaking an unconstitutional law. Although most states disapproved the resolutions, their passage demonstrated the potential for disunion in the late 1790s.

In 1799 a minor insurrection called the Fries Rebellion broke out when crowds of Pennsylvania German farmers released prisoners jailed for refusing to pay taxes to fund military expansion. Federal troops quickly quashed the disturbance.

National leaders acted as if a crisis were imminent. Vice President Jefferson hinted that events might push the southern states into secession from the Union; President Adams hid guns in his home. The election of 1800 would take place in an atmosphere charged with tension.

The Election of 1800

In the election campaign, the parties once again rallied around the Federalist Adams and the Republican Jefferson. Moderate leadership in both parties ensured that the nation would survive the tumultuous election. Jefferson and Madison discouraged radical activity, while Adams rejected demands that he ensure victory by deliberately sparking an insurrection or asking for a declaration of war against France.

"Nothing but an open war can save us," declared a High Federalist. But when the president discovered the French willing to seek peace in 1799, he proposed a special diplomatic mission. "Surprise, indignation, grief & disgust followed each other in quick succession," reported a Federalist senator. Adams obtained Senate approval for his envoys only by threatening to resign and so make Jefferson president. High Federalists tried unsuccessfully to dump Adams. Hamilton denounced him as a fool, but this tactic backfired when most New Englanders rallied around the president.

Adams's negotiations with France did not achieve a settlement until 1801, but the expectation of normal relations prevented Federalists from exploiting charges of Republican sympathy for the enemy. With the immediate threat of war removed, voters grew resentful that in just two years taxes had soared 33 percent to support an army that had done virtually nothing. As the danger of war receded, voters gave Federalists less credit for standing up to France and more blame for ballooning the national debt by $10 million.

High Federalists spitefully withheld the backing that Adams needed to win the presidency. Republicans successfully mobilized voters in Philadelphia and New York who were ready to forsake the Federalists. Voter turnouts more than doubled those of 1788, rising from 15 percent to 40 percent, and in hotly contested New York and Pennsylvania more than one-half the eligible voters participated. Con-

veniently overlooking Adams's own unconventional religious views, Federalists urged citizens to vote for "GOD—AND A RELIGIOUS PRESIDENT" and rejected "JEFFERSON—AND NO GOD!" Nonetheless thousands of Baptists, Methodists, and other dissenters voted for Jefferson.

Adams lost the presidency by just eight electoral votes, but Jefferson's election was not assured. Because all seventy-three Republican electors voted for Jefferson and his running mate, Aaron Burr of New York, the electoral college deadlocked in a Jefferson-Burr tie. The deadlock put the election into the House of Representatives, where six days and thirty-five ballots produced no result. Burr, now dreaming of becoming president himself, looked for Federalist support but was thwarted by Alexander Hamilton, who saw Jefferson as "by far not so dangerous a man." One Federalist abandoned Burr and gave Jefferson the presidency by history's narrowest margin.

hc Primary Source: Jefferson Campaign Poster

ECONOMIC AND SOCIAL CHANGE

During the new nation's first twelve years, the spread of economic production for markets transformed the lives of many Americans in ways whose outcome remained uncertain in 1800. At the same time, many Americans were rethinking questions of gender and race in American society.

Households and Market Production

For centuries the family household had been the scene of virtually all economic production. Family members, apprentices, servants, and even slaves were all part of this household economy; nearly everyone worked at what was either temporarily or permanently "home." The idea of "going to work" would have seemed odd indeed.

In the late eighteenth century, the vast majority of households consisted of a farmer and his family, which usually included seven children. Husband

and sons worked in the fields while wives, daughters, and young sons maintained the barns and gardens near the house and provided food and clothing for the family. Women bore and reared the children as well. Most families produced only what they needed and a small surplus for barter.

After the American Revolution, this began to change in heavily settled regions of the Northeast. Prosperous farmers began to sell their surplus produce to urban customers. Poorer farmers found other ways to produce for commercial markets. Young men and young couples moved west, while unmarried daughters frequently remained at home and spun and wove cloth. Enterprising merchants began catering to an emerging urban market for cloth as well as selling to southerners who wanted the cheapest possible material for slave clothing. Merchants would supply raw flax (for linen), wool, and cotton to mothers and daughters in farm households, returning in a few weeks to pay the women cash for their handiwork. A similar system emerged in the shoe industry, where prosperous shoemakers began supplying leather to others and paying them for the finished product.

White Women and the Republic

Along with the growing importance of women's economic roles, discussions of republicanism raised larger questions of women's equality. Neither the Revolution nor republican state constitutions had substantially altered the legal position of white women. Some states made it easier for women to obtain divorces, but only New Jersey allowed women to vote. However in 1807 New Jersey disenfranchised both women and free blacks.

Throughout American life, social change and republican ideology combined to challenge traditional attitudes toward women's rights. Americans increasingly recognized the right of a woman to choose her husband. In the Northeast, young women increasingly became pregnant as a way to force their fathers' consent to marriage. Marriage allowed young women to gain economic support in a region where the westward exodus of young men was increasingly leaving a growing number of women single.

White women also had fewer children than their mothers and grandmothers. Both declining farm sizes and urbanization contributed to the shrinkage; in one Massachusetts town, for example, the average number of children a woman bore declined from nine per marriage in 1750 to six by 1800. Some women were clearly finding relief from the nearly endless cycle of pregnancy and nursing that had consumed their grandmothers.

Republican notions of male-female relations began to change. "I object to the word 'obey' in the marriage-service," wrote one woman, "because it is a general word, without limitations of definitions. . . . The obedience between man and wife is, or ought to be mutual." Divorce petitions filed by women increasingly cited lack of mutuality as the cause for divorce.

The subordination of women to men increasingly became the subject of debate. Poet and essayist Judith Sargent Murray wrote that both genders had equal intellectual ability and deserved equal education. "We can only reason from what we know," she argued, "and if an opportunity of acquiring knowledge hath been denied us, the inferiority of our sex cannot fairly be deduced from there." Women should not rush into marriage but should first improve their minds so that they could instill republican ideals in their children.

The idea of "republican motherhood" emphasized the necessity of educating white women so they could inculcate republican virtues in their children, male as well as female. In the 1780s private academies for women began to emerge in cities. In 1789 Massachusetts forbade any town to exclude girls from its elementary schools.

By itself the expansion of educational opportunities for white women had a limited effect since women were generally still confined to "the narrow circle of domesticity." Republican assertions of male and female equality provoked scattered calls for political equality, although the great struggle for women's political rights would begin only in the next century.

Women could indeed be virtuous wives and mothers, but the world outside their homes offered them few opportunities to apply their educations.

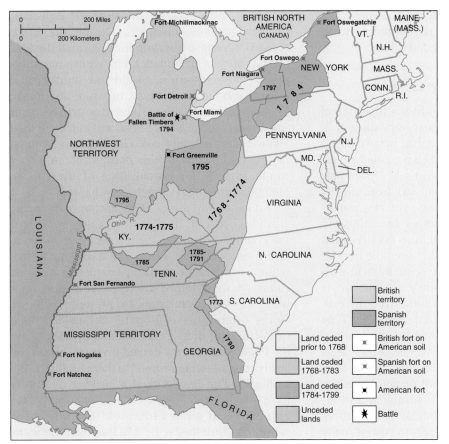

MAP 7.1
Indian Land Cessions, 1768–1799
During the last third of the eighteenth century, Native Americans were forced to give up extensive homelands throughout the eastern backcountry and further west in the Ohio and Tennessee River Valleys.

hc Interactive Map: Western Land Claims

Native Americans in the New Republic

Native Americans were tragically excluded from this growing prosperity. By 1795 most eastern Indian tribes had suffered severe reductions in population and territory, owing to battle, famine, and disease. From 1775 to 1795 the Cherokees declined from 16,000 to 10,000 and the Iroquois from 9,000 to 4,000. Between 1775 and 1800 Indians forfeited more land than the area inhabited by whites in 1775. Settlers crowded Indians onto reservations (often illegally), liquor dealers and criminals trespassed on Indian lands, and government agents and missionaries pressured Indians to abandon their lands and cultures. Indians who sold land to whites, or worked

for them, received an unfamiliar medium, cash, and found little to use the cash for except liquor.

Demoralized and unable to strike back, Indians often sank into alcoholism, and their settlements were plagued by despair and violence. Beginning in 1799 a Seneca Iroquois prophet, Handsome Lake, led his people in a creative effort to resolve the crisis. He preached against alcoholism among the Iroquois by appealing to their religious traditions. He welcomed Quaker missionaries who taught Euro-American agricultural methods to Iroquois men no longer able to hunt and trade. Many Iroquois men welcomed the change. Iroquois women who resisted because they stood to forfeit their collective ownership of farmland, their control of the food supply, and their place in tribal councils were accused of witchcraft. Among the Iroquois as with most Indians, the conflict between tradition and new ways proceeded fitfully.

Redefining the Color Line

The Republic's first years marked the high tide of African-Americans' Revolutionary-era success in bettering their lot. Although racism persisted, Jefferson's eloquent words "all men are created equal" awakened many white consciences. In 1790, 8 percent of African-Americans enjoyed freedom. By 1800, 11 percent were free. State reforms meanwhile attempted to improve slaves' conditions. In 1791 the North Carolina legislature declared that the "distinction of criminality between the murder of a white person and one who is equally an human creature, but merely of a different complexion, is disgraceful to humanity" and authorized the execution of whites who murdered slaves. By 1794 most states had outlawed the Atlantic slave trade.

Hesitant measures to ensure free blacks' legal equality appeared in the 1780s and early 1790s. Most states dropped restrictions on their freedom of movement, protected their property, and allowed them to enroll in the militia. All but three states either permitted free blacks to vote or made no specific attempts to exclude them. But before the 1790s ended, the trend toward lessening the social and legal distances between the races ended. Abolitionist sentiment ebbed, slavery became more entrenched, and whites demonstrated reluctance to accept free blacks as fellow citizens.

Federal law led the way in restricting the rights of African-Americans. In 1790 congressional procedures for naturalizing aliens limited eligibility to foreign whites. The federal militia law of 1792 allowed states to exclude free blacks. The navy and marine corps forbade nonwhite enlistments in 1798. By 1807 Delaware, Maryland, Kentucky, and New Jersey had stripped free blacks of the vote. Although free blacks enjoyed rights in some areas, the number of places treating them as the political equals of whites dropped sharply in the early 1800s.

Faced with growing constriction on their freedom and opportunities, free African-Americans turned to one another for support, especially through religious channels. During the 1780s Richard Allen and Absalom Jones formed the Free African Society of Philadelphia, whose members pooled their resources to aid one another and other blacks in need. When the white-dominated Methodist church they attended restricted black worshippers to the gallery, Allen and Jones and their followers formed their own congregation. Comparable developments in other northern communities would lead to the establishing of the African Methodist Episcopal Church (see Chapter 9).

An especially revealing symptom of changing attitudes occurred in 1793 when Congress passed the Fugitive Slave Law. The law required judges to award possession of a runaway slave on a formal request by a master or his representative. Accused runaways were denied jury trials and sometimes were refused permission to present evidence. Slaves' legal status as property disqualified them from claiming these constitutional privileges, but the Fugitive Slave Law denied even *free* blacks the legal protections guaranteed to them under the Bill of Rights. The law marked a striking departure from the atmosphere of the 1780s, when state governments had given whites and free blacks the same legal privileges. By 1793 white Americans clearly found it easy to forget that the Constitution had not limited citizenship to their race.

The bloody slave revolt on Saint Domingue undermined the trend toward abolition and reinforced the kind of fears that spawned racism. Reports of the slaughter of French slaveholders made white Americans more reluctant to criticize slavery and helped to transform the image of blacks from that of victims of injustice to one of potential menaces. In August 1800 a planned insurrection of more than 1,000 slaves in Richmond, Virginia, kindled smoldering white fears. The militia put down the conspiracy and executed 35 slaves, including the leader, Gabriel. "I have ventured my life in endeavoring to obtain the liberty of my countrymen, and I am a willing sacrifice to their cause," said one rebel before his execution.

Isolated uprisings occurred in the United States for years after "Gabriel's Rebellion," and rumors

Chronology

1789	First Congress convenes in New York. George Washington sworn in as first president. Judiciary Act. French Revolution begins.
1790	Alexander Hamilton submits his Reports on Public Credit and National Bank to Congress. Treaty of New York.
1791	Bank of the United States is granted a twenty-year charter. Vermont admitted to the Union. Bill of Rights ratified. Slave uprising begins in French colony of Saint Domingue. Hamilton submits his Report on Manufactures to Congress.
1792	Washington reelected president. Kentucky admitted to the Union.
1793	Fugitive Slave Law. *Chisholm* v. *Georgia*. French planters flee slave rebellion in Saint Domingue for the United States. France declares war on Britain and Spain. Washington's Neutrality Proclamation. Citizen Genet arrives in United States. First Democratic societies established.
1794	Whiskey Rebellion in western Pennsylvania. General Anthony Wayne's forces defeat Shawnees in the Battle of Fallen Timbers.
1795	Treaty of Greenville. Jay's Treaty with Britain ratified.
1796	Tennessee admitted to the Union.
1797	Treaty of San Lorenzo (Pinckney's Treaty) ratified. Washington's Farewell Address. John Adams elected president.
1798	XYZ Affair. Alien and Sedition Acts. Eleventh Amendment to the Constitution ratified.
1798–1799	Virginia and Kentucky Resolutions.
1798–1800	United States fights Quasi-War with France.
1799	Fries Rebellion in Pennsylvania.
1800	Gabriel's Rebellion in Virginia. Thomas Jefferson elected president.

persisted that a massive revolt was brewing. Antislavery sentiment diminished rapidly. The antislavery movement would not recover from the damage inflicted by the Saint Domingue revolt until the early 1830s.

A technological development strengthened slavery. In the 1790s demand in the British textile industry stimulated the cultivation of cotton in coastal South Carolina and Georgia. Here the soil and climate were ideal for growing long-staple cotton, whose fibers could be separated easily from its seed. In the South's upland and interior regions, however, only short-staple cotton thrived. Its seed clung tenaciously to the fibers and defied cleaning. It was as if southerners had discovered gold but could not mine it. In 1793 a New Englander, Eli Whitney, rescued the South by inventing a cotton gin that efficiently cleaned short-staple cotton. Improved by others, Whitney's machine removed a major obstacle to cotton cultivation, gave plantation slavery a new lease on life, and undermined the doubts of those who considered slavery economically outmoded. Thus by the time Thomas Jefferson became president in 1801, free blacks had suffered a subtle erosion of their political gains, and slaves stood no closer to freedom.

CONCLUSION   *hc* ACE Practice Test

The new nation's survival was by no means assured in the early years of the Constitution. Hamilton pushed through a series of bold measures that strengthened the federal government by giving it responsibility for the nation's debt and for overseeing a national bank. Jefferson, Madison, and others opposed these measures, which they said favored northeastern commercial interests and threatened liberty by concentrating political and economic power in a few hands. Spain and Britain hampered westward expansion, while both France and Britain each tried to force the new republic to take its side in their war with one another. Bitterly divided, white elites split into Republican and Federalist parties. Only when power transferred smoothly from Federalists to Republicans in the election of 1800 could long-term political stability be taken for granted.

While some whites granted limited recognition of women's independence, most abandoned the Revolution's loftiest goals for nonwhites, placing new restrictions on blacks and creating new obstacles to Native Americans' physical and cultural survival.

FURTHER READING

Ron Chernow, *Alexander Hamilton* (2004). A new portrait by a master of biography.

Douglas R. Egerton, *Gabriel's Rebellion: The Virginia Slave Conspiracies of 1800 and 1802* (1993). A thorough, well-written narrative that presents slave resistance against the backdrop of post-Revolutionary society and politics.

Stanley Elkins and Eric McKitrick, *The Age of Federalism: The Early American Republic, 1788–1800* (1993). A magisterial account of politics and diplomacy through the decisive election of 1800.

Joseph J. Ellis, *Founding Brothers: The Revolutionary Generation* (2000). A vivid study of personalities and personal relationships among political leaders in shaping the new union.

Joanne B. Freeman, *Affairs of Honor: National Politics in the New Republic* (2001). An insightful discussion of politics in the 1790s and the passions that underlay them.

Ramon A. Gutierrez and Richard J. Orsi (eds.), *Contested Eden: California and the Gold Rush* (1998). A fine collection of essays, introducing the history of the Pacific colony under Spanish and Mexican rule.

Joan M. Jensen, *Loosening the Bonds: Mid-Atlantic Farm Women, 1750–1850* (1986). A study of the interplay of women's roles and commercialization in what was then America's most dynamic agricultural region.

Gary B. Nash, *Forging Freedom: The Formation of Philadelphia's Black Community, 1720–1840* (1988). A landmark study of how North America's largest African-American community formed and survived in the face of racism and poverty.

Claudio Saunt, *A New Order of Things: Property, Power, and the Transformation of the Creek Indians, 1733–1816* (1999). A pathbreaking account of how eastern North America's most powerful Indian nation adapted to political, economic, and cultural change, and of the price its people paid for their survival.

Alan Taylor, *William Cooper's Town: Power and Persuasion on the Frontier of the Early American Republic* (1995). A compelling account of the fall of one elite Federalist in the face of the Republicans' rise to power.

Laurel Thatcher Ulrich, *A Midwife's Tale: The Life of Martha Ballard, Based on Her Diary, 1785–1812* (1990). A Pulitzer Prize-winning study of a woman's life in rural America.

Jeffersonianism and the Era of Good Feelings, 1801–1824

Portrait of Samuel Chester Reid, by John Wesley Jarvis, 1815

CHAPTER OUTLINE

The Age of Jefferson

The Gathering Storm

The War of 1812

The Awakening of American Nationalism

 This icon will direct you to additional study and research resources at http://college.hmco.com/history/us/boyer/enduring_concise/5e/students/index.html

On March 4, 1801, Thomas Jefferson walked from his boarding house to the Capitol for his inauguration, ostentatiously avoiding the pomp and ceremony he thought had grown out of hand under Washington and Adams.

Adams himself, still bitter after the tumultuous election of 1800, was not in Washington for the ceremony.

In his inaugural address, Jefferson struck a conciliatory note, assuring the Federalists that their rights would be respected. Despite the divisiveness of the recent election, he proclaimed that "we are all republicans, we are all federalists." He referred, not to the contending political parties, but to his hope that all Americans who accepted the federal

This chapter focuses on five major questions:

▶ How did Jefferson's philosophy of government shape his policies concerning public expenditures, the judiciary, and the Louisiana Purchase?

▶ What divisions split the Republican party during Jefferson's second term?

▶ Why did the United States go to war in 1812?

▶ How did the War of 1812 influence American politics?

▶ To what extent did Jefferson's legacy persist into the Era of Good Feelings? To what extent was it discarded?

union and representative government could work harmoniously.

Jefferson's ideal cast a lengthy shadow over the period from 1801 to 1825. His purchase of the Louisiana Territory nearly doubled the size of the United States. And his successors, James Madison and James Monroe, ruled under his belief that governments were strong only to the extent that they earned the affection of a contented people. The Federalist party, deserted by voters, collapsed and disintegrated.

But harmony proved elusive. Events in Europe continued to roil American politics. Even ending all trade with Europe did not allow the United States to remain clear of European wars; the policy, in fact, led to war between Britain and the United States in 1812.

With the Federalist party a declining force, factionalism tore at the Republican party. Some criticized President Jefferson for deserting his own principles, others for not creating a strong enough central government. And, ominously, in 1819 and 1820 Republicans split along sectional lines over the extension of slavery into Missouri.

THE AGE OF JEFFERSON

Narrowly elected, Jefferson saw his popularity rise in his first term as he scaled down seemingly unnecessary government expenditures. Increasingly confident of public support, he worked to loosen the Federalist grip on appointed offices, especially in the judiciary, and purchased Louisiana. Both political calculation and also his philosophy of government, known as Jeffersonianism, guided his moves.

Jefferson and Jeffersonianism

A man of extraordinary attainments, Jefferson spoke fluent French, read Latin and Greek, and studied several Native American languages. For more than twenty years he was president of America's foremost scientific society, the American Philosophical Society. He designed Monticello, his mountaintop mansion in Virginia, and spent 40 years overseeing its construction. Fascinated by gadgets, he invented a device for duplicating his letters and a revolving book stand. His personal library of 7,000 books was the foundation of the Library of Congress. His public career was luminous: principal author of the Declaration of Independence, governor of Virginia, ambassador to France, secretary of state, vice-president, and ultimately president.

Yet Jefferson was, and remains, a controversial figure. In 1802 a former supporter, James Callender, wrote a newspaper account in which he named Sally Hemings, a house slave at Monticello, as Jefferson's mistress. The light-skinned and lovely slave was the daughter of Jefferson's own father-in-law. Recent DNA tests have led most scholars to think it likely that Jefferson, a widower, was the father of at least one of her four surviving children.

Callender's story did Jefferson little damage in Virginia. Jefferson acted according to the rules of white Virginia gentlemen by never acknowledging any of Sally's children as his own. Although he freed two of her children (the other two ran away), he never freed Sally, nor did he ever mention her in his correspondence. Yet the story of Sally fed the charge that Jefferson was a hypocrite, for throughout his career he condemned the "race mixing" that he seems to have practiced.

Jefferson did not believe that blacks and whites could live permanently side by side, and he greatly feared a race war so vicious that it could be suppressed only by a dictator. Only by colonizing blacks in Africa could America avert revolution and chaos.

High taxes, standing armies, and public corruption could also threaten American liberty, he believed, by making government the master rather than the servant of the people. To prevent the United States from sinking into tyranny, Jefferson advocated that state governments retain great authority because they were immediately responsive to popular will.

Popular liberty required popular virtue, he believed, virtue being the disposition to place public good above private interest and to exercise vigilance in keeping government under control. To Jefferson, the most vigilant and virtuous people were educated farmers, accustomed to acting and thinking with sturdy independence. Least vigilant were the inhabitants of cities, which he saw as breeding grounds for mobs and as menaces to liberty. When Americans "get piled upon one another in large cities, as in Europe," he warned, "they will become corrupt as in Europe."

Although opponents labeled him a dreamy philosopher incapable of governing, Jefferson was in fact intensely practical. He studied science not for its abstract theories but because scientific advances would augment human happiness. Jefferson's practical cast of mind revealed itself in his inventions—including an improved plow and a gadget for duplicating letters—and in his presidential agenda.

Jefferson's "Revolution"

Jefferson described his election as a revolution, but the revolution he sought was to restore the liberty and tranquillity that (he thought) the United States had enjoyed in its earliest years and to reverse what he saw as a drift into despotism. The $10 million growth in the national debt under the Federalists alarmed Jefferson and his secretary of the treasury, Albert Gallatin. They rejected Alexander Hamilton's argument that debt strengthened the government by giving creditors a stake in its health. Just paying interest on the debt would re-

quire taxes, which would suck money from industrious farmers, the backbone of the Republic. The money would then fall into the hands of creditors, parasites who lived off interest payments. Increased tax revenues might also tempt the government to create a standing army, always a threat to liberty.

To Jefferson and Gallatin, federal economy outweighed the importance of military preparedness; Gallatin calculated that by holding the line on

Man of the People
Jefferson thought of himself as a working politician and man of the people, not as an aristocratic figurehead. Foreign diplomats in the United States were often shocked when Jefferson greeted them dressed in everyday working clothes and carpet slippers.

expenditures, the government could pay off the national debt in sixteen years. A lull in the war between France and England that had threatened American shipping in the 1790s convinced Jefferson that minimal military preparedness was a sound policy. "We can now proceed without risks in demolishing useless structures of expense . . . and fortifying the principles of free government," he wrote.

While cutting back funds for the army, Jefferson was ready to use the navy to gain respect for the American flag. In 1801 he ordered a naval squadron into action against the so-called Barbary Pirates of North Africa. Jefferson calculated that going to war would be cheaper than continuing to pay tribute to protect peace. In 1805 the United States concluded a peace treaty with Tripoli; the war had cost roughly half of the annual tribute fee.

Jefferson and the Judiciary

Conflicts over the judiciary derailed Jefferson's hopes of conciliation with moderate Federalists. The first sticking point was the Judiciary Act of 1801, which reduced the size of the Supreme Court and created sixteen new federal judgeships, all of which John Adams had filled with Federalists in last-minute "midnight appointments." Given the bitterness created by Federalist zeal in enforcing the Alien and Sedition Acts, to Jefferson this was further proof that his opponents saw the court system as a battering ram to attack Republicanism. Although he won repeal of the Judiciary Act in 1802, Jefferson remained suspicious of the judiciary system and its Federalist judges.

Chief Justice John Marshall, an arch-Federalist appointed by John Adams and the reputed author of the Judiciary Act of 1801, did little to erase Jefferson's suspicions. In *Marbury* v. *Madison* (1803), Marshall and the Court ruled that Congress had exceeded its constitutional authority in writing the Judiciary Act of 1789. This decision was the first time that the Court had overturned an act of Congress, an important step on the way to establishing the principle of judicial review. Jefferson had no quarrel with the principle of judicial review, but he found it galling that Marshall had used the deci-

sion to indirectly lecture him on the moral responsibilities of the presidency.

Even as the *Marbury* decision was pending, Republicans had taken the offensive against the judiciary, moving to impeach (charge with wrongdoing) two Federalist judges, John Pickering and Samuel Chase. Pickering, an insane alcoholic, was an easy call, and he was quickly removed from office, but Chase presented difficulties. He was an ardent Federalist who had zealously enforced the Alien and Sedition Acts. Nonetheless, the Constitution specified that judges could be impeached only for treason, bribery, and "high Crimes and Misdemeanors." Was impeachment a solution for excessive political partisanship, Chase's fundamental sin? Ultimately Chase was impeached in 1804, but the Senate narrowly failed to convict him, in part because moderate Republicans had begun to doubt that impeachment was the cure for judicial partisanship.

Chase's acquittal ended Jefferson's skirmishes with the judiciary. Unlike his radical followers, Jefferson objected neither to judicial review nor to an appointed judiciary; he merely challenged Federalist use of judicial power for political goals. Yet there was always a gray area between law and politics. To Federalists, there was no conflict between protecting the Constitution and advancing their party's cause. Nor did Federalists use their domination of the courts to undo Jefferson's "revolution" of 1800; the Marshall court, for example, upheld the constitutionality of the repeal of the Judiciary Act of 1801. In turn, Jefferson never proposed impeaching Marshall. And in the Pickering and Chase cases, Jefferson had merely tried to make the judiciary more responsive to popular will by challenging judges who had behaved outrageously. No other federal judge would be impeached for more than fifty years.

The Louisiana Purchase, 1803

Jefferson's goal of avoiding foreign entanglements would remain beyond reach as long as European powers held large territories in North America. In the Treaty of San Ildefonso (1800), a weakened Spain had returned the vast Louisiana Territory to

MAP 8.1

The Louisiana Purchase and the Exploration of the West

The explorations of Lewis and Clark demonstrated the vast extent of the area purchased from France.

hc Interactive Map: Louisiana Purchase

France, which, under Napoleon Bonaparte, was emerging as Europe's strongest military power. Jefferson was appalled.

The president had long imagined that the inevitable expansion of a free and virtuous American people would create an "empire of liberty." Spain was no obstacle, but Napoleonic France posed a real danger; Jefferson knew that Bonaparte's capacity for mischief was boundless. If Bonaparte gave England a free hand in the Mediterranean in exchange for a license for French expansion in North America, the United States could be sandwiched between British Canada and French Louisiana. And if Britain refused to cooperate with France, the British might seize Louisiana, trapping the Americans between two large British territories.

Bonaparte's real goal was different but no less dangerous to American interests. Sure of his destiny as a conqueror, he dreamed of re-creating a French New World empire bordering the Caribbean and the Gulf of Mexico. The island of Santo Domingo (modern Haiti and the Dominican Republic) would be the fulcrum of the empire and Louisiana its breadbasket. Before this dream could become reality, however, the French would have to subdue Santo Domingo, where a bloody slave rebellion had led to the creation of a government under the black statesman Toussaint L'Ouverture. Napoleon accordingly dispatched an army to reassert French control and to reestablish slavery, but yellow fever and fierce resistance by the former slaves doomed the French forces.

In the short run, Jefferson worried most about New Orleans, the only outlet for farmers along the Mississippi and Ohio river systems. Spain had temporarily granted Americans the right to park their produce there while waiting transfer to seagoing vessels.

Concern turned to alarm when the Spanish colonial administrator in New Orleans prohibited the deposit of American produce in that city for transshipment to foreign lands. Because American farmers west of the Appalachians depended on access to the sea via New Orleans, the Spanish order was a major provocation. Most Americans assumed (wrongly) that the order had come from Napoleon, who had not yet taken formal possession of Louisiana. A concerned Jefferson wrote that "the day that France takes possession of N. Orleans . . . we must marry ourselves to the British fleet and nation."

The combination of France's failure to subdue Santo Domingo and the termination of the American right of deposit at New Orleans stimulated two crucial decisions, one by Jefferson and the other by Napoleon, that led to the American purchase of Louisiana. First, Jefferson nominated James Monroe and Robert R. Livingston to negotiate with France for the purchase of New Orleans and as much of the Floridas as possible. (Because West Florida had repeatedly changed hands among France, Britain, and Spain, no one was sure who owned it.) Meanwhile, Napoleon had concluded that his Caribbean empire was not worth the cost. In addition, he planned to resume war in Europe and needed cash—so he decided to sell *all* of Louisiana. The American commissioners and the

French government settled on a price of $15 million. Thus the United States bought this immense, uncharted territory. No one knew its exact size, but the Louisiana Purchase virtually doubled the area of the United States.

Unsure of his constitutional authority to acquire Louisiana, Jefferson drafted an amendment that would have given him that power. But few Republicans shared his reservations, and Jefferson soon began to worry that the long process of ratifying an amendment might give Napoleon time to change his mind. In addition, aware that most Federalists opposed the Louisiana Purchase because it would decrease the relative importance of their eastern-seaboard strongholds, the Republican Jefferson saw no reason to hand the Federalists an issue by dallying over ratification. The president quietly dropped the amendment, and the Senate quickly ratified the purchase.

The Election of 1804

The main threat to Jefferson's reelection in 1804 was not the Federalists, who were dispirited and lacked a popular national issue, but Aaron Burr, his own vice president, who had tried to take advantage of a tie in the electoral college to gain the presidency in 1800. The Twelfth Amendment had clarified the electoral process but had not eliminated Burr's conniving; he had spent much of his vice presidency intriguing with the Federalists. The Republicans dispensed with the threat by unceremoniously dumping him from the ticket in 1804 in favor of George Clinton. In the election the Federalist nominees, Charles C. Pinckney and Rufus King, carried only two states. Jefferson's overwhelming victory brought his first term to a fitting close; between 1801 and 1804 the United States had doubled its territory, started to pay off its debt, and remained at peace. President Jefferson basked in the sun of success.

The Lewis and Clark Expedition

Louisiana dazzled Jefferson's imagination. Americans knew virtually nothing about the immense territory, not even its western boundary. A case could be made for the Pacific Ocean, but Jefferson was content to claim that Louisiana extended at least to the mountains west of the Mississippi, mountains that few Americans had seen. Thus the Louisiana Purchase was both a bargain and a surprise package.

Even before the purchase, Jefferson had planned an exploratory expedition. He had chosen Lieutenant Meriwether Lewis, his personal secretary, as commander and had sent him to Philadelphia for a crash course in zoology, astronomy, and botany. Lewis was to trace the Missouri River to its source, cross the western highlands, and follow the best water route to the Pacific. Although Jefferson stressed commercial possibilities in requesting congressional funding for the expedition, he probably cared more about advancing scientific knowledge. His instructions to Lewis focused on obtaining accurate measurements of latitude and longitude, gathering information about Native American languages and customs, and studying climate, volcanoes, and plant and animal life.

Leaving St. Louis in May 1804, Lewis, his second-in-command, William Clark, and about fifty others followed the Missouri and then the Snake and Columbia rivers. In the Dakota Country they hired a French-Canadian fur trader, Toussaint Charbonneau, as guide and interpreter. Charbonneau proved less than ideal, but his shortcomings were offset by his wife, Sacajawea, a sixteen-year-old Shoshone stolen by a rival tribe and then married to Charbonneau. During the expedition the presence of Sacajawea's newborn son helped to persuade skeptical tribes of Lewis and Clark's peaceful intent; she also showed the whites how to forage for wild plants, often their only food, by raiding rodent dens.

After reaching the Pacific in November 1805, the expedition returned to St. Louis. The explorers had collected vast amounts of scientific information, including the disturbing fact that more than 300 miles of mountains separated the Missouri from the Columbia. Nonetheless, the Lewis and Clark expedition stimulated interest in the West. The expedition also produced a sprinkling of tall tales about gigantic Indians, a mountain composed of salt, and soil too rich to grow trees.

Nonetheless, the expedition's drawings of the geography of the region led to more accurate maps and heightened interest in the West.

THE GATHERING STORM

In gaining Louisiana, the United States had benefited from the European powers' preoccupation with their own struggles. But between 1803 and 1814, the Napoleonic Wars turned the United States into a pawn in a chess game played by others and made Jefferson's second term far less successful than his first.

Europe was not Jefferson's only problem. He had to deal with a plot to dismantle the United States hatched in the inventive and perverse mind of Aaron Burr as well as face down challenges from within his own party.

Challenges on the Home Front

Aaron Burr suffered a string of reverses in 1804. Dropped from the 1804 ticket, he began to intrigue with a faction of extreme, or High, Federalists who were scheming to form a "Northern Confederacy" that would include Nova Scotia, New England, New York, and even Pennsylvania. To advance their plot, the Federalists helped Burr to gain the Federalist nomination for governor of New York. Alexander Hamilton, who had thwarted Burr's grab for the presidency in 1800 by supporting Jefferson, now foiled Burr a second time by allowing publication of his "despicable opinion" of Burr. After his defeat in the New York election, Burr challenged Hamilton to a duel and mortally wounded him at Weehawken, New Jersey, on July 11, 1804.

Indicted in two states for murdering Hamilton, Burr next hatched a scheme so audacious that not even his opponents could believe that he was capable of such treachery. Burr allied himself with General James Wilkinson, the military governor of the Louisiana Territory, who had been taking Spanish money since the 1780s. Their plot had several dimensions: they would create an independent confederacy of western states, conquer Mexico, and invade West Florida. The scheming duo presented the plot imaginatively. To westerners, they said that it had the covert support of the Jefferson administration; to the British, that it was a way to attack Spanish lands; and to the Spanish, that it would open the way to dividing up the United States.

In the fall of 1806 Burr and some sixty followers made their way down the Ohio and Mississippi rivers to join Wilkinson at Natchez. Wilkinson was not there. In October Jefferson, who described Burr as a crooked gun that never shot straight, denounced the conspiracy. Wilkinson abandoned the conspiracy and proclaimed himself a loyal Jeffersonian. Former vice president Burr panicked, tried to flee to West Florida but was captured and returned to Richmond to stand trial for treason. Chief Justice John Marshall presided and advised the jury that the prosecution had to prove actual treasonable acts—an impossible task because the conspiracy had never reached fruition. Jefferson was furious, but Marshall followed the clear wording of the Constitution, which deliberately made treason difficult to prove. The jury returned a "not proved" verdict, which Marshall entered as "not guilty." Still under indictment for the murder of Hamilton, Burr fled to Europe, where he tried but failed to involve Napoleon in a grand scheme that would be the prelude to a proposed Anglo-French invasion of the United States. Burr returned to the United States in 1812 and practiced law in New York. Upholding his reputation as a womanizer, he fathered two illegitimate children in his seventies and was divorced for adultery at eighty. Perhaps the most puzzling man in American history, Aaron Burr died in 1836.

Jefferson also faced a challenge from a group a fellow Republicans known as the Quids.* Their leader was John Randolph of Virginia, an eccentric man of acerbic wit. Randolph still subscribed to the "country ideology" of the 1770s, which celebrated the wisdom of the farmer against rulers and warned against governments' tendency to encroach on liberty. Originally, Jefferson had shared these beliefs, but he had recognized them as an ideology of opposition, not of power; once in office, he therefore

* Quid: a name taken from the Latin *tertium quid,* or "third thing"; roughly, a dissenter.

compromised. In contrast, Randolph remained frozen in the 1770s, denouncing every change as decline and proclaiming that he would throw all politicians to the dogs if he had less respect for dogs.

Not surprisingly, Randolph turned on Jefferson. First, he blasted the president for backing a compromise in the Yazoo land scandal. In 1795 the Georgia legislature had sold the huge Yazoo tract (35 million acres composing most of present-day Alabama and Mississippi) for a fraction of its value to land companies that had bribed virtually the entire legislature. The next legislature canceled the sale, but many investors had already bought land, some of them in good faith. The scandal was a moral challenge to Jefferson because of the good-faith purchases and a political dilemma as well, for some buyers were northerners whom Jefferson hoped to woo to the Republican party. In 1802 a federal commission compromised with an award of 5 million acres to the Yazoo investors. To Randolph, the compromise was itself a scandal—further evidence of the decay of republican virtue.

The Suppression of American Trade and Impressment

Burr's acquittal and Randolph's taunts shattered the aura of invincibility that had surrounded Jefferson. Now foreign affairs posed even sharper challenges. As Britain and France resumed their war, the United States prospered at Britain's expense by carrying sugar and coffee from French and Spanish Caribbean colonies to Europe. This trade not only provided Napoleon with supplies but also drove down the price of sugar and coffee from British colonies by adding to the glut of these commodities on the world market. The British concluded that their economic problems stemmed from American prosperity.

Fueling this boom was the reexport trade, which created conflicts with Britain. According to the British Rule of 1756, any trade closed during peacetime could not be opened during war. For example, France usually restricted the sugar trade to French ships during peacetime and thus could not open it to American ships during war. The U.S. response to the Rule of 1756 was the "broken voyage," by which U.S. ships would carry French sugar or coffee to American ports, unload it, pass it through customs, and then reexport it as *American* produce. Britain tolerated this dodge for nearly a decade but in 1805 initiated a policy of total war toward France, including the strangulation of French trade. In the *Essex* case (1805), a British court declared broken voyages illegal.

Next came a series of British trade decrees ("Orders in Council"), through which Britain intended to blockade part of continental Europe and thus staunch the flow of any products that might aid the French war effort. French counterdecrees, proclaiming the British Isles blockaded, followed. In effect, if Americans obeyed the British regulations, they would violate the French rules, and vice versa. In total war, however, there was no room for neutrality, so both Britain and France seized U.S. ships. The British captures were far more humiliating and infuriating, for although most French seizures took place in European ports, many British takeovers occurred within sight of the U.S. coastline.

To these provocations the British added impressment. At issue was Britain's seizing purported Royal Navy deserters from American merchant ships and subsequently forcing them back into service. British sailors had reason to be discontented with their navy. Discipline on the Royal Navy's "floating hells" was often brutal, and the pay low; sailors on American ships earned up to five times more than those on British ships. At a time when war raised the demand for sailors, the Royal Navy suffered a high rate of desertion to American ships. In 1807, 149 of the 419 sailors on the USS *Constitution* were British subjects.

Impressed sailors led harrowing lives that included frequent escapes and recaptures. One seaman endured impressment eleven times. Another, facing his third recapture, drowned himself rather than spend another day in the Royal Navy. Impressment was, moreover, galling to American pride, for even though many deserters had become American citizens, the British impressed them anyway. The British also impressed U.S.-born seamen, including those who could prove their American birth; between 1803 and 1812, 6,000 Americans were impressed.

The *Chesapeake* incident heightened British-American tensions. In June 1807 a British warship, HMS *Leopard,* attacked an American frigate, the USS *Chesapeake,* just off Virginia. The British boarded the vessel and seized four supposed deserters. One, an actual deserter, was later hanged; the other three, former Britons, had "deserted" only from impressment and were now American citizens. Never before had the British claimed the right to seize deserters off government ships. Public outrage mounted; Jefferson claimed that he had not seen so belligerent a spirit in America since 1775. Yet while making some preparations for a possible war, Jefferson sought peace, first by engaging in fruitless negotiations with Britain to gain redress for the *Chesapeake* and then by steering the Embargo Act through Congress in December 1807.

hc Primary Source: British Impressment

The Embargo Act of 1807

By far the most controversial legislation of Jefferson's presidency, the Embargo Act prohibited vessels from leaving American harbors for foreign ports. Technically, it prohibited only exports, but it stopped imports as well, for few foreign ships would enter American ports if they had to leave empty. An amazed British newspaper called the embargo "little short of an absolute secession from the rest of the civilized world."

Jefferson defended the embargo as "peaceable coercion," a way of forcing France and, especially, Britain to respect American neutrality. But it did not work. Although British trade with the United States plummeted, the British opened new markets in South America. France's Napoleon, for his part, treated the act as a joke, seizing American ships and then informing the United States that he was only helping to enforce the embargo. Furthermore, the discovery of a major loophole that allowed American ships blown off course to put in at European ports led to an epidemic of U.S. captains reporting that adverse winds had forced them across the Atlantic.

The Brig *Reaper*, 1809
Although damaged by the embargo, shipbuilding was among the principal industries of New England. Here the hull of the brig *Reaper* is readied for launch in Medford, Massachusetts. Shipwrights spread tallow on the launching way so that the ship could slide into the water. The small box on the left was used to steam oak panels to make them pliable for installation.

The United States itself felt the harshest effects. Thirty thousand seamen lost their jobs, hundreds of merchants went bankrupt, and debtors swelled the jail population. Unable to export produce or to sell it at a decent price in the cities, farmers suffered as well. Land speculators discovered that cash-starved farmers could not buy land. "I live and that is all," wrote one New York speculator. "I am doing no business, cannot sell anybody property, nor collect any money." New England suffered most; in Massachusetts, which accounted for a third of foreign trade, the embargo was a calamity.

Yet there were benefits. Unable to export goods, merchants used their capital to begin manufacturing. In 1808 the United States had only fifteen cotton textile mills; by the end of 1809 eighty-seven more had been built. But merchants already ruined or seamen driven to soup kitchens took little comfort. Nor could New Englanders forget that the source of their misery was one of the "Virginia lordlings," "Mad Tom" Jefferson, who knew little about New England and loathed cities, the foundation of the region's prosperity. A Massachusetts poet wrote:

Our ships all in motion once whitened the ocean,
They sailed and returned with a cargo;
Now doomed to decay they have fallen a prey
To Jefferson, worms, and embargo.

James Madison and the Failure of Peaceable Coercion

With Jefferson's blessing, the Republicans nominated James Madison and George Clinton for the presidency and vice presidency in 1808. The Federalists renominated Charles C. Pinckney and Rufus King, the same ticket that had failed in 1804. In 1808 the Federalists staged a modest comeback, but Madison handily won the presidency, and the Republicans continued to control Congress.

The Federalists' revival, modest as it was, rested on two factors. First, the Embargo Act gave them the national issue that they had long lacked. Second, younger Federalists had abandoned their elders' "gentlemanly" disdain for campaigning and deliberately imitated vote-winning techniques such as barbecues and mass meetings that had worked for the Republicans.

To some contemporaries, "Little Jemmy" Madison, five feet four inches tall, seemed a weak, shadowy figure compared to Jefferson. In fact, Madison's intelligence and capacity for systematic thought equaled Jefferson's. Like Jefferson, Madison believed that American liberty rested on the virtue of the people and that virtue was critically tied to the growth and prosperity of agriculture. Madison also recognized that agricultural prosperity depended on trade—farmers needed markets. The British West Indies, dependent on the United States for much lumber and grain, struck Madison as both a natural trading partner and a tempting target. Britain alone could not fully supply the West Indies. By embargoing its own trade with the Indies, Madison reasoned, the United States could force Britain to its knees before Americans would suffer severe losses.

The American embargo, however, was coercing no one. Increased trade between Canada and the West Indies made a shambles of Madison's plan to pressure Britain. On March 1, 1809, Congress replaced the Embargo Act with the weaker, face-saving Non-Intercourse Act, which opened U.S. trade to all nations except Britain and France and authorized the president to restore trade with either of those nations if it stopped violating neutral rights. But neither nation complied. Meanwhile, American shippers kept up their profitable trade with the British and French, despite the restrictions. In May 1810 Congress substituted a new measure, Macon's Bill No. 2, for the Non-Intercourse Act. This legislation reopened trade with both belligerents, France and Britain, and then offered a clumsy bribe to each: if either nation repealed its restrictions on neutral shipping, the United States would halt all trade with the other. None of these steps worked. France and Britain believed that when great powers (such as themselves) went to war, there could be no neutrals. Weak nations like the United States should stop babbling about moral ideals and neutral rights and seek the protection of a great power. Neither Napoleon nor the British intended to accommodate the United States.

As peaceable coercion became a fiasco, Madison came under fire from militant Republicans demanding more aggressive policies. Primarily southerners and westerners, the militants were infuriated by insults to the American flag. In addition, economic recession between 1808 and 1810 had convinced the firebrands that British policies were wrecking their regions' economies. The election of 1810 brought several young militants, christened "war hawks," to Congress. Led by Henry Clay of Kentucky, who preferred war to the "putrescent pool of ignominious peace," the war hawks included John C. Calhoun of South Carolina, Richard M. Johnson of Kentucky, and William R. King of North Carolina—all future vice presidents. Clay was elected Speaker of the House.

Tecumseh and the Prophet

More emotional and pugnaciously nationalistic than Jefferson or Madison, the war hawks called for expelling Britain from Canada and Spain from the Floridas. Their demands merged with westerners' fears that the British in Canada were recruiting Indians to halt the march of United States settlement. In reality, American policy, not British meddling, was the source of bloodshed on the frontier.

Jefferson believed that Indians and whites could live peacefully together if the Indians became farmers—and farmers required far less land than nomadic hunters. Jefferson and Madison insisted that Indians be compensated fairly for ceded land and that only Indians with a claim to the land they were ceding should conclude treaties. However, the march of white settlement was steadily shrinking Indian hunting grounds, and some Indians were willing to sign away land in return for blankets, guns, and liquor.

No American was more eager to acquire Indian lands than William Henry Harrison, governor of Indiana Territory. Harrison realized that Indiana would not become a state without more residents, and the best way to attract more residents was to offer them Indian land. In September 1809 Harrison rounded up a delegation of half-starved Indi-

Tecumseh
No fully authenticated portrait of Tecumseh exists, but whites described him as handsome and dominant. Believing that Indian lands were not the possession of individual tribes to negotiate away but collectively belonged to all the Indians, Tecumseh was a formidable opponent of white expansion.

ans who ceded millions of acres of land along the Wabash River for two cents an acre; none of the Indians actually lived on the land.

This treaty, the Treaty of Fort Wayne, outraged numerous tribes. Among the angriest were Tecumseh, the Shawnee chief, and his brother Lalawéthica. In 1805 Lalawéthica had had a frightening dream, a vision of drunken Indians who were tormented for eternity. Overnight he was transformed from a drunken misfit into a preacher. He gave up liquor and began beseeching surrounding tribes to return to the old ways and avoid contact with whites. Now known as the Prophet, he took a new name, Tenskwatawa, the "open door" through which Indians could achieve salvation. Shawnees responded to his message.

In the meantime, Tecumseh had tried to build a coalition of several tribes to stem the tide of white settlement. He insisted that Indian lands belonged collectively to all the tribes and could not be sold by splinter groups. Failing to reach a settlement with Tecumseh or the Prophet, Harrison concluded that it was time to attack the Indians. His target was a Shawnee encampment near the mouth of the Tippecanoe River. With Tecumseh absent, recruiting more followers, the Prophet launched an attack on Harrison's forces in November 1811. Outnumbered two to one and short of ammunition, Tenskwatawa's force was beaten off after inflicting heavy casualties.

Although a small engagement, the Battle of Tippecanoe had far-reaching effects. Harrison became a national hero and ultimately rode his reputation to the White House. The Prophet was discredited, but his brother Tecumseh became recognized as a leader among the western tribes. Finally, Tecumseh concluded that an alliance with the British was the only way to stop the spread of American settlement.

Congress Votes for War

By spring 1812 President Madison had concluded that war was inevitable, and he sent a war message to Congress on June 1. Ironically, an economic slump prompted Britain to repeal its Orders in Council on June 23, but by then Congress had declared war. Neither the war hawks nor westerners

held the key to the vote in favor of war; the votes of Republicans in states like Pennsylvania, Maryland, and Virginia were the decisive force in propelling the declaration of war through Congress. Opposition came mainly from Federalist strongholds in New England and New York. Party affiliation rather than sectional interests shaped the vote; in general southern Federalists opposed the war declaration while northern Republicans supported it.

In short, the vote for war followed party, rather than sectional, lines. Much like the president, most Republicans had not wanted war but had been led to demand it by an accumulation of grievances.

Madison, in his war message, listed impressment, the presence of British ships in U.S. waters, and British violation of neutral rights as wrongs that justified war. None of these complaints fully explains why America declared war in 1812. Neither do continuing Indian problems (blamed on the British) along the frontier. A more important underlying cause for the war was the economic recession that affected the South and West after 1808. Finally, the fact that Madison, rather than Jefferson, was president was vitally important. Jefferson had believed that Britain was motivated primarily by its desire to defeat Napoleon; time was on America's side, Jefferson thought, for once the war in Europe ended, the provocations would stop. Madison held that Britain's real motive was to strangle American trade and thus to eliminate the United States as a trading rival. European war or not, Madison saw Britain as a menace to America. In his war message he stated flatly that Britain was meddling with U.S. trade not because of the European war but because it "frustrated the monopoly which she [Britain] covets for her own commerce and navigation."

THE WAR OF 1812

Although American warships would win a few sensational duels with British men-of-war, the U.S. Navy simply could not challenge the Royal Navy on the high seas, or even prevent a British blockade of the American coast. Madison thus shifted his sights to Canada, whose small population made it seem an easy mark. Jefferson, for example, saw the conquest of Canada as "a mere matter of marching."

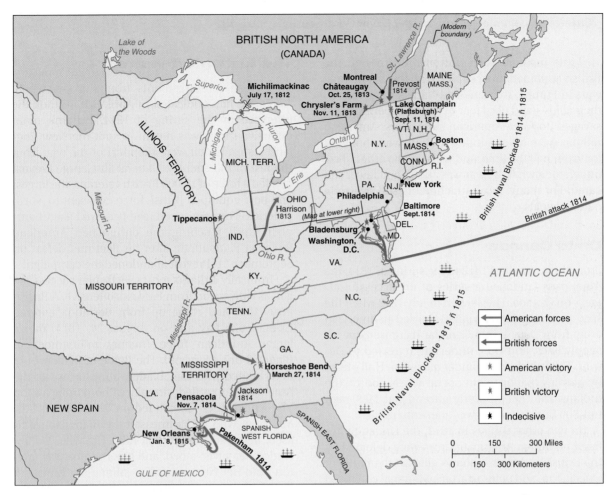

BRITISH NORTH AMERICA
(CANADA)

Michilimackinac
July 17, 1812

Montreal
Châteaugay
Oct. 25, 1813

Prevost
1814

Chrysler's Farm
Nov. 11, 1813

MAINE
(MASS.)

Lake Champlain
(Plattsburgh)
Sept. 11, 1814

VT. N.H.

Boston

MASS.

CONN.
R.I.

New York

Philadelphia

Baltimore
Sept.1814

Bladensburg
Washington,
D.C.

DEL.
MD.

PA.
N.J.

OHIO
Harrison
1813

(Map at lower right)

IND.

Tippecanoe

VA.

KY.

N.C.

TENN.

S.C.

GA.

MISSISSIPPI
TERRITORY

Horseshoe Bend
March 27, 1814

Pensacola
Nov. 7, 1814

Jackson
1814

LA.

New Orleans
Jan. 8, 1815

Pakenham 1814

SPANISH
WEST FLORIDA

SPANISH EAST FLORIDA

NEW SPAIN

GULF OF MEXICO

ILLINOIS
TERRITORY

MICH. TERR.

MISSOURI TERRITORY

Lake of
the Woods

L. Superior

L. Michigan

L. Huron

L. Ontario

L. Erie

Missouri R.

Mississippi R.

Ohio R.

St. Lawrence R.

(Modern
boundary)

British Naval Blockade 1814 – 1815

British attack 1814

ATLANTIC OCEAN

British Naval Blockade 1813 – 1815

→ American forces

→ British forces

* American victory

* British victory

* Indecisive

| 0 | 150 | 300 Miles |
| 0 | 150 | 300 Kilometers |

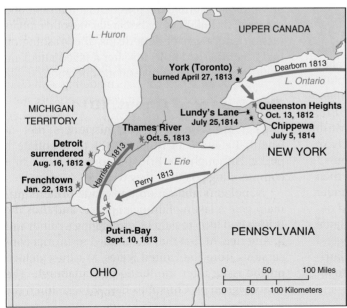

L. Huron

UPPER CANADA

York (Toronto)
burned April 27, 1813

Dearborn 1813

L. Ontario

MICHIGAN
TERRITORY

Lundy's Lane
July 25,1814

Queenston Heights
Oct. 13, 1812

Thames River
Oct. 5, 1813

Chippewa
July 5, 1814

Detroit
surrendered
Aug. 16, 1812

NEW YORK

Harrison 1813

Frenchtown
Jan. 22, 1813

L. Erie

Perry 1813

Put-in-Bay
Sept. 10, 1813

PENNSYLVANIA

OHIO

| 0 | 50 | 100 Miles |
| 0 | 50 | 100 Kilometers |

MAP 8.2
Major Battles of the
War of 1812

Most of the war's major engagements occurred on or
near the United States' northern frontier, but the Royal
Navy blockaded the entire Atlantic coast and the
British army penetrated as far south as Washington
and New Orleans.

MAP 8.3

Little justified such optimism. Although the British remained preoccupied with the Napoleonic wars in Europe, they enlisted Native Americans as their allies—and used fear of these "uncontrollable savages" to force American surrenders. American militias were often Sunday soldiers who "hollered for water half the time, and whiskey the other." Few understood what the war was about, and fewer still cared. For many, local attachments still overrode national goals.

On to Canada

From the summer of 1812 to the spring of 1814, the Americans launched a series of unsuccessful attacks on Canada. They began in July 1812 when the sixty-year-old general William Hull led an American army from Detroit into Canada. Tecumseh cut his supply lines, and Hull, unnerved, retreated to Detroit. The British commander played on Hull's fears by warning that he might not be able to control the Indians, and Hull promptly surrendered 2,000 men to 1,300 British and Native American troops.

In two other thrusts in 1812, the United States fared no better. American forces were defeated by the British and their Mohawk allies at the Battle of Queenston, and plans to attack Montreal collapsed when the New York militia refused to advance into Canada.

Renewed U.S. offensives and subsequent reverses in 1813 convinced the Americans that they could not retake Detroit while the British controlled Lake Erie. During winter 1812–1813 U.S. captain Oliver Hazard Perry built ships and outfitted them with captured cannon, and on September 10, 1813, the homemade American fleet destroyed a British squadron at Put-in-Bay on the western end of Lake Erie; "we have met the enemy, and they are ours," Perry triumphantly reported. The British then pulled out of Detroit, but American forces under General William Henry Harrison overtook and defeated a combined British-Indian force at the Battle of the Thames on October 5. Tecumseh, a legend among whites, died in the battle. Perry's and Harrison's victories cheered Americans, but efforts to invade Canada continued to falter.

The British Offensive

With fresh reinforcements from Europe, where Napoleon had abdicated in April, Britain took the offensive in the spring of 1814. Britain's main offensive thrust was meant to split the New England states, which were skeptical of the war, from the rest of the country. General Sir George Prevost headed a force of 10,000 British veterans, the largest and best-equipped British force ever sent to North America. They advanced readily down Lake Champlain until reaching the entrenched American forces at Plattsburgh; after his fleet met defeat on September 11, Prevost abandoned the campaign.

Ironically, Britain's most spectacular success began as a diversion from Prevost's offensive. A British army that had come up from Bermuda entered Chesapeake Bay and on August 24, 1814, met a larger American force (mainly militiamen) at Bladensburg, Maryland. The Battle of Bladensburg deteriorated into the "Bladensburg Races" as the American troops fled, virtually without firing a shot. The British then descended on Washington, D.C. Madison, who had witnessed the Bladensburg fiasco, fled into the Virginia hills. His wife, Dolley, loaded her silver, a bed, and a portrait of Washington onto her carriage before joining her husband. British troops ate the supper prepared for the Madisons and then burned the presidential mansion and other public buildings in the capital. Beyond embarrassing and angering Americans, the Washington raid accomplished little, for after a failed attack on Baltimore, the British broke off the operation.

The Treaty of Ghent, 1814

English and American commissioners met at Ghent, Belgium, in August 1814 to negotiate a peace. Although the British appeared to be in a commanding position, they were not.

Napoleon's abdication had made Britain's primary goal a lasting European peace, and thus the British had little to gain by prolonging a minor war in America. At first they demanded territorial concessions from the United States, but they yielded on the issue after the Battle of Plattsburgh. The treaty, signed on Christmas Eve, 1814, restored the *status quo ante bellum:** the United States neither gained nor lost territory. The fixing of the Canadian-American border was referred to a joint commission for future settlement. Impressment was left hanging, but the end of the European war made neutral rights a dead issue.

Ironically, America's most dramatic victory came on January 8, 1815, two weeks after the treaty had been signed but before word of it had reached America. A British force had descended on New Orleans. U.S. troops commanded by General Andrew ("Old Hickory") Jackson, legendary as a fierce Indian fighter, shredded the line of advancing redcoats, inflicting more than 2,000 casualties while suffering only 13 of their own.

The Hartford Convention

Although it meant nothing in terms of the war, the Battle of New Orleans proved devastating for the Federalist party. The Federalists' comeback had continued into the election of 1812, when their candidate, DeWitt Clinton, an antiwar Republican, had carried all of New England except Vermont, along with New York and New Jersey. American military setbacks had intensified Federalist disdain for Madison. He seemed to epitomize a decade of Republican misrule at New England's expense. The Louisiana Purchase, constitutionally dubious, had reduced the importance of New England, the Embargo Act had nearly destroyed the region's commerce, and "Mr. Madison's War" had brought fresh misery in the form of the British blockade. A few New England Federalists began to talk of secession from the Union.

In late 1814 a special Federalist convention met in Hartford, Connecticut. Although some supported secession, moderates took control and passed a series of resolutions expressing New England's grievances. Convinced that New England was becoming a permanent minority in a nation dominated by southern Republicans who failed to understand the region's commercial interests, the

---

* *Status quo ante bellum:* Latin for "the state of affairs before the war."

convention leaders proposed a series of constitutional amendments: to abolish the three-fifths clause, which allowed southerners to count slaves as a basis for representation; to require a two-thirds vote of Congress to declare war and to admit new states into the Union; to limit the president to a single term; to prohibit the election of two successive presidents from the same state; and to bar embargoes lasting more than sixty days. These proposals were as bold as their timing was disastrous. News of the peace and of Jackson's victory at New Orleans dashed Federalist hopes of gaining popular support, while the states' rights emphasis of the convention smelled of treason to many delegates. The restoration of peace stripped the Federalists of their primary grievance. In the presidential election of 1816, James Monroe, Madison's hand-picked successor and another Virginia Republican, swept the nation over negligible Federalist opposition. Four years later he would receive every electoral vote but one. The Federalists were finished as a force in national politics.

THE AWAKENING OF AMERICAN NATIONALISM

The United States emerged from the War of 1812 bruised but intact. In its first major war since independence, the American republic had demonstrated that it could fight on even terms against a major power and that republics could conduct wars without becoming despots. The war also produced several major symbols of American nationalism: the presidential mansion, whitewashed to hide smoke damage, became the White House; Britain's failed attack on Fort McHenry in Baltimore Harbor inspired Francis Scott Key's "Star-Spangled Banner"; and the Battle of New Orleans made Andrew Jackson a national hero and reinforced legends about the prowess of American frontier people and their "long rifles." Much of the legend spun around the Battle of New Orleans was untrue, but Americans loved it nonetheless, especially because it confirmed their conviction that amateur soldiers and militiamen could outfight a professional army.

Madison's Nationalism and the Era of Good Feelings, 1817–1824

The War of 1812 had three major political consequences. First, it eliminated the Federalists as a national political force. Second, it went far toward convincing the Republicans that the nation was strong and resilient, capable of fighting a war while maintaining liberty. Third, with political rivals removed, the Republicans began to embrace some Federalist ideas. Both President Madison and Henry Clay became advocates of federal support for internal improvements, tariff protection for new industries, and the creation of a new national bank; Clay christened these ideas the American System and proclaimed that they would make the nation economically self-sufficient. In 1816 Congress chartered the Second Bank of the United States and enacted a moderate tariff, but federally supported internal improvements were more difficult. Madison vetoed an internal improvements bill in 1817, believing that a constitutional amendment was necessary to authorize such improvements.

As Republicans adopted positions they once had disdained, an "Era of Good Feelings" dawned. Coined by a Boston newspaper editor, the term describes both of James Monroe's presidential administrations. Compared to Jefferson and Madison, Monroe was neither brilliant, polished, nor wealthy, but he wanted to heal America's political divisions, and he tried to avoid political controversies. Yet the good feelings were paper-thin, and Madison's veto of the internal improvements bill showed that disagreements lingered about the role of the federal government under the Constitution. The continuation of slavery was arousing sectional animosities that no phrase could paper over. Not surprisingly, the postwar consensus unraveled rapidly.

John Marshall and the Supreme Court

In 1819 Jefferson's old antagonist John Marshall, still chief justice, issued two opinions that stunned Republicans. The first case, *Dartmouth College* v. *Woodward*, focused on New Hampshire's attempt to transform a private corporation, Dartmouth College, into a state university. Marshall concluded that Dartmouth's original charter was a contract and thus was protected under the constitutional prohibition against state interference in contracts. Marshall's ruling had enormous implications. In effect, Marshall said that once a state had chartered a college or business, that state surrendered its power to alter the charter and, in large measure, its authority to regulate the beneficiary.

A few weeks later the chief justice handed down an even more momentous decision in *McCulloch* v. *Maryland.* At issue was whether the state of Maryland had the power to tax a national corporation, specifically the Baltimore branch of the Second Bank of the United States. Marshall focused on two issues. First, did Congress have power to charter a national bank? The Constitution, Marshall conceded, did not explicitly grant this power, but the broad sweep of enumerated powers implied the power to charter a bank. This was a clear enunciation of a broad, or "loose," construction (interpretation) of the Constitution. The second issue revolved around whether a state could tax an agency of the federal government that was located within its borders. Marshall argued that any power of the national government, enumerated or implied, was supreme within its sphere. States could not interfere with the exercise of federal power; thus Maryland's attempt to tax the bank was plainly unconstitutional.

The *McCulloch* decision dismayed many Republicans. The bank, initially supported by Madison and Monroe, had triggered the Panic of 1819 by tightening credit. Distressed western farmers angrily blamed the bank for their dilemmas. And now Marshall's decision placed the hated bank beyond the reach of any state government. The Constitution, Marshall said, was the creation not of state governments but of the people of *all* the states and thus overrode state laws. The decision was as much an attack on state sovereignty as a defense of the bank itself.

Like Jefferson, most Republicans considered the Union a compact among states and saw state governments as the guarantors of popular liberty. In Republican eyes, the *Dartmouth* and *McCulloch* cases stripped state governments of the power to impose the will of their people on corporations and thus threatened liberty.

The Missouri Compromise, 1820–1821

The controversy over statehood for Missouri highlighted the fragility of the Era of Good Feelings. Carved from the Louisiana Purchase, Missouri had attracted many southerners who expected to use slaves to grow cotton and hemp. By 1819 slaves made up 16 percent of the territory's inhabitants. Three slave states—Louisiana, Mississippi, and Alabama—had already been created out of the Louisiana Purchase without controversy. Missouri would be very different.

In February 1819 the House of Representatives considered a bill to admit Missouri as a slave state. A New York Republican offered an amendment that prohibited the further introduction of slaves into Missouri and provided for the emancipation, at age twenty-five, of all slave offspring born after Missouri joined the Union. Following rancorous debate, the House accepted the amendment and the Senate rejected it. Both chambers voted along sectional lines.

Virtually every issue that would wrack the Union in the next forty years was present in the Missouri controversy: southern charges that the North was conspiring to destroy the Union and to end slavery; northern accusations that southerners were conspiring to extend slavery. For a while

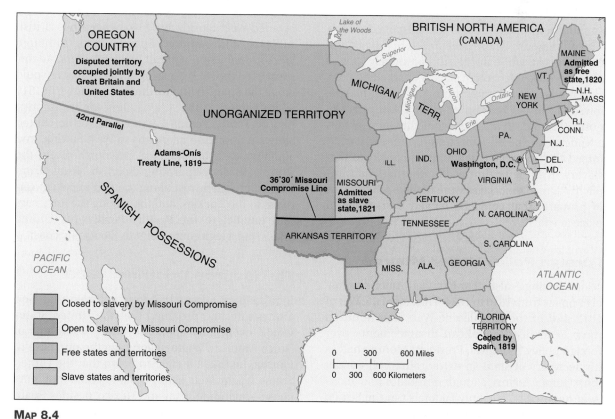

MAP 8.4
The Missouri Compromise, 1820–1821
The Missouri Compromise temporarily quelled controversy over slavery by admitting Maine as a free state and Missouri as a slave state and by prohibiting slavery in the remainder of the Louisiana Purchase north of 36°30'.

leaders doubted that the Union would survive the crisis; the words *disunion* and *civil war* were freely uttered, Henry Clay wrote.

A series of congressional agreements known collectively as the Missouri Compromise resolved the crisis. To balance the number of slave states and free states, Congress in 1820 admitted Maine as a free state and Missouri as a slave state; to forestall a further crisis, it also prohibited slavery in the remainder of the Louisiana Purchase north of 36°30', Missouri's southern border. An attempt by Missourians to bar free blacks from entering the territory nearly undid the compromise, but in 1821 a second Missouri Compromise opened the way for Missouri's admission by prohibiting Missouri from discriminating against citizens of other states, without stating whether free blacks were citizens.

The Missouri Compromise was widely viewed as a southern victory. The South had gained admission of Missouri, whose acceptance of slavery was controversial, while the North had merely gained Maine, whose rejection of slavery sparked no controversy. But at the same time, the South had allowed slavery to be banned from a vast territory north of 36°30´, an area that would not long remain a wilderness. The Missouri Compromise also reinforced the principle that Congress could prohibit slavery in some territories. Southerners had implicitly agreed that slaves were not like other forms of property that could be moved from place to place at will.

Foreign Policy Under Monroe

"Good feelings" also characterized American foreign policy from 1816 to 1824. The end of the War of 1812 and of the Napoleonic Wars had removed most Federalist-Republican disagreements over foreign policy. Moreover, President Monroe had as his secretary of state an extraordinary diplomat, John Quincy Adams, a tough negotiator and an ardent nationalist. The only Federalist in the Senate to support the Louisiana Purchase and the son of the last Federalist president, Adams had backed the embargo, joined the Republican party, and helped to negotiate the Treaty of Ghent.

Adams moved quickly to strengthen the peace with Great Britain. During his term the Rush-Bagot Treaty of 1817 demilitarized the Great Lakes and the British-American Convention of 1818 fixed the Canadian-American boundary and restored U.S. fishing rights off Newfoundland. With its northern border secure, the United States could turn its attention southward and westward.

Adams was equally successful with the Spanish, who still owned East Florida and claimed West Florida. It had never been clear whether the Louisiana Purchase included West Florida. Acting as if it did, the United States in 1812 had simply added a slice of West Florida to the state of Louisiana and another piece to the Mississippi Territory. Using the pretext that it was a base for Seminole Indian raids and a refuge for fugitive slaves, Andrew Jackson, now a military commander in the South, invaded West Florida in 1818, hanged two British subjects, and captured Spanish forts. Although Jackson had acted without explicit orders, Adams supported the raid, guessing correctly that it would panic the Spanish into further concessions. In 1819 Spain agreed to the Adams-Onís (or Transcontinental) Treaty, ceding East Florida to the United States, renouncing all claims to West Florida, and agreeing to a border that ran north along the Sabine River (separating Spanish Texas from Louisiana), then west along the Red and Arkansas rivers to the Rockies, and then along the forty-second parallel to the Pacific. Finally, the United States had a legitimate claim to the Pacific coast.

The Monroe Doctrine, 1823

John Quincy Adams had long believed that God and nature had ordained that the United States would eventually span the entire continent of North America. While negotiating the purchase of Florida, he made it clear to Spain that the United States might well seize what it could not purchase—including Texas and Mexico. Besides, Spain had other pressing concerns, primarily anticolonial revolutions that had erupted in South America. The failing imperial power sought aid in crushing the revolts from the Holy Alliance, which had

Chronology

1801	Thomas Jefferson's inauguration.		**1813**	Battle of the Thames.
1802	Repeal of the Judiciary Act of 1801. Yazoo land compromise.		**1814**	British burn Washington, D.C. Hartford Convention. Treaty of Ghent signed.
1803	*Marbury* v. *Madison.* Conclusion of the Louisiana Purchase.		**1815**	Battle of New Orleans.
1804	Impeachment of Justice Samuel Chase. Aaron Burr kills Alexander Hamilton in a duel. Jefferson elected to a second term.		**1816**	James Monroe elected president. Second Bank of the United States chartered.
1804–1806	Lewis and Clark expedition.		**1817**	Rush-Bagot Treaty.
1805	British court declares broken voyages illegal.		**1818**	British-American Convention of 1818 sets U.S.–Canada border in West. Andrew Jackson invades East Florida.
1807	*Chesapeake* affair. Embargo Act passed.		**1819**	Adams-Onís (Transcontinental) Treaty. *Dartmouth College* v. *Woodward.* *McCulloch* v. *Maryland.*
1808	James Madison elected president.		**1820**	Monroe elected to a second term.
1809	Non-Intercourse Act passed; Embargo Act repealed.		**1820–1821**	Missouri Compromise.
1810	Macon's Bill No. 2.		**1823**	Monroe Doctrine.
1811	Battle of Tippecanoe.			
1812	United States declares war on Britain. Madison reelected to a second term. General William Hull surrenders at Detroit. Battle of Queenston.			

been formed in Europe in 1815 to quash revolutions in the name of Christian principles. However, Britain had not joined the alliance. Its foreign minister, George Canning, now proposed a joint U.S.-British statement opposing European interference in South America and pledging that neither nation would annex any part of Spain's New World empire.

Adams shared Canning's opposition to European intervention in the New World, but rejected his insistence on a joint Anglo-American pledge never to annex any of Spain's former territories. The American secretary of state wanted to keep open the possibility of annexing Texas or Cuba.

This was the background of the Monroe Doctrine, as President Monroe's message to Congress on December 2, 1823, became known. Largely written by Adams, the message announced three key principles: that U.S. policy was to avoid European wars unless American interests were involved, that the "American continents" were not "subjects for future colonization by any European power," and that the United States would construe any European attempt at colonization as an "unfriendly act."

Europeans widely derided the Monroe Doctrine as a unilateral pronouncement by a United States that could not enforce it. Fear of Britain's Royal Navy, not the Monroe Doctrine, prevented European intervention in South America. Nonetheless, the doctrine had two major implications. First, in pledging not to interfere in European wars, the United States in effect declined to support any future revolutionary movements in Europe. Second, by keeping open options to annex territory in the Americas itself, the United States was claiming for itself a preeminent position in the New World.

CONCLUSION *hc* ACE Practice Test

Jefferson's philosophy left a strong imprint on his age. He had moved quickly to slash federal spending and contest Federalist control of the judiciary. His purchase of Louisiana reflected his view that American liberty depended on the perpetuation of agriculture. As the Federalist party waned, Jefferson had to face down challenges from his own party: the mischief of Aaron Burr and the charge from die-hard old Republicans that he was abandoning pure Republican principles.

After 1803 the Napoleonic Wars and the threat to American neutrality preoccupied Jefferson and his Republican successors, Madison and Monroe. The War of 1812 destroyed the Federalists, who committed political suicide at the Hartford Convention, and led Madison to call for a new national bank, federal support for internal improvements, and protective tariffs. The Monroe Doctrine warning Europeans not to meddle in the Western Hemisphere expressed America's increasingly assertive nationalism.

Conflict bubbled just below the surface throughout the Era of Good Feelings. Lacking Federalist opposition, the Republicans began to fragment into sectional factions, especially in the conflict over Missouri.

FURTHER READING

Stephen Ambrose, *Undaunted Courage* (1997). Fine new study of the Lewis and Clark expedition.

Joseph J. Ellis, *American Sphinx: The Character of Thomas Jefferson* (1997). A prize-winning attempt to unravel Jefferson's complex character.

Jan Ellen Lewis and Peter S. Onuf, eds., *Sally Hemings and Thomas Jefferson* (1999). An excellent compilation of current scholarship on the relationship between Jefferson and Sally Hemings.

Drew R. McCoy, *The Last of the Fathers: James Madison and the Republican Legacy* (1989). The best recent book on Madison.

Merrill Peterson, *Thomas Jefferson and the New Nation: A Biography* (1970). The best one-volume biography of Jefferson.

J. C. A. Stagg, *Mr. Madison's War: Politics, Diplomacy, and Warfare in the Early Republic* (1983). An important reinterpretation of the causes of the War of 1812.

John Sugden, *Tecumseh: A Life* (1997). A biography that illuminates the culture of the western Indians as they fought the Americans' advance.

Edward White, *The Marshall Court and Cultural Change, 1815–1835* (1991). A seminal reinterpretation of the Supreme Court under John Marshall.

9

Color Panorama of Detroit

The Transformation of American Society, 1815–1840

CHAPTER OUTLINE

Westward Expansion

The Growth of the Market Economy

Industrial Beginnings

Equality and Inequality

The Revolution in Social Relationships

 This icon will direct you to additional study and research resources at http://college.hmco.com/history/us/boyer/enduring_concise/5e/students/index.html

T he years 1815 to 1840 saw rapid, often disorienting changes that affected both those who followed the frontier westward and those who stayed in the East. A revolution in transportation stimulated interregional trade and migration and encouraged an unprecedented development of towns and cities. The new urban dwellers provided a market not only for agricultural produce but also for the manufactures of the industries springing up in New England and major northeastern cities.

Viewed superficially, these changes might seem to have had little effect on the way Americans lived. Whether in 1815 or in 1840, most Americans dwelled outside the cities, practiced agriculture for a living, and traveled on foot or by

This chapter focuses on five major questions:

▶ What caused the upsurge of westward migration after the War of 1812?

▶ What changes were linked to the rise of the market economy?

▶ How did the rise of canals affect where Americans lived and how they made their living?

▶ What caused the rise of industrialization?

▶ How did the rise of the market economy and industrialization change relationships within families and communities?

horse. In 1831 two young Frenchmen, Alexis de Tocqueville and Gustave de Beaumont, arrived in the United States, ostensibly to prepare a report on American prisons but actually to learn as much as they could about the "half-civilized, half-wild" American republic. Tocqueville's two-volume *Democracy in America*, published in 1835 and 1840, is still considered a masterpiece of insight into the American character.

Tocqueville and Beaumont had come at a time when everything seemed to be changing for these restless Americans, who appeared to live in the middle of "an always moving stream." Improvements in transportation were stimulating interregional trade and migration to the trans-Appalachian west, encouraging an unprecedented development of towns and cities, and transforming social relationships. Farmers increasingly raised crops to sell in distant markets, while the new urban dwellers formed a market for farm products as well as the products of the new factories that were springing up in the industrializing East.

To Tocqueville, Americans seemed to have only one goal: "that of getting rich." White Americans were an industrious and democratic people, but they treated nonwhites harshly. While recognizing slavery as a blot on American society, Tocqueville noted that whites treated each other as equals and that they all shared a passion for getting ahead.

WESTWARD EXPANSION

In 1790 the vast majority of the non-Indian population of the United States lived east of the Appalachian Mountains; by 1840 one-third were living between the Appalachians and the Mississippi River, defined as the West. These Americans rapidly developed a distinctive western culture.

A handful of Americans moved west for adventure, and these few usually headed to and beyond the Rocky Mountains. Most, however, came west dreaming of a better version of the life they had known in the East. Several factors fed this dream: the growing power of the federal government; its often ruthless removal of Indians from the path of white settlements; and a boom in the prices of agricultural commodities.

The Sweep West

This westward movement occurred in several thrusts. Americans leapfrogged the Appalachians after 1791 to bring four new states into the Union by 1803: Vermont, Kentucky, Tennessee, and Ohio. From 1816 to 1821 momentum carried settlers farther west, even across the Mississippi River, and six more states entered: Indiana, Mississippi, Illinois, Alabama, Maine, and Missouri. Ohio's population soared from 45,000 in 1800 to more than 1.5 million by 1840, and Michigan's from 5,000 in 1810 to 212,000 in 1840.

Pioneers usually migrated as families. In order to get their crops to markets, at first most clustered along the Ohio-Mississippi River system. Only when canals spread in the 1820s and 1830s did they venture any distance from rivers. In addition, pioneers often clustered with people who hailed from the same region back east. For example, when New Englanders found southerners already well entrenched in Indiana, they chose to settle in Michigan.

Western Society and Customs

These new westerners craved sociability. Even before towns sprang up, farm families joined their neighbors for sports and festivities. Men met for games that tested strength and agility: wrestling, lifting weights, pole jumping (for distance, not height), and hammer throwing. The games could be brutal. In gander pulling, riders competed to pull the head off a gander whose neck had been stripped of feathers and greased. Women usually combined work and play in quilting and sewing bees, carpet tackings, and even goose and chicken pluckings. At "hoedowns" and "frolics," the settlers danced to a fiddler's tune.

Western farm households usually practiced a clear gender division of labor. Men performed the heavy work such as cutting down trees and plowing fields. Women cooked, spun and wove, sewed, milked, and tended their large families. They also often helped with the butchering—slitting the hog's throat while it was still alive, bleeding it, scooping out the innards, washing the heart and liver, and hanging the organs to dry. Daintiness had been left behind, east of the mountains.

Most western sports and customs were eastern transplants, but the West developed a character of its own. Eastern elegance yielded to western lack of refinement—and made westerners targets for easterners' contemptuous jibes.

Westerners responded that they at least were honest democrats, not soft would-be aristocrats. Pretension got short shrift. A sojourner at a tavern who hung a blanket to cover his bed from public gaze might find it ripped down, a woman who sought privacy in a crowded room might be dismissed as "uppity," and a politician who came to a rally in a buggy, rather than on horseback, might lose votes.

The Far West

Exploration carried some Americans even farther west. Zebulon Pike explored the Spanish Southwest in 1806, sighting the Colorado peak later named after him. By 1811, in the wake of Lewis and Clark, the New York merchant John Jacob Astor had founded a fur-trading post at the mouth of the Columbia River in the Oregon Country. At first whites relied on the Native Americans for furs, but in the 1820s such "mountain men" as Kit Carson and Jedediah Smith penetrated deep beyond the Rockies.

Smith typified these men and their exploits. Originally from western New York, he had moved west as far as Illinois by 1822. That year he signed on with an expedition bound for the upper Missouri River. In the course of this and later explorations, Smith nearly fell victim to a grizzly bear in South Dakota's Black Hills, crossed the Mojave Desert into California and explored the San Joaquin Valley, and hiked back across the Sierras and the Great Basin to the Great Salt Lake, a forbidding trip. His thirst for adventure led to his early death at the hands of Comanche Indians in 1831.

The Federal Government and the West

The federal government's growing strength spurred westward expansion. Under the Articles of Confederation, several states had ceded western lands to the national government, creating a bountiful public domain. The Land Ordinance of 1785 had provided for the survey and sale of these lands, and the Northwest Ordinance of 1787 had established a mechanism for transforming them into states. The Louisiana Purchase had brought the entire Mississippi River under American control, and the Adams-Onís Treaty had wiped out the remnants of Spanish control east of the Mississippi. Six million acres of public land had been promised to volunteers during the War of 1812. The National Road, a highway begun in 1811 in Cumberland, Maryland, stretched farther westward, reaching Wheeling, Virginia, in 1818 and Vandalia, Illinois, by 1838. People crowded along it. One traveler wrote, "We are seldom out of sight, as we travel on this grand track toward the Ohio, of family groups before and behind us."

The same governmental strength that aided whites brought misery to the Indians. Virtually all the foreign policy successes of the Republicans

Barroom Dancing by John Lewis Krimmel, 1820
We can only guess what George Washington, looking soberly down from the wall, would have thought of these tipsy celebrants at a country tavern.

worked to the Native Americans' disadvantage. The Louisiana Purchase and Adams-Onís Treaty had stripped them of Spanish protection, and the War of 1812 had deprived them of British protection. Lewis and Clark bluntly told the Indians that they should "shut their ears up to the counsels of bad birds" and listen only to the Great White Father in Washington.

The Removal of the Indians

Westward-moving white settlers found in their path sizable numbers of Native Americans, especially in the South, home to the "Five Civilized Tribes"—the Cherokees, Creeks, Choctaws, Chickasaws, and Seminoles. Years of commercial dealings and intermarriage with Europeans had created in these tribes influential minorities of mixed-bloods who had embraced Christianity and agriculture. The Cherokees had adopted Anglo-American culture to a greater extent than any other tribe. Among them were farmers, millers, and even

slave owners; they also had a written form of their language, written laws, and their own bilingual newspaper, the *Cherokee Phoenix*.

Such "civilization" had little effect on southern whites, who viewed the Civilized Tribes with contempt and their lands with envy. A handful of tribes had sold their lands to the federal government and accepted removal west of the Mississippi River by 1830, but most clung to their land and customs. They wanted to remain near the burial grounds of their ancestors. When the Creek mixed-blood chief William McIntosh sold most of the Indians' land to the federal government, the tribal council executed him.

In the 1820s white squatters moved onto tribal lands; southern legislatures, loath to restrain white settlers, moved to expropriate Indian lands. State laws extended state jurisdiction over the tribes and excluded Indians from serving as witnesses in court cases involving whites, which effectively made it virtually impossible for Indians to collect debts owed them by whites.

President Andrew Jackson relished such measures. Himself a frontiersman contemptuous of Native Americans, Jackson believed that the tribes must be subject to the laws of the states, not exist as independent nations. Jackson's belief that Indians should be subject to state laws spelled doom for the Indians, who could neither vote nor hold office. In 1834 Cherokee chief John Ross got a taste of what that meant: Georgia, without consulting him, put his house up as a prize in the state lottery.

In 1830 President Jackson secured passage of the Indian Removal Act, authorizing him to exchange western territory for tribal lands. The real costs of removal were much greater. During Jackson's eight years in office, the federal government forced Indians to exchange 100 million acres of their eastern lands for 32 million acres of public lands. The Choctaws, Creeks, and Chickasaws began their "voluntary" migration in the late 1820s. In

1836 Creeks who clung to their homes were forcibly removed, often in chains. The bitter war to remove the Seminoles from their Florida lands lasted seven years and cost the federal government $20 million.

Ironically, the Cherokees, often considered the "most civilized" tribe, suffered the most. Pursuing their claims before the Supreme Court, they won two favorable decisions from Chief Justice John Marshall. In *Cherokee Nation* v. *Georgia* (1831), Marshall recognized the Cherokees as a "domestic dependent nation" with a legitimate claim to their lands in Georgia. A year later, in *Worcester* v. *Georgia*, Marshall declared them a "distinct" political community entitled to federal protection against Georgia's claims.

President Andrew Jackson reportedly sneered, "John Marshall has made his decision; now let him enforce it," and ignored the ruling. Then in 1835

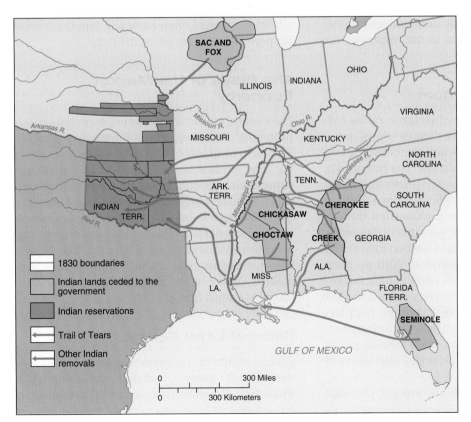

MAP 9.1

The Removal of the Native Americans to the West, 1820–1840

The so-called Trail of Tears, followed by the Cherokees, was one of several routes along which various tribes migrated on their forced removal to reservations west of the Mississippi.

hc Interactive Map: Removal of Native Americans

the U.S. government negotiated the fraudulent Treaty of New Echota with a handful of unauthorized individuals. It ceded most remaining Cherokee lands to the United States for $5.6 million and the Indians' transportation west. The principal signers were killed by other Cherokees in 1839, but by then the tribe's fate was sealed. Sixteen thousand Cherokees straggled west to the Indian Territory between 1835 and 1838 along the so-called Trail of Tears. A total of perhaps 4,000 died along the trail itself and within a year of the initial roundup and hard journey.

Indians in the Northwest Territory fared no better after they signed land-cession treaties. Two uprisings marked their westward removal. The first was quickly crushed, but the second, led by a Sac and Fox chief, Black Hawk, raged along the frontier in Illinois until federal troops and state militiamen virtually annihilated the Indians in 1832. After Black Hawk's defeat, the other northwestern tribes agreed to removal. Between 1832 and 1837 the United States consequently acquired nearly 190 million acres of Indian land in the Northwest for $70 million.

The Agricultural Boom

In clearing the Indians from their territory, the federal government was responding to whites' pressures for land. Depleted soil and overcrowding had long driven farmers west, but after the War of 1812 soaring agricultural commodity prices and rising demand for western foodstuffs sharpened the land hunger. England and France, exhausted by war, were importing substantial amounts of American wheat and corn; New England needed food for its burgeoning industrial population. With produce prices skyrocketing, western farmers took advantage of the Ohio-Mississippi river system to ship their grain to foreign markets through New Orleans. In short, federal Indian policy, although devastating to Native Americans, made farming possible in the West, and high prices and high demand made it attractive.

Cotton, and Eli Whitney's cotton gin, provided the impetus for settlement of the Old Southwest, especially Alabama and Mississippi. Indeed, the explosive westward thrust of southern farmers and planters after the War of 1812 resembled a gold rush. By 1817 land prices had shot up from $30 to $50 an acre. By 1820 Alabama and Mississippi produced half the nation's cotton. With a seemingly unlimited British market for raw cotton, production tripled between 1816 and 1831. Between 1831 and 1836 the value of cotton exports rose 300 percent, and cotton accounted for two-thirds of U.S. exports.

THE GROWTH OF THE MARKET ECONOMY

The high prices of agricultural commodities such as wheat and cotton tempted a growing number of farmers to add a cash crop, thus venturing into commercial agriculture or the market economy. In the South, the sale of slaves from older states to the new cotton belt accelerated rapidly after 1815. However, farmers often launched into the market economy without weighing the risks.

The Risks of the Market Economy

The new commercial farmers encountered serious problems, including wildly fluctuating markets. They also routinely had to borrow money to cover the long interval between harvest and sale. Thus commercial agriculture forced farmers to accept short-term debt in hope of reaping long-term profits. This debt was frequently worse than expected, particularly because many western farmers had also borrowed money to buy their land. The root of this indebtedness was the federal government's inability to figure how to transfer the public domain directly to small farmers.

Federal Land Policy

Federal efforts in this period to put the public domain into the hands of small farmers floundered. In the face of partisan and sectional pressures, the federal government passed various land laws in quick succession, each intended to undo the damage caused by its predecessors.

During the 1790s politics undermined the expectations of the framers of the Ordinance of 1785. The ordinance had aimed to ensure the orderly settlement of the public domain by creating townships of thirty-six square miles, divided into 640-acre sections. Because ordinary farmers could not afford such large purchases, the assumption was that they would pool their money to buy sections. It was also assumed that a population of compatible settlers living on adjoining lots would be easier to govern than one of isolated settlers on scattered homesteads. Federalists, with their political base in the East, were reluctant to encourage western settlement. They were, nevertheless, eager to sell land in order to raise revenue for the government. They reconciled their conflicting goals by selling huge tracts of land to speculators who waited for its value to rise and then sold off parcels to farmers. A federal land law of 1796 reflected Federalist goals by setting the minimum purchase at 640 acres at $2 an acre and allowing only one year for payment. Few small farmers could buy that much land at that price.

Jefferson and the Republicans, sure that the small farmer was the backbone of the Republic, took a different tack. The land law of 1800 dropped the minimum purchase to 320 acres and allowed up to four years for payment. By 1832 the minimum purchase had shrunk to 40 acres and the price to $1.25 an acre.

Long before then, speculators were already selling land in 40-acre parcels, a size that the small farmer could handle both financially and physically. The land they purchased was usually forested, and a new landowner could clear only 10 to 12 acres a year.

The growing availability of credit after the War of 1812 fed speculation. The chartering of the Second Bank of the United States in 1816 increased the amount of money in circulation and stimulated the growth of state banks. Between 1812 and 1817 bank notes in circulation soared from $45 million to $100 million. Stockholders and officers saw banks less as investments than as agencies that could lend them money for land speculation. The result was an orgy

of speculation; by 1819 the dollar value of sales of public lands was more than 1,000 percent greater than the average from 1800 to 1814.

The Speculator and the Squatter

Despite these problems, most of the public domain found its way into the hands of small farmers. The desire to recoup investments led speculators to sell quickly, as did the proliferation of squatters.

Squatters had long helped themselves to western land. Proud and independent, they hated land speculators and pressured Congress to allow "preemption" rights—that is, the right to purchase at the minimum price the land that they already lived on and had improved. After passing a series of limited preemption laws, Congress acknowledged a general right of preemption in 1841.

But these laws were of little use to farmers who had to purchase land from speculators. For them, interest rates ranged as high as 40 percent. Many western farmers, drowning in debt, had to skimp on food and plant cash crops in the hope of paying off creditors. Having moved west to fulfill dreams of self-sufficiency, they found themselves caught in the cash-crop economy, which quickly exhausted their land and forced them to move farther westward in search of new land. Abraham Lincoln's parents, who migrated from the East through several farms in Kentucky and then to Indiana, typified this "moving frontier."

The Panic of 1819

In 1819 the land boom collapsed like a house of cards, the victim of a financial panic. State banks' loose practices played a major role in causing the panic. These state banks issued their own bank notes, little more than a promise to pay the bearer a certain amount of specie (gold and silver coin) on demand. Such notes were plentiful and had helped fuel the land boom after 1815. Farmers also borrowed to buy more land and plant more crops, certain that sales to Europe would enable them to repay loans. But even as American farmers were becoming more dependent on agricultural exports to repay their debts, bumper crops in Europe combined with an economic slump in England to trim foreign demand for U.S. crops.

The result was a cascade of economic catastrophes. In the summer of 1819 the Bank of the United States, holder of large amounts of state bank paper, began to insist that the state banks redeem this paper in specie. To pay these debts, state banks demanded that farmers and land speculators repay their loans—in specie. Credit contracted sharply throughout the nation, particularly in the West.

Land speculators suffered as credit dried up and land prices tumbled. Hard-pressed farmers could not pay their debts, speculators could not collect their money, and land values collapsed. Land speculators were the biggest losers as land prices plummeted from nearly $70 an acre to barely $2. Prices for commodities such as wheat, corn, cotton, and tobacco sank by 50 percent or more. Unable to get much cash for their crops, farmers were unable to pay the speculators for the land they had bought, and land prices in general collapsed.

The significance of the Panic lay not only in its economic bite but also in the conclusions many Americans reached. First, the Panic left a bitter taste about banks, especially the Bank of the United States, widely blamed for the crash. Second, it demonstrated how dependent farmers had become on distant markets and the extent to which farmers had become entrepreneurs. This in turn accelerated the search for better, cheaper ways to get crops to market.

The Transportation Revolution: Steamboats, Canals, and Railroads

The transportation systems available in 1820 had serious weaknesses. The great rivers west of the Appalachians ran primarily north to south and hence could not by themselves connect western farmers to eastern markets. Roads were expensive to maintain, and horse-drawn wagons were slow and limited in range. Consequently, after 1820 attention and investment shifted to the development of waterways.

In 1807 Robert R. Livingston and Robert Fulton introduced the steamboat *Clermont* on the Hudson River. They soon gained a monopoly from the New York legislature to run a New York–New Jersey ferry service. Spectacular profits lured competitors, who secured a license from Congress and then filed suit to break the Livingston-Fulton monopoly. In 1824 Chief Justice John Marshall handed down his decision in what was known as the *Gibbons* v. *Ogden* case. Marshall ruled that Article I, Section 8, of the Constitution, which empowered Congress to regulate interstate commerce, applied to navigation as well. In this case, he wrote, the power of Congress to regulate interstate commerce had to prevail over the power of New York; thus the Livingston-Fulton monopoly was void. In the aftermath of this decision, other state-granted monopolies collapsed and steamboat traffic increased rapidly. The number of steamboats operating on western rivers jumped from 17 in 1817 to 727 by 1855.

Steamboats assumed a vital role along the Mississippi-Ohio river system. They were far more useful than rafts, which journeyed only one way, or keelboats, which took up to four months to travel upstream from New Orleans to Louisville; in 1817 a steamboat made the identical trip in just twenty-five days. The development of long, shallow hulls permitted navigation of the Mississippi-Ohio system even when hot, dry summers lowered the river level. Steamboats became more ornate as well as more practical, offering luxurious cabins and lounges, called saloons. The immense saloon of one steamboat, the *Eclipse,* featured skylights, chandeliers, and velvet-covered mahogany furniture.

While steamboats proved their value, canals replaced roads and turnpikes as the focus of popular enthusiasm and financial speculation. Although the cost of canal construction was mind-boggling—Jefferson dismissed the idea of canals as "little short of madness"—canals offered the possibility of connecting the Mississippi-Ohio system with the Great Lakes and even the East Coast.

A canal boom followed the completion in 1825 of the Erie Canal, which stretched 363 miles from Buffalo to Albany. For example, Ohio built a network of canals that enabled farmers to ship wheat by water to Lake Erie; the wheat was then shipped to Rochester for milling and finally traveled via the Erie Canal and the Hudson River to New York City. Shipping costs via the canal network were 10 percent of costs via road.

Railroads soon were competing with canals and gradually overtook them. In 1825 the first railroad for general transportation began operation in England. The new technology quickly reached the United States, and by 1840 there were 3,000 miles of railroad track, equal to the total canal mileage. Faster, cheaper to build, and able to reach more places, railroads enjoyed obvious advantages over canals, but Americans realized their potential only slowly.

Early railroads connected eastern cities rather than crossing the mountains and carried more passengers than freight. Not until 1849 did freight revenue exceed passenger revenue, and not until 1850 did railroads link the East Coast to Lake Erie. There were two main reasons for this slow pace of development. First, unlike canals, most railroads were built by private companies that tended to skimp on costs, as a result producing lines requiring constant repair. In contrast, canals needed little maintenance. Second, shipping bulky commodities such as iron, coal, and grain was cheaper by canal than by rail.

The Growth of the Cities

The transportation revolution accelerated the growth of towns and cities. Indeed, the forty years before the Civil War, 1820 to 1860, saw the most rapid urbanization in U.S. history. By 1860 New York City's population had rocketed from 124,000 to 800,000. Even more spectacular was the transformation of sleepy villages into bustling towns. For example, the Erie Canal turned Rochester, New York, from a small village into the Flour City, a boom town of 9,000 residents.

Urban growth was particularly fast in the West. The War of 1812 stimulated manufacturing and transformed villages into towns, as did the agricultural boom and the introduction of steamboats after 1815. Virtually all the major western cities were river ports. Of these, Pittsburgh, Cincinnati, Louisville, and New Orleans were the largest and most prominent. Pittsburgh was a manufacturing center, but the others were basically commercial hubs flooded by people eager to make money.

What the transportation revolution gave, it could also take away. The completion of the Erie Canal gradually shifted the center of western economic activity away from the river cities and toward the Great Lakes; Buffalo, Cleveland, Detroit, Chicago, and Milwaukee were the ultimate beneficiaries of the canal. In 1830 nearly 75 percent of western city dwellers lived in the river ports of New Orleans, Louisville, Cincinnati, and Pittsburgh, but by 1840 the proportion had dropped to 20 percent. The advent of modern manufacturing would multiply the effect of the transportation revolution on the growth of cities.

INDUSTRIAL BEGINNINGS

Industrialization gave an added boost to the growth of cities and towns. Americans sought to counter Britain's full generation lead in building factories in any way possible; Britain in turn banned the emigration of its skilled mechanics. However, one of those mechanics, Samuel Slater, was able to reach the United States in 1789. He helped design and build the first cotton mill in the United States the following year. The mill's work force mushroomed from nine to one hundred, and his mills multiplied. The pace of industrialization quickened in the 1810s and 1820s, especially in cotton textiles and shoes.

Industrialization was uneven. There was little in the South, where planters preferred to invest in land and slaves, and much in New England, where poor soil made agriculture an even poorer investment. Generally, industrialization involved three steps: the subdivision of tasks, the gathering of workers in large factories, and the use of high-speed machines to replace handwork.

Industrialization changed lives. Many benefited from industrialization, as former luxury goods became cheaper. And while cheap machine-made goods brought luxuries within the reach of working people, they also undermined skilled artisans. Most early factory workers were recruited from farms, where they had set their own pace and taken breaks as tasks were completed. In contrast, machines and the clock dictated the factory worker's pace. Finally, industrialization led to specialization; farmers could now concentrate on farming and buy clothes, shoes, and other products they had previously made.

Causes of Industrialization

Multiple factors stimulated industrialization. Merchants barred from foreign trade by the Embargo Act of 1807 redirected their capital into factories. After the War of 1812, acceptance of tariffs was widespread. Protected from foreign competition, New England's textile output rose from 4 million yards in 1817 to 323 million yards by 1840. And the transportation revolution gave manufacturers easier access to markets in the South and West.

Problems in New England's rural economy also stimulated industrialization. Many farm families had always engaged in small-scale manufacturing, and many of these gradually deserted farming worn-out soils for full-time manufacturing.

Technology played a major role. Confronted with a chronic labor shortage, Americans copied English machines or invented their own. For example, Eli Whitney, inventor of the cotton gin, gained a government contract to produce ten thousand muskets within a two-year period by using interchangeable parts. Although Whitney missed his deadline by more than a decade, his idea captured the imagination of many American leaders and foreshadowed the rise of a full-scale industrial economy.

Textile Towns in New England

New England became America's first industrial region. The trade wars leading up to the War of 1812 had devastated the Northeast's traditional economy and stimulated capital investment in manufacturing. New England's many swift-flowing rivers were ideal sources of waterpower for mills. The westward migration of New England's young men, unable to wrest a living from rocky soil, left a surplus of young women, who supplied cheap industrial labor. The establishment of the Boston Manufacturing Company in 1813 opened a new chapter in U.S. manufacturing. Backed by ample capital, the Boston Company built textile mills in the Massachusetts towns of Lowell and Waltham; by 1836 the company employed more than 6,000 workers.

Unlike Slater's mills, the Waltham and Lowell factories turned out more finished products, thus elbowing aside Slater's cottage industry. Slater had tried to preserve tradition by hiring entire families to work at his mills—the men to raise crops, the women and children to toil in the mills. In contrast, 80 percent of the workers in the Lowell and Waltham mills were unmarried women fifteen to thirty years old. Hired managers and company regulations, rather than families, provided discipline. Workers had to live in company boarding houses or approved private homes, attend Sabbath services, observe a 10 p.m. curfew, and accept the company's "moral police." These regulations were designed to give mills a good reputation so that families would continue to send their daughters to work there.

To prevent threads from snapping, the factories had to be kept humid; windows were nailed shut, and water was sprayed in the air. Flying dust and deafening noise were constant companions. In the 1830s conditions worsened as competition and recession led mill owners to reduce wages and speed up work schedules. The system's impersonality intensified the harshness of the work environment. Owners rarely visited factories; their agents, all men, gave orders to the workers, mainly women. In 1834 and again in 1836 women at the Lowell mills quit work to protest low wages. The largest strikes in American history to that point, they not only pitted workers against management but also women against men.

The size of the mills was not typical of industrial development in this era; as late as 1860, the average industrial establishment employed only eight workers. Outwork characterized most industries other than textiles. For example, prior to the introduction of sewing machines in the 1850s, women often sewed parts of shoes at home and then sent the piecework to factories for finishing.

New York and Philadelphia became major industrial centers, and their high population density made them especially suited to the piecework system. Instead of grouping workers in factories, middlemen subcontracted out tasks to widows, immigrants, and others who would fashion parts of shoes or saddles or dresses anywhere that light would enter.

Artisans and Workers in Mid-Atlantic Cities

The skilled artisans of New York City and Philadelphia tried to protect their interests by forming trade unions and "workingmen's" political parties. Initially, they sought to restore privileges and working conditions that artisans had once enjoyed, but gradually they joined forces with unskilled workers. When coal heavers in Philadelphia struck for a ten-hour day in 1835, carpenters, cigar makers, leather workers, and other artisans joined in what became the first general strike in the United States. The emergence of organized worker protests underscored the mixed blessings of economic development. Where some people prospered, others found their economic position deteriorating. By 1830 many Americans were questioning whether their nation was truly a land of equality.

Mill Girls
New England's humming textile mills were a magnet for untold numbers of independence-seeking young women in antebellum America.

EQUALITY AND INEQUALITY

Visitors to the United States sensed changes sweeping the country but could neither describe them nor agree on their direction. One of the most astute of these observers, the French nobleman Alexis de Tocqueville, whose *Democracy in America* (1835, 1840) is a classic, cited the "general equality of condition among the people" as the fundamental shaping force of American society. But Tocqueville also was keenly aware of inequalities in that society, inequalities less visible but no less real

than those in France. The United States might not have a permanent servant class, but it surely had its rich and its poor.

Even today historians disagree about the meaning and extent of inequality in antebellum (pre–Civil War) America. Nonetheless, we have a more detailed and complete understanding of that society than did its contemporaries, such as Tocqueville. The following discussion applies mainly to northern society; we examine the South's distinctive social structure in Chapter 12.

Growing Inequality: The Rich and the Poor

The gap between rich and poor continued to widen in the first half of the nineteenth century. Although striking inequalities separated rich and poor farmers, the inequalities were far greater in the cities, where a small fraction of the people owned a huge share of the wealth. In Boston the richest 4 percent of the people owned almost 70 percent of the wealth by 1848, whereas 81 percent of the population owned only 4 percent of the wealth. New York and other major cities mirrored these statistics.

hc Primary Source: Robert Owen's Alternative

Although commentators celebrated the self-made man and his rise "from rags to riches," few actually fit this pattern. Less than 5 percent of the wealthy had started life poor; almost 90 percent of well-off people had been born rich. Clearly, the old-fashioned way to wealth was to inherit it, to marry more of it, and to invest it wisely. Occasional rags-to-riches stories like that of John Jacob Astor and his fur-trading empire sustained the myth, but it was mainly a myth.

Splendid residences and social clubs also set the rich apart. In New York half the city's wealthy families lived on only eight streets, and they belonged to the same clubs. Tocqueville noted these facts and also observed that the rich feigned respect for equality, at least in public. They rode in ordinary carriages, brushed elbows with the less privileged, and avoided the conspicuous display of wealth that marked their private lives.

At the opposite end of the social ladder were the poor. By today's standards most antebellum Americans were poor; they depended on their children's labor to meet expenses, had little money for medical care or recreation, and suffered frequent unemployment. In 1850 an estimated three out of eight males over twenty owned little more than their clothing. In dealing with economic statistics, it is important to remember that the accumulation of wealth takes place over a lifetime. With its high birthrate, America was a nation of young people with little property. But many of them would gain wealth as they grew older.

Antebellum Americans distinguished between poverty, a common condition, and *pauperism,* which meant both poverty and dependency—the inability to care for oneself. The elderly, the ill, and the widowed often fell into the category of pauperism, although they were not seen as a permanent class. Pauperism caused by illness, old age, or circumstance would not pass from generation to generation.

Moralists' assumption that the United States would be free of a permanent class of paupers was comforting but misleading. The poorest white immigrants were from Ireland, where English landlords had evicted peasants from the land in the eighteenth century. The Irish became a nation of wanderers; "the poor Irishman," it was said, "the wheelbarrow is his country." These Irish immigrants played key roles in canal construction; others clustered in the Five Points area of New York City, which became the worst slum in America.

As Catholics, the Irish had little claim on the kindly impulses of American Protestants, but even Protestant poor suffered in the years from 1815 to 1840. As some Americans convinced themselves that success lay within everyone's grasp, they also tended to believe that the poor were responsible for their own poverty. Ironically, even as many Americans blamed the poor for being poor, discrimination mired some groups in enduring poverty. Among the chief victims were northern free blacks.

Free Blacks in the North

Prejudice against African-Americans was deeply ingrained in white society throughout the nation. Although slavery had largely disappeared in the North by 1820, discriminatory laws remained. The voting rights of African-Americans were severely restricted; for example, New York eliminated property requirements for whites but kept them for blacks. There were attempts to bar free blacks from migrating. And segregation prevailed in northern schools, jails, and hospitals. By 1850 blacks could vote on equal terms with whites in only one city, Boston.

Other laws restricted the movement of free blacks. Cities often barred free blacks from public transportation and either excluded them from

Richard Allen
First bishop of the African Methodist Episcopal Church, Richard Allen spent much of his time traveling, organizing societies of black Methodists, preaching on Sundays, and cutting wood on other days to earn his living.

public schools or forced them into segregated schools. Northern jails, almshouses, and hospitals were also segregated.

Most damaging of all to free blacks was the social pressure that forced them into unskilled, low-paying jobs throughout the northern cities. Recalling his youth as a free black in Rhode Island, William J. Brown wrote, "To drive carriages, carry a market basket after the boss, and brush his boots, or saw wood and run errands was as high as a colored man could rise." Although a few free blacks accumulated moderate wealth, free blacks in general were only half as likely as other city dwellers to own real estate.

One important black response to discrimination was the establishment of their own churches. When a group of free blacks was ejected from a Philadelphia church, they ultimately established the first black-run Protestant denomination, the African Methodist Episcopal Church, in 1816. The A.M.E. rapidly expanded to encompass a territory bounded by Washington, D.C., Pittsburgh, and New York City. Its members campaigned against slavery, provided education for black children, and formed mutual-aid societies.

The "Middling Classes"

Most antebellum Americans were neither fabulously rich nor grindingly poor but part of the "middling classes." Even though the wealthy owned an increasing proportion of wealth, per capita income grew at 1.5 percent annually between 1840 and 1860, and the standard of living generally rose after 1800.

Americans applied the term *middling classes* to farmers and artisans, who held the ideal of self-employment and were considered steady and dependable. Often, however, farmers and artisans led lives considerably less stable than this ideal. Allan Melville, the father of novelist Herman Melville, was an enterprising import merchant with boundless faith in the inevitable triumph of honesty and prudence who did well until the late 1820s, when his business sagged. By 1830 he was "destitute of resources and without a shilling—without immediate assistance I know not what will become of me." Despite loans of $3,500, Melville's downward spiral continued, and he died two years later, broken in spirit.

Artisans shared the perils of life in the middling classes. During the colonial period many had attained the ideal of self-employment, owning their tools, taking orders, making their products, and training their children and apprentices in the craft. By 1850 this self-sufficient artisan class had split into two distinct groups. The few artisans who had access to capital became entrepreneurs who hired journeymen to do the actual work. Without capital, most remained journeymen, working for the artisans-turned-entrepreneurs with little prospect of self-employment.

The emerging middling classes shared with the poor a high degree of transience. Even professionals such as judges and lawyers spent part of each year riding from one county courthouse to another. The itinerant clergyman mounted on an old nag and riding the countryside to visit the faithful was a familiar figure.

Transience would affect the lives of most Americans. Farmers exhausted their land by intensive cultivation of cash crops and then moved on. City dwellers moved frequently as they changed jobs—public transportation lagged far behind the spread of the cities. A survey on September 6, 1851, found that on that day 41,729 entered the city of Boston while 42,313 left. Most of these were searching for work, a frequent necessity for the middling classes as well as the poor.

THE REVOLUTION IN SOCIAL RELATIONSHIPS

Following the War of 1812 the growth of interregional trade, commercial agriculture, and manufacturing disrupted traditional social relationships and forged new ones. Two broad changes took place. First, Americans began to question traditional forms of authority and to embrace individualism; wealth, education, and social position no longer received automatic deference. Second, Americans created new foundations for authority. For example, women developed the idea that they possessed a "separate sphere" of authority in the home, and individuals formed voluntary associations to influence the direction of society.

The Attack on the Professions

An intense criticism of lawyers, physicians, and ministers exemplified the assault on and erosion of traditional authority. Between 1800 and 1840 the wave of religious revivals known as the Second Great Awakening (see Chapter 10) sparked fierce attacks on the professions. Revivalists blasted the clergy for creating complex theologies, drinking expensive wines, and fleecing the people. One revivalist accused physicians of inventing fancy Latin and Greek names for diseases to disguise their inability to cure them.

These attacks on the learned professions peaked between 1820 and 1850. Samuel Thomson led a successful movement to eliminate all barriers to entry into the medical profession, including educational requirements. By 1845 every state had repealed laws requiring licenses or education to practice medicine. In religion ministers found little job security as finicky congregations dismissed clergymen whose theology displeased them. In turn, ministers became more ambitious and more inclined to leave poor, small churches for large, wealthy ones.

The increasing commercialization of the economy led to both more professionals and more attacks on them. In 1765 America had one medical school; by 1860 there were sixty-five. The newly minted doctors and lawyers had neither deep roots in the towns where they practiced nor convincing claims to social superiority. "Men dropped down into their places as from clouds," one critic wrote. "Nobody knew who or what they were, except as they claimed." A horse doctor would hang up a sign as "Physician and Surgeon" and "fire at random a box of his pills into your bowels, with a vague chance of killing some disease unknown to him, but with a better prospect of killing the patient."

This questioning of authority was particularly sharp on the frontier. Easterners sneered that every man in the West claimed to be a "judge," "general," "colonel," or "squire." In a society in which *every* person was new, titles were easily adopted and just as readily challenged. Would-be gentlemen substituted an exaggerated sense of personal honor for legal or customary claims of authority. Obsessed with their fragile status, these "gentlemen" could react testily to the slightest insult, and consequently duels were common on the frontier.

The Challenges to Family Authority

Meanwhile, children quietly questioned parental authority. The era's economic change forced many young people to choose between staying at home to help their parents and venturing out on their own. Writing to her parents just before beginning work at a Lowell textile mill, eighteen-year-old Sally Rice explained:

> I must of course have something of my own before many more years have passed over my head, and where is that something coming from if I go home and earn nothing. You may think me unkind, but how can you blame me if I want to stay here. I have but one life to live and I want to enjoy myself as I can while I live.

This desire for independence fueled westward migration as well. Restless single men led the way. Two young men from Virginia put it succinctly: "All the promise of life now seemed to us to be at the other end of the rainbow—somewhere else—anywhere else but on the farm. . . . All our youthful plans had as their chief object the getting away from the farm."

As young antebellum Americans tried to escape close parental supervision, courtship and marriage patterns also changed. No longer dependent on parents for land, young people wanted to choose their own mates. Romantic love, rather than parental preference, increasingly determined marital decisions. Colonial Puritans had advised young people to choose marriage partners whom they *could* love; but by the early 1800s young men and women viewed romantic love as the indispensable basis for successful marriage.

One clear sign of lessening parental control over courtship and marriage was the number of women marrying out of their birth order. Traditionally, fathers had wanted their daughters to marry in the order of their birth to avoid suspicion that there was something wrong with any of them. Another mark of the times was the growing popularity of long engagements; young women were reluctant to tie the knot, fearing that marriage would snuff out their independence. Equally striking was the increasing number of young women who chose not to marry. Catharine Beecher, for example, the daughter of minister Lyman Beecher, broke off her engagement to a young man during the 1820s, later renewed the engagement, and after her fiancé's death remained single.

Thus young people lived more and more in a world of their own. Moralists reacted with alarm and flooded the country with books of advice to youth, all of which stressed the same message: that the newly independent young people should develop rectitude, self-control, and "character." The self-made adult began with the self-made youth.

Wives and Husbands

Another class of advice books counseled wives and husbands about their rights and duties. These books were a sign that relations between spouses were also changing. Young men and women accustomed to making their own decisions would understandably approach marriage as a compact among equals. Although inequalities within marriage remained—especially the legal tradition that married women could not own property—the trend was toward a form of equality.

One source of this change was the rise of the doctrine of separate spheres. The traditional view of women as subordinate in all ways yielded to a separate-but-equal doctrine that portrayed men as superior in making money and governing the world and women as superior in exerting moral influence on family members. Most important was the shift of responsibility for child rearing from fathers to mothers. Advice books instructed mothers to discipline children by withdrawing love rather than using corporal punishment. A whipped child might obey but would remain sullen and bitter. The gentler methods advocated in manuals promised to penetrate the child's heart, to make the child want to do the right thing.

The idea of a separate women's sphere blended with the image of family and home as secluded refuges from a disorderly society. Popular culture painted an alluring portrait of the pleasures of home in such sentimental songs as "Home, Sweet Home" and poems such as "A Visit from St. Nicholas." Even the physical appearance of houses changed; one prominent architect published plans for peaceful single-family homes to offset the hurly-burly of daily life. "There should be something to love," he wrote. "There must be nooks about it, where one would love to linger; windows, where one can enjoy the quiet landscape at his leisure; cozy rooms, where all fireside joys are invited to dwell."

But reality diverged far from this ideal. Ownership of a quiet single-family home lay beyond the reach of most Americans, even much of the middle class. Farm homes, far from tranquil, were beehives of activity, and city dwellers often had to sacrifice privacy by taking in boarders to supplement family income.

The decline of cottage industry and the growing number of men (merchants, lawyers, brokers) who worked outside the home gave women more time to lavish on children. Married women found these ideals sources of power: the doctrine of separate spheres subtly implied that women should control not only the discipline but also the number of children.

In 1800 the United States had one of the highest birthrates ever recorded. Statistically, the average woman bore 7.04 children. Children were valuable for the labor they provided and for the relief from the burdens of survival that they could bring to aging parents. The more children, the better, most couples assumed. However, the growth of the market economy raised questions about children's economic value. Unlike a farmer, a merchant or lawyer could not send his children to work at the age of seven or eight. The birthrate gradually dropped, especially in towns and cities, so that statistically, by 1900 the average woman would bear 3.98 children. Birthrates remained higher among African-Americans and immigrants and in the rural West, where land was plentiful.

Abstinence, *coitus interruptus* (the withdrawal of the penis before ejaculation), and abortion were common birth-control methods. Remedies for "female irregularity"—unwanted pregnancy—were widely advertised. The rubber condom and vaginal diaphragm were familiar to many Americans by 1865. Whatever the method, husbands and wives jointly decided to limit family size. Economic and ideological considerations blended together. Husbands could note that the economic value of chil-

dren was declining; wives, that having fewer children would give them more time to nurture each one and thereby to carry out their womanly duties.

Most supporters of the ideal of separate spheres did not advocate full legal equality for women. Indeed, the ideal of separate spheres was an explicit *alternative* to legal equality. But the concept enhanced women's power within marriage by giving them influence in such vital issues as child rearing and the frequency of pregnancies.

Horizontal Allegiances and the Rise of Voluntary Associations

As some forms of authority weakened, Americans devised new ways by which individuals could extend their influence over others. The antebellum era witnessed the widespread substitution of *horizontal* allegiances for *vertical* allegiances. In vertical allegiances, authority flows from the top down, and people in a subordinate position identify their interests with those of superiors rather than others in the same subordinate roles. The traditional patriarchal family is an example of vertical allegiance, as is the traditional apprentice system. When social relationships assumed a horizontal form, new patterns emerged. Vertical relationships remained but became less important. New relationships linked those who were in a similar position: for example, in the large textile mills, operatives realized they had more in common with one another than with their supervisors. Wives tended to form associations that bound them with other married women, and young men developed associations with other young men.

Voluntary associations encouraged sociability as transients and newcomers came together, usually in associations based on gender or race. These associations served as vehicles for members to assert their influence. Temperance societies fought to abolish alcohol, while moral-reform societies combated prostitution; both in effect enhanced women's power over men. Horizontal allegiances among like-minded Americans increased markedly.

Chronology

1790	Samuel Slater opens his first Rhode Island mill.	**1820–1850**	Growth of moral-reform societies.
1793	Eli Whitney invents the cotton gin.	**1820s**	Expansion of New England textile mills.
1807	Robert R. Livingston and Robert Fulton introduce the steamboat *Clermont* on the Hudson River.	**1824**	*Gibbons* v. *Ogden*.
1811	Construction of the National Road begins at Cumberland, Maryland.	**1830**	Indian Removal Act passed by Congress.
1813	Incorporation of the Boston Manufacturing Company.	**1831**	*Cherokee Nation* v. *Georgia* Alexis de Tocqueville begins visit to the United States to study American penitentiaries.
1816	Second Bank of the United States chartered.	**1832**	*Worcester* v. *Georgia*.
1817–1825	Construction of the Erie Canal started. Mississippi enters the Union.	**1834**	First strike at the Lowell mills.
		1835–1838	Trail of Tears.
1819	Economic panic, ushering in four-year depression. Alabama enters the Union.	**1840**	System of production by interchangeable parts perfected.

CONCLUSION *hc* ACE Practice Test

The westward flow of population after 1815 transformed the lives of Americans. The boom that followed the War of 1812 was all too quickly followed by its collapse in 1819, demonstrating vividly how dependent farmers had become on distant markets. The transportation revolution that followed encouraged a turn to commercial occupations as well as the growth of towns and cities. Merchants plunged capital into manufacturing enterprises ranging from textile mills to urban sweatshops, laying the foundation for America's emergence as a major industrial power by the end of the nineteenth century.

These changes brought prosperity to some, penury to others. They challenged traditional hierarchies and encouraged Americans to form voluntary associations. In such organizations, based on shared interests or opinions, footloose Americans found new identities to parallel or supplant older ones based on family and place of birth.

FURTHER READING

Edward J. Balleisen, *Navigating Failure: Bankruptcy and Commercial Society in Antebellum America* (2001). An important study of the risks spawned by the American economy.

Rowland Berthoff, *An Unsettled People: Social Order and Disorder in American History* (1971). A stimulating interpretation of American social history.

Carl Degler, *At Odds: Women and the Family in America from the Revolution to the Present* (1980). A fine overview of the economic and social experiences of American women.

John Lauritz Larson, *Internal Improvement: National Public Works and the Promise of Popular Government in the Early United States* (2001). An overview of road and canal projects that shows how local and regional rivalries frustrated plans for a nationally integrated system of improvements.

Harry N. Scheiber, *The Ohio Canal Era: A Case Study of Government and the Economy, 1820–1861* (1969). An analysis that speaks volumes about economic growth in the early republic.

Charles Sellers, *The Market Revolution: Jacksonian America, 1815–1846* (1991). A major, and controversial, reinterpretation of the period.

Alan Taylor, *William Cooper's Town* (1995). A compelling portrait of the New York frontier in the late eighteenth and early nineteenth centuries.

Peter Way, *Common Labour* (1993). Insightful book on the lives of canal workers.

Sean Wilentz, *Chants Democratic: New York City and the Rise of the American Working Class, 1788–1850* (1983). A stimulating synthesis of economic, social, and political history.

10

Politics, Religion, and Reform in Antebellum America

First State Election in Michigan

CHAPTER OUTLINE

The Rise of Democratic Politics, 1824–1832

The Bank Controversy and the Second Party System, 1833–1840

The Rise of Popular Religion

The Age of Reform

 This icon will direct you to additional study and research resources at http://college.hmco.com/history/us/boyer/enduring_concise/5e/students/index.html

The 1820s were a period of transition. As the Revolutionary generation passed from the scene—both Thomas Jefferson and John Adams died on July 4, 1826—new generations of Americans grappled with new problems born of westward migration, growing economic individualism, and increasing sectional conflict over slavery. Massive social and economic change shattered old assumptions and created a vigorous new brand of politics.

This transformation led to the birth of a second American party system, with Democrats and Whigs replacing Republicans and Federalists. The changes went far beyond names. The new parties organized grassroots support, molded government in response to the people's will, and welcomed conflict as a way to sustain interest in political issues.

192

Reform movements paralleled, and sometimes replaced, politics as idealistic men and women worked for temperance, abolition, education reform, and equality for women. Strongly held religious beliefs, often the product of evangelism and nontraditional sects, impelled reformers into these and other crusades, and they soon discovered that their success rested on their ability to influence politics.

Both the political and the reform agendas of the 1820s and 1830s diverged from those of the nation's founders. Those leaders had feared popular participation in politics, left an ambiguous legacy on slavery, and displayed little interest in women's rights. Yet even as Americans shifted their political and social priorities, they continued to venerate the founders. Histories of the United States, biographies of Revolutionary patriots, and torchlight parades that bore portraits of Washington and Jefferson alongside depictions of Andrew Jackson reassured the men and women of the young nation that they were remaining loyal to their heritage.

This chapter focuses on five major questions:

▶ How did American politics become more democratic from 1800 to 1840?

▶ Why was Andrew Jackson so popular? How did his policies contribute to the rise of the Whig party?

▶ How did the Panic of 1837 and its aftermath solidify the two-party system?

▶ What new assumptions about human nature underlay religious and reform movements?

▶ To what extent did the reform movements aim at extending equality to all Americans? How did they attempt to forge a more orderly society?

THE RISE OF DEMOCRATIC POLITICS, 1824–1832

In 1824 Andrew Jackson and John Quincy Adams were both members of Jefferson's Republican party; by 1834 Jackson was a Democrat and Adams a Whig. Tensions spawned by industrialization, the rise of the Cotton South, and westward expansion split Jefferson's old party. Generally, supporters of states' rights joined the Democrats, and advocates of national support for economic development became Whigs.

Democrat or Whig, leaders had to adapt to the rising notion that politics should be an expression of the will of the common people rather than an activity that gentlemen conducted on the people's behalf. Americans still looked up to their political leaders, but those leaders could no longer look down on the people.

Democratic Ferment

Democratizing forces in politics took several forms. One of the most common was the abolition of the requirement that voters own property; no western states had such a requirement, and eastern states gradually liberalized their laws. Moreover, written ballots replaced the custom of voting aloud, which had enabled elites to influence others at the polls. And appointive offices became elective. The selection of members of the electoral college shifted gradually from state legislatures to the voters, and by 1832 only South Carolina followed the old custom.

The fierce tug of war between Republicans and Federalists in the 1790s and early 1800s had taught both parties to court voters and listen to their will. At grand party-run barbecues from Maine to Maryland, potential voters washed down free clams and oysters with free beer and whiskey. Republicans sought to expand suffrage in the North, and Federalists did likewise in the South, each in hopes of transforming itself into a majority party in that section.

The pace of political democratization was uneven, however. The parties were still run from the top down as late as 1820, with candidates nominated by caucus, that is, a meeting of party members in the legislature. However, political democracy did not extend to allowing either women or free blacks the right to vote.

The Election of 1824

Sectional politics shattered the harmony of the Era of Good Feelings. In 1824 five candidates, all Republicans, battled for the presidency. John Quincy Adams emerged as the New England favorite. John C. Calhoun and William Crawford fought to represent the South. Henry Clay of Kentucky assumed that his leadership in promoting the American System would endear him to the East as well as to his native West. Tennessean Andrew Jackson stunned the four by emerging as a favorite of frontier people, southerners, and some northerners as well.

Most Republicans in Congress refused to support Crawford, the caucus's choice, and a paralyzing stroke soon removed him from the race. Impressed by Jackson's support, Calhoun withdrew to run unopposed for the vice presidency. Jackson won the popular and electoral vote but failed to win the majority electoral vote required by the Constitution. When the election went to the House of Representatives, Clay threw his support, and thus the presidency, to Adams; Adams then promptly appointed Clay secretary of state. Jackson's supporters raged that a "corrupt bargain" had cheated their candidate, "Old Hickory," of the presidency. Although no evidence of any outright deal was uncovered, the widespread belief in a corrupt bargain hung like a cloud over Adams's presidency.

John Quincy Adams as President

Failing to understand the changing political climate, Adams made several other miscalculations that would cloak his presidency in controversy. For example, he proposed federal support for internal improvements, although strict Jeffersonians had continued to attack them as unconstitutional. Adams then infuriated southerners by proposing to send American delegates to a conference of newly independent Latin American nations. Southerners opposed U.S. participation because it would imply recognition of Haiti, the black republic created by slave revolutionaries. Both the sharp debate over Missouri and the discovery of Denmark Vesey's conspiracy to ignite a slave rebellion in South Carolina had shaken southern slaveholders. Instead of building new bases of support, Adams clung to the increasingly obsolete view of the president as custodian of the public good, aloof from partisan politics. He alienated his supporters by appointing his opponents to high office and wrote loftily, "I have no wish to fortify myself by the support of any party whatever." Idealistic though his view was, it guaranteed him a single-term presidency.

The Rise of Andrew Jackson

As Adams's popularity fell, Andrew Jackson's rose. His victory over the British at the Battle of New Orleans made him a national hero, and southerners admired him as a Tennessee slaveholder, a renowned Indian fighter, and an advocate of Indian removal. Also, southerners praised Jackson's demand that they be allowed a free hand in pushing

The Election of 1824

Candidate	Party	Electoral Vote	Popular Vote	Percentage of Popular Vote
John Quincy Adams	Democratic-Republican	84	108,740	30.5
Andrew Jackson	Democratic-Republican	99	153,544	43.1
William H. Crawford	Democratic-Republican	41	46,618	13.1
Henry Clay	Democratic-Republican	37	47,136	13.2

the Indians westward as a noble application of Jeffersonian ideals of states' rights—and a way to satisfy their land hunger. Veteran politicians distrusted Jackson's notoriously hot temper and his penchant for duels, but ordinary people seemed to have no such objections. As the only candidate in 1824 not linked to the Monroe administration, Jackson was also in a position to capitalize on discontent after the Panic of 1819. To many Americans, Jackson, who as a boy had fought in the Revolution, was a living link to a more virtuous past.

By 1826 towns and villages across the country buzzed with political activity. Because supporters of Jackson, Adams, and Clay all still called themselves Republicans, few realized that a new political system was being born. The man most alert to the new currents was Martin Van Buren, who would be Jackson's vice president and then president.

Van Buren exemplified a new breed of politician. A tavernkeeper's son, he had worked his way up through New York politics and created a powerful statewide machine, the Albany Regency, composed of men like himself from the middling and lower ranks. A genial man who befriended even his political rivals, Van Buren loved the game of politics and possessed an uncanny ability to sense which way the political winds were shifting.

The election of 1824 had convinced Van Buren of the need for two-party competition. Without the discipline imposed by party competition, the Republicans had splintered into sectional factions. The country would be better served, he thought, by reducing the shades of opinion in the country to just two so that parties could clash and a clear winner emerge. Jackson was the logical leader, and presidential nominee, of one new party, becoming known as the Democratic party; its opponents, calling themselves National Republicans, nominated Adams. The second American party system was taking shape.

The Election of 1828

The 1828 campaign was a vicious, mudslinging affair. The National Republicans attacked Jackson as a murderer, a drunken gambler, and an adulterer.

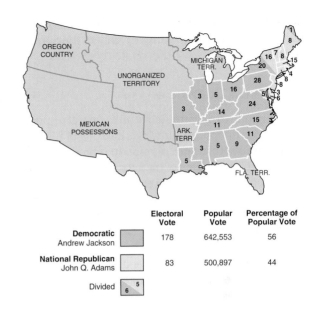

	Electoral Vote	Popular Vote	Percentage of Popular Vote
Democratic Andrew Jackson	178	642,553	56
National Republican John Q. Adams	83	500,897	44
Divided	5 6		

MAP 10.1
The Election of 1828

He had in fact killed several men in duels and had several more executed militarily; and in 1791 he had married Rachel Robards, erroneously believing that her divorce from her first husband had become final. Jackson supporters retaliated that Adams was rich and in debt, had tried to gain favor with the Russian tsar by providing him with a beautiful American prostitute, and—perhaps worst of all to westerners—wore silk underwear.

The Adams supporters' charges that Jackson was an illiterate backwoodsman backfired and endeared "Old Hickory" to ordinary people. Jackson's mudslingers, moreover, had the better aim. They proclaimed that Jackson was the common man incarnate—his mind unclouded by learning, his morals simple and true, his will fierce and resolute. Adams, in contrast, was an aristocrat, a scholar whose learning obscured the truth, a man who could write but not fight.

The election swept Jackson into office with twice Adams's electoral votes. The popular vote, much closer, reflected the strong sectional bases of the new parties. Adams doubled Jackson's vote in New England, while Jackson doubled Adams's vote in the South and nearly tripled it in the Southwest.

Jackson in Office

Jackson rode to the presidency on a wave of opposition to corruption and privilege, and one of his first moves was to institute "rotation in office"—the removal of officeholders of the rival party. Nearly half of the higher-ranking civil servants were summarily fired. In fact, so many homes were suddenly up for sale that the Washington housing market slumped.

Although his opponents called it the "spoils system," Jackson defended rotation in office on the basis of democracy: the duties of most officeholders were so simple that as many plain people as possible should have the chance to work for the government. However, under Martin Van Buren and his successors, federal jobs would become rewards for loyalty to the victorious party.

Andrew Jackson, by Ralph Earl
Jackson during the Nullification Crisis, looking serene in the uniform of a major-general and determined to face down the greatest challenge to his presidency.

Jackson's use of the spoils system ruffled feathers, but the issues of internal improvements and tariffs ignited real controversy. Like most southerners, Jackson believed that federal support for internal improvements was simply a lavish give-away. He thought that such funding violated the Constitution, which stated that Congress could appropriate money only for national purposes, not for the benefit of particular sections or interests. Accordingly, in 1830 Jackson vetoed a bill to provide federal support for a road in Kentucky between Maysville and Lexington.

The Maysville Road Bill veto and the almost simultaneous Indian Removal Act enhanced Jackson's popularity in the South. The tariff issue, however, would test southern loyalty. In 1828 while Adams was still president, Congress passed a high protective tariff favorable to western agriculture and New England manufacturing. Southerners fumed at the tariff, which raised the price of manufactured goods and also created the threat of retaliatory tariffs against southern cotton exports. To the surprise of Jackson and his followers, he, rather than Adams, bore the brunt of southern ire.

Nullification

The 1828 tariff, the "Tariff of Abominations," laid the foundation for a split between Jackson and his vice president, John C. Calhoun. Although he had entered Congress as a "war hawk" and had championed nationalism early in his career, Calhoun had gradually become a states' rights sectionalist. He had supported the tariff of 1816 but would fiercely oppose that of 1828.

Calhoun burned with ambition to be president. Jackson had stated that he would serve only one term and as vice president Calhoun assumed that he would succeed Jackson. To do so, he needed to maintain the support of the South, which was increasingly taking an antitariff stance. Calhoun's own state, South Carolina, had suffered economic decline throughout the 1820s; its citizens blamed protective tariffs for driving up the price of manufactured goods and for threatening cotton prices by lowering American demand for British cotton cloth, which was spun and woven from southern cotton. Whereas New Englanders, among them Senator Daniel Webster of Massachusetts, supported the tariff and protectionism, southerners responded with militant hostility.

Calhoun also accepted the Virginia and Kentucky Resolutions of 1798–1799, which defined the Union as a compact among the states, an association conferring limited powers on the central government. He insisted that the only constitutional tariff was one that raised money for the common national defense, not one that favored a particular section at the expense of others. Calhoun expressed these views anonymously in the widely circulated *South Carolina Exposition and Protest* (1828), which argued not only that the 1828 tariff was unconstitutional but also that states had the right to nullify that tariff within their borders.

More was at stake than the price of manufactured goods. Southerners feared that a government capable of passing tariffs favoring one section over another might also pass laws meddling with slavery. Although this idea seemed far-fetched—Jackson himself was a slaveholder—South Carolina's whites were edgy about the safety of slavery. African-Americans composed a majority of their state's population, the slave Nat Turner's bloody rebellion in Virginia in 1831 raised fears of a similar threat to South Carolina, and William Lloyd Garrison's new newspaper, *The Liberator,* advocated immediate abolition. To many South Carolinians, these were ominous signs warning that a line had to be drawn against tariffs and possible future interference with slavery.

Like Calhoun, Jackson was strong-willed and proud. Unlike Calhoun, he already was president and the leader of a national party that included supporters of the tariff. To mollify both protariff and antitariff forces, he devised two policies.

First, he distributed surplus federal revenue, largely derived from the tariff duties, to the states, hoping to remove the taint of sectional injustice from the tariff. Second, he tried to ease tariffs down from the sky-high 1828 rates, and Congress passed

John C. Calhoun, by Charles Bird King, c. 1825
Jackson, defeated in the presidential election of 1824, won handily four years later. The magnetic Calhoun, Jackson's vice president, broke with Jackson over nullification and the Peggy Eaton affair and resigned the vice presidency in 1832.

slight reductions in 1832. But these measures did little to satisfy Calhoun and the South Carolinians.

By the time the somewhat lower tariff was passed, other issues had ruptured relations between the president and vice president. Jackson learned that in 1818, then–Secretary of War Calhoun had urged that Jackson be punished for his unauthorized raid into Spanish Florida. Combined with the snubbing by Calhoun's wife, Floride, of Peggy Eaton, the scandal-tainted spouse of Jackson's ally and secretary of war, John H. Eaton, this revelation convinced Jackson that he had to "destroy [Calhoun] regardless of what injury it might do me or my administration." A Jefferson Day dinner in April 1830 featured a symbolic confrontation between Jackson and Calhoun. Jackson proposed the toast "Our Union: It must be preserved." Calhoun responded, "The Union next to Liberty the most dear. May we always remember that it can only be preserved by distributing equally the benefits and burdens of the Union."

The stage was set for the president and vice president to clash over nullification. In November 1832 a South Carolina convention, citing Calhoun's states' rights doctrine, nullified the tariffs of 1828 and 1832 and forbade the collection of customs duties within the state. Jackson reacted quickly. He despised nullification as an "abominable doctrine" that would reduce the government to anarchy and denounced the South Carolinians as "unprincipled men who would rather rule in hell than be subordinate in heaven." He sent arms to Unionists in South Carolina and issued a proclamation that lambasted nullification as unconstitutional; the Constitution, he emphasized, had established "a single nation," not a league of states.

In March 1833 the crisis eased as President Jackson signed "the olive branch and the sword," in one historian's words. The Compromise Tariff of 1833, the olive branch or peace offering, provided for a gradual but significant lowering of tariff duties from 1833 to 1842. The Force Bill, the sword, authorized the president to use arms to collect customs duties in South Carolina. Although South Carolina did not abandon the principle of nullification—in fact, it petulantly nullified the Force Bill—it accepted the Compromise Tariff and rescinded its nullification of the tariffs of 1828 and 1832.

This so-called Compromise of 1833 grew out of a mixture of partisanship and statesmanship. Its chief architect was Henry Clay of Kentucky, who had long favored high tariffs. Clay not only feared the outbreak of civil war but also wanted to keep control of the tariff issue away from the Jacksonians, even if that meant a lower tariff. The nullifiers, recognizing that no other states had supported them, preferred giving Clay, not Jackson, credit for defusing the crisis; they therefore supported the Compromise Tariff and rescinded the nullification proclamation. Americans everywhere hailed Henry Clay as the Great Compromiser.

The Bank Veto and the Election of 1832

Jackson recognized that the gap between rich and poor was widening. While he did not object to wealth earned by hard work, he believed that the wealthy too often enjoyed privileges granted by corrupt legislatures. Additionally, disastrous speculation early in his life led him to distrust all banks, paper money, and monopolies—and the Bank of the United States was guilty on all counts.

The Bank of the United States had received a twenty-year charter from Congress in 1816. As a creditor of state banks, the Bank of the United States in effect restrained their printing and lending of money by its ability to demand the redemption of state notes in specie (gold or silver coin). Many other aspects of the Bank of the United States made it controversial. For example, it was widely blamed for the Panic of 1819. Second, as the official depository for federal revenue, it was a privileged institution at a time when privilege was coming under fierce attack. The bank had far greater lending capacity than state banks and thus dominated them. Its capital of $35 million was more than double yearly federal expenditures. Third, although chartered by the federal government, the bank was controlled by its stockholders, who were private citizens—"moneyed capitalists" in Jackson's view. Finally, its location in Philadelphia, rather than Washington, symbolized the bank's independence of supervision by the national government. The bank's president, the aristocratic Nicholas Biddle, saw himself as a public servant duty-bound to keep the bank above politics.

Aware of Jackson's opposition, Biddle sought an early rechartering of the bank, urged on by Henry Clay, who hoped to ride the probank bandwagon into the White House in 1832. Congress passed, and Jackson promptly vetoed, the recharter bill. The president denounced the bank as a private and privileged monopoly that drained the West of specie, was immune to taxation by states, put inordinate power in the hands of a few men, and made "the rich richer and the potent more powerful."

By 1832 Jackson had made clear his views on major issues. He was simultaneously a strong defender of states' rights *and* a staunch Unionist. Although he cherished the Union, Jackson believed the states far too diverse to accept strong direction from the federal government. The safest course was to allow the states considerable freedom so that they would remain contentedly within the Union and would reject such a dangerous doctrine as nullification.

Throwing aside earlier promises to retire, Jackson ran for the presidency again in 1832, with Martin Van Buren as his running mate. Henry Clay ran on the National Republican ticket, stressing his American System of protective tariffs, national banking, and federal support for internal improvements. Jackson's overwhelming personal popularity swamped Clay, 219 to 49 electoral votes. Secure in office for another four years, Jackson was ready to finish dismantling the Bank of the United States.

THE BANK CONTROVERSY AND THE SECOND PARTY SYSTEM, 1833–1840

Jackson's Bank veto ignited a searing controversy that threatened to engulf all banks. One major problem was that the United States had no paper currency of its own. Instead, private bankers (widely viewed as sinister figures) issued paper notes, which they promised to redeem in specie. These IOUs fueled economic development by making credit easy. But if a banknote depreciated, wage earners paid in paper would suffer. Further, paper money encouraged speculation, which multiplied both profit and risk. For example, farmers could now buy land on credit in the belief that its value would rise; if it did, they could sell the land at a profit, but if its value fell, the farmers became mired in debt. Would the United States embrace swift economic development at the price of allowing some people to get rich quickly while others languished? Or would the nation undergo more modest growth in traditional molds, anchored by "honest" manual work and frugality?

Before the answer to these questions was clear, the banking issue dramatically transformed politics. It contributed both to the growth of opposition to the Democrats and to the steady expansion of popular interest in politics.

The War on the Bank

Jackson could have allowed the Bank of the United States, "the monster," as he termed it, to die a natural death when its charter expired, but he and his followers believed that if the bank escaped with a breath of life, "it will soon recover its wonted strength, its whole power to injure us, and all hope of its destruction must forever be renounced." When Biddle began calling in bank loans and contracting credit to forestall further moves by Jackson, Jacksonians saw their darkest fears confirmed. The bank, Jackson said, "is trying to kill me, but I will kill it." So the president began removing federal deposits from the Bank of the United States and putting them into private banks chartered by individual states.

In turn, this policy raised new problems. State banks that were depositories for federal funds could use these moneys as the basis for issuing more notes and extending more loans. Jackson hoped to head off the danger of a credit-fueled speculative economy by limiting the number of state banks used for federal revenue. But he discovered that doing so was impossible; indeed, by the end of 1833 there were twenty-three "pet banks," chosen in part for their loyalty to the Democratic party. Jackson could not stem the rapid economic expansion fueled by paper money and by foreign specie flowing in to purchase cotton. In 1836 the president reluctantly signed the Deposit Act, increasing the number of deposit banks and lessening federal control over them.

The Democratic party split between advocates of soft money (paper) and hard money (specie). The two Democratic camps agreed that the Bank of the United States was evil, but for different reasons. Soft-money Democrats, especially strong in the West, resented the bank's restriction of credit and wanted more paper money. Hard-money Democrats, typically wage-earning urban workers, disliked the speculative economy based on paper money and easy credit, and they deeply feared inflation.

The Rise of Whig Opposition

During Jackson's second term the National Republicans changed their name to the Whig party and broadened their base of support in both the North and the South. As Jackson's policies became clearer and sharper, the opposition attracted people alienated by his positions.

For example, Jackson's crushing of nullification led some southerners to the Whigs in order to oppose Jackson. Jackson's war against the Bank of the United States and his opposition to federal aid for internal improvements alienated other southerners and drove them to the Whigs as well. Most of the South remained Democratic, but the Whigs made substantial inroads nonetheless. Northern reformers also joined the Whigs, who were far more willing than the Democrats to effect social change by government intervention. And supporters of Henry Clay's American System joined advocates of public education and temperance in seeking a more activist, interventionist national government.

Meanwhile, social reformers in the North were infusing new vitality into the opposition to Jackson. These reformers wanted to end slavery and the sale of liquor, improve public education, and elevate public morality. While most Democrats opposed any government attempt to impose uniform standards on the diverse American society, Whigs tended to accept active government intervention, and thus reformers gravitated to the Whig party. At the same time, reform agitation and its association with the Whigs drove Irish immigrants into the arms of the Democratic party. In turn, many native-born Protestants, contemptuous of the Irish, turned Whig.

One remarkable source of Whig strength was Anti-Masonry, a protest movement against the secrecy of Masonic lodges, which had long provided prominent men with fraternal fellowship and exotic rituals. In 1826 William Morgan, a stonemason from Genesee County, New York, was kidnapped after threatening to expose Masonic secrets. Efforts to solve the mystery of Morgan's disappearance foundered because local officials, themselves Masons, obstructed the investigation. Rumors spread that Masonry was a conspiracy of the rich to suppress liberty, a secret order of men who loathed Christianity, and an exclusive retreat for drunkards.

By 1836 the Whigs had become a national party with widespread appeal. Whigs everywhere assailed Andrew Jackson as an imperious dictator, "King Andrew I"; and the name "Whigs" evoked memories of the American patriots who had opposed George III in 1776.

The Election of 1836

Andrew Jackson was a hard act to follow. Democrats nominated Martin Van Buren, proclaiming that he and the Democratic party were Jackson's heirs, the perfect embodiment of the popular will. The Whigs ran four candidates from different sections of the country. The Democrats accused the Whigs of attempting to split the vote and throw the election into the House, where they could wheel and deal as in 1824, but in fact the Democrats overestimated their opponents. The Whigs had no strategy, much less such a devious one, and Van Buren carried the popular vote. His margin was narrow, however, and, in an ominous sign, the Democrats carried barely half the southern vote—they had won two-thirds of it only four years earlier.

The Panic of 1837

Jackson left office in 1837 in a burst of glory. Yet he bequeathed to his successor a severe depression.

In the speculative boom of 1835 and 1836, born of Jackson's policy of placing federal funds in state banks, the total number of banks doubled, the value of bank notes in circulation nearly tripled, and both commodity and land prices soared skyward. But the overheated economy began to cool rapidly in May 1837 as prices tumbled and as bank after bank suspended specie payments. After a short rally, 1839 saw a second crash as banks across the nation again suspended specie payments.

The ensuing depression was far more severe and prolonged than the Panic of 1819. Wages fell by one-third between 1836 and 1842. Desperate, many workers turned to the teachings of William Miller, who was convinced that the end of the world was imminent. Dressed in black coats and stovepipe hats, Miller's followers roamed urban sidewalks and rural villages in search of converts. Many purchased white robes and made ready for the last day, calculated as October 2, 1843. The day came and went, but it was not the last.

The prolonged depression had a deeper root. Domestically, a directive from Congress in 1836, declaring that only gold and silver could be used to purchase public lands, cut credit. International events played a role as well, especially ultimate declines in London's flow of specie.

The Search for Solutions

Van Buren, known affectionately as "the little magician" for his political shrewdness, used those skills to ride out the depression, which was battering ordinary citizens and the Democratic party alike. The administration called for the creation of an independent treasury that would hold government revenues and keep them from the grasp of corporations. When Van Buren finally signed the Independent Treasury Bill into law on July 4, 1840, his supporters hailed it as a second Declaration of Independence.

The Independent Treasury reflected the basic Jacksonian suspicion of an alliance between the federal government and banking. However, the Independent Treasury Act failed to address banking on the state level, where newly chartered state banks—more than 900 in number by 1840—lent money to farmers and businessmen, fueling the speculative economy feared by Jacksonians.

Whigs and Democrats differed sharply in their approach to the multiplication of state banks. Whigs, convinced that Jackson's Specie Circular, not banks themselves, had brought on the depression, supported policies allowing any group to start a bank as long as its members met state

requirements. Democrats, who tended to blame banks and paper money for the depression, adopted the hard-money position favored by Jackson and his advisers. After 1837 the Democrats were in effect an antibank, hard-money party.

The Election of 1840

Despite the depression, the Democrats renominated Van Buren. Avoiding the mistake of 1836, the Whigs nominated a single candidate, Ohio's William Henry Harrison, and ran John Tyler of Virginia for vice president. The Whigs chose Harrison, sixty-seven years old, largely because he had few enemies.

Early in the campaign the Democrats made a big mistake, ridiculing Harrison as "Old Granny" who desired only to spend his declining years in a cabin sipping cider. In so doing, they handed the Whigs the most famous campaign symbol in American history. The Whigs saluted Harrison as a simple frontiersman, the hero of the Battle of Tippecanoe, and a defender of all those people raised in log cabins. Disdaining a platform, the

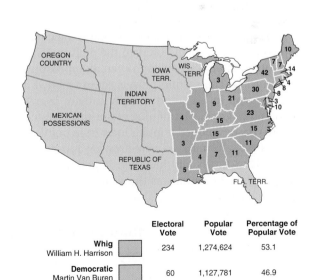

MAP 10.2
The Election of 1840

	Electoral Vote	Popular Vote	Percentage of Popular Vote
Whig William H. Harrison	234	1,274,624	53.1
Democratic Martin Van Buren	60	1,127,781	46.9

Whigs ran a "hurrah" campaign using log cabins for headquarters, singing log cabin songs, and ladling out log cabin cider. Instead of a platform, they trumpeted, "Tippecanoe and Tyler, too!" and attacked Van Buren as an aristocrat who lived in "regal splendor."

Harrison was elected in a clear victory. The depression would have made it difficult for any Democrat to win, and Van Buren lacked the halo of military glory that gleamed around Jackson and Harrison. However, many of Van Buren's problems stemmed from his style of campaign. While the Whigs ran a rousing race aimed directly at the "common man," Van Buren quietly wrote letters of encouragement to key supporters. Ironically, the Whigs beat the master politician at his own game.

The Second Party System Matures

The strong contrasts between the two parties and the sharp choices they presented jolted the American electorate. Nearly 2.4 million people voted in 1840, up an astonishing 60 percent from 1836. Most of that change was in the number of people who chose to vote; prior to 1840 the proportion of white males who voted had ranged from 55 to 58 percent; in 1840 it rose to 80 percent.

Both the depression and the frenzied log cabin campaign had brought voters to the polls in 1840, but voter turnouts stayed high even after prosperity returned. The second party system reached a high plateau in 1840 and remained there over a decade. The gradual hardening of the line between the two parties piqued popular interest in politics.

By 1840 reform issues were drawing as many to the polls as tariffs and banking. Religion, rather than politics, however, was the source of many of these reforms.

THE RISE OF POPULAR RELIGION

In *Democracy in America,* Alexis de Tocqueville called religion "the foremost of the political institutions" in the United States. "In France I had almost always seen the spirit of religion and the spirit of freedom pursuing courses dramatically opposed to each other; but in America I found that they were intimately united, and that they reigned in common over the same country."

Tocqueville was referring to the way religious impulses reinforced democracy and liberty. Just as Americans demanded that politics be accessible to average people, they insisted ministers preach doctrines that appealed to ordinary men and women. Successful ministers used plain language to move the heart, not theological complexity to dazzle the intellect. Increasingly, Americans put individuals in charge of their own religious destiny, thrusting aside Calvinist predestination in favor of the belief that anyone could attain heaven. A series of religious revivals known as the Second Great Awakening contributed to the growing harmony between religion and politics and to the growing conviction that heaven itself was democratic.

The Second Great Awakening

The Second Great Awakening first flared in Connecticut in the 1790s, and during the following half century it set ablaze one section of the nation after another. As the revivals moved westward, they underwent striking changes, typified by the rise of camp meetings. Here the members of several denominations gathered together in sprawling open-air camps to hear revivalists proclaim that the Second Coming of Jesus was near and that the time for repentance was now. The most famous camp meeting took place at Cane Ridge, Kentucky, in August 1801. A huge crowd gathered on a hillside to listen to thunderous sermons, sing hymns, and experience divine grace.

The Cane Ridge revival was part of the Great Kentucky Revival of 1800–1801. These frontier revivals featured "exercises" in which men and women rolled around like logs, jerked their heads furiously, and grunted like animals. Critics blasted the frontier frenzy for encouraging fleshly lust and complained that "more souls were begot than saved" at the camp meetings. But although these early frontier revivals challenged traditional reli-

The ensuing depression was far more severe and prolonged than the Panic of 1819. Wages fell by one-third between 1836 and 1842. Desperate, many workers turned to the teachings of William Miller, who was convinced that the end of the world was imminent. Dressed in black coats and stovepipe hats, Miller's followers roamed urban sidewalks and rural villages in search of converts. Many purchased white robes and waited anxiously for the last day, calculated as October 22, 1843. The day came and went, but it was not the last.

The prolonged depression had multiple roots. Domestically, Jackson's Specie Circular of July 1836, declaring that only specie, not paper money, could be used to purchase public lands, dried up credit. International causes played a large role as well, especially Britain's decision in 1836 to halt the flow of specie from its shores to the United States.

The Search for Solutions

Van Buren, known as "the sly fox" and "the little magician" for his political craftiness, would need those skills to confront the depression, which was battering ordinary citizens and the Democratic party alike. The president called for the creation of an independent treasury that would hold government revenues and keep them from the grasp of corporations. When Van Buren finally signed the Independent Treasury Bill into law on July 4, 1840, his supporters hailed it as a second Declaration of Independence.

The Independent Treasury reflected the basic Jacksonian suspicion of an alliance between the federal government and banking. However, the Independent Treasury Act failed to address banking on the state level, where newly chartered state banks—more than 900 in number by 1840—lent money to farmers and businessmen, fueling the speculative economy feared by Jacksonians.

Whigs and Democrats differed sharply in their approach to the multiplication of state banks. Whigs, convinced that Jackson's Specie Circular, not banks themselves, had brought on the depression, supported policies allowing any group to start a bank as long as its members met state requirements. Democrats, who tended to blame banks and paper money for the depression, adopted the hard-money position favored by Jackson and his advisers. After 1837 the Democrats were in effect an antibank, hard-money party.

The Election of 1840

Despite the depression, the Democrats renominated Van Buren. Avoiding the mistake of 1836, the Whigs nominated a single candidate, Ohio's William Henry Harrison, and ran John Tyler of Virginia for vice president. The Whigs chose Harrison, sixty-seven years old, largely because he had few enemies.

Early in the campaign the Democrats made a fatal mistake, ridiculing Harrison as "Old Granny" who desired only to spend his declining years in a log cabin sipping cider. In so doing, they handed the Whigs the most famous campaign symbol in American history. The Whigs saluted Harrison as a rugged frontiersman, the hero of the Battle of Tippecanoe, and a defender of all those people who lived in log cabins. Disdaining a platform, the

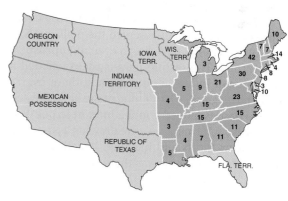

		Electoral Vote	Popular Vote	Percentage of Popular Vote
Whig William H. Harrison		234	1,274,624	53.1
Democratic Martin Van Buren		60	1,127,781	46.9

MAP 10.2
The Election of 1840

Whigs ran a "hurrah" campaign using log cabins for headquarters, singing log cabin songs, and ladling out log cabin cider. Instead of a platform, they trumpeted, "Tippecanoe and Tyler, too!" and attacked Van Buren as an aristocrat who lived in "regal splendor."

Harrison was elected in a clear victory. The depression would have made it difficult for any Democrat to win, and Van Buren lacked the halo of military glory that gleamed around Jackson and Harrison. However, many of Van Buren's problems stemmed from his style of campaign. While the Whigs ran a rousing race aimed directly at the "common man," Van Buren quietly wrote letters of encouragement to key supporters. Ironically, the Whigs beat the master politician at his own game.

The Second Party System Matures

The strong contrasts between the two parties and the sharp choices they presented jolted the American electorate. Nearly 2.4 million people voted in 1840, up an astonishing 60 percent from 1836. Most of that change was in the number of people who chose to vote; prior to 1840 the proportion of white males who voted had ranged from 55 to 58 percent; in 1840 it rose to 80 percent.

Both the depression and the frenzied log cabin campaign had brought voters to the polls in 1840, but voter turnouts stayed high even after prosperity returned. The second party system reached a high plateau in 1840 and remained there over a decade. The gradual hardening of the line between the two parties piqued popular interest in politics.

By 1840 reform issues were drawing as many to the polls as tariffs and banking. Religion, rather than politics, however, was the source of many of these reforms.

THE RISE OF POPULAR RELIGION

In *Democracy in America,* Alexis de Tocqueville called religion "the foremost of the political institutions" in the United States. "In France I had almost always seen the spirit of religion and the spirit of freedom pursuing courses dramatically opposed to each other; but in America I found that they were intimately united, and that they reigned in common over the same country."

Tocqueville was referring to the way religious impulses reinforced democracy and liberty. Just as Americans demanded that politics be accessible to average people, they insisted ministers preach doctrines that appealed to ordinary men and women. Successful ministers used plain language to move the heart, not theological complexity to dazzle the intellect. Increasingly, Americans put individuals in charge of their own religious destiny, thrusting aside Calvinist predestination in favor of the belief that anyone could attain heaven. A series of religious revivals known as the Second Great Awakening contributed to the growing harmony between religion and politics and to the growing conviction that heaven itself was democratic.

The Second Great Awakening

The Second Great Awakening first flared in Connecticut in the 1790s, and during the following half century it set ablaze one section of the nation after another. As the revivals moved westward, they underwent striking changes, typified by the rise of camp meetings. Here the members of several denominations gathered together in sprawling open-air camps to hear revivalists proclaim that the Second Coming of Jesus was near and that the time for repentance was now. The most famous camp meeting took place at Cane Ridge, Kentucky, in August 1801. A huge crowd gathered on a hillside to listen to thunderous sermons, sing hymns, and experience divine grace.

The Cane Ridge revival was part of the Great Kentucky Revival of 1800–1801. These frontier revivals featured "exercises" in which men and women rolled around like logs, jerked their heads furiously, and grunted like animals. Critics blasted the frontier frenzy for encouraging fleshly lust and complained that "more souls were begot than saved" at the camp meetings. But although these early frontier revivals challenged traditional religious customs—indeed, the most successful preachers were farmers and artisans who had experienced powerful conversions and scorned those whose religion came from books—the revivalists promoted law, order, and morality.

Methodists, the most successful frontier denomination, became the largest American Protestant denomination, soaring from 70,000 members in 1800 to more than 1 million in 1844. The Methodists emphasized that religion was a matter of the heart rather than the head and relied on itinerant circuit riders, young, unmarried men who traveled ceaselessly and preached in houses, open fields, or wherever else listeners would gather. After the Methodist circuit riders left, their converts held weekly "classes" to provide mutual encouragement and to chastise members for drunkenness, fighting, gossiping, fornication, and even shrewd business practices.

Eastern Revivals

By the 1820s the Second Great Awakening had begun to shift back to the East. The hottest revival fires blazed in an area of western New York known as the Burned-Over District. No longer a frontier, western New York teemed with descendants of Puritans who hungered for religious experience and with people drawn by the hope of wealth after the completion of the Erie Canal. It was a fertile field of high expectations and bitter discontent. The man who harnessed these anxieties to religion was Charles Grandison Finney, a lawyer-turned-Presbyterian minister. His greatest "harvest" came in the thriving canal city of Rochester in 1830–1831.

Finney's innovations at the Rochester revival justified his reputation as the "father of modern revivalism." First, he pioneered in generating cooperation among Protestants, and all denominations participated in his revivals. In addition, he introduced such novelties as the "anxious seat," a bench where those ready for conversion could be made objects of special prayer, and the "protracted meeting," which ran nightly for a week or more. Finally, although a Presbyterian, Finney rejected the Calvinist doctrine of total depravity, humankind's irre-

sistible inclination to sin. Instead, he proclaimed, sin was a voluntary act, and those who willed themselves to sin could just as readily will themselves not to sin. In theory, men and women could live perfect lives, free of sin. Those converted by Finney or other evangelists believed that they were cleansed of past guilt and were beginning a new life. "I have been born again," a young convert wrote. "I am three days old when I write this letter."

Originally controversial, Finney's ideas came to dominate "evangelical" Protestantism, which focused on the need for an emotional religious conversion. He succeeded because he told people what they wanted to hear: that their destinies were in their own hands. A society that celebrated the "self-made" individual embraced Finney's assertion that even in religion people could make of themselves what they chose. Finney multiplied his success by emphasizing the role of women, who outnumbered male converts nearly two to one. Finney encouraged women to give public testimonials of their conversion, and he often converted men by first winning over their wives and daughters.

Critics of Revivals: The Unitarians

Although some praised revivals for saving souls, others doubted their lasting effects. The Unitarians were a small but influential group of critics. Although their basic doctrine—that Jesus Christ was less than fully divine—had gained acceptance among religious liberals in the eighteenth century, Unitarianism became a formal denomination only in the early nineteenth century. Hundreds of New England Congregational churches were torn apart by the withdrawal of socially prominent families who had embraced Unitarianism and by legal battles over which group, Congregationalists or Unitarians, could occupy church property. Unitarians won few converts outside New England, but their tendency to attract the wealthy and educated gave them influence beyond their numbers.

Unitarians criticized revivals as uncouth emotional exhibitions and argued that "character building" was more effective than sudden emotional conversion. Yet they and the revivalists agreed in rejecting the Calvinist emphasis on human wickedness. Christianity had only one purpose, a Unitarian leader proclaimed: "the perfection of human nature, the elevation of men into nobler beings."

The Rise of Mormonism

Far more controversial than the Unitarians were the Mormons and their church, the Church of Jesus Christ of Latter-day Saints, another new denomination of the 1820s. Joseph Smith, its founder, grew up in the heart of the Burned-Over District. Conflict among the various religious denominations that thrived in the region left Smith confused: "Some were contending for the Methodist faith, some for the Presbyterian, and some for the Baptists," he later wrote. He wondered who was right and who wrong or whether they were "all wrong together."

Smith resolved this conflict, which was not uncommon in the Burned-Over District, in a unique way. He claimed that an angel had led him to a buried book of revelation and to special stones for use in translating it. The Book of Mormon, which Smith translated, tells the story of an ancient Hebrew prophet, Lehi, whose descendants migrated to America and created a prosperous civilization. Jesus had appeared and performed miracles in the New World, but Lehi's descendants had departed from the Lord's ways and quarreled among themselves. God had cursed some of these defectors with dark skin; these were the American Indians, who had long since forgotten their history.

Smith quickly gathered followers. Mormonism's appeal lay partly in its placing America at the center of Christian history and partly in its resolving the conflicting claims within Protestantism by additional revelations beyond those in the Bible. The Mormons moved steadily west, both to escape persecution and to draw closer to the Indians, whom they wished to convert. Smith's claim of a new revelation guaranteed a hostile reception for the Mormons wherever they went because it undermined the authority of the Bible, which, along with the Constitution, contained the ideals on which the American republic rested.

In 1843 Smith added fuel to the fire by proclaiming yet another revelation, this one sanctioning polygyny, the practice of taking multiple wives. Smith's claims that he was a prophet, the "Second Mohammed," also intensified the controversy that boiled around Mormonism. He proclaimed that Mormonism would be to Christianity what Christianity had been to Judaism: a grand, all-encompassing, and higher form of religion. Smith called himself "Prophet of the Kingdom of God." But in 1844 the state of Illinois charged him with treason and jailed him in the town of Carthage. There, in June 1844, a mob murdered Smith and his brother.

Mormonism is one of the few religions to originate in the United States. Smith initially hoped that Americans would respond to his call, but hostility from non-Mormons soon convinced Smith that the future of Mormonism lay in separation from society. In this respect it mirrored the efforts of several religious communal societies, among them the Shakers, whose members likewise set themselves apart from society.

The Shakers

The founder of the Shakers (who derived their name from a convulsive religious dance that was part of their ceremony) was Mother Ann Lee, the illiterate daughter of an English blacksmith. Lee and her followers had established a series of tightly knit agricultural-artisan communities in America after her arrival in 1774. Shaker artisanship, particularly in furniture, had quickly gained renown for its simple lines, beauty, and strength. Shaker advances in the development of new farm tools and seed varieties would be a boon to the growing market economy. However, the Shakers were fundamentally otherworldly and hostile to materialism. Lee had insisted that her followers abstain from sexual intercourse, believed that the end of the world was imminent, and derived many of her doctrines from trances and visions. She had also taught that at the Second Coming, Jesus would take the form of a woman.

Shaker missionaries took advantage of revivalism's appeal. At Cane Ridge and other revivals, Shaker proselytizers attracted converts whom the revivals had loosened from their traditional religious moorings. By the 1830s the Shakers numbered about 6,000.

Although the Shakers and the Mormons lived apart from traditional society, most evangelical Protestants taught that religion and the pursuit of wealth were compatible. Revivalists taught that getting ahead in the world was acceptable as long as people were honest, temperate, and bound by their consciences. By encouraging involvement in society, evangelism provided a powerful stimulus to the multiple social reform movements of the 1820s and 1830s.

THE AGE OF REFORM

During the 1820s and 1830s unprecedented numbers of men and women joined organizations aimed at improving society. The abolition of slavery, women's rights, temperance, better treatment of criminals and the insane, public education, and even the establishment of perfect, utopian communities were on the various reformers' agenda. At a time when women and blacks alike could not vote, the major parties sidestepped controversial issues such as slavery and women's rights. Reform movements offered both groups the opportunity to influence public issues. White male reformers generally viewed politics as a sorry spectacle that rewarded the sacrifice of principle with victory at the polls. Although they occasionally cooperated with political parties, especially the Whigs, reformers gave their loyalty to their causes, not to parties.

Religious revivalism intensified the righteousness of reformers, who believed that they were on God's side of any issue. Abolitionists and temperance reformers tended to come from evangelical backgrounds, but others, school reformers and women's rights advocates particularly, were often hostile or indifferent to revivals. Yet even reformers opposed to revivalism borrowed evangelical preachers' language and psychology by painting drunkenness, ignorance, and inequality as sins calling for immediate repentance and change. Reform movements lacked a national scope. New England and those parts of the Midwest settled by New Englanders were hotbeds of reform, while southerners actively suppressed abolition, displayed only mild interest in temperance and educational reform, ignored women's rights, and saw utopian communities as proof of the mental instability of northern reformers.

The War on Liquor

Agitation for temperance (either total abstinence from alcoholic beverages or moderation in their use) intensified during the second quarter of the nineteenth century. Alcohol abuse was a growing problem: per capita consumption of rum, whiskey, gin, and brandy had risen steadily until it exceeded seven gallons per year by 1830, nearly triple today's rate. The average adult male downed a half pint of liquor a day, and reformers saw alcohol excess as a male indulgence whose bitter consequences (for example, spending money on liquor instead of food) fell on women and children. Not surprisingly, millions of women marched behind the temperance banner.

The movement took off in 1825 when the popular evangelist Lyman Beecher, in six widely acclaimed lectures, thundered against all use of alcohol. Evangelical Protestants established the American Temperance Society the following year, and by 1834 it enjoyed some 5,000 state and local affiliates. The American Temperance Society demanded total abstinence and flooded the country with tracts denouncing the "amazing evil" of strong drink.

The laboring class became a chief target for temperance reformers. Passing a jug around the workplace every few hours had been a time-honored way to relieve on-the-job fatigue, but large factories demanded a more disciplined, sober work force. Manufacturers quickly supported the evangelical temperance reformers. Uninterested in temperance at first, workers flocked to reform after the Panic of 1837, forming the Washington Temperance Societies beginning in 1840. Many workers who joined the Washingtonians were reformed drunkards who had concluded that hard times required temperance and frugality. Because so many of the forces dislocating workers in the late 1830s were beyond their control, they looked to something that they could control: drinking. Take care of temperance, a Washingtonian told his audience, and the Lord would take care of the economy.

As temperance won new supporters, the crusaders shifted their emphasis from the individual drinker to the entire community and demanded that towns and even states ban all traffic in liquor. By the late 1830s prohibition was scoring victories, especially in New England. The steady rise of alcohol consumption halted in the early 1830s and then began to fall; by the 1840s the rate of consumption was less than half that in the 1820s.

Public-School Reform

Like temperance crusaders, school reformers worked to encourage orderliness and thrift in the common people. Rural "district" schools were a main target. Here students ranging in age from three to twenty crowded into a single room and learned to read and count, but little more.

District schools enjoyed considerable support from rural parents. However, reformers insisted that schools had to equip children for the emerging competitive and industrial economy. In 1837 Horace Mann of Massachusetts, the most articulate and influential of the reformers, became the first secretary of his state's newly created board of education. He presided over sweeping reforms to transform schools from loose organizations into highly structured institutions that occupied most of a child's time and energy. Mann's goals included shifting financial support of schools from parents to the state, compelling attendance, extending the school term, introducing standardized textbooks, and grading schools (that is, classifying students by age and attainment).

School reformers sought to spread uniform cultural values as well as to combat ignorance. Requiring students to arrive at a set time would teach punctuality, and matching children against their peers would stimulate the competitiveness needed in an industrializing society. Children would read the same books and absorb the same moral lessons. The McGuffey readers, which sold 50 million copies between 1836 and 1870, preached industry, honesty, sobriety, and patriotism.

Mann's reforms took root primarily in the North, despite challenges from farmers satisfied with the district school, from Catholics objecting to anti-Catholic and anti-Irish barbs in the textbooks, and from the working poor, who widely saw compulsory education as a menace to families dependent on children's wages. He and other school reformers prevailed in part because their opponents could not cooperate with each other and in part because the reformers attracted influential allies, including urban workers, manufacturers, and women. Many people doubted that a woman could control a one-room school with students of widely variant ages, but managing a classroom of eight-year-olds was different. Reformers predicted that school reform would make teaching a suitable profession for women, and they were right. By 1900, 70 percent of the nation's teachers were women.

School reform also appealed to native-born Americans alarmed by the swelling tide of immigration. The public school became a vehicle for forging a common American culture out of an increasingly diverse society. However, few reformers stressed the integration of black and white children. When black children got any schooling, it was usually in segregated schools; black children in integrated schools encountered such virulent prejudice that African-American leaders in northern cities often preferred segregated schools.

Abolition

Antislavery sentiment had flourished among whites during the Revolutionary era but faded in the early nineteenth century. The American Colonization Society, founded in 1817, was the main antislavery organization of this period. It proposed gradual emancipation, compensation for slave owners when slaves became free, and the shipment to Africa of freed blacks. Although these proposals attracted some support from slave owners in the Upper South, they were unrealizable. The growing cotton economy had made slavery more attractive than ever to most southerners, and few owners would have freed their slaves, even if compensated. The U.S. slave population, fed by natural increase, soared in the early nineteenth century, from 1.2 million in 1810 to more than 2 million by 1830, but only 1,400 blacks migrated to Africa, and most were already free.

Radical antislavery views flourished primarily among African-Americans themselves. Opposing colonization in Africa—for most American blacks were native born—they formed scores of abolition societies. One free black, David Walker of Boston, even called for a rebellion to crush slavery.

In 1821 Benjamin Lundy, a white Quaker, began a newspaper, the *Genius of Universal Emancipation,* that trumpeted repeal of the Constitution's three-fifths clause, the outlawing of the internal slave trade, and the abolition of slavery in U.S. territories. Seven years later Lundy hired a young New Englander, William Lloyd Garrison, as an editorial assistant. The prematurely bald, bespectacled Garrison looked like a genial schoolmaster, but he would become a potent force in the antislavery movement.

In 1831 Garrison launched a newspaper, *The Liberator,* to spread his radical antislavery message. "I am in earnest," he wrote. "I will not equivocate—I will not excuse—I will not retreat a single inch—AND I WILL BE HEARD." His battle cry was "immediate emancipation"; his demand, civil and legal equality for African-Americans. However, even Garrison did not believe that all slaves could be freed overnight. People first had to realize that slavery was sinful and its continued existence intolerable.

Black abolitionists supported Garrison; in its early years three-fourths of *The Liberator*'s subscribers were African-American. Other blacks were emerging as powerful writers and speakers. Frederick Douglass, an escaped slave, could rivet an audience with an opening line: "I appear before the immense assembly this evening as a thief and a robber. I stole this head, these limbs, this body from my master, and ran off with them."

Relations between white and black abolitionists were often stormy. Many white abolitionists called for legal, but not civil and social, racial

A is an Abolitionist—
A man who wants to free
The wretched slave—and give to all
An equal liberty.

B is a Brother with a skin
Of somewhat darker hue,
But in our Heavenly Father's sight,
He is as dear as you.

C is the Cotton-field, to which
This injured brother's driven,
When, as the white man's *slave,* he toils
From early morn till even.

D is the Driver, cold and stern,
Who follows, whip in hand,
To punish those who dare to rest,
Or disobey command.

The Antislavery Alphabet

Viewing children as morally pure and hence as natural opponents of slavery, abolitionists produced antislavery toys, games, and, as we see here, alphabet books.

hc Interactive Map: Escape from Slavery

equality; preferred light-skinned to dark-skinned blacks; and hesitated to admit African-Americans to antislavery societies. And widespread white prejudice made the life of any abolitionist precarious. Mobs attacked abolitionists often; one angry crowd, in Alton, Illinois, murdered abolitionist editor Elijah Lovejoy in 1837.

Abolitionists drew on the language of revivals to describe slavery as sin, but Protestant churches did not rally solidly behind abolition. Lyman Beecher roared against the evils of strong drink but whimpered about those of slavery. When he tried to suppress abolitionists at Cincinnati's Lane Theological Seminary, Theodore Dwight Weld led a mass withdrawal of students, who went on to establish Oberlin College.

As if external hostility were not enough, abolitionists differed passionately with one another. The largest national abolition group, the American Anti-Slavery Society, founded in 1833, was split by disagreements over whether abolitionists should form their own political party and about what role women should play in antislavery. Abolitionists from the Midwest and the Burned-Over District, most with ties to Charles Grandison Finney, formed the antislavery Liberty party in 1840 and ran a presidential slate. In contrast, Garrison increasingly rejected *all* laws and government. Embracing the doctrine of "nonresistance," he established the New England Non-Resistance Society in 1838. Like slavery, Garrison and his extremist followers argued, all government depended on force, and because force was the opposite of Christian love, Christians should refuse to vote, to hold office, or to have anything to do with government.

Equally divisive to the abolitionist cause were questions over the role of women in the movement. In 1837 Angelina and Sarah Grimké, the daughters of a South Carolina slaveholder, made an antislavery lecture tour of New England. Women had become deeply involved in antislavery societies by then, but always in female auxiliaries. The Grimké sisters were controversial because they spoke to audiences of both men and women at a time when it was thought indelicate for women to address male audiences. Clergymen chastised the Grimké sisters for lecturing men rather than obeying them.

Such criticism backfired, turning the Grimkés and others to the cause of women's rights. In 1838 Sarah wrote *Letters on the Condition of Women and the Equality of the Sexes;* Angelina penned her equally classic *Letters to Catharine E. Beecher* (a militant opponent of female equality). Many male abolitionists tried to dampen the feminist flames, including the poet John Greenleaf Whittier, who dismissed women's grievances as "paltry" compared to the "great and dreadful wrongs of slavery." Even Theodore Dwight Weld, who married Angelina Grimké, wanted to subordinate women's rights to antislavery. Garrison, welcoming the controversy, promptly espoused women's rights and urged that women be given positions equal to men in the American Anti-Slavery Society. In 1840 the election of Abby Kelley to a previously all-male committee split the American Anti-Slavery Society, with many profeminists splintering off to form their own groups. The split, however, did little to derail the antislavery crusade because local societies—more than 1,500 of them—continued to function more or less independently.

One of the most disruptive abolitionist tactics was to flood Congress with petitions calling for an end to slavery in the District of Columbia. Lacking time to consider the petitions, Congress in effect deprived citizens of their right to have the petitions heard. Then in 1836 southerners secured passage of the "gag rule," which automatically tabled abolitionist petitions and thus prevented congressional discussion of them. In the ensuing battle over the gag rule, congressmen with little sympathy for abolition attacked southerners for suppressing the constitutional right of petition. Ex-president John Quincy Adams, at the time a representative from Massachusetts, led the struggle against the gag rule until it was lifted in 1845.

Women's Rights

Women occupied a paradoxical position in the 1830s. They could not vote and, if married, had no right to own property or to keep their own wages.

At the same time, reform movements gave women unprecedented opportunities for public activity within their own "sphere"; for example, by suppressing liquor, women could claim that they were transforming wretched homes into nurseries of happiness.

The argument that women were natural guardians of family life was double-edged. It justified reform activities on behalf of the family but undercut women's demands for legal equality. So deeply ingrained was sexual inequality that most women came reluctantly to the issue of women's rights as a result of their experience in other reform movements, especially abolitionism. Among the early women's rights advocates who started their reform careers as abolitionists were the Grimké sisters, Lucretia Mott, Lucy Stone, and Abby Kelley.

Like abolitionism, the women's rights cause emphasized that differences of race and gender were unimportant. "Men and women," wrote Sarah Grimké, "are CREATED EQUAL! They are both moral and accountable beings, and whatever is *right* for a man to do, is *right* for woman." The most articulate and aggressive advocates of women's rights tended to gravitate to William Lloyd Garrison, who stressed the degradation of women under slavery; the entire South was a vast brothel, Garrison wrote, in which slave women were "treated with more indelicacy and cruelty than cattle." **hc** Primary Source: Ohio Associationist

The discrimination within the abolition movement infuriated women and drove them to make women's rights a separate cause. When Lucretia Mott and other American women attended the World Anti-Slavery Convention in London in 1840, they were relegated to a screened-off section. The incident made a deep impression on Mott and on Elizabeth Cady Stanton. In 1848 they organized a women's rights convention at Seneca Falls, New York. The convention issued a Declaration of Sentiments that began, "All men and all women are created equal." The participants passed a series of resolutions, including a call for the right of women to vote, which would become the centerpiece of women's rights activity after the Civil War.

Lucretia Mott
A co-organizer of the Seneca Falls convention, Mott recalled growing up "thoroughly imbued with women's rights." The daughter of a sea captain, she was raised in a Quaker family in the whaling community of Nantucket, Massachusetts. With their husbands and fathers often absent on voyages, Nantucket women took over many practical responsibilities. As a Quaker, Mott was taught that men and women had equal spiritual gifts.

Women's rights had less immediate impact than most other reforms. Temperance and school reform were far more popular, and antislavery created more commotion. Women would not secure the right to vote throughout the nation until 1920, fifty-five years after the Thirteenth Amendment had abolished slavery. One reason for the relatively slow advance of women's rights was that piecemeal gains, such as married women's securing the right to own property in several states before the Civil War, satisfied many women. The cult of domesticity also slowed feminism's advance; by sanctioning women's involvement in other reforms, it provided women with pursuits beyond the family and thus blunted demands for full equality.

Penitentiaries and Asylums

Nineteenth-century reformers operated from radically new assumptions about the causes of poverty, crime, and insanity. Rather than seeing such deviant behavior as the result of defects in human nature, as earlier Americans had, these reformers concluded that it stemmed from drunken fathers and broken homes. At the root of all evil lay the failure of parental discipline, not the will of God or the wickedness of human nature. Thus secular reformers, like religious revivalists, concluded that the right combination of moral influences could change human nature.

To cure crime, for example, reformers created highly ordered and disciplined penitentiaries as substitutes for failed parental discipline. Sincere reformation, rather than simple incarceration, became the goal. Solitary confinement would purge offenders' violent habits, reformers believed; at new prisons in Auburn and Ossining, New York, prisoners could neither speak nor look at one another during the day and spent their nights in small, windowless cells. Critics of the "Auburn system" preferred the "Pennsylvania system," in which each prisoner was isolated in a single cell and received no news or visits from the outside.

Antebellum America also witnessed a transformation in the treatment of the poor. The infirm poor crowded into almshouses, while the able-bodied poor entered workhouses. Idealistic reformers argued that taking the poor from demoralizing surroundings and putting them into such highly regimented institutions could change them into virtuous, productive citizens. But the results were often dismal. In 1833 a legislative committee found that inmates of the Boston House of Industry were packed seven to a room and included unwed mothers, the sick, and the insane as well as the poor.

Many of the insane were confined in prisons. In 1841 an idealistic Unitarian schoolteacher, Dorothea Dix, discovered insane people kept in an unheated room at the East Cambridge, Massachusetts, jail. After visiting other jails and almshouses, an appalled Dix reported that the insane were confined "in *cages, closets, cellars, stalls, pens! Chained, naked, beaten with rods, and lashed into obedience.*" Supported by Horace Mann and other reformers, she encouraged legislatures to create separate insane asylums, and by 1860, twenty-eight

states, four cities, and the federal government had built public mental institutions.

Penitentiaries, workhouses, and insane asylums all reflected the optimistic belief that deviancy could be erased by providing the right environment. Reformers believed that the unfettered freedom and individualism of American society were defects and that the poor, criminal, and insane needed regimentation. Later generations would questions these assumptions.

Utopian Communities

The belief in the perfectibility of human nature and conduct found its most extreme expression in the "utopian" communities that flourished during the reform years. Most of these, founded by intellectuals, were meant to be alternatives to the prevailing competitive economy and models whose success would inspire others.

American interest in utopian communities began in the 1820s. In 1825 British industrialist Robert Owen founded the New Harmony community in Indiana. As a mill owner, Owen had improved his workers' living conditions and educational opportunities; he was convinced that the problems of the early industrial age were social, not political. Vice and misery would vanish if social arrangements were perfected, he thought. The key was the creation of small, planned communities—"Villages of Unity and Mutual Cooperation"—with a perfect balance of occupational, religious, and social groups.

New Harmony was to provide a model for the United States; by 1827, Owen predicted, northern states would embrace its principles. Unfortunately, by 1827 there was little left to embrace, for the community, a magnet for idlers and fanatics, had fallen apart. However, Owen's belief that environment shaped character and that cooperation was superior to competition survived and influenced urban workers in particular throughout the nineteenth century.

Experimental communities with hopeful names such as Fruitlands, Hopedale, and Brook Farm proliferated amid the economic chaos of the late 1830s and 1840s. Brook Farm, which was

Chronology

1824	John Quincy Adams elected president by the House of Representatives.	1834	Whig party organized.
1826	American Temperance Society organized.	1836	Specie Circular. Martin Van Buren elected president.
1828	Andrew Jackson elected president. "Tariff of Abominations." John Calhoun anonymously writes *South Carolina Exposition and Protest.*	1837	Horace Mann becomes secretary of the Massachusetts Board of Education Elijah Lovejoy murdered by proslavery mob. Grimké sisters set out on lecture tour of New England.
1830	Jackson's Maysville Road Bill veto. Indian Removal Act.	1838	Garrison's New England Non-Resistance Society founded. Sarah Grimké's *Letters on the Condition of Women and the Equality of the Sexes* and Angelina Grimké's *Letters to Catharine E. Beecher.*
1830–1831	Charles G. Finney's Rochester revival.		
1831	William Lloyd Garrison starts *The Liberator.*		
1832	Jackson vetoes recharter of the Bank of the United States. Jackson reelected president. South Carolina Nullification Proclamation.	1840	Independent Treasury Act passed. William Henry Harrison elected president. First Washington Temperance Society started.
1833	Force Bill. Compromise Tariff. American Anti-Slavery Society founded. South Carolina nullifies the Force Bill.	1841	Dorothea Dix begins exposé of prison conditions. Brook Farm community founded.
		1848	Seneca Falls Convention.

founded near Boston in 1841, was the creation of a group of religious philosophers called transcendentalists. Most transcendentalists, including Ralph Waldo Emerson, had started as Unitarians but then tried to revitalize Christianity by proclaiming the infinite spiritual capacities of ordinary men and women. Brook Farm, like other utopias, was both a retreat and a model. Sure that the competitive commercial life of the cities was unnatural, philosophers spent their evenings in lofty musings after a day perspiring in the cabbage patch. Brook Farm attracted several renowned writers, including Emerson and Nathaniel Hawthorne, and its literary magazine, *The Dial,* disseminated transcendentalist ideas about philosophy, art, and literature (see Chapter 11).

The most controversial of the antebellum experiments in communitarian utopianism, the Oneida community in New York State, established in 1848, challenged conventional notions of the family by permitting sexual intercourse between all male and female members. Although contemporaries dismissed its founder, John Humphrey Noyes, as a licentious crackpot, Oneida achieved considerable economic prosperity and attracted new members long after less radical utopian experiments such as Brook Farm had collapsed. Widely derided as fit only for cranks, utopias exemplified in extreme form the idealism and hopefulness that permeated reform in the Jacksonian era.

CONCLUSION *hc* ACE Practice Test

The voice of the people resounded through politics and religion during the 1820s and 1830s. Mass political parties and "hurrah" campaigns replaced the surface harmony of the Era of Good Feelings. Revivalists all but abandoned the doctrine of human depravity by stressing Americans' capacity to remake themselves.

The louder the people spoke, the less unified they became. Andrew Jackson, seemingly the embodiment of the people's will, plunged into divisive contests about internal improvements, tariffs, nullification, and banking. Likewise the revivals that sought to unite Americans in a religion of the heart spawned new and controversial sects such as the Mormons and Shakers.

Seeking to forge order out of chaos, reformers built regimented institutions to cultivate the basic goodness of human nature. They disdained politics as corrupt even as they denounced liquor, ignorance, and slavery; yet these same reformers organized an abolitionist political party, for in a mass democracy, sooner or later everything became political.

FURTHER READING

Lee Benson, *The Concept of Jacksonian Democracy: New York as a Test Case* (1961). A major revisionist interpretation of the period.

Catherine A. Brekus, *Strangers and Pilgrims: Female Preaching in America, 1740–1845* (1998). An informative overview of how female preachers shaped religious practices in early America.

Donald B. Cole, *The Presidency of Andrew Jackson* (1993). Fine account, incorporating the latest scholarship.

William W. Freehling, *Prelude to Civil War* (1966). A major study of the nullification crisis.

Michael Holt, *The Rise and Fall of the American Whig Party* (1999). A comprehensive and masterful study.

Richard R. John, *Spreading the News: The American Postal System from Franklin to Morse* (1995). Provides excellent insight into the role of communications in the public life of American democracy.

Paul E. Johnson and Sean Wilentz, *The Kingdom of Matthias* (1994). A significant attempt to illuminate issues of urbanization, gender, and class during the 1820s through an investigation of the career of a cult leader, Matthias the Prophet.

Steven Mintz, *Moralists and Modernizers* (1995). A clearly written overview that stresses the modernizing features of antebellum reform movements.

Robert V. Remini, *Henry Clay: Statesman for the Union* (1991). An important new biography of the leading Whig statesman of the period.

Arthur M. Schlesinger Jr., *The Age of Jackson* (1945). A classic study, now dated in some of its interpretations but still highly readable.

Chilton Williamson, *American Suffrage: From Property to Democracy, 1760–1860* (1960). The standard study of changing requirements for voting.

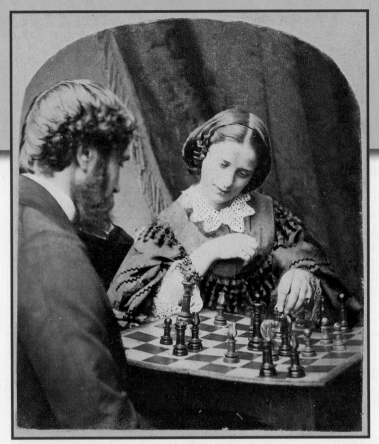

Chess Game, mid-1860s
From the Collections of Henry Ford Museum and Greenfield Village

Technology, Culture, and Everyday Life, 1840–1860

 This icon will direct you to additional study and research resources at http://college.hmco.com/history/us/boyer/enduring_concise/5e/students/index.html

In the mid-nineteenth century, most Americans believed that technology—a word coined in 1829 to describe the application of science to improving the conditions of life—was God's chosen instrument of progress. For example, they forecast that the telegraph, a major invention of the age, would bring about world peace.

But progress had a darker side. Revolvers were useless for hunting or in battle, but excellent for the violent settling of private scores. Farmwomen who had traditionally earned money sewing by hand in their homes gave way to women who sewed by machine in sweatshops. Philosophers and artists began to worry about the despoliation of

This chapter focuses on five major questions:

▶ What technological improvements increased the productivity of American industry between 1840 and 1860?

▶ In what ways did technology transform the lives of ordinary Americans?

▶ Technological change brought about both new kinds of national unity and new kinds of social division. How?

▶ How did the ways in which Americans passed their free time change during this period?

▶ What did American writers and artists see as the distinguishing features of their nation? How did these ideas find expression in literature, painting, and landscape architecture?

the landscape by factories, and conservationists launched conscious efforts to preserve enclaves of nature as parks and retreats.

TECHNOLOGY AND ECONOMIC GROWTH

To optimistic Americans, technology was both democratic and progressive. Machines would advance civilization because they could perform the work of ten people without needing food or clothing, Daniel Webster contended. A Lowell mill girl wrote, "It is emphatically the age of improvement. The arts and sciences have been more fully developed and the great mass of society are feeling its improvement."

The technology that transformed life in antebellum America included the steam engine, the cotton gin, the reaper, the use of interchangeable

parts in manufacturing, the sewing machine, and the telegraph. Some of these inventions originated in Europe, but Americans had a flair for investing in others' inventions and perfecting their own. Sadly, these advances did not benefit everyone. The cotton gin, for example, riveted slavery firmly in place by intensifying southern dependence on cotton. By rendering traditional skills obsolete, technology also undercut the position of artisans. Nonetheless, the improved transportation and increased productivity that technology made possible raised the living standards of many free Americans between 1840 and 1860.

Agricultural Advancement

Although few settlers ventured onto the treeless, semiarid Great Plains before the Civil War, settlement edged west after 1830 from the woodlands of Ohio and Kentucky into parts of Indiana, Michigan, and Illinois where flat grasslands (prairies) alternated with forests. The prairies' matted soil was difficult to break for planting, but in 1837 John Deere invented a steel-tipped plow that halved the labor required to clear prairie for planting. Timber for housing and fencing was available near the prairies, and settlement occurred rapidly.

Wheat quickly became the Midwest's major cash crop. Technology eased the task of harvesting wheat. The traditional hand sickle consumed enormous amounts of time and labor and collecting and binding the cut wheat, even more. Experiments with horse-drawn machines to replace sickles had failed until Cyrus McCormick of Virginia developed the mechanical reaper. In 1834 McCormick patented his machine; in 1847 he opened a factory in Chicago, and by 1860 he had sold 80,000 reapers. During the Civil War McCormick made immense profits by selling 250,000 reapers. The mechanical reaper, which harvested grain seven times faster than traditional methods with half the labor force, guaranteed that wheat would dominate the midwestern prairies.

Ironically, just as Connecticut Yankee Eli Whitney's cotton gin had created the Old South's economy, an invention by Cyrus McCormick, a proslavery Democrat, would help the Union win the Civil War. Northern agriculture took advantage of his reaper and copies of it to raise agricultural production; southerners, reliant on slave labor, had little reason to mechanize. The reaper would keep northern agricultural production high despite the mobilization of hundreds of thousands of northern men.

Although Americans generally remained wasteful farmers—abundant cheap land made it more "practical" to move west than to try to improve played-out soil—a movement for more efficient cultivation developed before the Civil War, primarily in the East. Because eastern soils could not compete with fertile western lands, eastern farmers had little choice. For example, some farmers in Orange County, New York, fed their cattle only clover and bluegrass; combining better feed with an emphasis on cleanliness in processing dairy products, they could then charge twice as much as others for the superior butter they marketed. Virginia wheat growers fertilized their soil with plaster left over from construction of the James River Canal and raised their average yield 250 percent between 1800 and 1860. In the 1840s cotton planters began importing guano, the dropping of sea birds on islands off Peru, for use as a fertilizer. By applying fertilizers, eastern cotton growers could close the gap created by the superior fertility of soils in the Southwest.

Technology and Industrial Progress

The early growth of U.S. manufacturing relied primarily on imported technology. That dependence lessened during the 1830s as American industries became more innovative.

Eli Whitney had pioneered in the application of interchangeable parts in the United States in 1798, but the manufacture of guns and other products using interchangeable parts still required a great deal of handwork before the components could be fitted together. By the 1840s, however, American factories had eliminated the need for hand-fitting by improving the quality of machine tools. In 1853 the superintendent of the Springfield, Massachu-

Woman at Singer Sewing Machine
Asked to repair a sewing machine that did not do continuous stitching, Isaac M. Singer invented one that did. Patented in 1851, the Singer machine quickly dominated the market. Although most early sewing machines were used in factories, some had made their way into households by 1860.

setts, armory staged a spectacular demonstration of interchangeable parts for a British commission investigating American technology. Rifles produced in ten consecutive years were stripped and their parts easily reassembled at random.

The American system of manufacturing offered multiple advantages. Damaged machines no longer had to be discarded but could be repaired simply by installing new parts. Improved machine tools allowed entrepreneurs to mass-produce new inventions rapidly, and the speed of production attracted investors. By the 1850s Connecticut firms, among them Smith and Wesson, were mass-producing the revolving pistol, which Samuel Colt had invented in 1836. Sophisticated machine tools made it possible to increase production "by confining a worker to one particular limb of a pistol until he had made two thousand." Elias Howe's sewing machine, invented in 1846, entered mass production only two years later.

After Samuel F. B. Morse transmitted the first telegraph message, Americans eagerly seized on the telegraph's promise to eliminate the constraints of time and place. They formed telegraph companies and strung lines with stunning speed. By 1852 more than fifteen thousand miles of line connected cities as distant as Quebec, New Orleans, and St. Louis. The first transcontinental line was completed in 1860. **h c** Primary Source: American Technology as an Influence Abroad

The Railroad Boom

Even more than the telegraph, the railroad dramatized technology's democratic promise. In 1790 even European royalty could travel no faster than fourteen miles an hour and that only with frequent changes of horses. By 1850 an ordinary American could travel three times as fast on a train. The swift, comfortable transportation that American railroads provided for the common person dramatized technology's democratic promise. U.S. railroads offered only one class of travel, in contrast to the several classes on European railroads. With the introduction of adjustable upholstered seats that could serve as couches at night, every American in effect traveled first class—except for African-Americans, who often were forced to sit separately.

Americans loved railroads "as a lover loves his mistress," one Frenchman wrote, but there was little to love about the earliest railroads. Sparks from locomotives showered the passengers riding in open cars, which were common. Travelers sometimes had to get out and pull trains to stations. Lacking lights, trains rarely ran at night. Before the introduction of standard time zones in 1883 (see Chapter 18), scheduling was a nightmare; at noon in Boston it was twelve minutes before noon in New York City. Delays were frequent, for trains on single-track lines had to wait on sidings for other trains to pass. Because a train's location was a mystery once it had left the station, these waits could seem endless.

Between 1840 and 1860 the size of the rail network and the power and convenience of trains were stunningly transformed. Railroad track went from 3,000 to 30,000 miles, flat-roofed coaches replaced open cars, kerosene lamps made night

MAP 11.1
Railroad Growth, 1850–1860
Rail ties between the East and the Midwest greatly increased during the railroad "boom" of the 1850s.
h c Interactive Map: Population Distribution, 1790 & 1850.

travel possible, and powerful engines let trains climb steep hills. Fifty thousand miles of telegraph wire enabled dispatchers to communicate with trains en route and thus to reduce delays.

Problems nonetheless lingered. Sleeping accommodations remained crude, and schedules erratic. Because individual railroads used different gauge track, frequent changes of train were necessary: there were eight changes between Charleston and Philadelphia in the 1850s. Yet nothing slowed the advance of railroads or cured America's mania for them. By 1860 the United States had more track than all the rest of the world.

Railroads spearheaded the second phase of the transportation revolution. Canals remained in use, but railroads, both faster and less vulnerable to winter freezes, gradually overtook them, first in passengers and then in freight. By 1860 the value of goods transported by railroads greatly exceeded that carried by canals.

During the 1850s the nation's rail net grew by 22,000 miles, and most of the expansion took place east of the Mississippi River. Cities such as Chicago, Chattanooga, and Atlanta boomed because of the railroads. Most important, the railroads crossed the Appalachian Mountains to link the East and the Midwest. The New York Central and the Erie railroads joined New York City to Buffalo; the Pennsylvania Railroad connected Philadelphia and Pittsburgh; and the Baltimore and Ohio Railroad linked the Chesapeake Bay to the Ohio-Mississippi system at Wheeling, Virginia (now West Virginia). Trunk lines tied these routes to cities farther west. By 1860 rail routes ran from Buffalo to Cleveland, Toledo, and Chicago; from Pittsburgh to Fort Wayne; and from Wheeling to Cincinnati and St. Louis.

Chicago's growth illustrates the impact of these rail links. In 1849 it was a village of a few hundred people with virtually no rail service. By 1860 it had become a metropolis of 100,000, served by eleven railroads. Farmers in the upper Midwest no longer had to send their grain, livestock, and dairy products down the Mississippi to New Orleans; they could now ship their products directly east. Chicago supplanted New Orleans as the interior's main commercial hub.

The east-west rail lines stimulated the settlement and agricultural development of the Midwest. By 1860 Illinois, Indiana, and Wisconsin had replaced Ohio, Pennsylvania, and New York as the leading wheat-growing states. Enabling farmers to speed their produce to the East, railroads increased the value of farmland and promoted additional settlement. In turn, this population growth stimulated industrial development in cities such as Chicago and Minneapolis, for the new settlers needed lumber for fences and houses and mills to grind wheat into flour. Railroads also spurred the

growth of small towns along their midwestern routes. Some lines, such as the Illinois Central, made profits from real-estate speculation. After purchasing land for stations along its route, the Illinois Central laid out towns around the stations and even stipulated street names. By the Civil War, few viewed the Midwest as a frontier or its inhabitants as pioneers.

As the nation's first big business, railroads transformed the conduct of business, particularly in finance. State money had helped to finance many lines, but by the 1840s it began to dry up. Federal aid would not be widely available until the Civil War. Although local and county governments tried to fill the void, the dramatic expansion of the rail net in the 1850s required new sources of financing. Private investors had long purchased railroad stock, but the large trunk lines of the 1850s needed far more capital than small investors could generate. Thus the railroads turned to the capital market in New York City. The railroad boom helped to make Wall Street the nation's greatest capital market, as the securities of all the leading railroads were traded on the floor of the New York Stock Exchange. New York also became the center of modern investment firms. These companies evaluated securities issued by railroads in Toledo or Chattanooga and then found purchasers in New York, Paris, London, and Amsterdam. Controlling the flow of funds to the railroads, investment bankers soon influenced their internal affairs. A Wall Street analyst noted in 1851 that railroad men seeking financing "must remember that money is power, and that the [financier] can dictate to a great extent his own terms."

Rising Prosperity

Technology also improved life by lowering prices. Clocks that cost $50 to make by hand in 1800 could be produced for 50¢ by 1850. Widespread use of steam power led to a 25 percent rise in the average worker's real income (purchasing power) between 1840 and 1860; unlike water wheels, steam engines could run in all seasons, and so workers did not have to face long winter layoffs. Although cotton textile workers saw little gain in hourly wages, their average annual wages rose from $160 to $201 between 1830 and 1869.

The growth of towns and cities also contributed to the upward trend in average annual wages. In contrast to rural farming areas, with their heavily seasonal labor, urban settings offered jobs year-round. Towns and cities also provided women and children—who seldom were paid for farm labor—new opportunities for paid work. Children's wages played an important role in family finances for working-class families. An average New York or Philadelphia working-class family spent $500 to $600 per year on food, rent, clothing, and fuel. However, an average male head of household earned $300 a year. Clearly, the survival of many families depended on the wages of children and wives.

The average urban worker was marginally better off than the average rural worker, primarily because of seasonal fluctuations in agricultural work. Most antebellum Americans continued to see farming as the ideal occupation, but comparatively few could raise the $500 or so in cash necessary to purchase, clear, and stock a farm and then wait three to five years for any reward. The economic advantages of urban life explain in part why so many Americans moved to urban areas in the first half of the nineteenth century. So does the unprecedented range of comforts and conveniences that the city offered.

THE QUALITY OF LIFE

Subtle but critical changes in the quality of daily life accompanied the large-scale transformations in transportation, production, and income in the two decades before the Civil War. These changes occurred within the home and affected routine activities such as eating, drinking, and washing. Americans became far more comfortable as machine-made furniture, stoves, and fresh food entered the home.

But change occurred unevenly. Technology made it possible for the middle class to enjoy luxu-

ries formerly reserved for the rich, yet it widened the gulf between middle class and poor. As middle-class homes became increasingly lavish, the urban poor crowded into cramped tenements. And some critical elements—medicine, for example—lagged far behind in the technological explosion. Nevertheless, Americans embraced the benefits of progress and ignored its limitations. Lacking medical advances, Americans embraced popular health movements that stressed diet and regimen over doctors.

Dwellings

During the early 1800s the unattached and distinctive wood-frame houses dotting colonial urban skylines yielded to quickly constructed, uniform-looking brick row houses. In response to rising land values, row houses were typically built with narrow facades, and they were often twice as long from front to back as they were from side to side, a design that tended to shut out light. As land values soared (as much as 750 percent in Manhattan between 1785 and 1815), renting, rather than owning, homes became common. By 1815 more than half of the homes in large cities were rented. Skyrocketing land values also led to the subdivision of row houses for occupancy by several families. The worst of these, known as tenements, were the usual habitats of Irish immigrants and free blacks.

Fashionable urban residences usually faced small parks and boasted a *Park* or *Square* address, not the plebeian *Street*. The wealthy enjoyed elegant doors, curved staircases, carved columns, and fancifully shaped rooms, all beyond the reach of the middle class. However, the rise of mass-produced furniture brought furnishings in the elaborately ornamented French style known as rococo into middle-class homes by 1860. Such furniture featured ornate carved wooden frames supporting heavily upholstered backs and seats topped with medallions; vines, leaves, and flowers covered both wooden and upholstered surfaces. Mirrors with intricate gilded moldings depicting birds, flowers, and young women were often so heavy that they threatened to tumble from the wall. Technological advances in furniture making tended to level taste between the middle and upper classes while marking those classes off from everyone else.

In rural areas the quality of housing depended as much on the date of settlement as on social class. In recently settled areas the standard dwelling was a one-room log cabin with split-log floors that allowed in drafts, roofs that let in snow, crude chimneys made of sticks and clay, and windows covered by oiled paper or cloth. As rural communities matured, log cabins gave way to frame houses of two or more rooms with glass windows and better insulation.

Conveniences and Inconveniences

To us, everyday life in the 1840s and 1850s was primitive; but to contemporaries it was constantly improving. Stoves made it possible to cook several dishes at once, and railroads brought fresh vegetables to the city, an unobtainable luxury in the 1830s. Urban waterworks carried fresh water from rivers and reservoirs to hydrants. In 1823 Philadelphia completed the first urban water-supply system; by 1860 sixty-eight public water systems were operating in the United States.

Such new conveniences existed side by side with squalor. Coal stoves belched out soot to pollute the air and blacken new-fallen snow. Only the rich could afford fruits out of season. And so few homes had iceboxes that salt remained the principal way of preserving meat; Americans ate more pork than beef because salt destroyed the flavor of beef more than that of pork. Although public waterworks were engineering marvels, their impact was uneven; few urban houses had running water, and so families carried water from street hydrants into their homes. Because hot running water was rare, the water had to be heated on the stove before one could take a bath. Not surprisingly, people rarely bathed.

Infrequent baths meant pungent body odors, but they mingled with a multitude of strong scents.

Even fashionable residential streets contained stables backed by mounds of manure. Street cleaning was left to private contractors, who often discharged their duties casually, and so urban Americans relied on hogs, which they let roam freely to scavenge, for cleaning public thoroughfares. Outdoor privies added to the stench. Flush toilets were rare outside cities, and within cities sewer systems lagged behind water systems. Boston had only 5,000 flush toilets in 1860 for a population of 178,000, a far higher ratio of toilets to people than most cities. Expensive conveniences such as running water and flush toilets widened the gap between the haves and have-nots. They also sharpened gender differences. Freed from making articles for home consumption, women were now expected to make every house a "glorious temple" of spotlessly clean floors and gleamingly polished furniture. A writer skeptical of this rush toward fastidiousness warned women against "ultra-housewifery."

Disease and Health

Despite the slowly rising living standard, Americans remained vulnerable to disease. Epidemic disease swept through antebellum American cities and felled thousands. Yellow fever and cholera killed one-fifth of New Orleans's population in 1832–1833, and cholera alone killed 10 percent of St. Louis's population in 1849.

Ironically, the transportation revolution increased the danger of epidemic diseases. The cholera epidemic of 1832, the first truly national epidemic, followed shipping routes: one branch of the epidemic ran from New York City up the Hudson River, across the Erie Canal to Ohio, and down the Ohio River to the Mississippi and New Orleans; the other branch followed shipping up and down the East Coast from New York.

Major outbreaks of cholera or yellow fever intensified public calls for the establishment of municipal health boards. However, even when such agencies were formed, they were often powerless to require the reporting of diseases.

The inability of physicians to explain epidemic diseases led to general distrust of the medical profession and to the making of public health a low-priority issue (see Chapter 9). No one understood that bacteria caused cholera and yellow fever. Instead, doctors debated the "contagion" theory versus the "miasm" theory of disease. Contagionists, who believed that touch spread disease, called for quarantines of affected areas. Supporters of the miasm theory argued that poisonous gases (miasms) emitted by rotten vegetation or dead animals carried disease through the air. They concluded that swamps had to be drained and streets cleaned. It quickly became apparent that neither theory worked.

Although epidemic disease baffled antebellum physicians, the discovery of anesthesia opened the way for advances in surgery. Laughing gas (nitrous oxide) had long provided partygoers who inhaled it enjoyable sensations of giddiness and painlessness, but it was difficult to handle. Crawford Long, a Georgia physician who had attended laughing gas frolics in his youth, employed sulfuric ether (an easily transportable liquid with the same properties as nitrous oxide) during surgery. Long did not follow up his discovery, but in 1846 William T. G. Morton, a dentist, successfully employed sulfuric ether during an operation at Massachusetts General Hospital. Within a few years ether was widely used.

The discovery of anesthesia improved the public image of surgeons, who had long been viewed as brutes hacking away at agonized patients. It also permitted longer and thus more careful operations. However, the failure of most surgeons to recognize the importance of clean hands and sterilized instruments partially offset the value of anesthesia. As early as 1843, Oliver Wendell Holmes Sr., a poet and physician, published a paper on how unclean hands spread puerperal fever among women giving birth, but disinfection was accepted only gradually. Operations remained as dangerous as the conditions they tried to heal. The mortality rate for amputations hovered around 40 percent, and during the Civil War 87 percent of soldiers who suffered abdominal wounds died from them.

Popular Health Movements

Doubtful of medicine and skeptical of the benefits of public health, antebellum Americans turned to various therapies that promised a longer, healthier life. Hydropathy, the "water cure," offered "an abundance of water of dewy softness and crystal transparency, to cleanse, renovate, and rejuvenate the disease-worn and dilapidated system." Well-to-do women flocked to hydropathic sanitoriums both to relieve pain and to enjoy relaxation and exercise in a congenial gathering place.

Sylvester Graham, a temperance reformer turned health advocate, popularized dietary changes as the way to better health. He urged Americans to eat less; to substitute vegetables, fruits, and wholegrain bread (called Graham bread) for meat; to abstain from spices, coffee, tea, and alcohol; and to avoid sexual "excess" (by which he meant most sex).

Reformers became enthusiastic proponents of Graham's ideas. Abolitionists and others agreed with Graham that Americans' unnatural cravings, whether for red meat or sex, stimulated violence and aggressive impulses. But Graham's doctrines also attracted a broad audience beyond the reform movements. His books sold well, and his public lectures were thronged. His commonsense ideas appealed to Americans wary of orthodox medicine, and he used familiar religious terms to describe disease, which was hell, and health, which amounted to a kind of heaven on earth. Graham provided simple assurances to an audience as ignorant as he was of disease's true causes.

Phrenology

The belief that each person was master of his or her own destiny underlay not only evangelical religion and health movements but also the most popular of the antebellum scientific fads: phrenology. Created by a Viennese physician, Franz J. Gall, phrenology rested on the idea that the human mind comprised thirty-seven distinct faculties, or "organs," each localized in a different part of the brain. Phrenologists thought that the degree of each organ's development determined skull shape, so that they could accurately analyze an individual's character by examining the bumps and depressions of the skull.

In the United States two brothers, Orson and Lorenzo Fowler, became the chief promoters of phrenology in the 1840s. Orson Fowler opened a publishing house (Fowlers and Wells) that marketed phrenology books everywhere. The Fowlers met criticisms that phrenology was godless by pointing out a huge organ called "Veneration" to prove that people were naturally religious, and they answered charges that phrenology was pessimistic by claiming that exercise could improve every desirable mental organ. Lorenzo Fowler reported that several of his own skull bumps had grown.

Phrenology appealed to Americans as a "practical" science. In a mobile, individualistic society, it promised a quick assessment of others. Merchants sometimes used phrenological charts to hire clerks, and some young women even induced their fiancés to undergo a phrenological analysis before marriage.

Phrenologists had close ties to popular health movements. Fowlers and Wells published the *Water-Cure Journal* and Sylvester Graham's *Lectures on the Science of Human Life*. Orson Fowler filled his popular phrenological books with tips on the evils of coffee, tea, meat, spices, and sex that could have been plucked from Graham's writings.

Easily understood and practiced, and filled with the promise of universal betterment, phrenology was ideal for antebellum America. Just as Americans had invented machines to better their lives, they could invent "sciences" that promised human betterment.

DEMOCRATIC PASTIMES

Between 1830 and 1860 technology transformed recreation into a commodity that could be purchased in the form of cheap newspapers and novels and equally cheap tickets to plays, museums,

and lectures. Fortunes awaited entrepreneurs who could sense what kind of entertainment people wanted and who could use available technology to satisfy them. James Gordon Bennett, one of the founders of the penny press, and P. T. Barnum, the greatest showman of the century, made the public want what they had to sell.

Bennett and Barnum saw themselves as purveyors of democratic entertainment: they sold their wares cheaply to anyone. Barnum's American Museum in New York City catered to varied social classes that paid to see paintings, dwarfs, mammoth bones, and other attractions. By marketing his museum as a family entertainment, Barnum helped to break down barriers between pastimes of husband and wife. Racy news stories in Bennett's *New York Herald* provided a vast audience with common information and topics of conversation.

Technology also changed the way Americans amused themselves. People had long found ways to enjoy themselves, and even the gloomiest Puritans had indulged in games and sports. After 1830, however, individuals increasingly became spectators rather than creators of amusements, relying on entrepreneurs who supplied entertainment.

Newspapers

In 1830 the typical American newspaper was four pages long, with the front and back pages filled almost completely with advertisements. The interior pages contained editorials, reprints of political speeches, notices of political events, and information about shipping. Even the most prominent papers had a daily circulation of only 1,000 to 2,000; subsidies from political parties or factions supported them. "Journalists," a contemporary wrote, "were usually little more than secretaries dependent upon cliques of politicians, merchants, brokers, and office seekers for their prosperity and bread."

Because they could be profitable without being popular, most early newspapers had limited appeal. Priced at six cents an issue, the average paper was too expensive for a worker who earned less than a dollar a day. Moreover, with few eye-catching news stories or illustrations, papers seemed little more than bulletin boards.

In the 1830s technology began to transform newspapers. Cheaper paper and steam-driven presses drastically lowered production costs, and enterprising journalists, among them James Gordon Bennett, saw the implications: slash prices, boost circulation, and reap vast profits. In 1833 New York's eleven daily newspapers had a combined daily circulation of only 26,500. Two years later the combined circulation of the three largest "penny" newspapers had soared to 44,000. From 1830 to 1840 national newspaper circulation rose from 78,000 to 300,000, and the number of weekly newspapers more than doubled.

The penny press also revolutionized the marketing and format of newspapers. Newsboys hawked the penny papers on busy street corners, and reporters filled the papers with gripping news stories designed to attract readers. As sociologist Michael Schudson observes, "The penny press invented the modern concept of 'news'." The penny papers also used the telegraph to speed both news and human-interest stories to readers.

Some penny papers were little more than scandal sheets, but others, such as Bennett's *New York Herald* and Horace Greeley's *New York Tribune,* pioneered modern financial and political reporting. The *Herald* featured a daily "money article" that analyzed and interpreted financial events. "The spirit, pith, and philosophy of commercial affairs is what men of business want," Bennett wrote. The relentless snooping by the *Tribune*'s Washington reporters outraged politicians. In 1841 *Tribune* correspondents were temporarily barred from the House of Representatives for reporting that an Ohio representative ate his lunch in the House chamber, picked his teeth with a jackknife, and wiped his greasy hands on his pants and coat.

The Theater

Like newspapers, theaters increasingly appealed to a mass audience. Antebellum theaters were large and crowded; cheap seats drew a democratic throng of lawyers and merchants and their wives, artisans and clerks, sailors and noisy boys, and a sizable body of prostitutes. The presence of prostitutes in the audience was only one of many factors that made theaters vaguely disreputable. Theater audiences were notoriously rowdy: they stamped their feet, hooted at villains, and threw potatoes and garbage at the stage when they disliked the characters or the acting.

Actors developed huge followings. In 1849 a long-running feud between leading American actor Edwin Forrest and popular British actor William Macready ended with a riot in New York City that left twenty people dead. The Astor Place riot demonstrated theater's broad popularity. Forrest's supporters included Irish workers who loathed the British and who appealed to "working men" to rally against the "aristocrat" Macready. Macready, projecting a polished, intellectual image, attracted the better-educated classes. Had not all classes patronized the theater, the riot probably never would have occurred.

The plays themselves were as diverse as the audiences. Melodramas, whose plots resembled those of sentimental novels, were popular; vice was punished, virtue was rewarded, and the heroine married the hero. Yet the single most popular dramatist was William Shakespeare. In 1835 Philadelphia audiences witnessed sixty-five performances of his plays. Shakespeare himself might not have recognized some of these performances, adapted as they were for popular audiences. Theatrical managers highlighted swordfights and assassinations, cut long speeches, and changed tragic endings to happy ones. Producers arranged for short performances or demonstrations between acts. In the middle of *Macbeth,* the audience might see an impersonation of Tecumseh or of Aaron Burr, jugglers and acrobats, a drummer beating twelve drums at once, or a three-year-old who weighed one hundred pounds.

Minstrel Shows

The minstrel shows that Americans flocked to see in the 1840s and 1850s forged enduring stereotypes that buttressed white Americans' sense of superiority by diminishing blacks. The shows arose in northern cities in the 1840s as blackfaced white men took the stage to present an evening of songs, dances, and humorous sketches.

Although the performances featured elements of African-American culture, especially dance steps, most of the songs were from white culture. Stephen Foster's "Camptown Races" and "Massa's in the Cold, Cold Ground," first performed in minstrel shows, reflected whites' notions of how blacks sang, not authentic black music. The images of blacks projected by minstrelsy catered to the prejudices of the working-class whites who dominated the audiences. Minstrel troupes depicted blacks as stupid, clumsy, and obsessively musical and emphasized their Africanness. At a time of intensifying political conflict over race, minstrel shows planted images and expectations about blacks' behavior through stock characters such as Uncle Ned, the tattered, humble, and docile slave; and Zip Coon, the arrogant urban free black who paraded around in a high hat and long-tailed coat and lived off his girlfriends' money.

By the 1850s cities from New York to San Francisco had minstrel theaters, and touring professionals brought minstrelsy to small towns and villages. The craze for minstrelsy even brought minstrels to the White House to entertain Presidents John Tyler, James K. Polk, Millard Fillmore, and Franklin Pierce.

Dan Bryant, the Minstrel
Bryant was one of many antebellum popularizers of black minstrelsy. One of the earliest known minstrelsy performances occurred in Boston in 1799 when a white man, Gottlieb Graupner, reportedly made up as a black, sang and accompanied himself on the banjo.

P. T. Barnum

No one understood better than P. T. Barnum how to turn the public's craving for entertainment into a profitable business. He was simultaneously a hustler who cheated his customers before they could cheat him and an idealist who founded a newspaper to attack wrongdoing and who thought of himself as a public benefactor.

After moving to New York City in 1834, Barnum began his career as an entrepreneur of entertainment. His first venture exhibited an African-American woman, Joyce Heth, whom Barnum billed as the 169-year-old former slave nurse of George Washington. In Barnum's mind, the truth or falsehood of the claim was irrelevant. What mattered was that people would pay. It was the start of a lifelong game between Barnum and the public.

In 1841 Barnum purchased a run-down museum in New York City, rechristened it the American Museum, and opened a new chapter in the history of popular entertainment. Avoiding the educational slant of other museums, Barnum concentrated on curiosities and faked exhibits; he wanted to interest people, not to educate them. The American Museum included ventriloquists, magicians, albinos, a five-year-old midget named Tom Thumb, and the "Feejee Mermaid," a shrunken oddity "taken alive in the Feejee Islands." By 1850 Barnum's entertainment emporium was the best-known museum in the nation.

A genius at publicity, Barnum recognized that newspapers could invent as well as report news. Thus he frequently wrote letters (under various names) to newspapers hinting that the scientific world was agog over some astonishing curiosity that the public could soon view at the American Museum. Barnum's success rested on more than people's curiosity, however. A temperance advocate, he provided lectures on the evils of alcohol and gave the place a reputation as a center for safe family amusement. In addition, Barnum tapped the public's insatiable appetite for natural wonders. At a time when each year brought new technological marvels, Americans would believe in anything, even the Feejee Mermaid.

THE QUEST FOR NATIONALITY IN LITERATURE AND ART

Europeans paid no attention to American poetry or fiction before the 1820s. While Americans could point with pride to Washington Irving's tales of Sleepy Hollow and Rip Van Winkle, they also had to admit that Irving had done most of his work while living in England.

After 1820 the United States experienced a literary flowering known as "the American Renaissance." Leading figures of this burst of creativity included James Fenimore Cooper, Ralph Waldo Emerson, Henry David Thoreau, Margaret Fuller, Walt Whitman, Nathaniel Hawthorne, Herman Melville, and Edgar Allan Poe. In 1830, 40 percent of books published in the United States were written by Americans; by 1850 this had increased to 75 percent.

Novels left room for interpretation. They might have lessons to teach, but the reader was likely more interested in plot and characters than in the moral.

Roots of the American Renaissance

Two broad movements, one economic and the other philosophical, contributed to this development. First, the transportation revolution created a national market for books, especially fiction. First to benefit from this new market was Sir Walter Scott, a British author whose historical novels became wildly popular in the United States and showed that there was a huge market for fiction. Scott became a model for many American authors, including James Fenimore Cooper.

Second, a new philosophical movement, romanticism, saturated the American Renaissance. Romantics emphasized emotion and inner feelings, focusing on the individual and his or her unique response to nature and emotion. This new emphasis on emotion created a more democratic literature, accessible to virtually everyone (unlike earlier classicism, which demanded a knowledge of ancient history and mythology). Women entered the fiction market in large numbers; although barred from higher education and the classics, they could easily access their emotions and tweak the emotions of their readers. Harriet Beecher Stowe's massive best-seller, *Uncle Tom's Cabin*, illustrates how successful women authors were in tugging at their readers' heartstrings. Novels also possessed a subversive quality, a freedom of plot and character not available to the essayist.

Cooper, Emerson, Thoreau, Fuller, and Whitman

James Fenimore Cooper was a trailblazer in the development of a national literature with distinctively American themes. In his frontiersman Natty Bumppo, "Leatherstocking," Cooper created an American archetype. Natty first appears in *The Pioneers* (1823) as an old man, a former hunter, who blames the farmers for wantonly destroying upstate New York's game and turning the silent and majestic forests into deserts of tree stumps. As a spokesman for nature against the march of civilization, Natty became a highly popular figure, and his life unfolded in several other enormously popular novels, such as *The Last of the Mohicans* (1826), *The Pathfinder* (1840), and *The Deerslayer* (1841).

During the 1830s Ralph Waldo Emerson emerged as the most influential spokesman for those who sought a national literature and art. Emerson, who served briefly as a Unitarian minister and then became a popular lecturer, voiced American intellectual ambitions in his 1837 address "The American Scholar," which called on American writers to break free of European standards.

As the leader of transcendentalism, the American offshoot of romanticism, Emerson contended that ideas of God and freedom were innate, not the result of reason. Knowledge was like sight—an instantaneous and direct perception of truth. Anyone, whether a learned university professor or a common farmer, could glimpse truth by following the promptings of his heart. Thus the United States, young and democratic, could produce as noble a literature and art as any tradition-bound European nation. "Our day of independence, our long apprenticeship to the learning of other lands draws to a close," he proclaimed. Let "the single man plant himself indomitably on his instincts and . . . the huge world will come around to him."

Although he admired Cooper's fiction, Emerson expressed his own version of literary nationalism in essays characterized by a homely reliance on the individual as well as an interest in broad philosophical questions. The true scholar, he stressed, must be independent. "Let him not quit his belief that a popgun is a popgun, though the ancient and honorable of the earth affirm it to be the crack of doom." Emerson's essays did not rely upon systematic arguments and evidence; with his conviction that truth was intuitive and individual, he relied on a sequence of vivid if unconnected assertions whose truth the reader would instantly see. One of his readers remarked that listening to Emerson was like trying to see the sun in a heavy fog; one could see light but never the sun itself.

Emerson had a magnetic attraction for young intellectuals ill at ease in conventional society.

Henry David Thoreau, born in 1817, typified the younger Emersonians. Unlike Emerson, whose adventurousness was largely intellectual, Thoreau was both a thinker and a doer. At one point he went to jail rather than pay poll taxes that would support the Mexican War, a conflict that he saw as part of a southern conspiracy to extend slavery. The experience of jail led Thoreau to write *Civil Disobedience* (1849), in which he defended disobedience of unjust laws.

In spring 1845 Thoreau moved a few miles from Concord into the woods near Walden Pond. He constructed a simple cabin on land owned by Emerson and spent the next two years providing for his wants away from civilization. Thoreau's stated purpose for his retreat to Walden was to write a book about a canoe trip that he and his brother had taken, but he soon discovered a larger purpose and undertook a much more important book. *Walden* (1854), although it abounded with descriptions of nature and wildlife, carried a larger, transcendentalist message. Thoreau proclaimed that his woodland retreat had taught him that only a few weeks' work was needed to satisfy material needs; most of the year could be used to examine life's purpose. The problem with Americans, he wrote, was that they turned themselves into "mere machines" to acquire wealth without asking why. Thoreau prodded Americans with the uncomfortable truth that material progress and moral progress were not as intimately related as they liked to think.

One of the most remarkable figures in Emerson's circle was Margaret Fuller, an intellectual whose status distanced her from conventional society. Her father gave her the sort of education a young man might have received at Harvard; she read Latin and Greek, the modern German romantics, and the English literary classics. Transcendentalism, with its emphasis on the free life of the spirit and the need for each person to discover truth on his or her own, opened a new world for Fuller. For five years she supported herself by presiding over "conversations" by Boston's elite men and women. Transcendentalism also reinforced her feminist ideas; in *Women in the Nineteenth*

Century (1845) she cast aside the doctrine of "separate spheres" and contended that no woman could achieve personal fulfillment without developing her intellectual abilities and overcoming her fear of being called masculine.

Another unconventional thinker with whom Emerson sympathized was the poet Walt Whitman, who was self-taught, exuberant, outgoing, and in love with everything American except slavery. A journalist and fervent Democrat, Whitman had an intimate, affectionate knowledge of ordinary Americans. His reading of Emerson nurtured his belief that the United States would be the cradle of a new citizen in whom natural virtue would flourish. The threads of Whitman's early career came together in his major work, *Leaves of Grass,* a book of poems first published in 1855.

Leaves of Grass shattered existing poetic conventions. Whitman composed in free verse, and his blunt, often lusty words assailed "delicacy." He wrote of "the scent of these armpits finer than prayer" and "winds whose soft-tickling genitals rub against me." Whitman became the subject as well as the writer of his poems, especially in "Song of Myself." He saw himself—crude, plain, self-taught, passionately democratic—as the personification of the American people.

To some contemporary critics, *Leaves of Grass* seemed the work of an escaped lunatic. One derided it as a "heterogeneous mass of bombast, egotism, vulgarity, and nonsense." Emerson and a few others, however, reacted enthusiastically. Emerson had long awaited the appearance of "the poet of America" and knew immediately that Whitman was that poet.

Hawthorne, Melville, and Poe

Three major writers of the 1840s and 1850s strayed far from Emerson's ideals. Nathaniel Hawthorne, Herman Melville, and Edgar Allan Poe wrote fiction that paid little heed to Emerson's call for a literature treating the everyday experiences of ordinary Americans. Hawthorne, for example, set *The Scar-*

Edgar Allan Poe
Hounded by poverty, Poe scratched out a living as an ill-paid "magazinist." Today, his reputation easily outdistances that of many of his better-paid contemporaries.

let Letter (1850) in New England's Puritan past, *The House of the Seven Gables* (1851) in a mansion haunted by memories of the past, and *The Marble Faun* (1859) in Rome. Poe set several of his short stories in Europe; and Melville's novels *Typee* (1846), *Omoo* (1847), and *Mardi* (1849) took place in the exotic South Seas, and his masterpiece, *Moby-Dick* (1851), aboard a whaler.

In part, these three writers felt that American life lacked the materials for great fiction. Hawthorne bemoaned the difficulty of writing about a country "where there is no shadow, no antiquity, no mystery, no picturesque and gloomy wrong." Psychology, not society, fascinated these writers. Each probed the depths of the human mind rather than the intricacies of social relationships. Their work displayed an underlying pessimism about the human condition and the fundamental irrationality of human nature.

Pessimism led them to create characters obsessed by pride, guilt, a desire for revenge, or a quest for perfection and then to set their stories along the byways of society, where they could explore the complexities of human motivation without the jarring intrusions of everyday life. For example, in *The Scarlet Letter* Hawthorne returned to the Puritan era in order to examine the psychological and moral consequences of the adultery committed by Hester Prynne and the minister Arthur Dimmesdale, although he devoted little attention to depicting the Puritan village in which the action takes place. Melville, in *Moby-Dick,* created the frightening Captain Ahab, whose relentless pursuit of a white whale fails to fill the chasm in his soul and brings death to all his crew except the narrator. Poe, in his short story "The Fall of the House of Usher" (1839), interwove the symbol of a crumbling mansion with the mental agony of a crumbling family.

Although these three authors ignored Emerson's call to write about the ordinary life of their fellow Americans, they fashioned a distinctively American fiction. Their works, preoccupied with analysis of moral dilemmas and psychological states, fulfilled Tocqueville's prediction that writers in democratic nations, while rejecting traditional sources of fiction, would explore the abstract and universal questions of human nature.

Literature in the Marketplace

The suspicion that commercialism would corrupt art did not entirely vanish in nineteenth-century America, but it certainly withered. The brilliant poet Emily Dickinson made little or no attempt to publish her work at all. But other authors, hardstrapped for cash, entered the marketplace. Poe, for example, scratched out a meager living writing short stories for popular magazines. Thoreau

turned to Walden only after he failed to market his poems in New York City.

Emerson helped to promote the lyceum, a new institution aimed at bringing culture to a broad public. Local organizations for sponsoring lectures, lyceums blossomed rapidly between the late 1820s and 1860. Taking advantage of the emergence of the railroad, Emerson worked the lyceum circuit, presenting most of his essays as lectures before publishing them, and relied on lecture fees as his principal source of income. Herman Melville said that "if they will pay my expenses and give a reasonable fee, I am ready to lecture in Labrador or on the Isle of Desolation off Patagonia."

Although few women traveled the lyceum circuit, they discovered other ways to tap into the growing market for literature. Writing fiction was the most lucrative occupation open to women prior to the Civil War.

Sentimental novels dominated popular fiction in the 1840s and 1850s. Susan Warner, one of the most popular writers, used such tearjerkers to elevate herself from poverty to luxury. In her *The Wide, Wide World,* the heroine wept, on the average, every other page for two volumes. Women's fiction could also be subversive, challenging the image of men as steadfast providers and women as delicate dependents. In a typical novel, a female orphan or a spoiled rich girl was thrown into hard times by a drunken father and learned to prevail. The moral was clear: women could overcome trials and improve their lives.

This sea of popular culture threatened to swamp Emerson, Hawthorne, Poe, and Melville. Emerson competed on the lecture circuit against P. T. Barnum, Hawthorne complained bitterly about "female scribblers," and Poe maintained that the public's judgment of a writer's merit was nearly always wrong. Nonetheless, society by and large did not ignore these major writers. Emerson's lectures made him famous, *The Scarlet Letter* enjoyed strong sales, and Poe's *The Raven* was so popular that some suggested that the raven replace the eagle as America's national bird. These writers, like other lesser lights, discovered that to make a living with their pens they had to meet certain popular expectations. *The Scarlet Letter,* a love story, was what the public wanted; *Moby-Dick,* with its all-male cast and high-seas exploits, was not.

American Landscape Painting

American painters between 1820 and 1860 also sought to develop nationality in their work. Lacking a mythic past of gods and goddesses, they subordinated historical and figure painting to landscape painting. The American landscape, though barren of the "poetry of decay" that Europe's ruined castles and crumbling temples provided, was fresh and relatively unencumbered by the human imprint. These conditions posed a challenge to the painters of the Hudson River school, which flourished from the 1820s to the 1870s. Its best-known representatives—Thomas Cole, Asher Durand, and Frederic Church—painted scenes of the unspoiled region around the Hudson River.

Although all three men compared the majesty of the Hudson to that of the Rhine, none was exclusively a landscapist. Some of Cole's most popular paintings were allegories, such as *The Course of Empire,* a sequence of five canvases depicting the rise and fall of an ancient city; it implied that luxury doomed republican virtue. Nor did these men paint only the Hudson; for example, Church painted the Andes Mountains. And the Hudson River school clearly influenced Albert Bierstedt in his monumental canvases of the Rockies.

The works of Washington Irving and the opening of the Erie Canal had piqued interest in the Hudson during the 1820s. Then, after 1830 Emerson and Thoreau lauded primitive nature; "in wildness is the preservation of the world." Thoreau wrote. By this time, much of the original American forest already had fallen to pioneer axes, and one writer urgently concluded that "it behooves our artists to rescue from [civilization's] grasp the little that is left before it is too late."

The Hudson River painters did more than preserve a passing wilderness; they also emphasized emotional effect. Cole's rich colors; billowing clouds; massive, gnarled trees; towering peaks; and deep chasms so heightened the dramatic impact of his paintings that poet William Cullen Bryant compared them to "acts of religion." In powerful, evocative canvases, American artists aimed to capture the natural grandeur of their land.

Like Cole, George Catlin tried to preserve a vanishing America through his art. His goal was to paint as many Native Americans as possible in their pure and "savage" state. By 1837 he had created 437 oil paintings and thousands of sketches of faces and customs from nearly fifty tribes. Catlin's romantic view of the Indians as noble savages was a double-edged sword. His admirers delighted in his dignified portrayals of Indians but shared his foreboding that the march of progress had already doomed these noble creatures to oblivion.

Landscape architects tried to create small enclaves of nature to provide spiritual refreshment to harried city dwellers. "Rural" cemeteries with pastoral names such as Harmony Grove, placed near major cities, became tourist attractions, designed as much for the living as for the dead. On a grander scale Frederick Law Olmsted and Calvert Vaux designed New York City's Central Park to look like undisturbed countryside. Drainage pipes carried water to man-made lakes, and trees screened out the surrounding buildings. Central Park became an idealized version of nature, meant to remind visitors of landscapes that they had seen in pictures. Thus nature was made to mirror art.

CONCLUSION *hc* ACE Practice Test

Technology transformed American life from 1840 to 1860. Mechanical reapers increased wheat production and enabled agriculture to keep pace with population growth. Steam power stretched out the employment season and increased productivity and income. Railroads created new communities and brought greater variety to the American diet. Technology gave rise to the penny press and the inexpensive novel and widened the reading public. Advocates of progress hailed these developments as instruments of ever-rising popular happiness.

Chronology

1820	Washington Irving, *The Sketch Book.*	**1850**	Nathaniel Hawthorne, *The Scarlet Letter.*
1823	Philadelphia completes the first urban water-supply system. James Fenimore Cooper, *The Pioneers.*	**1851**	Hawthorne, *The House of the Seven Gables.* Herman Melville, *Moby-Dick.* Erie Railroad completes its line to the West.
1826	Cooper, *The Last of the Mohicans.*	**1852**	Pennsylvania Railroad completes its line between Philadelphia and Pittsburgh.
1833	The *New York Sun,* the first penny newspaper, is established.	**1853**	Ten small railroads are consolidated into the New York Central Railroad.
1834	Cyrus McCormick patents the mechanical reaper.	**1854**	Henry David Thoreau, *Walden.*
1835	James Gordon Bennett establishes the *New York Herald.*	**1855**	Walt Whitman, *Leaves of Grass.*
1837	Ralph Waldo Emerson, "The American Scholar."	**1856**	Pennsylvania Railroad completes Chicago link. Illinois Central completed between Chicago and Cairo, Illinois.
1841	P. T. Barnum opens the American Museum.		
1842	Edgar Allan Poe, "The Murders in the Rue Morgue."	**1857**	Baltimore–St. Louis rail service completed.
1844	Samuel F. B. Morse patents the telegraph. Poe, "The Raven."	**1858**	Frederick Law Olmsted is appointed architect in chief for Central Park.
1846	W. T. G. Morton successfully uses anesthesia. Elias Howe Jr., patents the sewing machine.		
1849	Second major cholera epidemic. Astor Place theater riot leaves twenty dead.		

But progress had a price. As it narrowed the gap between the wealthy and the middle class, it widened the gap between these fortunate classes and the poor. Progress also posed moral and spiritual challenges and threatened unspoiled nature. As Hawthorne and Melville realized, progress would not necessarily liberate Americans from the dilemmas of the human condition.

FURTHER READING

Lawrence Buell, *New England Literary Culture* (1986). An excellent study of the relationship between writers and their culture.

Mary Kupiec Cayton, *Emerson's Emergence: Self and Society in the Transformation of New England* (1989). A sensitive interpretation of the major figure in the American Renaissance.

Ruth S. Cowan, *A Social History of American Technology* (1997). An excellent survey.

Ann Douglas, *The Feminization of American Culture* (1977). An analysis of the role of the middle-class women and liberal ministers in the cultural sphere during the nineteenth century.

Richard R. John, *Spreading the News: The American Postal System from Franklin to Morse* (1996). A revealing look at the age.

Judith A. McGaw, ed., *Early American Technology* (1994). A collection of fine essays on technology from the colonial era to 1850.

Barbara Novak, *Nature and Culture: American Landscape Painting, 1825–1875* (1982). An insightful study of the relationships between landscape painting and contemporary religious and philosophical currents.

Gwendolyn Wright, *Building the Dream: A Social History of Housing in America* (1981). An exploration of the ideologies and policies that have shaped American housing since Puritan times.

12

The Old South and Slavery, 1830–1860

 This icon will direct you to additional study and research resources at http://college.hmco.com/history/us/boyer/enduring_concise/5e/students/index.html

African-American Family Group in Virginia, by Larkin Mead, 1861 or 1862

Slipping through the swampy woodlands of Southampton County, Virginia, in the early morning of August 22, 1831, a band of slaves led by Nat Turner embarked on a grisly campaign of liberation. As the death count rose, so did the number of slaves following Turner; by noon more than sixty slaves had taken up axes, hatchets, and muskets, and more than sixty whites had been shot, clubbed, or hacked to death.

Despite Southampton County's isolation, word of the slave uprising soon reached the capital, Richmond, and neighboring North Carolina counties, and thousands of militia and vigilantes poured into the area. Shocking destruction greeted them; dismembered bodies and fresh blood testified to the rage unleashed by the rebels. In turn the slaves would fall victim to white rage, as scores of blacks were killed, whether or not they had actually been involved. Most of Turner's followers were either shot on sight or jailed, tried, and hanged. Turner himself eluded capture until late October; after a trial, he too was hanged.

White Virginians were stunned. What had gone wrong? Slavery in Virginia, they believed, was relatively mild, certainly in comparison to the harsh conditions in Alabama and Mississippi. And Nat Turner's background at first glance offered no answers—he did not claim that he had been mistreated by his owners. Far more was known about Nat Turner than any other black slave because of his "Confessions," recorded by his court-appointed attorney.

What the "Confessions" did reveal was in many ways more troubling than a simple litany of mistreatment and resentment. The Nat Turner of the "Confessions" was an intelligent and deeply religious man who had learned to read and write in childhood. Although Virginians, like most southerners, thought that Christianity would make slaves more docile, Nat Turner had focused on biblical passages threatening death to anyone who "stealeth" a man, a fair description of slavery. A mystic and prophet, Turner claimed that in his childhood he had seen heavenly visions of black and white spirits fighting each other. A solar eclipse had been, he thought, God's signal that the time had come for him to lead his people to freedom by killing slaveholders.

Asked shortly before his death whether he had been mistaken, Nat Turner replied, "Was not Christ crucified?" White southerners read his confessions and shuddered; many concluded that they were living on a "smothered volcano."

Before Turner, white Virginians had worried little about a slave rebellion. When whites first heard of trouble Southside, many whites jumped to the conclusion that the British were invading and only gradually realized that the slaves were rebelling.

In the short term, Nat Turner's rebellion triggered a fierce debate over emancipation of slaves in the Virginia legislature of 1831–1832; in the long

run, it hardened the hold that slavery had on the South. Once Virginia rejected emancipation, the word all but disappeared from the southern vocabulary. As northern states one by one jettisoned slavery, southern states clung to it more fiercely. Although the Upper and Lower South differed tremendously, slavery forged the two sections into a single entity known as the Old South.

KING COTTON

In 1790 the South was essentially stagnant. Tobacco, its primary cash crop, had lost its economic vitality even as it had depleted the once-rich southern soils, and neither rice nor cotton could replace tobacco's economic importance. Three out of four southerners still lived along the Atlantic seaboard, specifically in the Chesapeake and the Carolinas. One of three resided in Virginia alone.

This chapter focuses on four major questions:

▶ How did the rise of cotton cultivation affect the population and economy of the Old South? How did northerners' image of the Old South differ from the way southerners saw themselves?

▶ What major social divisions segmented the white South?

▶ How did slavery affect social relations in the white South? Why did nonslaveholding whites see their futures tied to the survival of slavery?

▶ What conditions in the Old South made it possible for a distinctive culture to develop among slaves? What were the predominant features of this culture?

The contrast between that South and the dynamic South of 1850 was stunning. By 1850 southerners had moved south and west—now only one of seven southerners lived in Virginia—and cotton reigned as king, shaping this new South. The growth of the British textile industry had created a huge demand for cotton, while Indian removal had made way for southern expansion into the "Cotton Kingdom," a broad swath of land that stretched from South Carolina, Georgia, and northern Florida in the east through Alabama, Mississippi, central and western Tennessee, and Louisiana, and from there on to Arkansas and Texas.

The Lure of Cotton

To the British traveler Basil Hall, southerners talked incessantly of cotton. "Every flow of wind from the shore wafted off the smell of that useful plant; at every dock or wharf we encountered it in huge piles or pyramids of bales, and our decks were soon choked with it. All day . . . the captain, pilot, crew, and passengers were talking of nothing else." A warm climate, wet springs and summers, and relatively dry autumns made the Lower (or Deep) South ideal for cultivating cotton. A cotton farmer needed neither slaves nor cotton gins nor the capital required for sugar cultivation. Indeed, perhaps 50 percent of farmers in the "Cotton Belt" owned no slaves, and to process their harvest, they could turn to the widely available commercial gins. In short, cotton profited everyone; it promised to make poor men prosperous and rich men kings.

Yet large-scale cotton cultivation and slavery grew together as the southern slave population nearly doubled between 1810 and 1830. Three-fourths of all southern slaves worked in the cotton economy in 1830. Owning slaves enabled a planter to harvest vast fields of cotton speedily, a crucial advantage because a sudden rainstorm at harvest time could pelt cotton to the ground and soil it.

Cotton offered an added advantage: it was compatible with corn production. Corn could be planted either earlier or later than cotton and harvested before or after. Because the cost of owning a slave remained the same regardless of whether he or she was working, corn production allowed slaveholders to shift slave labor between corn and cotton. By 1860 the acreage devoted to corn in the Old South actually *exceeded* that devoted to cotton. Economically, corn and cotton gave the South the best of two worlds. Intense demand in Britain and New England kept cotton prices high and money flowing into the South. Because of southern self-sufficiency in growing corn and raising hogs that thrived on the corn, money did not drain away to pay for food. In 1860 the twelve wealthiest counties in the United States were all in the South.

Ties Between the Lower and Upper South

Two giant cash crops, sugar and cotton, dominated agriculture in the Lower South. The Upper South, a region of tobacco, vegetable, hemp, and wheat growers, depended far less on the great cash crops. Nevertheless, a common dependence on slavery unified the Upper and the Lower South and made the Upper South identify more with the Lower South than with the nation's free states.

A range of social, political, and psychological factors promoted this unity. First, many settlers in the Lower South had come from the Upper South. Second, all white southerners benefited from the Constitution's three-fifths clause, which let them count slaves as a basis for congressional representation. Third, abolitionist attacks on slavery stung all southerners and bound them together. Fourth, economic ties linked the two Souths. The profitability of cotton and sugar increased the value of slaves throughout the South. The sale of slaves from the declining plantation states of the Upper South to the booming Lower South was a huge business. Eliminate the slave trade, one Virginian argued, and "Virginia will be a desert."

The North and South Diverge

However, the changes responsible for the dynamic growth of the South widened the distance between it and the North. The South remained predomi-

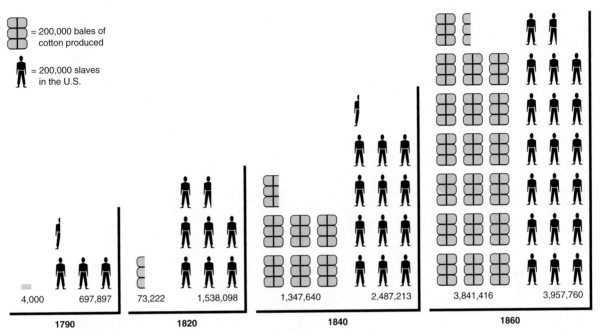

= 200,000 bales of cotton produced

= 200,000 slaves in the U.S.

1790	1820	1840	1860
4,000	73,222	1,347,640	3,841,416
697,897	1,538,098	2,487,213	3,957,760

Growth of Cotton Production and the Slave Population, 1790–1860
Cotton and slavery rose together in the Old South.

nantly rural as the North became more and more urban.

Lack of industry kept the South rural; by 1850 it had one-third of the U.S. population but accounted for only a tenth of the nation's manufacturing. In 1850 the industrial output of the entire South was less than a third that of Massachusetts alone.

Some southerners advocated and created factories in the South, but they were a minority. By 1860 cotton-textile mills were scattered throughout the South, and Richmond boasted the nation's fourth-largest producer of iron products, the Tredegar Iron Works. Despite these successes, industrial output in the South trailed far behind that of the New England and Middle Atlantic states. Southern factories were small; they produced mainly for nearby markets, and they were closely tied to agriculture. While northern factories manufactured cloth and shoes, southern factories turned grain into flour, corn into meal, and trees into lumber.

Slavery posed a major obstacle to southern industrialization, but not because slaves were unfit for factories; the Tredegar Iron Works was among many factories that employed slaves. However, the prospect of industrial slavery troubled slaveholders. Away from the strict discipline and supervision possible on a plantation, slaves sometimes behaved as if they were free, shifting jobs, working overtime, and even negotiating better working conditions. A Virginia planter summed up whites' lamentations about urban, industrial slaves: they "got the habit of roaming about and *taking care of themselves.*"

But the chief brake on southern industrialization was money, not labor. To raise the capital needed to build factories, planters would have had to sell their slaves. They seldom did. Cash crops such as cotton and sugar were proven, but the

Port and City of New Orleans
In the late 1850s New Orleans was the largest city and port in the South. Cotton bales, sometimes protected by a tarpaulin, awaited loading on sailing ships for transport to Europe or New England. Steamships were used mainly for carrying traffic on the Mississippi River rather than for ocean voyages.

benefits of industrialization were remote and doubtful. Successful industrialization also would disrupt social relations, a southerner contended, by introducing "filthy, overcrowded, licentious factories" and attracting abolitionists. As long as southerners believed that the cash-crop economy remained profitable, they had little reason to plunge into the uncertainties of industrialization.

In education, as in industry, the South lagged behind the North. Where northerners recognized the benefits of an educated work force for their growing manufacturing economy, agriculturally oriented southerners rejected compulsory education and were reluctant to tax property to support schools. They abhorred the thought of educating slaves, and southern lawmakers made it a crime to teach slaves to read. For most whites, the only available schools were private. White illiteracy thus remained high in the South as it declined in the North.

The primary reason for the South's failure to develop effective public schools was widespread indifference. Agricultural, self-sufficient, and independent, the middling and poor whites of the South remained unconvinced of the need for public education. They had little dependency on the printed word, few complex commercial transactions, and infrequent dealings with urban people. Planters did not need an orderly and disciplined white work force; they already had a black one that they were determined to keep illiterate lest it acquire ideas about freedom.

Because the South diverged so sharply from the North, outsiders often dismissed it as backward. A northern journalist wrote of white southerners in the 1850s, "They work little, and that little, badly; they earn little, they sell little; they buy little, and have little—very little—of the common comforts and consolations of civilized life."

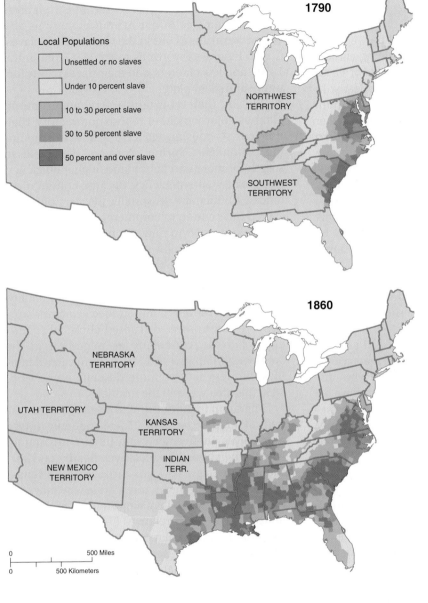

MAP 12.1

Distribution of Slaves, 1790 and 1860

In 1790 the majority of slaves resided along the southeastern seaboard. By 1860, however, slavery had spread throughout the South, and slaves were most heavily concentrated in the Deep South states. *Source:* Reprinted with permission of the McGraw-Hill Companies, from *Ordeal by Fire: The Civil War and Reconstruction*, Second Edition, by James M. McPherson. Copyright © 1992 by the McGraw-Hill Companies. *hc* Interactive Map: The Legal Status of Slavery, from the Revolution to the Civil War

But the South did not lack progressive features. By 1860 white per capita income in the South exceeded the national average. And although southerners lagged behind northerners in general technology, they did advance in the area that concerned them most: scientific agriculture.

Thus the Old South was not economically backward—it was merely different. Cotton was a wonderful crop, and southerners could hardly be blamed for making it their ruler. As a southern senator wrote in 1858, "You dare not make war upon cotton; no power on earth dares to make war upon it. Cotton is king."

THE SOCIAL GROUPS OF THE WHITE SOUTH

There was wide diversity within and between the South's slaveholding and nonslaveholding classes. Although some planters owned hundreds of slaves and lived lavishly, most lived more modestly. In 1860, one-fourth of all white families in the South owned slaves; nearly half of those owned fewer than five slaves, and three-fourths had fewer than ten slaves. Only 12 percent owned twenty or more slaves, and only 1 percent a hundred or more. Non-slaveholders were equally diverse. Most owned farms and drew on the labor of family members, but other whites squatted on land in the pine barrens or piney woods and scratched out a living by raising livestock, hunting, fishing, and planting a few acres of corn, oats, or sweet potatoes.

Planters, small slaveholders, family farmers, and pine-barrens folk composed the South's four main white groups. Many southerners—lawyers, physicians, merchants, and artisans—did not fall into any of these four, but they tended to identify their interests with one or another of the agricultural groups. Urban merchants and lawyers depended on the planters and shared their views on most issues, whereas rural artisans and merchants dealt with, and were thus attuned to, the family farmers, or yeomen.

Planters and Plantation Mistresses

The plantation, with its porticoed mansion and fields teeming with slaves, stands at the center of the popular image of the Old South. This romanticized view, reinforced by novels and movies such as *Gone with the Wind,* is not entirely false, for the South did contain plantations that travelers found "superb beyond description." Abundant slaves, the division of labor they afforded, and plentiful land allowed large plantations to generate incomes of $20,000 or more a year, an immense sum in those years.

In the eighteenth century during the initial flush of settlement in the piedmont and trans-Appalachian South, even well-off planters generally had lived in humble log cabins. After 1810, however, elite planters competed with one another to build stately mansions. Yet most planters counted their wealth not in grand mansions and elegant furnishings but in the value of their slaves. A field hand was worth as much as $1,700 in the 1850s, and few planters sold their slaves to buy furniture and silver plate.

But in their constant worry about profit, planters enjoyed neither repose nor security. High fixed costs—housing and feeding slaves, maintaining cotton gins, hiring overseers—led them to search for more and better land, higher efficiency, and greater self-sufficiency. Because cotton prices tended to fluctuate seasonally, planters often assigned their cotton to commercial agents in cities, who held the cotton until the price was right. The agents extended credit so that the planters could pay their bills before the cotton was sold. Indebtedness became part of the plantation economy and intensified the planters' quest for profitability. Psychological strains compounded economic worries. Frequent moves disrupted circles of friends and relatives, particularly as migration to the Southwest (Alabama and Mississippi) carried families into less settled, more desolate areas. Until 1850 this area was still the frontier.

Migration to the Southwest often deeply unsettled plantation women. They suddenly found themselves in frontier conditions with neither friends, neighbors, nor relatives nearby and surrounded by slaves. "I am sad tonight, sickness preys upon my frame," wrote a bride who moved to Mississippi in 1833. "I am alone and more than 150 miles from any near relatives in the wild woods of an Indian nation." Frequent absences by husbands, whether they were looking for new land, supervising outlying plantations, or conducting business in the city, intensified wives' loneliness.

Planters and their wives found various ways of coping with their isolation. Employing overseers to run the plantation, some lived in cities; in 1850 one-half the planters in the Mississippi Delta lived in New Orleans or Natchez. Most planters acted as their own overseers, however, and dealt with the problems of harsh living conditions by opening their homes to visitors. The responsibility for such hospitality fell heavily on wives, who might have to entertain as many as fifteen people for breakfast and attend to the needs of visitors who stayed for days. Plantation wives also bore the burdens of raising their children, supervising house slaves, making clothes and carpets, looking after smoke-houses and dairies, planting gardens, and, often, keeping the plantation accounts. Plantation wives were anything but the delicate idlers of legend.

Among the heaviest sorrows of some plantation mistresses was the presence of mulatto children, constant reminders of their husbands' infidelities. Charlestonian Mary Boykin Chesnut, a famous diarist, observed tartly, "Any lady is ready to tell you who is the father of all the mulatto children in everybody's household but her own. These, she seems to think, drop from clouds." Southern men insisted on sexual purity for white women but allowed themselves a looser standard. The father of abolitionist sisters Sarah and Angelina Grimké fathered three mulatto children after his wife's death. The gentlemanly code usually tolerated such transgressions.

Yet isolation, drudgery, and humiliation did not turn planters' wives against the system. Indeed, when the Civil War came, they supported the Confederacy as enthusiastically as any group. However much they might have hated living as white islands in a sea of slaves, they recognized that their wealth and position depended on slavery.

The Small Slaveholders

In 1860, 88 percent of all slaveholders owned fewer than twenty slaves, and most possessed fewer than ten. One out of every five slaveholders worked outside of agriculture, as a lawyer, physician, merchant, or artisan.

Small slaveholders experienced conflicting loyalties and ambitions. In upland regions they absorbed the outlook of the more numerous yeomen (nonslave owning small farmers); they owned only a few slaves and rarely aspired to become large planters. In contrast, in the plantation-dominated low country and delta regions, small slaveholders often aspired to planter status. There someone with ten slaves could realistically look forward to owning thirty. And ambitious, acquisitive individu-

als equated success with owning more slaves. The logic of slavery remained the same: the only way to justify the investment in slaves was to set them to work on profitable crops. Such crops demanded more and better land, and both the planters and the small slaveholders of the deltas were restless and footloose.

The social structure of the deltas was fluid. In the early antebellum period large planters had been reluctant to risk transporting their hundreds of valuable slaves in a still turbulent region. It was small slaveholders who led the initial westward push into the Cotton Belt in the 1810s and 1820s. Gradually, large planters, too, moved westward, buying up the land that the small slave owners had developed and turning the region from Vicksburg to Natchez into large plantations. Small slave owners took the profits from selling their land, bought more slaves, and moved on. They gradually transformed the region from Vicksburg to Tuscaloosa, Alabama, into a belt of medium-sized farms with a dozen or so slaves on each.

The Yeomen

Nonslaveholding family farmers, or yeomen, composed the largest single group of southern whites. Most owned land, and many hired slaves to help at harvest. In areas of poor soil, such as eastern Tennessee, yeomen were typically subsistence farmers, but most yeomen grew some cash crops. Their land-holdings were comparatively small, ranging from 50 to 200 acres. Yeomen generally inhabited uplands, such as the piedmont of the East or the hilly upcountry of the Southwest, far from the rich coastal plains and deltas. Young, landless yeomen lived with and worked for relatives.

Above all, the yeomen valued self-sufficiency. Unlike planters, who were driven to acquire more land and to plant more cash crops, the yeomen devoted much of their acreage to subsistence crops such as corn, sweet potatoes, and oats. The planter's ideal was profit with modest self-sufficiency; the yeoman's goal, self-sufficiency with modest profit.

Yeomen living in planter-dominated regions were often dismissed as "poor white trash," but in the upland regions that they dominated, the yeomen were highly respected. Upland slaveholders tended to own only a few slaves; like the yeomen, they were essentially family farmers. With or without the aid of slaves, yeomen fathers and sons cleared the land and cultivated the fields. Wives and daughters planted and tended vegetable gardens, helped at harvest, occasionally cared for livestock, cooked, and made the family's clothes.

Unlike southern planters, yeomen marketed their cash crops locally, trading cotton, wheat, and tobacco for goods and services from nearby artisans and merchants. In some areas yeomen sold their surplus corn to drovers and herdsmen who specialized in raising hogs. Along the French Broad River in eastern Tennessee, for example, 20,000 to 30,000 hogs a year were fattened for market. At peak season a traveler would see 1,000 hogs a mile. The hogs were penned at night in huge stock stands—veritable hog hotels—and fed with corn supplied by the local yeomen.

The People of the Pine Barrens

Independent whites of the wooded "pine barrens" were one of the most controversial groups in the Old South. About 10 percent of southern whites, they usually squatted on the land; put up crude cabins; cleared some acreage, where they planted corn between tree stumps; and grazed hogs and cattle in the woods. They neither raised cash crops nor engaged in the daily routine of orderly work that characterized family farmers. With their ramshackle houses and handful of stump-strewn acres, they appeared lazy and shiftless.

Abolitionists cited the pine-barrens people as proof that slavery degraded whites, but southerners responded that, while the pine-barrens folk were poor, they could at least feed themselves, unlike the paupers of northern cities. In general, the people of the pine barrens were both self-sufficient and fiercely independent. Pine-barrens men were reluctant to hire themselves out as laborers to do "slave" tasks, and the women refused to become servants.

Neither victimized nor oppressed, these people generally lived in the pine barrens by choice. The

grandson of a farmer who had migrated from Emanuel County, Georgia, to the Mississippi pine barrens explained his grandfather's decision: "The turpentine smell, the moan of the winds through the pine trees, and nobody within fifty miles of him, [were] too captivating . . . to be resisted, and he rested there."

SOCIAL RELATIONS IN THE WHITE SOUTH

Antislavery northerners often charged that slavery warped the South's entire social structure. By creating a permanent black underclass of bond servants, they alleged, slavery robbed lower-class whites of the incentive to work, reduced them to shiftless misery, and rendered the South a premodern throwback in an otherwise progressive era. Southerners retorted that the real center of white inequality was the North, where merchants and financiers paraded in fine silks and never soiled their hands with manual labor.

In reality, the white South mixed aristocratic and democratic, premodern and modern features. Although the South featured considerable class inequality, property ownership was widespread. Rich planters dominated social life and the legislature, but they did not necessarily get their way, and often their political agenda paralleled that of other whites. Like white northerners, white southerners were restless, acquisitive, eager to make money, and skillful at managing complex commercial enterprises. Yet practices such as slaveholding and dueling thrived in the South when they were dying out elsewhere.

Conflict and Consensus in the White South

Planters tangled with yeomen on several issues. With extensive economic dealings and need for credit, planters inclined toward the Whig party, which generally supported economic development. The independent yeomen, cherishing their self-sufficiency, tended to be Democrats.

Yet few conflicts arose between these groups. An underlying political unity reigned in the South. Geography was in part responsible: planters, small slaveowners, yeomen, and pine-barrens folk tended to cluster in different regions, each independent of the others. In addition, with landownership widespread and factories sparse, few whites worked for other whites, and so friction among whites was minimized.

The white South's political structure was sufficiently democratic to prevent any one group from gaining exclusive control over politics. Planters dominated state legislatures, but they owed their election to the popular vote. And the democratic currents that had swept northern politics between 1815 and 1860 had affected the South as well; newer southern states entered the Union with democratic constitutions that included universal white manhood suffrage—the right of all adult white males to vote.

Although yeomen often voted for planters, the nonslaveholders did not give their elected representatives a blank check to govern as they pleased. During the 1830s and 1840s Whig planters who favored banks faced intense and often successful opposition from Democratic yeomen. These yeomen blamed banks for the Panic of 1837 and pressured southern legislatures to restrict bank operations. The nonslaveholders got their way often enough to nurture their belief that they, not the slaveholders, controlled politics.

Conflict over Slavery

Nevertheless, considerable *potential* existed for conflict between slaveholders and nonslaveholders. The southern white carpenter who complained in 1849 that "unjust, oppressive, and degrading" competition from slave labor depressed his wages surely had a point. Between 1830 and 1860 the slaveholding class shrank in size in relation to the total white population, but its share of total wealth increased. As a Louisiana editor wrote in 1858, "The present tendency of supply and demand is to concentrate all the slaves in the hands of the few, and thus excite the envy rather than cultivate the sympathy of the people."

Yet although pockets of opposition dotted the South, slavery did not create profound or lasting divisions between slaveholders and nonslaveholders. For example, antagonism to slavery flourished in parts of Virginia up to 1860, but proposals for emancipating the slaves dropped from the state's political agenda after 1832. Kentucky had a history of antislavery activity dating back to the 1790s, but after calls for emancipation suffered a crushing defeat in an 1849 referendum, slavery ceased to be a political issue there.

The rise and fall of pro-emancipation sentiment in the South raises a key question: as most white southerners were nonslaveholders, why did they not attack slavery more consistently? To look ahead, why were so many southerners willing to fight ferociously and to die bravely during the Civil War in defense of an institution in which they apparently had no real stake? There are several reasons. First, some nonslaveholders hoped to become slaveholders. Second, most southerners accepted the racist assumptions on which slavery rested; they dreaded the likelihood that emancipation would encourage "impudent" blacks to entertain ideas of social equality with whites. Slavery appealed to whites as a legal, time-honored, and foolproof way to enforce the social subordination of blacks. Third, no one knew where the slaves, if freed, would go or what they would do. Colonizing freed blacks in Africa was unrealistic, southerners concluded, but they also believed that without colonization, emancipation would lead to a race war. In 1860 Georgia's governor sent a blunt message to his constituents, many of them nonslaveholders: "So soon as the slaves were at liberty thousands of them would leave the cotton and rice fields . . . and make their way to the healthier climate of the mountain region [where] we should have them plundering and stealing, robbing and killing."

The Proslavery Argument

Between 1830 and 1860 southerners constructed a defense of slavery as a positive good rather than a necessary evil. St. Paul's injunction that servants obey their masters became a biblical justification for some. Others looked to the classical past to argue that slavery was both an ancient and classical institution; the slave society of Athens, they said, had produced Aristotle and Plato, and Roman slaveholders had laid the foundations of Western civilization. George Fitzhugh of Virginia contrasted the plight of the northern "wage slaves," callously discarded when they became too ill or too old to work, with the lot of southern slaves, cared for by masters who attended to their health, their clothing, and their discipline.

At the same time, southerners increasingly suppressed any open discussion of slavery within the South. Proslavery writers warned that abolitionists wanted to destroy the family as well as slavery by undermining the "natural" submission of children to parents, wives to husbands, and slaves to masters. In the 1830s proslavery southerners seized abolitionist literature from southern mails and burned it. Although Kentucky abolitionist Cassius Marcellus Clay protected his press with two cannons, in 1845 a mob dismantled it anyway. By 1860 any southerner found with a copy of Hinton R. Helper's antislavery *The Impending Crisis* might well fear for his life.

The rise of the proslavery argument coincided with a shift in the position of southern churches on slavery. During the 1790s and early 1800s some Protestant ministers had assailed slavery as immoral, but by the 1830s most clergymen had convinced themselves that slavery was both compatible with Christianity and necessary for the proper exercise of Christian religion. Slavery, they proclaimed, displayed Christian responsibility toward one's inferiors, and it helped African-Americans to develop Christian virtues such as humility and self-control. Southerners increasingly attacked antislavery evangelicals in the North for disrupting the "superior" social arrangement of the South. In 1837 southerners and conservative northerners had combined forces to drive antislavery New School Presbyterians out of that denomination's main body, in 1844 the Methodist Episcopal Church split into northern and southern wings, and in 1845 Baptists formed a separate Southern Convention. In effect, southern evangelicals seceded from national church organizations long be-

fore the South seceded from the Union.
hc Primary Source: Religion as Social Control

Violence in the White South

Throughout the colonial and antebellum periods, violence deeply colored the daily lives of white southerners. In the 1760s a minister described back-country Virginians "biting one anothers Lips and Noses off, and gowging one another—that is, thrusting out anothers Eyes, and kicking one another on the Cods [genitals], to the great damage of many a Poor Woman." Gouging out eyes became a specialty of sorts among poor southern whites. On one occasion a South Carolina judge entered his court to find a plaintiff, a juror, and two witnesses all missing one eye. Stories of eye gougings and ear bitings became part of Old South folklore. Mike Fink, a legendary southern fighter and hunter, boasted that he was so mean in infancy that he refused his mother's milk and howled for whiskey. Yet beneath the folklore lay the reality of violence that gave the Old South a murder rate as much as ten times higher than that of the North.

The Code of Honor and Dueling

At the root of most violence in the white South lay intensified feelings of personal pride that reflected the inescapable presence of slaves. White southerners saw slaves degraded, insulted, and powerless to resist. In turn, whites reacted violently to even trivial insults to demonstrate that they had nothing in common with slaves.

Among gentlemen this exaggerated pride took the form of a code of honor, with honor defined as an extraordinary sensitivity to one's reputation. Northern moralists celebrated a rival idea, character, the quality that enabled an individual to behave in steady fashion regardless of how others acted toward him or her. In the honor culture of the Old South, however, even the slightest insult, as long as it was perceived as intentional, could become the basis for a duel.

Formalized by French and British officers during the Revolutionary War, dueling gained a secure niche in the Old South as a means by which gentlemen dealt with affronts to their honor. Seemingly trivial incidents—a harmless brushing against the side of someone at a public event, a hostile glance—could trigger a duel. Yet dueling did not necessarily lead to violence. Gentlemen viewed dueling as a refined alternative to the random violence of lower-class life. Instead of leaping at his antagonist's throat, a gentleman remained cool, settled on a weapon with his opponent, and agreed to a meeting place. In the interval, friends of the parties negotiated to clear up the "misunderstanding" that had provoked the challenge. Most confrontations ended peaceably rather than on the field of honor at dawn.

Although dueling was as much a way of settling disputes peacefully as of ending them violently, the ritual could easily end in death or maiming. Dueling bypassed the court system, which would have guaranteed a peaceful result; in disputes involving honor, recourse to the law struck many southerners as cowardly and shameless.

Dueling rested on the assumption that gentlemen could recognize each other and know when to respond to a challenge. Nothing in the code of honor compelled a person to duel with someone who was not a gentleman, for such a person's opinion hardly mattered. An insolent porter who insulted a gentleman might get a whipping but did not merit a duel. Yet it was often difficult to determine who was a gentleman. Indeed, the Old South teemed with would-be gentlemen. A clerk in a country store in Arkansas in 1850 found it remarkable that ordinary farmers who hung around the store talked of their honor, and that the proprietor, a German Jew, carried a dueling pistol.

The Southern Evangelicals and White Values

With its emphasis on the personal redress of grievances and its inclination toward violence, the ideal of honor conflicted with the values preached by the southern evangelical churches, notably the Baptists, Methodists, and Presbyterians. These denominations stressed humility and self-restraint, virtues that sharply contrasted with the culture of display that buttressed the extravagance and violence of the Old South.

By the 1830s, however, southern evangelicals had begun to change. They no longer made an effort to reach out to women, blacks, and the poor; instead, women were now expected to remain silent in church, while urban blacks increasingly formed their own churches. Both Methodists and Baptists began to attract the well-to-do, a tendency that increased with the opening of colleges such as Randolph-Macon and Wake Forest. More and more, southern gentry and evangelicals shared values, including a prickly regard for their honor and reputation. By the 1860s the South counted many gentlemen like the Bible-quoting Presbyterian general Thomas J. "Stonewall" Jackson, fierce in a righteous war but a sworn opponent of strong drink, gambling, and dueling.

LIFE UNDER SLAVERY

Slavery, the institution at the root of the code of honor and other distinctive features of the Old South, has long inspired controversy among historians. Some have seen slavery as a benevolent institution in which African-Americans lived contentedly under kindly masters; others, as a brutal system that drove slaves into constant rebellion. Neither view is accurate, but both contain a germ of truth. There were kind masters, and some slaves developed genuine affection for their owners. Yet slavery inherently oppressed its African-American victims by forcibly appropriating their life and labor. Even kind masters exploited blacks in order to earn profits. And kindness was a double-edged sword; the benevolent master expected grateful affection from his slaves and interpreted that affection as loyalty to slavery itself. When northern troops descended on the plantations during the Civil War, masters were genuinely surprised and dismayed to find many of their most trusted slaves deserting to Union lines.

The kindness or cruelty of masters was important, but three other factors primarily determined slaves' experience: the kind of agriculture in which they worked, whether they resided in rural or urban areas, and what century they lived in. The experiences of slaves working on cotton plantations in the 1830s differed drastically from those of slaves in 1700, for reasons unrelated to the kindness or brutality of masters.

The Maturing of the Plantation System

Slavery changed significantly between 1700 and 1830. In 1700 the typical slave was a man in his twenties, recently arrived from Africa or the Caribbean, who worked on an isolated small farm. Drawn from different regions of Africa, few slaves spoke the same language. Because slave ships carried twice as many men as women, and because slaves were widely scattered, blacks had difficulties finding partners and creating a semblance of family life. Severe malnutrition sharply limited the number of children slave women bore. Without continuing importations, the number of slaves in North America would have declined between 1710 and 1730.

In contrast, by 1830 the typical North American slave was as likely to be female as male, had been born in America, spoke English, and worked beside numerous other slaves on a plantation. The rise of plantation agriculture in the eighteenth century was at the heart of the change. Plantation slaves found mates more easily than slaves on scattered farms. The ratio between slave men and women fell into balance, and marriage between slaves on the same or nearby plantations increased. The native-born slave population soared after 1750. The importation of African slaves declined, and in 1808 Congress banned it.

Work and Discipline of Plantation Slaves

In 1850 the typical slave worked on a large farm or plantation with at least ten other slaves. Almost three-quarters of all slaves belonged to masters with ten or more slaves, and just over one-half lived in units of twenty or more slaves. Thus understanding the life of a typical slave requires examining plantation routines.

An hour before sunrise, a horn or a bell awakened the slaves. After a sparse breakfast, they marched to the fields. A traveler in Mississippi described such a procession: "First came, led by an old driver carrying a whip, forty of the largest and strongest women I ever saw together; they were all in a simple uniform dress of bluish check stuff, the skirts reaching little below the knee; their legs and feet were bare; they carried themselves loftily, each having a hoe over the shoulder, and walking with a free, powerful swing." The plow hands followed, "thirty strong, mostly men, but few of them women. . . . A lean and vigilant white overseer, on a brisk pony, brought up the rear."

Slave men and women worked side by side in the fields. Those female slaves who did not labor in the fields remained busy. A former slave, John Curry, described how his mother milked cows, cared for children whose mothers worked in the fields, cooked for field hands, washed and ironed for her master's household, and looked after her own seven children. Plantations never lacked tasks for slaves of either gender. As former slave Solomon Northup noted, "Ploughing, planting, picking cotton, gathering the corn, and pulling and burning stalks, occupies the whole of the four seasons of the year. Drawing and cutting wood, pressing cotton, fattening and killing hogs, are but incidental labors." In any season the slave's day stretched from dawn to dusk. When darkness made field work impossible, slaves toted cotton bales to the ginhouse, gathered wood for supper fires, and fed the mules. Weary from their labors, they slept in log cabins on wooden planks.

Although virtually all antebellum Americans worked long hours, no others experienced the combination of long hours and harsh discipline that slave field hands endured. Northern factory workers did not live in fear of drivers walking among them with a whip. Repulsive brutality pervaded American slavery. For example, pregnant slave women were sometimes forced to lie in depressions in the ground and endure whipping on their backs, a practice that supposedly protected

Black Women and Men on a Trek Home, South Carolina
Much like northern factories, large plantations made it possible to impose discipline and order on their work force. Here African-American women loaded down with cotton join their men on the march home after a day in the fields.
(© Collection of The New York Historical Society, ID 47843)

the fetus while abusing the mother. Masters often delegated discipline and punishment to white overseers and black drivers. The barbaric discipline meted out by others twinged the consciences of many masters, but most justified it as their Christian duty to ensure the slaves' proper "submissiveness." Frederick Douglass recalled that his worst master had been converted at a Methodist camp meeting. "If religion had any effect on his character at all," Douglass related, "it made him more cruel and hateful in all his ways."

Despite the system's brutality, some slaves advanced—not to freedom but to semiskilled or skilled indoor work. Some became blacksmiths, carpenters, or gin operators, and others served as cooks, butlers, and dining-room attendants. These house slaves became legendary for their disdain of field hands and poor whites. Slave artisans and house slaves generally enjoyed higher status than the field hands.

The Slave Family

Masters thought of slaves as naturally promiscuous and flattered themselves into thinking that they alone held slave marriages together. Masters had powerful incentives to encourage slave marriages: bringing new slaves into the world and discouraging slaves from running away. James Henry Hammond, governor of South Carolina and a large slaveholder, noted in his diary how he "flogged Joe Goodwyn and ordered him to go back to his wife. Ditto Gabriel and Molly and ordered them to come together."

This picture of benevolent masters holding together promiscuous slaves is misleading. Slavery itself posed the keenest challenge to slave families. Conditions on small farms and new plantations discouraged the formation of families, and even on large plantations slaves were often dispersed to different sites without any consideration of marriage or family ties. Slave adults were far less likely than whites to marry, and slave children more likely to live with a single parent or even with neither parent. The law provided neither recognition of nor protection for the slave family. Masters reluctant to break slave marriages by sale could neither bequeath their reluctance to heirs nor avoid economic hardship that might force them to sell slaves. The reality, one historian has calculated, was that on average a slave would see eleven family members sold during his or her lifetime.

Inevitably, the buying and selling of slaves disrupted attempts to create a stable family life. Poignant testimony to the effects of sale on slave families appeared in advertisements for runaway slaves. An 1851 North Carolina advertisement said that a particular fugitive was probably "lurking in the neighborhood of E. D. Walker's, at Moore's Creek, who owns most of his relatives, or Nathan Bonham's who owns his mother; or perhaps, near Fletcher Bell's, at Long Creek, who owns his father." Small wonder that a slave preacher pronounced a couple married "until death or *distance* do you part."

Other factors disrupted slave marriages. The marriage of a slave woman did not protect her against the sexual demands of her master or, indeed, of any white. Slave children of white masters sometimes became targets for the wrath of white mistresses. Sarah Wilson, the daughter of a slave and her white master, remembers that as a child she was "picked on" by her mistress until the master ordered his wife to let Sarah alone because she "got big, big blood in her." Field work kept slave mothers from their children, who were cared for by the elderly or by the mothers of other children.

Despite these enormous obstacles, relationships within slave families were often intimate and, where possible, long lasting. Lacking legal protection, slaves developed their own standards of family morality. A southern white woman observed that slaves "did not consider it wrong for a girl to have a child before she married, but afterwards were extremely severe upon anything like infidelity on her part." Given the opportunity, slaves solemnized their marriages before members of the clergy. White clergymen who accompanied Union armies into Mississippi and Louisiana during the Civil War conducted thousands of marriage rites for slaves who had long viewed themselves as married and desired a formal ceremony and registration.

On balance, slave families differed profoundly from white families. Many planters divided their holdings into several farms and distributed slaves among them without regard to marriage ties. Conditions on small farms and new plantations discouraged the formation of families. Spouses were always vulnerable to being sold. Slaves were more likely than whites to never marry or to marry late, and slave children were more likely to live with a single parent, usually the mother, or with neither parent.

Broad kinship patterns—close ties between children and grandparents, aunts, and uncles as well as parents—had marked West African cultures, and they were reinforced by the separation of children and parents that routinely occurred under slavery. Frederick Douglass never knew his father and saw his mother rarely, but he vividly remembered his grandmother. In addition, slaves often created "fictive" kin networks, naming friends as their uncles, aunts, brothers, or sisters. In this way they helped to protect themselves against the disruption of family ties and established a broader community of obligation. When plantation slaves greeted each other as "brother," they were not making a statement about actual kinship but about obligations to each other.

The Longevity, Health, and Diet of Slaves

Of the 10 million to 12 million Africans imported to the New World between the fifteenth and nineteenth centuries, North America received only 550,000 of them (about 5 percent), whereas Brazil received 3.5 million (nearly 33 percent). Yet by 1825, 36 percent of all slaves in the Western Hemisphere lived in the United States, and only 31 percent in Brazil. The reason for this difference is that slaves in the United States reproduced faster and lived longer than those in Brazil and elsewhere in the Western Hemisphere.

Several factors account for U.S. slaves' longer lives and higher rates of reproduction. First, with the gender ratio among slaves equalizing more rapidly in North America, slaves there married earlier and had more children. Second, because raising corn and livestock was compatible with growing cotton, the Old South produced plentiful food. Slaves generally received a peck of cornmeal and three to four pounds of fatty pork a week, which they often supplemented with vegetables grown on small plots and with catfish and game.

Slaves enjoyed greater immunity from malaria and yellow fever than whites but suffered more from cholera, dysentery, and diarrhea. Lacking privies, slaves usually relieved themselves behind bushes, and consequently urine and feces contaminated the sources of their drinking water. Slave remedies for stomach ailments, though commonly ridiculed by whites, often worked. For example, slaves ate white clay to cure dysentery and diarrhea. We now know that white clay contains kaolin, a remedy for these disorders.

Nonetheless, slaves experienced a higher mortality rate than whites. The very young suffered most; infant mortality among slaves was double that among whites, and one in three African-American children died before age ten. Plantations in the disease-ridden lowlands had the worst overall mortality rates, but overworked field hands often miscarried or bore weakened infants even in healthier areas.

Slaves Off Plantations

Greater freedom from supervision and greater opportunities awaited slaves who worked off plantations in towns and cities. Most southern whites succumbed to the lure of cotton and established small farms; the resulting shortage of white labor created a steady demand for slaves outside the plantation economy. Driving wagons, working as stevedores on the docks, manning river barges, and toiling in mining and lumbering gave slaves an opportunity to work somewhere other than the cotton fields. Other African-Americans served as engineers for sawmills or artisans for ironworks. African-American women and children constituted the main labor force for the South's fledgling textile industry.

The draining of potential white laborers from southern cities also provided opportunity for slaves to become skilled artisans. Slave or free, blacks found it easier to pursue skilled occupations in southern cities than in northern ones, where immigrant laborers competed with blacks for work.

Despite slavery's stranglehold, urban African-Americans in the South enjoyed opportunities denied their counterparts in the North. Generally, slaves who worked in factories, mining, or lumbering were hired out by their masters rather than owned by their employers. If working conditions for hired-out slaves deteriorated badly, masters would refuse to provide employers with more slaves. Consequently, working conditions for slaves off the plantation generally stayed at a tolerable level. Watching workers load cotton onto a steamboat, Frederick Law Olmsted was amazed to see slaves sent to the top of the bank to roll the bales down to Irishmen who stowed them on the ship. Asking the reason for this arrangement, Olmsted was told, "The niggers are worth too much to be risked here; if the Paddies [Irish] are knocked overboard, or get their backs broke, nobody loses anything."

Life on the Margin: Free Blacks in the Old South

Free blacks were likelier than southern blacks in general to live in cities. In 1860 one-third of the free blacks in the Upper South and more than half in the Lower South were urban.

Urban specialization allowed free blacks the chance to become carpenters, coopers (barrel makers), barbers, and small traders. Most of the meat, fish, and produce in an antebellum southern market was prepared for sale by free blacks. Urban free blacks formed their own fraternal orders and churches; in New Orleans free blacks also had their own opera and literary journals. In Natchez a free black barber, William Tiler Johnson, invested profits from his shop in real estate, acquired stores that he rented out, and bought a plantation and slaves.

Despite such successes, free blacks were vulnerable in southern society. They continued to increase in absolute numbers (a little more than 250,000 free people of color lived in the South in 1860), but the rate of growth of the free black population slowed radically after 1810. Fewer masters freed their slaves after that time, and following the Nat Turner rebellion in 1831, states legally restricted the liberties of free blacks. Every southern state forbade free blacks to enter, and in 1859 Arkansas ordered all free blacks to leave.

Although a free-black culture flourished in certain cities, that culture did not reflect the conditions under which the majority of blacks lived. Most free blacks dwelled in rural areas, where whites lumped them together with slaves, and a much higher percentage of blacks were free in the Upper South than in the Lower South.

Many free blacks were mulattos, the product of white masters and black women, and looked down on "darky" field hands and laborers. But as discrimination against free people of color intensified during the late antebellum period, many free blacks realized that whatever future they had was as blacks, not whites. Feelings of racial solidarity increased during the 1850s, and after the Civil War, the leaders of the ex-slaves were usually blacks who had been free before the war.

Slave Resistance

Fear of slave insurrection haunted the Old South. In lowland and delta plantation areas slaves often outnumbered whites. In the cities free blacks could have provided leadership for rebellions. Rumors of slave conspiracies flew within the southern white community, and all whites knew of the massive black revolt that had destroyed French rule in Santo Domingo.

But Nat Turner's revolt remained the only slave rebellion that actually resulted in white deaths. Most slave rebellions were conspiracies that never materialized. For example, in 1800 a Virginia slave named Gabriel Prosser plotted an uprising but was betrayed by other slaves and executed. In 1822 Denmark Vesey and his followers planned to attack Charleston, South Carolina, and seize the city's arms and ammunition, but other slaves informed the authorities, and the conspirators were executed.

Several factors explain this apparent tranquillity. First, although slaves formed a majority in South Carolina and a few other areas, they did not constitute a *large* majority in any state. Second, unlike Caribbean slave owners, most southern masters lived on their plantations; they possessed armed force and were willing to use it. Third, family ties among U.S. slaves made them reluctant to

risk death and thereby to orphan their children. Finally, slaves who ran away or plotted rebellion had no allies. Southern Indians routinely captured runaway slaves and claimed rewards for them; some Indians even owned slaves.

Unable to rebel, many slaves tried to escape to freedom in the North. Some light mulattos who passed as whites succeeded. More often, slaves borrowed, stole, or forged passes from plantations or obtained papers describing them as free. Frederick Douglass borrowed a sailor's papers to make his escape from Baltimore to New York City. Some former slaves, including Harriet Tubman and Josiah Henson, returned to the South to assist others to escape. Despite legends of an "Underground Railroad" of abolitionists helping slaves to freedom, fugitive slaves owed little to abolitionists. The "safe houses" of white sympathizers in border states were better known to slave-catchers than to runaways.

Escape to freedom was a dream rather than a realistic alternative for most blacks. Out of millions of slaves, probably fewer than a thousand actually escaped to the North. Slaves who did run away often were not seeking freedom but the chance to visit spouses or escape punishment; most remained in the South. During the eighteenth century, African slaves had often run away in groups and tried to create the sort of villages they had known in Africa. But the American acquisition of Florida deprived potential runaways of their major haven; few uninhabited places to which they could flee remained.

Despite poor prospects for permanent escape, slaves could disappear for prolonged periods into the free-black communities of southern cities. Slaves enjoyed a fair degree of practical freedom to drive wagons to market and to come and go when they were off plantations. Slaves sent to a city might overstay their leave and pass themselves off as free. This kind of practical freedom did not change slavery's underlying oppressiveness, but it did give slaves a sense of having certain rights, and it helped to channel slave resistance into activities that were furtive and relatively harmless rather than open and violent. Theft, for example, was so common that planters kept tools, smokehouses, and closets under lock and key. Overworked field hands might leave tools out to rust, feign illness, or simply refuse to work. Slaves could not be fired for such malingering or negligence. And Frederick Law Olmsted even found masters afraid to punish a slave "lest [he or she] should abscond, or take a sulky fit and not work, or poison some of the family, or set fire to the dwelling." Indeed, not all furtive resistance was harmless. Arson and poisoning, both common forms of vengeance in African culture, flourished in the Old South. So did fear. Masters afflicted by dysentery never knew for sure that they had not been poisoned.

Arson, poisoning, theft, work stoppage, and negligence acted as alternatives to violent rebellion, but their goal was not freedom. Their object was merely to make slavery bearable. Most slaves would have preferred freedom but settled for less. "White folks do as they please," an ex-slave said, "and the darkies do as they can."

THE EMERGENCE OF AFRICAN-AMERICAN CULTURE

Enslaved blacks combined elements of African and American culture to create a distinctive culture of their own.

The Language of Slaves

Before slaves could develop a common culture, they needed a common language. During the colonial period African-born slaves, speaking a variety of languages, had developed a "pidgin"—that is, a language that has no native speakers but in which people with different native languages can communicate. Many African-born slaves spoke English pidgin poorly, but their American-born descendants used it as their primary language.

Like all pidgins, English pidgin was a simplified language. Slaves usually dropped the verb *to be* (which had no equivalent in African tongues) and ignored or confused genders. Instead of saying "Mary is in the cabin," they typically said, "Mary, he

in cabin." They substituted *no* for *not,* as in "He no wicked." Some African words, among them *banjo,* moved from pidgin to standard English, and others, such as *goober* (peanut), entered southern white slang. Although many whites ridiculed pidgin, and black house servants struggled to speak standard English, pidgin proved indispensable for communication among slaves.

African-American Religion

Religion played an equally important role in forging an African-American culture. Africa contained rich and diverse religious customs and beliefs. Despite the presence of a few Muslims and Christians in the early slave population, most of the slaves brought from Africa followed one of many native African religions. Most of these religions drew little distinction between the spiritual and natural worlds—storms, illnesses, and earthquakes were all assumed to stem from supernatural forces. God, spirits that inhabited woods and waters, and ancestor spirits all constituted these supernatural forces. The religions of West Africa, the region where most American slaves originated, attached special significance to water, which symbolized life and hope.

However, African religions did not unify American slaves. African religions differed greatly, and the majority of slaves in the colonial period were young men who had not absorbed this religious heritage. Remnants of African religion remained, however, in part because before the 1790s whites made few attempts to convert slaves to Christianity. When whites' conversion efforts increased, dimly remembered African beliefs such as the reverence for water may have aided Christian missionaries in influencing slaves to accept Christianity and to undergo baptism. Evangelical Christianity, like African religions, drew few distinctions between the sacred and the worldly. Just as Africans believed that droughts and plagues resulted from supernatural forces, revivalists knew in their hearts that every drunkard who fell off his horse and every Sabbath breaker struck by lightning had experienced a deliberate, direct punishment from God.

Mary Edmonia Lewis and
Forever Free
Named Wildfire by her Chippewa mother and black father, Mary Edmonia Lewis adopted a Christian name upon entering Oberlin College. Later she studied sculpture in Boston and Rome. Her "Forever Free" (1867) commemorated the abolition of slavery.

By the 1790s African-Americans formed about a quarter of the membership of the Methodist and Baptist denominations. The fact that converted slaves played significant roles in the South's three slave rebellions reinforced whites' fears that a Christian slave would be a rebellious slave. These slave uprisings, especially the Nat Turner rebellion, spurred Protestant missionaries to intensify their efforts among slaves. They pointed to the self-taught Turner as proof that slaves could learn about Christianity and claimed that only organized efforts at conversion would ensure that the slaves were taught correct versions of Christianity. After Methodists, Baptists, and Presbyterians split into northern and southern wings, missionaries argued that it was safe to convert slaves, for the southern churches had rid themselves of antislavery elements. Between 1845 and 1860 the number of African-American Baptists doubled.

Christian blacks' experience in the Old South illustrates the contradictions of life under slavery. Urban blacks often had their own churches, but rural blacks and slaves worshiped in the same churches as whites. Although African-Americans sat in segregated sections, they heard the same service as whites. Churches became the most interracial institutions in the Old South, and biracial churches sometimes disciplined whites for abusing black Christian members. But Christianity was not a route to black liberation. Ministers went out of their way to remind slaves that spiritual equality was not the same as civil equality. The conversion of slaves succeeded only to the extent that it did not challenge the basic inequality of southern society.

However, slaves listening to the same sermons as whites often came to different conclusions. For example, slaves drew parallels between their captivity and that of the Jews, the Chosen People. Like the Jews, slaves concluded, they were "de people of de Lord." If they kept the faith, they would reach the Promised Land.

"The Promised Land" could refer to Israel, to heaven, or to freedom. Whites agreed that Israel and heaven were the only permissible meanings, but some African-Americans thought of freedom as well. Many plantations had black preachers, slaves trained by white ministers to spread Christianity among blacks. In the presence of masters or ministers, African-American preachers repeated the familiar biblical command "Obey your master." Often, however, slaves met for services apart from whites, and then the message changed.

Some slaves privately interpreted Christianity as a religion of liberation, but most recognized that their prospects for freedom were slight. Generally, Christianity neither turned blacks into revolutionaries nor made them model slaves. It did provide slaves with a view of slavery different from their masters' outlook. Masters argued that slavery was a benign and divinely ordained institution, but Christianity told slaves that the institution was an affliction, a terrible and unjust system that God had allowed in order to test their faith. For having endured slavery, he would reward slaves. For having created it, he would punish masters.

Black Music and Dance

African-American culture expressed blacks' feelings. Long after white rituals had grown sober and sedate, the congregation in African-American religious services shouted "Amen" and let their body movements reflect their feelings. Slaves also expressed their emotions in music and dance. Southern law forbade them to own "drums, horns, or other loud instruments, which may call together or give sign or notice to one another of their wicked designs and intentions." Instead, slaves made rhythmical clapping, called "patting juba," an indispensable accompaniment to dancing. Slaves also played an African instrument, the banjo, and beat tin buckets as substitutes for drums. Slave music was tied to bodily movement; slaves expressed themselves in a dance that was African in origin, emphasizing shuffling steps and bodily contortions rather than quick footwork and erect backs as in whites' dances.

Whether at work or prayer, slaves liked to sing. Work songs usually consisted of a leader's chant and a choral response. Masters encouraged such songs, believing that singing induced slaves to work harder and that the innocent content of work

songs proved that slaves were happy. However, Frederick Douglass, recalling his own past, observed that "slaves sing most when they are most unhappy. The songs of the slave represent the sorrows of his heart; and he is relieved by them, only as an aching heart is relieved by its tears."

Blacks also sang religious songs, later known as spirituals, which reflected the powerful emphasis that slave religion placed on deliverance from earthly travails. Whites took a dim view of spirituals and tried to make slaves sing "good psalms and hymns" instead of "the extravagant and nonsensical chants, and catches, and hallelujah songs of their own composing." But enslaved blacks clung to their spirituals, drawing hope from them that "we will soon be free, when the Lord will call us home," as one spiritual promised.

CONCLUSION _hc_ ACE Practice Test

The cotton gin revitalized southern agriculture and lured southerners to the new Cotton Belt states. As the Old South became more dependent on cotton, it also became more dependent on slave labor.

Slavery did much to shape social relations among the Old South's major groups: planters, small slaveholders, yeomen, and the people of the pine barrens. And the presence of slaves fed the exaggerated notions of personal honor that made white southerners so violent.

Slavery both shaped and distorted the Old South. Although most whites did not own slaves, virtually all whites believed that southern prosperity, and their very lives, depended on perpetuating slavery. On the other hand, northerners believed that slavery had thwarted progress in the South and turned it into a region of "sterile lands and bankrupt estates."

To southerners, the North, especially the industrial Northeast, was the region clearly out of step. Agriculture made the South a far more comfortable place to live than the industrial North. As northerners assaulted slavery, southerners responded by portraying it as a benevolent response to the natural inequality of whites and blacks. After all, they argued, slaves were well fed, they were Christian, and they were fond of their masters.

Chronology

1800	Gabriel Prosser plans a slave rebellion in Virginia.
1808	Congress prohibits external slave trade.
1816–1819	Boom in cotton prices stimulates settlement of the Southwest.
1819–1820	Missouri Compromise.
1822	Denmark Vesey's conspiracy is uncovered in South Carolina. Nat Turner leads a slave rebellion in Virginia.
1832	Virginia legislature narrowly defeats a proposal for gradual emancipation.
1844–1845	Methodist and Baptist churches split over slavery into northern and southern wings.
1849	Sugar production in Louisiana reaches its peak.
1849–1860	Period of high cotton prices.
1857	Hinton R. Helper, *The Impending Crisis of the South*
1859	John Brown's raid on Harpers Ferry.
1860	South Carolina secedes from the Union.

Although comforting, such images were dead wrong. Few slaves accepted slavery; they did not openly rebel, but they engaged in many acts of covert resistance. The Christianity they embraced was far different from that of the whites. To whites, the Christian gospel taught slaves to be submissive; to slaves, the gospel taught the injustice of human bondage and the promise of eventual deliverance.

FURTHER READING

John Ashworth, *Slavery, Capitalism, and Politics in the Antebellum Republic* (1995). A reinterpretation of the causes of the Civil War from a Marxist perspective.

Orville Vernon Burton, *In My Father's House Are Many Mansions: Family and Community in Edgefield, South Carolina* (1985). An extremely valuable study of the South Carolina upcountry.

Bruce Collins, *White Society in the Antebellum South* (1985). A very good, brief synthesis of southern white society and culture.

William J. Cooper, *Liberty and Slavery: Southern Politics to 1860* (1983). A valuable synthesis and interpretation of recent scholarship on the antebellum South in national politics.

Clement Eaton, *The Growth of Southern Civilization, 1790–1860* (1985). A fine survey of social, economic, and political change.

Robert W. Fogel, *Without Consent or Contract: The Rise and Fall of American Slavery* (1989). A comprehensive reexamination of the slaves' productivity and welfare.

Robert W. Fogel and Stanley L. Engerman, *Time on the Cross: The Economics of American Negro Slavery* (1974). A controversial book that uses mathematical models to analyze the profitability of slavery. (Fogel won the Nobel Prize in Economics in 1993.)

Eugene D. Genovese, *Roll, Jordan, Roll: The World the Slaves Made* (1974). The most influential work on slavery in the Old South written during the last twenty-five years; a penetrating analysis of the paternalistic relationship between masters and slaves.

Peter Kolchin, *Unfree Labor: American Slavery and Russian Serfdom* (1987). A comparative study that sets American slavery within the context of unfree labor in the early nineteenth century.

Stephanie McCurry, *Masters of Small Worlds* (1995). An illuminating and influential account of race, class, and gender relations in the South Carolina low country.

James Oakes, *The Ruling Race: A History of American Slaveholders* (1982). An important attack on the ideas of Eugene D. Genovese.

U. B. Phillips, *American Negro Slavery* (1918) and *Life and Labor in the Old South* (1929). Works marred by racial prejudice but containing a wealth of information about slavery and the plantation system.

Kenneth M. Stampp, *The Peculiar Institution: Slavery in the Antebellum South* (1956). A standard account of the African-American experience under slavery.

Miners in the Sierras, by Charles Christian Nahl, 1851–1852

Immigration, Expansion, and Sectional Conflict, 1840–1848

CHAPTER OUTLINE

Newcomers and Natives

The West and Beyond

The Politics of Expansion, 1840–1846

The Mexican-American War and Its Aftermath, 1846–1848

 This icon will direct you to additional study and research resources at http://college.hmco.com/history/us/boyer/enduring_concise/5e/students/index.html

The Mormons who trekked westward between 1845 and 1847 were part of the great flood of Americans washing across the continent in the spirit of "Manifest Destiny." Although their goal was the construction of a separate Mormon society, which they achieved in "Deseret," as they called the Utah emptiness where they established their colony, the Mormons shared the American dream of expansion and the fervent belief that they could create a better life by moving beyond the boundaries and constraints of eastern settlements.

"Americans regard this continent as their birthright," thundered Sam Houston of Texas; Indians and Mexicans had to make way for "our mighty march." In barely a

This chapter focuses on four major questions:

▶ How did the massive immigration of the 1840s influence the balance of power between Whigs and Democrats?

▶ What economic and political forces fed westward expansion in the 1840s?

▶ How did President James K. Polk unite the Democrats behind a program of westward expansion? How did the Democrats "sell" the annexation of Texas to the North in the election of 1844?

▶ How did the outcome of the Mexican-American War intensify intersectional conflict? Why did it split the Democratic party?

thousand days during James K. Polk's administration (1845–1849), the United States expanded by 50 percent. It annexed Texas, gained half of the vast Oregon territory through negotiations with Britain, and claimed California and New Mexico after deliberately provoking war. At the same time immigrants poured into the United States, largely from Europe.

Expansion and immigration were linked. Most immigrants gravitated to the ardently expansionist Democratic party. In turn, Democrats concluded that the solution to widening sectional and ethnic conflict was more expansion. By bringing more land into cultivation, they believed, America could recapture its Jeffersonian ideal as a nation of self-sufficient farmers. And expansion would offer something for everyone: Oregon would gratify the North; Texas, the South; and California, every region.

It didn't work out that way. In fact, expansion heated sectional antagonisms to the boiling point, split the Democratic party along sectional lines, and set the nation on the path to the Civil War.

NEWCOMERS AND NATIVES

Between 1815 and 1860, 5 million European immigrants reached the United States. Of these, 4.2 million arrived between 1840 and 1860, and 3 million crowded in just from 1845 to 1854, the largest immigration relative to population in U.S. history. The Irish and the Germans dominated this wave of newcomers; by 1860 three-fourths of foreign-born Americans were Irish or German.

Expectations and Realities

Although a desire for religious freedom drew some immigrants to U.S. shores, hopes of economic betterment lured the majority. Travelers' accounts and relatives' letters assured Europeans that America was an ideal world, a utopia. Yet, typically, emigrants faced hard times. Because ships sailed irregularly, many were forced to spend their small savings in waterfront slums while awaiting departure. Squalid cargo ships carried most of the emigrants, who endured wretched conditions in quarters as crowded as those of slave ships.

For many, the greatest shock came after landing. In the depression years of the 1840s, immigrants quickly discovered that farming in America was a perilous prospect, radically different from what they had known in Europe. Unlike the compact farming communities of Europe, American agricultural areas featured scattered farms, and Americans' individualism led them to speculate in land and to move frequently.

Clear patterns emerged amid the shocks and dislocations of immigration. For example, most Irish immigrants lacked the capital to purchase land and consequently crowded into urban areas of New England, New York, New Jersey, and Pennsylvania, where they could find jobs. German immigrants often arrived at southern ports, but slavery, climate, and lack of economic opportunity gradually drove them north to settle in Illinois, Ohio, Wisconsin, and Missouri.

Cities, rather than farms, attracted most antebellum immigrants; by 1860 German and Irish newcomers constituted half or more of the population of St. Louis, New York, Chicago, Cincinnati, Milwaukee, Detroit, and San Francisco. These fast-growing cities needed people with strong backs willing to work for low wages. Irish construction gangs built the houses, streets, and aqueducts that were changing the face of urban America and dug the canals and railroads that linked these cities. In addition to jobs, cities provided immigrants with the community life lacking in farming areas.

The Germans

In 1860 there was no German nation-state, only a collection of principalities and kingdoms. Immigrants from this area thought of themselves as Bavarians, Westphalians, or Saxons, not Germans. They included Catholics, Protestants, Jews, and freethinkers who denounced all religions.

German immigrants spanned a wide spectrum of class and occupation. Most were farmers, but professionals, artisans, and tradespeople made up a sizable minority. For example, Levi Strauss, a Jewish tailor from Bavaria, reached the United States in 1847. When gold was discovered in California the next year, Strauss gathered rolls of cloth and sailed for San Francisco. There he fashioned tough work overalls from canvas. Demand soared, and Strauss opened a factory to produce his cheap overalls, later known as blue jeans or Levi's.

A common language transcended the differences among German immigrants and bound them together. They clustered in the same neighborhoods, formed their own militia and fire companies, and established German-language parochial schools and newspapers. The diversity of the German-speaking population further fostered solidarity. Because Ger-

German Winter Gardens
A well-known beer hall on lower Manhattan's Bowery, the German Winter Gardens were famous for music and sociability.

The Metropolitan Museum of Art, The Edward W. C. Arnold Collection of New York Prints, Maps and Pictures, Bequest of Edward W. C. Arnold, 1954. 54.90.166 Photograph © 1993 The Metropolitan Museum of Art, New York.

mans supplied their own lawyers, doctors, teachers, and merchants from their midst, they had no need to go outside their neighborhoods. Native-born Americans simultaneously admired German industriousness and resented German self-sufficiency, which they interpreted as clannishness. In a vicious cycle, the Germans responded by becoming even more clannish. In effect, they isolated themselves from gaining the political influence that Irish immigrants acquired.

The Irish

There were three waves of Irish immigration. Between 1815 and the mid-1820s, most Irish immigrants were Protestants, small landowners and tradespeople drawn by enthusiastic veterans of the War of 1812 who reported that America was a paradise where "all a man needed was a gun and sufficient ammunition to be able to live like a prince." From the mid-1820s to the mid-1840s, Irish immigration became both more Catholic and poorer, primarily comprising tenant farmers evicted by Protestant landlords as "superfluous." Rich or poor, Protestant or Catholic, nearly a million Irish crossed the Atlantic to the United States between 1815 and 1845.

Then, between 1845 and the early 1850s the character of Irish immigration changed dramatically. In Ireland blight destroyed harvest after harvest of potatoes, virtually the only food of the peasantry, and triggered one of the most gruesome famines in history. The Great Famine killed a million people. Those who survived, a landlord wrote, were "famished and ghastly skeletons." To escape suffering and death, 1.8 million Irish migrated to the United States in the decade after 1845.

Overwhelmingly poor and Catholic, these newest Irish immigrants entered the work force at the bottom. Paddy with his pickax and Bridget the maid were simultaneously stereotypes and realities. While Irish men dug streets and canals and railroads, Irish women worked as maids and textile workers. Poverty drove women to work at early ages, and the outdoor, all-season labor performed by their husbands turned many of them into work-

ing widows. Because the Irish usually married late, almost half the Irish immigrants were single adult women, many of whom never married. Most of these Irish-Americans lived a harsh existence. One immigrant described the life of the average Irish-born laborer as "despicable, humiliating, [and] slavish"; there was "no love for him—no protection of life—[he] can be shot down, run through, kicked, cuffed, spat upon—and no redress." Nevertheless, a few Irish struggled up the social ladder, becoming foremen in factories or small storeowners.

It sometimes seemed that no matter what the Irish did, they clashed with other Americans. The poorer Irish who dug canals, took in laundry, or worked as domestics competed with equally poor free blacks. The result was Irish animosity toward blacks and Irish hatred of abolitionists. At the same time, the Irish who secured skilled or semiskilled jobs clashed with native-born white workers.

Anti-Catholicism, Nativism, and Labor Protest

Hostility toward Irish immigrants often took the form of anti-Catholicism, a latent impulse among American Protestants since early Puritan days. The surge of Irish immigrants in the second quarter of the nineteenth century revived anti-Catholic fever. For example, a mob, fueled by rumors that a Catholic convent in Charlestown, Massachusetts, contained torture chambers, burned the building to the ground. A groundswell of anti-Catholic publications climaxed with Maria Monk's best-selling *Awful Disclosures of the Hotel Dieu Nunnery in Montreal*, which vividly described wild sexual relations between nuns and priests. Although she claimed to be a former nun, Maria Monk was actually a former prostitute.

The surge of Catholic immigration in the 1840s also had political ramifications. Protestants formed anti-immigrant societies with names like the American Republicans and the United Order of Americans. One such secret society, the Order of the Star-Spangled Banner, would become the "Know-Nothing," or American, party, a major political force in the 1850s.

In the 1840s nativist parties prospered during flare-ups over local issues, such as whether the Protestant or Catholic version of the Bible should be used in predominantly Catholic schools. In 1844, for example, the "Bible Riots" in Philadelphia, spurred on by the electoral success of American Republican party candidates, led to the deaths of sixteen people and the destruction of thirty buildings at the hands of Protestant mobs.

An explosive mixture of fears and discontents fueled nativism. Protestants generally saw their doctrines such as the responsibility of each individual to interpret scripture as far more democratic than Catholicism, which made doctrine the province of the pope and the hierarchy. Native-born artisans and journeymen, already hard pressed by the subdivision of tasks and the aftermath of the Panic of 1837, feared that desperately poor Catholic immigrants represented threats to their jobs. Nativism fed on such fears and anxieties.

Demands for land reform joined nativism as a proposed solution to workers' economic woes. Land reformers argued that workers' true interests could never be met by an industrial order in which factory workers sold their labor for wages and thus abandoned any hope of economic independence. However, the appeal of land reform was limited. Most factory workers dreaded "the horrors of wilderness life;" as they could not afford the farm animals or the equipment they needed. The idea of solving industrial problems by resettling factory workers on farms seemed a pipe dream.

Labor unions appealed to workers left cold by the promises of the land reformers. For example, desperately poor Irish immigrants, refugees from an agricultural society, believed that they could gain more through unions and strikes than through farming. Even women workers organized unions in these years; the leader of a seamstresses' union proclaimed, "Too long have we been bound down by tyrant employers."

Probably the most important development for workers in the 1840s was a state court decision. In *Commonwealth* v. *Hunt* (1842), the Massachusetts Supreme Court ruled that labor unions were not illegal monopolies that restrained trade. However,

because less than 1 percent of the work force at that time belonged to unions, their impact was sharply limited. Thus Massachusetts employers easily brushed aside the *Commonwealth* decision, firing union agitators and replacing them with cheap immigrant labor. "Hundreds of honest laborers," a labor paper reported in 1848, "have been dismissed from employment in the manufactories of New England because they have been suspected of knowing their rights and daring to assert them." This repression effectively blunted agitation for a ten-hour workday in an era when the twelve- or fourteen-hour day was typical.

Ethnic and religious tensions also split the antebellum working class during the 1830s and 1840s. Friction between native-born and immigrant workers inevitably became intertwined with the political divisions of the second party system.

hc Primary Source: Philadelphia Mechanics Respond to New Pressures

Labor Protest and Immigrant Politics

Few immigrants had voted before reaching America, and even fewer had fled political persecution. Political upheavals had erupted in Austria and some German states in the turbulent year 1848, but among the 1 million German immigrants to the United States, only 10,000 were political refugees, or "Forty-Eighters." Once settled in the United States, however, many immigrants became politically active. They discovered that urban political organizations could help them to find housing and jobs—in return for votes. Both the Irish and the Germans identified overwhelmingly with the Democratic party. By 1820 the Irish controlled Tammany Hall, the New York City Democratic organization; Germans became staunch Democrats in Milwaukee, St. Louis, and other cities.

Immigrants' fears about jobs partly explained their widespread Democratic support. Former president Andrew Jackson had given the Democratic party an antiprivilege, anti-aristocratic coloration, making the Democrats seem more sympathetic than the Whigs to the common people. In addition, antislavery was linked to the Whig party, and the Irish loathed abolitionism because they feared that freed slaves would become their economic competitors. Moreover, the Whigs' moral and religious values seemed to threaten those of the Irish and Germans. Hearty-drinking Irish and German immigrants shunned temperance-crusading Whigs, many of whom were also rabid anti-Catholics. Even public-school reform, championed by the Whigs, was perceived as a menace to the Catholicism of Irish children and as a threat to the integrity of German language and culture.

The Bible Riots illustrate both the interplay of nativism, religion, and politics and the way in which local issues shaped the immigrants' political loyalties. Both Democrats and Whigs became adept at attracting voters initially drawn to politics by local issues such as liquor regulations and school laws. Nativists usually voted for Whig candidates rather than those of overtly nativist parties, while immigrants followed the Democratic party from local battles into national politics. There the Democrats taught immigrants to revere George Washington, Thomas Jefferson, and Andrew Jackson; to view "moneyed capitalists" as parasites who would tremble when the people spoke; and to think of themselves as Americans. During the 1830s the Democrats had persuaded immigrants that such national issues as the Bank of the United States and the tariff were vital to them. Similarly, in the 1840s the Democrats would try to convince immigrants that national territorial expansion would advance their interests.

THE WEST AND BEYOND

As late as 1840 the American West meant the area between the Appalachian Mountains and the Mississippi River or just beyond. West of that lay the inhospitable Great Plains. A semiarid treeless plateau, the Plains sustained huge buffalo herds and the nomadic Indians who lived off the buffalo. Because the Great Plains presented would-be farmers with formidable obstacles, public interest shifted toward the Far West, the fertile region beyond the Rockies.

The Far West

By the Transcontinental (or Adams-Onís) Treaty of 1819, the United States had relinquished to Spain its claims to Texas west of the Sabine River and in return Spain renounced its claims to the Oregon Country north of California. Two years later the Mexican Revolution had brought Mexico independence from Spain and possession of all North American territory claimed by Spain—Texas, California, and the southwest quadrant of the continent. In 1824 and 1825 Russia yielded its claims to Oregon south of Alaska, and in 1827 the United States and Great Britain revived an earlier agreement for the joint occupation of the Oregon Territory. Texas, New Mexico, California, and Oregon stretched over an area larger than Britain, France, and Germany combined. Although this vast region should have tempted them, in the 1820s Mexico, the United States, and Britain all viewed the Far West as a remote and shadowy frontier. The American line of settlement reached only to Missouri, a 2,000-mile trek (allowing for mountains) from the West Coast.

Far Western Trade

After sailing around South America and up the Pacific coast, early merchants had established American and British outposts on the West Coast. Between the late 1790s and the 1820s, for example, Boston merchants had built a thriving trade, exchanging goods from the eastern United States for western sea-otter fur, cattle, hides, and tallow (rendered from cattle fat and used for making candles and soap). The British Hudson's Bay Company developed a similar trade in Oregon and northern California. The California trade generated little friction with Mexico. Californians were as eager to buy as the traders were to sell. Traders who settled in California, such as the Swiss-born John Sutter, learned to speak Spanish and became assimilated into Mexican culture.

Also during the 1820s, trading links developed between St. Louis and Santa Fe. Each spring, midwesterners loaded wagon trains with tools, cloth-

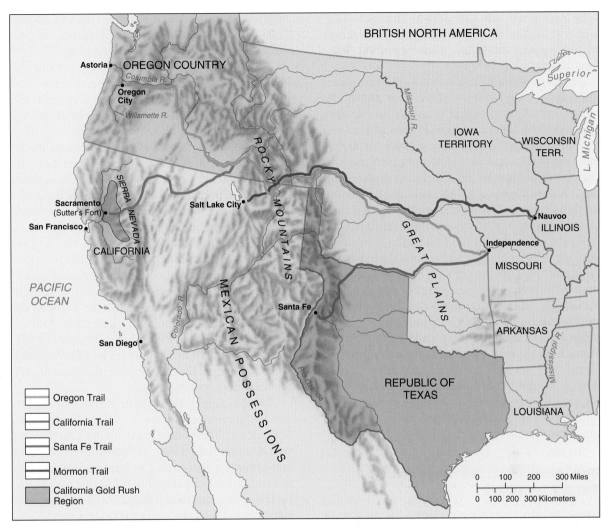

MAP 13.1
Trails to the West, 1840
By 1840 several trails carried pioneers from Missouri and Illinois to the West.

ing, and household sundries and rumbled westward to Santa Fe, where they traded their goods for mules and silver. Mexico welcomed the trade. By the 1830s more than half the goods trucked west along the Santa Fe Trail trickled into the mineral-rich Mexican provinces of Chihuahua and Sonora and were exchanged for Mexican silver pesos, which became the principal medium of exchange in Missouri.

Some Americans ventured north from Santa Fe to trap beaver in what is today western Colorado and eastern Utah. Americans from St. Louis soon found themselves competing with both the Santa Fe traders and the agents of the Hudson's Bay Company for lucrative beaver pelts. In 1825 William Ashley of St. Louis initiated an annual rendezvous along the Green River in Mexican territory, where midwestern traders could exchange beaver pelts for supplies and thereby save themselves the long trip back to St. Louis. Gradually, the St. Louis traders wrested the beaver trade from their Santa Fe competitors.

For the most part, American traders and trappers operating on the northern Mexican frontier in the 1820s and 1830s provided a service to Mexico's provinces. The Mexican people of New Mexico and California depended on American trade for manufactured goods, and the Mexican government in both provinces needed revenues from customs duties. The New Mexican government often had to wait until the caravan of American traders arrived from St. Louis before it could pay its officials and soldiers.

Yet despite the mutually beneficial relations between Mexicans and Americans, the potential for conflict was always present. Spanish-speaking, Roman Catholic, and accustomed to a hierarchical society, the Mexicans formed a striking contrast to the Protestant, individualistic Americans. Furthermore, American traders returned to the United States with glowing reports about the fertility and climate of Mexico's northern provinces. Consequently, by the 1820s American settlers were moving into eastern Texas. At the same time, the ties binding Mexico's government to its northern provinces were fraying.

The American Settlement of Texas to 1835

Spain, and later Mexico, recognized that the key to controlling their frontier provinces lay in promoting settlement there by Spanish-speaking people— Spaniards, Mexicans, and Indians who had embraced Catholicism and agriculture. Thus by the early nineteenth century, Spanish missions, which had long been the chief instrument of Spanish expansion, stretched up the California coast as far as San Francisco and into the interior of New Mexico and Texas.

The Spanish missions combined political, economic, and religious goals. Paid by the government, the Franciscan priests who staffed the missions tried to convert Native Americans and to settle them on mission lands. By 1823 more than 20,000 Indians lived on the lands of the twenty-one California missions, most of them protected by a fort, or presidio, like that at San Francisco.

In the late 1820s the mission system began to decline, the victim of Mexican independence and the new government's decision to secularize the missions by distributing their lands to ambitious government officials and private ranchers. Many of the Native Americans who fled the missions joined the nomads who had always resisted conversion; lawlessness surged, and few Mexicans ventured into the vast and threatening emptiness of the frontier.

In 1824 the Mexican government began to encourage American colonization of the region as a way to bring in manufactured goods and to gain protection against Indian attacks on lands further south and west. The government bestowed generous land grants on agents known as *empresarios* to recruit peaceful American settlers for Texas, as the Anglo region of Coahuila-Tejas became known. Stephen F. Austin, the most successful of the *empresarios,* brought in 300 families by 1825. By 1830, 7,000 Americans lived in Texas, more than double the Mexican population there.

Trouble quickly developed. Most of the American settlers were southerners, many of them slaveholders. Mexico abolished slavery in 1829; the next year it closed its borders to importation of slaves and to further American immigration. Neither ban worked. Americans continued to pour into Texas: by 1836 Texas contained 30,000 Anglo-Americans, 5,000 black slaves, and only 4,000 Mexicans.

At the same time, the Mexican government grew more and more erratic. When Antonio López de Santa Anna became president of Mexico in 1834, he restricted the power of the individual states, including Coahuila-Tejas. His actions ignited a series of rebellions in the Mexican states, the most important of which became the Texas Revolution.

The Texas Revolution, 1836

At first the insurgent Anglo-Texans sought the restoration of the liberal Constitution of 1824 and greater autonomy for Texas, not independence. But Santa Anna's brutal treatment of the rebels

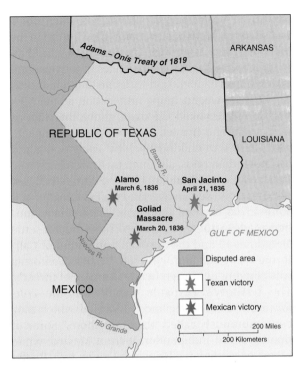

Map 13.2
Major Battles in the Texas Revolution, 1835–1836
Sam Houston's victory at San Jacinto was the decisive action of the war and avenged the massacres at the Alamo and Goliad.

alarmed the initially moderate Austin and others. When Santa Anna invaded Texas in fall 1835, Austin cast his lot with the radicals who wanted outright independence.

Santa Anna's armies met with initial success. In February 1836, 4,000 of his men laid siege to San Antonio, where 200 rebels had retreated into an abandoned mission, the Alamo. On March 6—four days after Texas had declared its independence, although they did not know about it—the defenders of the Alamo were overwhelmed by Mexican troops. Under Santa Anna's orders, the Mexican army killed all the Alamo's defenders, including the wounded. A few weeks later Mexican troops massacred 350 Texas prisoners at Goliad.

Even before the Alamo and Goliad, Texas delegates had met to proclaim Texas independent of Mexico. They chose Sam Houston, already a military leader, as their first president. A giant man who wore leopard-skin vests, Houston retreated east to pick up recruits, many of them Americans who crossed the Sabine River border to fight Santa Anna. On April 21, 1836, Houston's army turned and surprised the complacent Mexican forces under Santa Anna, which had encamped on a prairie just to the east of what is now the city of Houston. Shouting, "Remember the Alamo!" and "Remember Goliad!" Houston's army of 1,200 tore through the Mexican lines, killing nearly half of Santa Anna's men in fifteen minutes and capturing the general himself. This engagement, the Battle of San Jacinto, gave Texas its independence from Mexico, although the Mexican government never ratified the treaty that Santa Anna signed.

American Settlements in California, New Mexico, and Oregon

Before 1840 California and New Mexico, both less accessible than Texas, exerted only a mild attraction for American settlers. That year a mere 100 Americans lived in New Mexico and perhaps 400 in California. According to a contemporary, these Americans "are scattered throughout the whole Mexican population, and most of them have Spanish wives. . . . They live in every respect like the Spanish."

Yet the beginnings of change were evident. During the 1840s Americans streamed into the Sacramento Valley, lured by favorable reports of the region and welcomed by the Hispanic population as a way to encourage economic development. To these land-hungry settlers, geographically and culturally separated from the Mexican population, no sacrifice was too great if it led to California.

To the north, Oregon's abundant farmland beckoned settlers from the Mississippi Valley. By 1840 some 500 Americans had settled there, in what was described as a "pioneer's paradise" where "the pigs are running around under the great acorn trees, round and fat and already cooked, with knives and forks sticking in them so that you can cut off a slice whenever you are hungry." To some, Oregon was more attractive than California, especially because the joint British-American occupation seemed to herald eventual U.S. annexation.

The Overland Trails

Whether bound for California or Oregon, Americans faced a four-month ordeal crossing terrain little known in reality but vividly depicted in fiction as an Indian killing ground. Cautious pioneers stocked up on enough guns to equip an army in jump-off towns such as Independence and St. Joseph, Missouri. In fact, they were more likely to shoot one another than to be shot by the usually cooperative Indians and much more likely to be scalped by Independence or St. Joseph merchants selling their goods at inflated prices.

Along the Overland Trail the emigrants faced hardships and hazards; ornery mules that kicked, bit, and balked; oxen that collapsed from thirst; and overloaded wagons that broke down. Trails were difficult to follow and too often marked by the debris of broken wagons and the bleached bones of oxen. Guidebooks were more like guessbooks. In

1846 the Donner party, following one such book, lost so much time that it became snowbound in the High Sierras and survived by turning to cannibalism. Emigrants met the challenges of the overland trail by close cooperation with one another, traveling in huge wagon trains rather than alone. Men yoked and unyoked the oxen, drove the wagons and stock, and hunted. Women packed, cooked, and assisted in childbirths. Men also stood guard against Indian raids, although these were rare.

Between 1840 and 1848, an estimated 11,500 pioneers followed an overland trail to Oregon, and some 2,700 reached California. Such small numbers made a difference, for the British did not settle Oregon at all and the Mexican population of California was small and scattered. By 1845 California was clinging to Mexico by the thinnest of threads. The territory's Hispanic population, the *californios,* felt little allegiance to Mexico, which they contemptuously called "the other shore." Some of them wanted independence from Mexico, while others contemplated British or French rule. By the mid-1840s these *californios,* with their tenuous allegiances, faced a growing number of American settlers with definite political sympathies.

Emigrant Wagon Train Bedding Down for the Night

Men, women, and children divided the tasks—caring for oxen, feeding horses, drawing water, preparing supper, washing clothes— on the basis of gender and age.

Benjamin F. Reinhart, *An Evening Halt—Emigrants Moving to the West in 1840,* 1867, oil on canvas, 40 × 70 in. In the Collection of the Corcoran Gallery of Art, Washington, D.C. Gift of Mr. and Mrs. Lansdell K. Christie, 59.21.

THE POLITICS OF EXPANSION, 1840–1846

Westward expansion raised the question of whether the United States should annex Texas. In the 1840s the Texas issue sparked political passions and became entangled with other unsettling issues about the West. Between 1846 and 1848 a war with Mexico and a dramatic confrontation with Britain settled these questions on terms favorable to the United States.

At the start of the 1840s western issues received little attention in a nation concerned with issues relating to economic recovery—tariffs, banking, and internal improvements. Only after politicians failed to address the economic problems coherently did opportunistic leaders thrust expansion-related issues to the top of the political agenda.

The Whig Ascendancy

The election of 1840 brought the Whig candidate William Henry Harrison to the presidency and installed Whig majorities in both houses of Congress. The Whigs proposed to replace Van Buren's Independent Treasury (see Chapter 10) with some sort of national fiscal agency such as the Bank of the United States. The Whig party also favored a revised tariff that would increase government revenues but remain low enough to permit the importation of foreign goods. According to the Whig plan, the states would then receive tariff-generated revenues for internal improvements.

The Whig program might well have breezed into law. But Harrison died after only a month in office, and his successor, John Tyler, a Virginia aristocrat put on the ticket for his southern appeal, proved a disaster for the Whigs. A former Democrat, Tyler continued to favor the Democratic philosophy of states' rights. As president, he used the veto to shred his new party's program. In August 1841 a Whig measure to create a new national bank fell to Tyler's veto, as did a subsequent modification.

Tyler also played havoc with Whig tariff policy by vetoing one bill to lower tariffs to 20 percent in accord with the Compromise Tariff and rejecting

another to distribute revenue from a higher tariff to the states. Whig leaders were understandably furious; some Whigs talked of impeaching Tyler. In August 1842 the president, needing money to run the government, signed a new bill that maintained some tariffs above 20 percent but abandoned distribution to the states.

Tyler's erratic course confounded and disrupted his party. By maintaining some tariffs above 20 percent, the tariff of 1842 satisfied northern manufacturers, but by abandoning distribution, it infuriated southerners and westerners. The issue cut across party lines. In the congressional elections of 1842, the Whigs paid a heavy price for failing to enact their program; they lost control of the House to the Democrats. Now the nation had one party controlling the Senate, another controlling the House, and a president who appeared to belong to neither.

Tyler and the Annexation of Texas

Although disowned by his party, Tyler ardently desired a second term as president. Domestic issues offered him little hope of building a popular following, but foreign policy was another matter. In 1842 Tyler's secretary of state, Daniel Webster, concluded the Webster-Ashburton Treaty with Great Britain, settling a long-festering dispute over the Maine-Canadian border. Tyler reasoned that if he could follow the treaty, which was highly popular in the North, with the annexation of Texas, he could build a national following.

The issue of slavery clouded every discussion of Texas. Antislavery northerners saw proposals to annex Texas as part of a southern conspiracy to extend American territory into Mexico, Cuba, and Central America. Thus an unlimited number of new slave states could be created, but British Canada would eliminate the possibility of free states expanding to the north. And some southerners talked openly of carving Texas into four or five slave states.

Nevertheless, in summer 1843 Tyler launched a campaign for Texas annexation. He justified his crusade by reporting that he had learned of an attempt to make Texas a British, rather than an American, ally. John C. Calhoun, who became secretary of state in 1844, embroidered these reports with his own theories of British plans to use abolition as a way to destroy rice, sugar, and cotton production in the United States.

In spring 1844 Tyler and Calhoun submitted to the Senate a treaty annexing Texas. Accompanying the treaty was a letter from Calhoun to the British minister in Washington defending slavery as beneficial to African-Americans, the only way to protect them from "vice and pauperism." Abolitionists now had evidence that the annexation of Texas was linked to a conspiracy to extend slavery. Consequently, both Whig and Democratic leaders came out in opposition to the annexation of Texas, and the treaty went down to crushing defeat in the Senate. But however ostensibly decisive, the Senate vote simply dumped the annexation question into the upcoming presidential election.

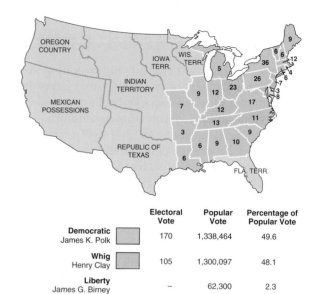

	Electoral Vote	Popular Vote	Percentage of Popular Vote
Democratic James K. Polk	170	1,338,464	49.6
Whig Henry Clay	105	1,300,097	48.1
Liberty James G. Birney	–	62,300	2.3

MAP 13.3
The Election of 1844

The Election of 1844

Tyler's ineptitude turned the presidential campaign into a free-for-all. Unable to gather support as an independent, he dropped out of the race. Henry Clay had a secure grip on the Whig nomination, but Martin Van Buren's apparently clear path to the head of the Democratic ticket vanished as the issue of annexation split his party. A deadlocked Democratic party finally turned to James K. Polk of Tennessee, the first "dark-horse" nominee in American history.

Jeering "Who is James K. Polk?" the Whigs derided the nomination. However, Polk, a wily campaigner, convinced many northerners that annexation of Texas would benefit them. In an imaginative scenario, Polk and his supporters argued that if Britain succeeded in abolitionizing Texas, slavery would not be able to move westward, racial tensions in existing slave states would intensify, and the chances of a race war would increase. However farfetched, this argument played effectively on northern racial phobias and helped Polk to detach annexation from Calhoun's narrow, prosouthern defense.

In contrast to the Democrats, whose position was clear, Clay and the Whigs wobbled. After several shifts Clay finally came out against annexation, but not until September. His wavering alienated his southern supporters and prompted some of his northern supporters to bolt the Whigs for the antislavery Liberty party, formed in 1840. The Whigs also infuriated Catholic immigrant voters by nominating Theodore Frelinghuysen for the vice presidency. A supporter of temperance and an assortment of other causes, Frelinghuysen confirmed fears that the Whigs were the orthodox Protestant party. Catholic immigrants turned out in large numbers to vote for the Democrats.

On the eve of the election in New York City, so many Irish marched to the courthouse to be qualified for voting that the windows had to be opened to allow people to enter and leave. "Ireland has reconquered the country which England lost," moaned an embittered Whig. Polk won the electoral vote 170–105, but his margin in the popular vote was only 38,000 out of 2.6 million votes cast. A shift of 6,000 votes in New York, where the immigrant vote and Whig defections to the Liberty party had hurt Clay, would have given Clay the state and the presidency.

Manifest Destiny, 1845

The election of 1844 demonstrated the strength of national support for the annexation of Texas. The surging popular sentiment for expansion reflected a growing conviction that America's natural destiny was to expand into Texas and all the way to the Pacific Ocean.

Expansionists emphasized extending the "area of freedom" and talked of "repelling the contaminating proximity of monarchies upon the soil that we have consecrated to the rights of man." For young Americans such as Walt Whitman, such restless expansionism knew few limits. "The more we reflect upon annexation as involving a part of Mexico, the more do doubts and obstacles resolve themselves away," Whitman wrote. "Then there is California, on the way to which lovely tract lies Santa Fe; how long a time will elapse before they shine as two new stars in our mighty firmament?" Americans needed only a phrase to capture this ebullient spirit. In 1845 John L. O'Sullivan, a New York Democratic journalist, supplied that phrase when he wrote of "our manifest destiny to overspread and to possess the whole of the continent which Providence has given us for the development of the great experiment of liberty and federated self-government entrusted to us."

Advocates of Manifest Destiny used lofty language and invoked God and nature to justify expansion. Because most champions of Manifest Destiny were Democrats who favored annexing Texas, northern Whigs dismissed Manifest Destiny as a smoke screen to conceal an evil intent to extend slavery. In fact, many expansionists supported neither slavery nor annexation. Most had their eyes not on Texas but on Oregon and California. Blaming the post-1837 depression on the failure of Americans to find markets for their agricultural surplus, they saw California and Oregon as solutions. A Missouri Democrat observed that "the ports of Asia are as convenient to Oregon as the ports of Europe are to the eastern slope of our confederacy, with an infinitely better ocean for naviga-

tion." An Alabama Democrat praised California's "safe and capacious harbors," which "invite to their bosoms the rich commerce of the East."

More than trade was at stake. To many, expansion presented an opportunity to preserve the agricultural character of the American people and thus to safeguard democracy. Fundamentally Jeffersonian, expansionists equated industrialization and urbanization with social stratification and class strife. To avoid the "bloated wealth" and "terrible misery" that afflicted Britain, the United States *had to* expand.

Democrats saw expansion as a logical complement to their support of low tariffs and their opposition to centralized banking. High tariffs and banks tended to "favor and foster the factory system," but expansion would provide farmers with land and with access to foreign markets. Americans would continue to be farmers, and the foundations of the Republic would remain secure.

This message, trumpeted by the penny press, made sense to the working poor, many of them Irish immigrants. Expansion would open economic opportunity for the common people and thwart British plans to free American slaves, whom the poor viewed as potential competition for already scarce jobs.

Expansionism drew on the ideas of Thomas Jefferson, John Quincy Adams, and other leaders of the early Republic who had proclaimed the American people's right to displace any people, uncivilized or European, from their westward path. Early expansionists had feared that overexpansion might create an ungovernable empire, but their successors had no such qualms. Although they pointed with alarm to the negative effects of industrialization, the expansionists also relied on the technology of industrialization. The railroad and the telegraph, they said, had annihilated the problem of distance and made expansion safe.

Polk and Oregon

The growing spirit of Manifest Destiny intensified the Oregon issue. To soften northern criticism of the pending annexation of Texas, the Democrats had included in their 1844 platform the assertion

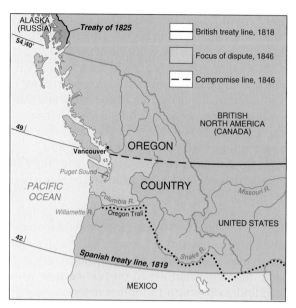

MAP 13.4
Oregon Boundary Dispute
Although demanding that Britain cede the entire Oregon Territory south of 54°40', the United States settled for a compromise at the forty-ninth parallel.

that American title "to the whole of the Territory of Oregon is clear and unquestionable." Taken literally, this statement, which Polk repeated in his inaugural address, pressed an American claim to the entire Oregon Territory between California and 54°40', the southern boundary of Alaska, a claim never before advanced.

Polk's objectives in Oregon were far subtler than his language. He knew that it would take a war with Britain for the United States to claim the entire Oregon Territory, and he wanted to avoid war. He hoped the belligerent language would persuade the British to accept what they had previously rejected, a division of Oregon at the forty-ninth parallel. This settlement would give the United States the superb deep-water harbor of Puget Sound and the southern tip of Vancouver Island.

Polk's position succeeded in rousing furious interest in the nation's acquiring the entire territory. Mass meetings adopted such resolutions as "The Whole or None!" Each year brought new American

settlers into Oregon. John Quincy Adams, though no supporter of the annexation of Texas or the 54°40' boundary for Oregon, believed that American settlements gave the United States a stronger claim than discovery and exploration had given the British. The United States, not Britain, he contended, was destined "to make the wilderness blossom as the rose, to establish laws, to increase, multiply, and subdue the earth," all "at the first behest of God Almighty."

In April 1846 Polk forced the issue by notifying Britain that the United States was terminating the joint British-American occupation of Oregon. In effect, this message was that the British could either go to war over the American claims to 54°40' or negotiate. They chose to negotiate. Although raging against "that illregulated, overbearing, and aggressive spirit of American democracy," Britain faced too many other problems to wage war over "a few miles of pine swamp." The ensuing treaty divided Oregon at the forty-ninth parallel, although Britain retained all of Vancouver Island and navigation rights on the Columbia River. On June 15, 1846, the Senate ratified the treaty, stipulating that Britain's navigation rights on the Columbia were temporary.

THE MEXICAN-AMERICAN WAR AND ITS AFTERMATH, 1846–1848

Between 1846 and 1848 the United States successfully fought a war that cost Mexico its claims to Texas and the provinces of New Mexico and California. While many Americans rejoiced over this victory, others foresaw that questions over the status of slavery in the newly acquired territories boded ill for the future.

The Origins of the Mexican-American War

While Polk challenged Britain over Oregon, the United States and Mexico moved toward war. The conflict had both immediate and remote causes. One long-standing grievance lay in the failure of the Mexican government to pay $2 million in debts owed to U.S. citizens. Bitter memories of the Alamo and of the Goliad massacre, moreover, reinforced American loathing of Mexico. Above all, the issue of Texas poisoned relations. Mexico still hoped to regain Texas or to keep it independent of the United States.

Still politically unstable—the presidency changed hands twenty times from 1829 to 1844—Mexico was afraid that an aggressive United States would trample on anyone in its path while disguising its intentions with high-sounding phrases. Once in control of Texas, Mexicans feared, the United States might seize other provinces, or even Mexico itself, and treat Mexicans as it treated slaves.

Polk's election increased the strength of the pro-annexationists, as his campaign had persuaded many northerners that Texas's annexation would bring national benefits. In February 1845 both houses of Congress responded to popular sentiment by passing a resolution annexing Texas. However, Texans balked, in part because some feared that union with the United States would provoke a Mexican invasion and war on Texas soil.

Polk moved rapidly. To sweeten the pot for Texans, he supported their claim that the Rio Grande constituted Texas's southern border, despite Mexico's contention that the Nueces River, 100 miles farther north, bounded Texas. Because the Rio Grande meandered west and north nearly 2,000 miles, it encompassed a huge territory, including part of modern New Mexico. The Texas that Polk proposed to annex thus was far larger than the Texas that had gained independence from Mexico. On July 4, 1845, reassured by Polk's support, Texas voted to accept annexation. To counter Mexican belligerency, Polk ordered American troops under General Zachary Taylor to the edge of the disputed territory. Taylor deployed his army at Corpus Christi, south of the Nueces River, in territory still claimed by Mexico.

California and its fine harbors influenced Polk's actions, for he had entered the White House with the firm intention of extending American control over that province, too. If Mexico went to war with the United States over Texas, Polk's supporters claimed, "the road to California will be open to us." Reports from American agents convinced Polk that the way lay open for California to join the United States as Texas would—by revolution and then annexation.

Continued turmoil in Mexican politics further complicated this complex situation. In early 1845 a new Mexican government agreed to negotiate with the United States, and Polk decided to give negotiations a chance. In November 1845 he dispatched John Slidell to Mexico City with instructions to gain Mexican recognition of the annexation of Texas with the Rio Grande border. In exchange, the U.S. government would assume the debt owed by Mexico to American citizens. Polk also authorized Slidell to offer up to $25 million for California and New Mexico. However, by the time Slidell reached Mexico City, the government there had become too weak to make concessions to the United States, and its head, General José Herrara, refused to receive Slidell. Polk then ordered Taylor to move southward to the Rio Grande, hoping to provoke a Mexican attack and to unite the American people behind war.

The Mexican government, however, dawdled over taking the bait. Polk was about to send a war message to Congress when word finally arrived that Mexican forces had crossed the Rio Grande and attacked the U.S. army. *"American blood has been shed on American soil!"* Polk's followers jubilantly proclaimed. On May 11, 1846, Polk informed Congress that war "exists by the act of Mexico herself" and called for $10 million to fight the war.

Polk's disingenuous assertion that the United States was already at war provoked furious opposition in Congress. For one thing, the Mexican attack on Taylor's troops had taken place on land never before claimed by the United States. Equally grievous, in announcing that war already existed, Polk seemed to undercut congressional power to declare war. He was using a mere border incident as a pretext to plunge the nation into a general war to acquire more slave territory. Whig papers warned readers that Polk was "precipitating you into a fathomless abyss of crime and calamity." But Polk had backed the Whigs into a corner. They could not afford to appear unpatriotic—they remembered vividly what opposition to the War of 1812 had cost the Federalists—so they swallowed their outrage and supported war.

Polk's single-minded pursuit of his goals had prevailed. A humorless, austere man who banned dancing and liquor at White House receptions, Polk inspired little personal warmth. But he had clear objectives and pursued them unflinchingly. He triumphed over all opposition, in part because of his opponents' fragmentation, in part because of expansion's popular appeal, and in part because of his foreign antagonists' weakness. Reluctant to fight over Oregon, Britain had negotiated. Too weak to negotiate, Mexico chose to fight over territory that it had already lost (Texas) and where its hold was feeble (California and New Mexico).

The Mexican-American War

Most European observers expected Mexico to win the war. Its army was four times the size of the American forces, and it was fighting on home ground. The United States, having botched its one previous attempt to invade a neighbor, Canada in 1812, now had to sustain offensive operations in an area remote from American settlements. American expansionists, however, hardly expected the Mexicans to fight at all. Racism and arrogance convinced many Americans that the Mexican people, degraded by their mixed Spanish and Indian population, were "as sure to melt away at the approach of [American] energy and enterprise as snow before a southern sun," as one newspaper publisher insisted.

In fact, the Mexicans fought bravely and stubbornly, although unsuccessfully. In May 1846 Taylor, "Old Rough and Ready," routed the Mexican army in Texas and pursued it across the Rio Grande, eventually to capture the major city of Monterrey in September. War enthusiasm surged in the United States, and recruiting posters blared, "Here's to old Zach! Glorious Times! Roast Beef, Ice Cream, and Three Months' Advance!" After taking Monterrey, Taylor, starved for supplies, halted and granted Mexico an eight-week armistice. Eager to

Patriotism and the Mexican-American War
U.S. soldiers commonly wore tall hats known as shako caps during the Mexican-American War. The caps were adorned with decorative plates showing the eagle spreading its wings, the symbol of Manifest Destiny.

undercut Taylor's popularity—the Whigs were already touting him as a presidential candidate—Polk stripped him of half his forces and reassigned them to General Winfield Scott. He was to mount an amphibious attack on Vera Cruz and proceed on to Mexico City, following the path of Cortés and his *conquistadores*. Events outstripped Polk's scheme, however, when Taylor defeated a far larger Mexican army at the Battle of Buena Vista, on February 22–23, 1847.

Farther north, American forces took advantage of the shakiness of Mexican rule to strip away New Mexico and California. In spring 1846 Colonel Stephen Kearny led an army from Fort Leavenworth, Kansas, toward Santa Fe. Having overcome immense natural obstacles to reach New Mexico, Kearny took the territory by a combination of bluff, bluster, and, perhaps, bribery. The Mexican governor, who had said that "it is better to be thought brave than to be so," fled at Kearny's approach. Once he had suppressed a brief rebellion by Mexicans and Indians, Kearny controlled New

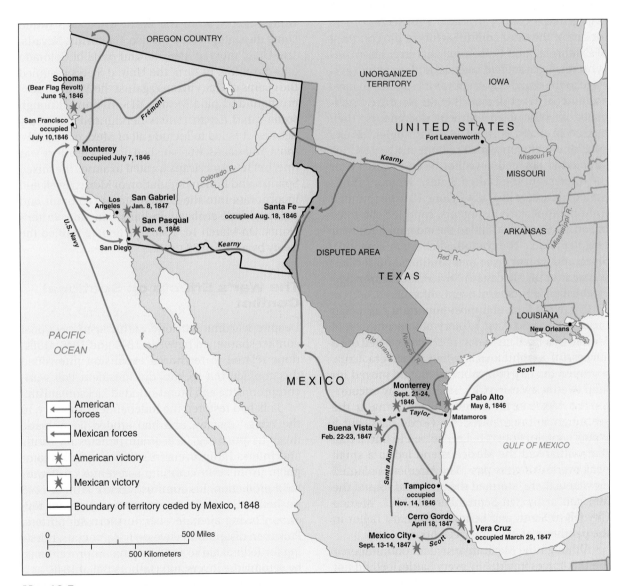

MAP 13.5
Major Battles of the Mexican War
The Mexican-American War's decisive campaign began with General Winfield Scott's capture of Vera Cruz and ended with his conquest of Mexico City. *hc* Interactive Map: The Mexican War

Mexico securely enough that he could dispatch part of his army south into Mexico to support Taylor at Buena Vista.

California also fell easily into American hands. In 1845 Polk had ordered the Pacific Squadron under Commodore John D. Sloat to occupy California's ports in event of war. The president had also dispatched a courier overland with secret orders for one of the most colorful actors in the conquest of California, John C. Frémont. A Georgia-born adventurer, Frémont had taken advantage of his marriage to the daughter of a powerful senator to have accounts of his explorations in the Northwest published as official government documents, then basked in glory as "the Great Pathfinder." Polk's courier caught up with Frémont in Oregon. Instructed to proceed to California and "watch over the interests of the United States," Frémont interpreted his orders liberally. In June 1846 he rounded up some American insurgents, captured the town of Sonoma, and proclaimed the independent "Bear Flag Republic." The combined efforts of Frémont, Sloat, and Kearny (who had continued on to California after his successful New Mexico campaign) established U.S. control over California.

The war's final and most important campaign brought Winfield Scott to glory in the conquest of Mexico City itself. In March 1847 Scott carried out a successful amphibious landing near Vera Cruz, pounded the city into submission, and moved inland to attack Mexico City. The U.S. army encountered a Mexican force under Santa Anna at the seemingly impregnable Cerro Gordo pass, but a young captain, Robert E. Lee, helped to find a trail that outflanked the Mexicans and led to a small peak overlooking the pass. The Americans planted howitzers there, stormed the pass, and routed the Mexican army. On September 13, 1847, Mexico City fell to Scott, and he joined Zachary Taylor in the pantheon of new American heroes.

Although the Mexican army had outnumbered the U.S. forces in virtually every battle, it could not match the superior artillery or the superior logistics and organization of the "barbarians of the North." American soldiers died like flies from yellow fever, and they carried into battle the agonies of venereal disease, which they picked up (and left) in every Mexican town they captured, but they benefited enormously from the unprecedented quality of their weapons, supplies, and organization.

By the Treaty of Guadalupe-Hidalgo (February 2, 1848), Mexico ceded Texas with the Rio Grande boundary, New Mexico, and California to the United States; from the Mexican cession would come the states of New Mexico, California, Nevada, and Utah, most of Arizona, and parts of Colorado and Wyoming. In turn, the United States assumed the claims of U.S. citizens against the Mexican government and paid Mexico $15 million. Although some rabid expansionists denounced the treaty because it failed to include all of Mexico, Polk, like most Americans, was satisfied. Empty territory was fine, but few Americans wanted to annex the mixed Spanish and Indian population of Mexico itself and incorporate into the United States "ignorant and indolent half-civilized Indians," in one writer's words. On March 10, 1848, the Senate ratified the treaty by a vote of 38 to 10.

The War's Effects on Sectional Conflict

Despite wartime patriotic enthusiasm, sectional conflict sharpened between 1846 and 1848. Questions related to territorial expansion intensified this conflict, but so, too, did President Polk's uncompromising and literal-minded Jacksonianism.

Polk had restored the Independent Treasury, to the Whigs' dismay, and had eroded Democratic unity by pursuing Jacksonian policies on tariffs and internal improvements. Despite Polk's campaign promise to combine a revenue tariff with mild protection, his administration's Tariff of 1846 slashed duties to the minimum necessary for revenue. Having alienated his northern supporters, Polk then disappointed western Democrats, thirsting for federal aid to fund internal improvements, by vetoing the Rivers and Harbors Bill of 1846.

Important as these issues were, territorial expansion generated the Polk administration's major battles. To Polk, it mattered little whether new territories were slave or free. Expansion would meet its purposes by dispersing the population, weakening dangerous tendencies toward centralized government, and ensuring the agricultural and democratic character of the United States. Focusing attention on slavery in the territories struck him as "not only unwise but wicked." To Polk, the Missouri Compromise, prohibiting slavery north of 36°30', embodied a simple, permanent solution to the question of territorial slavery.

But many northerners were coming to see slavery in the territories as a profoundly disruptive issue that neither could nor should be solved simply by extending the 36°30' line. Abolitionist Whigs, who opposed any expansion of slavery on moral grounds, posed a lesser threat to Polk than northern Democrats who feared that extending slavery into New Mexico and California would deter free laborers from settling those territories. Those Democrats argued that competition with slavery degraded free labor, that the westward extension of slavery would create a barrier to the westward migration of free labor, and that such a barrier would intensify social problems already evident in the East: excessive concentration of population, labor protest, class strife, and social stratification.

The Wilmot Proviso

A young Democratic congressman from Pennsylvania, David Wilmot, galvanized these disaffected northern Democrats. In August 1846 he introduced an amendment to an appropriations bill. This amendment, which became known as the Wilmot Proviso, stipulated that slavery be prohibited in any territory acquired by the negotiations. Wilmot represented the Democrats who had supported annexing Texas on the assumption that it would be the last slave state. Like other northern Democrats, he believed that Polk had made an implicit bargain: Texas for slaveholders, California and New Mexico for free labor. But Polk and southern Democrats opposed any barrier to the expansion of slavery south of the Missouri Compromise line; they believed that the westward expansion of slavery would reduce the concentration of slaves in older southern regions and thus lessen the chances of a slave revolt.

The proviso raised unsettling constitutional questions. Calhoun and other southerners contended that because slaves were property, the Constitution protected slaveholders' right to carry their slaves wherever they chose. This position led to the conclusion that the Missouri Compromise was unconstitutional. On the other side, many northerners cited the Northwest Ordinance of 1787, the Missouri Compromise, and the Constitution itself, which gave Congress the power to "make all needful rules and regulations respecting the territory or other property belonging to the United States," as justification for congressional legislation over slavery in the territories.

The Election of 1848

The Whigs watched in dismay as prosperity returned under Polk's program of an independent treasury and low tariffs. Never before had Henry Clay's American System of national banking and high tariffs seemed so irrelevant. But the Wilmot Proviso gave the Whigs a political windfall; originating in the Democratic party, it allowed the Whigs to portray themselves as the South's only dependable friends.

These considerations inclined the majority of Whigs toward Zachary Taylor. As a Louisiana slaveholder, he had obvious appeal to the South. As a political newcomer, he had no loyalty to a discredited American System. And as a war hero, he had broad national appeal. Nominating Taylor as presidential candidate in 1848, the Whigs presented him as an ideal man "without regard to creeds or principles" and ran him without any platform.

The Democrats faced a greater challenge because David Wilmot was one of their own. They could not ignore the issue of slavery in the territories, but if they embraced the positions of either Wilmot or Calhoun, the party would split along sectional lines. When Polk declined to run for reelection, the Democrats nominated Lewis Cass of Michigan, who had formulated the doctrine of "squatter sovereignty," or popular sovereignty as it was later called. Cass argued that Congress should let the question of slavery in the territories be

"Union" Woodcut by Thomas W. Strong, 1848
This 1848 campaign poster for Zachary Taylor reminded
Americans of his military victories, unmilitary bearing (note the
civilian dress and straw hat), and deliberately vague promises.
As president, Taylor finally took a stand on slavery in the
Mexican cession, but his position angered the South.

Free-Soil party. Declaring their dedication to "Free
Trade, Free Labor, Free Speech, and Free Men," the
Free-Soilers nominated Martin Van Buren on a
platform opposing any extension of slavery.

Zachary Taylor benefited from the opposition's
alienation of key northern states over the tariff issue, from Democratic disunity over the Wilmot
Proviso, and from his war-hero stature. He captured a majority of electoral votes in both North
and South. Although it failed to carry any state, the
Free-Soil party ran well enough in the North to
demonstrate the grassroots popularity of opposition to the extension of slavery. By showing that
opposition to the spread of slavery had far more
appeal than outright abolitionism, the Free-Soilers
sent both Whigs and Democrats a message that
they would be unable to ignore in future elections.

The California Gold Rush

When Wilmot had introduced his proviso, the issue
of slavery in the West was more abstract than immediate, for Mexico had not yet ceded any territory. The picture quickly changed when an American carpenter discovered gold while building a
sawmill in the foothills of California's Sierra
Nevada only nine days before the Treaty of
Guadalupe-Hidalgo was signed. A frantic gold rush
erupted. A San Francisco paper complained that
"the whole country from San Francisco to Los An-
geles, and from the shore to the base of the Sierra
Nevada, resounds with the sordid cry to *GOLD,
GOLD, GOLD!* while the field is left half-planted,
the house half-built, and everything neglected but
the manufacture of shovels and pickaxes." By December 1848 pamphlets with such titles as *The Emigrant's Guide to the Gold Mines* had hit the streets
of New York City, and the gold rush was on. Overland emigrants to California rose from 400 in 1848
to 44,000 in 1850.

Arriving by land as well as by sea, gold-rushers
swelled California's population from 15,000 in the
summer of 1848 to 250,000 by 1852. They came
from every corner of the world; one journalist reported that when she walked through a miners'
camp she heard English, Italian, French, Spanish,

decided by the people who settled there. Squatter
sovereignty appealed to many because of its arrest-
ing simplicity and vagueness; it neatly dodged the
explosive question of whether Congress actually
possessed power to prohibit territorial slavery. In
fact, few Democrats wanted definitive answers. As
long as the doctrine remained vague, northern and
southern Democrats alike could interpret it to their
respective benefit.

In the campaign both parties tried to avoid the
issue of slavery in the territories, but neither succeeded. A pro-Wilmot faction of the Democratic
party linked up with the abolitionist Liberty party
and antislavery "Conscience" Whigs to form the

Chronology

1822	Stephen F. Austin founds the first American community in Texas.	1846	The United States declares war on Mexico. John C. Frémont proclaims the Bear Flag Republic in California. Congress votes to accept a settlement of the Oregon boundary issue with Britain. Tariff of 1846. Colonel Stephen Kearny occupies Santa Fe. Wilmot Proviso introduced. Taylor takes Monterrey.
1830	Mexico closes Texas to further American immigration.		
1835	Santa Anna invades Texas.		
1836	Texas declares its independence from Mexico. Fall of the Alamo. Goliad massacre. Battle of San Jacinto.		
1840	William Henry Harrison elected president.	1847	Taylor defeats Santa Anna at the Battle of Buena Vista. Vera Cruz falls to Winfield Scott. Mexico City falls to Scott. Lewis Cass's principle of "squatter sovereignty."
1841	Harrison dies; John Tyler becomes president.		
1842	Webster-Ashburton Treaty.		
1844	James K. Polk elected president.	1848	Gold discovered in California. Treaty of Guadalupe-Hidalgo signed. Taylor elected president.
1845	Congress votes by joint resolution to annex Texas. Mexico rejects Slidell mission.		

German, and Hawaiian. Clashes between Anglo-Americans and Hispanics were frequent. Anglo-Americans particularly resented the Chinese who flooded into California in the 1850s as contract laborers. Rampant prejudice did not stop Americans from hiring Chinese workers, however.

The gold rush transformed the Hispanic hamlet of Yerba Buena into the "pandemonium" city of San Francisco; population soared from 150 to 50,000. No other American city boasted people from more parts of the world. The ethnic and racial tensions of the gold fields spilled over into the city and in 1851 merchants organized a Committee of Vigilance to patrol the streets, deport undesirables, and try and hang alleged thieves and murderers.

The gold rush made the issue of slavery in the West an immediate, practical concern. The newcomers to California included Mexicans, free blacks, and slaves brought by southern planters. White prospectors loathed the idea of competing with these groups and wanted to drive them from the gold fields. Violence mounted, and demands grew for a strong civilian government to replace the ineffective military government left over from the war.

The gold rush guaranteed that the question of slavery in the Mexican cession would be the first item on the agenda for Polk's successor and the nation.

CONCLUSION *hc* ACE Practice Test

The massive immigration of the 1840s changed the face of American politics. Angry at Whig nativism and anti-Catholicism, German and Irish immigrants swelled the Democratic party. The Whigs unraveled. President John Tyler, a Democrat in Whig's clothing, vetoed key Whig measures. Combined, these developments led to the surprise election of James K. Polk, a Democrat and an ardent expansionist, in 1844.

Wrapped in the language of Manifest Destiny, expansion appealed to Americans. It promised trade routes to the Pacific, more land for farming, and, in the case of Texas, more slave states. Polk gave Manifest Destiny direction by annexing Texas, provoking a crisis with Britain over Oregon, and provoking the Mexican-American War.

But even as the war began, cracks were showing in Polk's support. The Wilmot Proviso exposed deep sectional divisions that would explode in the secession of Free-Soil Democrats in 1848. Victorious over Mexico and enriched by the discovery of gold in California, Americans simultaneously counted the blessings of expansion and feared its costs.

FURTHER READING

Peter J. Blodgett, *Land of Golden Dreams* (1999). A vivid account of California during the gold rush and the settlement of the Far West.

William R. Brock, *Parties and Political Conscience: American Dilemmas, 1840–1850* (1979). An excellent interpretive study of the politics of the 1840s.

William H. Goetzmann, *When the Eagle Screamed: The Romantic Horizon in American Diplomacy, 1800–1860* (1966). A lively overview of antebellum expansionism.

Maldwyn A. Jones, *American Immigration* (1960). An excellent brief introduction to immigration.

Michael A. Morrison, *Slavery and the American West: The Eclipse of Manifest Destiny and the Coming of the Civil War* (1997). An important recent study.

Malcolm J. Rorabaugh, *Days of Gold: The California Gold Rush and the American Nation* (1997). Emphasizes how the discovery of gold in California reaffirmed the American belief that, regardless of family name or education, anyone who worked hard in America could grow rich.

Charles G. Sellers, *James K. Polk: Continentalist, 1843–1846* (1966). An outstanding political biography.

Henry Nash Smith, *Virgin Land: The American West as Symbol and Myth* (1950). A classic study of westward expansion in the American mind.

The Last Moments of John Brown by Thomas Hovdenden, 1884 (detail)

The Metropolitan Museum of Art, Gift of Mr. and Mrs. Carl Stoekel, 1897. (97.5).
Photograph © 1982 The Metropolitan Museum of Art, New York.

From Compromise to Secession, 1850–1861

 This icon will direct you to additional study and research resources at http://college.hmco.com/history/us/boyer/enduring_concise/5e/students/index.html

In early July 1859 a man calling himself Isaac Smith rented a dilapidated farmhouse a few miles from Harpers Ferry, Virginia, the site of a federal armory. Before long others arrived, including two young women; soon they were busy unloading fifteen boxes of what Smith termed "hardware." Although the men seemed reclusive, the young women were amiable, chatting with their neighbors, to whom everything seemed normal.

In fact, nothing was normal. "Smith" was actually John Brown, a brooding abolitionist with a price on his head for

This chapter focuses on four major questions:

▶ Was the Compromise of 1850 a genuine meeting of the minds between northerners and southerners? How did the Fugitive Slave Act and the election of 1852 undo the Compromise?

▶ Why did the Whig party collapse in the wake of the Kansas-Nebraska Act? Why wasn't the Democratic party as badly split?

▶ How did "Bleeding Kansas" influence the rise of the Republican party? How did the Republican party unify the North?

▶ Why did southerners conclude that the North intended not just to restrict the expansion of slavery but to destroy it everywhere—even in the South?

the murder of proslavery settlers in Kansas three years earlier in the Pottawatomie Massacre. Brown believed that God had ordained him to "purge this land with blood" to eradicate the evil of slavery. Joining him were a daughter, a daughter-in-law, three of his sons, and a mixed crew of white idealists, free blacks, and fugitive slaves. The "hardware" consisted of rifles and revolvers, which Brown and his followers intended to use to raid the Harpers Ferry arsenal—and ignite a slave insurrection throughout the South.

Abolitionists viewed Brown as a "doer," someone who could handle any rough stuff necessary to wipe out slavery. He fascinated many eastern abolitionists, themselves pacifists, who were beginning to suspect that only violence would end slavery. Although they supported him financially, they knew nothing of his plans for Harpers Ferry.

On the moonless evening of October 16, 1859, Brown and his army of eighteen seized the arsenal and armory at Harpers Ferry and waited for slaves to

rally around them and begin a massive rebellion. Two days later a contingent of Marines under the command of Colonel Robert E. Lee stormed the armory and killed or mortally wounded almost all of Brown's followers. A handful escaped but were eventually captured and executed. Brown himself was seriously wounded and captured. The anticipated—and feared—slave rebellion never happened.

Although prominent northern abolitionists tried to distance themselves from the event, correspondence unearthed at the farmhouse clearly linked them to Brown. During his trial, Brown rejected his own lawyers' claims that he was insane and instead told his captors that he had rendered to God the "greatest service man can." Gradually northern opinion became more and more sympathetic to Brown, seeing him as a martyr. Such opinion reached its apotheosis with the respected Ralph Waldo Emerson, who said that Brown's execution would "make the gallows as glorious as the cross."

Southerners saw matters quite differently. Brown may have botched the operations, but his plan to provoke a slave insurrection was reminiscent of Nat Turner's rebellion a generation earlier. To slaveholders, Brown's vision of uniting nonslaveholding whites, free blacks, and slaves was all too plausible; Brown was not a lunatic but a tool of the abolition movement that would drench the South in blood.

THE COMPROMISE OF 1850

Ralph Waldo Emerson's grim prediction that a U.S. victory in the Mexican War would be like swallowing arsenic proved disturbingly accurate. When the war ended in 1848, the United States contained an equal number (fifteen each) of free and slave states, but the vast territory gained by the war threatened to upset this balance. Any solution to the question of slavery in the Mexican cession—a free-soil policy, extension of the Missouri Compromise line, or popular sovereignty—ensured controversy. The prospect of free soil angered southerners, while extension of the Missouri Compromise line antagonized free-soil northerners as well as southern extremists who proclaimed that Congress could not bar slavery's expansion. Popular sovereignty offered the greatest hope for compromise by taking the question of slavery out of national politics and handing it to each territory, but this notion pleased neither free-soil nor proslavery extremists.

As the rhetoric escalated, events plunged the nation into crisis. Utah and then California, both acquired from Mexico, sought admission to the Union as free states. Texas, admitted to the Union as a slave state in 1845, aggravated matters by claiming the eastern half of New Mexico, thus potentially opening the door to slavery's extension into other newly acquired territory.

By 1850 other issues had become intertwined with territorial questions. Northerners had grown increasingly unhappy with slavery in the District of Columbia, within the shadow of the Capitol; southerners complained about lax enforcement of the Fugitive Slave Act of 1793. Any broad compromise would have to take both matters into account.

Zachary Taylor at the Helm

President Zachary Taylor believed that the South must not kindle the issue of slavery in the territories because neither New Mexico nor California was suited for slavery. In 1849 he asserted that "the people of the North need have no apprehension of the further extension of slavery."

Taylor's position differed significantly from the thinking behind the still controversial Wilmot Proviso, which proposed that Congress bar slavery in the territories ceded by Mexico. Taylor's plan, in contrast, left the decision to the states. He prompted California to apply for admission as a free state, bypassing the territorial stage, and hinted that he expected New Mexico (where the Mexican government had abolished slavery) to do the same. This strategy appeared to offer a quick, practical solution to the problem of extending slavery. The North would gain two new free states, and the South would gain acceptance of the right of the individual state to bar or to permit slavery.

But southerners rejected Taylor's plan. Not only would it yield the Wilmot Proviso's goal—the banning of slavery from the lands acquired from Mex-

ico—but it rested on the shaky assumption that slavery could never take root in California or New Mexico. Southerners also protested the addition of two new free states. "If we are to be reduced to a mere handful . . . wo, wo, I say to this Union," John C. Calhoun warned. Disillusioned with Taylor, a slaveholder from whom they had expected better, nine southern states agreed to send delegates to a convention to meet in Nashville in June 1850.

Henry Clay Proposes a Compromise

Had Taylor held a stronger position in the Whig party, he might have blunted mounting southern opposition. But many leading Whigs had never accepted this political novice, and in early 1850 Kentucky senator Henry Clay challenged Taylor's leadership by forging a compromise bill to resolve the whole range of contentious issues. Clay proposed (1) the admission of California as a free state; (2) the division of the remainder of the Mexican cession into two territories, New Mexico and Utah, without federal restrictions on slavery; (3) the settlement of the Texas–New Mexico boundary dispute on terms favorable to New Mexico; (4) as a pot-sweetener for Texas, an agreement that the federal government would assume the state's large public debt; (5) continuation of slavery in the District of Columbia but abolition of the slave trade; and (6) a more effective fugitive slave law.

Clay rolled all these proposals into a single "omnibus" bill. The debates over the compromise bill during late winter and early spring 1850 marked the last major appearance on the public stage of Clay, Calhoun, and Webster, the trio who had stood at the center of American political life since the War of 1812. Clay, the conciliator as ever, warned the South against the evils of secession and assured the North that nature would check the spread of slavery. Gaunt and gloomy, the dying Calhoun listened as another senator read Calhoun's address for him, a repetition of his warnings that only if the North treated the South as an equal could the Union survive. Webster spoke vividly in favor of compromise, "not as a Massachusetts man, nor as a Northern man, but as an American," and chided the North for trying to "reenact the will of God" by excluding slavery from the Mexican cession. Strident voices countered these attempts at conciliation. The antislavery Whig William Seward of New York enraged southerners by talking of a "higher law than the Constitution"—namely, the will of God against the extension of slavery. Clay's compromise faltered as Clay broke with President Taylor, who attacked him as a glory hunter.

Even as the Union faced its worst crisis since 1789, events in summer 1850 eased the way toward resolution. When the Nashville convention met in June, only nine of the fifteen slave states, primarily in the Lower South, sent delegates. Despite the reckless pronouncements of the "fire-eaters" (extreme advocates of "southern rights"), moderates dominated. Then Zachary Taylor celebrated too extravagantly on July 4 and died five days later of a stomach ailment. His successor, Millard Fillmore of New York, supported Clay's compromise. Finally, Senator Stephen A. Douglas of Illinois took over stewardship of the compromise. He broke the omnibus into a series of individual measures; to secure Democratic support Douglas proposed that popular sovereignty settle the slavery issue in New Mex-

ico and Utah. These tactics worked. By summer's end the Compromise of 1850 had become reality.

Assessing the Compromise

Although President Fillmore hailed the compromise as a final settlement of sectional issues, it failed to bridge the underlying differences between North and South. Southerners had voted against the admission of California and northerners against the Fugitive Slave Act. Only shifting alliances between moderates and northerners or southerners on specific issues had achieved passage of the compromise.

Each section could claim victories from the compromise. Northern victories were clear: admission of California and abolition of the slave trade in the District of Columbia. However, southern victories, such as the stricter fugitive slave law, were clouded by the legislators' failure to resolve the issue of congressional authority over slavery in territories outside the Mexican cession.

Southerners therefore reacted ambivalently to the Compromise of 1850. In state elections during fall 1850 and 1851, procompromise candidates generally thrashed the law's opponents. At the same

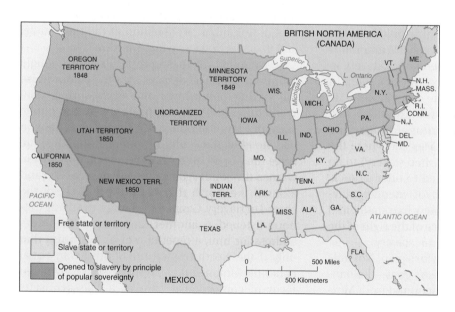

MAP 14.1

The Compromise of 1850

The Compromise of 1850 admitted California as a free state. Utah and New Mexico were left open to slavery or freedom according to the principle of popular sovereignty.

time, even Unionists in Georgia wrote the celebrated Georgia platform, which threatened secession if Congress prohibited slavery in the Mexican cession or repealed the Fugitive Slave Act. And the South's one clear victory, the passage of a new, more stringent fugitive slave law, quickly proved a mixed blessing. Few slaves had been taken into the Mexican cession, so the question of slavery there had a hypothetical quality. But the issues raised by the new fugitive slave law were concrete: real southerners would pursue real fugitives—on northern soil. Average northerners to whom slavery had been an abstraction would respond to this new reality with fury.

Enforcement of the Fugitive Slave Act

Northern moderates accepted the Fugitive Slave Act of 1850 as the price of saving the Union, but the law outraged antislavery northerners. It denied alleged fugitives the right of trial by jury, forbade them to testify at their own trial, permitted their return to slavery merely on the testimony of a claimant, and enabled court-appointed commissioners to collect ten dollars if they ruled for the slaveholder but only five if they ruled for the fugitive. As one commentator noted, the law threatened to turn the North into "one vast hunting ground." It targeted *all* runaways, putting at risk even fugitives who had lived as free blacks for thirty years or more. Above all, the law brought home to northerners the uncomfortable truth of their own complicity in slavery's continuation. By legalizing the activities of slave-catchers on northern soil, the law reminded northerners that slavery was a national problem, not merely a southern institution. Antislavery northerners assailed the law in such terms as the "vilest monument of infamy of the nineteenth century."

Efforts to catch and return runaways inflamed emotions in both North and South. In 1854 a Boston mob aroused by antislavery speeches killed a courthouse guard in an abortive effort to rescue fugitive slave Anthony Burns. Determined to enforce the law, President Franklin Pierce sent federal troops to escort Burns to the harbor, where a ship carried him back to slavery. As five platoons of

Frederick Douglass
Born into slavery, Frederick Douglass became a commanding orator and writer in the 1840s and 1850s. He bitterly attacked the Fugitive Slave Act. The only way to make the law a "dead letter," he vowed, was to make "half a dozen or more dead kidnappers." In an Independence Day speech in 1852, he reminded white Americans that "This Fourth of July is yours, not mine."

troops marched Burns to the ship, 50,000 people lined the streets. One Bostonian hung from his window a black coffin bearing the words "the funeral of liberty." The Burns incident shattered the complacency of conservative supporters of the Compromise of 1850. "We went to bed one night old fashioned conservative Compromise Union Whigs," textile manufacturer Amos A. Lawrence wrote, "and waked up stark mad Abolitionists." A Boston committee later purchased Burns's freedom, but other fugitives had worse fates. Margaret Garner, about to be captured and sent back to Kentucky as a slave, tried to kill her children rather than witness their return to slavery.

Northerners devised ways to interfere with the enforcement of the Fugitive Slave Act. "Vigilance" committees spirited endangered blacks to Canada, lawyers dragged out hearings to raise slave-catchers' expenses, and "personal liberty laws" hindered state officials' enforcement of the law. These obstructionist tactics convinced southerners that opposition to slavery boiled just beneath the surface of northern opinion. The southern "victory" represented by the passage of the Fugitive Slave Act seemed increasingly illusory.

Uncle Tom's Cabin

Harriet Beecher Stowe's novel *Uncle Tom's Cabin* (1852) drummed up wide northern support for fugitive slaves. Stowe, the daughter of famed evangelical Lyman Beecher, greeted the Fugitive Slave Act with horror. In one of the novel's most memorable scenes, she depicted the slave Eliza, clutching her infant son, bounding across ice floes on the Ohio River to freedom. Slavery itself was Stowe's main target. Much of her novel's power derives from its view that good intentions mean little in the face of so evil an institution. The good intentions of a kindly slave owner die with him, and Uncle Tom is sold to the vicious Yankee Simon Legree, who whips Tom to death. Stowe also played effectively to the emotions of her audience by demonstrating how slavery ripped slave families apart.

Three hundred thousand copies of *Uncle Tom's Cabin* were sold in 1852, and 1.2 million by summer 1853. Stage dramatizations reached perhaps fifty times as many people as the novel did. As a play, *Uncle Tom's Cabin* enthralled working-class audiences normally indifferent or hostile to abolitionism. Yet the impact of *Uncle Tom's Cabin* cannot be precisely measured. Although it hardly lived up to the prediction of one abolitionist leader that it would convert 2 million people to abolitionism, it did push many waverers toward an aggressive antislavery stance. As historian David Potter concluded, the northern attitude toward slavery "was never quite the same after *Uncle Tom's Cabin*."

The Election of 1852

The Fugitive Slave Act fragmented the Whig party. Northern Whigs took the lead in defying the law, and southern Whigs had a difficult time explaining away the power of vocal free-soil Whigs.

In 1852 the Whigs' nomination of Mexican-American War hero General Winfield Scott as their presidential candidate widened the sectional split in the party. Although a Virginian, Scott owed his nomination to the northern free-soil Whigs. His single, feeble statement endorsing the Compromise of 1850 undercut southern Whigs trying to portray the Democrats as the party of disunion and themselves as the party of both slavery and the Union.

The Democrats bridged their own sectional division by nominating Franklin Pierce of New Hampshire, a dark-horse candidate whose chief attraction was that no faction of the party violently opposed him. The "ultra men of the South," a friend of his noted, "say they can cheerfully go for him, and none, none say they cannot." Northern and southern Democrats alike rallied behind the Compromise of 1850 and behind the ideal of popular sovereignty, and Pierce won a smashing victory. In the most one-sided election since 1820, he carried twenty-seven of the thirty-one states and collected 254 of 296 electoral votes. Following the Whigs' devastating defeats throughout the South in both presidential and local elections, one stalwart lamented "the decisive breaking-up of our party."

THE COLLAPSE OF THE SECOND PARTY SYSTEM, 1853–1856

Franklin Pierce was the last presidential candidate of the nineteenth century to carry the popular and electoral vote in both North and South. Not until Franklin D. Roosevelt swept into office in 1932 would another president do so. Pierce also became the last president to hold office under the second party system—Whigs against Democrats. Within four years of Pierce's election, the Whig party would disintegrate, to be replaced by two newcomers, the American (Know-Nothing) party and the Republican party.

Unlike the Whigs, the Republican party was a purely sectional, northern party, drawing its support from both former Whigs and discontented

Democrats. The Democrats survived as a national party, but with a base so shrunken in the North that the newborn Republican party captured two-thirds of the free states in the election of 1856.

For decades the second party system had kept the conflict over slavery in check by providing Americans other issues to argue about—banking, internal improvements, tariffs, and temperance. By the 1850s the debate over slavery extension overshadowed such issues and exposed raw divisions in each party. Whigs, with their larger, more aggressive free-soil wing, were much more vulnerable to disruption than the Democrats. Thus when Stephen A. Douglas put forth a proposal in 1854 to organize the vast Nebraska territory with no restrictions on slavery, he ignited a fire-storm that consumed the Whig party.

The Kansas-Nebraska Act

Signed in late May 1854, the Kansas-Nebraska Act shattered the already weakened second party system and triggered renewed sectional strife. The bill's roots lay in the seemingly uncontroversial desire of farmers to organize the large territory west of Iowa and Missouri. Railroad enthusiasts who dreamed of a rail line linking the Midwest to the Pacific also wanted the territory organized.

In January 1854 Democratic senator Stephen A. Douglas of Illinois proposed a bill to organize Nebraska as a territory. Douglas believed that a railroad to the Pacific would bring national benefits, including a continuous line of settlement, and thought that a railroad-based western expansion would unite the splintering Democratic factions.

Two sources of potential conflict loomed. First, some southerners advocated a southern-based Pacific route rather than a midwestern one. Second, Nebraska lay north of the Missouri Compromise line in the Louisiana Purchase, a region closed to slavery. Under Douglas's bill, the South would lose the Pacific rail route *and* face the possibility of more free territory in the Union. To placate southerners and win their votes, Douglas made two concessions. First, he proclaimed the Missouri Compromise now void, superseded by the Compromise of 1850 and its doctrine of popular sovereignty. Second, Douglas agreed to divide the territory into northern and southern parts, Nebraska and Kansas. Implicit in this, at least to southerners,

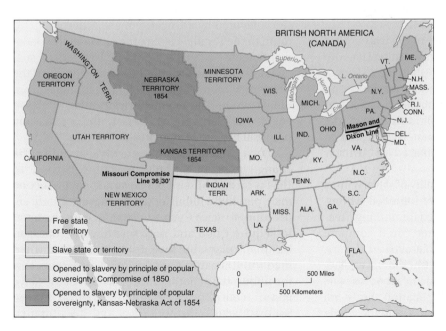

MAP 14.2

The Kansas-Nebraska Act, 1854

Kansas and Nebraska lay within the Louisiana Purchase, north of 36°30', and hence were closed to slavery until Stephen A. Douglas introduced his bills in 1854.

hc Interactive Map: The Kansas–Nebraska Act, 1854

was the idea that Nebraska would be free soil but Kansas would be open to slavery.

These modifications to Douglas's original bill set off a storm of protest. Despite Douglas's belief that national expansion was the critical issue, most attention focused on the extension of slavery. Antislavery northerners assailed the bill as "an atrocious plot" to violate the Missouri Compromise and to turn Kansas into a "dreary region of despotism, inhabited by masters and slaves." Their anger provoked an equal response among southerners and added the issue of regional pride to the already volatile mix of expansion and slavery.

Despite the uproar, Douglas guided the bill easily through the Senate. Matters were far more tumultuous in the House, where the bill passed by a narrow margin. Ominously, not a single northern Whig in the House voted for the bill, and northern Democrats split evenly.

The Surge of Free Soil

Amid the clamor over his bill, Douglas ruefully observed that he could now travel to Chicago by the light of his own burning effigies. Neither a fool nor a political novice, he was the victim of a political bombshell—free soil—that exploded under his feet.

Support for free soil united many who agreed on little else. Many free-soilers were racists who opposed allowing any African-Americans, slave or free, into the West. Others repudiated slavery on moral grounds and rejected blatantly racist legislation. However, as one abolitionist noted, the free-soil convictions of many westerners rested on a "perfect, if not supreme" hatred of African-Americans.

Although split over the morality of slavery, most free-soilers agreed that slavery impeded whites' progress. Because a slave worked for nothing, free-soilers claimed, no free laborer could compete with a slave. In any territory that allowed slavery, free labor would therefore vanish. Wherever slavery appeared, a free-soiler argued, "labor loses its dignity; industry sickens; education finds no schools; religion finds no churches, and the whole land of slavery is impoverished." Free-soilers also used an early version of the domino theory to blast the idea that slavery had natural limits. "Slavery is as certain to invade New Mexico and Utah, as the sun is to rise," insisted a free-soiler. If slavery secured a toehold in Kansas, free-soilers warned, Minnesota would fall to slavery as well.

The Kansas-Nebraska Act, in free-soilers' opinion, was "a part of a continuous movement of slaveholders to advance slavery over the entire North." Free-soilers saw southern planters, southern politicians, and their northern dupes, such as Stephen A. Douglas, entangled in a gigantic conspiracy to extend slavery.

The Ebbing of Manifest Destiny

The uproar over the Kansas-Nebraska Act embarrassed the Pierce administration. It also doomed Manifest Destiny, the one issue that had held the Democrats together in the 1840s.

Franklin Pierce had come to office championing Manifest Destiny, but increasing sectional rivalries sidetracked his efforts. In 1853 his emissary James Gadsden negotiated the purchase of a strip of land south of the Gila River (now southern Arizona and part of southern New Mexico), an acquisition favored by advocates of a southern railroad route to the Pacific. Fierce opposition to the Gadsden Purchase revealed mounting free-soilers' suspicions of expansion, and the Senate approved the treaty only after slashing 9,000 square miles from the purchase. The sectional rivalries beginning to engulf the Nebraska bill clearly threatened any proposal to gain new territory.

Cuba provided even more vivid proof of the change in public attitudes toward expansion. In 1854 a former Mississippi governor, John A. Quitman, planned a filibuster (an unofficial military expedition) to seize Cuba from Spain. Pierce wanted to acquire Cuba and may first have encouraged Quitman's plans, but the president backed down in the face of northern opposition. Northerners saw the filibuster as another manifestation of the Slave Power's conspiracy to grab more territory for the South's "peculiar institution."

Events, however, slipped out of Pierce's control. In October 1854 the American ambassadors to Great Britain, France, and Spain, two of them southerners, met in Belgium and issued the unofficial Ostend Manifesto, calling on the United States to acquire Cuba by any means, including force. Beset by the storm over the Kansas-Nebraska Act and northern fury over Quitman's proposed filibuster, Pierce repudiated the manifesto.

Despite the Pierce administration's disavowal of the Ostend Manifesto, the idea of expansion into the Caribbean continued to attract southerners, including the Tennessee-born adventurer William Walker. Between 1853 and 1860, the year a firing squad in Honduras executed him, Walker led a succession of filibustering expeditions into Mexico and Nicaragua. Taking advantage of civil chaos in Nicaragua, he made himself the chief political force there, reinstituted slavery, and talked of making Nicaragua a U.S. colony.

Although some southerners were against expansion—among them the Louisiana sugar planters who opposed acquiring Cuba because Cuban sugar would compete with their product—southern expansionists stirred up enough commotion to worry antislavery northerners that the South aspired to establish a Caribbean slave empire. Like a card in a poker game, the threat of expansion southward was all the more menacing for not being played. As long as the debate on the extension of slavery focused on territories in the continental United States, slavery's prospects for expansion were limited. However, adding Caribbean territory to the equation changed all calculations.

The Whigs Disintegrate, 1854–1855

While straining Democratic unity, the Kansas-Nebraska Act wrecked the Whig party. Although Democrats lost ground in the 1854 congressional elections, the Whigs failed to benefit. No matter how furious the free-soil Democrats were at Douglas for introducing the act, they could not forget that southern Whigs had supported him. Northern Whigs split into two camps: antislavery "Con-

science" Whigs, led by Senator William Seward of New York, and conservatives, led by former president Millard Fillmore. The conservatives believed that the Whig party had to adhere to the Compromise of 1850 to maintain itself as a national party.

This deep division within the Whig party repelled antislavery Democrats and prompted antislavery Whigs to look for an alternative party. By 1856 the new Republican party would become home for these antislavery refugees; however, in 1854 and 1855 the American, or Know-Nothing, party emerged as the principal alternative to the faltering established parties.

The Rise and Fall of the Know-Nothings, 1853–1856

The Know-Nothings evolved out of a nativist organization, the Order of the Star-Spangled Banner. (The party's popular name derived from its members' standard response to inquiries about its activities: "I know nothing.") One of many nativist societies that had mushroomed in response to the immigration boom of the 1840s, the Order of the Star-Spangled Banner had pressured existing parties to nominate and appoint only native-born Protestants. It had also urged lengthening the naturalization period before immigrants could vote.

Winfield Scott's compaign for the presidency in 1852 had alienated many nativists, who had previously voted Whig. Trying to revitalize his badly split party, Scott had courted the traditionally Democratic Catholic vote. Most Catholics had voted for Franklin Pierce, but many nativists bailed out of the Whig party. The Kansas-Nebraska Act cemented nativist allegiance to the Know-Nothings, opposed both to the extension of slavery and to Catholicism. An obsessive fear of conspiracies unified the Know-Nothings. They simultaneously denounced a papal conspiracy against the American republic and a Slave Power conspiracy reaching its tentacles throughout the United States.

The Know-Nothings enjoyed a meteoric rise and an equally rapid fall. For example, in 1854 they captured the governorship, almost the entire state legislature, and all the congressional seats of

Massachusetts. Such Know-Nothing successes wrecked Whig hopes of capitalizing on hostility to the Kansas-Nebraska Act.

By 1856 the Know-Nothings had become a falling star soon to plummet below the horizon. They proved as vulnerable to sectional conflicts over slavery as the Whigs. In 1855 southern Know-Nothings, mainly proslavery former Whigs, combined with northern conservatives to make acceptance of the Kansas-Nebraska Act part of the Know-Nothing platform, blurring the attraction of Know-Nothingism to northern voters more antislavery than anti-Catholic. One such former Whig, Illinois congressman Abraham Lincoln, asked pointedly, "How can anyone who abhors the oppression of negroes be in favor of degrading classes of white people?" Most Know-Nothings eventually concluded that, as one observer put it, "neither the Pope nor the foreigners ever can govern the country or endanger its liberties, but the slavebreeders and slavetraders *do* govern it, and threaten to put an end to all government but theirs." Chief beneficiary of the Know-Nothing dilemma was the emerging Republican party, which had no southern wing to blunt its antislavery message.

The Republican Party and the Crisis in Kansas, 1855–1856

Born in the chaotic aftermath of the Kansas-Nebraska Act, the Republican party would become the main opposition to the Democratic party by 1856 and would win each presidential election from 1860 until 1884. In 1855, however, few might have predicted such a bright future. Although united in opposition to the Kansas-Nebraska Act, the fledgling party was host to conservatives who wanted to restore the Missouri Compromise, radicals who had been part of the Liberty party abolitionists, and a sizable middle of free-soilers.

Building organizations at the state level was essential, for state issues often shaped voters' allegiances. The Know-Nothings, for example, linked support for temperance, strong at the state level, with anti-Catholicism and antislavery. Frequently antislavery voters were also protemperance and anti-Catholic, believing that addiction to alcohol and submission to the pope were both forms of enslavement to be eradicated. Competing with the Know-Nothings for these intensely moralistic voters at the state level, Republicans faced a dilemma: if they attacked the Know-Nothings for stressing anti-Catholicism over antislavery, they might well alienate the voters, but if they compromised with the Know-Nothings, they might well lose their own identity as a party.

Alternately attacking and conciliating, the Republicans succeeded in some state elections in 1855 but lost ground as popular ire against the Kansas-Nebraska Act cooled. By the start of 1856 they were organized in only half the northern states and lacked any national organization. The Republicans desperately needed something to make voters more concerned about the Slave Power than about rum or Catholicism. Salvation for the nascent party came in the form of violence in Kansas, which quickly became known as Bleeding Kansas. This violence united the party around its free-soil center, intensified antislavery feelings, and boosted Republican fortunes.

In the wake of the Kansas-Nebraska Act, Boston abolitionists had organized a company to send antislavery settlers into Kansas, but most of the territory's early settlers came from Missouri or other parts of the Midwest. Few of these opposed slavery on moral grounds. Some supported slavery; others wanted to keep all African-Americans out of Kansas. "I kem to Kansas to live in a free state," exclaimed one clergyman, "and I don't want niggers atrampin' over my grave."

Despite most settlers' racist leanings and hatred of abolitionists, Kansas became a battleground between proslavery and antislavery forces. In March 1855 thousands of proslavery Missouri "border ruffians" crossed into Kansas to vote illegally in the first elections for the territorial legislature. Drawing revolvers, they quickly silenced judges who challenged their right to vote in Kansas. Ironically, proslavery forces probably would have won an honest election. But the proslavery legislature established in 1855 in Lecompton, Kansas, operated under a cloud of fraud. "There is not a proslavery man of my acquaintance in Kansas," wrote the antislavery wife of a farmer, "who does not acknowledge that the Bogus Legislature was the result of a gigantic and well-planned fraud, that the elections were carried by an invading mob from Missouri." The Lecompton legislature shredded what little good reputation it had by passing a series of outrageous laws, punishing the harboring of fugitive slaves by ten years' imprisonment, and making the circulation of abolitionist literature a capital offense.

The legislature's actions set off a chain reaction. In summer 1855 free-staters, including many aroused to oppose the Lecompton legislature, organized a rival government at Topeka. In May 1856 the Lecompton government dispatched a posse to Lawrence, where some free-staters were organizing a militia. The Lecompton posse, bearing banners emblazoned "southern rights" and "let yankees tremble and abolitionists fall," tore through Lawrence, burning buildings and destroying two printing presses. There were no deaths, but Republicans immediately dubbed the incident "the sack of Lawrence."

The next move belonged to John Brown, a Connecticut-born abolitionist with an overpowering sense of divinely ordained mission. The "sack" of Lawrence convinced Brown that God now beckoned him "to break the jaws of the wicked." In late May Brown led seven men, including his four sons and his son-in-law, toward Pottawatomie Creek near Lawrence. They shot to death one man associated with the Lecompton government and hacked four others to pieces with broadswords. Brown's "Pottawatomie Massacre" terrified southerners and transformed "Bleeding Kansas" into a battleground between North and South. Supporters of slavery armed themselves for, as one South Carolinian wrote, "no Proslavery man knows when he is safe in this Ter[ritory]."

Popular sovereignty had failed in Kansas. Instead of resolving the issue of the extension of slavery, popular sovereignty had institutionalized the division over slavery by creating two rival governments. The Pierce administration compounded its problems, and Kansas's, by denouncing the anti-slavery Topeka government and recognizing the proslavery Lecompton government, thus forcing northern Democrats into the awkward appearance of supporting the "Bogus Legislature" at Lecompton. Nor did popular sovereignty keep the slavery issue out of politics. On the day before the proslavery attack on Lawrence, Republican senator Charles Sumner of Massachusetts delivered a wrathful speech, "The Crime Against Kansas," in which he verbally lashed the Senate for its complicity in slavery. Sumner singled out Senator Andrew Butler of South Carolina for making "the harlot, slavery" his mistress. The speech stunned the Senate. Two days later a relative of Butler, Democratic representative Preston Brooks of South Carolina, strode into the Senate chamber and beat Sumner with a cane. The hollow cane broke after five or six blows, but Sumner, who required stitches, took three years to recuperate. Brooks immediately became a hero in the South.

Now "Bleeding Kansas" and "Bleeding Sumner" united the North. The "sack" of Lawrence, President Pierce's recognition of the proslavery Lecompton government, and Brooks's actions seemed to clinch the Republican argument that an aggressive slaveocracy was in power and holding white northerners in contempt. By denouncing the Slave Power rather than slavery, the Republicans sidestepped the divisive question of slavery's morality. Instead, they focused on portraying planters as arrogant aristocrats, the natural enemies of the laboring people of the North.

The Election of 1856

The presidential race of 1856 revealed the scope of the political realignment of the preceding few years. The Republicans, in their first presidential contest, nominated John C. Frémont, the "pathfinder" of California "Bear State" fame. Northern Know-Nothings also endorsed Frémont, while southern Know-Nothings nominated Millard Fillmore, the last Whig president. The Democrats dumped the battered Pierce for James Buchanan of Pennsylvania, who had had the luck to be out of the country (as minister to Great Britain) during the Kansas-Nebraska furor. A signer of the Ostend Manifesto, Buchanan was popular in the South.

The campaign became two separate races: Frémont versus Buchanan in the free states and Fillmore versus Buchanan in the slave states. Buchanan in effect was the only national candidate. Although Frémont attracted wide support in the North and Fillmore equal support in the South, Buchanan carried enough votes in both North and South to win the presidency.

The election of 1856 made three facts clear. First, the American party was finished as a major national force. Having worked for the Republican Frémont, most northern Know-Nothings joined that party. Fillmore's dismal showing in the South convinced southern Know-Nothings to abandon their party and seek a new political affiliation. Second, although in existence for barely a year, lacking any base in the South, and running a political novice, the Republican party did very well. A purely sectional party had nearly captured the presidency. Third, as long as the Democrats could unite behind a single national candidate, they would be hard to defeat. To achieve unity, however, the Democrats would have to find more James Buchanans— "doughface" moderates acceptable to southerners and northerners alike.

THE CRISIS OF THE UNION, 1857–1860

No one ever accused James Buchanan of impulsiveness or fanaticism. Although a moderate who wished to avoid controversy, Buchanan would preside over one of the most controversy-ridden administrations in American history. A Supreme Court decision concerning Dred Scott, a Missouri slave who had resided in free territory for several years; the creation of the proslavery Lecompton constitution in Kansas; the raid by John Brown on Harpers Ferry, Virginia; and secession itself would wrack Buchanan's administration. The forces driving the nation apart were spinning out of control by 1856, and Buchanan could not stop them. By his

inauguration, southerners saw creeping abolitionism in the guise of free soil and northerners detected an ever more insatiable Slave Power. Once these potent images took hold in the minds of the American people, politicians could do little to erase them.

The Dred Scott Case, 1857

Pledged to congressional "noninterference" with slavery in the territories, Buchanan looked to the courts for resolution of the vexatious issue of slavery's extension. A case that appeared to promise a solution had been winding its way through the courts for years; on March 6, 1857, two days after Buchanan's inauguration, the Supreme Court handed down its decision in *Dred Scott* v. *Sandford*.

During the 1830s his master had taken Dred Scott, a slave, from the slave state of Missouri into Illinois and the Wisconsin Territory, both closed to slavery. After his master's death, Scott sued for his freedom on the grounds of his residence in free territory. Scott's case reached the Supreme Court in 1856.

The Court faced two key questions. Did Scott's residence in free territory during the 1830s make him free? Did Scott, again enslaved in Missouri, have the right to sue in the federal courts? The Supreme Court could have neatly sidestepped controversy by ruling that Scott had no right to sue, but it chose not to.

Instead, Chief Justice Roger B. Taney, a seventy-nine-year-old Marylander, handed down a sweeping decision that touched off another fire-storm. First, Taney wrote, Scott, a slave, could not sue for his freedom. Further, no black, whether a slave or a free descendant of slaves, could become a U.S. citizen. Continuing his incendiary opinion, Taney ruled that even had Scott been entitled to sue, his residence in free territory did not make him free because the Missouri Compromise, whose provisions prohibited slavery in the Wisconsin Territory, was itself unconstitutional. The compromise, declared Taney, violated the Fifth Amendment's protection of property (including slaves).

The *Dred Scott* decision, instead of settling the issue of expansion of slavery, touched off another blast of controversy. The antislavery press flayed it as "willful perversion" filled with "gross historical falsehoods." Republicans saw the decision as further evidence that the fiendish Slave Power gripped the nation. The Slave Power, a northern paper bellowed, "has marched over and annihilated the boundaries of the states. We are now one great homogeneous slaveholding community."

Like Stephen A. Douglas after the Kansas-Nebraska Act, James Buchanan now appeared as another northern dupe of an evil slaveocracy. Republicans restrained themselves from open defiance of the decision only by insisting that it did not bind the nation; Taney's comments on the constitutionality of the Missouri Compromise, they contended, were opinions unnecessary to settling the case and therefore technically not binding.

The savage reaction to the decision provided more proof that no "judicious" or nonpartisan solution to slavery was possible. Any doubter needed only to read the fast-breaking news from Kansas.

The Lecompton Constitution, 1857

While the Supreme Court wrestled with the abstract issues raised by the expansion of slavery, President Buchanan sought a concrete solution to the problem of Kansas, where the free-state government at Topeka and the officially recognized proslavery government at Lecompton regarded each other with profound distrust. Buchanan's plan for Kansas looked simple: an elected territorial convention would draw up a constitution that would either prohibit or permit slavery; Buchanan would submit the constitution to Congress; Congress would then admit Kansas as a state.

Unfortunately, the plan exploded in Buchanan's face. Popular sovereignty, the essence of the plan, demanded fair play, a commodity scarce in Kansas. The territory's history of fraudulent elections left both sides reluctant to commit their fortunes to the polls. In June 1857 an election for a constitutional convention took place, but free-staters, by now a majority in Kansas, boycotted the election on grounds that the proslavery forces would rig it. A constitutional convention dominated by proslavery delegates then met and drew up the Lecompton constitution, which protected the rights of slaveholders already residing in Kansas and provided for a referendum to decide whether to allow more slaves into the territory.

Buchanan faced a dilemma. A supporter of popular sovereignty, he had favored letting Kansas voters decide the slavery issue. But now he confronted a constitution drawn up by a convention chosen by less than 10 percent of the eligible voters, a referendum that would not allow voters to remove slaves already in Kansas, and the prospect that the proslavery side would conduct the referendum no more honestly than it had other elections. However, there were compelling reasons to accept the Lecompton constitution. The South, which had provided Buchanan's winning margin in the 1856 election, supported it. To Buchanan, the wrangling over slavery in Kansas was a case of extremists' turning minor issues into major ones, especially because only about 200 slaves resided in Kansas and because prospects for slavery in the remaining territories were slight. The admission of Kansas to the Union as free or slave seemed the quickest way to end the commotion, and so in December 1857 Buchanan endorsed the Lecompton constitution.

Stephen A. Douglas and other northern Democrats broke with Buchanan. To them, the Lecompton constitution, in allowing voters to decide only whether more slaves could enter Kansas, violated the spirit of popular sovereignty. "I care not whether [slavery] is voted down or voted up," Douglas proclaimed, but refusal to allow any vote on slavery amounted to "a system of trickery and jugglery to defeat the fair expression of the will of the people."

Meanwhile, the turbulent swirl of events continued in Kansas. The newly elected territorial legislature called for a referendum on the Lecompton constitution and thus for a referendum on slavery itself. Two elections followed. In December 1857 the referendum called by the constitutional convention took place. Free-staters boycotted it, and the Lecompton constitution passed overwhelmingly. Two weeks later the election called by the territorial legislature took place. This time proslavery forces boycotted, and the constitution went down to crushing defeat. Buchanan tried to ignore this second election, but when he attempted to bring Kansas into the Union under the Lecompton constitution, Congress blocked him and forced yet another referendum. In this third election Kansas could accept or reject the entire constitution, with the proviso that rejection would delay statehood. However, Kansans voted down the Lecompton constitution.

Buchanan simultaneously had failed to tranquilize Kansas and alienated northerners in his own party, who now more than ever believed that the southern Slave Power pulled all the important strings in the Democratic party. Douglas emerged as a hero for northern Democrats but saw his cherished formula of popular sovereignty become a prescription for strife rather than harmony.

The Lincoln-Douglas Debates, 1858

Despite the acclaim that he received for his stand against the Lecompton constitution, Douglas faced a stiff challenge in the 1858 Illinois senatorial election. Of his Republican opponent, Abraham Lincoln, Douglas remarked: "I shall have my hands full. He is the strong man of his party—full of wit, facts, and dates—and the best stump speaker with his droll ways and dry jokes, in the West."

Physically and ideologically, the two candidates presented a striking contrast. Tall and gangling, Lincoln possessed energy, ambition, and a passion for self-education that had carried him from the Kentucky log cabin where he was born into law and politics in his adopted Illinois. First elected as a Whig, he joined the Republican party in 1856. The New England–born Douglas stood a foot shorter than Lincoln, but to the small farmers of southern

origin who populated the Illinois flatlands, he was the "little giant," the personification of the Democratic party in the West.

Despite Douglas's position against the Lecompton constitution, Lincoln saw him as author of the Kansas-Nebraska bill and a man who cared not whether slavery was voted up or down as long as the vote was honest. Opening his campaign with his famous "House Divided" speech ("this government cannot endure permanently half *slave* and half *free*"), Lincoln stressed the gulf between his free-soil position and Douglas's popular sovereignty. Douglas dismissed the house-divided doctrine as an invitation to secession. What mattered to him was not slavery but the continued expansion of white settlement. Both men wanted to keep slavery out of the path of white settlement, but Douglas believed that popular sovereignty was the surest way to do so without disrupting the Union.

The high point of the campaign came in a series of seven debates held from August to October 1858. Douglas used the debates to portray Lincoln as a virtual abolitionist and advocate of racial equality. Lincoln replied that Congress had no constitutional authority to abolish slavery in the South. He also asserted that "I am not, nor ever have been in favor of bringing about the social and political equality of the white and black man."

In the debate at Freeport, Illinois, Lincoln tried to make Douglas squirm by asking how popular sovereignty could be reconciled with the *Dred Scott* decision. Douglas responded that, although the Supreme Court had ruled that Congress could not exclude slavery from the territories, the voters in a territory could do so by refusing to enact laws that gave legal protection to slave property. This "Freeport doctrine" salvaged popular sovereignty but did nothing for Douglas's reputation among southerners, who preferred the guarantees of *Dred Scott* to the uncertainties of popular sovereignty. Trying to move beyond debates on free soil and popular sovereignty, Lincoln shifted in the closing debates to attacks on slavery as "a moral, social, and political evil." *hc* Primary Source: Lincoln the Pragmatist responds to Civil Disorder

Stephen A. Douglas
Douglas's politics was founded on his unflinching conviction that most Americans favored national expansion and would support popular sovereignty as the fastest and least controversial way to achieve it. Douglas's self-assurance blinded him to rising northern sentiment for free soil.

Abraham Lincoln
Clean-shaven at the time of his famous debates with Douglas, Lincoln would soon grow a beard to give himself a more distinguished appearance.

Neither man scored a clear victory in the debates, and the senatorial election, which Douglas won, settled no major issues. Nonetheless, the candidates' contest was crucial. It solidified the sectional split in the Democratic party and made Lincoln famous in the North—and infamous in the South.

The Legacy of Harpers Ferry

Although Lincoln explicitly rejected abolitionism, he called free soil a step toward the "ultimate extinction" of slavery. Many southerners ignored the differences between free soil and abolitionism, seeing them as inseparable components of an unholy alliance against slavery. To many in the South, the entire North seemed locked in the grip of demented leaders bent on civil war.

Two things reinforced southerners' dire image of the North: the evidence of northern complicity in the Harpers Ferry raid in 1859 and the virtual canonization of John Brown by northern preachers. Convinced that many northerners endorsed the use of violence to end slavery, some southerners began refusing to associate with northerners and northern institutions. For example, about 250 southerners studying medicine in Philadelphia withdrew from the city's medical schools and enrolled in southern medical schools. Although Republicans, including Lincoln and Senator William Seward of New York, denounced Brown's raid, southerners suspected that they regretted the conspiracy's failure more than the attempt itself.

Brown's abortive raid also rekindled southern fears of a slave insurrection. Rumors flew around the South, and vigilantes turned out to battle conspiracies that existed only in their own minds. Volunteers, for example, mobilized to defend northeastern Texas against thousands of abolitionists supposedly on their way to pillage Dallas and its environs. The hysteria generated by such rumors played into the hands of the extremists known as fire-eaters, who encouraged the witch hunts in order to gain political support.

Although fears of a slave insurrection proved groundless, they strengthened southern anxieties about abolitionism. More and more southerners concluded that the Republican party itself directed abolitionism and deserved blame for John Brown's plot as well. After all, had not influential Republicans assailed slavery, unconstitutionally tried to ban it, and spoken of an "irrepressible conflict" between slavery and freedom? The Tennessee legislature reflected southern views when it passed resolutions declaring that the Harpers Ferry raid was "the natural fruit of this treasonable 'irrepressible conflict' doctrine put forth by the great head of the Black Republican party and echoed by his subordinates."

The South Contemplates Secession

A pamphlet published in 1860 embodied a growing southern conviction: *The South Alone Should Govern the South.* Most southerners, however, reached this conclusion gradually and reluctantly. In 1850, insulated from the main tide of immigration, southerners thought themselves the most American of Americans. The events of the 1850s led growing numbers of southerners to conclude that the North had deserted the principles of the Union and had virtually declared war on the South by using such headline-grabbing phrases as "irrepressible conflict" and "a higher law." To southerners, the North, not slavery, was the problem. For some, venturing into the North became entering "enemy territory" and "a totally different country."

As sectional ties frayed, John Brown's raid electrified southern opinion. Secession made no sense as a tactic to win concrete goals, but logic had yielded to emotion in much of the South. Fury at what southerners considered the irresponsible, unconstitutional course taken by Republicans in attacking slavery drove the talk of secession, and so did the belief that the North treated the South as inferior, even as a slave. "Talk of Negro slavery," wrote one angry southerner, "is not half so humiliating and disgraceful as the slavery of the South to the North." White southerners, certain that slavery made it possible for them to enjoy unprecedented freedom and equality, took great pride in their homeland. They bitterly resented Republican portrayals of the South as a region of arrogant planters and degraded common whites.

THE COLLAPSE OF THE UNION, 1860–1861

As long as the pliant James Buchanan occupied the White House, southerners only talked of secession.

However, once Buchanan declined to seek reelection, they anxiously awaited the next presidential election. By 1860 voters were deciding not just an election but also the fate of the Union. Lincoln's election began the parade out of the Union by southern states. Initially only the Lower South seceded, encouraging moderates to search for a compromise to save the Union. But the time for compromise had passed.

The Election of 1860

Republicans had done well in the elections of 1856 as a single-issue, free-soil party, but they had to broaden their base in order to win in 1860. Republican leaders needed an economic program to complement their advocacy of free soil. A severe economic slump following the Panic of 1857 provided them an opening. The depression shattered a decade of prosperity and thrust economic concerns to the fore. In response, the Republicans developed an economic program based on support for a protective tariff, federal aid for internal improvements, and grants to settlers of free 160-acre homesteads carved from public lands. By proposing to open homesteading to immigrants who were not yet citizens, the Republicans took a giant step to shed lingering vestiges of nativism—and to bring those immigrants into the Republican party.

To broaden their appeal, the Republicans chose Abraham Lincoln as their presidential candidate over the better-known William H. Seward. Lincoln offered a stronger possibility of carrying key states such as Pennsylvania and his home state of Illinois and projected a more moderate image than Seward, whose penchant for phrases like "irrepressible conflict" and "higher law" made him appear radical. In contrast, Lincoln repeatedly had said that Congress had no constitutional right to interfere with slavery in the South and had rejected the "higher law" doctrine.

The Democrats, still clinging to national party status, had to bridge their own sectional divisions. The *Dred Scott* decision and the conflict over the Lecompton constitution had weakened northern Democrats and strengthened southern Democrats.

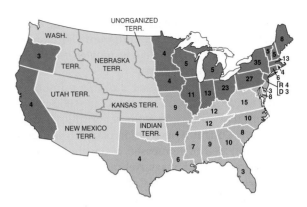

	Electoral Vote	Popular Vote	Percentage of Popular Vote
Republican Abraham Lincoln	180	1,865,593	39.8
Democratic, Southern John C. Breckinridge	72	848,356	18.1
Democratic, Northern Stephen A. Douglas	12	1,382,713	29.5
Constitutional Union John Bell	39	592,906	12.6
Divided			

MAP 14.3
The Election of 1860

While Douglas still desperately defended popular sovereignty, southern Democrats stretched *Dred Scott* to conclude that Congress now had to protect slavery in the territories.

The Democratic party's internal turmoil boiled over at its Charleston convention in spring 1860. Failing to win a platform guaranteeing the federal protection of slavery in the territories, delegates from the Lower South stormed out. The convention adjourned to Baltimore, where a new fight erupted over whether to seat the pro-Douglas delegates hastily chosen to replace the absent delegates from the Lower South. When the convention voted to seat these new delegates, representatives from Virginia and the Upper South walked out. What remained of the original Democratic convention nominated Douglas, but the seceders marched off to yet another hall in Baltimore and nominated Buchanan's vice president, John C. Breckinridge of Kentucky, on a platform calling for the congressional protection of slavery in the territories. The spectacle of two different Democratic candidates for the presidency signaled the complete disruption of the party.

The South still contained a sizable number of moderates, often former Whigs. In 1860 these southern moderates joined former northern Whigs in the new Constitutional Union party. They nominated John Bell of Tennessee, a slaveholder who had opposed the Kansas-Nebraska Act and the Lecompton constitution. Calling for the Union's preservation, the new party took no stand on slavery's extension.

The four candidates presented a relatively clear choice. At one end of the spectrum, Lincoln conceded that the South had the constitutional right to preserve slavery, but he demanded that Congress prohibit its extension. At the other end, Breckinridge insisted that Congress had to protect slavery anywhere it existed. In the middle were Bell and Douglas, the latter still trying to salvage popular sovereignty. In the end Lincoln won 180 electoral votes; his three opponents, only 123. However, Lincoln's popular votes, 39 percent of the total, came almost completely from the North. Douglas, the only candidate to run in both sections, ran second in the popular vote but carried only Missouri. Bell won most of the Upper South, and Breckinridge took Maryland and the Lower South.

The Movement for Secession

Southerners faced a dilemma. The president-elect was so unpopular in the South that his name had not even appeared on the ballot in many southern states. Lincoln's victory struck many southerners as a calculated insult. The North, a South Carolina planter said, "has got so far toward being abolitionized as to elect a man avowedly hostile to our institutions." Few southerners believed that Lincoln

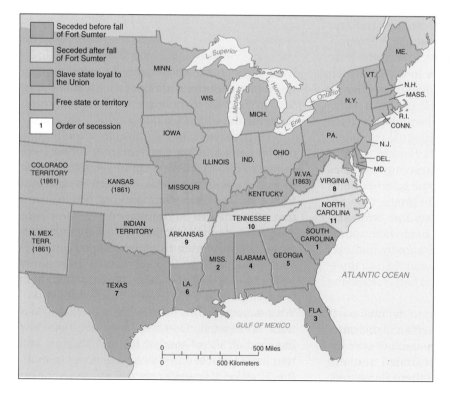

MAP 14.4
Secession
Four key states—Virginia, Arkansas, Tennessee, and North Carolina—did not secede until after the fall of Fort Sumter. The border slave states of Maryland, Delaware, Kentucky, and Missouri stayed in the Union.

would fulfill his promise to protect slavery in the South, and most feared that he would act as a tool for more John Browns.

Some southerners had threatened secession at the prospect of Lincoln's election, and now the moment of decision had arrived. On December 20, 1860, a South Carolina convention voted unanimously for secession; in short order Alabama, Mississippi, Florida, Georgia, Louisiana, and Texas followed. On February 4, 1861, delegates from these seven states met in Montgomery, Alabama, and established the Confederate States of America. But uncertainty colored the secession movement. Many southerners, even in the Deep South, had resisted the fire-eaters' call to leave the Union. Jefferson Davis, inaugurated in February 1861 as president of the Confederacy, was a reluctant secessionist who had remained in the Senate two weeks after his own state of Mississippi had seceded.

At first the Upper South rejected secession completely. More economically dependent on the North, it had proportionately fewer slaves and more nonslaveholders, whose loyalty in case of secession was dubious. Finally, if secession precipitated a war, the Upper South was the likely battleground. Consequently, the secession movement that South Carolina had begun so boldly in December 1860 seemed to be falling apart by March 1861.

The Search for Compromise

The lack of southern unity confirmed the view of most Republicans that the secessionists were more bluster than substance. Seward described secession as the work of "a relatively few hotheads," and Lincoln believed that the loyal majority of southerners would soon wrest control from the fire-eating minority.

This perception stiffened Republican resolve to resist compromise. Moderate John J. Crittenden of Kentucky suggested compensation for owners of runaway slaves, repeal of northern personal-liberty laws, a constitutional amendment to prohibit the federal government from interfering with slavery in southern states, and another amend-

ment to restore the Missouri Compromise line. But in the face of adamant Republican opposition, the Crittenden plan collapsed.

Lincoln's faith in a "loyal majority" of southerners exaggerated both their numbers and their dedication to the Union. Many southern opponents of the fire-eating secessionists sat on the fence, waiting for major concessions from the North; their allegiance to the Union thus was conditional. But compromise would have meant the abandonment of free soil, a basic principle on which the Republican party had been founded, and Lincoln, who misread southern opinion, resisted.

Beyond the issue of compromise, the precipitous secession of the Lower South had changed the question that Lincoln faced. The issue no longer revolved around slavery's extension but around secession. The Lower South had left the Union in the face of losing a fair election. For Lincoln to cave in to such pressure would violate majority rule, the sacred principle on which the nation had been founded.

The Coming of War

By the time Lincoln took office in March 1861, only a spark was needed to set off a war. Lincoln pledged in his inaugural address to "hold, occupy, and possess" federal property in the states that had seceded, a statement that committed him to the defense of Fort Pickens in Florida and Fort Sumter in the harbor of Charleston, South Carolina. Accordingly, the president informed South Carolina's governor of his intention to supply Fort Sumter with provisions but neither reinforcements nor ammunition. Shortly before dawn on April 12, 1861, Confederate shore batteries bombarded the fort, which surrendered the next day.

Proclaiming an insurrection in the Lower South, Lincoln called for 75,000 militia to suppress the rebellion. The outbreak of hostilities ended fence-sitting in the Upper South. "I am a Union man," one southerner wrote, "but when they [the Lincoln administration] send men south it will change my notions. I can do nothing against my own people." In quick succession Virginia, North

Chronology

1848	Treaty of Guadalupe-Hidalgo ends Mexican War. Free-Soil party formed. Zachary Taylor elected president.	**1856**	The "sack" of Lawrence, Kansas. John Brown's Pottawatomie Massacre. James Buchanan elected president.
1849	California seeks admission to the Union as a free state.	**1857**	*Dred Scott* decision. President Buchanan endorses the Lecompton constitution in Kansas.
1850	Nashville convention assembles to discuss the South's grievances. Compromise of 1850.	**1858**	Congress refuses to admit Kansas to the Union under the Lecompton constitution. Lincoln-Douglas debates.
1852	Harriet Beecher Stowe, *Uncle Tom's Cabin*. Franklin Pierce elected president.	**1859**	John Brown's raid on Harpers Ferry.
1854	Ostend Manifesto. Kansas-Nebraska Act.	**1860**	Abraham Lincoln elected president. South Carolina secedes from the Union.
1854–1855	Know-Nothing and Republican parties emerge.	**1861**	The remaining Lower South states secede. Confederate States of America established. Crittenden compromise plan collapses. Lincoln takes office. Firing on Fort Sumter; Civil War begins. Upper South secedes.
1855	Proslavery forces steal the election for a territorial legislature in Kansas. Proslavery Kansans establish a government in Lecompton. Free-soil government established in Topeka, Kansas.		

Carolina, Arkansas, and Tennessee joined the Confederacy. Acknowledging that "I am one of those dull creatures that cannot see the good of secession," Robert E. Lee resigned from the U.S. Army rather than lead troops against his native Virginia.

The North, too, was ready for a fight, less to abolish slavery than to punish secession. Stephen Douglas, exhausted by his efforts to find a peaceable solution to the issue of slavery extension, assaulted "the new system of resistance by the sword and bayonet to the results of the ballot-box" and affirmed, "I deprecate war, but if it must come I am with my country, under all circumstances, and in every contingency."

CONCLUSION   *hc* ACE Practice Test

Most American political leaders thought that the Compromise of 1850 had finally settled the contro-versy over the expansion of slavery. After all, the majority of Americans did not want to abolish slavery in the southern states; they were only divided over slavery's expansion, and the Compromise provided a solution. Stephen A. Douglas, certain of his reading of public opinion, believed that the furor over slavery would quickly subside.

He was wrong.

The problem was that northerners and southerners had very different understandings of liberty. To northerners it was freedom to pursue their self-interest without competition from slaves; to southerners it was freedom to dispose of slaves, their legally acquired property, as they chose. Thus the Compromise soon began to come apart at the seams. Northerners resented and resisted enforcement of the Fugitive Slave Act and saw southern support of the Kansas-Nebraska bill as proof that southerners still wanted to extend slavery. In turn, Southerners angered by northern defiance of the

Fugitive Slave Act interpreted northern outrage against Douglas's bill as further evidence of the North's disrespect for the law.

By the mid-1850s sectional tensions were spinning out of control. The Whig party collapsed, and ties between northern and southern Democrats frayed. "Bleeding Kansas" pushed many former Whigs and northern Democrats toward the new— and purely sectional—Republican party. Even as southerners wavered on the idea of secession, northern hostility toward the *Dred Scott* decision and sympathy for John Brown seemed to prove that the North's real design was to destroy slavery— and the South.

Secession capped a decade in which a shared political heritage had driven both sides to different conclusions. North and South alike subscribed to the rule of law, and each accused the other of deserting that principle. War finally erupted between siblings who claimed the same heritage but had become strangers to each other.

FURTHER READING

Eric Foner, *Free Soil, Free Labor, Free Men: The Ideology of the Republican Party Before the Civil War* (1970). An outstanding analysis of the thought, values, and components of the Republican party.

William W. Freehling, *The Road to Disunion: Secessionists at Bay, 1776–1854* (1990). A major study that traces the roots of secession.

William E. Gienapp, *The Origins of the Republican Party, 1852–1856* (1988). A major recent study of the party's formative period.

Michael F. Holt, *The Political Crisis of the 1850s* (1978). A lively reinterpretation of the politics of the 1850s.

Allan Nevins, *The Ordeal of the Union* (Vols. 1–2, 1947). A very detailed, highly regarded account of the coming of the Civil War.

David Potter, *The Impending Crisis, 1848–1861* (1976). The best one-volume overview of the events leading to the Civil War.

Mark Stegmaier, *Texas, New Mexico, and the Compromise of 1850* (1996). A good study of the significance of the Texas–New Mexico boundary dispute for the sectional crisis.

15

Crucible of Freedom: Civil War, 1861–1865

CHAPTER OUTLINE

Mobilizing for War

In Battle, 1861–1862

Emancipation Transforms the War, 1863

War and Society, North and South

The Union Victorious, 1864–1865

 This icon will direct you to additional study and research resources at http://college.hmco.com/history/us/boyer/enduring_concise/5e/students/index.html

Soldiers' Photographs, 1861–1865

Soldiers on both sides claimed the ideals of liberty, loyalty, and patriotism as their own, and like them, too, most Americans in 1861 harbored false expectations. Few volunteers expected a long war, and none anticipated the carnage that the war would bring.

One out of every five soldiers who fought in the Civil War died in it. The 620,000 American soldiers killed between 1861 and 1865 nearly equaled the number of U.S. soldiers killed in all other American wars combined. As it became clear that a few battles would not decide the war, leaders on both sides contemplated, and often adopted, previously unthinkable strategies. The Confederacy, despite its states' rights basis, had to draft men into its army and virtually extort supplies from civilians. By the end of the war, the Confederacy was even prepared to arm slaves in a desperate effort to save a society founded on slavery. The North, which began the war with the objective of overcoming secession, explicitly disclaiming any intention of interfering with slavery, found that in order to win, it had to destroy slavery.

MOBILIZING FOR WAR

Neither North nor South was prepared for war. In April 1861 most of the Union's small army, a scant 16,000 men, was scattered across the West. One-third of its officers had resigned to join the Confederacy. The nation had not had a strong president since James K. Polk in the 1840s, and many viewed the new president, Abraham Lincoln, as a yokel. It seemed doubtful that such a government could marshal its people for war. The Confederacy was even less prepared: it had no tax structure, no navy, only two tiny gunpowder factories, and poorly equipped, unconnected railroad lines.

During the first two years of war, both sides would have to overcome these deficiencies, raise and supply large armies, and finance the war. In each region mobilization would expand the powers of the central government to a degree that few had anticipated.

Recruitment and Conscription

The Civil War armies were the largest organizations ever created in America; by the end of the war, more than 2 million men had served in the Union army and 800,000 in the Confederate army. In the first flush of enthusiasm for war, volunteers rushed to the colors. "War and volunteers are the only topics of conversation or thought," an Oberlin College student wrote to his brother in April 1861. "I cannot study. I cannot sleep. I cannot work."

At first the raising of armies was a local, rather than a national or state, effort. Regiments usually consisted of volunteers from the same locale. Southern cavalrymen provided their own horses, and uniforms were left to local option. In both

This chapter focuses on five major questions:

▶ What major advantages did each side possess at the start of the Civil War?

▶ How successfully did the Union and the Confederacy respond to the pressures of war?

▶ How did the issues of slavery and emancipation transform the war?

▶ What factors determined the military outcome of the war?

▶ In what lasting ways did the Civil War change the United States?

armies the troops themselves elected officers up to the rank of colonel. This informal, democratic way of raising and organizing soldiers reflected the nation's political traditions but could not withstand the stresses of the Civil War. As early as July 1861 the Union began examinations for officers. With casualties mounting, moreover, military demand exceeded the supply of volunteers. The Confederacy felt the pinch first and in April 1862 enacted the first conscription law in American history, requiring all able-bodied white men aged eighteen to thirty-five to serve in the military. (By war's end the limits would be seventeen and fifty.) The Confederacy's Conscription Act aroused little enthusiasm. A later amendment exempting owners or overseers of twenty or more slaves evoked complaints about "a rich man's war but a poor man's fight."

Despite opposition, the Confederate draft became increasingly difficult to evade, and this fact stimulated volunteering. Only one soldier in five was a draftee, but four out of every five eligible white southerners served in the Confederate army. An 1862 law requiring all soldiers to serve for the duration of the war ensured that a high proportion of Confederate soldiers would be battle-hardened veterans.

Once the army was raised, the Confederacy had to supply it. At first the South imported arms and ammunition from Europe or relied on weapons taken from federal arsenals and captured on the battlefield. Gradually, the Confederacy assigned contracts to privately owned factories such as the Tredegar Iron Works in Richmond, provided loans to establish new plants, and created government-owned industries such as the giant Augusta Powder Works in Georgia. The South lost few, if any, battles for want of munitions.

Supplying troops with clothing and food proved more difficult. When the South invaded Maryland in 1862, thousands of Confederate soldiers remained behind because they could not march barefoot on Maryland's gravel-surfaced roads. Late in the war, Robert E. Lee's Army of Northern Virginia ran out of food but never out of ammunition. Supply problems had several sources: railroads that fell into disrepair or were captured, an economy that grew more cotton and tobacco than food, and Union capture of the livestock and grain-raising districts of central Tennessee and Virginia. Close to desperation, the Confederate Congress in 1863 passed the Impressment Act, authorizing army officers to take food from reluctant farmers at prescribed rates. One provision, bitterly resented, empowered agents to impress slaves into labor for the army. Slave owners were willing to give up their relatives to military service, a Georgia congressman noted, "but let one of their negroes be taken and what a howl you will hear."

The industrial North more easily supplied its troops with arms, clothes, and food, but keeping a full army was another matter. When the initial tide of enthusiasm for enlistment ebbed, Congress turned to conscription with the Enrollment Act of March 1863. Every able-bodied white male citizen aged twenty to forty-five faced the draft.

The Enrollment Act provided some exemptions and offered two ways of escaping the draft: substitution, or paying another man to serve; and commutation, or paying a $300 fee to the government. As enrollment districts competed for volunteers by

offering cash bounties, "bounty jumpers" repeatedly enrolled and then deserted after collecting their payment. Democrats denounced conscription as a violation of individual liberties and states' rights, and ordinary citizens resented the substitution and commutation privileges and leveled their own "poor man's fight" charges. Nevertheless, as in the Confederacy, the law stimulated volunteering: only 8 percent of all Union soldiers were draftees or substitutes.

Financing the War

The recruitment and supply of huge armies lay far beyond the capacity of American public finance at the start of the war. During the 1840s and 1850s federal spending had averaged only 2 percent of the gross national product.* With such meager expenditures, the federal government met its revenue needs from tariff duties and income from the sale of public lands. During the war, however, as annual federal expenditures rose to 15 percent of the gross national product, the need for new sources of revenue became urgent. When neither additional taxes nor war bond sales produced enough revenue, the Union and the Confederacy began to print paper money. Early in 1862 President Lincoln signed into law the Legal Tender Act, authorizing the issue of $150 million in paper "greenbacks." Although the North's financial officials distrusted paper money, they resorted to it because, as the Union's treasury secretary bluntly put it, *The Treasury is nearly empty.* Unlike gold and silver, which had established market values, the value of paper money depended on the public's confidence in the government that issued it. To bolster that confidence, Union officials made the greenbacks legal tender (that is, acceptable in payment of most public and private debts).

In contrast, the Confederacy never made paper money legal tender, and so suspicions arose that

---

* Gross national product (GNP): the sum, measured in dollars, of all goods and services produced in a given year. By contrast, in the 1980s the federal budget averaged about 25 percent of GNP.

the southern government had little faith in its own money. The fact that the Confederacy raised little of its wartime revenue from taxes compounded the problem. Northern invasions and poor internal transportation made collecting taxes difficult, and ultimately the South raised less than 5 percent of its wartime revenue from taxes (compared to 21 percent in the North).

Confidence in the Confederacy's paper money quickly evaporated, and the value of paper money in relation to gold plunged. The Confederate response—printing more paper money—merely accelerated inflation. Prices in the North rose 80 percent during the war, but those in the South soared more than 9,000 percent.

By raising taxes, floating bonds, and printing paper money, both North and South broke with the hard-money, minimal-government traditions of American public finance. In the North, Republicans took advantage of the departure of southern Democrats to push through Congress a measure that they and their Whig predecessors had long advocated: a national banking system. Passed in February 1863, the National Bank Act allowed banks to obtain federal charters and to issue national bank notes (backed by the federal government). The North's ability to revolutionize its system of public finances reflected both its greater experience with complex financial transactions and its stronger political cohesion.

Political Leadership in Wartime

The Civil War pitted rival political systems as well as armies and economies against each other. The South entered the war with several apparent political advantages. Lincoln's call for militiamen to suppress the rebellion had transformed southern waverers into secessionists. "Never was a people more united or more determined," wrote a New Orleans resident. "There is but one mind, one heart, one action." Southerners had a strong leader in Jefferson Davis, the president of the Confederacy, who possessed experience, honesty, courage, and what one commentator called "a jaw sawed in *steel.*"

Abraham Lincoln
When Lincoln became president in March 1861, he faced more severe problems than any predecessor. Washington photographer Matthew Brady captured this image of the solemn president-elect on February 23, 1861, a few weeks after the formation of the Confederacy and shortly before Lincoln's inauguration.

In contrast, the Union's list of political liabilities appeared lengthy. Loyal but contentious northern Democrats wanted no conscription, no National Bank, and no abolition of slavery. Even within the Republican party, Lincoln, with little national experience, had trouble commanding respect. A small but vocal group of Republicans known as the Radicals—including Secretary of the Treasury

Salmon P. Chase, Senator Charles Sumner of Massachusetts, and Representative Thaddeus Stevens of Pennsylvania—vigorously criticized Lincoln. First they focused on his failure to make the slaves' emancipation a war goal, and later they would lash him for being too eager to readmit the conquered rebel states into the Union.

Lincoln's style of leadership both encouraged and disarmed opposition within the Republican party. Keeping his counsel to himself until ready to act, he met criticism with homespun anecdotes that threw his opponents off guard. Caught between Radicals and conservatives, Lincoln used his cautious reserve to maintain open communications with both wings of the party and to fragment his opposition. He also co-opted some members of the opposition, including Chase, by bringing them into his cabinet.

In contrast, Jefferson Davis had a knack for making enemies. A West Pointer, he would rather have led the army than the government, and he used his sharp tongue to win arguments rather than friends. Davis's cabinet suffered frequent resignations; for example, the Confederacy had five secretaries of war in four years. Relations between Davis and his vice president, Alexander Stephens of Georgia, were disastrous. Stephens left Richmond, the Confederate capital, in 1862 and spent most of the war in Georgia sniping at Davis as "weak and vacillating, timid, petulant, peevish, obstinate."

The clash between Davis and Stephens involved not just personalities but also the ideological divisions that lay at the heart of the Confederacy. The Confederate Constitution explicitly guaranteed the sovereignty of the Confederate states and prohibited the government from enacting protective tariffs or supporting internal improvements. For Stephens and other influential Confederate leaders, the Confederacy existed to protect slavery and to enshrine states' rights. For Davis, the overriding objective of the Confederacy was to secure the independence of the South from the North, if necessary at the expense of states' rights.

This difference between Davis and Stephens somewhat resembled the discord between Lincoln and the northern Democrats. Lincoln believed that winning the war demanded increasing the central government's power; like Stephens, northern Democrats resisted centralization. But Lincoln could control his opponents more effectively than Davis controlled his. By temperament Lincoln was more suited to reconciliation than Davis was, and the different nature of party politics in the two sections favored him as well.

In the South the Democrats and the remaining Whigs agreed to suspend party politics for the war's duration. Although intended to encourage unity, this decision led to discord. As southern politics disintegrated along personal and factional lines, Davis found himself without organized political support. In contrast, in the Union northern Democrats' opposition to Lincoln tended to unify the Republicans. After Democrats won control of five states in the election of 1862, Republicans swallowed a bitter lesson: no matter how much they disdained Lincoln, they had to rally behind him or risk being driven from office. Ultimately, the Union developed more political cohesion than the Confederacy not because it had fewer divisions but because it managed those divisions more effectively.

Securing the Union's Borders

Even before large-scale fighting began, Lincoln moved to safeguard Washington, which was bordered by two slave states (Virginia and Maryland) and filled with Confederate sympathizers. A week after Fort Sumter's fall, a Baltimore mob attacked a Massachusetts regiment bound for Washington, but enough troops slipped through to protect the capital. Lincoln then dispatched federal troops to Maryland and suspended the writ of habeas corpus;* federal troops could now arrest Marylanders without formally charging them with specific offenses. Both Maryland and Delaware, another border slave state, voted down secession.

---

* Habeas corpus: a court order requiring that the detainer of a prisoner bring the person in custody to court and show cause for his or her detention.

Next Lincoln authorized the arming of Union sympathizers in Kentucky, a slave state with a Unionist legislature, a secessionist governor, and a thin chance of staying neutral. Lincoln also stationed troops just across the Ohio River from Kentucky, in Illinois, and when a Confederate army invaded Kentucky early in 1862, those troops drove it out. Officially, at least, Kentucky became the third slave state to declare for the Union. Four years of murderous fighting ravaged the fourth, Missouri, as Union and Confederate armies and bands of guerrillas clashed. Despite savage fighting and the divided loyalties of its people, Missouri never left the Union.

By holding the border slave states in the Union, Lincoln kept open his lines to the free states and gained access to the river systems in Kentucky and Missouri that led into the heart of the Confederacy. Lincoln's firmness, particularly in the case of Maryland, scotched charges that he was weak-willed.

IN BATTLE, 1861–1862

The Civil War was the first war in which both sides relied extensively on railroads, the telegraph, mass-produced weapons, joint army-navy tactics, iron-plated warships, rifled guns and artillery, and trench warfare. Thus there is some justification for its description as the first modern war.

Armies, Weapons, and Strategies

Compared to the Confederacy's 9 million people, who included 3 million slaves, the Union had 22 million people in 1861. The North also enjoyed 3.5 times as many white men of military age, 90 percent of all U.S. industrial capacity, and two-thirds of its railroad track. But the North faced a daunting challenge: to force the South back into the Union. The South, in contrast, fought only for independence. To subdue the Confederacy, the North would have

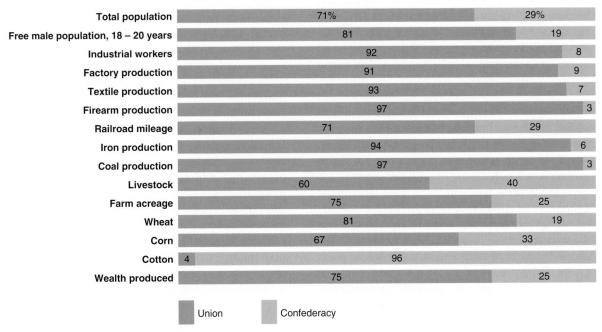

	Union	Confederacy
Total population	71%	29%
Free male population, 18 – 20 years	81	19
Industrial workers	92	8
Factory production	91	9
Textile production	93	7
Firearm production	97	3
Railroad mileage	71	29
Iron production	94	6
Coal production	97	3
Livestock	60	40
Farm acreage	75	25
Wheat	81	19
Corn	67	33
Cotton	4	96
Wealth produced	75	25

Comparative Population and Economic Resources of the Union and the Confederacy, 1861
At the start of the war, the Union enjoyed huge advantages in population, industry, railroad mileage, and wealth, and, as it would soon prove, a superior ability to mobilize its vast resources. The Confederacy, however, enjoyed the many advantages of fighting a defensive war.

to sustain offensive operations over an area comparable in size to the part of Russia that Napoleon had invaded in 1812 with disastrous results.

Measured against this challenge, the North's advantages in population and technology shrank. The North had more men but needed them to defend long supply lines and to occupy captured areas. Consequently, it could commit a smaller proportion of its overall force to combat. The South, relying on slaves for labor, could assign a higher proportion of its white male population to combat. And although the Union had superior railroads, it had to move its troops and supplies huge distances, whereas the Confederacy could shift its troops relatively short distances within its defense area without railroads. The South's poor roads hampered the supply-heavy northern forces as well. Finally, southerners had an edge in morale, for Confederate troops usually fought on home ground.

The Civil War witnessed experiments with a variety of new weapons, including the submarine, the repeating rifle, and the multibarreled Gatling gun, the predecessor of the machine gun. Whereas smoothbore muskets had an effective range of 80 yards, the Springfield or Enfield rifles widely in use by 1863 were accurate at 400 yards. The rifle's development posed a challenge to long-accepted military tactics, which stressed the mass infantry charge. Armed with muskets, defenders could fire only a round or two before being overwhelmed. Armed with rifles, however, defenders could fire several rounds before closing with the enemy.

As the fighting wore on, both sides recognized the value of trenches, which offered defenders protection against withering rifle fire. In addition, the rifle forced generals to depend less on cavalry. Traditionally, cavalry had been among the most prestigious components of an army, in part because cavalry charges were often devastatingly effective and in part because the cavalry helped to maintain class distinctions within the army. More accurate rifles reduced the cavalry's effectiveness, for the bullet that missed a rider could hit his horse. Thus the cavalry increasingly was relegated to reconnaissance and raids.

Nonetheless, the introduction of the rifle did not fundamentally change military tactics. An attacking army still had a good chance of success if it surprised its enemy, and the lush forests of the South offered abundant opportunities for surprise. Lacking the element of surprise could well doom an attacking army. For example, at the Battle of Fredericksburg in December 1862, Confederate forces virtually annihilated Union forces charging uphill over open terrain. Generals believed that surprise was their best route to success; thus they attempted to strike an unwary or weakened enemy with all the troops they could muster.

Much like previous wars, the Civil War was fought basically in a succession of battles during which exposed infantry traded volleys, charged, and countercharged. The side that withdrew first from the battlefield was considered the loser, even though it frequently sustained lighter casualties than the "victor." The defeated army usually moved back a few miles to lick its wounds; the winners stayed in place to lick theirs. Although politicians raged at generals for not pursuing a beaten foe, they seldom understood the difficulties that a mangled victor faced in gathering horses, mules, supply trains, and exhausted soldiers for an attack. Not surprisingly, generals on both sides concluded that the best defense was a good offense.

What passed for long-range Union strategy in 1861 was the Anaconda plan, which called for the Union to blockade the southern coast and to thrust, like a huge snake, down the Mississippi River. In theory, sealing off and severing the Confederacy would make the South recognize the futility of secession and end the war as bloodlessly as possible. However, the lack of adequate ships and men to seize the Mississippi in 1861 prevented the implementation of this ambitious plan.

Early in the war the need to secure the border slave states, especially Kentucky and Missouri, dictated Union strategy in the West, sending northern armies plunging southward from Kentucky into Tennessee. The Appalachian Mountains tended to separate this western theater from the eastern theater.

MAP 15.1
The War in the East, 1861–1862
Union advances on Richmond were turned back at Fredericksburg and the Seven Days' Battles, and the Confederacy's invasion of Union territory was stopped at Antietam. **h c** Interactive Map: The Anaconda Plan & the Battle of Antietam

Stalemate in the East

East of the mountains, the Confederates' decision to locate their capital in Richmond, Virginia, shaped Union strategy. "Forward to Richmond!" became the Union's first war cry. But before Union troops could reach Richmond, one hundred miles southwest of Washington, they would have to dislodge a Confederate army brazenly encamped at

Manassas Junction, Virginia, only twenty-five miles from the Union capital. Lincoln ordered General Irvin McDowell to attack the rebel force. In the resulting First Battle of Bull Run (or First Manassas*),

---

* Because the North often named battles after local landmarks, usually bodies of water, and the South after the nearest town, some Civil War battles are known by two names.

Scenes of Antietam

A painting of the Antietam battlefield by James Pope, a Union soldier of the Second Vermont Infantry, shows three brigades of Union troops advancing under Confederate fire. In the photograph of Antietam, dead rebel gunners lie next to the wreckage of their battery. The building in both painting and photograph, a Dunker church, was the scene of furious fighting.

amateur armies clashed in bloody chaos under a blistering sun in July 1861 as well-dressed, picnicking Washington dignitaries watched the carnage. The Confederates routed the larger Union army.

After Bull Run, Lincoln appointed General George B. McClellan to replace McDowell as commander of the Union's Army of the Potomac. McClellan, a master of administration and training, transformed a ragtag mob into a disciplined fighting force. His soldiers adored him, but Lincoln became disenchanted. To the president, the key to victory lay in launching simultaneous attacks on several fronts so that the North could exploit its

advantages in manpower and communications. McClellan, a proslavery Democrat, hoped for a series of relatively bloodless victories that would result in the readmission of southern states into the Union with slavery still intact.

In spring 1862 McClellan got a chance to demonstrate the value of his strategy. After Bull Run, the Confederates had pulled back behind the Rappahannock River to block a Union march toward Richmond. McClellan decided to go around the southerners by transporting his troops down the Chesapeake Bay to the tip of the peninsula formed by the York and James rivers and then to attack Richmond from the rear.

At first McClellan's Peninsula Campaign unfolded smoothly. But after luring the Confederacy to the brink of defeat, he hesitated, refusing to launch the final attack without the reinforcements he expected. Confederate forces under General Thomas "Stonewall" Jackson had turned back the reinforcements. As McClellan delayed, General Robert E. Lee assumed command of the Confederacy's Army of Northern Virginia. An opponent of secession, a man so courteous that he seemed almost too gentle, Lee nevertheless was McClellan's opposite, bold and willing to accept casualties.

Lee immediately took the offensive, attacking the much larger Union forces in the Seven Days' Battles (June–July 1862). Raging through forests east of Richmond, the battles cost the Confederacy nearly twice as many men as the Union, but McClellan, not Lee, blinked. Unnerved by mounting casualties, he sent a series of panicky reports to Washington. Lincoln, who cared little for McClellan's peninsula strategy, ordered him to call off the campaign and return to Washington.

With McClellan out of the picture, Lee and his lieutenant, Stonewall Jackson, pushed north, routing a Union army at the Second Battle of Bull Run (Second Manassas) in August 1862. Lee followed up this victory with a bold stroke: he took his army across the Potomac and northward into Maryland, hoping that the fall harvest could provide him with desperately needed supplies. McClellan met Lee at the Battle of Antietam (Sharpsburg) on September 17, 1862. North and South together suffered 24,000 casualties in this bloodiest day of the war. Tactically, the battle was a draw, but strategically it constituted a major Union victory because it forced Lee to withdraw south of the Potomac. Most important, Antietam provided Lincoln the occasion to issue the Emancipation Proclamation, freeing all slaves under rebel control. Lincoln complained that McClellan had "the slows" and faulted him for not pursuing Lee after Antietam. McClellan's replacement, General Ambrose Burnside, thought himself unfit for high command. He was right. In December 1862 he led 122,000 federal troops against 78,500 Confederates at the Battle of Fredericksburg (Virginia). Burnside captured the town but then sacrificed his army in futile charges up the heights west of the town. The carnage shook even Lee. "It is well that war is so terrible—we should grow fond of it," he told an aide during the battle. Richmond remained, in the words of a southern song, "a hard road to travel." The war in the East had become a stalemate.

h c Primary Source: A Union Soldier's Opinion of the War

The War in the West

The Union fared better in the West. Unlike the geographically limited eastern theater, the war in the West shifted over a vast terrain that provided access to rivers leading directly into the South. The West also spawned new leadership in the person of an obscure Union general, Ulysses S. Grant. A West Point graduate with a reputation for heavy drinking, and a failed farmer and businessman, Grant soon proved one of the Union's best leaders.

In 1861–1862 Grant had stabilized control of Missouri and Kentucky and then moved south to attack Corinth, Mississippi, a major rail junction. In early April 1862 Confederate forces staged a surprise attack on Grant's army, encamped at Shiloh Church in southern Tennessee. Driven back on the first day, Union forces counterattacked on the second day and drove the Confederate army from the field. Of 77,000 men who fought at Shiloh, 23,000 were killed or wounded. Perhaps the most important casualty was General Albert Sydney Johnston, whose death deprived the Confederacy of its best commander west of the Appalachians. Defeated at Shiloh, the Confederates evacuated Corinth.

For the Corinth-Shiloh Campaign, the Confederacy had stripped New Orleans of its defenses, leaving its largest city guarded by only 3,000 militia. A combined land-sea force under Union general Benjamin Butler and Admiral David G. Farragut took advantage of the weakened defenses and captured New Orleans in late April. Farragut continued up the Mississippi as far as Natchez. When a Union flotilla moved down the river in June and took Memphis, the North controlled the great river except for a 200-mile stretch between Port Hudson, Louisiana, and Vicksburg, Mississippi.

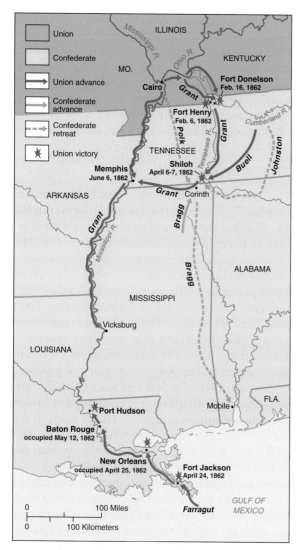

MAP 15.2
The War in the West, 1861–1862
By the end of 1862 the North held New Orleans and the entire Mississippi River except for the stretch between Vicksburg and Port Hudson.

Mexico. A thousand miles to the east, opposing armies battled for control of the crucial Missouri River. In Pea Ridge, Arkansas, in March 1862, northern troops scattered a Confederate force of 16,000.

These Union victories changed the Trans-Mississippi war. As the rebel threat faded, western volunteers who had mobilized to crush Confederates turned to fighting Indians. Conflict between Union forces and Native Americans erupted in Minnesota, Arizona, Nevada, Colorado, and New Mexico. After 1865 federal troops moved west to complete the rout of the Indians that had begun during the Civil War.

The Soldiers' War

Civil War soldiers were typically volunteers from farms and small towns who joined companies of recruits from their area. Not only local loyalties spurred enrollment; so too did ideas of honor and valor. Soldiers on both sides believed that military life was a transforming experience that turned citizens into warriors and boys into men.

Recruits were meshed into regiments and then sent to training camps. Military training was notoriously poor, and much of army life was tedious and uncomfortable. Union troops ate beans, bacon, salt pork, pickled beef, and hardtack—biscuits almost impossible to crack. Confederate forces ate bacon and cornmeal, and they often ran out of that, as well as blankets, shoes, socks, and clothes. Both sides suffered from a multitude of lice, fleas, ticks, flies, and rats, and from the diseases they carried.

Dreams of military glory faded swiftly for most. It was a war of appalling casualties, and soldiers quickly learned to inure themselves to the stench of death. The high casualty rates came not from improved technology, such as the rifle, but from the armies' inability to use such technology well. Too often a battle meant both sides standing and shooting at one another at close range until one or the other gave up and fell back.

The motives of these soldiers varied widely. Some Confederates joined in order to preserve slavery, and some Union soldiers fought in order to

In 1862 Union and Confederate forces also clashed in the Transmississippi West, a vast region that stretched from the Midwest to the Pacific Coast. On the banks of the Rio Grande, Union volunteers and Mexican-American companies drove a Confederate army from Texas out of New destroy it. As the war ground on, more and more Union soldiers came to see emancipation as their goal, often as a practical rather than a moral matter; as an Indiana soldier said, "Every negro we get strengthens us and weakens the rebels."

Ironclads and Cruisers: The Naval War

By plunging the navy into the Confederacy like a dagger, the Union exploited one of its clearest advantages. The North began the war with more than forty active warships—the South had none—and by 1865 northern industrial advantages had given the United States the largest navy in the world. Steamships could penetrate the South's river systems from any direction. Yet the Union navy faced an extraordinary challenge in its efforts to blockade the South's 3,500 miles of coastline. Sleek Confederate blockade runners darted in and out of southern harbors with little chance of capture early in the war. Their chances of success gradually diminished, however, as the North tightened the blockade and began to capture key southern ports. In 1861 almost 90 percent of blockade runners made it through; by 1865 the rate had sunk to 50 percent.

Despite meager resources, the South made impressive efforts to offset the North's naval advantages. Early in the war the Confederates raised a scuttled Union frigate, the *Merrimac;* sheathed its sides in iron; rechristened it the *Virginia;* and deployed it to attack wooden Union ships at Hampton Roads, Virginia. The *Virginia's* success ended on March 9, 1862, when it tangled with the hastily built Union ironclad *Monitor* in the first battle ever fought between ironclads. The battle ended in a draw, but the South eventually lost the naval war because it could not build enough ships to overcome the northern lead. Even successful commerce raiders, such as the British-built *Alabama* and the *Florida,* although they wreaked havoc on the Union's merchant marine, did comparatively little to tip the balance in the South's favor because the North did not depend on imports for war materiel. The South lost the naval war.

The Diplomatic War

While armies and navies clashed in 1861–1862, conflict developed on a third front: diplomacy. At the war's start southerners had confidently opened a campaign to gain swift diplomatic recognition for the Confederacy. They were sure of the support of Britain and France's upper classes and even more certain that Britain, dependent on the South for four-fifths of its cotton, would have to break the Union blockade.

In 1861 Confederate diplomats James Mason and John Slidell sailed for Europe to lobby for recognition of an independent South, but their ship, the *Trent,* fell into Union hands. When the pair ended up as prisoners in Boston, British tempers exploded. Considering one war at a time quite enough, President Lincoln ordered Mason and Slidell released. But settling the *Trent* affair did not eliminate friction between the United States and Britain. Union diplomats protested the construction of Confederate commerce raiders such as the *Alabama* and the *Florida* in British shipyards and threatened war if two British-built ironclads were turned over to the Confederacy. Britain gave in and purchased the vessels for its own navy.

The South fell far short of its diplomatic objectives. Neither Britain nor France ever recognized the Confederacy as a nation. Southerners had badly overestimated the leverage of "cotton diplomacy" and the power of King Cotton, exaggerating the impact of their threats to withhold raw cotton supplies. Britain had an enormous cotton surplus on hand when the war began and developed other sources of cotton during the war, especially in India and Egypt. Although the South's share of England's cotton imports plummeted from 77 percent to 10 percent during the war, Britain's textile industry never faltered.

Lincoln's issuance of the Emancipation Proclamation, freeing the slaves, effectively preempted any British or French move toward recognition of the Confederacy. By transforming the war into a struggle about slavery, Lincoln won wide support among liberals and the working class in Britain. The proclamation, wrote Henry Adams (diplomat

Charles Francis Adams's son) from London, "has done more for us here than all of our former victories and all our diplomacy."

EMANCIPATION TRANSFORMS THE WAR, 1863

"I hear old John Brown knocking on the lid of his coffin and shouting 'Let me out! Let me out!'" abolitionist Henry Stanton wrote to his wife after the fall of Fort Sumter. "The Doom of Slavery is at hand." In 1861 this prediction seemed wildly premature. In the inaugural address Lincoln had stated bluntly, "I have no purpose, directly or indirectly, to interfere with the institution of slavery in the states where it exists." Yet within two years both necessity and ideology made emancipation a primary northern goal.

The rise of emancipation as a war goal reflected the changing character of the conflict itself. As the fighting raged on, demands for the prosecution of a "total war" intensified in the North, and many people who were unconcerned about the morality of slavery accepted abolition as a military necessity.

From Confiscation to Emancipation

The Union's policy on emancipation developed in several stages. As soon as northern troops invaded the South, questions arose about captured rebel property, including slaves. Generally, slaves who fled behind Union lines were considered "contraband"—enemy property liable to seizure—and were put to work for the Union army. In August 1861 Congress passed the first Confiscation Act, which authorized the seizure of all property, including slaves, used in military aid of the rebellion. This law did not free slaves, nor did it apply to those who had not worked for the Confederate army.

Several factors determined the Union's cautious approach. For one thing, Lincoln maintained that the South could not legally secede and thus argued that the Constitution's protection of property still applied. Second, Lincoln did not want to alienate slaveholders in the border states and pro-

slavery Democrats. In December 1861 he assured Congress that the war would not become a "remorseless revolutionary struggle." At the same time, however, the Radical Republicans pressured Lincoln to make the Civil War a second American Revolution, one that would abolish slavery. Thaddeus Stevens urged that the Union "free every slave—slay every traitor—burn every Rebel mansion, if these things be necessary to preserve this temple of freedom." Radicals agreed with African-American abolitionist Frederick Douglass that "to fight against slaveholders without fighting against slavery, is but a half-hearted business."

Emancipation also took on military significance with each Union setback, as northerners began to recognize that slavery permitted the South to commit a higher percentage of its white men to battle. In July 1862 Congress therefore passed the second Confiscation Act, which authorized the seizure of property belonging to all rebels, stipulated that slaves who entered Union lines "shall be forever free," and authorized the use of blacks as soldiers.

Nevertheless, Lincoln continued to stall. "My paramount object in this struggle *is* to save the Union, and is *not* either to save or destroy slavery," Lincoln averred. "If I could save the Union without freeing *any* slave, I would do it, and if I could save it by freeing *all* the slaves, I would do it; and if I could save it by freeing some and leaving others alone, I would also do that." But Lincoln, who had always loathed slavery, gradually came around to the view that the war had to lead to abolition. Reluctant to push the issue while Union armies reeled in defeat, he drafted a proclamation of emancipation and waited for the right moment to announce it. After the Union victory at Antietam, Lincoln issued the Preliminary Emancipation Proclamation (September 1862), which declared all slaves under rebel control free as of January 1, 1863. The final Emancipation Proclamation, issued on January 1, 1863, declared "forever free" all slaves in areas in rebellion.

The proclamation had limited practical impact. It applied only to areas in which it could not be enforced, those still in rebellion, and did not touch slavery in the border states. But the Emancipation Proclamation was a brilliant political stroke. By making it a military measure, Lincoln pacified northern conservatives, and by issuing the proclamation himself, he stole the initiative from the Radical Republicans. Through the proclamation, moreover, Lincoln mobilized support for the Union among European liberals, pushed the border states toward emancipation (both Missouri and Maryland abolished slavery before the war's end), and increased slaves' incentives to escape as Union troops neared. Fulfilling the worst of Confederate fears, the proclamation also enabled African-Americans to join the Union army.

The Emancipation Proclamation did not end slavery everywhere or free "*all* the slaves," but it changed the war. From 1863 on the war for the Union was also a war against slavery.

Crossing Union Lines

The attacks and counterattacks of the opposing armies turned many slaves into pawns of the war, free when Union troops overran their area, slaves again if the Confederates regained control. One North Carolina slave celebrated his liberation twelve different times. By 1865 about 500,000 former slaves were in Union hands.

Although in the first year of the war masters could retrieve slaves from Union armies, after 1862 slaves who crossed Union lines were considered free. The continual influx of freed slaves created a huge refugee problem for army commanders. Many freed slaves served in army camps as cooks, teamsters, and laborers. Some worked for pay on abandoned plantations or were leased out to planters who swore allegiance to the Union. Whether in camps or on plantations, freedmen questioned the value of liberation. Deductions for clothing and food ate up most of their earnings, and labor contracts bound them for long periods of time. Moreover, the freedmen encountered fierce prejudice among Yankee soldiers, who widely feared that emancipation would propel blacks northward after the war. The best solution to the widespread "question of what to do with the darkies," wrote one northern soldier, "would be to shoot them."

But this was not the whole story. Contrabands who aided the Union as spies and scouts helped to break down bigotry. "The sooner we get rid of our foolish prejudice the better for us," a Massachusetts soldier wrote home. In March 1865 Congress established the Freedmen's Bureau to provide relief, education, and work for the former slaves. The same law also provided that forty acres of abandoned or confiscated land could be leased to each freedman or southern Unionist, with an option to buy after three years. This was the first and only time that Congress provided for the redistribution of confiscated Confederate property.

Black Soldiers in the Union Army

During the first year of the war the Union had rejected African-American soldiers. Only after the Emancipation Proclamation did the large-scale enlistment of blacks begin. Prominent blacks, including Frederick Douglass, worked as recruiting agents in northern cities. Douglass clearly saw the link between military service and citizenship. "Once let the black man get upon his person the brass letters, U.S.; let him get an eagle on his button, and a musket on his shoulder and bullets in his pocket, and there is no power on earth which can deny that he has earned the right to citizenship." By the war's end 186,000 African-Americans had served in the Union army, one-tenth of all Union soldiers. One-half came from the Confederate states.

White Union soldiers commonly objected to the new recruits on racial grounds. Others, including Colonel Thomas Wentworth Higginson, a liberal minister and former John Brown supporter who led a black regiment, welcomed the black soldiers. "There is a fierce energy about them [in battle] beyond anything of which I have ever read, except it be the French Zouaves [troops in North Africa]," he observed. Even Union soldiers who held African-Americans in contempt came to approve of "anything that will kill a rebel." Black recruitment offered opportunities for whites to secure commissions, for blacks served in separate regiments under white officers. For most of the

COME AND JOIN US BROTHERS.

PUBLISHED BY THE SUPERVISORY COMMITTEE FOR RECRUITING COLORED REGIMENTS
1210 CHESTNUT ST. PHILADELPHIA.

Come and Join
A recruitment poster urges black men to enlist in the Union Army. African-American volunteers served in black regiments led by white officers.

war, black soldiers earned far less pay than whites. "We have come out Like men and Expected to be Treated as men but we have bin Treated more Like Dogs then men," an African-American soldier complained. Not until June 1864 did Congress belatedly equalize the pay of black and white soldiers.

African-American soldiers also suffered a far higher mortality rate than whites. Seldom committed to combat, they were far more likely to die of disease in bacteria-ridden garrisons. The Confederacy refused to treat captured black Union soldiers as prisoners of war; instead they were sent back to the states from which they had come to be reenslaved or executed. In an especially gruesome incident, when Confederate troops captured Fort Pillow, Tennessee, in 1864, they massacred 262 blacks.

Although fraught with inequities and hardships, military service symbolized citizenship for African-Americans. And the Union's use of African-American soldiers, especially former slaves, struck a military as well as psychological blow at the Confederacy. "They will make good soldiers," General Grant wrote in 1863, "and taking them from the en-emy weakens him in the same proportion they strengthen us."

Slavery in Wartime

Anxious white southerners on the home front felt as if they were perched on a volcano. To maintain control over their 3 million slaves, they tightened slave patrols, spread scare stories among slaves, and sometimes even moved entire plantations to relative safety in Texas. "The whites would tell the colored people not to go to the Yankees, for they would harness them to carts . . . in place of horses," remembered one African-American fugitive.

Some slaves remained faithful to their owners, hiding treasured belongings from marauding Union soldiers. Others were torn between loyalty and desire for freedom; one body servant, for example, accompanied his master to war, rescued him when he was wounded, and then escaped on his master's horse. Given the chance to flee to Union lines, most slaves did. Freedom was irresistible. But the majority of southern slaves stayed on their plantations under the nominal control of their masters. Despite the fears of southern whites, no general slave uprising occurred, and the Confederate war effort continued to utilize slave labor. Thousands of slaves worked in war plants, toiled as teamsters and cooks in army camps, and served as nurses in field hospitals. However, wartime conditions reduced overall slave productivity. The women and boys who remained on plantations complained of hard-to-control slaves who refused to work, worked inefficiently, or even destroyed property.

Whether slaves fled to freedom or merely stopped working, they effectively undermined the plantation system. Slavery disintegrated even as the Confederacy fought to preserve it. By 1864 a desperate Confederate Congress considered impressing slaves into the army in exchange for their freedom at the war's end. Although Robert E. Lee himself favored making slaves into soldiers, others were adamantly opposed. "If slaves will make good soldiers," a Georgia general argued, "our whole theory of slavery is wrong." In March 1865 the Confederate Congress passed a bill to arm 300,000 slave soldiers.

Although the plan to arm the slaves never took effect, the debate over it damaged southern morale by revealing deep internal divisions over war goals. Even before these conflicts had become obvious, the South's military position had deteriorated.

The Turning Point of 1863

In summer and fall 1863 Union fortunes improved dramatically in every theater of the war. However, the spring had gone badly as General Joseph "Fighting Joe" Hooker, a windbag fond of issuing pompous proclamations to his troops, suffered a crushing defeat at Chancellorsville, Virginia, in May 1863. Although Chancellorsville cost the South dearly—Stonewall Jackson was accidentally killed by his own troops—it humiliated the North, whose forces had outnumbered the Confederate troops two to one. "What will the country say?" Lincoln moaned. Reports from the West brought no better news: Grant was still unable to take Vicksburg, and the rebels clung to a vital 200-mile stretch of the Mississippi.

Union fortunes rose when Lee determined to invade the North. The decision provoked dissension within the Confederate government, but Lee needed supplies that war-racked Virginia could no longer provide. He also hoped that Lincoln would move troops from Vicksburg back into the eastern theater, and he believed that a major Confederate victory on northern soil could tip the balance to propeace northern Democrats and gain European recognition for the Confederacy. Lee led his 75,000 men into Maryland and then pressed forward into southern Pennsylvania. Lincoln, rejecting Hooker's plan to attack a virtually unprotected Richmond, replaced him with General George G. Meade.

MAP 15.3
The War in the East, 1863
Victorious at Chancellorsville in May 1863, Lee again invaded Union territory but was decisively stopped at Gettysburg.

Early in July 1863 Lee's offensive ground to a halt at a Pennsylvania road junction, Gettysburg. Confederates foraging for shoes in the town stumbled into Union cavalry, and both sides called for reinforcements. Thus began the war's greatest battle. The Union fielded 90,000 troops against Lee's 75,000, and the struggle raged for the first three days of July. On the afternoon of the third day, Lee ordered a direct frontal assault on the Union lines, and 15,000 men under General George E. Pickett charged across the open field, flags bright in the brilliant sunshine. Union rifles poured volley after volley into the onrushing Confederates, whose line wavered and then broke. More than one-half of Pickett's force lay dead, dying, or captured. When Lee withdrew to Virginia the next day, July 4, he had lost seventeen generals and more than one-third of his army. Total Union and Confederate casualties numbered 50,000. Although Meade failed to pursue the retreating rebels, the Union men rejoiced that they had parried Lee's stab northward.

Almost simultaneously, the North won a strategically vital battle in the West, at Vicksburg. After arduous maneuvering, Grant had besieged Vicksburg, the key to the Mississippi. After six weeks, during which southern soldiers and civilians alike survived by eating mules and even rats, the Confederate commander surrendered his 30,000-man garrison to Grant on July 4, the day that Lee began his withdrawal from Pennsylvania. Port Hudson, the last Confederate stronghold on the Mississippi, soon surrendered. "The Father of Waters flows unvexed to the sea," Lincoln proclaimed.

A second crucial Union victory in the West soon followed as armies stormed back and forth across Tennessee. By November 1863 the Union forces had finally captured and held Chattanooga, and the way lay open for a Union strike into Georgia.

Coming on the heels of reverses that had driven northern morale to its lowest point of the war, Union successes in the second half of 1863 stiffened the North's will to continue fighting and plunged some Confederate leaders into despair. After the fall of Vicksburg, chief of ordnance Josiah Gorgas lamented, "Yesterday we rode the pinnacle of success—today absolute ruin seems our portion. The Confederacy totters to its destruction."

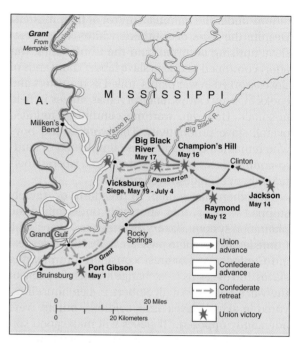

MAP 15.4

The War in the West, 1863: Vicksburg
Grant first moved his army west of Vicksburg to a point on the Mississippi south of the town. Then he marched northeast, taking Jackson, and finally west to Vicksburg.

Totter it might, but the South was far from falling. Lee and his Army of Northern Virginia still defended Virginia and Richmond. Although the loss of Vicksburg had cut the Confederacy in half, southern states west of the Mississippi could still provide soldiers. And the heart of the Confederacy—the Carolinas, Georgia, Florida, Mississippi, and Virginia—remained in southern hands. Few contemporaries thought that the fate of the Confederacy had been sealed.

WAR AND SOCIETY, NORTH AND SOUTH

The Civil War, engulfing two economies and societies, extended far beyond the battlefields. By 1863 the contrasts between North and South were stark:

superior resources enabled the Union to meet wartime demands that the imperiled Confederacy could not. But both sides confronted similar problems: labor shortages, inflation, and disunity and dissent. The war disrupted and dislocated families in the Union and Confederacy alike but especially in the South. Women on both sides took on new roles at home, in the workplace, and in relief efforts.

The War's Economic Impact: The North

The war had a wildly uneven effect on the Union's economy. Deprived of southern markets, the shoe industry in Massachusetts declined; deprived of raw cotton, the textile industry went into a tailspin. But northern industries directly related to the war effort, such as the manufacture of arms and uniforms, benefited from huge government contracts. Railroads flourished. Now an overwhelming majority in Congress, and with no need to balance southern interests against those of the North, the Republican party carried through a vigorous probusiness legislative agenda. Congress hiked the tariff in 1862 and again in 1864 to protect domestic industries. In July 1862 it passed the Pacific Railroad Act to build a transcontinental railroad. The government chartered the Union Pacific and Central Pacific corporations and gave each large land grants and generous loans, a total of 60 million acres of land and $20 million. The issuance of greenbacks and the creation of a national banking system brought a measure of uniformity to the nation's financial system.

The Republicans designed these measures to help all social classes and partially succeeded. The Homestead Act (passed in May 1862), embodying the party's ideal of "free soil, free labor, free men," granted 160 acres of public land to settlers after five years of residence on the land. By 1865, 20,000 homesteaders had occupied new land in the West under this act. To bring higher education within the reach of the common people, the Morrill Land Grant Act of July 1862 gave states proceeds from public land to establish universities emphasizing "such branches of learning as are related to agriculture and mechanic arts [engineering]."

Despite the idealistic goals underlying such laws, the war benefited the wealthy more than the average citizen. Corrupt contractors grew rich by selling the government substandard merchandise such as the notorious "shoddy," clothing made from compressed rags, which quickly disintegrated. Speculators made millions in the gold market, profiting more from Union defeats than from Union victories. Dealers with access to scarce commodities reaped astonishing profits. Manpower shortages in agricultural areas stimulated demand for Cyrus McCormick's mechanical reaper. McCormick redoubled his profits by investing in pig iron and watching as wartime demand drove the price of iron from $23 to $40 a ton.

Ordinary workers suffered. Protective tariffs, wartime excise taxes, and inflation bloated the price of finished goods, while wages lagged 20 percent or more behind cost increases. As boys and women poured into government offices and factories to replace men serving in the army, they drew lower pay, and the threat that employers could hire more youths and females undercut the bargaining power of men remaining in the labor force.

Workers complained about their low wages and a handful formed unions, a practice that would accelerate after the war. Employers denounced work complaints as unpatriotic hindrances to the war effort, and in 1864 troops were diverted from combat to put down protests in war industries.

The War's Economic Impact: The South

The war shattered the South's economy. In fact, if both regions are considered together, the war retarded *American* economic growth. For example, the U.S. commodity output, which had increased 51 percent and 62 percent in the 1840s and 1850s, respectively, rose only 22 percent during the 1860s. Even this modest gain depended wholly on the North, for during that same decade commodity output in the South *declined* 39 percent.

Multiple factors offset the South's substantial wartime industrial growth. For example, the war destroyed the South's railroads. Cotton production plunged from 4 million bales in 1861 to 300,000 in 1865. Southern food production also declined because of Union occupation and a shortage of manpower. Food scarcities occurred late in the war. "The people are subsisting on the ungathered crops and nine families out of ten are left without meat," lamented one Mississippian.

Part of the blame for the South's food shortage rested with the planters. Despite government pleas to grow more food, many planters continued to raise cotton. To feed its hungry armies, the Confederacy impressed food from civilians. Farms and plantations run by the wives of active soldiers provided the easiest targets for food-impressment agents, and the women sent desperate pleas to their husbands to return home. By late 1864, half the Confederacy's soldiers were absent from their units.

The manpower drain that hampered food production reshaped the lives of southern white women; with three of every four white men in the military during the war, southern women faced new challenges and chronic shortages. With manufactured goods in short supply, women wove cloth and improvised replacements for unavailable goods, such as ink, dye, coffee, shoes, and candles. The war made refugees of many women; Texas became an appealing haven for those who sought to preserve their slave property. For most women and their families, however, refugee life was disorienting and demoralizing.

In one respect the persistence of cotton growing aided the South as cotton became the basis for the Confederacy's flourishing trade with the enemy. In July 1861 the U.S. Congress virtually legalized this trade by allowing northern commerce with southerners loyal to the Union. In practice, it proved impossible to tell loyalists from rebels, and northern traders happily swapped bacon, salt, blankets, and other necessities with whoever would sell them southern cotton. By 1864 traffic through the lines was providing the South with enough food daily to feed Lee's Army of Northern Virginia. To one disenchanted northern congressman, it seemed that the Union's policy was "to feed an army and fight it at the same time."

Trading with the enemy alleviated the South's food shortages but intensified its morale problems. The prospect of traffic with the Yankees gave planters an incentive to keep growing cotton, and it fattened merchants and middlemen. "Oh! the extortioners," complained a War Office clerk in Richmond. "Our patriotism is mainly in the army and among the ladies of the South. The avarice and cupidity of men at home could only be exceeded by ravenous wolves."

Dealing with Dissent

Both wartime governments faced mounting dissent and disloyalty. Within the Confederacy, dissent assumed two basic forms. First, a vocal group of states' rights supporters persistently attacked Jefferson Davis's government as a despotism. Second, loyalty to the Union flourished among the nonslaveholding small farmers who lived in the Appalachian region. To these people, the Confederate rebellion was a slave owners' conspiracy. An Alabama farmer complained of the planters, "All they want is to get you pupt up and to fight for their infurnal negroes and after you do there fighting you may kiss there hine parts for o they care." On the whole, the South responded mildly to such popular disaffection. In 1862 the Confederate Congress gave President Davis the power to suspend the writ of habeas corpus, but he used it sparingly.

Lincoln faced similar challenges in the North, where the Democratic minority opposed both emancipation and the wartime growth of centralized power. One faction, the "Peace Democrats" (called Copperheads by their opponents, to suggest a resemblance to a species of easily concealed poisonous snakes), demanded a truce and a peace conference. They charged that the administration's war policy would "exterminate the South," make reconciliation impossible, and spark "terrible social change and revolution" nationwide.

Strongest in the border states, the Midwest, and northeastern cities, the Democrats mobilized farmers of southern background and the urban working class, especially recent immigrants, who feared losing their jobs to free blacks. In 1863 this volatile mix of political, ethnic, racial, and class antagonisms exploded into antidraft protests in several cities. By far the most violent eruption occurred in July 1863 in New York City, where mobs of Irish working-class men and women roamed the streets for four days until federal troops suppressed them. The Irish loathed the idea of being drafted to fight a war on behalf of slaves who, once freed, might compete with them for jobs. They also bitterly resented the provision of the draft law that allowed the rich to purchase substitutes. The mobs' targets reflected their grievances: the rioters lynched at least a dozen blacks, injured hundreds more, and burned draft offices and the homes of wealthy Republicans.

President Lincoln's speedy dispatch of federal troops to quash these riots typified his forceful response to dissent. Lincoln imposed martial law with far less hesitancy than Davis; he suspended the writ of habeas corpus nationwide in 1863 and authorized the arrest of rebels, draft resisters, and anyone engaged in "any disloyal practice." The responses of Davis and Lincoln to dissent underscored the differences between the two regions' wartime political systems. Lincoln and the Republicans used dissent to rally patriotic fever against the Democrats, but Davis lacked the institutionalization of dissent provided by party conflict and thus had to tread lightly lest he be branded a despot.

Yet Lincoln did not unleash a reign of terror against dissent. In general, the North preserved freedom of the press, speech, and assembly. In 1864 the Union became the first warring nation in history to hold a contested national election. Moreover, most of the 15,000 civilians arrested in the North were quickly released. A few cases aroused concern. In 1864 a military commission sentenced an Indiana man to be hanged for an alleged plot to free Confederate prisoners. Two years later in *Ex parte* Milligan (1866), the Supreme Court overturned the conviction, ruling that military courts could not try civilians when civil courts were open. The arrest of outspoken dissident politicians raised protests as well. Clement L. Vallandigham, an Ohio Peace Democrat, challenged the administration, denounced the suspension of habeas corpus, and proposed an armistice. In 1863 a military commission sentenced him to jail for the duration of the war; when Ohio Democrats nominated him for governor, Lincoln changed the sentence to banishment. Escorted to enemy lines in Tennessee, Vallandigham was left in the hands of bewildered Confederates and escaped to Canada. The Supreme Court refused to review his case.

The Medical War

The Union and the Confederacy alike witnessed remarkable wartime patriotism that propelled civilians, especially women, to work tirelessly to alleviate soldiers' suffering. The United States Sanitary Commission, organized in June 1861 to assist the Union's medical bureau, depended on women volunteers. Described by one woman as a "great artery that bears the people's love to the army," the commission raised funds, bought and distributed supplies, and ran special kitchens to supplement army rations. One widow, Mary Ann "Mother" Bickerdyke, served sick and wounded Union soldiers as both nurse and surrogate mother.

Women also reached out to aid the battlefront through the nursing corps. Some 3,200 women served the Union and the Confederacy as nurses. Dorothea Dix, famed for her campaigns on behalf of the insane, became head of the Union's nursing corps. Clara Barton, an obscure clerk in the Patent Office, found ingenious ways of channeling medicine to the sick and wounded. Catching wind of Union movements before the Battle of Antietam, she showed up at the battlefield on the eve of the clash with a wagonload of supplies. When army surgeons ran out of bandages and started to dress wounds with corn husks, she raced forward with lint and bandages. In 1881 she would found the American Red Cross. The Confederacy also had extraordinary nurses, among them Belle Boyd, who served as both nurse and spy and once dashed through a field, waving her bonnet, to give Stonewall Jackson information. Nurses witnessed horrible sights. One reported, "About the amputating table lay large piles of human flesh—legs, arms, feet, and hands."

Pioneered by British reformer Florence Nightingale in the 1850s, nursing was a new vocation for women. In the eyes of critics, it marked a brazen departure from women's proper sphere. Male doctors were unsure about how to react to female nurses and sanitary workers. Some saw a potential for mischief in women's presence in male hospital wards. But other physicians viewed nursing and sanitary work as useful. The miasm theory of disease (see Chapter 11) won wide respect among physicians and stimulated valuable sanitary measures. In partial consequence, the ratio of disease to battle deaths was much lower in the Civil War than in the Mexican-American War. Nonetheless, for every soldier killed during the Civil War, two died of disease. The germ theory of disease was unknown, and arm and leg wounds often led to gangrene or tetanus. Typhoid, malaria, diarrhea, and dysentery were rampant in army camps.

Prison camps posed a special problem. The two sides had far more prisoners than they could handle, and prisoners on both sides suffered gravely. The worst conditions plagued the southern camps. Squalor and insufficient rations turned the Confederate prison camp at Andersonville, Georgia, into a virtual death camp; 3,000 prisoners a month (out of a total of 32,000) were dying there by August 1864. After the war an outraged northern public demanded, and got, the execution of Andersonville's commandant. Although the commandant was partly to blame, the deterioration of the southern economy was primarily responsible for such wretched conditions. Union prison camps were only marginally better.

The War and Women's Rights

Nurses and Sanitary Commission workers were not the only women to serve society in wartime. In North and South alike, women took over jobs vacated by men. In rural areas, where manpower shortages were most acute, women often plowed, planted, and harvested.

Northern women's rights advocates hoped that the war would yield equality for women as well as for slaves. A grateful North, they contended,

should reward women for their wartime service and recognize the link between black rights and women's rights. In 1863 feminists Elizabeth Cady Stanton and Susan B. Anthony organized the National Woman's Loyal League. Its members principally gathered signatures on petitions calling for a constitutional amendment to abolish slavery, but Stanton and Anthony used the organization to promote woman suffrage as well. Despite high expectations, the war did not bring women significantly closer to economic or political equality. Nor did it much change the prevailing definition of women's sphere. Men continued to dominate the medical profession, and for the rest of the century the census classified nurses as domestic help.

This failure to win the vote for women by capitalizing on the rising sentiment for abolition keenly disappointed women's rights advocates. The North had compelling reasons to abolish slavery, but northern politicians saw little practical value in woman suffrage. The *New York Herald*, which supported the Loyal League's attack on slavery, dismissed its call for woman suffrage as "nonsense and tomfoolery." Stanton wrote bitterly, "So long as woman labors to second man's endeavors and exalt his sex above her own, her virtues pass unquestioned; but when she dares to demand rights and privileges for herself, her motives, manners, dress, personal appearance, and character are subjects for ridicule and detraction."

THE UNION VICTORIOUS, 1864–1865

Successes at Gettysburg and Vicksburg in 1863 notwithstanding, the Union stood no closer to taking Richmond at the start of 1864 than in 1861, and most of the Lower South remained under Confederate control. The North's persistent inability to destroy the main Confederate armies eroded the Union's will to attack. War weariness strengthened the Democrats and jeopardized Lincoln's reelection in 1864.

The year 1864 was crucial for the North. A Union army under General William Tecumseh

Sherman captured Atlanta in September, boosting northern morale and helping to reelect Lincoln. Sherman then marched unimpeded across Georgia and into South Carolina and devastated the states. In Virginia, Grant backed Lee into trenches around Petersburg and Richmond and forced the evacuation of both cities—and ultimately the Confederacy's collapse.

The Eastern Theater in 1864

Early in 1864 Lincoln made Grant the commander of all Union armies and promoted him to lieutenant general. At first glance, the stony-faced, cigar-puffing Grant seemed an unlikely candidate for so exalted a rank, held previously only by George Washington. But Grant's successes in the West had made him the Union's most popular general. He moved his headquarters to the Army of the Potomac in the East and mapped a strategy for final victory.

Grant shared Lincoln's belief that the Union had to coordinate its attacks on all fronts to exploit its numerical advantage. He planned a sustained offensive against Lee in the East while ordering Sherman to attack the rebel army in Georgia. Sherman's mission was "to break it [the Confederate army] up, and to get into the interior of the enemy's country . . . inflicting all the damage you can."

In early May 1864 Grant led 118,000 men against Lee's 64,000 in a forested area near Fredericksburg, Virginia, called the Wilderness. The Union army fought the Army of Northern Virginia in a series of bloody engagements in May and June. These battles ranked among the war's fiercest; at Cold Harbor, Grant lost 7,000 men in one hour. Instead of recoiling from such an immense "butcher's bill," Grant pressed on, forcing Lee to pull back to trenches guarding Petersburg and Richmond.

Once entrenched, Lee could not threaten the Union rear with rapid moves as he had done for three years. Lee sent General Jubal A. Early on raids down the Shenandoah Valley, which served the Confederacy as a granary and as an indirect way to menace Washington. Grant countered by ordering General Philip Sheridan to march down the valley from the north and lay it waste. By September 1864 Sheridan controlled the devastated valley.

While Grant and Lee grappled in the Wilderness, Sherman led 98,000 men into Georgia. Opposing him with 53,000 men (later reinforced to 65,000), General Joseph Johnston slowly retreated toward Atlanta, conserving his strength for a defense of the city. Dismayed by this defensive strategy, President Davis replaced Johnston with the adventurous John B. Hood. He gave Davis what he wanted, a series of attacks on Sherman, but Sherman pressed relentlessly forward against Hood's increasingly depleted army. Unable to defend Atlanta, Hood evacuated the city, which Sherman took on September 2, 1864.

The Election of 1864

Atlanta's fall came at a timely moment for Lincoln, in the thick of a tough campaign for reelection. Radical Republicans opposed his renomination, largely because of his desire to restore occupied parts of the Confederacy to the Union, and rallied around Secretary of the Treasury Salmon P. Chase. The Democrats, meanwhile, had never forgiven Lincoln for making emancipation a war goal, and now the Copperheads demanded an immediate armistice followed by negotiations.

Lincoln, however, benefited from his own resourcefulness and his foes' problems. Chase's challenge failed, and by the time of the Republican convention, Lincoln's managers controlled the nomination. To isolate the Peace Democrats, the Republicans formed a temporary organization, the National Union party, and chose a southern Unionist, Democratic senator Andrew Johnson of Tennessee, for the vice presidency. The Democrats nominated George B. McClellan, former commander of the Army of the Potomac, who advocated military victory and tried to distance himself from the Democratic platform, which called for peace without victory.

Lincoln doubted that he would be reelected, but the fall of Atlanta provided an enormous boost. With 55 percent of the popular vote and 212 out of 233 electoral votes, he swept to victory.

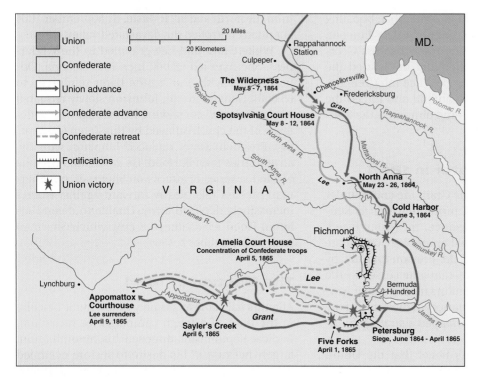

MAP 15.5
The Final Virginia Campaign, 1864–1865
Refusing to abandon his campaign in the face of enormous casualties, Grant finally pushed Lee into defensive fortifications around Petersburg, whose fall doomed Richmond. When Lee tried to escape to the west, Grant cut him off and forced his surrender.

The convention that nominated Lincoln also endorsed a constitutional amendment to abolish slavery, which Congress passed early in 1865. The Thirteenth Amendment would be ratified by the end of the year.

Sherman's March Through Georgia

Meanwhile, Sherman gave the South a lesson in total war. Refusing to chase Hood back into Tennessee, he decided to abandon his own supply lines, to march his army across Georgia to Savannah, and to live off the countryside. He would break the South's will to fight, terrify its people, and "make war so terrible . . . that generations would pass before they could appeal to it again."

Sherman began by burning much of Atlanta and forcing the evacuation of its civilian population. This harsh measure freed him of the need to feed and garrison the city. Then he led the bulk of his army, 62,000 men, out of Atlanta toward Savan-

nah. Four columns of infantry, augmented by cavalry squads and followed by thousands of jubilant slaves, moved on a front sixty miles wide and at a pace of ten miles a day, destroying everything that could aid the Confederacy—arsenals, railroads, munitions plants, cotton gins, crops, and livestock. This ruin far exceeded Sherman's orders. Although told not to destroy civilian property, foragers ransacked and demolished homes. Indeed, havoc seemed a vital part of Sherman's strategy. By the time he occupied Savannah, he estimated that his army had destroyed $100 million worth of property. After taking Savannah in December 1864, Sherman's army wheeled north toward South Carolina and advanced unimpeded to Columbia, where fires set by looters, slaves, soldiers of both sides, and liberated Union prisoners razed the city. Sherman headed for North Carolina. By spring 1865 his army had left behind 400 miles of ruin. Other Union armies controlled the entire Confederacy, except Texas and Florida, and destroyed its wealth. "War is cruelty and you cannot refine it,"

Sherman wrote. "Those who brought war into our country deserve all the curses and maledictions a people can pour out."

Toward Appomattox

While Sherman headed north, Grant renewed his assault on the entrenched Army of Northern Virginia. His main objective was Petersburg, a railroad hub south of Richmond. The fall of Atlanta and the devastation wrought by Sherman's army took a heavy toll on Confederate morale. Desertions reached epidemic proportions. Late in March 1865 Grant, reinforced by Sheridan, swung his army around the western flank of the Petersburg defenders. Lee could not stop him. On April 2 a courier brought the grim news to Jefferson Davis, attending church in Richmond: "General Lee telegraphs that he can hold his position no longer."

Davis left his pew, gathered his government, and fled. On the morning of April 3 Union troops entered Richmond, pulled down the Confederate flag, and raised the Stars and Stripes over the capital. Explosions set by retreating Confederates left the city "a sea of flames." Union troops liberated the jail, which held slaves awaiting sale, and its rejoicing inmates poured into the streets. On April 4 Lincoln toured the city and, for a few minutes, sat at Davis's desk with a dreamy expression on his face.

Lee led a last-ditch effort to escape westward to Lynchburg and its rail connections. But Grant and Sheridan choked off the route, and on April 9 Lee bowed to the inevitable. He asked for terms of surrender and met Grant in a private home in the village of Appomattox Courthouse, east of Lynchburg. As stunned troops gathered outside, Lee appeared in full dress uniform, complete with sword. Grant entered in his customary disarray, smoking a cigar. The final surrender came four days later as Lee's troops laid down their arms between federal ranks. "On our part," wrote a Union officer, "not a sound of trumpet . . . nor roll of drum; not a cheer . . . but an awed stillness rather." Grant paroled Lee's 26,000 men and sent them home with the horses and mules "to work their little farms." Within a month the remnants of Confederate resistance collapsed.

Grant headed back to Washington. On April 14 he turned down a theater date with the Lincolns; his wife found Mrs. Lincoln overbearing. That night at Ford's Theater an unemployed pro-Confederate actor, John Wilkes Booth, entered Lincoln's box and shot him in the head. Assassination attempts on the secretary of state and vice president failed, and Booth escaped. Within two weeks Union troops hunted him down and shot him to death (or he shot himself). Four accused accomplices were hanged, and four more were imprisoned. On April 15 Lincoln died and Andrew Johnson became president. Six days later Lincoln's funeral train left Washington on its mournful journey to Springfield, Illinois. Crowds of thousands gathered at stations to weep as the black-draped train passed.

The Impact of the War

The Civil War took a larger human toll than any other war in American history. More than 600,000 persons died during the tragic four years of war. Most families in the nation suffered losses. Vivid reminders remained well into the twentieth century. For many years armless and legless veterans gathered at regimental reunions, and thousands of communities built monuments to the dead.

The war's costs were high, but only the southern economy was destroyed. By war's end the North had most of the nation's wealth and industrial capacity. Spurring economic modernization, the war provided opportunities for industrial development and capital investment. No longer the largest slave-owning power in the world, the United States would become a major industrial nation.

The war had political ramifications as well. States never regained their antebellum range of powers. The national banking system gradually supplanted state banks, and greenbacks provided a national currency. The war also promoted large-scale organization in both the business world and public life.

Finally, the Civil War fulfilled abolitionists' prophecies as well as Union goals, producing the very sort of radical upheaval within southern society that Lincoln had tried to avoid. Beaten Confederates

Chronology

1861	President Abraham Lincoln calls for volunteers to suppress the rebellion (April). Virginia, Arkansas, Tennessee, and North Carolina join the Confederacy (April–May). Lincoln imposes a naval blockade on the South (April). U.S. Sanitary Commission formed (June). First Battle of Bull Run (July). First Confiscation Act (August).
1862	Legal Tender Act (February). George B. McClellan's Peninsula Campaign (March–July). Battle of Shiloh (April). Confederate Congress passes the Conscription Act (April). David G. Farragut captures New Orleans (April). Homestead Act (May). Seven Days' Battles (June–July). Pacific Railroad Act (July). Morrill Land Grant Act (July). Second Confiscation Act (July). Second Battle of Bull Run (August). Battle of Antietam (September). Preliminary Emancipation Proclamation (September). Battle of Fredericksburg (December).
1863	Emancipation Proclamation issued (January). Lincoln suspends writ of habeas corpus nationwide (January). National Bank Act (February). Congress passes the Enrollment Act (March). Battle of Chancellorsville (May). Battle of Gettysburg (July). Surrender of Vicksburg (July). New York City draft riots (July).
1864	Ulysses S. Grant given command of all Union armies (March). Battle of the Wilderness (May). Battle of Cold Harbor (June). Surrender of Atlanta (September). Lincoln reelected (November). William Tecumseh Sherman's march to the sea (November–December).
1865	Congress passes the Thirteenth Amendment (January). Sherman moves through South Carolina (January–March). Grant takes Richmond (April). Robert E. Lee surrenders at Appomattox (April). Lincoln dies (April).

wondered whether blacks and Yankees would permanently take over the South. "Hello, massa," an African-American Union soldier called out when he spotted his former owner among Confederate prisoners whom he was guarding. "Bottom rail top dis time." The nation now shifted its attention to the reconstruction of the conquered South and the fate of 3.5 million newly freed slaves.

CONCLUSION   *hc* ACE Practice Test

When the Civil War began, each side faced major challenges. The North had to conquer large areas of the South, cripple the South's resources, and destroy its armies. The South in turn had to fight a defensive war on its own soil and hold out long enough to convince the North that further war was futile.

Both sides faced the challenge of raising armies and funds. To this end they each drafted troops, imposed taxes, and printed paper money. Political dissent assaulted both governments. However, the Union possessed far greater resources in terms of manpower and industrial production than the South. As the war progressed, slavery began to disintegrate, thus weakening the South even more.

The North came to see the abolition of slavery as a military measure. The Emancipation Proclamation, which Lincoln issued on January 1, 1863, met multiple purposes. It not only freed the slaves but also changed the nature of the Civil War: the war to save the Union became a war to end slavery.

Historians continue to debate the war and its causes. One school holds that internal weaknesses in the Confederacy were the primary cause of the Union victory, while the other school stresses the unpredictability of war itself and sees the South's defeat as a near thing.

The impact of the war is clear. It boosted the northern economy, strengthened the national government, confirmed the triumph of the Republican party and its commitment to industrialization, and it ended slavery. Emancipation and a sense of nationalism were the war's chief legacy. The nation would now turn its attention to the restoration of the conquered South and to deciding the future of the former slaves.

FURTHER READING

David H. Donald, *Lincoln* (1995). A compelling biography that reveals connections between Lincoln's private and public lives.

Drew Gilpin Faust, *Mothers of Invention: Women of the Slave-holding South in the American Civil War* (1996). Examines elite women's relation to slavery, southern culture, and the deprivations of war.

Gary W. Gallagher, *The Confederate War* (1997). Shows how Confederate leaders pursued promising strategies; explores links between morale and the battlefield.

Leon Litwack, *Been in the Storm So Long: The Aftermath of Slavery* (1979). A prize-winning examination of slaves' responses to the process of emancipation, continuing into the Reconstruction era.

James M. McPherson, *Battle Cry of Freedom: The Civil War Era* (1988). An award-winning study of the war years, skillfully integrating political, military, and social history.

James M. McPherson, *For Cause and Comrades: Why Men Fought in the Civil War* (1997). Uses soldiers' letters to explore motivation and responses to combat.

George C. Rable, *The Confederate Republic: A Revolt Against Politics* (1994). Discusses the tension between nationalism and individualism in Confederate political life.

Charles Royster, *The Destructive War: William Tecumseh Sherman, Stonewall Jackson, and the Americans* (1991). An insightful exploration of the meaning of violence and nationality in the Civil War era.

Lyde Cullen Sizer, *The Political Work of Northern Women Writers and the Civil War, 1850–1870* (2000). Shows how northern women responded to national issues of the Civil War era, including slavery and emancipation.

Michael Vorenberg, *Final Freedom: The Civil War, the Abolition of Slavery, and the Thirteenth Amendment* (2001). Considers the framing and ratification of the Thirteenth Amendment and the political context in which emancipation became law.

Former slaves in Jacksonville, Florida

The Crises of Recon-struction, 1865–1877

hc This icon will direct you to additional study and research resources at http://college.hmco.com/history/us/boyer/enduring_concise/5e/students/index.html

"We was all walking on golden clouds," said Felix Heywood, describing the day he and his fellow slaves learned of emancipation. "We all felt like heroes. . . . We was free!" Almost no slaves in Texas had known about emancipation until the arrival of a Union army after the war; to this day, "Juneteenth" (June 19, 1865) is still celebrated by African-Americans in Texas.

Heywood, twenty years old at the war's end, had been owned by a rancher in Bexar County, Texas, not too far from the Alamo, Texas's great symbol of freedom. Many of his friends and relatives moved away when freedom came, he recalled. "Right off colored folks started on the move. They seemed to want to get closer to freedom so they'd know what it was." Heywood and his family stayed in Bexar County, where their former owners gave them ranchland

This chapter focuses on five major questions:

▶ How did Radical Republicans gain control of Reconstruction politics?

▶ What impact did federal Reconstruction policy have on the former Confederacy and ex-Confederates?

▶ In what ways did newly freed slaves reshape their lives after emancipation?

▶ What factors contributed to the end of Reconstruction in the 1870s? Which was most significant?

▶ Was Reconstruction a success or a failure? Why?

and cattle. Ultimately he left ranching and moved to San Antonio, where he worked on the waterworks.

In old age, Heywood looked back to remember the arrival of emancipation. "We know'd freedom was on us, but we didn't know what was to come with it," he recalled. "We thought we was goin' to be richer and better off than the white folks. . . . But it didn't turn out like that. We soon found out that freedom could make folks proud but it didn't make 'em rich."

For the nation, as for Felix Heywood and his fellows, the end of the Civil War was a time of uncharted possibilities—and unresolved conflicts. While former slaves exulted over their freedom, their former owners were often as grim as the ravaged southern landscape. Several thousand fled to Brazil, Mexico, or Europe, but most remained.

After most wars victors care little for the mood of the vanquished, but the Civil War was different. The Union had sought not merely victory but the return of national unity. The federal government faced unprecedented questions. How could the Union be restored and the South reintegrated? Who would control the process—Congress or the

president? Should Confederate leaders be tried for treason? Most important, what would happen to the 3.5 million former slaves? The freedmen's future was *the* crucial postwar issue, for emancipation had set in motion the most profound upheaval in the nation's history. Slavery had been both a labor system and a means of racial control; it had determined the South's social, economic, and political structure. The end of the Civil War, in short, posed two huge challenges that had to be addressed simultaneously: readmitting the Confederate states to the Union and defining the status of free blacks in society.

Between 1865 and 1877, the nation faced major and often divisive challenges and crises. Conflict characterized Congressional debates, the former Confederacy, and the industrializing postwar North. These crises of Reconstruction—the restoration of the former Confederate states and the fate of the former slaves—reshaped the legacy of the Civil War.

RECONSTRUCTION POLITICS, 1865–1868

The end of the Civil War offered multiple possibilities for chaos and vengeance. The federal government could have imprisoned Confederate leaders; former rebel troops could have become guerrillas; freed slaves could have waged a racial war against their former masters. None of this happened. Instead, intense *political* conflict dominated the immediate postwar period. The political upheaval, sometimes attended by violence, produced new constitutional amendments, an impeachment crisis, and some of the most ambitious domestic legislation ever enacted by Congress, the Reconstruction Acts of 1867–1868. It culminated in something that few expected, the enfranchisement of African-American men.

In 1865 only a handful of Radical Republicans advocated African-American suffrage. Any plan to restore the Union, Representative Thaddeus Stevens of Pennsylvania proclaimed, would have to "revolutionize Southern institutions, habits, and manners . . . or all our blood and treasure have been spent in vain." In the complex political battles of Reconstruction, the Radicals won broad support for their program, including African-American male enfranchisement. Just as the Civil War had led to emancipation, so Reconstruction led to African-American suffrage.

Lincoln's Plan

Conflict over Reconstruction began even before the war ended. In December 1863 President Lincoln issued the Proclamation of Amnesty and Reconstruction, which allowed southern states to form new governments if at least 10 percent of those who had voted in the 1860 elections swore an oath of allegiance to the Union and accepted emancipation. This plan excluded most Confederate officials and military officers, who would have had to apply for presidential pardons, as well as African-Americans, who had not voted in 1860. Lincoln hoped both to undermine the Confederacy and to build a southern Republican party.

Radical Republicans in Congress wanted a slower readmission process that would exclude even more ex-Confederates from political life. The Wade-Davis bill, passed by Congress in July 1864, provided that a military government would rule each former Confederate state and that at least one-half of the eligible voters would have to swear allegiance before they could choose a convention to repeal secession and abolish slavery. In addition, to qualify as a voter or a delegate, a southerner would have to take the "ironclad" oath, swearing that he had never voluntarily supported the Confederacy. The Wade-Davis bill would have delayed readmission of southern states almost indefinitely.

Lincoln pocket-vetoed* the Wade-Davis bill, and an impasse followed. Arkansas, Louisiana, Tennessee, and parts of Virginia moved toward readmission under variants of Lincoln's plan, but Congress refused to seat their delegates. Lincoln hinted that he might be moving toward a more rigorous policy than his original one, a program that

---

* Pocket-vetoed: failed to sign the bill within ten days of Congress's adjournment.

would include African-American suffrage. But his death foreclosed the possibility that he and Congress might draw closer to agreement, and Radicals now looked with hope to the new president, Andrew Johnson.

Presidential Reconstruction Under Johnson

At first glance, Andrew Johnson seemed a likely ally for the Radicals. The only southern senator to remain in Congress when his state seceded, Johnson had taken a strong anti-Confederate stance and had served as military governor of Tennessee for two years. Self-educated, an ardent Jacksonian, a foe of the planter class, a supporter of emancipation—Johnson carried impeccable credentials. However, as a lifelong Democrat he had his own political agenda, sharply different from that of the Radicals.

In May 1865, with Congress out of session, Johnson shocked Republicans by announcing his own program, A Proclamation of Amnesty and Reconstruction, to bring the southern states still without Reconstruction governments—Alabama, Florida, Georgia, Mississippi, North Carolina, South Carolina, and Texas—back into the Union. Virtually all southerners who took an oath of allegiance would receive pardon and amnesty, and all their property except slaves would be restored to them. Confederate civil and military officers would still be disqualified, as would well-to-do former Confederates (anyone owning taxable property worth $20,000 or more). By purging the plantation aristocracy, Johnson claimed, he would aid "humble men, the peasantry and yeomen of the South, who have been decoyed . . . into rebellion." Oath takers could elect delegates to state conventions, which would call regular elections, proclaim secession illegal, repudiate debts incurred under the Confederacy, and ratify the Thirteenth Amendment, which abolished slavery.

This presidential Reconstruction took effect in summer 1865, with unforeseen results. Johnson handed out pardons liberally (some 13,000) and dropped his plans for the punishment of treason. By the end of 1865 all seven states had created new

King Andrew

This Thomas Nast cartoon, published just before the 1866 congressional elections, conveyed Republican antipathy to Andrew Johnson. The president is depicted as an autocratic tyrant. Radical Republican Thaddeus Stevens, upper right, has his head on the block and is about to lose it. The Republic sits in chains.

civil governments that in effect restored the *status quo ante bellum*. Confederate officers and large planters resumed state offices, and former Confederate congressmen and generals won election to Congress. Because many of these new representatives were former Whigs who had not supported secession, southerners believed that they genuinely had elected "Union" men. Some states refused to repudiate their Confederate debts or to ratify the Thirteenth Amendment.

Most infuriating to the Radicals, every state passed a "black code" intended to ensure a landless, dependent black labor force—to "secure the services of the negroes, teach them their place," in the words of one Alabamian. These codes, which replaced earlier slave codes, guaranteed the freedmen some basic rights—marriage, ownership of property, the right to testify in court against other blacks—but also restricted freedmen's behavior. Some states established segregation, and most prohibited racial intermarriage, jury service by blacks, and court testimony by blacks against whites. Most harmful, black codes included economic restrictions to prevent blacks from leaving the plantation, usually through labor contracts that stipulated anyone who had not signed a labor contract was a vagrant and subject to arrest.

hc Primary Source: Louisiana Black Code

These codes left freedmen no longer slaves but not really liberated. Although many of their provisions never actually took effect—for example, the Union army and the Freedmen's Bureau suspended the enforcement of the racially discriminatory laws—the black codes reflected white southern attitudes and showed what "home rule" would have been like without federal intervention.

To many northerners, both the black codes and the election of former Confederates to high office reeked of southern defiance. "What can be hatched from such an egg but another rebellion?" asked a Boston newspaper. When the Thirty-ninth Congress convened in December 1865, it refused to seat the southern delegates and prepared to dismantle the black codes and to lock ex-Confederates out of power.

Congress Versus Johnson

Southern blacks' status became the major issue in Congress. With Congress split into four blocs—Democrats, and radical, moderate, and conservative Republicans—a politically adroit president could have protected his program. Ineptly, Johnson alienated the moderates and pushed them into the Radicals' arms by vetoing some key moderate measures.

In late 1865 Congress voted to extend the life of the Freedmen's Bureau for three more years. Staffed mainly by army officers, the bureau provided relief, rations, and medical care; built schools for former slaves; put them to work on abandoned or confiscated lands; and tried to protect their rights as laborers. To strengthen the bureau, Congress had voted to allow it to run special military courts that would settle labor disputes and invalidate labor contracts forced on African-Americans under the black codes. In February 1866 Johnson vetoed the bill; the Constitution, he declared, neither sanctioned military trials of civilians in peacetime nor supported a system to care for "indigent persons." Then in March 1866 Congress passed the Civil Rights Act of 1866, which made African-Americans U.S. citizens with the same civil rights as other citizens and authorized federal intervention to ensure African-Americans' rights in court. Johnson vetoed this measure also, arguing that it would "operate in favor of the colored and against the white race." In April Congress overrode his veto, and in July it enacted the Supplementary Freedmen's Bureau Act over another presidential veto.

These vetoes puzzled many Republicans, for the new laws did not undercut the basic structure of presidential Reconstruction. Although the vetoes gained support for Johnson among northern Democrats, they cost him dearly among moderate Republicans, who began to ally with the Radicals. Was Johnson a political incompetent, or was he merely trying, unsuccessfully, to forge a centrist coalition? Whatever the case, he drove moderate and Radical Republicans together toward their next step: the passage of a constitutional amendment to protect the new Civil Rights Act.

The Fourteenth Amendment, 1866

In April 1866 Congress adopted the Fourteenth Amendment, its most ambitious attempt to deal with the problems of Reconstruction and the freed slaves. In the first clause, the amendment proclaimed that all persons born or naturalized in the United States were citizens and that no state could abridge their rights without due process of law or deny them equal protection under the law. Second, the amendment guaranteed that if a state denied suffrage to any male citizen, its representation in Congress would be proportionally reduced. Third, the amendment disqualified from state and national offices *all* prewar officeholders who had supported the Confederacy. Finally, it repudiated the Confederate debt and maintained the validity of the federal debt. In effect, the Fourteenth Amendment nullified the *Dred Scott* decision, threatened southern states that deprived African-American men of the right to vote, and invalidated most of the pardons that President Johnson had ladled out. Beyond demonstrating widespread receptivity to the Radicals' demands, including African-American male suffrage, the Fourteenth Amendment represented the first national effort to limit the states' control of civil and political rights.

Passage of the amendment created a firestorm. Abolitionists said that it did not go far enough to protect African-American voting rights, southerners blasted it as vengeful, and President Johnson denounced it. The president's unwillingness to compromise solidified the new alliance between moderate and Radical Republicans and transformed the congressional elections of 1866 into a referendum on the Fourteenth Amendment.

Over the summer Johnson set off on a whistle-stop train tour campaigning against the amendment. Humorless and defensive, the president made fresh enemies, however, and doomed his hope of creating a new political party, the National Union party, opposed to the amendment. Meanwhile, the moderate and Radical Republicans defended the amendment, condemned President Johnson, and branded the Democratic party "a common sewer . . . into which is emptied every element of treason, North and South."

Republicans carried the congressional elections of 1866 in a landslide, winning nearly two-thirds of the House and three-fourths of the Senate. They had secured a mandate for the Fourteenth Amendment and their own Reconstruction program.

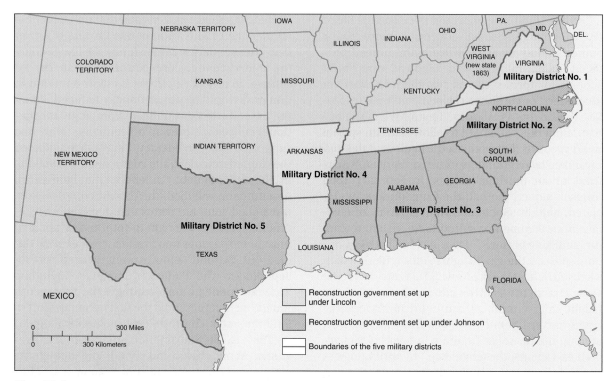

MAP 16.1
The Reconstruction of the South
The Reconstruction Act of 1867 divided the former Confederate states, except Tennessee, into five military districts and set forth the steps by which new state governments could be created. **hc** Interactive Map: The Reconstruction

Congressional Reconstruction, 1866–1867

The congressional debate over reconstructing the South began in December 1866 and lasted three months. Radical leaders, anxious to stifle a resurgence of Confederate power, called for African-American suffrage, federal support for public schools, confiscation of Confederate estates, and extended military occupation of the South. Moderate Republicans accepted part of this plan. The lawmakers debated every ramification of various legislative proposals, and in February 1867, after complex political maneuvers, Congress passed the Reconstruction Act of 1867. Johnson vetoed it, and on March 2 Congress passed the law over his veto. Three more Reconstruction acts, passed in 1867

and 1868 over presidential vetoes, refined and enforced the first act.

The Reconstruction Act of 1867 invalidated the state governments formed under the Lincoln and Johnson plans; only Tennessee, which had already ratified the Fourteenth Amendment and had been readmitted to the Union, escaped further Reconstruction. The new law divided the other ten former Confederate states into five military districts. It provided that voters—all black men, plus whites not disqualified by the Fourteenth Amendment—could elect delegates who would write a new state constitution granting African-American suffrage. After congressional approval of the state constitution, and after the state legislature's ratification of the Fourteenth Amendment, Congress would readmit the state into the Union. The enfranchisement of African-Americans and disfranchisement of so many ex-Confederates made the Reconstruction Act of 1867 far more radical than Johnson's program. Even then, however, it provided only temporary military rule, made no provisions to prosecute Confederate leaders for treason, and neither confiscated nor redistributed property.

Radical Republican leader Thaddeus Stevens had proposed confiscation of large Confederate estates to "humble the proud traitors" and to provide land for the former slaves. He hoped to create a new class of self-sufficient African-American yeomen farmers. Because political independence rested on economic independence, he contended, land grants would be far more valuable to African-Americans than the vote. But moderate Republicans and others backed away from Stevens's proposal. Tampering with property rights in the South might well jeopardize them in the North, they argued, and could endanger the entire Reconstruction program. Thus Congress rejected the most radical parts of the Radical Republican program.

Congressional Reconstruction took effect in spring 1867, but Johnson impeded its implementation by replacing pro-Radical military officers with conservative ones since Reconstruction could not be enforced without military power. Furious and more suspicious than ever of the president, congressional moderates and Radicals again joined forces to block Johnson from further hampering Reconstruction.

The Impeachment Crisis, 1867–1868

In March 1867, responding to Johnson's obstructionist tactics, Republicans in Congress passed two laws to restrict presidential power. The Tenure of Office Act prohibited the president from removing civil officers without Senate consent. Its purpose was to protect Secretary of War Edwin Stanton, a Radical ally needed to enforce the Reconstruction acts. The other law banned the president from issuing military orders except through the commanding general, Ulysses S. Grant, who could not be removed without the Senate's consent. Not sat-

isfied with clipping the president's wings, Radicals also began to look for grounds for impeachment and conviction to remove all possible obstacles to Reconstruction. Intense investigations by the House Judiciary Committee and private detectives turned up no impeachable offenses, but Johnson himself soon provided the charges that his opponents needed.

In August 1867 Johnson suspended Stanton and in February 1868 tried to remove him. The president's defiance of the Tenure of Office Act drove moderate Republicans back into alliance with the Radicals. The House approved eleven charges of impeachment, nine of them based on violation of the Tenure of Office Act and the other two accusing Johnson of being "unmindful of the high duties of the office," of seeking to disgrace Congress, and of not enforcing the Reconstruction acts.

Johnson's trial by the Senate, which began in March 1868, riveted public attention for eleven weeks. Seven congressmen, including leading Radicals, served as prosecutors, or "managers." Johnson's lawyers maintained that he was merely seeking a court test of the Tenure of Office Act, a law that he believed unconstitutional, by violating it. They also contended that the law did not protect Stanton because Lincoln, not Johnson, had appointed him. And they asserted that Johnson was guilty of no crime indictable in a regular court.

The congressional "managers" countered that impeachment was a political process, not a criminal trial, and that Johnson's "abuse of discretionary power" constituted an impeachable offense. Some Senate Republicans wavered, fearful that the removal of a president would destroy the balance of power within the federal government. They also were reluctant to see Benjamin Wade, a Radical Republican who was president pro tempore of the Senate, become president, as the Constitution then provided.

Intense pressure weighed on the wavering Republican senators. Ultimately, seven Republicans risked political suicide by voting with the Democrats against removal, and the Senate failed by one vote to convict Johnson. In so doing, the legislators set two critical precedents: in the future, no president would be impeached on political grounds, nor would he be impeached because two-thirds of Congress disagreed with him. In the short term, nonetheless, the anti-Johnson forces achieved their goals, for Andrew Johnson had no future as president. Republicans in Congress could now pursue their last major Reconstruction objective: guaranteeing African-American male suffrage.

The Fifteenth Amendment and the Question of Woman Suffrage, 1869–1870

African-American suffrage was the linchpin of congressional Reconstruction. Only with the support of African-American voters could Republicans secure control of the southern states. The Reconstruction Act of 1867 had forced southern states to enfranchise black men in order to reenter the Union, but most northern states still refused to grant suffrage to African-Americans. The Fifteenth Amendment, drawn up by Republicans and ap-

proved by Congress in 1869, aimed both to protect black suffrage in the South and to extend it to the northern and border states, on the assumption that newly enfranchised African-Americans would gratefully vote Republican. The amendment prohibited the denial of suffrage by the states to anyone on account of race, color, or previous condition of servitude.

Democrats opposed the amendment on the grounds that it violated states' rights, but they did not control enough states to prevent its ratification. However, to some southerners, the amendment's omissions made it acceptable; as a Richmond newspaper pointed out, it had "loopholes through which a coach and four horses can be driven." Indeed, the new amendment did not guarantee African-American officeholding, nor did it prohibit restrictions on suffrage such as property requirements and literacy tests, both of which might be used to deny African-Americans the vote.

The debate over black suffrage drew new participants into the fray. Women's rights advocates had tried to promote both black suffrage and

The Reconstruction Amendments

Amendment and Date of Congressional Passage	Provisions	Ratification
Thirteenth (January 1865)	Prohibited slavery in the United States.	December 1865
Fourteenth (June 1866)	Defined citizenship to include all persons born or naturalized in the United States.	July 1868, after Congress made ratification a prerequisite for readmission of ex-Confederate states to the Union.
	Provided proportional loss of congressional representation for any state that denied suffrage to any of its male citizens.	
	Disqualified prewar officeholders who supported the Confederacy from state or national office.	
	Repudiated the Confederate debt.	
Fifteenth (February 1869)	Prohibited the denial of suffrage because of race, color, or previous condition of servitude.	March 1870; ratification required of Virginia, Texas, Mississippi, and Georgia for readmission to the Union.

woman suffrage, but Radical Republicans rejected any linkage between the two, preferring to concentrate on black suffrage. Supporters of women's rights were themselves divided. Frederick Douglass argued that black suffrage had to receive priority. "If the elective franchise is not extended to the Negro, he is dead," explained Douglass. "Woman has a thousand ways by which she can attach herself to the ruling power of the land that we have not." Women's rights leaders Elizabeth Cady Stanton and Susan B. Anthony disagreed. If the Fifteenth Amendment did not include women, they emphasized, it would establish an "aristocracy of sex" and increase the disabilities under which women already labored. The argument fractured the old abolition–women's rights coalition and would lead to the development of an independent women's rights movement.

The battle over black suffrage and the Fifteenth Amendment split women's rights advocates into two rival suffrage associations, both founded in 1869. The Boston-based American Woman Suffrage Association sought state-by-state suffrage, while the more radical National Woman Suffrage Association, based in New York and led by Stanton and Anthony, promoted a constitutional amendment for woman suffrage.

Throughout the 1870s the two groups competed for support. Two western states, Wyoming and Utah, extended the vote to women, but the suffrage movement had little to do with it. In 1872 Susan B. Anthony mobilized about seventy women to vote nationwide; she was indicted, convicted, and fined. One of the would-be voters, Virginia Minor, brought suit with her husband against the registrar who had refused to allow her to vote. In *Minor v. Happersett* (1875), the Supreme Court ruled that a state could deny women the right to vote. Woman suffrage advocates braced for a long struggle.

By the time the Fifteenth Amendment was ratified in 1870, Congress could look back on five years of momentous achievement. Three constitutional amendments had broadened the scope of democracy by abolishing slavery, affirming the rights of citizens, and prohibiting the denial of suffrage on the basis of race. Congress had readmitted the for-

mer Confederate states into the Union. At the same time, momentum had slowed at the federal level. In 1869 the center of action shifted to the South, where tumultuous change was under way.

RECONSTRUCTION GOVERNMENTS

During the years of presidential Reconstruction, 1865–1867, the southern states faced formidable tasks: creating new governments, reviving war-torn economies, and dealing with the impact of emancipation. Racial tensions flared as freedmen organized political meetings to protest ill treatment and demand equal rights, and deadly race riots erupted in major southern cities. In May 1866 white crowds attacked African-American veterans in Memphis and rampaged through African-American neighborhoods, killing forty-six people. Two months later in New Orleans, whites assaulted black delegates on their way to a political meeting and left forty people dead.

Congressional Reconstruction, supervised by federal troops, began in spring 1867 with the dismantling of existing governments and the formation of new state governments dominated by Republicans. By 1868 most former Confederate states had rejoined the Union, and within two years the process was complete.

But Republican rule did not long endure in the South. Opposition from southern Democrats, the landowning elite, vigilantes, and most white voters proved insurmountable. Nevertheless, these Reconstruction governments were unique because African-American men, including former slaves, participated in them. Slavery had ended in other societies, too, but only in the United States had freedmen gained democratic political rights.

A New Electorate

The Reconstruction laws of 1867–1868 transformed the southern electorate by temporarily disfranchising 15 percent of potential white voters and by enfranchising more than 700,000 freed slaves. Black voters outnumbered whites by

100,000 overall and held voting majorities in five states.

This new electorate provided a base for the Republican party, which had never existed in the South. To scornful Democrats, the Republicans comprised three types of scoundrels: northern "carpetbaggers" who had come south for wealth and power; southern scalawags, poor and ignorant, looking to profit from Republican rule; and hordes of uneducated freedmen, easily manipulated. In fact, the hastily assembled Republican party, crossing racial and class lines, constituted a loose coalition of diverse factions with often contradictory goals.

To northerners who moved south after the war, the former Confederacy was an undeveloped region, ripe with possibilities. The carpetbaggers included many former Union soldiers who hoped to buy land, open factories, build railroads, or simply enjoy the warmer climate. Holding almost one in three state offices, they wielded disproportionate political power.

A handful of scalawags (white southerners who supported the Republicans) were old Whigs, but most were small farmers from the mountain regions of North Carolina, Georgia, Alabama, and Arkansas. Former Unionists who had owned no slaves and who felt no loyalty to the old plantation elite, they wanted to improve their economic position and cared little one way or the other about black suffrage. Scalawags held the most political offices during Reconstruction but proved the least stable element of the Republican coalition. Many drifted back into the Democratic fold.

Freedmen, the backbone of southern Republicanism, provided eight out of ten Republican votes. They sought land, education, civil rights, and political equality and remained loyal Republicans. "We know our friends," an elderly freedman said. Although Reconstruction governments depended on African-American votes, freedmen held at most one in five political offices and constituted a legislative majority only in South Carolina, whose population was more than 60 percent black. No African-Americans won the office of governor, and only two served in the U.S. Senate. A mere 6 percent of south-ern members of the House were African-American, and almost 50 percent came from South Carolina.

A significant status gap divided high-level African-American officials from African-American voters. Most freedmen cared mainly about their economic future, especially about acquiring land, whereas African-American officeholders concerned themselves far more with attaining equal rights. Still, both groups shared high expectations and prized enfranchisement.

Republican Rule

Large numbers of African-Americans participated in government for the first time in the state constitutional conventions of 1867–1868. The South Carolina convention had an African-American majority, and in Louisiana one-half the delegates were freedmen. In general, these conventions instituted democratic changes such as universal manhood suffrage and public-school systems but failed to provide either integrated schools or land reform. Wherever proposed, plans for the confiscation and redistribution of land failed.

Once civil power shifted to the new state governments, Republican administrations began ambitious public-works programs. They built roads and bridges, promoted railroad development, and funded institutions to care for orphans, the insane, and the disabled. Republican regimes also expanded state government and formed state militia in which African-Americans often were heavily represented. Finally, they created public-school systems, almost nonexistent in the antebellum South.

These reforms cost millions, and state debts and taxes skyrocketed. During the 1860s taxes rose 400 percent. Although northern tax rates still exceeded southern tax rates, southerners, particularly landowners, resented the new levies. In their view, Reconstruction strained the pocketbooks of the properties in order to finance the vast expenditures of Republican legislatures, the "no property herd."

Opponents of Reconstruction viewed Republican rule as wasteful and corrupt, the "most stupendous system of organized robbery in history." Indeed, corruption did permeate some state governments, as in Louisiana and South Carolina. The main profiteers were government officials who accepted bribes and railroad promoters who doled them out. But neither group was exclusively Republican. In fact, corruption increasingly characterized government *nationally* in these years and was both more flagrant and more lucrative in the North. But such a comparison did little to quiet the critics of Republican rule.

Counterattacks

For ex-Confederates, African-American enfranchisement and the "horror of Negro domination" created nightmares. As soon as congressional Reconstruction began, it fell under attack. Democratic newspapers assailed delegates to the North Carolina constitutional convention as an "Ethiopian minstrelsy . . . baboons, monkeys, mules . . . and other jackasses." They demeaned Louisiana's constitution as "the work of ignorant Negroes cooperating with a gang of white adventurers."

But Democrats delayed any political mobilization until the readmission of the southern states was completed. Then they swung into action, often calling themselves Conservatives to attract former Whigs. At first, they pursued African-American votes, but when that initiative failed, they switched tactics. In every southern state the Democrats contested elections, backed dissident Republican factions, elected some Democratic legislators, and lured scalawags away from the Republican party.

Vigilante efforts to reduce black votes bolstered Democratic campaigns to win white ones. Antagonism toward free blacks, long present in southern life, grew increasingly violent. As early as 1865 Freedmen's Bureau agents itemized a variety of outrages against blacks, including shooting, murder, rape, arson, and "severe and inhuman beating." White vigilante groups sprang up in all parts of the former Confederacy, but one organization became dominant. In spring 1866 six young Confederate war veterans in Tennessee formed a social club, the Ku Klux Klan, distinguished by elaborate rituals, hooded costumes, and secret passwords. New Klan dens spread rapidly. By the election of

The Ku Klux Klan
The menacing disguise characterized the Ku Klux Klan's campaign of intimidation during Reconstruction. The Klan strove to end Republican rule, restore white supremacy, and obliterate, in a southern editor's words, "the preposterous and wicked dogma of negro equality."

1868, when African-American suffrage had become a reality, the Klan had become a terrorist movement directed against potential African-American voters.

The Klan sought to suppress black voting, to reestablish white supremacy, and to topple the Reconstruction governments. It targeted Union League officers, Freedmen's Bureau officials, white Republicans, black militia units, economically successful blacks, and African-American voters. Some Democrats denounced Klan members as "cut-throats and riff-raff," but some prominent Confederate leaders, including General Nathan Bedford Forrest, were active Klansmen. Vigilantism united southern whites of different social classes and drew on the energy of many Confederate veterans.

Republican legislatures tried to outlaw vigilantism, but when state militia could not enforce the laws, state officials turned to the federal government for help. In response, between May 1870 and February 1871 Congress passed three Enforcement Acts, each progressively more stringent. The First Enforcement Act protected African-American voters. The Second Enforcement Act provided for federal supervision of southern elections, and the Third Enforcement Act (also known as the Ku Klux Klan Act) authorized the use of federal troops and the suspension of habeas corpus. Although thousands were arrested under the Enforcement Acts, most terrorists escaped conviction.

By 1872 the federal government had effectively suppressed the Klan, but vigilantism had served its purpose. A large military presence in the South could have protected black rights, but instead troop levels fell steadily. Congress allowed the Freedmen's Bureau to die in 1869, and the Enforcement Acts became dead letters. White southerners, a Georgia politician explained in 1871, could not discard "a feeling of bitterness, a feeling that the Negro is a sort of instinctual enemy of ours." The battle over Reconstruction was in essence a battle over the implications of emancipation, and it had begun as soon as the war had ended.

THE IMPACT OF EMANCIPATION

"The master he says we are all free," a South Carolina slave declared in 1865. "But it don't mean we is white. And it don't mean we is equal." Yet despite the daunting handicaps they faced—illiteracy, lack of property, lack of skills—most former slaves found the exhilaration of freedom overwhelming. Emancipation had given them the right to their own labor and a sense of autonomy, and during Reconstruction they asserted their independence by casting off white control and shedding the vestiges of slavery.

Confronting Freedom

For the ex-slaves, mobility was often liberty's first fruit. Some left the slave quarters; others fled the plantation completely. "I have never in my life met with such ingratitude," a South Carolina mistress exclaimed when a former slave ran off.

Emancipation stirred waves of migration within the former Confederacy. Some slaves headed to the Deep South, where desperate planters would pay higher wages for labor, but more moved to towns and cities. Urban African-American populations doubled and tripled after emancipation. The desire to find lost family members drove some migrations. "They had a passion, not so much for wandering as for getting together," explained a Freedmen's Bureau official. Parents sought children who had been sold; husbands and wives who had been separated reunited; and families reclaimed children who were being raised in masters' homes. The Freedmen's Bureau helped former slaves to get information about missing relatives and to travel to find them, and bureau agents also tried to resolve entanglements over the multiple alliances of spouses who had been separated under slavery.

Not all efforts at reunion succeeded. Some fugitive slaves had died during the war or were untraceable. Other ex-slaves had formed new partnerships and could not revive old ones. But the success stories were poignant. "I's hunted an' hunted till I track you up here," one freedman told the wife whom he found twenty years after their separation by sale.

Once reunited, freed blacks quickly legalized unions formed under slavery, sometimes in mass ceremonies of up to seventy couples. Legal marriage had a tangible impact on family life. In 1870 eight out of ten African-American families in the cotton-producing South were two-parent families, about the same proportion as white families. Men asserted themselves as household heads, and their wives and children often withdrew from the work force. Thus severe labor shortages followed immediately after the war because women had made up half of all field workers. However, by Reconstruction's end, many African-American women had rejoined the work force out of economic necessity, either in the fields or as cooks, laundresses, and domestic servants.

Black Institutions

The freed blacks' desire for independence also led to the growth of African-American churches. The African Methodist Episcopal Church, founded by Philadelphia blacks in the 1790s, gained thousands of new southern members. Negro Baptist churches, their roots often in plantation "praise meetings" organized by slaves, sprouted everywhere.

The influence of African-American churches extended far beyond religion. They provided relief, raised funds for schools, and supported Republican policies. African-American ministers assumed leading political roles. Even after southern Democrats excluded most freedmen from political life at Reconstruction's end, ministers remained the main pillars of authority within African-American communities.

Schools, too, played a crucial role for freedmen as the ex-slaves sought literacy for themselves and above all for their children. At emancipation, African-Americans organized their own schools, which the Freedmen's Bureau soon supervised. Northern philanthropic organizations paid the wages of instructors, half of whom were women. In 1869 the bureau reported more than 4,000 African-American schools in the former Confederacy.

The Freedmen's School
Supported by the Freedmen's Bureau, northern freedmen's aid societies, and African-American denominations, freedmen's schools reached about 12 percent of school-age African-American children in the South by 1870. Here, a northern teacher poses with her students at a school in rural North Carolina.

Within three more years each southern state had a public-school system, at least in principle, generally with separate schools for blacks and whites. The Freedmen's Bureau and others also helped to establish Howard, Atlanta, and Fisk Universities in 1866–1867 and Hampton Institute in 1868. Nonetheless, African-American education remained limited. Few rural blacks could reach the schools, and those who tried were sometimes the targets of vigilante attacks. Thus by the end of Reconstruction, more than 80 percent of the African-American population remained illiterate, although literacy was rising among children.

Not only school segregation but also other forms of racial separation were taken for granted. Whether by law or by custom, segregation continued on streetcars and trains as well as in churches, theaters, and restaurants. In 1875 Congress passed the Civil Rights Act, banning segregation except in schools, but in the 1883 *Civil Rights Cases,* the Supreme Court threw the law out. The Fourteenth Amendment did not prohibit discrimination by individuals, the Court ruled, only that perpetrated by the state.

White southerners adamantly rejected the prospect of racial integration, which they insisted would lead to racial amalgamation. "If we have social equality, we shall have intermarriage," contended one white southerner, "and if we have intermarriage, we shall degenerate." Urban blacks occasionally protested segregation, but most freed blacks were less interested in "social equality" than in African-American liberty and community. Moreover, the new black elite—teachers, ministers, and politicians—served African-American constituencies and thus had a vested interest in separate black institutions. Too, rural blacks had little desire to mix with whites; rather, they sought freedom from white control. Above all, they wanted to secure personal independence by acquiring land.

Land, Labor, and Sharecropping

"The sole ambition of the freedman," a New Englander wrote from South Carolina in 1865, "appears to be to become the owner of a little piece of land, there to erect a humble home, and to dwell in peace and security, at his own free will and pleasure." Indeed, to free blacks everywhere, "forty acres and a mule" promised emancipation from plantation labor, white domination, and cotton, the "slave crop." Landownership signified economic independence. "We want to be placed on land until we are able to buy it and make it our own," an African-American minister told General Sherman in Georgia during the war.

But the freedmen's visions of landownership failed to materialize, for large-scale land reform never occurred. A few slaves did obtain land, either through the pooling of resources or through the Southern Homestead Act. In 1866 Congress passed this law, setting aside 44 million acres of land in five southern states for freedmen; but the land was poor, and few slaves had resources to survive until their first harvest. About 4,000 blacks claimed homesteads, though few could establish farms. By the end of Reconstruction, only a fraction of former slaves owned working farms. Without large-scale land reform, barriers to African-American landownership remained overwhelming.

Three obstacles impeded African-American landownership. Freedmen lacked capital to buy land or tools. Furthermore, white southerners generally opposed selling land to blacks. Most important, planters sought to preserve a cheap labor force and forged laws to ensure that black labor would remain available on the plantations.

The black codes written during presidential Reconstruction were designed to preserve a captive labor force. Under labor contracts in effect in 1865–1866, freedmen received wages, housing, food, and clothing in exchange for field work. But cash was scarce, and wages often became a small share of the crop, typically one-eighth or less, to be divided among the entire work force. Freedmen's Bureau agents encouraged African-Americans to sign the contracts, seeing wage labor as a step toward economic independence. "You must begin at the bottom of the ladder and climb up," bureau head O. O. Howard told the freedmen.

Problems arose immediately. Freedmen disliked the new wage system, especially the use of gang labor, which resembled the work pattern under

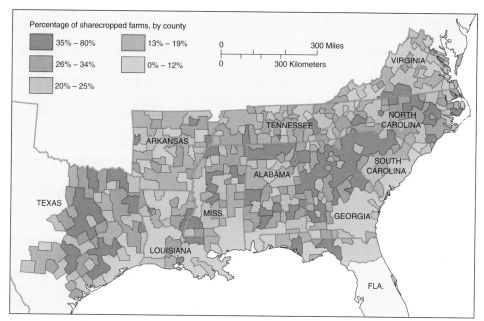

MAP 16.2
Southern Sharecropping, 1880

The depressed economy of the late 1870s caused poverty and debt, increased tenancy among white farmers, and forced many renters, black and white, into sharecropping. By 1880 the sharecropping system pervaded most southern counties, with highest concentrations in the Cotton Belt from South Carolina to eastern Texas. *Source:* U.S. Census Office, Tenth Census, 1880, Report of the Production of Agriculture (Washington, D.C.: Government Printing Office, 1883), Table 5.

slavery. Moreover, postwar planters had to compete for labor even as many scorned African-American workers as lazy or inefficient. One landowner estimated that workers accomplished only "two-fifths of what they did under the old system." As productivity fell, so did land values. Plummeting cotton prices and poor harvests in 1866 and 1867 combined with these other factors to create an impasse: landowners lacked labor, and freedmen lacked land.

Southerners began experimenting with new labor schemes, including the division of plantations into small tenancies. Sharecropping was the most widespread arrangement. Under this system, landowners subdivided large plantations into farms of thirty to fifty acres and rented them to freedmen under annual leases for a share of the crop, usually one-half. Freedmen liked this decentralized system, which let them use the labor of

family members and represented a step toward independence. A half share of the crop far exceeded the fraction that they had received under the black codes. Planters benefited, too, for the leases gave them leverage over their tenants and tenants shared the risk of poor harvests with them. Most important, planters retained control of their land. The most productive land thus remained in the hands of a small group of owners; in effect sharecropping helped to preserve the planter elite.

Although the wage system continued on sugar and rice plantations, by 1870 the plantation tradition had yielded to sharecropping in the cotton South. A severe depression in 1873 drove many blacks and independent white farmers into sharecropping. By 1880 sharecroppers, white and black, farmed 80 percent of the land in cotton-producing states. In fact, white sharecroppers outnumbered black, although a higher proportion of southern blacks, almost 75 percent, were involved in the system. Changes in marketing and finance, meanwhile, made the sharecroppers' lot increasingly precarious.

Toward a Crop-Lien Economy

Before the Civil War planters had depended on factors, or middlemen, who sold them supplies, extended credit, and marketed their crops through urban merchants. Because the high value of slave property had backed these long-distance credit arrangements, this system collapsed with the end of slavery. The postwar South, with its hundreds of thousands of tenant farmers and sharecroppers, needed a local credit system.

Into this gap stepped rural merchants, who advanced supplies to tenants and sharecroppers on credit and sold their crops to wholesalers. Because renters had no property to serve as collateral, merchants secured their loans with a lien, or claim, on each farmer's next crop. Exorbitant interest rates, 50 percent or more, quickly forced many tenants and sharecroppers into a cycle of indebtedness. The sharecropper might well owe part of his crop to the landowner and another part (the rest of his crop, or more) to the merchant. Illiterate tenants who could not keep track of their financial arrangements were at the mercy of sometimes unscrupulous merchants. "A man that didn't know how to count would always lose," an Arkansas freedman explained. Once a tenant's real or alleged debts exceeded the value of his crop, he was tied to the land, to cotton, and to sharecropping.

By the end of Reconstruction, sharecropping and crop liens had bound the South to easily marketable cash crops such as cotton and prevented crop diversification. Soil depletion, land erosion, and outmoded equipment stranded capital-short planters in a cycle of poverty. Postwar changes in southern agriculture left the region with bleak economic prospects.

Trapped in perpetual debt, tenant farmers became the chief victims of the new agricultural order. Cotton remained the only survival route open to poor farmers, regardless of race, but low income

from cotton locked them into sharecropping and crop liens. African-American tenants, for whom neither landownership nor economic independence ever materialized, saw their political rights dwindle as rapidly as their hopes for economic freedom. When Reconstruction ended, neither state governments nor the national government offered them protection, for northern politicians were preoccupied with their own problems.

NEW CONCERNS IN THE NORTH, 1868–1876

The nomination of Ulysses S. Grant for president in 1868 launched a chaotic era in national politics. His eight years in office featured political scandals, a party revolt, a massive depression, and a steady retreat from Reconstruction. By the mid-1870s northern voters cared more about economics, unemployment, labor unrest, and currency problems than the "southern question." Eager to end sectional conflict. Republicans turned their backs on the freedmen.

Grantism

Republicans had good reason to nominate General Grant. A war hero, he was endorsed by veterans, admired throughout the North, and unscathed by the bitter feuds of Reconstruction politics. To oppose Grant, the Democrats nominated Horatio Seymour, arch-critic of the Lincoln administration and an opponent of Reconstruction and greenbacks. Grant ran on his personal popularity more than on issues. Although he carried all but eight states, the popular vote was close; newly enfranchised freedmen provided Grant's margin in the South. When he was inaugurated, Grant pledged to execute all the laws, whether he agreed with them or not, to support sound money, and to follow a humane policy toward the Indians.

Grant's presidential leadership proved as weak as his war leadership had been strong. He had little political skill; his cabinet appointments were at best mediocre, and a string of scandals plagued his administration. In 1869 financier Jay Gould and his partner Jim Fisk attempted to corner the gold market with the help of Grant's brother-in-law. When gold prices tumbled, investors were ruined, and Grant's reputation was tarnished. Near the end of Grant's first term, his vice president, Schuyler Colfax, got caught up in the Crédit Mobilier scandal, an elaborate scheme to skim off the profits of the Union Pacific Railroad. Then in 1875 Grant's personal secretary, Orville Babcock, was found guilty of accepting bribes from the "whiskey ring," distillers who preferred bribery to payment of federal taxes. And in 1876 voters learned that Grant's secretary of war, William E. Belknap, had taken bribes to sell lucrative Indian trading posts in Oklahoma.

Although Grant was not personally involved in the scandals, he did little to restrain such activities, and "Grantism" came to stand for fraud, bribery, and corruption in office. Such evils, however, spread far beyond Washington. The New York City press in 1872 revealed that Democrat boss William M. Tweed led a ring that had looted the city treasury and collected some $200 million in kickbacks and bribes. When Mark Twain and coauthor Charles Dudley Warner published their scathing satire *The Gilded Age* (1873), readers recognized the novel's speculators, self-promoters, and maniacal opportunists as familiar types in public life.

Grant did enjoy some foreign policy successes. In 1872 his administration engineered the settlement of the *Alabama* claims with England: an international tribunal ordered Britain to pay $15.5 million to the United States in compensation for damage inflicted by Confederate-owned but British-built raiders. But the administration went astray when it tried to add nonadjacent territory to the Union. In 1867 the Johnson administration had purchased Alaska from Russia at the bargain price of $7.2 million. The purchase had rekindled expansionists' hope, and in 1870 Grant decided to annex the Caribbean island nation of Santo Domingo (the modern Dominican Republic). The president believed that annexation would promote Caribbean trade and provide a haven for persecuted southern blacks. Despite speculators' hopes for windfall profits, the Senate rejected the annexation treaty and further diminished Grant's reputation.

As the election of 1872 approached, dissident Republicans feared that "Grantism" would ruin the party. Former Radicals and other Republicans left out of Grant's "Great Barbecue" formed their own party, the Liberal Republicans.

The Liberals' Revolt

The Liberal Republican revolt split the Republican party and undermined Reconstruction. Liberals demanded civil service reform to bring the "best men" into government. In the South they demanded an end to "bayonet rule" and argued that African-Americans, now enfranchised, could fend for themselves. Corruption in government posed a greater threat than Confederate resurgence, the Liberals claimed, and they demanded that the "best men" in the South, ex-Confederates barred from holding office, be returned to government.

New York Tribune editor Horace Greeley, inconsistently supporting both a stringent Reconstruction policy and leniency toward the ex-Confederates, received the Liberal Republican nomination, and the Democrats endorsed Greeley as well. Republican reformers found themselves allied with the party that they had recently castigated as a "sewer" of treasonable sentiments.

Despite Greeley's arduous campaigning (he literally worked himself to death on the campaign trail and died a few weeks after the election), Grant carried 56 percent of the popular vote and won the electoral vote handily. But his victory had come at a high price: to nullify the Liberals' issues, "regular" Republicans passed an amnesty act allowing all but a few hundred ex-Confederates to resume office. And during Grant's second term Republicans' desire to discard the "southern question" grew as a depression gripped the nation.

The Panic of 1873

The postwar years brought accelerated industrialization, rapid economic expansion, and frantic speculation as investors rushed to take advantage of seemingly unlimited opportunities. Railroads led the speculative boom. The transcontinental line reached completion in 1869 (see Chapter 17), and by 1873 almost 400 railroads crisscrossed the Northeast. But in addition to transforming the northern economy, the railroad boom led entrepreneurs to overspeculate, with drastic results.

In 1869 Philadelphia banker Jay Cooke took over a new transcontinental line, the Northern Pacific. For four years Northern Pacific securities sold briskly, but in 1873 construction costs outran bond sales. In September Cooke, his bank vaults stuffed with unsalable bonds, defaulted on his obligations. His bank, the largest in the nation, shut down. Then the stock market collapsed and smaller banks and other firms followed; and the Panic of 1873 plunged the nation into a devastating five-year depression. Thousands of businesses went bankrupt. By 1878 unemployment had risen to more than 3 million. Labor protests mounted, and industrial violence spread (see Chapter 18). The depression of the 1870s demonstrated ruthlessly that conflicts born of industrialization had replaced sectional divisions.

The depression also fed a dispute over currency that had begun in 1865. During the Civil War Americans had used greenbacks, a paper currency not backed by a specific weight in gold. "Sound-money" supporters demanded the withdrawal of greenbacks from circulation as a means of stabilizing the currency. Their opponents, "easy-money" advocates such as farmers and manufacturers dependent on easy credit, wanted to expand the currency by issuing additional greenbacks. The deepening depression created even more demand for easy money, and the issue split both major parties.

Controversy over the type of currency was compounded by the question of how to repay the federal debt. In wartime the Union government had borrowed astronomical sums through the sale of war bonds. Bond holders wanted repayment in "coin," gold or silver, even though many of them had paid for the bonds in greenbacks. The Public Credit Act of 1869 promised payment in coin.

Senator John Sherman, the author of the Public Credit Act, put together a series of compromises to satisfy both "sound-money" and "easy-money" advocates. Sherman's measures, exchanging Civil War

bonds for new ones payable over a longer period of time and defining "coin" as gold only, preserved the public credit, the currency, and Republican unity. His Specie Resumption Act of 1875 promised to put the nation back on the gold standard by 1879.

But Sherman's measures, however ingenious, did not placate the Democrats, who gained control of the House in 1875. Many Democrats, and a few Republicans, were "free-silver" advocates who wanted the silver dollar restored in order to expand the currency and end the depression. The Bland-Allison Act of 1878 partially restored silver coinage by requiring the government to buy and coin several million dollars' worth of silver each month. In 1876 other expansionists formed the Greenback party to keep the paper money in circulation for the sake of debtors, but they enjoyed little success. As the depression receded, the clamor for "easy money" subsided, only to return in the 1890s (see Chapter 20). Although never settled, the controversial "money question" diverted attention away from Reconstruction and thus contributed to its demise.

Reconstruction and the Constitution

During the 1870s the Supreme Court also played a role in weakening northern support for Reconstruction as new constitutional questions surfaced.

Would the Court support laws to protect freedmen's rights? The decision in *Ex Parte* Milligan (1866) had suggested not. In *Milligan,* the Court had ruled that a military commission could not try civilians in areas where civilian courts were functioning, thus dooming the special military courts that had been established to enforce the Supplementary Freedmen's Bureau Act. Would the Court sabotage the congressional Reconstruction plan? In 1869 in *Texas* v. *White,* the Court had let Reconstruction stand, ruling that Congress had the power to ensure each state a republican form of government and to recognize the legitimate government in any state.

However, during the 1870s the Supreme Court backed away from Reconstruction. The process began with the *Slaughterhouse* decision of 1873. In this case the Court ruled that the Fourteenth Amendment protected the rights of *national* citizenship, such as the right to interstate travel, but that it did not protect the civil rights that individuals derived from *state* citizenship. The federal government, in short, did not have to safeguard such rights against violation by the states. The *Slaughterhouse* decision effectively gutted the Fourteenth Amendment, which was intended to secure freedmen's rights against state encroachment.

The Supreme Court retreated even further from Reconstruction in two cases involving the Enforcement Act of 1870. In *U.S.* v. *Reese* (1876), the Court threw out the indictment of Kentucky officials who had barred African-Americans from voting. Another decision that same year, *U.S.* v. *Cruikshank,* again weakened the Fourteenth Amendment. In the *Cruikshank* case, the Court ruled that the amendment barred *states,* but not *individuals,* from encroaching on individual rights.

Continuing this retreat from Reconstruction, the Supreme Court in 1883 invalidated both the Civil Rights Act of 1875 and the Ku Klux Klan Act of 1871. Taken cumulatively, these decisions dismantled Republican Reconstruction and confirmed rising northern sentiment that Reconstruction's egalitarian goals were unenforceable.

Republicans in Retreat

The Republicans gradually disengaged from Reconstruction, beginning with the election of Grant as president in 1868. Grant, like most Americans, hesitated to approve the use of federal authority in state or local affairs.

In the 1870s Republican idealism waned. Instead, commercial and industrial interests dominated both the Liberal and "regular" wings of the party, and few had any taste left for further sectional strife. When Democratic victories in the House of Representatives in 1874 showed that Reconstruction had become a political liability, the Republicans prepared to abandon it.

By 1875, moreover, the Radical Republicans had virtually disappeared. The Radical leaders Chase, Stevens, and Sumner had died, and others

had grown tired of "waving the bloody shirt," or defaming Democratic opponents by reviving wartime animosity. Party leaders reported that voters were "sick of carpet-bag government" and tired of the "southern question" and the "Negro question." It seemed pointless to prop up southern Republican regimes that even President Grant found corrupt. Finally, Republicans generally agreed with southern Democrats that African-Americans were inferior. To insist on black equality, many party members believed, would be a thankless, divisive, and politically suicidal course that would quash any hope of reunion between North and South. The Republican retreat set the stage for Reconstruction's end in 1877.

RECONSTRUCTION ABANDONED, 1876–1877

"We are in a very hot political contest just now," a Mississippi planter wrote his daughter in 1875, "with a good prospect of turning out the carpetbag thieves by whom we have been robbed for the past six to ten years." Indeed, an angry white majority had led a Democratic resurgence throughout the South in the 1870s, and by the end of 1872 four ex-Confederate states had already returned the Democrats to power. By 1876 Republican rule survived in only three southern states. Democratic victories in state elections that year and political bargaining in Washington in 1877 ended what little remained of Reconstruction.

Redeeming the South

After 1872 the Republican collapse in the South accelerated. Congressional amnesty enabled virtually all ex-Confederate officials to regain office, divided Republicans lost their grip on the southern electorate, and attrition diminished Republican ranks. Carpetbaggers returned North or joined the Democrats, and scalawags deserted the Republicans in large numbers. Tired of northern interference and seeing the possibility of "home rule," scalawags decided that staying Republican meant going down with a sinking ship. Unable to win new white votes or retain the old ones, the fragile Republican coalition crumbled.

Meanwhile, the Democrats mobilized formerly apathetic white voters. Although still faction-ridden—businessmen who dreamed of an industrialized "New South" had little in common with the old planter elite, the so-called Bourbons—the Democrats shared one goal: kicking the Republicans out. The Democrats' tactics varied. In several Deep South states Democrats resorted to violence. In Vicksburg in 1874 rampaging whites slaughtered about 300 blacks and terrorized thousands of potential voters. Vigilante groups in several southern states disrupted Republican meetings and threatened blacks who had registered to vote. "The Republicans are paralyzed through fear and will not act," the carpetbag governor of Mississippi wrote his wife. "Why should I fight a hopeless battle?"

Terrorism did not completely squelch black voting, but it did deprive Republicans of enough African-American votes to win state elections. Throughout the South economic pressures reinforced intimidation; labor contracts included clauses barring attendance at political meetings, and planters threatened to evict sharecroppers who stepped out of line.

Redemption, the word that Democrats used to describe their return to power, introduced sweeping changes. States rewrote constitutions, cut expenses, lowered taxes, eliminated social programs, limited the rights of tenants and sharecroppers, and shaped laws to ensure a stable African-American labor force. Legislatures restored vagrancy laws, strengthened crop-lien statutes, and remade criminal law. New criminal codes directed at African-Americans imposed severe penalties for what formerly were misdemeanors: stealing livestock or wrongly taking part of a crop became grand larceny, punishable by five years at hard labor. By Reconstruction's end, a large African-American convict work force had been leased out to private contractors.

Freedmen whose hopes had been raised by Republicans saw their prospects destroyed by the redeemers. The new laws, Tennessee blacks stated at

The Duration of Republican Rule in the Ex-Confederate State

Former Confederate States	Readmission to the Union Under Congressional Reconstruction	Democrats (Conservatives) Gain Control	Duration of Republican Rule
Alabama	June 25, 1868	November 14, 1874	6 1/2 years
Arkansas	June 22, 1868	November 10, 1874	6 1/2 years
Florida	June 25, 1868	January 2, 1877	8 1/2 years
Georgia	July 15, 1870	November 1, 1871	1 year
Louisiana	June 25, 1868	January 2, 1877	8 1/2 years
Mississippi	February 23, 1870	November 3, 1875	5 1/2 years
North Carolina	June 25, 1868	November 3, 1870	2 years
South Carolina	June 25, 1868	November 12, 1876	8 years
Tennessee	July 24, 1866*	October 4, 1869	3 years
Texas	March 30, 1870	January 14, 1873	3 years
Virginia	January 26, 1870	October 5, 1869†	0 years

*Admitted before the start of Congressional Reconstruction.†Democrats gained control before readmission. *Source:* Reprinted by permission from John Hope Franklin. *Reconstruction After the Civil War* (Chicago: University of Chicago Press, 1962), 231.

an 1875 convention, imposed "a condition of servitude scarcely less degrading than that endured before the late civil war." In the late 1870s an increasingly oppressive political climate gave rise to an "exodus" movement among African-Americans. Nearly 15,000 African-American "exodusters" from the Deep South moved to Kansas and set up homesteads. But scarce resources left most of the freed slaves stranded. Not until the twentieth century would the mass migration of southern blacks to the Midwest and North gain momentum.

The Election of 1876

By autumn 1876, with redemption almost complete, both parties were moving to discard the animosity left by the war and Reconstruction. The Republicans nominated Rutherford B. Hayes, the governor of Ohio, for president. Popular with all factions and untainted by the Grant scandals, Hayes, a "moderate," favored "home rule" in the South and civil and political rights for all—clearly contradictory goals. The Democrats nominated Governor Samuel J. Tilden of New York, a political reformer known for his assaults on the Tweed Ring that had plundered New York's City's treasury. Both candidates were fiscal conservatives, favored sound money, endorsed civil service reform, and decried corruption.

Tilden won the popular vote by a small margin, but the Republicans challenged pro-Tilden electoral votes from South Carolina, Florida, and Louisiana. Giving those nineteen electoral votes to Hayes would make him the winner. The Democrats, for their part, requiring a single electoral vote to put Tilden in the White House, challenged one electoral vote from Oregon. But Southern Republicans managed to throw out enough Democratic ballots in the contested states to proclaim Hayes the winner.

The nation now faced an unprecedented dilemma. Each party claimed victory, and each accused the other of fraud. In fact, both sets of southern votes were fraudulent: Republicans had discarded legitimate Democratic ballots, and Democrats had illegally prevented freedmen from voting. In January 1877 Congress created a special electoral commission to resolve the conflict. The commission originally consisted of seven Republicans, seven Democrats, and one independent, but when the independent resigned, a Republican replaced him. The commission gave the Republican Hayes the election by an 8–7 vote.

Congress now had to certify the new electoral vote. But the Democrats controlled the House, and some planned to forestall approval of the electoral vote. For many southern Democrats, regaining control of their states was far more important than electing a Republican president—*if* the new Republican administration would leave the South alone. Republican leaders, for their part, were willing to bargain, for Hayes wanted not just victory but also southern approval. Informal negotiations followed, with both parties exchanging promises. Ohio Republicans and southern Democrats agreed that if Hayes won the election, he would remove federal troops from all southern states. Other negotiations led to the understanding that southerners would receive federal patronage, federal aid to railroads, and federal support for internal improvements. In

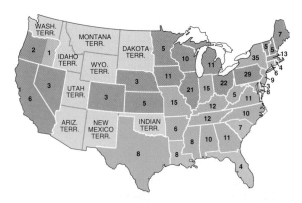

	Uncontested Electoral Vote	Electoral Vote	Popular Vote	Percentage of Popular Vote
Republican Rutherford B. Hayes	165	185	4,034,311	48.0
Democratic Samuel J. Tilden	184	184	4,288,546	51.0
Greenback Peter Cooper	–	–	75,973	1.0
	Disputed			

MAP 16.3
The Disputed Election of 1876

Chronology

1863	President Abraham Lincoln issues Proclamation of Amnesty and Reconstruction.
1864	Wade-Davis bill passed by Congress and pocket-vetoed by Lincoln.
1865	Freedmen's Bureau established. Civil War ends. Lincoln assassinated. Andrew Johnson becomes president. Johnson issues Proclamation of Amnesty and Reconstruction. Ex-Confederate states hold constitutional conventions (May–December). Thirteenth Amendment added to the Constitution. Presidential Reconstruction completed.
1866	Congress enacts the Civil Rights Act of 1866 and the Supplementary Freedmen's Bureau Act over Johnson's vetoes. Ku Klux Klan founded in Tennessee. Tennessee admitted to the Union. Race riots in southern cities. Republicans win congressional elections.
1867	Reconstruction Act of 1867. William Seward negotiates the purchase of Alaska. Constitutional conventions meet in the ex-Confederate states. Howard University founded.
1868	President Johnson is impeached, tried, and acquitted. Fourteenth Amendment added to the Constitution. Ulysses S. Grant elected president.
1869	Transcontinental railroad completed.
1870	Congress readmits the four remaining southern states to the Union. Fifteenth Amendment added to the Constitution. Enforcement Act of 1870.
1871	Second Enforcement Act. Ku Klux Klan Act.
1872	Liberal Republican Party formed. Amnesty Act. *Alabama* claims settled. Grant reelected president.
1873	Panic of 1873 begins (September–October), setting off a five-year depression.
1874	Democrats gain control of the House of Representatives.
1875	Civil Rights Act of 1875. Specie Resumption Act.
1876	Disputed presidential election: Rutherford B. Hayes versus Samuel J. Tilden.
1877	Electoral commission decides election in favor of Hayes. The last Republican-controlled state governments fall in Florida, South Carolina, and Louisiana.
1879	"Exodus" movement spreads through several southern states.

turn, southerners promised to accept Hayes as president and to treat the freedmen fairly.

Congress thus ratified Hayes's election. Once in office, Hayes fulfilled many of the agreements made by his colleagues. Republican rule toppled in Louisiana, South Carolina, and Florida. But some of the bargains struck in the so-called Compromise of 1877 fell apart, particularly Democratic promises to treat the freedmen fairly and Hayes's pledges to ensure the freed slaves' rights. "When you turned us loose, you turned us loose to the sky, to the storm, to the whirlwind, and worst of all . . .

to the wrath of our infuriated masters," Frederick Douglass had charged at the 1876 Republican convention. "The question now is, do you mean to make good to us the promises in your Constitution?" By 1877 the answer was clear: "No."

CONCLUSION   *hc* ACE Practice Test

Between 1865 and 1877, the United States underwent a series of crises. President Johnson and Congress clashed over his moderate plan for restoring the South. Radicals in Congress impeached the president, and the Radicals took over Reconstruction. Emancipation reshaped black communities as former slaves sought their identity as free people, and transformed the southern economy as a new labor system replaced slavery. The North hurtled headlong into an era of industrial growth, labor unrest, and financial crisis. By the mid-1870s northern politicians were ready to turn their backs on Reconstruction; in the South, Republican regimes toppled and were replaced by Democratic control. Reconstruction's collapse in 1877 reflected not only a waning of northern resolve but also a successful campaign of violence, intimidation, and protest waged by ex-Confederates.

Both political parties were glad to see Reconstruction go. Republicans shed the burden of the "southern question," while Democrats returned to power in the South and would remain entrenched there for more than a century. Reconstruction's end also signified a triumph for nationalism and the spirit of reunion.

Reconstruction's reputation sank. By the early twentieth century it was viewed as a fiasco fashioned by carpetbaggers, scalawags, and Radical Republicans. Historians saw Reconstruction as a failure.

Today historians have a different take on Reconstruction: it was a democratic experiment that did not go far enough. Congress failed to promote freedmen's independence through land reform, leaving southern blacks without the economic power to defend their interests. Additionally, the federal government failed to back reconstruction with military force. Given the choice between protecting blacks' rights at whatever cost or promoting reunion, the government opted for reunion. Thus Reconstruction's failure was essentially the federal government's failure to fulfill its own goals and create a biracial democracy in the South. In many ways the problems of Reconstruction have continued into the twenty-first century.

Reconstruction left a significant legacy in the Fourteenth and Fifteenth amendments, which remain monuments to the democratic zeal that swept Congress in the 1860s. African-Americans created their own monuments in those years in the form of reunited families, newly founded institutions such as schools and churches, and participation, however brief, in government.

But in the 1880s most white Americans left Reconstruction to history and turned their energies to their own economic future—to railroads, factories, and mills, and to the exploitation of the country's bountiful natural resources.

FURTHER READING

David W. Blight, *Race and Reunion: The Civil War in American Memory* (2001). Explores competing views on the significance of the Civil War in the Reconstruction era and in later decades.

Ellen Carol DuBois, *Feminism and Suffrage: The Emergence of an Independent Women's Movement in America, 1848–1869* (1978). Shows how the woman suffrage movement developed in the context of Reconstruction politics.

Eric Foner, *Reconstruction: America's Unfinished Revolution, 1863–1877* (1988). A thorough exploration of Reconstruction that draws on recent scholarship and stresses the centrality of the African-American experience.

Tera W. Hunter, *To 'Joy My Freedom: Southern Black Women's Lives and Labors After the Civil War* (1997). Explores the experience of women workers in Atlanta from Reconstruction into the twentieth century.

Leon Litwack, *Been in the Storm So Long: The Aftermath of Slavery* (1979). A comprehensive study of the African-American response to emancipation in 1865–1866.

Heather Cox Richardson, *The Death of Reconstruction: Race, Labor, and Politics in the Post–Civil War North, 1865–1901* (2004). Explores northern disenchantment with Reconstruction policies and dwindling of northern support for freed blacks in the South.

Kenneth M. Stampp, *The Era of Reconstruction, 1865–1877* (1965). A classic revisionist interpretation of Reconstruction, focusing on the establishment and fall of Republican governments.

Joel Williamson, *The Negro in South Carolina During Reconstruction, 1861–1877* (1965). A pioneer study of African-American life and institutions after emancipation.

Appendix

DECLARATION OF INDEPENDENCE

IN CONGRESS, JULY 4, 1776

The Unanimous Declaration of the Thirteen United States of America

When, in the course of human events, it becomes necessary for one people to dissolve the political bands which have connected them with another, and to assume, among the powers of the earth, the separate and equal station to which the laws of nature and of nature's God entitle them, a decent respect to the opinions of mankind requires that they should declare the causes which impel them to the separation.

We hold these truths to be self-evident: That all men are created equal; that they are endowed by their Creator with certain unalienable rights; that among these are life, liberty, and the pursuit of happiness; that, to secure these rights, governments are instituted among men, deriving their just powers from the consent of the governed; that whenever any form of government becomes destructive of these ends, it is the right of the people to alter or to abolish it, and to institute new government, laying its foundation on such principles, and organizing its powers in such form, as to them shall seem most likely to effect their safety and happiness. Prudence, indeed, will dictate that governments long established should not be changed for light and transient causes; and accordingly all experience hath shown that mankind are more disposed to suffer, while evils are sufferable, than to right themselves by abolishing the forms to which they are accustomed. But when a long train of abuses and usurpations, pursuing invariably the same object, evinces a design to reduce them under absolute despotism, it is their right, it is their duty, to throw off such government, and to provide new guards for their future security. Such has been the patient sufferance of these colonies; and such is now the necessity which constrains them to alter their former systems of government. The history of the present King of Great Britain is a history of repeated injuries and usurpations, all having in direct object the establishment of an absolute tyranny over these states. To prove this, let facts be submitted to a candid world.

He has refused his assent to laws, the most wholesome and necessary for the public good.

He has forbidden his governors to pass laws of immediate and pressing importance, unless suspended in their operation till his assent should be obtained; and, when so suspended, he has utterly neglected to attend to them.

He has refused to pass other laws for the accommodation of large districts of people, unless those people would relinquish the right of representation in the legislature, a right inestimable to them, and formidable to tyrants only.

He has called together legislative bodies at places unusual, uncomfortable, and distant from the depository of their public records, for the sole purpose of fatiguing them into compliance with his measures.

He has dissolved representative houses repeatedly, for opposing, with manly firmness, his invasions on the rights of the people.

He has refused for a long time, after such dissolutions, to cause others to be elected; whereby the legislative powers, incapable of annihilation, have returned to the people at large for their exercise;

the state remaining, in the mean time, exposed to all the dangers of invasions from without and convulsions within.

He has endeavored to prevent the population of these states; for that purpose obstructing the laws of naturalization of foreigners; refusing to pass others to encourage their migration hither, and raising the conditions of new appropriation of lands.

He has obstructed the administration of justice, by refusing his assent to laws for establishing judiciary powers.

He has made judges dependent on his will alone, for the tenure of their offices, and the amount and payment of their salaries.

He has erected a multitude of new offices, and sent hither swarms of officers to harass our people and eat out their substance.

He has kept among us, in times of peace, standing armies, without the consent of our legislatures.

He has affected to render the military independent of, and superior to, the civil power.

He has combined with others to subject us to a jurisdiction foreign to our constitution, and unacknowledged by our laws, giving his assent to their acts of pretended legislation:

For quartering large bodies of armed troops among us;

For protecting them, by a mock trial, from punishment for any murders which they should commit on the inhabitants of these states;

For cutting off our trade with all parts of the world;

For imposing taxes on us without our consent;

For depriving us, in many cases, of the benefits of trial by jury;

For transporting us beyond seas, to be tried for pretended offenses;

For abolishing the free system of English laws in a neighboring province, establishing therein an arbitrary government, and enlarging its boundaries, so as to render it at once an example and fit instrument for introducing the same absolute rule into these colonies;

For taking away our charters, abolishing our most valuable laws, and altering fundamentally the forms of our governments;

For suspending our own legislatures, and declaring themselves invested with power to legislate for us in all cases whatsoever.

He has abdicated government here, by declaring us out of his protection and waging war against us.

He has plundered our seas, ravaged our coasts, burned our towns, and destroyed the lives of our people.

He is at this time transporting large armies of foreign mercenaries to complete the works of death, desolation, and tyranny already begun with circumstances of cruelty and perfidy scarcely paralleled in the most barbarous ages, and totally unworthy of the head of a civilized nation.

He has constrained our fellow-citizens, taken captive on the high seas, to bear arms against their country, to become the executioners of their friends and brethren, or to fall themselves by their hands.

He has excited domestic insurrection among us, and has endeavored to bring on the inhabitants of our frontiers the merciless Indian savages, whose known rule of warfare is an undistinguished destruction of all ages, sexes, and conditions.

In every stage of these oppressions we have petitioned for redress in the most humble terms; our repeated petitions have been answered only by repeated injury. A prince, whose character is thus marked by every act which may define a tyrant, is unfit to be the ruler of a free people.

Nor have we been wanting in our attentions to our British brethren. We have warned them, from time to time, of attempts by their legislature to extend an unwarrantable jurisdiction over us. We have reminded them of the circumstances of our emigration and settlement here. We have appealed to their native justice and magnanimity; and we have conjured them by the ties of our common kindred, to disavow these usurpations, which would inevitably interrupt our connections and correspondence. They, too, have been deaf to the voice of justice and of consanguinity. We must, therefore, acquiesce in the necessity which denounces our separation, and hold them, as we hold the rest of mankind, enemies in war, in peace friends.

We, therefore, the representatives of the United States of America, in General Congress assembled, appealing to the Supreme Judge of the world for the rectitude of our intentions, do, in the name and by the authority of the good people of these colonies, solemnly publish and declare, that these United Colonies are, and of right ought to be, FREE AND INDEPENDENT STATES; that they are absolved from all allegiance to the British crown, and that all political connection between them and the state of Great Britain is, and ought to be, totally dissolved; and that, as free and independent states, they have full power to levy war, conclude peace, contract alliances, establish commerce, and do all other acts and things which independent states may of right do. And for the support of this declaration, with a firm reliance on the protection of Divine Providence, we mutually pledge to each other our lives, our fortunes, and our sacred honor.

JOHN HANCOCK [*President*]
[*and fifty-five others*]

CONSTITUTION OF THE UNITED STATES OF AMERICA

PREAMBLE

We the people of the United States, in order to form a more perfect union, establish justice, insure domestic tranquility, provide for the common defense, promote the general welfare, and secure the blessings of liberty to ourselves and our posterity, do ordain and establish this CONSTITUTION for the United States of America.

ARTICLE I

Section 1. All legislative powers herein granted shall be vested in a Congress of the United States, which shall consist of a Senate and a House of Representatives.

Section 2. The House of Representatives shall be composed of members chosen every second year by the people of the several States, and the electors in each State shall have the qualifications requisite for electors of the most numerous branch of the State Legislature.

No person shall be a Representative who shall not have attained to the age of twenty-five years, and been seven years a citizen of the United States, and who shall not, when elected, be an inhabitant of that State in which he shall be chosen.

Representatives and direct taxes shall be apportioned among the several States which may be included within this Union, according to their respective numbers, *which shall be determined by adding to the whole number of free persons, including those bound to service for a term of years and excluding Indians not taxed, three-fifths of all other persons.* The actual enumeration shall be made within three years after the first meeting of the Congress of the United States, and within every subsequent term of ten years, in such manner as they shall by law direct. The number of Representatives shall not exceed one for every thirty thousand, but each State shall have at least one Representative; *and until such enumeration shall be made, the State of New Hampshire shall be entitled to choose three, Massachusetts eight, Rhode Island and Providence Plantations one, Connecticut five, New York six, New Jersey four, Pennsylvania eight, Delaware one, Maryland six, Virginia ten, North Carolina five, South Carolina five, and Georgia three.*

When vacancies happen in the representation from any State, the Executive authority thereof shall issue writs of election to fill such vacancies.

The House of Representatives shall choose their Speaker and other officers; and shall have the sole power of impeachment.

Section 3. The Senate of the United States shall be composed of two Senators from each State, *chosen by the legislature thereof,* for six years; and each Senator shall have one vote.

Immediately after they shall be assembled in consequence of the first election, they shall be divided as equally as may be into three classes. The seats of the Senators of the first class shall be vacated at the expiration of the second year, of the second class at the expiration of the fourth year, and of the third class at the expiration of the sixth year, so that one-third may be chosen every second year; and if vacancies happen by resignation or otherwise, during the recess of the legislature of any State, the Executive thereof may make temporary appointments until the next meeting of the legislature, which shall then fill such vacancies.

No person shall be a Senator who shall not have attained to the age of thirty years, and been nine years a citizen of the United States, and who shall not, when elected, be an inhabitant of that State for which he shall be chosen.

The Vice President of the United States shall be President of the Senate, but shall have no vote, unless they be equally divided.

Note: Passages no longer in effect are printed in italic type.

The Senate shall choose their other officers, and also a President *pro tempore,* in the absence of the Vice President, or when he shall exercise the office of the President of the United States.

The Senate shall have the sole power to try all impeachments. When sitting for that purpose, they shall be on oath or affirmation. When the President of the United States is tried, the Chief Justice shall preside: and no person shall be convicted without the concurrence of two-thirds of the members present.

Judgment in cases of impeachment shall not extend further than to removal from the office, and disqualification to hold and enjoy any office of honor, trust or profit under the United States; but the party convicted shall nevertheless be liable and subject to indictment, trial, judgment and punishment, according to law.

Section 4. The times, places and manner of holding elections for Senators and Representatives shall be prescribed in each State by the legislature thereof; but the Congress may at any time by law make or alter such regulations, except as to the places of choosing Senators.

The Congress shall assemble at least once in every year, and such meeting *shall be on the first Monday in December, unless they shall by law appoint a different day.*

Section 5. Each house shall be the judge of the elections, returns and qualifications of its own members, and a majority of each shall constitute a quorum to do business; but a smaller number may adjourn from day to day, and may be authorized to compel the attendance of absent members, in such manner, and under such penalties, as each house may provide.

Each house may determine the rules of its proceedings, punish its members for disorderly behavior, and with the concurrence of two-thirds, expel a member.

Each house shall keep a journal of its proceedings, and from time to time publish the same, excepting such parts as may in their judgment require secrecy; and the yeas and nays of the members of either house on any question shall, at the desire of one-fifth of those present, be entered on the journal.

Neither house, during the session of Congress, shall, without the consent of the other, adjourn for more than three days, nor to any other place than that in which the two houses shall be sitting.

Section 6. The Senators and Representatives shall receive a compensation for their services, to be ascertained by law and paid out of the treasury of the United States. They shall in all cases except treason, felony and breach of the peace, be privileged from arrest during their attendance at the session of their respective houses, and in going to and returning from the same; and for any speech or debate in either house, they shall not be questioned in any other place.

No Senator or Representative shall, during the time for which he was elected, be appointed to any civil office under the authority of the United States, which shall have been created, or the emoluments whereof shall have been increased, during such time; and no person holding any office under the United States shall be a member of either house during his continuance in office.

Section 7. All bills for raising revenue shall originate in the House of Representatives; but the Senate may propose or concur with amendments as on other bills.

Every bill which shall have passed the House of Representatives and the Senate, shall, before it become a law, be presented to the President of the United States; if he approve he shall sign it, but if not he shall return it with objections to that house in which it originated, who shall enter the objections at large on their journal, and proceed to reconsider it. If after such reconsideration two-thirds of that house shall agree to pass the bill, it shall be sent, together with the objections, to the other house, by which it shall likewise be reconsidered, and, if approved by two-thirds of that house, it shall become a law. But in all such cases the votes of both houses shall be determined by yeas and nays, and the names of the persons voting for and against the bill shall be entered on the journal of each house respectively. If any bill shall not be returned by the President within ten days (Sundays excepted) after it shall have been presented to him, the same shall be a law, in like manner as if he had signed it, unless the Congress by their adjournment prevent its return, in which case it shall not be a law.

Every order, resolution, or vote to which the concurrence of the Senate and House of Representatives may be necessary (except on a question of adjournment) shall be presented to the President of the United States; and before the same shall take effect, shall be approved by him, or being disapproved by him, shall be repassed by two-thirds of the Senate and House of Representatives, according to the rules and limitations prescribed in the case of a bill.

Section 8.   The Congress shall have power

To lay and collect taxes, duties, imposts, and excises, to pay the debts and provide for the common defense and general welfare of the United States; but all duties, imposts and excises shall be uniform throughout the United States;

To borrow money on the credit of the United States;

To regulate commerce with foreign nations, and among the several States, and with the Indian tribes;

To establish an uniform rule of naturalization, and uniform laws on the subject of bankruptcies throughout the United States;

To coin money, regulate the value thereof, and of foreign coin, and fix the standard of weights and measures;

To provide for the punishment of counterfeiting the securities and current coin of the United States;

To establish post offices and post roads;

To promote the progress of science and useful arts by securing for limited times to authors and inventors the exclusive right to their respective writings and discoveries;

To constitute tribunals inferior to the Supreme Court;

To define and punish piracies and felonies committed on the high seas and offenses against the law of nations;

To declare war, grant letters of marque and reprisal, and make rules concerning captures on land and water;

To raise and support armies, but no appropriation of money to that use shall be for a longer term than two years;

To provide and maintain a navy;

To make rules for the government and regulation of the land and naval forces;

To provide for calling forth the militia to execute the laws of the Union, suppress insurrections, and repel invasions;

To provide for organizing, arming, and disciplining the militia, and for governing such part of them as may be employed in the service of the United States, reserving to the States respectively the appointment of the officers, and the authority of training the militia according to the discipline prescribed by Congress;

To exercise exclusive legislation in all cases whatsoever, over such district (not exceeding ten miles square) as may, by cession of particular States, and the acceptance of Congress, become the seat of government of the United States, and to exercise like authority over all places purchased by the consent of the legislature of the State, in which the same shall be, for erection of forts, magazines, arsenals, dock-yards, and other needful buildings;—and

To make all laws which shall be necessary and proper for carrying into execution the foregoing powers, and all other powers vested by this Constitution in the government of the United States, or in any department or officer thereof.

Section 9.   *The migration or importation of such persons as any of the States now existing shall think proper to admit shall not be prohibited by the Congress prior to the year 1808; but a tax or duty may be imposed on such importation, not exceeding $10 for each person.*

The privilege of the writ of habeas corpus shall not be suspended, unless when in cases of rebellion or invasion the public safety may require it.

No bill of attainder or ex post facto law shall be passed.

No capitation, or other direct, tax shall be laid, unless in proportion to the census or enumeration herein before directed to be taken.

No tax or duty shall be laid on articles exported from any State.

No preference shall be given by any regulation of commerce or revenue to the ports of one State over those of another; nor shall vessels bound to, or from, one State, be obliged to enter, clear, or pay duties in another.

No money shall be drawn from the treasury, but in consequence of appropriations made by law; and a regular statement and account of the receipts and expenditures of all public money shall be published from time to time.

No title of nobility shall be granted by the United States: and no person holding any office of profit or trust under them, shall, without the consent of the Congress, accept of any present, emolument, office, or title, of any kind whatever, from any king, prince, or foreign state.

Section 10. No State shall enter into any treaty, alliance, or confederation; grant letters of marque and reprisal; coin money; emit bills of credit; make anything but gold and silver coin a tender in payment of debts; pass any bill of attainder, ex post facto law, or law impairing the obligation of contracts, or grant any title of nobility.

No State shall, without the consent of Congress, lay any imposts or duties on imports or exports, except what may be absolutely necessary for executing its inspection laws: and the net produce of all duties and imposts, laid by any State on imports or exports, shall be for the use of the treasury of the United States; and all such laws shall be subject to the revision and control of the Congress.

No State shall, without the consent of Congress, lay any duty of tonnage, keep troops or ships of war in time of peace, enter into any agreement or compact with another State, or with a foreign power, or engage in war, unless actually invaded, or in such imminent danger as will not admit of delay.

ARTICLE II

Section 1. The executive power shall be vested in a President of the United States of America. He shall hold his office during the term of four years, and, together with the Vice President, chosen for the same term, be elected as follows:

Each state shall appoint, in such manner as the legislature thereof may direct, a number of electors, equal to the whole number of Senators and Representatives to which the State may be entitled in the Congress; but no Senator or Representative, or person holding an office of trust or profit under the United States, shall be appointed an elector.

The electors shall meet in their respective States, and vote by ballot for two persons, of whom one at least shall not be an inhabitant of the same State with themselves. And they shall make a list of all the persons voted for, and of the number of votes for each; which list they shall sign and certify, and transmit sealed to the seat of government of the United States, directed to the President of the Senate. The President of the Senate shall, in the presence of the Senate and the House of Representatives, open all the certificates, and the votes shall then be counted. The person having the greatest number of votes shall be the President, if such number be a majority of the whole number of electors appointed; and if there be more than one who have such majority, and have an equal number of votes, then the House of Representatives shall immediately choose by ballot one of them for President; and if no person have a majority, then from the five highest on the list said house shall in like manner choose the President. But in choosing the President the votes shall be taken by States, the representation from each State having one vote; a quorum for this purpose shall consist of a member or members from two-thirds of the States, and a majority of all the States shall be necessary to a choice. In every case, after the choice of the President, the person having the greatest number of votes of the electors shall be the Vice President. But if there should remain two or more who have equal votes, the Senate shall choose from them by ballot the Vice President.

The Congress may determine the time of choosing the electors and the day on which they shall give their votes; which day shall be the same throughout the United States.

No person except a natural-born citizen, *or a citizen of the United States at the time of the adoption of this Constitution,* shall be eligible to the office of President; neither shall any person be eligible to that office who shall not have attained to the age of thirty-five years, and been fourteen years a resident within the United States.

In case of the removal of the President from office or of his death, resignation, or inability to discharge the powers and duties of the said office, the same shall devolve on the Vice President, and the Congress may by law provide for the case of removal, death, resignation, or inability, both of the President and Vice President, declaring what officer shall then act as President, and such officer shall act accordingly, until the disability be removed, or a President shall be elected.

The President shall, at stated times, receive for his services a compensation, which shall neither be increased nor diminished during the period for which he shall have been elected, and he shall not receive within that period any other emolument from the United States, or any of them.

Before he enter on the execution of his office, he shall take the following oath or affirmation:—"I do solemnly swear (or affirm) that I will faithfully execute the office of the President of the United States, and will to the best of my ability preserve, protect and defend the Constitution of the United States."

Section 2.   The President shall be commander in chief of the army and navy of the United States, and of the militia of the several States, when called into the actual service of the United States; he may require the opinion, in writing, of the principal officer in each of the executive departments, upon any subject relating to the duties of their respective offices, and he shall have power to grant reprieves and pardons for offenses against the United States, except in cases of impeachment.

He shall have power, by and with the advice and consent of the Senate, to make treaties, provided two-thirds of the Senators present concur; and he shall nominate, and by and with the advice and consent of the Senate, shall appoint ambassadors, other public ministers and consuls, judges of the Supreme Court, and all other officers of the United States, whose appointments are not herein otherwise provided for, and which shall be established by law: but Congress may by law vest the appointment of such inferior officers, as they think proper, in the President alone, in the courts of law, or in the heads of departments.

The President shall have power to fill up all vacancies that may happen during the recess of the Senate, by granting commissions which shall expire at the end of their next session.

Section 3.   He shall from time to time give to the Congress information of the state of the Union, and recommend to their consideration such measures as he shall judge necessary and expedient; he may, on extraordinary occasions, convene both houses, or either of them, and in case of disagreement between them, with respect to the time of adjournment, he may adjourn them to such time as he shall think proper; he shall receive ambassadors and other public ministers; he shall take care that the laws be faithfully executed, and shall commission all the officers of the United States.

Section 4.   The President, Vice President and all civil officers of the United States shall be removed from office on impeachment for, and on conviction of, treason, bribery, or other high crimes and misdemeanors.

ARTICLE III

Section 1.   The judicial power of the United States shall be vested in one Supreme Court, and in such inferior courts as the Congress may from time to time ordain and establish. The judges, both of the Supreme and inferior courts, shall hold their offices during good behavior, and shall, at stated times, receive for their services a compensation which shall not be diminished during their continuance in office.

Section 2.   The judicial power shall extend to all cases, in law and equity, arising under this Constitution, the laws of the United States, and treaties made, or which shall be made, under their authority;—to all cases affecting ambassadors, other public ministers and consuls;—to all cases of admiralty and maritime jurisdiction;—to controversies to which the United States shall be a party;—to controversies between two or more States;—*between a State and citizens of another State;*—between citizens of different States;—between citizens of the same State claiming lands under grants of different States, and between a State, or the citizens thereof, and foreign states, citizens or subjects.

In all cases affecting ambassadors, other public ministers and consuls, and those in which a State shall be party, the Supreme Court shall have original jurisdiction. In all the other cases before mentioned, the Supreme Court shall have appellate jurisdiction, both as to law and fact, with such exceptions, and under such regulations, as the Congress shall make.

The trial of all crimes, except in cases of impeachment, shall be by jury; and such trial shall be held in the State where said crimes shall have been committed; but when not committed within any State, the trial shall be at such place or places as the Congress may by law have directed.

Section 3.   Treason against the United States shall consist only in levying war against them, or in adhering to their enemies, giving them aid and comfort. No person shall be convicted of treason unless on the testimony of two witnesses to the same overt act, or on confession in open court.

The Congress shall have power to declare the punishment of treason, but no attainder of treason shall work corruption of blood, or forfeiture except during the life of the person attainted.

ARTICLE IV

Section 1.   Full faith and credit shall be given in each State to the public acts, records, and judicial proceedings of every other State. And the Congress may by general laws prescribe the manner in which such acts, records, and proceedings shall be proved, and the effect thereof.

Section 2.   The citizens of each State shall be entitled to all privileges and immunities of citizens in the several States.

A person charged in any State with treason, felony, or other crime, who shall flee from justice, and be found in another State, shall on demand of the executive authority of the State from which he fled, be delivered up, to be removed to the State having jurisdiction of the crime.

No person held to service or labor in one State, under the laws thereof, escaping into another, shall, in consequence of any law or regulation therein, be discharged from such service or labor, but shall be delivered up on claim of the party to whom such service or labor may be due.

Section 3.   New States may be admitted by the Congress into this Union; but no new State shall be formed or erected within the jurisdiction of any other State; nor any State be formed by the junction of two or more States, or parts of States, without the consent of the legislatures of the States concerned as well as of the Congress.

The Congress shall have power to dispose of and make all needful rules and regulations respecting the territory or other property belonging to the United States; and nothing in this Constitution shall be so construed as to prejudice any claims of the United States, or of any particular State.

Section 4.   The United States shall guarantee to every State in this Union a republican form of government, and shall protect each of them against invasion; and on application of the legislature, or of the executive (when the legislature cannot be convened); against domestic violence.

ARTICLE V

The Congress, whenever two-thirds of both houses shall deem it necessary, shall propose amendments to this Constitution, or, on the application of the legislatures of two-thirds of the several States, shall call a convention for proposing amendments, which, in either case, shall be valid to all intents and purposes, as part of this Constitution, when ratified by the legislatures of three-fourths of the several States, or by conventions in three-fourths thereof, as the one or the other mode of ratification may be proposed by the Congress; provided *that no amendments which may be made prior to the year one thousand eight hundred and eight shall in any manner affect the first and fourth clauses in the ninth section of the first article;* and that no State, without its consent, shall be deprived of its equal suffrage in the Senate.

ARTICLE VI

All debts contracted and engagements entered into, before the adoption of this Constitution, shall be as valid against the United States under this Constitution, as under the Confederation.

This Constitution, and the laws of the United States which shall be made in pursuance thereof; and all treaties made, or which shall be made, under the authority of the United States, shall be the supreme law of the land; and the judges in every State shall be bound thereby, anything in the Constitution or laws of any State to the contrary notwithstanding.

The Senators and Representatives before mentioned, and the members of the several State legislatures, and all executive and judicial officers, both of the United States and of the several States, shall be bound by oath or affirmation to support this Constitution; but no religious test shall ever be required as a qualification to any office or public trust under the United States.

ARTICLE VII

The ratification of the conventions of nine States shall be sufficient for the establishment of this Constitution between the States so ratifying the same.

Done in Convention by the unanimous consent of the States present, the seventeenth day of September in the year of our Lord one thousand seven hundred and eighty-seven and of the Independence of the United States of America the twelfth. In witness whereof we have hereunto subscribed our names.

[Signed by]
G° WASHINGTON
Presidt and Deputy from Virginia
[*and thirty-eight others*]

AMENDMENTS TO THE CONSTITUTION

AMENDMENT I*

Congress shall make no law respecting an establishment of religion, or prohibiting the free exercise thereof; or abridging the freedom of speech, or of the press; or the right of the people peaceably to assemble, and to petition the government for a redress of grievances.

AMENDMENT II

A well-regulated militia being necessary to the security of a free State, the right of the people to keep and bear arms shall not be infringed.

---

* The first ten Amendments (Bill of Rights) were adopted in 1791.

AMENDMENT III

No soldier shall, in time of peace, be quartered in any house without the consent of the owner, nor in time of war, but in a manner to be prescribed by law.

AMENDMENT IV

The right of the people to be secure in their persons, houses, papers, and effects, against unreasonable searches and seizures, shall not be violated, and no warrants shall issue but upon probable cause, supported by oath or affirmation, and particularly describing the place to be searched, and the persons or things to be seized.

AMENDMENT V

No person shall be held to answer for a capital, or otherwise infamous crime, unless on a present-ment or indictment of a grand jury, except in cases arising in the land or naval forces, or in the militia, when in actual service in time of war or public dan-ger; nor shall any person be subject for the same offense to be twice put in jeopardy of life or limb; nor shall be compelled in any criminal case to be a witness against himself, nor be deprived of life, lib-erty, or property, without due process of law; nor shall private property be taken for public use with-out just compensation.

AMENDMENT VI

In all criminal prosecutions, the accused shall en-joy the right to a speedy and public trial, by an im-partial jury of the State and district wherein the crime shall have been committed, which district shall have been previously ascertained by law, and to be informed of the nature and cause of the accu-sation; to be confronted with the witnesses against him; to have compulsory process for obtaining wit-nesses in his favor, and to have the assistance of counsel for his defense.

AMENDMENT VII

In suits at common law, where the value in contro-versy shall exceed twenty dollars, the right of trial by jury shall be preserved, and no fact tried by a jury shall be otherwise reexamined in any court of the United States, than according to the rules of the common law.

AMENDMENT VIII

Excessive bail shall not be required, nor excessive fines imposed, nor cruel and unusual punish-ments inflicted.

AMENDMENT IX

The enumeration in the Constitution, of certain rights, shall not be construed to deny or disparage others retained by the people.

AMENDMENT X

The powers not delegated to the United States by the Constitution, not prohibited by it to the States, are reserved to the States respectively, or to the people.

AMENDMENT XI   [*Adopted 1798*]

The judicial power of the United States shall not be construed to extend to any suit in law or equity, commenced or prosecuted against one of the United States by citizens of another State, or by cit-izens or subjects of any foreign state.

AMENDMENT XII   [*Adopted 1804*]

The electors shall meet in their respective States, and vote by ballot for President and Vice President, one of whom, at least, shall not be an inhabitant of the same State with themselves; they shall name in their ballots the person voted for as President, and in distinct ballots the person voted for as Vice Pres-ident, and they shall make distinct lists of all per-sons voted for as President, and of all persons voted for as Vice President, and of the number of votes for each, which lists they shall sign and cer-tify, and transmit sealed to the seat of government of the United States, directed to the President of the Senate;—the President of the Senate shall, in the presence of the Senate and House of Represen-tatives, open all the certificates and the votes shall then be counted;—the person having the greatest number of votes for President shall be the Presi-dent, if such number be a majority of the whole number of electors appointed; and if no person have such majority, then from the persons having the highest numbers not exceeding three on the list of those voted for as President, the House of Representatives shall choose immediately, by bal-lot, the President. But in choosing the President, the votes shall be taken by States, the representa-tion from each State having one vote; a quorum for this purpose shall consist of a member or members from two-thirds of the States, and a majority of all the States shall be necessary to a choice. And if the House of Representatives shall not choose a President whenever the right of choice shall devolve upon them, before *the fourth day of March* next following, then the Vice President shall act as President, as in the case of the death or other constitutional disability of the President.

The person having the greatest number of votes as Vice President shall be the Vice President, if such a number be a majority of the whole number of electors appointed; and if no person have a majority, then from the two highest numbers on the list the Senate shall choose the Vice President; a quorum for the purpose shall consist of two-thirds of the whole number of Senators, and a majority of the whole number shall be necessary to a choice. But no person constitutionally ineligible to the office of President shall be eligible to that of Vice President of the United States.

AMENDMENT XIII   [*Adopted 1865*]

Section 1.   Neither slavery nor involuntary servitude, except as a punishment for crime whereof the party shall have been duly convicted, shall exist within the United States, or any place subject to their jurisdiction.

Section 2.   Congress shall have power to enforce this article by appropriate legislation.

AMENDMENT XIV   [*Adopted 1868*]

Section 1.   All persons born or naturalized in the United States, and subject to the jurisdiction thereof, are citizens of the United States and of the State wherein they reside. No State shall make or enforce any law which shall abridge the privileges or immunities of citizens of the United States; nor shall any State deprive any person of life, liberty, or property, without due process of law; nor deny to any person within its jurisdiction the equal protection of the laws.

Section 2.   Representatives shall be apportioned among the several States according to their respective numbers, counting the whole number of per-

sons in each State, excluding Indians not taxed. But when the right to vote at any election for the choice of Electors for President and Vice President of the United States, Representatives in Congress, the executive and judicial officers of a State, or the members of the legislature thereof, is denied to any of the male inhabitants of such State, being twenty-one years of age and citizens of the United States, or in any way abridged, except for participation in rebellion, or other crime, the basis of representation therein shall be reduced in the proportion which the number of such male citizens shall bear to the whole number of male citizens twenty-one years of age in such State.

Section 3.   No person shall be a Senator or Representative in Congress or Elector of President and Vice President, or hold any office, civil or military, under the United States, or under any State, who, having previously taken an oath, as a member of Congress, or as an officer of the United States, or as a member of any State legislature, or as an executive or judicial officer of any State, to support the Constitution of the United States, shall have engaged in insurrection or rebellion against the same, or given aid and comfort to the enemies thereof. Congress may, by a vote of two-thirds of each house, remove such disability.

Section 4.   The validity of the public debt of the United States, authorized by law, including debts incurred for payment of pensions and bounties for services in suppressing insurrection or rebellion, shall not be questioned. But neither the United States nor any State shall assume or pay any debt or obligation incurred in aid of insurrection or rebellion against the United States, or any claim for the loss or emancipation of any slave; but all such debts, obligations, and claims shall be held illegal and void.

Section 5.   The Congress shall have the power to enforce, by appropriate legislation, the provisions of this article.

AMENDMENT XV   [*Adopted 1870*]

Section 1.   The right of citizens of the United States to vote shall not be denied or abridged by the United States or by any State on account of race, color, or previous condition of servitude.

Section 2.   The Congress shall have power to enforce this article by appropriate legislation.

AMENDMENT XVI   [*Adopted 1913*]

The Congress shall have power to lay and collect taxes on incomes, from whatever source derived, without apportionment among the several States, and without regard to any census or enumeration.

AMENDMENT XVII   [*Adopted 1913*]

Section 1.   The Senate of the United States shall be composed of two Senators from each State, elected by the people thereof, for six years; and each Senator shall have one vote. The electors in each State shall have the qualifications requisite for electors of [voters for] the most numerous branch of the State legislatures.

Section 2.   When vacancies happen in the representation of any State in the Senate, the executive authority of such State shall issue writs of election to fill such vacancies: Provided, that the Legislature of any State may empower the executive thereof to make temporary appointments until the people fill the vacancies by election as the Legislature may direct.

Section 3.   This amendment shall not be so construed as to affect the election or term of any Senator chosen before it becomes valid as part of the Constitution.

AMENDMENT XVIII
[*Adopted 1919; repealed 1933*]

Section 1.   *After one year from the ratification of this article the manufacture, sale, or transportation of intoxicating liquors within, the importation*
thereof into, or the exportation thereof from the United States and all territory subject to the jurisdiction thereof, for beverage purposes, is hereby prohibited.

Section 2.   *The Congress and the several States shall have concurrent power to enforce this article by appropriate legislation.*

Section 3.   *This article shall be inoperative unless it shall have been ratified as an amendment to the Constitution by the legislatures of the several States, as provided by the Constitution, within seven years from the date of the submission thereof to the States by the Congress.*

AMENDMENT XIX   [*Adopted 1920*]

Section 1.   The right of citizens of the United States to vote shall not be denied or abridged by the United States or by any State on account of sex.

Section 2.   The Congress shall have the power to enforce this article by appropriate legislation.

AMENDMENT XX   [*Adopted 1933*]

Section 1.   The terms of the President and Vice President shall end at noon on the 20th day of January, and the terms of Senators and Representatives at noon on the 3d day of January, of the years in which such terms would have ended if this article had not been ratified; and the terms of their successors shall then begin.

Section 2.   The Congress shall assemble at least once in every year, and such meeting shall begin at noon on the 3d day of January, unless they shall by law appoint a different day.

Section 3.   If, at the time fixed for the beginning of the term of the President, the President-elect shall have died, the Vice President-elect shall become President. If a President shall not have been chosen before the time fixed for the beginning of his term, or if the President-elect shall have failed to qualify, then the Vice President-elect shall act as President until a President shall have qualified; and the Congress may by law provide for the case wherein neither a President-elect nor a Vice President-elect shall have qualified, declaring who shall then act as President, or the manner in which one who is to act shall be selected, and such persons shall act accordingly until a President or Vice President shall have qualified.

Section 4. The Congress may by law provide for the case of the death of any of the persons from whom the House of Representatives may choose a President whenever the right of choice shall have devolved upon them, and for the case of the death of any of the persons from whom the Senate may choose a Vice President whenever the right of choice shall have devolved upon them.

Section 5. Sections 1 and 2 shall take effect on the 15th day of October following the ratification of this article.

Section 6. This article shall be inoperative unless it shall have been ratified as an amendment to the Constitution by the Legislatures of three-fourths of the several States within seven years from the date of its submission.

AMENDMENT XXI [Adopted 1933]

Section 1. The eighteenth article of amendment to the Constitution of the United States is hereby repealed.

Section 2. The transportation or importation into any State, Territory, or Possession of the United States for delivery or use therein of intoxicating liquors, in violation of the laws thereof, is hereby prohibited.

Section 3. This article shall be inoperative unless it shall have been ratified as an amendment to the Constitution by conventions in the several States, as provided in the Constitution, within seven years from the date of submission thereof to the States by the Congress.

AMENDMENT XXII [Adopted 1951]

Section 1. No person shall be elected to the office of President more than twice, and no person who has held the office of President, or acted as President, for more than two years of a term to which some other person was elected President shall be elected to the office of President more than once. But this article shall not apply to any person holding the office of President when this article was proposed by the Congress, and shall not prevent any person who may be holding the office of President, or acting as President, during the term within which this article becomes operative from holding the office of President or acting as President during the remainder of such term.

Section 2. This article shall be inoperative unless it shall have been ratified as an amendment to the Constitution by the legislatures of three-fourths of the several States within seven years from the date of its submission to the States by the Congress.

AMENDMENT XXIII [Adopted 1961]

Section 1. The District constituting the seat of Government of the United States shall appoint in such manner as the Congress may direct:

A number of electors of President and Vice President equal to the whole number of Senators and Representatives in Congress to which the District would be entitled if it were a State, but in no event more than the least populous State; they shall be in addition to those appointed by the States, but they shall be considered for the purposes of the election of President and Vice President, to be electors appointed by a State; and they shall meet in the District and perform such duties as provided by the twelfth article of amendment.

Section 2. The Congress shall have the power to enforce this article by appropriate legislation.

AMENDMENT XXIV [Adopted 1964]

Section 1. The right of citizens of the United States to vote in any primary or other election for

President or Vice President, for electors for President or Vice President, or for Senator or Representative in Congress, shall not be denied or abridged by the United States or any State by reason of failure to pay any poll tax or other tax.

Section 2.   The Congress shall have the power to enforce this article by appropriate legislation.

AMENDMENT XXV   [*Adopted 1967*]

Section 1.   In case of the removal of the President from office or of his death or resignation, the Vice President shall become President.

Section 2.   Whenever there is a vacancy in the office of the Vice President, the President shall nominate a Vice President who shall take office upon confirmation by a majority vote of both Houses of Congress.

Section 3.   Whenever the President transmits to the President pro tempore of the Senate and the Speaker of the House of Representatives his written declaration that he is unable to discharge the powers and duties of his office, and until he transmits to them a written declaration to the contrary, such powers and duties shall be discharged by the Vice President as Acting President.

Section 4.   Whenever the Vice President and a majority of either the principal officers of the executive departments or of such other body as Congress may by law provide, transmit to the President pro tempore of the Senate and the Speaker of the House of Representatives their written declaration that the President is unable to discharge the powers and duties of his office, the Vice President shall immediately assume the powers and duties of the office as Acting President.

Thereafter, when the President transmits to the President pro tempore of the Senate and the Speaker of the House of Representatives his written declaration that no inability exists, he shall resume the powers and duties of his office unless the Vice President and a majority of either the principal officers of the executive department[s] or of such other body as Congress may by law provide,

transmit within four days to the President pro tempore of the Senate and the Speaker of the House of Representatives their written declaration that the President is unable to discharge the powers and duties of his office. Thereupon Congress shall decide the issue, assembling within forty-eight hours for that purpose if not in session. If the Congress, within twenty-one days after receipt of the latter written declaration, or, if Congress is not in session, within twenty-one days after Congress is required to assemble, determines by two-thirds vote of both Houses that the President is unable to discharge the powers and duties of his office, the Vice President shall continue to discharge the same as Acting President; otherwise, the President shall resume the powers and duties of his office.

AMENDMENT XXVI   [*Adopted 1971*]

Section 1.   The right of citizens of the United States, who are eighteen years of age or older, to vote shall not be denied or abridged by the United States or by any State on account of age.

Section 2.   The Congress shall have power to enforce this article by appropriate legislation.

AMENDMENT XXVII*   [*Adopted 1992*]

No law, varying the compensation for services of the Senators and Representatives, shall take effect, until an election of Representatives shall have intervened.

---

* Originally proposed in 1789 by James Madison, this amendment failed to win ratification along with the other parts of what became the Bill of Rights. However, the proposed amendment contained no deadline for ratification, and over the years other state legislatures voted to add it to the Constitution; many such ratifications occurred during the 1980s and early 1990s as public frustration with Congress's performance mounted. In May 1992 the Archivist of the United States certified that, with the Michigan legislature's ratification, the article had been approved by three-fourths of the states and thus automatically became part of the Constitution. But congressional leaders and constitutional specialists questioned whether an amendment that took 202 years to win ratification was valid, and the issue had not been resolved by the time this book went to press.

Presidential Elections, 1789–2004

Year	States in the Union	Candidates	Parties	Electoral Vote	Popular Vote	Percentage of Popular Vote
1789	11	GEORGE WASHINGTON	No party designations	69		
		John Adams		34		
		Minor candidates		35		
1792	15	GEORGE WASHINGTON	No party designations	132		
		John Adams		77		
		George Clinton		50		
		Minor candidates		5		
1796	16	JOHN ADAMS	Federalist	71		
		Thomas Jefferson	Democratic-Republican	68		
		Thomas Pinckney	Federalist	59		
		Aaron Burr	Democratic-Republican	30		
		Minor candidates		48		
1800	16	THOMAS JEFFERSON	Democratic-Republican	73		
		Aaron Burr	Democratic-Republican	73		
		John Adams	Federalist	65		
		Charles C. Pinckney	Federalist	64		
		John Jay	Federalist	1		
1804	17	THOMAS JEFFERSON	Democratic-Republican	162		
		Charles C. Pinckney	Federalist	14		
1808	17	JAMES MADISON	Democratic-Republican	122		
		Charles C. Pinckney	Federalist	47		
		George Clinton	Democratic-Republican	6		
1812	18	JAMES MADISON	Democratic-Republican	128		
		DeWitt Clinton	Federalist	89		
1816	19	JAMES MONROE	Democratic-Republican	183		
		Rufus King	Federalist	34		
1820	24	JAMES MONROE	Democratic-Republican	231		
		John Quincy Adams	Independent Republican	1		
1824	24	JOHN QUINCY ADAMS	Democratic-Republican	84	108,740	30.5
		Andrew Jackson	Democratic-Republican	99	153,544	43.1
		William H. Crawford	Democratic-Republican	41	46,618	13.1
		Henry Clay	Democratic-Republican	37	47,136	13.2
1828	24	ANDREW JACKSON	Democratic	178	642,553	56.0
		John Quincy Adams	National Republican	83	500,897	44.0
1832	24	ANDREW JACKSON	Democratic	219	687,502	55.0
		Henry Clay	National Republican	49	530,189	42.4
		William Wirt	Anti-Masonic	7	33,108	2.6
		John Floyd	National Republican	11		
1836	26	MARTIN VAN BUREN	Democratic	170	765,483	50.9
		William H. Harrison	Whig	73		
		Hugh L. White	Whig	26	739,795	49.1
		Daniel Webster	Whig	14		
		W. P. Mangum	Whig	11		

Because candidates receiving less than 1 percent of the popular vote are omitted, the percentage of popular vote may not total 100 percent.

Before the Twelfth Amendment was passed in 1804, the electoral college voted for two presidential candidates; the runner-up became vice president.

(cont.)

Year	States in the Union	Candidates	Parties	Electoral Vote	Popular Vote	Percentage of Popular Vote
1840	26	WILLIAM H. HARRISON	Whig	234	1,274,624	53.1
		Martin Van Buren	Democratic	60	1,127,781	46.9
1844	26	JAMES K. POLK	Democratic	170	1,338,464	49.6
		Henry Clay	Whig	105	1,300,097	48.1
		James G. Birney	Liberty		62,300	2.3
1848	30	ZACHARY TAYLOR	Whig	163	1,360,967	47.4
		Lewis Cass	Democratic	127	1,222,342	42.5
		Martin Van Buren	Free Soil		291,263	10.1
1852	31	FRANKLIN PIERCE	Democratic	254	1,601,117	50.9
		Winfield Scott	Whig	42	1,385,453	44.1
		John P. Hale	Free Soil		155,825	5.0
1856	31	JAMES BUCHANAN	Democratic	174	1,832,955	45.3
		John C. Frémont	Republican	114	1,339,932	33.1
		Millard Fillmore	American	8	871,731	21.6
1860	33	ABRAHAM LINCOLN	Republican	180	1,865,593	39.8
		Stephen A. Douglas	Democratic	12	1,382,713	29.5
		John C. Breckinridge	Democratic	72	848,356	18.1
		John Bell	Constitutional Union	39	592,906	12.6
1864	36	ABRAHAM LINCOLN	Republican	212	2,206,938	55.0
		George B. McClellan	Democratic	21	1,803,787	45.0
1868	37	ULYSSES S. GRANT	Republican	214	3,013,421	52.7
		Horatio Seymour	Democratic	80	2,706,829	47.3
1872	37	ULYSSES S. GRANT	Republican	286	3,596,745	55.6
		Horace Greeley	Democratic	*	2,843,446	43.9
1876	38	RUTHERFORD B. HAYES	Republican	185	4,034,311	48.0
		Samuel J. Tilden	Democratic	184	4,288,546	51.0
		Peter Cooper	Greenback		75,973	1.0
1880	38	JAMES A. GARFIELD	Republican	214	4,453,295	48.5
		Winfield S. Hancock	Democratic	155	4,414,082	48.1
		James B. Weaver	Greenback-Labor		308,578	3.4
1884	38	GROVER CLEVELAND	Democratic	219	4,879,507	48.5
		James G. Blaine	Republican	182	4,850,293	48.2
		Benjamin F. Butler	Greenback-Labor		175,370	1.8
		John P. St. John	Prohibition		150,369	1.5
1888	38	BENJAMIN HARRISON	Republican	233	5,477,129	47.9
		Grover Cleveland	Democratic	168	5,537,857	48.6
		Clinton B. Fisk	Prohibition		249,506	2.2
		Anson J. Streeter	Union Labor		146,935	1.3
1892	44	GROVER CLEVELAND	Democratic	277	5,555,426	46.1
		Benjamin Harrison	Republican	145	5,182,690	43.0
		James B. Weaver	People's	22	1,029,846	8.5
		John Bidwell	Prohibition		264,133	2.2
1896	45	WILLIAM MCKINLEY	Republican	271	7,102,246	51.1
		William J. Bryan	Democratic	176	6,492,559	47.7

*When Greeley died shortly after the election, his supporters divided their votes among the minor candidates.
Because candidates receiving less than 1 percent of the popular vote are omitted, the percentage of popular vote
may not total 100 percent.

(cont.)

Year	States in the Union	Candidates	Parties	Electoral Vote	Popular Vote	Percentage of Popular Vote
1900	45	WILLIAM MCKINLEY	Republican	292	7,218,491	51.7
		William J. Bryan	Democratic; Populist	155	6,356,734	45.5
		John C. Wooley	Prohibition		208,914	1.5
1904	45	THEODORE ROOSEVELT	Republican	336	7,628,461	57.4
		Alton B. Parker	Democratic	140	5,084,223	37.6
		Eugene V. Debs	Socialist		402,283	3.0
		Silas C. Swallow	Prohibition		258,536	1.9
1908	46	WILLIAM H. TAFT	Republican	321	7,675,320	51.6
		William J. Bryan	Democratic	162	6,412,294	43.1
		Eugene V. Debs	Socialist		420,793	2.8
		Eugene W. Chafin	Prohibition		253,840	1.7
1912	48	WOODROW WILSON	Democratic	435	6,296,547	41.9
		Theodore Roosevelt	Progressive	88	4,118,571	27.4
		William H. Taft	Republican	8	3,486,720	23.2
		Eugene V. Debs	Socialist		900,672	6.0
		Eugene W. Chafin	Prohibition		206,275	1.4
1916	48	WOODROW WILSON	Democratic	277	9,127,695	49.4
		Charles E. Hughes	Republican	254	8,533,507	46.2
		A. L. Benson	Socialist		585,113	3.2
		J. Frank Hanly	Prohibition		220,506	1.2
1920	48	WARREN G. HARDING	Republican	404	16,143,407	60.4
		James N. Cox	Democratic	127	9,130,328	34.2
		Eugene V. Debs	Socialist		919,799	3.4
		P. P. Christensen	Farmer-Labor		265,411	1.0
1924	48	CALVIN COOLIDGE	Republican	382	15,718,211	54.0
		John W. Davis	Democratic	136	8,385,283	28.8
		Robert M. La Follette	Progressive	13	4,831,289	16.6
1928	48	HERBERT C. HOOVER	Republican	444	21,391,993	58.2
		Alfred E. Smith	Democratic	87	15,016,169	40.9
1932	48	FRANKLIN D. ROOSEVELT	Democratic	472	22,809,638	57.4
		Herbert C. Hoover	Republican	59	15,758,901	39.7
		Norman Thomas	Socialist		881,951	2.2
1936	48	FRANKLIN D. ROOSEVELT	Democratic	523	27,752,869	60.8
		Alfred M. Landon	Republican	8	16,674,665	36.5
		William Lemke	Union		882,479	1.9
1940	48	FRANKLIN D. ROOSEVELT	Democratic	449	27,307,819	54.8
		Wendell L. Willkie	Republican	82	22,321,018	44.8
1944	48	FRANKLIN D. ROOSEVELT	Democratic	432	25,606,585	53.5
		Thomas E. Dewey	Republican	99	22,014,745	46.0
1948	48	HARRY S TRUMAN	Democratic	303	24,105,812	49.5
		Thomas E. Dewey	Republican	189	21,970,065	45.1
		Strom Thurmond	States' Rights	39	1,169,063	2.4
		Henry A. Wallace	Progressive		1,157,172	2.4

Because candidates receiving less than 1 percent of the popular vote are omitted, the percentage of popular vote may not total 100 percent.

(cont.)

Year	States in the Union	Candidates	Parties	Electoral Vote	Popular Vote	Percentage of Popular Vote
1952	48	DWIGHT D. EISENHOWER	Republican	442	33,936,234	55.1
		Adlai E. Stevenson	Democratic	89	27,314,992	44.4
1956	48	DWIGHT D. EISENHOWER	Republican	457	35,590,472	57.6
		Adlai E. Stevenson	Democratic	73	26,022,752	42.1
1960	50	JOHN F. KENNEDY	Democratic	303	34,227,096	49.7
		Richard M. Nixon	Republican	219	34,108,546	49.5
		Harry F. Byrd	Independent	15	502,363	.7
1964	50	LYNDON B. JOHNSON	Democratic	486	43,126,506	61.1
		Barry M. Goldwater	Republican	52	27,176,799	38.5
1968	50	RICHARD M. NIXON	Republican	301	31,770,237	43.4
		Hubert H. Humphrey	Democratic	191	31,270,533	42.7
		George C. Wallace	American Independent	46	9,906,141	13.5
1972	50	RICHARD M. NIXON	Republican	520	47,169,911	60.7
		George S. McGovern	Democratic	17	29,170,383	37.5
1976	50	JIMMY CARTER	Democratic	297	40,827,394	49.9
		Gerald R. Ford	Republican	240	39,145,977	47.9
1980	50	RONALD W. REAGAN	Republican	489	43,899,248	50.8
		Jimmy Carter	Democratic	49	35,481,435	41.0
		John B. Anderson	Independent		5,719,437	6.6
		Ed Clark	Libertarian		920,859	1.0
1984	50	RONALD W. REAGAN	Republican	525	54,451,521	58.8
		Walter F. Mondale	Democratic	13	37,565,334	40.5
1988	50	GEORGE H. W. BUSH	Republican	426	47,946,422	54.0
		Michael S. Dukakis	Democratic	112	41,016,429	46.0
1992	50	WILLIAM J. CLINTON	Democratic	370	43,728,275	43.2
		George H. W. Bush	Republican	168	38,167,416	37.7
		H. Ross Perot	Independent		19,237,247	19.0
1996	50	WILLIAM J. CLINTON	Democratic	379	47,401,185	49.2
		Robert Dole	Republican	159	39,197,469	40.7
		H. Ross Perot	Reform		8,085,294	8.4
2000	50	GEORGE W. BUSH	Republican	271	50,456,141	47.9
		Albert Gore Jr.	Democratic	266	50,996,039	48.4
		Ralph Nader	Green		2,882,807	2.7
2004	50	GEORGE W. BUSH	Republican	286	60,608,582	51.0
		John Kerry	Democratic	252	57,288,974	48.0
		Ralph Nader	Independent		406,924	1.0

Because candidates receiving less than 1 percent of the popular vote are omitted, the percentage of popular vote may not total 100 percent.

Photograph Credits

Chapter 1   *p. 1,* American Museum of Natural History; *p. 4,* Richard Alexander Cooke III; *p. 7,* Cahokia Mounds State Historic Site.

Chapter 2   *p. 13,* Courtesy of the John Carter Brown Library at Brown University; *p. 15,* Werner Forman/Art Resource, New York; *p. 21,* Copyright © The Trustees of The British Museum; *p. 26,* © George H.H. Huey Photography, Inc.; *p. 32,* Copyright The New York Public Library/Art Resource, New York.

Chapter 3   *p. 34,* Courtesy of Berkeley Castle Charitable Trust, Gloucestershire, England; *p. 37,* drawing from John Underhill's *News from America,* 1638; *p. 47,* Copyright The New York Public Library/Art Resource, New York; *p. 53,* Library of Congress; *p. 56,* Courtesy Museum of New Mexico, Neg. #11409.

Chapter 4   *p. 59,* Courtesy, Winterthur Museum; *p. 65,* Photograph Courtesy Peabody Essex Museum; *p. 68,* from the Collections of the Henry Ford Museum and Greenfield Village; *p. 79,* Courtesy of the Boston Public Library, Print Department.

Chapter 5   *p. 81,* Library of Congress; *p. 88,* Library of Congress; *p. 102,* photograph Courtesy of the Concord Museum, Concord, Massachusetts, *www.concordmuseum.org.*

Chapter 6   *p. 108,* from Joseph P. Tustin, *Diary of the American War: A Hessian Journal* by Captain Johann Ewald, Field Jager Corps. (New Haven, Connecticut: Yale University Press, 1979. By permission of Yale University Press; *p. 118,* Boston Athenaeum; *p. 126,* Colonial Williamsburg Foundation.

Chapter 7   *p. 133,* Terra Foundation for American Art, Daniel J. Terra Art Acquistion Endowment Fund, 2000.6. Photography Courtesy of Terra Foundation for American Art, Chicago; *p. 136,* © Archivio Iconografico, S.A./Corbis; *p. 143,* Chicago Historical Society, P&S-1914.0001.

Chapter 8   *p. 155,* Minneapolis Institute of Arts, William Hood Dunwoody Fund; *p. 157,* Library of Congress; *p. 164,* G.W. Blunt White Library, Manuscript Collection/Mystic Seaport Museum; *p. 165,* painting by Mathais Noheimer, photo by MPI/Getty Images.

Chapter 9   *p. 175,* Copyright The New York Public Library/Art Resource, New York; *p. 178,* Library of Congress; *p. 185,* University of Massachusetts–Lowell, Center for Lowell History; *p. 187,* Moorland-Spingarn Research Center, Howard University, Washington, D.C.

Chapter 10   *p. 192,* Gift of Mrs. Samuel T. Carson, Photograph ©1991 The Detroit Institute of Art (detail); *p. 196,* Memphis Brooks Museum of Art, Memphis, Tennessee, Memphis Park Commission Purchase 46.2; *p. 197,* National Portrait Gallery, Smithsonian Institution/Art Resource, New York; *p. 207,* Boston Athenaeum; *p. 209,* Chicago Historical Society, ICHi-22021.

Chapter 11   *p. 213,* from the Collections of The Henry Ford Museum and Greenfield Village; *p. 215* Library of Congress; *p. 223,* © Bettmann/Corbis; *p. 226,* Courtesy of the John Hay Library at Brown University, Harris Collection of American Poetry and Plays. Gift of Hortense Webster.

Chapter 12   *p. 230,* Library of Congress; *p. 234,* Historic New Orleans Collection, accession 1988.9; *p. 248,* (left) Schomberg Center, Copyright The New York Public Library/Art Resource, New York, (right) Howard University Gallery of Art, Washington, D.C.

Chapter 13   *p. 251,* The Hallmark Photographic Collection, Hallmark Cards, Inc., Kansas City, Missouri; *p. 266,* Chicago Historical Society, P&S-1920.0038; *p. 270,* Library of Congress.

Chapter 14   *p. 277,* National Portrait Gallery, Smithsonian Institution/Art Resource, New York; *p. 287,* (left) National Portrait Gallery, Smithsonian Institution/Art Resource, New York, (right) Library of Congress.

Chapter 15   *p. 294,* George Eastman House; *p. 297,* © Bettmann/Corbis; *p. 302,* (top) Library of Congress, (bottom) Antietam National Battlefield, Sharpsburg, Maryland; *p. 308,* Chicago Historical Society, ICHi-22051.

Chapter 16   *p. 320,* The William Gladstone Collection; *p. 323, Harper's Weekly,* 1866; *p. 330,* © Bettmann/Corbis; *p. 332,* The William Gladstone Collection.

Index

Crops: cash, 44, 50, 180, 231; in
Columbian exchange, 25; soil damage
and, 68–69; wheat, 69, 123, 214, 217. *See
also specific crop*
Crusades, 14
Cuba, 84, 280; Ostend Manifesto and, 281
Cult of domesticity, 209
Culture: of African-American slaves,
247–249; of early Americans, 3–8; Euro-
pean, 16, 18–19; Indian, 10–11; popular,
189–190, 227–228; school reform and,
206; of Southern free blacks, 245–246
Currency, disputes over, 338. *See also* Pa-
per money
Curry, John, 242
Customs duties, 92–93, 198. *See also*
Tariffs
Customs racketeering, 95–96

Da Gama, Vasco, 22
Daily life. *See* Lifestyle
Dakota country, 161
Dancing, 178; African-American, 249
Dartmouth College v. *Woodward,* 170
Dartmouth University, 78
Daughters of Liberty, 94–95
Davis, Jefferson, 291, 315, 317; leadership
style of, 297, 298, 312
Dawes, William, 101
Death: Indian burials and, 5–6; rates of, in
New England, 40
Debt, 73, 149; colonial, 85–86; farmer,
180, 181; Jefferson and, 157–158; Mexi-
can, 265; plantation economy and, 236;
Reconstruction and, 330; Texas, 275. *See
also* Credit; War debt
Declaration of Independence, 103–104,
117; document, A1–A3
Declaration of Sentiments, 209
Declaratory Act (1766), 90
Deere, John, 214
Deerslayer, The (Cooper), 225
Deforestation, 68; colonial New England,
41; in Europe, 18
Delaware: as border state, Civil War, 298;
colonial, 54
Delaware Indians, 52, 71, 84, 86, 98; land
taken from, 72, 123
Democracy, 120, 131, 144
Democracy in America (Tocqueville), 176,
185, 202
Democratic party, 195, 199, 201, 279; Civil
War dissenters (Copperheads), 312, 313,
315; expansion and, 252, 263; extension
of slavery and, 269, 270; Fifteenth
Amendment and, 328; immigrants in,
255, 256; post-Reconstruction, 339–340,
341; Reconstruction and, 330, 331; secession and, 289–290; in South, 238;
states' rights and, 261
Democratic (Republican) societies, 145

Deposit Act (1836), 199
Depression: following Panic of 1837,
200–201, 263; following Panic of 1857,
289; following Panic of 1873, 338; post-
Revolution, 122–123, 125. *See also* Re-
cession
De Soto, Hernando, 27, 55
Detroit, 71, 86, 175, 183; immigrants in,
253; in War of 1812, 167 (map), 168
Dial (magazine), 211
Diaphragm, vaginal, 190
Diarrhea, 245, 314
Días, Bartolomeu, 21
Dickinson, Emily, 227
Dickinson, John, 91, 93, 101, 121
Diet. *See* Food (diet)
Diplomacy: Civil War, 305–306; Constitu-
tion, 127; Revolutionary War, 112. *See
also* Foreign affairs; Treaties
Diptheria epidemic, 77
Disease, 45, 188, 219–220, 268; in colonial
cities, 69; diptheria epidemic, 77; Indi-
ans and, 24–25, 35, 36, 50, 86, 140;
slaves and, 245; small pox, 24–25, 86;
theories of, 220, 314; venereal, 140, 268;
in Virginia colony, 30–31
Dissent and dissenters: among Puritans,
37–38; Civil War, 312–313
District of Columbia. *See* Washington,
D.C.
Diversity, 34–35; in Middle colonies, 51,
54
Division of labor, by gender, 177, 260
Divorce, 150; in Puritan New England, 39
Dix, Dorothea, 210, 313
Doctors. *See* Medicine
Doeg Indians, Bacon's Rebellion and, 47
Domesticity, cult of, 209
Dominion of New England, 61
Donner party, 260
Douglas, Stephen A., 276, 285; debates with
Lincoln, 286–287; election of 1860 and,
289, 290; Kansas-Nebraska Act and,
279–280; portrait of, 287; secession and,
292
Douglass, Frederick, 207, 246, 306, 329,
342; on black soldiers, 307; photo of,
277; on slave life, 243, 244, 249
Draft (military), Civil War: in Confederacy,
295; riots against, 313; in Union, 296
Drake, Sir Francis, 28
Dred Scott v. Sandford, 284–285, 286, 289,
325
Drivers of slaves, 207, 242, 243
Dueling: Burr-Hamilton, 161; on frontier,
188; Jackson and, 195; in Old South,
240–241
Dunmore, Lord, 99
Durand, Asher, 228
Dutch (Netherlands), 112; New England
trade with, 60; rebellion against Spain,
26, 32; trade rivalry with England, 63;

West Indian colonies of, 49 (map). *See
also* New Netherland
Dysentery, 314; slaves and, 245

Earl, Ralph, 102, 196
Early, Jubal A., 315
East: farming techniques in, 215; revivals
in, 203
Eastern woodlands Indians, 5–7, 9 (map)
East Florida, 108, 116, 172
East India Company, 98–99
East Jersey, 53. *See also* New Jersey
Eaton, John and Peggy, 197
Eclipse (steamboat), 182
Economy: banks and, 199–200; cash crop,
180; colonial, 62–64; commercialization
of, 188; crop-lien, 336; Embargo Act
and, 163–164; in Europe, 18–19; Hamilton and, 136, 137–139; impact of Civil
War, 299, 311–312; Indians and, 119
(*See also* Fur trade); inequality and, 185;
in Louisiana, 71; market, 38, 149–150,
180–183; mercantilism and, 54–55,
63–64; New England and, 38; Panic of
1819, 170, 181–182; plantation, 50, 236;
in Plymouth Plantation, 31; in Salem,
42, 44; slavery, 48; technology and,
214–218; in urban areas, 69. *See also*
Depression; Finance
Education: African-American, 333–334;
colleges, 37, 78, 311, 334; literacy, 76,
234, 336; Protestantism and, 20; Puritan
New England, 36–37; reform in, 206; in
South, 234; for women, 150
Edwards, Jonathan, 77–78
Edward VI (England), 20
Egalitarianism, Revolutionary War and,
116–117. *See also* Equality and
inequality
Eighteenth Amendment, A13
Eighth Amendment, A11
Elections: of 1792, 135; of 1794, 145; of
1796, 146–147; of 1798, 147; of 1800,
149; of 1804, 160; of 1808, 164; of 1810,
165; of 1812, 169; of 1816, 169; of 1824,
194; of 1828, 195–196; of 1832, 198–199;
of 1836, 200; of 1840, 201, 261; of 1842,
261; of 1844, 262–263; of 1848, 269–270;
of 1850–1851, 276; of 1852, 278, 281; of
1854, 281; of 1855, 282; of 1856,
283–284; of 1860, 289–290; of 1864, 313,
315–316; of 1866, 325; of 1868, 336; of
1872, 337; of 1876, 341–342; Michigan,
193; presidential, A17–A21; of senators,
126, A-4, A-13. *See also* Voting and voting rights
Electoral College, 149
Electoral commission, election of 1876
and, 341
Electricity, Franklin and, 77
Eleventh Amendment, 135, A12
Eliot, John, 42